PILTDOWN
A scientific forgery

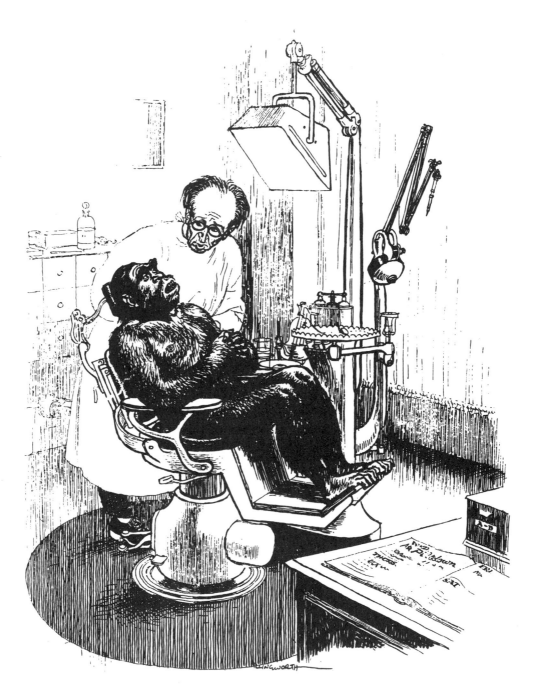

"This may hurt, but I'm afraid I'll have to remove the whole jaw."

(Collapse of 600,000-year-old party)

From PUNCH 2 December 1953

PILTDOWN

A Scientific forgery

FRANK SPENCER

Based on research by Ian Langham (1942–1984)

Natural History Museum Publications
Oxford University Press
LONDON OXFORD & NEW YORK

First published 1990 by
British Museum (Natural History)
Cromwell Road, London SW7 5BD

&

Oxford University Press, Walton Street, Oxford OX2 6DP
Oxford New York Toronto
Delhi Bombay Calcutta Madras Karachi
Petaling Java Singapore Hong Kong Tokyo
Nairobi Dar es Salaam Cape Town
Melbourne Auckland

and associated companies in
Beirut Berlin Ibadan Nicosia

Oxford is a trade mark of Oxford University Press

Published in the United States
by Oxford University Press, New York

© Frank Spencer
Department of Anthropology
Queens College CUNY, NY 11367–0904

British Library Cataloguing in Publication Data
Spencer, Frank, 1942–
Piltdown: a scientific forgery.
1.   Piltdown Man
I.   Title
573.3

ISBN 0–19–858522–5

Library of Congress Cataloging-in-Publication Data
Spencer, Frank, 1942–
Piltdown: a scientific forgery.
1. Piltdown forgery.   I. Title.
GN82.5.S63   1990   573.3   90–7688

ISBN 0–19–858522–5

9 8 7 6 5 4 3 2 1
Printed in the United States of America
on acid-free paper

Contents

Foreword

That the world loves a mystery is manifestly evident from the record-breaking run of "The Mousetrap", currently in its 38th year, and that other perennial 'whodunnit', "The Piltdown Hoax" which has been running almost as long. But there the similarity ends: the Mousetrap audiences leave the theatre knowing who did indeed do it, whereas the Piltdown drama is still being acted out. No detective novel has ever been invested with such a shoal of red herrings; and what a cast of suspects! One feels that the solution might defy even the remarkable powers of Sherlock Holmes himself (especially since his begetter, Sir Arthur Conan Doyle, has been adduced by some as being the hoaxer).

For my own part, I have a strong personal (even perverse in the light of the many troubled hours it afforded me) attachment to the Piltdown controversy. Chance ordained that I should be in the Keeper's (W N Edwards) room discussing a career in the British Museum (Natural History) when the Director, Sir Gavin de Beer, burst in full of arrangements for the meeting that evening of the Geological Society at which the Piltdown hoax was to be exposed . . . a meeting which I made sure I did not miss. Then, later, though the tide of interest in Piltdown ebbed and flowed, scarcely a year went by without some resurgence of the Piltdown controversy. I also had the privilege of discussing the possible protagonists and their motives with colleagues in the Museum and with investigators throughout the world who came to see the material and archives, for Piltdown had become an issue of international significance. Despite the great diversity of opinions and conclusions, I and many of my colleagues adhered to our possibly parochial views that the hoax was centred on the Museum and that its intended victim was Sir Arthur Smith Woodward, Keeper of Geology from 1901 to 1924 (though even he has been accused of being the perpetrator!).

One of the many Piltdown investigators, Dr Ian Langham of the University of Sydney, had been undertaking a lengthy and comprehensive review of the Museum's large Piltdown archive, and was near to the completion of his researches at the time of his tragic death in 1984. When it seemed that this would be yet another unresolved chapter in the Piltdown saga, it was with great relief and pleasure that I learned that Frank Spencer of the City University of New York had been asked by Ian's widow, Kathryn Langham, to bring her husband's work to completion and to reveal his solution on the identity of the Piltdown perpetrator(s). Aware of the fact that Dr Spencer had reached a similar conclusion (though from a somewhat different direction), I was delighted by his acceptance of Mrs Langham's invitation and his subsequent plan to write not only an historical narrative (as a vehicle for Langham's case), but also to prepare, in conjunction with this work, a summary of the Piltdown papers — both of which were to be published by the Museum. Since many of the earlier theories regarding the forgers' identities were evidently based either on an insufficient depth of research or understanding of the chronology of events, as well as the interrelationships of the various players, I was fully supportive of Frank Spencer's ambitious plan. That he succeeded in analysing, digesting and presenting such an extensive archival source in a relatively short time is a tribute to his industry and dedication. His work has resulted in the publication of two separate but closely interrelated books: *The Piltdown Papers* (in itself a very comprehensive and detailed study), which is an annotated collection of pertinent correspondence and other documents covering the period from 1909 through to 1955, and the present volume *Piltdown: a scientific forgery*, an analytical reconstruction of the history of the Piltdown affair and Langham's brief.

Piltdown: a scientific forgery is a scholarly and thoroughly absorbing work; providing a most diverting insight into the personalities, ambitions and motives of the protagonists, setting them in the centre of the scientific environment in which they worked some three-quarters of a century ago. And what of the conclusions? These are certainly as surprising and remarkable as any proposed hitherto, and I am sure will be just as controversial.

Is this the end of the Piltdown affair? Until such time as an unequivocal, signed and detailed confession comes to light (and one that can be shown to fit the facts as we now know them), I rather doubt it. However, anyone who wishes to dispute the evidence and conclusions drawn here will have to match both Spencer's scholarship and industry.

H W Ball
Keeper of Palaeontology 1966–1986

Introduction to a forgery

Phillip V Tobias

Director, Palaeo-anthropology Research Unit Department of Anatomy and Human Biology University of the Witwatersrand, Johannesburg

The story of Piltdown has long been one of the most fascinating episodes in the history of palaeoanthropology. Its spell is woven by a multitude of intertwined threads: Why was it done? Whence were the planted bones derived? How were the remains treated? When and how were the forged specimens lodged in the gravels of Piltdown? By whom and exactly when was each of the fraudulently deposited specimens uncovered? How did it come about that so many prominent scholars of the day were taken in by the Piltdown cache? Did the *paradigm*, created or strengthened by the Piltdown remains, play a major part in delaying the acceptance of R A Dart's claims for the Taung child-representative of *Australopithecus africanus*, on the basis that, "If Piltdown was an ancestor, Taung could not have been"? On the latter thinking, did the Piltdown forgery delay the advance of hominid evolutionary studies by a quarter of a century? Who first started suspecting that the Piltdown remains should be considered fraudulent? How and by whom was the fraud initially exposed? What effect did this entire 45-year history have on the practice of palaeoanthropology? Lastly, who perpetrated the forgery and what were the motives of the person or persons responsible?

These are some of the questions which this work explores in a most searching, comprehensive and erudite manner.

When I was a student and a young staff member under Professor Raymond A Dart about forty years ago, the remains of Piltdown I and II and of Barcombe Mills were still considered by most investigators as "respectable" fossils. In 1953 nine talks on "Africa's Place in the Human Story" were presented by the South African Broadcasting Corporation, with R A Dart as editor of the series. My talk entitled "The Very Ancient Human Inhabitants of Africa", was broadcast on Sunday evening 14 June 1953. In it I compared the African fossils with some from Europe and Asia, and so it came about that I made what might have been one of the last published statements about the Piltdown I remains before Joseph Weiner came to suspect that a hoax had been perpetrated.

> The Piltdown skull fragments ... were found between 1908 and 1913, with part of a lower jaw and an eye-tooth, which, in contrast with the skull, are like those of a chimpanzee. Indeed, some anatomists say the jaw belongs to a fossil ape which somehow became mixed up in the gravel deposit with the human skull fragments. Quite recently, Dr Kenneth Oakley has found that the fluorine content in both the skull and jaw are virtually identical and this indicates that the bones are of the same age. Of course, this does not prove that the bones belonged to the same individual and so, even today, the 40-year old puzzle of Piltdown Man remains unsolved. If the jaw really belongs to the skull, it is a most unexpected combination; if it does not belong to the skull, it is an almost unbelievable coincidence that the human and ape cranial bones should have remained so close together in the same gravel patch![1]

Only 46 days later, during a sleepless night on 30 July 1953, Joseph Weiner, at Oxford, lighted on the notion that the Piltdown mandible was probably a forgery. Less than four months later (21 November 1953), he with Kenneth Oakley and Sir Wilfrid Le Gros Clark published the evidence that it had indeed been a fake.

Perhaps it is worth placing on record here a much earlier reference and one which may well be the earliest published assertion, albeit unsupported, that the Piltdown fossils were forged.[2] The *Rand Daily Mail*, of 2 March 1925, published an antievolutionist letter by one A W Baker, of P O North Rand (near Johannesburg), in which it was claimed, without citing evidence, that the Piltdown man was a fake:

> I suppose the correspondent who cites the Piltdown man as one of the links in the assured facts of modern scientific discovery is aware that this wonderful man is a fake. Part of a frontal bone, part of a jawbone, and one tooth, found in a quarry, sufficed. With these the scientists built up all the rest of a body to suit their theory, making it as like as possible to what they conceived a missing link ought to be.
>
> It was then placed in a museum, and professors take their students to gaze upon their manufactured ancestor. Although several distinguished scientists have declared that the tooth and the jaw do not belong to the same creature as the frontal bone, this colossal fake is still exhibited in the name of modern science.[3]

It was in 1930, according to K P Oakley and C P Groves,[4] that Gerrit Miller, a zoologist at the Smithsonian Institution, Washington D.C., who had early (1915) interpreted the mandible as that of a new species of chimpanzee (*Pan vetus*), reached the conclusion that the jaw had been fraudulently altered. However, he did not have proof — nor had he ever examined the original specimens: hence his colleagues are said to have dissuaded him from publishing his conclusion![5] Oakley[6] reported also that C S Coon's suspicions had been aroused when, in 1951, he detected striae on the surface of the Piltdown molars. Apart from mentioning this observation to his wife, Coon did not publish his surmise that the furrows were artificial.

After my brief expression of the "almost unbelievable coincidence" posed by the dualistic interpretation of Piltdown I, my interest in the problem continued to be whetted over the years by conversations with W H L Duckworth at Cambridge, Kenneth Oakley in London, and Louis Leakey in Nairobi. During a lengthy discussion I had with 85 year-old Dr Duckworth in 1955, in his rooms at Jesus College, Cambridge, where he had lived almost uninterruptedly since 1885, the following emerged:

> He [Duckworth] told me that when Elliot Smith first came to Cambridge, he had shared a room with Dr. Duckworth in the Anatomy Department for three years (1895–7); at that time, Elliot Smith was working on the brain of the marsupial. They had been great friends. Later, Duckworth seems to have offended Sir Grafton, possibly over a letter Duckworth had written to Schwalbe at Strasburg. Duckworth had had a chance of seeing the Piltdown remains even before the Geological Society meeting and had spotted at once that the patina on the cranium and on the jaw differed. He had written volumes of unpublished observations and reflections on the Piltdown remains and had reasoned that if this jaw were that of a man, then it meant we were no longer able to distinguish between the mandible of an ape and that of a man! He had written a letter on the Piltdown question to Schwalbe. After Schwalbe's death, all his correspondence had been sent to Elliot Smith and, among this, Elliot Smith found the letter from Duckworth on Piltdown. Apparently, Elliot Smith considered that Duckworth had had no right to say what he did and he seems never to have forgiven Duckworth for this.

If his memory was not at fault, it is interesting to contemplate the possibility that Duckworth's suspicions might have been aroused when he first examined the

Piltdown remains[7], even though he tended to accept them when he spoke at the famous meeting of the Geological Society in December 1912. Did he give expression to his doubts in the letter to Schwalbe?

The discussions with Dr Louis S B Leakey, during the course of my visits to Nairobi between 1957 and 1972, frequently came around to Piltdown and his conviction that Teilhard de Chardin had been the forger, although his "evidence" was circumstantial. It is interesting to note, however, that in the second volume of his autobiography, *By the Evidence* (1974), Leakey himself makes no reference to Teilhard, though he discusses the forgery and the "forgers". He accepts that Charles Dawson was "one of the parties to the practical joke" and adds only the following:

> The other man, I suspect, dared not accept responsibility for revealing what had been done when the corroboration for his partner was no longer available [through Dawson's death in August 1916]. I imagine that this second person was the one who had acquired the various fragmentary fossils from North Africa and America, and was also the one whose knowledge of chemistry was sufficiently adept to enable him to undertake the necessary work to make the specimens look like fossils.[8]

On more than one occasion, Leakey recited to me his circumstantial reasons for suspecting Teilhard, and he told of a conversation he had with Teilhard in New York City, some time between the exposure of the hoax in 1953 and Teilhard's death on 10 April 1955. When Leakey asked Teilhard what he thought of Weiner's published claim that Dawson had perpetrated the fraud, Louis reported that Teilhard said, "I know who did the Piltdown hoax and it was not Charles Dawson". Teilhard gave a little smile, according to Louis, and said no more on the subject. As mentioned also by Cole,[9] Leakey told me that he wanted to publish a book on the Piltdown story, in which he would "expose" Teilhard's supposed role in the fraud, but Mary Leakey was present during this conversation and she immediately said, "O don't, Louis! You'll only make enemies . . ." and Louis said no more on the subject!

Early in April 1984, I received a telephone call from Ian Langham (Department of History at the University of Sydney), followed up by a letter on 26 April 1984. He wished to visit me on his way back to Australia and he wrote:

> My current research projects are (1) a biographical work on Sir Arthur Keith; (2) a revaluation of the events surrounding the Piltdown forgery. Project (2) is the thing that is burning a hole in my brain at present, as I have amassed evidence relating to the culpability question which is, I believe, an order of magnitude "harder" and less circumstantial than anything that anyone else has managed to come up with so far. And before I bring the wrath of God down upon myself by publishing it, I would like to first check it out with the *cognoscenti*.

So it came about that Langham and I spent Thursday, 24 May 1984, in a 7–8 hours' conversation on Piltdown and related matters. During this "chat" Ian divulged his theory as to the identity of the scientist-member of the two-team of forgers he was postulating. It struck me that as far as I knew this was about the only one of all the "Piltdown men" who had not so far been incriminated. I subjected his proposal to stringent criticism, on the one hand, and enthusiastic encouragement on the other. I drew attention to the dangers inherent in a two-person theory: each could have betrayed the other and the great man would have exposed himself to an enormous danger. "And", I speculated, "would there not have been more passing reference in some letter or diary entry, by one or the other?" I urged him of the importance of continuing with his researches and of writing up the fruits of his labours on original unpublished archival material in London, including the Keith papers.

As I was convinced that the acceptance of Piltdown by leading figures in British anthropology had played a major part in delaying the acceptance of Dart's (1925) claims for the Taung child, I invited Langham to attend the international symposium which was to take place early in 1985, on the 60th anniversary of the announcement of the discovery of *Australopithecus africanus*. Langham's subsequent letter to me, dated 31 May 1984, after his return to Australia, intimated he would be delighted to give a paper on "the history of hominid studies, with special reference to Piltdown and how it caused the African finds to be misinterpreted". He added:

> My Piltdown revelations should have appeared in print by then and I imagine that your Symposium would represent an unequalled opportunity to get oral feedback from the leading practitioners of the discipline.

In a subsequent letter to me, Ian, unable to raise the air fare, had to withdraw from the Taung Jubilee Symposium. He agreed on the difficulties I had raised about the two-man team of forgers and wrote:

> Actually I think I can show that the dynamics of the two-man system *were* unstable, and very nearly led to one man giving the game away.

In the same letter a few alarm signals appeared:

> I feel wretched about doing this [withdrawing from the Taung meeting] . . . My writing up of the Piltdown article has been going falteringly . . . [and] . . . this is being written under conditions of stress.

It was the last letter I received from him. His tragic death occurred on 29 July 1984.

Nearly a year later I received letters from Mrs Kathryn Langham, Dr Peter Cochrane and Dr Tim Murray, asking my view on their choice of Dr Frank Spencer of Queens College of the City University of New York, to bring Ian Langham's researches on the Piltdown forgery to completion.

Having known and admired Frank Spencer's (1979) two-volume study on Aleš Hrdlička and his other writings on the history of physical anthropology, I had no hesitation whatever in replying that Mrs Langham and Ian's colleagues could not have chosen a more reliable, conscientious and scholarly person than Spencer to develop, write up and publish Ian's unfinished tale. Moreover, Mrs Langham gave me permission to pass on to Dr Spencer the correspondence that had passed between her late husband and myself.

The book which has emerged from the pen of Frank Spencer is undoubtedly a most comprehensive and scholarly study of the subject. From his own researches on the Piltdown papers in the British Museum (Natural History), on the Keith Papers in the Royal College of Surgeons and on other original sources, Spencer has produced a penetrating study of Piltdown as an episode in the history of science, and has enabled us to see the events centred around Piltdown in an historical and philosophical perspective.

The Piltdown history shows that it was the sheer weight of newly-discovered evidence that made it utterly impossible to sustain the Piltdown *paradigm* after 1950 and led to its replacement. The hoax could succeed in hoodwinking and convincing many scientists in 1912, before Africa had thrown its ancient hominid fossil surprises into the melting pot, but it had become untenable by 1950 when men like Sir Wilfrid

Le Gros Clark had come finally to accept the hominid status of the australopithecine fossils from South Africa. It was against this background that Joe Weiner came up with the hypothesis that a forgery had been effected. As J Bronowski and others have pointed out, the assumption of truthfulness in science is the very leitmotif, almost the religion, of the scientist. We may think our colleagues have been mistaken, foolish, ignorant, ill-advised, pig-headed or simple minded, but the very last thing we tend to suspect them of is dishonesty.

For the last 37 years, ever since the uncovering of the hoax, amateur and professional sleuths have sought with diligence to expose the guilty party or parties. One of those who scoured the original sources for evidence, and did so probably more thoroughly than had ever before been done — was Ian Langham; and it was he who came up with the newest, the most surprising, nay, shocking, and the most seemingly logical conclusion as to the identity of the scientist-member of the team of forgers. Dr Spencer has done full justice to the work and reasoning of the late Dr Langham in presenting his brief on the hoaxer's identity. With typical thoroughness, Spencer has reworked all the original source material over a number of years, so that his presentation of Langham's theory in the final chapter is informed by his own researches and reasoning.

We do not know exactly how Ian Langham would have developed and presented his brief on the Piltdown *affaire*, but I cannot help believing he would have enthusiastically approved of the critical, objective yet supportive treatment that has been accorded by Dr Spencer, as reflected in Chapter 8 of this work.

The discipline of physical anthropology owes a great debt of gratitude to Dr Frank Spencer. He has produced a deeply analytical, wondrously satisfying and eminently readable work on an episode in the history of palaeoanthropology. Not only that, but he has furnished countless insights into aspects of the scientific process, as exemplified by the activities of those who devoted a staggering amount of time in the first half of this century to the forlorn attempt to place Piltdown into the scheme of human evolution. Finally he leads us to the historical inevitability that, as Geoffrey Chaucer wrote half a millenium ago, ''Murder will out''.

NOTES

[1] Tobias, P V (1954). The very ancient human inhabitants of Africa. *In*: R A Dart (Ed), *Africa's Place in the Human Story*. Johannesburg, S Afr Broadcasting Corp. pp. 23–26.

[2] We should of course remember William K Gregory's (1914) comment, made *en passant*, that it had been suspected by some that the Piltdown bones might represent a deliberate hoax ''to fool the scientists''. However, when stating this view, presumably for sake of completeness, Gregory dissociated himself from it ''in view of the circumstances of the discovery''. (see Chapter 7).

[3] ''Science and the Skull''. Letter from A W Baker to the Editor, *Rand Daily Mail* (Johannesburg) 2 March 1925.

[4] See Oakley & Groves (1970).

[5] See fn 37, Chapter 5.

[6] K P Oakley (1979). Suspicions about Piltdown man. *New Scientist*: p 1014. 21 June.

[7] As indicated in the present volume and the companion volume, *The Piltdown Papers* (Spencer 1990), there is no documentary evidence to support Duckworth's statement that he had viewed the specimens prior to the celebrated meeting at Burlington house on 18 December 1912. While the date of his examination of the originals remains uncertain it is clear from his communication with Woodward in June 1913 that not only was he experiencing some problems in his study of the Piltdown jaw but that he was also at this time in contact with Schwalbe (see Spencer 1990: 2.2.16 and 2.3.17).

[8] L S B Leakey (1974). *By the Evidence. Memoirs, 1932–1951*. New York. See page 23.

[9] See Cole (1975).

Preface

Following the exposure of the Piltdown forgery in 1953, a thorough investigation to determine the identity of the perpetrator(s) was undertaken by Joseph S Weiner of Oxford University (who had been largely responsible for bringing the forgery to light), assisted by Kenneth P Oakley and other staff members of the Department of Geology at the British Museum (Natural History) in South Kensington, London. The results of this inquiry were later summarized in Weiner's book *The Piltdown Forgery*, published in 1955. Although favourably inclined to the hypothesis that Charles Dawson, the principal discoverer at Piltdown, had been the perpetrator, Weiner admitted that the case against him was based largely on suspicion rather than positive and final proof. Yet, in spite of this, it was difficult to imagine that this complex deception, involving as it did a series of "discoveries" made between 1912 and 1915, could have been accomplished without Dawson's involvement. As Weiner acknowledged, there was the remote possibility that Dawson had either been duped, the innocent victim of an elaborate prank, or that he had been merely the passive instrument of a "shadow figure", who besides being the mastermind of the entire operation, might also have exerted some influence over Dawson. This latter idea was not without its attractions, and as Weiner's Piltdown notes and correspondence clearly reveal, he had, over the years prior to his death in 1982, pursued several lines of inquiry in an effort to establish such a case. Unable to demonstrate either a definite link between Dawson and any of the individuals he had targeted as possible candidates for the role of "shadow figure", or muster any reliable evidence that supported the "dupe" hypothesis, Weiner ultimately returned to his former position, namely that Dawson had acted alone. "We have tried to provide exculpatory interpretations of his entanglements in these events", he wrote in 1955:

> What emerges, however, is that it is not possible to maintain that Dawson could not have been the actual perpetrator; he had the ability, the experience, and whatever we surmise may have been the motive, he was at all material times in a position to pursue the deception throughout its various phrases. For anyone else to have played this complicated role is to raise a veritable Hyde to Dawson's Jekyll. Complementary, also, to the difficulty of excluding Dawson from the authorship — there is nothing that will serve to do this — is the difficulty of accepting his known activities as compatible with a complete unawareness of the real state of affairs.

Although during Weiner's lifetime there had been a string of attempts to place the blame elsewhere, the plausibility of these various cases had, without exception, been flawed by a palpable lack of supporting evidence and/or knowledge of events. Contrary to expectations, surprisingly few Piltdown sleuths had bothered to wade through the entire Piltdown archive at the British Museum (Natural History). One notable exception, however, was the late Dr Ian Langham, a senior lecturer in the history and philosophy of science at Sydney University, Australia.

Dr Langham's particular interest in the Piltdown affair had been prompted in part by the appearance of Ronald Millar's book *The Piltdown Men* which presented a highly contentious case against the Australian anatomist Sir Grafton Elliot Smith. When Millar's book appeared in the early 1970s, Langham was a Joseph Henry Fellow in the

History of Science at Princeton University, working on his doctoral thesis (completed in 1976). This work was expanded and revised for publication in 1981 under the title: *The Building of British Social Anthropology: W H R Rivers and his Cambridge Disciples in the Development of Kinship Studies, 1898–1931*. Besides being the first detailed and archivally based analysis of the early history of British social anthropology, Langham's book also included a comprehensive discussion of the school of cultural diffusionism and the role played by Elliot Smith in its popularization. Evidently, it was in the context of this concern with Smith's anthropology that Langham became intrigued by Millar's thesis that the Australian born anatomist had perpetrated the Piltdown hoax. Langham's subsequent researches at the British Museum (Natural History) in the early 1980s, however, quickly led him to abandon his own ingenious case against Smith (published in 1978).

While immersing himself in the Piltdown archives, Langham began looking for other archival resources in an attempt to grasp a more complete picture of the episode. Cognisant of Sir Arthur Keith's active participation in the Piltdown controversy, he had made a careful search of this worker's private and professional papers housed in the Library of the Royal College of Surgeons in London. Although Keith had destroyed much of his Piltdown related correspondence, his personal and professional diaries remained intact; it was here that Langham found evidence which viewed after his extensive archival researches at the South Kensington Museum cast a completely different light on both Keith and the entire Piltdown episode. At this time, however, Langham had several other projects brewing and had to decide whether to publish his findings immediately or to wait until he had more time to write a comprehensive account of the forgery, based on his work at the Royal College of Surgeons and the British Museum (Natural History), as a vehicle for his solution. He opted for the latter course. It was then, in 1983, that I arrived at the Royal College armed with a grant from the Wenner-Gren Foundation to work on the Keith papers.

My interest in the Keith papers dated back to the mid-1970s when I had examined them as part of my doctoral research on the life and work of the American physical anthropologist Aleš Hrdlička. Since Hrdlička had devoted a considerable amount of time and ink to the Piltdown problem, and remained convinced that the Piltdown cranial fragments had no business with the apelike jaw that had reportedly been found with them, I was naturally intrigued to know more about how Hrdlička's view had been received by his British counterparts, and especially Keith, with whom the American had a longstanding professional relationship. Of particular interest to me was Hrdlička's inquiry (dated 28 October 1912) of Keith regarding rumours of this discovery which had begun circulating some months before (see Spencer 1990: 1.2.16). Like Hrdlička, I was puzzled by Keith's tardy reply (dated 23 December 1912) and his admission that he had not been allowed to examine the remains until they were shown to the Geological Society of London at Burlington House on 18 December 1912. Yet, as Keith's diaries reveal, he had visited the South Kensington Museum to view the remains on at least two occasions before they were made public. Although this knowledge (among other things) served to further advance my nascent suspicions regarding Keith's culpability in the Piltdown episode, the full significance of what I had seen at the Royal College in the summer of 1976 remained obscured by a lack of precise knowledge of related events, documented in the archives of the British Museum (Natural History).

On hearing of my plan to work on the Keith papers, and knowing of my past interest in the Piltdown affair, Langham was obviously concerned that I might "beat [him] to the punch." While Piltdown and the question of the forger's identity was indeed an underlying motive for my presence at the Royal College, it was not, as

Langham learned, my sole purpose. Hence, under the impression that Ian's work on Piltdown was near to publication, it seemed both reasonable and logical for me to leave this matter in his capable hands while I continued with the task of cataloguing and organizing the Keith collection, and to advancing my knowledge of Keith's work in human palaeontology and his relationship with Hrdlička and other Anglo-American contemporaries.

The following year, in the summer of 1984, Ian Langham tragically died in Sydney. Soon thereafter his colleagues at the University of Sydney, Drs Peter Cochrane and Tim Murray, invited me to Sydney to discuss the prospect of my salvaging Ian's work and bringing his solution to the Piltdown forgery to light. Although aware of whom Ian considered responsible I was, to say the least, curious to know specifically what he had found (other than the provocative enteries in Keith's diaries I had seen earlier) and how he had orchestrated his belief. Unfortunately Ian had not at the time of his death formally committed his case to paper. Thus, in the absence of a manuscript and any synthetic notes, the full significance of the "evidence" documented in his Piltdown related papers was not immediately apparent. As a consequence I was initially faced with the task of retracing his footsteps in order to evaluate and understand precisely what it was that he had found. To this end I requested, and promptly received permission from the British Museum (Natural History) for their Piltdown archive to be microfilmed in order that I might study these documents in New York, and compare this body of data with what Langham had extracted from it, since much of the primary material I subsequently received from the University of Sydney had been drawn predominantly from this source. From the perspective of this protracted study I was then able, at last, to grasp not only the significance of what I had seen in 1976 (and subsequently), but more importantly the full meaning of Ian's notes and collected materials. A reconstruction of his brief is presented in the last chapter: "Beyond a Reasonable Doubt?"

It is clear from the extensive materials Langham had collected that he had intended to write a substantial history of the Piltdown affair. Thus, in undertaking this project, my aim has been not only to do justice to this intended goal, but also (if possible) to dispose once and for all of much of the confusion, as well as some of the myths that have been over the years accumulating around the entire affair. To this end, in collaboration with the British Museum (Natural History), it was decided to write and publish the present narrative simultaneously with a volume entitled *The Piltdown Papers*, the latter being an annotated selection of the primary correspondence and other documents relating to the history of the Piltdown affair.

The present work is divided into eight chapters, the first six of which document the history of the entire episode from the unveiling in 1912 through to 1953 when the forgery was finally detected. Although the organization and content of these chapters is self-evident, there are several points I feel compelled to mention. Recognizing that not everyone who will read this book will be familiar with the state of palaeo-anthropology at the beginning of the twentieth century, the first chapter endeavours to fill this gap — but I hasten to add that it does not pretend to be a definitive account of late nineteenth century palaeoanthropological method and theory. At the same time as introducing the nonspecialist reader to terms and concepts current to the period, this chapter also serves to provide insights into the theoretical expectations that had spawned and nurtured the Piltdown forgery. Hence the somewhat biased focus of this introductory overview.

The next five chapters present an impartial account of events as they unfolded, with a view to understanding the history of the Piltdown remains as normal scientific activity. There are several reasons for taking this tack. In the first place it is important not to lose sight of the obvious fact that until 1953, the Piltdown remains, while subject to various and conflicting interpretations, were generally viewed as genuine fossils. Hence rather than confuse this narrative with the forgery subplot, the events from 1912 through to 1953 are presented in strict chronological order, and from the perspective of the time period under consideration – thereby providing the reader with a clear view of the issues involved. At the same time as establishing a more secure position from which to judge subsequent propositions regarding the identity of the forger(s), this narrative permits the reader to understand more clearly the scientific arguments that led so many reputable scientists to endorse the now seemingly ludricous marriage of an orangutan mandible to a palpably modern human braincase. This approach also allows for the introduction of important insights into the inner dynamics of the Piltdown debate, which as will be seen in the last chapter are vital to understanding Langham's brief. And what is crucial here is the conjectural recognition that the forgery was not a practical joke that got out of hand, but rather one that had been tailored to withstand scientific scrutiny and thereby promote a particular interpretation of the human fossil record.

Given the particular focus of this historical narrative and the fact that it stops abruptly with the debunking of the Piltdown remains in 1953, the nonspecialist reader might infer from Chapter Five that everything thereafter was suddenly sweetness and light in palaeoanthropology. While there is little question that the removal of Piltdown set the stage for a major revision of human phylogeny (particularly with regard to the evolutionary expectations of the ancestral forms of the human lineage), it would be misleading to suppose that its departure resolved all of the problems attending the interpretation of the human fossil record as it stood in 1953. Furthermore, since 1953 there have been numerous, as well as often startling additions to the human fossil record, particularly from Africa, where it is now possible to document the broad evolutionary contours of the human lineage from its precursorial australopithecine stage through to a pithecanthropine-like phase, on to the emergence of anatomically modern humans. Although there is still considerable disagreement among specialists regarding the question of how the existing fossils of the australopithecines should be arranged (i.e. their phylogenetic relationship to one another and later hominid forms), there appears to be a general agreement (in the absence of a similar grade represented in either the European or Asian fossil assemblages) that the human lineage originated in Africa during the early Pliocene. But while there might well be a nascent consensus regarding this aspect of the human evolutionary scenario the same cannot be said of subsequent events leading to the emergence of the modern human form.

At the risk of oversimplifying a complex and ongoing debate, workers operating on this front separate into two distinct camps: those who favour the view that the modern human form sprung essentially from a single geographic source, namely Africa, versus those who argue that this transition occurred at different times and in different regions of the Old World. Where the former position contends that resident archaic hominid *Homo sapiens* in Europe and Asia were replaced by itinerant African populations (for which incidentally there is no direct evidence; indeed the cultural record from this period is surprisingly homogenous and gives no hint of an abrupt behavioural change in either Europe or Asia), the latter camp argues that the Pleistocene fossil record manifests a trend toward increasing morphological differentiation along geographic lines. Accordingly, in Africa, as in Europe and Asia, anatomically modern humans are said to have emerged independently from residential precursors. But until the scales are tipped by new and more compelling evidence the relative merits of these two divergent arguments must remain largely a matter of personal opinion.

Although, as noted in the fifth chapter, the period between the two World Wars witnessed the discovery of several important human fossils which contributed to the changing theoretical ethos of human palaeontology, it is contended that the recovery of the human cranial remains at Swanscombe, in Kent, England, by Alvan T Marston in 1935–6, and his subsequent attempts to equate this find with those at Piltdown had in fact been the prime mover in the eventual collapse of the Piltdown fraud. Indeed, had it not been for Marston's continuing agitations, it is conjectured that Kenneth Oakley might not have acted as quickly as he did to apply the fluorine dating technique first to the Galley Hill skeleton and then to Piltdown. While not wishing to detract from the importance of Oakley's contribution to the Piltdown solution, it is evident that over the years Weiner's critical role in the events of 1953 has been overshadowed by the utility of Oakley's work on the application of the fluorine technique. Chapter Six endeavours to adjust this view.

The accuracy of this historical reconstruction can be readily checked by consulting the primary archival materials presented in *The Piltdown Papers*. With this in mind, the chapter notes (located at the end of the book, pp 209–40), indicate where in *The Piltdown Papers* volume cited primary archival material can be located. For example, Joseph Weiner's transcript of the interview with Sir Arthur Keith on 21 November 1953, is cited as Spencer (1990: 6.3.5): The first number appearing after 1990 refers to the sixth section of the catalogue; while the second denotes the third subsection, and the last number indicates where the document appears in the subsection series. To further assist the reader in this regard I have supplied both works with a complimentary separate name and subject indexes. I have also made rather liberal use of the chapter notes not only to supply further background information but also, where indicated, appropriate subtextual commentaries on events or subjects under discussion. While many of these endnotes, particularly in the first six chapters, will, I am sure be of only peripheral interest to the nonspecialist reader, the same cannot be said for the remaining two chapters which deal with the intriguing subject of the forger(s).

The new solution presented in Chapter Eight is based largely on my reading of Ian Langham's surviving notes and materials, and it is evident from these papers that he too did not subscribe to the opinion that the forgery had been a malicious prank, but rather that it had been conceived and orchestrated with the specific intention of manipulating scientific opinion. Although every effort has been made to do justice to his brief, it must be stressed that no one knows how he ultimately intended to make his case. Hence for this reason I take full responsibility for the final synthesis presented here. While acknowledging that it is controversial and that there are some *possible* weaknesses particularly with regard to the evidence used to establish a pre-1912 connection between Keith and Dawson, I nevertheless believe the case not only hangs together and compliments known collateral facts and events, but it also makes considerable sense of both Keith's and Dawson's otherwise generally inexplicable behaviour during the height of the Piltdown controversy. In contrast to earlier attempts to establish the identity and responsibility for the forgery, it is contended that Langham's brief is firmly grounded in a body of direct and circumstantial evidence. However, the overriding question here is does this body of evidence prove guilt beyond a reasonable doubt? While I believe it does, it is for the reader to decide; and in reaching a verdict the reader is obliged to consider first, if the circumstances of the case have been satisfactorily established, and second, if the inferences drawn therefrom are consistent not only with the guilt of the parties involved but also inconsistent with their innocence.

ACKNOWLEDGEMENTS

For bringing this aspect of the Piltdown project to completion my sincere thanks go to Mrs Kathryn Langham for allowing me unrestricted access to her late husband's Piltdown related papers and her trust. I also thank Dr Peter Cochrane (Department of History, University of Sydney) and Dr Tim Murray (now of the Department of Anthropology, La Trobe University), who served as advisers to both Mrs Langham and the University of Sydney. In addition I would like to take this opportunity to thank the University of Sydney itself, and the many people (some of whom are listed below) who had assisted Ian Langham in his Piltdown researches.

Since much of the work on this narrative was intimately bound up with the preparation of *The Piltdown Papers*, it is necessary to repeat my thanks to a number of people from whom I received information and assistance (plus several others not mentioned in this latter work). They include: Ms Elizabeth Allen (Hunterian Museum, Royal College of Surgeons), Ms Stella Bellem (Curator, Bexhill Museum); Dr Ian Carmichael (City University of New York); Mr Eustace Cornelius (former Librarian, Royal College of Surgeons); Mr Geoffrey T Denton (Uckfield, Sussex); Mr K W Dickins (Archivist, Sussex Archaeological Society); Ms Gill Furlong (Archivist, Library, University College London); Professor Edgar Gregersen (Queens College of the City University of New York); Professor J de Heinzelin (Institut Royal des Sciences Naturelles de Belgique, Bruxelles); Dr Robin Harvey (Lincoln, England); Professor G Ainsworth Harrison (Oxford University); Mrs Margaret Hodgson (Canterbury, Kent); Dr Douglas Brandon-Jones (Hampstead, London); Mrs Robin Kenward (Piltdown, Sussex); Dr Jeffrey T Laitman (Mount Sinai School of Medicine, New York); Mr John Lynch (BBC London); Ms Monica McCullum (University of Melbourne); Dr Lawrence Martin (State University of New York, Stony Brook); Mr Giles Oakley (London); Mr Peter Ambrose Orchard (Otham, Kent); Dr Stanley S Raphael (Windsor, Ontario); Dr David B Scott (Sun City, Arizona); Dr Sydel Silverman (Wenner-Gren Foundation for Anthropological Research Inc., New York); Professor Fred H Smith (Northern Illinois University); Mr and Mrs Frank Spencer Snr (Rochester, Kent); Mr James Spirrell (Queens, New York); Professor Phillip V Tobias (University of the Witwatersrand, Johannesburg); Sig Franco Vivarelli (Livorno, Italia); Professor Sherwood L Washburn (University of California, Berkeley); Professor Richard G West (Cambridge University); and Mr Lionel Woodhead (Brighton, Sussex).

My thanks also go to Mrs Suzanne Katz and Ms Marianne Conti (interlibrary loan service) of the Rosenthal Library at Queens College CUNY for their ungrudging assistance in locating some of the more obscure publications I needed to consult.

I also take great pleasure in conveying my sincere gratitude to the numerous people at the British Museum (Natural History) who have assisted me over the past four years. In particular I would like to thank several members of the Department of Palaeontology, namely the former Keeper, William Ball and his successor Robin Cocks, as well as, Theya Molleson, Chris Stringer, Peter Andrews, and Robert Kruszynski. I am also greatly indebted to Ann Lum of the Palaeontology/Mineralogy Library for her patience and willingness to share with me her extensive knowledge of the Museum's Piltdown archive. And in the Museum's publication department special thanks must go to Myra Givans and her staff for their enthusiastic editorial assistance.

Last, but by no means least, I thank my wife Elena for her unfailing support and committment to this protracted project. Had it not been for her patience and assistance this book would certainly never have been completed.

Illustrations, unless otherwise stated are from the archives of the Palaeontology/ Mineralogy Library, British Museum (Natural History).

Frank Spencer
New York, April 1990

Dramatis Personae

The following is a list of major and some minor characters mentioned in the Piltdown narrative, arranged in alphabetical order for convenience of reference. The numeral in parentheses after each name indicates individual's age in 1912. The chapter of the narrative in which the listed individual is first mentioned is given in brackets at the end of each entry. For more complete biographical information, see appended references.

Abbott, William James Lewis (59): an early supporter and close associate of Benjamin Harrison of Ightham. In addition to conducting archaeological research in the Home Counties, Abbott had considerable influence on the early activities of several leading amateur scientists, most notably Alfred Kennard [1]. See *The Times* (12 August 1933; *Proc Geol Soc Lond* (1934) **90**: 50–1; Kennard (1947); Blinderman (1986: 192–218).

Barlow, Frank Orwell (32): technical assistant in the Department of Geology at the British Museum (Natural History), South Kensington. Barlow was responsible for preparing plaster replicas of the Piltdown skull as restored under Arthur Smith Woodward's direction. These replicas were later distributed by the R F Damon Company of Weymouth, of which Barlow was a partner [2]. See *Man* (1952) No 102.

Black, Davidson (28): Canadian anatomist. During a sabbatical leave from Case Western University in 1914 Black had assisted Dawson and Woodward at Piltdown. Later in 1919 Black secured a position at the Peking Union Medical College in China where he was intimately involved in the excavations at Choukoutien [4]. See Hood (1964) and Spencer (1979).

Boswell, Percy G H (26): professor of geology at Liverpool University from 1917 to 1929. Prior to obtaining a First Class B.Sc (External) at London University in 1912, Boswell taught at the Technical School in Ipswich where be began his researches into the stratigraphy of the Pliocene of Essex and Suffolk. During this time he had been a close associate of Reid Moir [1]. See *Biogr Mem Roy Soc Lond* (1961) **7**: 17–29.

Boucher de [Crévecouer de] Perthes, Jacques (d. 1868): former French diplomat and antiquarian. His archaeological studies in the Somme river valley during the 1840s and 1850s were largely responsible for establishing the fact that human beings had once coexisted with extinct mammalia [1]. See Grayson (1983) and Cohen & Hublin (1989).

Boule, Marcellin (51): French palaeontologist. An opponent of eolithic theory as well as an early critic of Woodward's interpretation of the Piltdown remains [1]. See *Man* (1943) No 24: 42–3 and Hammon (1982).

Breuil, Henri (35): French prehistoric archaeologist (and ordained priest), stationed at the Muséum National d'Histoire Naturelle from 1910 and at the Collège de France from 1929 to 1947 [4]. See Broderick (1963).

Broom, Robert (46): South African (b. Scotland) anatomist and palaeontologist. In addition to being an early and lasting supporter of Dart's interpretation of the Taung fossil, Broom remained loyal to Woodward's monistic restoration of the Piltdown remains [5]. See *S Afr J Sci* (1953) **48**: 3–19.

Burne, Richard H (44): Keith's assistant at the Royal College of Surgeons [8]. See *Obit Not Fellows Roy Soc Lond* (1954) **9**: 27–32; Cope (1959: 297).

Butterfield, William Ruskin (40): from 1909 through to the mid 1930s, Butterfield was Librarian of the Hastings Public Museum and Library. In this capacity he was on familiar terms with a number of local scientists linked with the Piltdown controversy. In particular, Charles Dawson and Lewis Abbot [6]. See *Hastings & E Sussex Nat* (1935) **5**: 57–61.

Clark, Wilfrid Edward Le Gros (17): British anatomist. From 1919 to 1924 he held the chair of anatomy at St Bartholomew's Hospital Medical College, whereupon he succeeded his former mentor F G Parsons at St Thomas'. Four years later he moved to the chair of anatomy in Oxford, in succession to Arthur Thomson (1861–1933). Clark's scientific interest lay primarily in comparative primate anatomy and phylogeny. After the war Clark became an enthusiastic supporter of Dart's views on the phylogenetic significance of the South African Australopithecines, and it was largely in this context that he resurrected a lapsed Readership in physical anthropology at Oxford — a move which brought Joseph Weiner from Johannesburg to Clark's department in late 1940s [5]. See *Biogr Mem Fellows Roy Soc Lond* (1973) **19**: 217–33.

Corner, Frank (50): London physician. An associate of Benjamin Harrison's Ightham Circle of eolithophiles [1]. See *Nature* (1939) **143**: 53.

Cunnington, William (d. 1906): a well-known English fossil collector. In the late 1890s he became an energetic critic of the British eolithic movement [1].

Dart, Raymond (19): professor of anatomy, University of the Witwatersrand, Johannesburg. Dart was responsible for describing the first Australopithecine fossil found in 1924 [5]. See Tobias (1984).

Dawkins, William Boyd (75): first professor of geology at Owens College [Manchester University] from 1874 to 1908, and confidant of his former student Arthur Smith Woodward. In addition to harbouring a deep scepticism of Darwinism, Dawkins was a fierce opponent of the British eolithic movement [1]. See *Proc Roy Soc Lond* **107**: xxiii–xxvi.

Dawson, Charles (48): the principal discoverer of the Piltdown remains. Dawson was a practising solicitor in Uckfield, Sussex where he held several public appointments. His primary scientific interests were in geology and archaeology [2]. See *Geol Mag* (1916) **3**: 477–9.

Doyle, Arthur Conan (53): physician and novelist. Practiced medicine from 1882 until 1890, whereupon he devoted himself full-time to his literary pursuits. Although a member of the Sussex Archaeological Society, Doyle's interests and knowledge of Wealden prehistory appears to have been rather superficial [6]. See Charles Dawson's pre-1912 correspondence in Spencer (1990).

Dubois, Eugène (54): Dutch physician who discovered, in Central Java in the early 1890s, the remains of an early hominid form which he claimed was a transitional form between man and ape [2]. See Theunisson (1989); *Nature* (1941) **147**: 473; *Man* (1944) **44**: 76.

Duckworth, Wynfrid Laurence Henry (42): Cambridge anatomist and physical anthropologist. A close friend and supporter of Arthur Keith [2]. See *Nature* (1956) [March] pp 505–6.

Edmunds, Francis H (19): British geologist attached to the Geological Survey. In the mid 1920s, while surveying the Wealden district, Edmunds determined that the elevation of the Piltdown gravel terrace was below 50ft, and not at the 100ft level as previously estimated. This piece of information later became a critical factor in evaluating the results of Kenneth Oakley's flourine tests on the Piltdown remains [5].

Evans, John (d. 1908): English antiquarian and numismatist. Along with Joseph Prestwich in 1859 he had played a central role in the establishment of human antiquity. Later, be became a leading antagonist of the British eolithic movement [1]. See Evans (1943).

Fraipont, Julien (d. 1910): a Belgian anatomist who described the Spy skeletons found in the mid 1880s, and thereby recognized that the Neanderthals represented a distinct Upper Palaeolithic population [1].

Geikie, James (73): Scottish geologist, and brother of Archibald Geikie who was former director-general of the Geological Survey of the United Kingdom (1882–1901). In addition to being an early supporter of eolithic theory, James Geikie was also responsible for popularising the idea that the Glacial Epoch [Pleistocene] had involved four major glacial advances punctuated by three mild inter-glacial periods [1]. See *Geol Mag* (1913) **10**: 241–8; *Geol Mag* (1915) [April] p 192.

Gregory, William King (36): vertebrate palaeontologist at the American Museum of Natural History and Henry Fairfield Osborn's "fidus Achates". Although initially supporting Gerrit Miller's dualist interpretation of the Piltdown remains, like Osborn he too eventually abandoned this position [4]. See *[U.S.] Nat Acad Sci. Biogr Mem* (1975) **46**: 91–133.

Harrison, Benjamin (75): British antiquarian and eolithophile. With the support of Joseph Prestwich he became a leading figure in the British eolithic movement during the last decades of the nineteenth century [1]. See Harrison (1928).

Haward, Frederick [James Nairn] (41): a mechanical engineer by training and a founding member of the Prehistoric Society of East Anglia. He was a close friend of Samuel H Warren with whom he shared a healthy scepticism of eolithic theory. See *Proc Geol Assoc (Lond)* (1954) **65**: 88–9.

Hinton, Martin A C (29): prior to his appointment as Deputy Keeper in the Department of Zoology at the British Museum (Natural History) in 1921, Hinton had been a volunteer worker specializing in fossil rodents. He also had a peripheral interest in archaeology and human palaeontology, and early in his career had done some important and collaborative work in this area with Alfred S. Kennard [4]. See *Biogr Mem Fellows Roy Soc Lond* (1963) pp 155–70.

Hrdlička, Aleš (43): Curator of physical anthropology at the U.S. National Museum of Natural History (Smithsonian Institution), Washington D.C. Like his associate in the Department of Mammals, Gerrit S. Miller, Hrdlička was strongly opposed to Woodward's monistic interpretation of the Piltdown remains [4]. See *Amer J Phys Anthropol* (1940) **26**: 3–40; *Nature* (1943) **152**: 349.

Huxley, Thomas Henry (d. 1895): a dominant figure in British science during the second half of the nineteenth century. Among other things he played an important role in the popularisation of Darwin's evolutionary thesis [1]. See *Fort Rev* (1895) **58**: 313–16; 317–22; *North Amer Rev* (1895) **161**: 279–86; *Nat Sci* (1895) **7**: 121–5; *Geol Mag* (1895) pp 337–41; *Nineteenth Cent* (1896) **40**: 274–92.

Jones, Thomas Rupert (d. 1911): a geologist and early supporter of the British eolithic movement [1]. See *Quart J Geol Soc Lond* (1912) **68**: lviii–lxi.

Keith, Arthur (46): anatomist and leading supporter of Tertiary Man in Britain. Prior to his appointment as conservator of the Hunterian Museum of the Royal College of Surgeons, Keith had served as demonstrator of anatomy at the London Hospital (1895–1908). He retired (in 1932) to become master of the Buckston Browne Institute, a research facility of the Royal College at Downe, near Farnborough, Kent. He died in 1955 [1]. See *Biogr Mem Fellows Roy Soc Lond* (1955) **I**: 145–62; *J Anat* (1955) **89**: 403–11.

Kennard, Alfred Santer (42): a London businessman and amateur palaeontologist. Although Kennard's particular interest was Pleistocene Mollusca, he was also an avid amateur archaeologist. In addition to a long-standing relationship with Lewis Abbott, with whom he shared an enthusiasm for eolithic theory, Kennard also did important collaborative work with Martin Hinton [1]. See *Quart J Geol Soc Lond* (1948) **104**: lvii–lviii, and *Proc Geol Assoc London* (1949) **60**: 80–1.

Kenward, Mabel (27): the daughter of Robert Kenward who was chief tenant Barkham Manor when the so-called Piltdown skull was found in a gravel pit located on this estate [7]. See Spencer (1990).

Lankester, Edwin Ray (65): in addition to being a former occupant of the chair of zoology at University College, London (1882–90), followed by the Linacre chair of comparative anatomy at Oxford (1890–8), Lankester had been Director of the British Museum and Keeper of Zoology at South Kensington from 1898 until his retirement in 1907. He was an early champion of Reid Moir's primordial flints and Woodward's interpretation of the Piltdown remains. Although an early supporter of the eolithic movement, by the early 1920s his enthusiasm for the great antiquity of these controversial flints was on the wane. See *Nature* (1929) **124**: 309–14, 345–7.

Leakey, Louis S B (b. 1903): an early pioneer in East African human palaeontology. Although a supporter of the idea of the great antiquity of the modern human form, he harboured a rather jaundiced view of the Piltdown remains [5]. See Clark (1976).

Lyne, W Courtney (d. 1949): practising dentist who endeavoured to discredit the canine tooth discovered at Piltdown in 1913 [4].

MacCurdy, George Grant (49): physical anthropologist at Yale University and close associate at Hrdlicka's. MacCurdy was an early supporter of Gerrit Miller's dualist interpretation of the Piltdown remains [4].

Marriott, Reginald A (55): a retired army Major living in Lewes, Sussex who devoted much of his sparetime to Wealden geology and archaeology. It appears that Marriott enjoyed the friendship of several prominent figures connected with the Piltdown controversy — in particular Charles Dawson and Arthur Keith [6]. See Weiner (1955).

Marston, Alvan T (23): London dentist and amateur archaeologist. His discovery in the mid 1930s of a Middle Pleistocene hominid cranium at Swanscombe set in motion a new phase in the Piltdown controversy [5].

Miller, Gerrit S (43): mammalogist working at the U.S. National Museum of Natural History (Smithsonian Institution), Washington D.C. In 1915 Miller endeavoured to demonstrate that Woodward's reconstruction of the Piltdown skull was erroneous. He claimed the jaw was not human but that of a fossil chimpanzee [4].

Moir, James Reid (33): a businessman from Ipswich, England with a consuming interest in prehistoric archaeology and an avid eolithophile. Among his most influential supporters were Edwin Ray Lankester and Arthur Keith [1]. See *Obit Not Fellows Roy Soc Lond* (1942–4) **4**: 733–45; *Nature* (1944) **153**: 368–9; *Proc Prehist Soc [Cambridge]* (1945) **XI**: 66–8.

Morris, Harry (d. *c.* 1947): an amateur archaeologist and avid eolithophile from Lewes, Sussex. In addition to being a member of the Sussex Archaeological Society, Morris appears to have enjoyed the confidence of Arthur Keith and several other notable scientists of the period. For reasons no longer clear Morris had become convinced that many of the remains found at Piltdown were not authentic, and that Charles Dawson had been responsible for these plants [6].

Mortillet, Gabriel de (d. 1898): a prominent French archaeologist and palaeontologist who was responsible for formalising the concept of an eolithic industry [1].

Newton, Edwin Tulley (72): a palaeontologist, who besides being a supporter of the British eolithic movement, was also responsible for providing the first description and evaluation of the controversial Galley Hill remains in 1895 [1]. See *Nature* (1930) **125**: 280–1.

Oakley, Kenneth P (1): a geologist and palaeontologist, who joined the British Museum (Natural History) in 1935. After World War II, Oakley developed criteria for dating fossils by comparing the fluorine content of modern, subfossil and fossil material of determined age. The development of this technique was crucial to the subsequent solution of the Piltdown problem [5]. Stearn (1981: 236, 244–7).

Osborn, Henry Fairfield (55): American palaeontologist; Director of the American Museum of Natural History, New York. Although initially supporting Gerrit Miller's dualist thesis, Osborn was subsequently persuaded otherwise by the discovery of Piltdown II. See *Geol Mag* (1917) **4**: 193–6; *Quart J Geol Soc Lond* (1936) **92**: xcii–xcv.

Parsons, Frederick Gymer (48): professor of anatomy at St Thomas' Hospital Medical

School during the height of the Piltdown debates (1912–17). It was Parsons who challenged Arthur Keith in 1914 to reconstruct a skull deliberately broken along the lines of the Piltdown cranium [3]. See Keith (1950).

Prestwich, Joseph (d. 1896): a London wine-merchant and geologist. Besides playing a central role in the establishing human antiquity in 1859, Prestwich was also a major figure in the British eolithic movement during the last quarter of the nineteenth century [1]. See G A Prestwich (1899).

Pycraft, William Plane (44): former assistant of Ray Lankester. After Lankester's departure from the British Museum (Natural History) Pycraft remained attached to the Department of Zoology as an osteologist. He appears to have been one of Woodward's main Museum consultants on the Piltdown remains [3]. See *Nature* (1942) **149**: 575; *Proc Lin Soc Lond* (1943) **154**: 293–4.

Reid, Clement (59): a London geologist (attached to the Geological Survey) and critic of the geological interpretation of the Piltdown gravel terrace [1]. See *Quart J Geol Soc Lond* (1917) **73**: lxi–lxiv; *Geol Mag* (1917) **4**: 47–8.

Rutot, A Louis (65): a Belgian geologist and leading advocate on the Continent of eolithic theory [1]. See *Acad Roy Sci Lett Beaux-Arts de Belgique. Annuaire.* (1966) pp 3–123.

St Barbe, Guy: an amateur archaeologist who lived in Uckfield, Sussex when the Piltdown remains were first described. In addition to being an associate of Charles Dawson, St Barbe was a close friend of Major Reginald Marriott of Lewes who was thought to have been an associate of the eolithophile Harry Morris [6].

Schoettensack, Otto (d. 1912): a German geologist (University of Heidelberg) who was responsible for describing and evaluating the hominid jaw found in the Mauer sandpits, near Heidelberg in 1907 [2]. See Kraatz & Querner (1967).

Schwalbe, Gustav (68): professor of anatomy at the University of Strasburg who made an influential study of the human fossil record as it existed at the turn of the century [2]. See *Anat Anz* (1916) **49**: 210–21; Smith (1987).

Seeley, Harry Govier (d. 1909): professor of geology and palaeontology at King's College, London during the last decades of the nineteenth century. In addition to being one of Woodward's mentors at King's, he later became his father-in-law [1]. See *Proc Roy Soc Lond* (1911) **83**: xv–xvii.

Smith, Grafton Elliott (41): British neuroanatomist and anthropologist (b. New South Wales). In 1912, Smith was Professor of anatomy at Manchester University. Later (1919), he moved to University college, London. He was responsible for describing the Piltdown endocranial cast [2]. See *Obit Not Fellows Roy Soc Lond* (1936–38) **2**: 323–33; Dawson (1938).

Smith, Reginald Allender (38): British antiquarian and eolithophile. During the Piltdown period he worked under Charles Hercules Read (1857–1929) in the Department of Ethnology and British Medieval Antiquites in the British Museum (Bloomsbury) [2]. See *Proc Geol Assoc* (1941) **52**: 74–5.

Sollas, William Johnson (63): professor of geology at Oxford University from 1897–1936. Although a supporter of Woodard's interpretation of the Piltdown skull, he was not an advocate (at least until the early 1920s) of the British eolithic movement [1]. See *Man* (1937) **36**: 212–13.

Strahan, Aubrey (60): a professional geologist, who following completion of his studies at Cambridge in 1870 became attached to the Geological Survey. In 1914, following a stint as president of the Geological Society (1912–14), he succeeded J J Harris Teall (1849–1924) as Director of the Geological Survey [1]. See *Geol Mag* (1915) **2**: 193–8.

Symington, Johnson (61): professor of anatomy in Queen's University, Belfast. In addition to harbouring some deep reservations about Woodward's monistic interpretation of the Piltdown remains, Symington was a vocal critic of Elliot Smith's reading of the Piltdown endocranial remains [4]. See *J Anat* (1924) **58**: 275–9.

Teilhard de Chardin, Pierre (31): French Jesuit priest and palaeontologist. While stationed in Hastings, England (1908–12), Teilhard became associated with Charles Dawson and Arthur Smith Woodward, and assisted them in their work at the Barkham Manor [Piltdown] site [2]. See Cuénot ([1958] 1968).

Thomas, Michael R Oldfield (54): An assistant Keeper (in charge of Mammals) in the Department of Zoology at the British Museum (Natural History). His primary interest was marsupials. He was a close friend of Martin Hinton, with whom he collaborated with in a number of published studies [7]. See *Proc Roy Soc Lond* (1930) **106**: i–v.

Underwood, Arthur Swayne (58): professor of dental surgery at King's College, London with a private practice in Harley Street. From all indications Underwood served as Woodward's primary consultant on dental matters pertaining to the reconstruction of the Piltdown skull [3].

Warren, Samuel Hazzledine (40): a London wholesale merchant with a passionate interest in geology and palaeontology. Although now best remembered for his description of the Clacton flint industry, Warren was a leading antagonist of the British eolithic movement [1]. See *Proc Geol Soc Lond* (1959): 153–5; *Proc Geol Assoc* (1961) **72**: 170.

Waterson, David (41): British anatomist and early critic of Arthur Smith Woodward's interpretation of the Piltdown cranial remains [2].

Weidenreich, Franz (39): German anatomist who after World War I became increasingly vocal in his criticism of the monistic interpretation of the Piltdown skull [5]. See *Amer J Phys Anthropol* (1949) **51**: 85–90.

Weiner, Joseph S (b. 1915): South African anatomist, who in 1953 held the Readership in physical anthropology at Oxford (see Clark). On seeing the original Piltdown remains at a Wenner-Gren symposium held in London in July 1953, Weiner had returned to Oxford convinced that they were forgeries. With the support of Le Gros Clark his hypothesis was investigated and proved [6]. See *Ann Human Biol* (1982) **9**: 583–592.

Willett, Edgar (56): prior to his early retirement in 1906, Willett had been Administrator of Anaesthetics at the Alexandra Hospital for Children and St Bartholomew's Hospital, London (1897–1906). In his retirement Willet evidently devoted his time to serving on the council of East Sussex and to the pursuit of a "keen interest" in prehistoric archaeology — as witness by his periodic communications to the Sussex Archaeological Society [7]. See *Lancet* (1928) [April] p 837.

Williams, James Leon (60): an American dental surgeon who assisted Arthur Keith in preparing a modified version of the Piltdown skull (1913). Shortly, thereafter Williams (who had been in England since 1887) suddenly returned to America [3]. See Clapp (1925).

Woodhead, Samuel Allinson (50): a chemistry instructor and later principal at Uckfield [Sussex] Argricultural College. A close friend of Charles Dawson, whom he occasionally assisted in the excavation of the Barkham Manor [Piltdown] site [2]. See *The Analyst [J Soc Public Analysts and other Analytical Chem]* (1943) **68**: 297.

Woodward, Arthur Smith (48): a vertebrate palaeontologist and Keeper of Geology at the British Museum (Natural History) from 1901 to 1924. In addition to assisting Charles Dawson in the excavation of the Barkham Manor [Piltdown] site, Woodward was responsible for the initial interpretation and reconstruction of the Piltdown skull [2]. See *Obit Not Fellows Roy Soc Lond* (1945–8) **5**: 79–112.

PILTDOWN
A scientific forgery

1 The search for Tertiary Man: a prologue to Piltdown

Where ... must we look for primaeval Man? Was the oldest Homo sapiens Pliocene or Miocene, or yet more ancient? In the still older strata do the fossilized bones of an Ape more anthropoid, or a Man more pithecoid, than any yet known await the researches of some unborn palaeontologist?[1]

Throughout the first half of the nineteenth century there had been scattered reports in England and on the Continent of human remains being found in association with those of extinct animals, but much of this evidence had come from caves, where, as it was repeatedly stressed, the intermixing of deposits by periodic flooding was an inherent problem. Furthermore, as these critics noted in their repeated denunciation of such evidence, caves had frequently been used in pre-Roman times as either sepulchres or habitation sites, thereby providing yet another opportunity for the "occasional admixture of fragments óf human skeletons, and the bones of modern quadrupeds, with those of extinct species, introduced at more early periods, and by natural causes".[2] Hence, for reasons such as these, and continuing adherence to the idea that the boundary of human history was set by biblical chronology, evidence for the coexistence of the human species with extinct mammals from cave sites had been generally rejected as being nothing more than a fortuitous association. There were, however, a few rare instances in which human relics had been found at open-air sites: such as the case of the stone implements found by the French antiquarian, Jacques Boucher de Perthes (1788–1868), during the early 1840s in the stratified terrace gravels of the Somme river valley in north-west France. But the significance of these and similar finds was not appreciated until 1859, when the English geologist Joseph Prestwich (1812–96), and a few of his geologist and antiquarian colleagues, was led to reconsider the earlier rejection of such evidence.[3]

By the beginning of 1860 the tide of scientific opinion had turned and was now generally inclined to the idea that the human species had once coexisted with extinct mammals and at a time that could no longer be accommodated by biblical chronology. In spite of the growing support for this new paradigm, there was no scientific consensus on the extent of human antiquity, and workers were not persuaded to embrace another contemporaneous and equally revolutionary idea, namely, that of evolution.[4] Indeed, many of those who had supported the movement for human antiquity were plainly suspicious of Charles Darwin's (1809–82) transmutational thesis. Yet whatever an individual's particular stance might have been with regard to evolutionism, it was widely accepted, by evolutionists and non-evolutionists alike, that the issue of antiquity was, as Darwin himself later acknowledged, "the indispensable basis" for understanding human origins.[5] Thus, it was in this developing context that scientific attention during the 1860s shifted to the problem of determining the extent of human antiquity and the task of establishing a reliable framework of relative chronology into which both human skeletal and cultural remains could be fitted.

Joseph Prestwich, a wine merchant and geologist. Played a central role in the establishment of human antiquity and was a major figure in the British eolithic movement.

THE CONTOURS OF A CONTROVERSY

Although in his landmark communication to the Royal Society on 26 May 1859, Joseph Prestwich had left little doubt in the minds of his audience as to the reality of the evidence found in the river terrace gravels at Abbeville in north-west France for the coexistence of man with extinct mammals, he had been reluctant to venture much beyond the point that stone artifacts had been extracted from undisturbed gravel deposits; that they were associated with the remains of extinct mammalia; and that these deposits had been laid down during a period anterior to the modern geological epoch. In fact when it came time to summarize these findings, he confessed to not being able to adequately explain the situation, and went on to suggest that:

> The evidence, in fact, as it present stands, does not seem to . . . necessitate the carrying of Man back in the past, so much as the bringing forward of the extinct animals towards our own time.[6]

This reluctance to assign a greater antiquity to the evidence was guided, it seems, not so much by the anticipated threat of censure, as by the inability to harmonize the implication of these findings with his then distinctly catastrophist orientation. "It might be supposed", Prestwich explained:

> that in assigning to Man an appearance [in the Postglacial epoch] . . . it would of necessity imply his existence during long ages beyond all calculations . . . The reasons on which such a view has been held have been,—the great lapse of time considered requisite for the dying out of so many species of great Mammals,—the circumstances that many of the smaller valleys have been excavated since they lived,—the presumed

non-existence of Man himself,—and the great extent of the later and more modern accumulations. But we have in this part of Europe no succession of strata to record the gradual dying out of the species, but much, on the contrary which points to an abrupt end ... [Yet, this Postglacial period] ... if the foregoing facts are truly interpreted, would seem nevertheless to have been marked, before its end, by the presence of Man, on a land clothed with a vegetation apparently similar to that now flourishing in like latitudes, and whose waters were inhabited by Testacea also of forms now living; while on the surface of that land there lived Mammalia, of which some species are yet the associates of Man, although accompanied by others, many of them of gigantic size, and of forms now extinct.[7]

Prior to 1830, the superficial gravels and loams in which Boucher de Perthes had found the bones of extinct mammals along with human industrial remains in the Somme river valley, were thought to represent the debris of the Noachian Flood. During the next two decades, however, the perception of these gravels changed. Where previously they had been thought of as the product of a single catastrophic event, it became increasingly apparent that their constituents exhibited considerable regional variation, indicating not only that they had been formed at different times, but also that water-action had not been the exclusive deposition mechanism. It was from the vantage point of this changing perspective that the Swiss zoologist, Louis Agassiz (1807–73), had proposed in the late 1830s the idea that the landscape of antediluvian Europe had been affected by an ice age. From his studies of erratic boulders and the movement of glaciers in the Jura mountains, Agassiz had argued that many of the deposits formerly attributed to the Noachian Flood were in fact products of large sheets of land ice and floating icebergs.[8] It was in recognition of the general validity of Agassiz's glacial hypothesis that the British geologist, Roderick Impey Murchison (1792–1871), had suggested that ''Drift'' was perhaps a more appropriate term than ''Diluvium'' to describe these deposits.[9]

At this juncture the Glacial epoch was believed to have been a single rather than a multiple event, and by the mid 1850s the ''Drift'' deposits had become widely recognized as an essentially postglacial phenomenon, which was understood to represent ''a vast lapse of time'' during which the final preparations of the world as a fit habitat for human beings were made. But where earlier in the century these same deposits had been thought of as the products of an abrupt and convulsive deluge that marked the onset of the modern geological epoch (an event that could be correlated with biblical chronology), the situation was now decidedly vague. It was no longer clear where the so-called Postglacial epoch ended and the Recent began. Thus, where previously the Diluvium had served to neatly partition the Recent from the then seemingly different and hostile world of the Antediluvium, the gradual dissolution of this conceptual barrier had unleashed the prospect of a period during the Postglacial epoch when modern and extinct animals not only shared the European landscape, but had also witnessed the appearance of the first human beings.

If human beings had coexisted with extinct animals, as Boucher de Perthes claimed, this meant that the Postglacial and Recent epochs were dovetailed, and not, as catastrophist theory demanded, discontinuous events. Although such a view was later seen to compliment the inherent principles of continuity and gradual development of Darwinism, Prestwich prudently avoided any discussion of the philosophical implications of his findings. In retrospect it is evident that he was, by now, inclined to the view that catastrophist geology had perhaps overemphasized the extent of the discontinuities between the Postglacial and the Recent, but he did not state it categorically at the time. Indeed it was only after a protracted study of the implement-bearing gravels of France and England that Prestwich finally ventured

The Differentiation of the Secondary and Tertiary formations in the nineteenth century

Era	Period	Epoch	Synonyms
CENOZOIC[a]	QUATERNARY[c]	Holocene[b] (Postglacial) Pleistocene[g] (Preglacial)[h]	Recent (Alluvium)[d] (Drift)[e] (Diluvium)[d]
	TERTIARY[f]	Pliocene[i] Miocene[i] Oligocene[j] Eocene[i] Palaeocene[k]	
MESOZOIC[a]	(SECONDARY[f]) Cretaceous[l] Jurassic[m] Triassic[n]		
PALAEOZOIC[a]	(SECONDARY[f]) Permian[o] Carboniferous[p] Devonian[q] Silurian[r] Ordovician[s] Cambrian[t] *		
ARCHAEOZOIC**	PRIMARY[f] Precambrian		

a: Phillips (1838); b: Gervais (1850); c: Desnoyers (1829); d: Mantell (1822); e: Sedgwick (1839); f: Arduino (1760); g: Lyell (1839); h: Prestwich (1861); i: Lyell (1833); j: Beyrich (1839); k: Schimper (1874); l: Omalius d'Halloy (1831); m: Humboldt (1795), cf. Buch (1839); n: Alberti (1834); o: Murchison (1841); p: Conybeare & Phillips (1822); q: Sedgwick & Murchison (1839); r: Murchison (1835); s: Lapworth (1879); t: *cf.* Sedgwick (1842). * The distinction between the Cambrian and Pre-Cambrian was not clear, and invariably referred to the Primary formations. ** More frequently referred to as simply Precambrian. NB: Terms enclosed in parentheses are now obsolete.

forth with an explanatory model which endeavoured to harmonize the catatrophist and evolutionist viewpoints.

The results of Prestwich's surveys of the major river systems of north-west France and south-east England were delivered to the Royal Society in 1862.[10] Here he argued against the proposition that the implement-bearing gravels in the Somme valley had been formed by a sudden influx from the sea. This was refuted, he said, by the presence of land and freshwater molluscs in both high an low-level valley gravels, as well as a general absence of marine shells except in those areas immediately adjacent to the coast. This also apeared to be the situation in England. At Hoxne in Suffolk, where some sixty years earlier John Frere (1740–1807) had found a series of flint implements in circumstances akin to those in France, Prestwich said these had clearly been found in melt-water gravels that overlie the widespread boulder clay, formed by the crushing action of an advancing sheet of land-ice. The implement-bearing gravels of the Thames valley had also seemingly been deposited after the river had begun eroding its way through the surrounding boulder clay. Similarly, Prestwich said he could find no evidence to support the claim that these river systems had been formed exclusively by either the bursting of inland lakes, swollen by the sudden melting of mountain snows and glaciers, or any "transitory passage of any body of water over the land". All of this, and much besides, told Prestwich that these river-valleys had been excavated during the Postglacial and that they had not been formed simply by a single cataclysmic force but rather the intense and progressive "river-action" and "periodical floods imparting a torrential character to the rivers".

Viewed in this light, the gravel terraces flanking a river valley served to mark catastrophic episodes in the progressive excavation of a valley. Accordingly, those deposits situated at the crown of a valley represented the commencement of the erosion process, and thus were the oldest; whereas those situated at lower elevations were regarded as more recent. This, linked with an earlier observation that many of the implements found by Boucher de Perthes had come from gravels situated well above the present floor of the river valley, led Prestwich to consider the possibility that the height of a gravel bed might serve as a means by which to compare and thereby determine its relative age. Without exception, the implement-bearing gravels at Abbeville and at other sites in the Somme river valley were found in "high-level gravels", situated between 50 and 100 feet above the present valley floor. Most of these high-level gravel terraces were found to contain the fossil remains of ancient elephants and other extinct animals. By contrast, many of the low-level gravel beds tended to be non-fossiliferous, though there were some notable exceptions, such as those at St Acheul and St Roche, near Amiens. Originally Prestwich had supposed that the former site was older than the latter, but subsequent work there indicated that the two sites were in fact contiguous. Since the elevation of these gravel deposits were some 30 feet above the river, Prestwich classified them as "intermediate" terraces.

While admitting that it was not always easy to determine the "high-level gravels" in some of the river valleys of south-eastern England, Prestwich was nevertheless able to demonstrate a similar state of affairs. For instance, the elevation of the implement-bearing beds in the Waveney valley near Hoxne was found to vary between 40 and 50 feet. Elsewhere in Suffolk, such as at Bury St Edmunds, where the remains of ancient

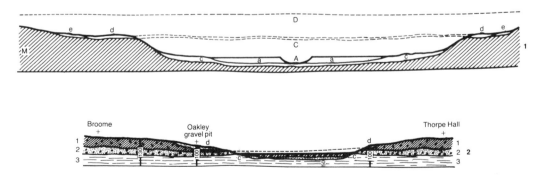

Prestwich's 'high and low level valley gravels' model. 1, cross-section of the Somme river valley: (M) General section of the valley; (D) original level prior to excavation; (A) present level of river channel; (a) recent alluvium; (c) low-level gravel terrace; (d) high- level gravel terrace; (e) non-fossiliferous drift on slopes of the major valley. Based on Prestwich (1863:264). The general height of the Somme valley ranges from 200 to 400 ft., and its mean width is less than a mile. 2, Cross-section of the Waveney river valley, near Hoxne, Suffolk: (1) boulder clay; (2) sands and gravels under boulder clay; (3) chalk; (a) alluvium; (c) low-level gravel terrace; (d) high-level gravel terrace. (Based on Prestwich, 1863:253)

elephants had been recovered, Prestwich found considerable evidence for intermediate terraces. Like those at Amiens, these terraces were invariably located at heights between 20 and 30 feet.

As Prestwich's surveys revealed, there was considerable variation in the kinds of animal bones represented in these river terraces. Collectively they presented a confusing array of animals. Some were species that were adapted to a temperate climate, such as bison and bear, and others were either tundra species (reindeer, mammoth and woolly rhinoceros), or sub-tropical forms (hippopotamus). In the absence of a more compelling argument, it was widely accepted at the time that seasonal migration might explain this confused picture; but while migration could account for some differences, it was hard to imagine hippopotamus and reindeer herds changing places every year. Although Prestwich did not specifically address this issue, the general results of his study did provide some support for the migration hypothesis. In this regard he noted the general concordance between the river valleys of north-west France and south-east England which, when compounded with the recognized identities between flora and fauna, reinforced the notion of the comparatively recent separation of the two countries. Precisely when this separation took place was still largely a matter of speculation. However, the presence of coastal "high-level" gravels on both sides of the Channel provided Prestwich with a means to determine the probable existence of a "contracted" sea channel between the two countries during the "high-level valley-gravel period".[11] But in making this argument he noted that this primal channel had in all probability been frozen in winter, and thus would not have been an insurmountable barrier to either man or beast. This traffic between the two landmasses, he conjectured, had, in all probability continued until at least the close of the "low-level valley-gravel period". By this time, not only had the sea-channel widened considerably, but also climatic conditions, as indicated by the faunal assemblages, were tending progressively to that of the Recent epoch.

Towards the end of the 1860s, the Scottish geologist, James Geikie (1839–1915), found evidence which led him to support the existence of an interglacial period in

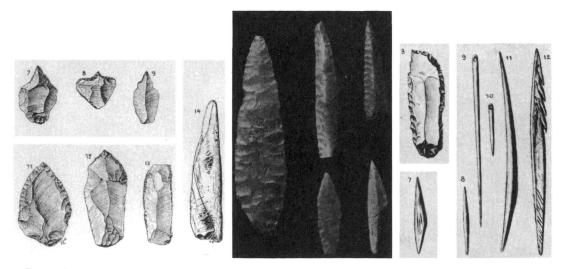

Examples of (left) Mousterian, (centre) Solutrean and (right) Magdalenian industries. (From Boule, 1923)

Scotland.[12] In marked contrast to neighbouring drift deposits which contained the remains of reindeer and mammoth, Geikie's "interglacial" bed had exclusively yielded the remains of temperate fauna. This, compounded with evidence furnished by other workers such as Searles V. Wood (1798–1880), Richard H. Tiddeman (1842–1917), John Dakyns (d. 1910) and John Aitken (1839–1919), convinced Geikie that many of the deposits which hitherto had been regarded as Postglacial drifts, were in fact attributable to the earlier warm period of the glacial epoch.[13]

By the mid 1870s, Geikie was in a position to synthesize the accumulated evidence and to produce a synopsis of the European "Great Ice Age", which was seen to have involved four major glacial advances and three mild interglacial periods. As a result the "high terraces" described by Prestwich were subsequently attributed to Geikie's First, Second and Third Glacial stages, while the "lower" terraces were recognized as being composed of materials belonging to the Fourth Glacial and Postglacial stages.[14] It was also at this juncture that workers began to adopt the terms Quaternary or Pleistocene to distinguish the complex post-Pliocene deposits (i.e. Glacial, Postglacial and Recent) from those of the Tertiary formations.

In the meantime, the crown of the 100 ft Terrace served as a convenient conceptual marker for the commencement of the Postglacial epoch that seemingly delineated the apparent extent of human prehistory. Although acknowledging that the processes he had described implied a greater amount of time than he had originally proposed for human antiquity, Prestwich still balked at the idea of it being computed in "hundreds of thousands of years". Such estimates, he declared, were both "unsafe" and, to say the least, "premature".

While Prestwich had been scaling the slopes of the 100 ft Terrace, his long time confrère Edouard Lartet (1801–71), a French lawyer-archaeologist, had endeavoured to establish a chronological framework into which both human skeletal and cultural remains could be fitted using the fossil animal bones recovered from French caves. Lartet's scheme, published in 1861, recognized four major subdivisions of Glacial, Postglacial and early Recent epochs, namely, the Ages of the Great Cave Bear (*Ursus spelaeus*), Mammoth (*Elephas primigenius*), Reindeer (*Cervus tarandus*) and Aurochs (*Bos taurus primigenius*). Several years later and largely on the basis of his work in the caves of the Dordogne region in south-west France, Lartet acknowledged that his Cave Bear and Mammoth periods were essentially inseparable, and thus sank the former in the latter.

In 1865, another of Prestwich's French colleagues, Félix Garrigou (1835–1920), pointed out that Lartet's scheme was biased to cold-adapted fauna and completely ignored a large component of the palaeontological record which contained a number of subtropical forms such as *Hippopotamus*, *Elephas antiquus* and Merck's rhinoceros (*Dicerorhinus kirkbergensis*). As such, Garrigou proposed that Lartet's scheme be modified by the addition of an "age" characterized by *Elephas antiquus*.[15]

Although in retrospect Garrigou's suggested modification is seen to have been a movement in the right direction, at the time it merely served to underscore the lack of agreement among workers regarding the utility of palaeontological remains as chronological markers. As critics were quick to note, representative fauna varied from region to region. Furthermore, it was argued that the assemblages recovered from the Dordogne caves and rock shelters might simply reflect the preferences of either the human occupants or some other animal predator, rather than a succession of faunal change. In fact it was not until Geikie's division of the Glacial epoch was put in place that much of this confusion was finally swept away and it was recognized that animal fossils could be utilized as reliable chronological markers, within certain limits.

Meanwhile, cognisant of the shortcomings of Lartet's faunal subdivision of the

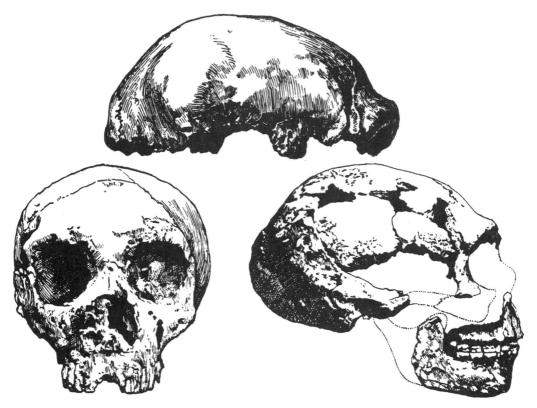

Three major Pleistocene hominids discovered in the nineteenth century: (above) the Neanderthal (Germany) calotte; (left) Gibraltar (Iberian peninsula) skull; (right) one of the Spy skulls (Belgium).

Quaternary, the French anthropologist Gabriel de Mortillet (1821–98) tendered a scheme of relative chronology based on the sequence of stone-tool industries found in France.

As the British antiquarian John Evans (1823–1908) had noted in 1859,[16] the stone implements found by Boucher de Perthes in the Somme river valley were significantly different from those attributed to Celtic (pre-Roman) Europe. Where the latter tended to "show traces of having been ground and polished, wholly or in part; those from the drift, on the contrary, [had] merely been roughly chipped out of flint, and in no case ground".[17] In 1865, the antiquarian John Lubbock [Lord Avebury] (1834–1913) formalized this observation by proposing that the older and crudely chipped stone-tool industries be referred to under the term "Palaeolithic", while the more recent polished stone artifacts should be grouped under the term "Neolithic".[18]

Lubbock's suggestion was attractive, particularly to Mortillet, who, unlike some of his more conservative Parisian colleagues, was an avid promoter of Darwinism.[19] Mortillet, like Lubbock, sought to link the progress manifest in the archaeological record with the evolutionary history of the human species. It seemed to these workers that our palaeolithic ancestors had used the simplest stone tools and then gradually progressed to the more sophisticated use of stone and bone, before passing on to the discovery of bronze and iron.[20]

Specifically, Mortillet recognized five industrial stages or "epochs" constituting the

Palaeolithic, named after the French sites where the industries were typically represented. His sequence commenced with the "Epoque de Chelles" or the Chellean. Here, at Chelles-sur-Marne, the remains of *Elephas antiquus* had been found in association with stone implements, similar to those found by Boucher de Perthes. While varying considerably in size, these Chellean implements were seen to be more or less amygaloid or almond-shaped, made by striking flakes from a flint or pebble so that the residual core formed the implement. Boucher de Perthes had called these core-tools, "haches", or hand-axes, whereas Mortillet characterized them as simple "hand-hammers" (*coup de poing*). Following this period came the "Epoque du Moustier", named after the rock shelter Le Moustier situated in the Dordogne region of south-west France, which had been excavated in the early 1860s, and was distinguished by the frequency with which tools were chipped out of flakes. Mortillet believed this industry represented the cultural bridge to the traditions of the Upper Palaeolithic: the Aurignacian, Solutrean and Magdalenian. These latter industries had likewise been recovered from caves in the Dordogne region, namely Aurignac, Solutré and La Madeleine respectively. In direct contrast to the preceding industries of the Lower Palaeolithic, the Upper Palaeolithic sequence was characterized by the use of flint blades, as well as by an increasing use of bone, antler and ivory, particularly during the Magdalenian, when flint was used less. In this latter period, these ivory and other bony artifacts were extensively worked and frequently displayed a high-level of artistry.

Late nineteenth century geological and cultural subdivisions of the Pleistocene (Quaternary)

Last Glaciation (= Würm)	Magdalenian Solutrean Aurignacian Mousterian	Upper Palaeolithic
Third Interglacial (= Riss-Würm)	Mousterian Late Acheulian	Middle Palaeolithic
Third Glaciation (= Riss)		
Second Interglacial (= Mindel-Riss)	Early Acheulian Chellean	Lower Palaeolithic
Pre-Glacial	Eolithic	

Although in the case of these Upper Palaeolithic industries it was clear from recovered skeletal material that they had been manufactured by a type of humanity that was not significantly different from the modern human form, the identity of the Lower Palaeolithic artisans was blurred. The expectation, at least among the evolutionists, was that as one proceeded back through time the anatomy of the modern human form would gradually dissolve into a mosaic of primitive features, and that eventually a point would be reached where this metamorphic form would in essence be indistinguishable from that of an anthropoid ape. While Lartet had described *Dryopithecus*, an ape-like fossil that had been found in the Miocene beds at Saint-Gaudens in 1856, it did not throw any significant light on the question of the earlier stages of human evolution.[21] At this time there was only a handful of human fossils available for study. All of them were of equivocal geological provenance and none had been found in Britain. Among the material available in the mid 1860s was the now recognized Upper Pleistocene hominids of Engis (Belgium), discovered in 1833; the Gibraltar skull, which had been found in 1848, but not described until 1865; and the celebrated Neanderthal skeleton that had been found in the Neander valley, Germany, in 1856. At this time, however, these fossils were regarded as merely examples of the "primitive races of man" that had once occupied Palaeolithic Europe prior to the commencement of the Recent epoch and which, from a strictly anatomical point of view, were considered not to be significantly removed from modern *Homo sapiens*. In fact the evolutionary significance of these fossils went unrecognized until the discovery of "two remarkable human skeletons" at Spy, near Goyet, in the Belgian province of Namur, in 1886. Their discovery in association with the remains of several extinct mammals and a collection of stone implements closely resembling the Palaeolithic industry known as the Mousterian, left little doubt as to their geological age and also permitted Julien Fraipont (1857–1910), the Belgian anatomist and palaeontologist (who had been invited to examine this material), to forge an anatomical connection between the Spy skeletons and the remains from the Neander valley. From this emerged the first composite picture of the European Neanderthals, whom Fraipont characterized as being short in stature, but powerfully built, with strong and curiously curved thigh bones which seemingly must have required them to walk with a bend at the knees. Their skulls were long and depressed with strongly developed eyebrow ridges and a heavy projecting face and jaw. In contrast to Upper Palaeolithic man, whose skeletons presented a much taller and more gracile form, the Neanderthals appeared brutish, if not "pithecoid", but like others before him Fraipont believed this ancient form of humanity did little to bridge the structural gap between man and ape.[22] In fact, when the British zoologist and anatomist, Thomas Henry Huxley (1825–95), reviewed the Engis and Neander material in 1863, he was driven to essentially the same conclusion. Referring to these crania, Huxley wrote:

> [They] in no sense . . . [can be] regarded as the remains of a human being intermediate between Men and Apes. At most, they demonstrate the existence of a Man whose skull may be said to revert somewhat towards the pithecoid type . . .[These crania thus form,] in reality, the extreme term of a series leading gradually to the highest and best developed of human crania.[23]

Furthermore, judging from the artifacts found at Abbeville and elsewhere, it appeared to him that not only were the "most ancient Races of men" morphologically indistinguishable from modern humans, but also that they had fashioned their implements in much the same way as "those fabricated by the lowest savages at the present day". Whether this meant that *Homo sapiens* had originated somewhere in the deep recesses of the Tertiary was still far from clear, but Huxley for one seemed to think it was a distinct possibility. Indeed throughout the 1860s there had been a mounting flood of published reports of human remains being found in Tertiary deposits. In some cases human bones had reportedly been found, though more often than not they were merely artifacts. Although this evidence drew considerable criticism, the movement nevertheless continued to gather momentum.

Among the first reports advocating a human presence in the Tertiary Era was that made by Jules Desnoyers (1800–87), a French geologist of some distinction, who early in the summer of 1863, announced the discovery of a series of extinct mammalian bones in the gravel deposits at Saint-Prest, near Chartres, bearing cut marks and other striae which he felt could only have been produced by a human agency.

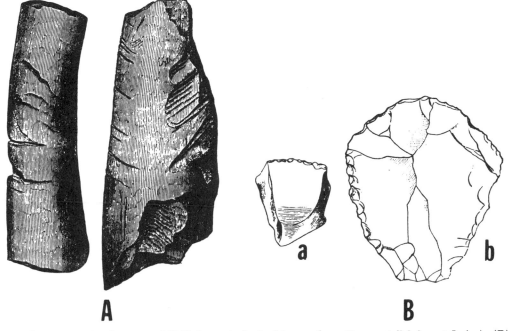

French Tertiary implements: (A) Delauny's incised bones from Pouancé (Maine-et-Loire). (B) Bourgeois' Tertiary 'grattoir' from Thenay (a) compared with one found by Boucher de Perthes in the Somme valley (b). (From Hamy, 1870:49)

Familiar with the Saint-Prest sites and respecting his long-time friend's achievements in geology, Charles Lyell (1797–1875), who was then the principal arbiter in British geology, approached this claim with considerable care and caution. Since the Saint-Prest deposits had not yielded any industrial remains until this time, Lyell wondered if the marks his friend had found on the animal bones, namely those of elephant, rhinoceros and hippopotamus, might have been made by another animal, such as *Trogontherium*, the extinct Pliocene giant beaver, whose bones had been found at Saint-Prest. To test this hypothesis, Lyell arranged for the radius of a horse and the humerus of an ox, both "entire and free from any superficial scratches", to be placed in a cage with four porcupines at the London Zoo. At the end of ten days the bones were removed and found to possess scratch marks similar to those found on the Saint-Prest bones. The only problem was that while the modern bones possessed numerous teeth marks, the Saint-Prest bones did not![24] There were of course other possible natural explanations, such as post-mortem dessication (resulting in splitting), or the movement *in situ* of the remains in an abrasive matrix; but the examined bones of a comparative age from other sites did not exhibit these same peculiar "incisions, striations and cuts". Thus, in concluding his investigations, Lyell wrote:

> I consider the art of deciphering the cuts and other markings observable on fossil bone to be at present so much in its infancy, that I must hesitate before assenting to M. Desnoyers' proposition, that the fossil of Saint-Prest demonstrate "the high probability of the existence of Man before the glacial epoch." But the facts and theory which he has set forth with so much ability will stimulate archaeologists and palaeontologists to make fresh enquiries, and to search diligently for works of art, wherever cut and striated bones occur. The detection of these markings at Saint-Prest

may lead to still more important investigations; and we may be on the eve of great discoveries, however indistinct and shadowy the proofs may now appear.[25]

Four years later, at the second International Congress of Anthropology & Prehistoric Archaeology held in Paris, a French antiquarian, the Abbé Delaunay, exhibited a small collection of bones of *Halitherium* (an extinct sea mammal) that bore cut marks similar to those described earlier by Desnoyers. These incised bones Delaunay said, had been recovered from a Miocene shell-bed of marine origin at Pouancé (Maine-et-Loire).[26] Of even greater interest, however, was the collection of stone artifacts which the Abbé Louis Bourgeois (1819–78) brought to the Congress. Bourgeois' collection had been recovered from the base of a Miocene deposit situated near Thenay, south of Orléans on the Loire River. Compared with the crudest scrapers from the Somme river valley, Bourgeois' "grattoirs" appeared to the uneducated eye to be nothing more than a pile of natural flint flakes. However, on closer inspection, so Bourgeois contended, these stones were seen to bear the tell-tale signs of "l'aurore de l'humanité".[27] These signs included a modicum of retouching, and more particularly, the apparent replication of a basic tool design (at least in the selection Bourgeois chose to exhibit in Paris).

The reaction to Bourgeois' exhibit was mixed. While many simply could not get beyond the fact that the Thenay specimens looked like natural objects, there were others who were persuaded otherwise. Bourgeois' case hung in the balance until 1872, when he surfaced again, this time in Brussels at the sixth International Congress of Anthropology & Prehistoric Archaeology. On this occasion, at his request, a committee of fifteen delegates was convened to examine the Thenay material. Although the conclusion was again not unanimous, the lion's share of the votes on this occasion went to Bourgeois. Nine of the committee reported in favour of some of the flints having been worked, while five dismissed the specimens as being natural and one remained undecided.

As some of Bourgeois' sympathizers noted at the time, and in particular Mortillet,[28] the crudity of the Thenay forms were not only in keeping with their antiquity, but also the expectation that their author had stood on the threshold of humanity. Like his British counterpart, John Lubbock,[29] Mortillet was convinced that human material culture was a mirror of biological evolution. As such it was both reasonable and logical to assume that as the stone implements of the Palaeolithic and Neolithic documented the gradual emergence of modern humanity, so the crude tools of the Tertiary represented the work of a transitional creature that stood betwixt man and the bestial apes.[30] Emboldened by similar finds made at Puy Courny in the Aurillac region of south-central France, and at a series of sites near Lisbon, Portugal[31], Mortillet was finally moved to postulate the existence of an European Tertiary man-ape. He rejected, however, the provocative idea that this transitional form of humanity had been *Dryopithecus*,[32] arguing instead for a form that stood between the apes and man: "[A]nimals of another genus, precursors of man on the chain of being", a precursor he gave the name *Anthropopithecus*. To characterize its primitive industry and the period to which it belonged, Mortillet had coined the term "Eolithique" or Dawn Stone Age.[33]

In Britain the idea of Tertiary Man met with strong resistance. Presiding over a symposium held in May 1877 at the Anthropological Institute in London to consider the "Present State of the Question of the Antiquity of Man", John Evans noted in his opening address that the situation had changed drastically since 1859:

It is now no longer difficult to get evidence accepted as to the antiquity of man. The danger rather lies in the other direction, and we are liable to have evidence brought forward relating to discoveries bearing upon the subject which is hardly trustworthy.[34]

With blatant scepticism Evans went on to review the evidence put forward to support a human presence in preglacial times. He argued that such claims were difficult to evaluate because "human bones, or humanly-worked implements may belong to far more recent periods than the deposits in which they are found", since "objects from the surface are . . . liable to get mixed in with those from lower beds, and we cannot always trust the observations of ordinary workmen". Because there were so many sources of doubt and error in the existing reports, Evans concluded by saying: "I cannot but think that our watchword for the present must be caution, caution, caution".[35]

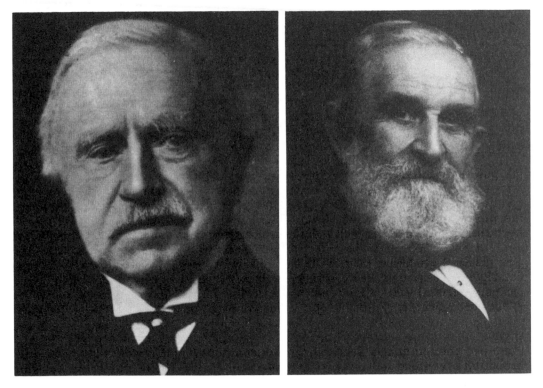

Left: William Boyd Dawkins, fierce opponent of the British eolithic movement. (Cave Science *5, 1963)*
Right: Joseph Evans, antiquarian, who with Joseph Prestwich played a key role in the establishment of human antiquity. (The Royal Anthropological Institute of Great Britain and Ireland)

These sentiments were echoed by William Boyd Dawkins (1837–1929), a professor of geology at Owens College (later the Victoria University, Manchester), who under the tutelage of Hugh Falconer (1808–65)[36] had established something of a reputation in British cave research and human prehistory. His contribution to the London symposium was sharply critical of both the idea of Tertiary Man and Geikie's glacial hypothesis. Recognizing that acceptance of the latter opened the temporal gates to the former, Dawkins endeavoured, on this occasion, to dismantle's Geikie's thesis by demonstrating that seasonal migration could more than adequately explain the co-mingling of northern (cold) and southern (warm) fauna so evident in British caves and river drifts. His argument was grounded in the fact that it was still unclear how much the northern glaciers had extended into southern England.[37] Favouring the view promoted at the symposium by Thomas McKenny Hughes (1832–1917), that the deposits in the south spoke of a postglacial scenario, Dawkins suggested that the glaciers had been confined essentially to northern latitudes and that throughout this period their position had fluctuated with changing temperatures.

In taking this position Dawkins and similarly inclined workers were favouring a comparatively simple and sequential account of human natural history. Indeed, three years later, Dawkins' book *Early Man in Britain* set the seal on this more orthodox view of human antiquity. Here Dawkins noted that with the onset of the Glacial Epoch large numbers of mammals that had previously prospered in the European Pliocene either perished or relocated. In particular he noted the disappearance of the apes from the European landscape and contended that, even if man had existed at this time, it was highly improbable that the most specialized organism in the animal kingdom would have survived this mass extinction at the beginning of the Pleistocene.[38]

While many British geologists and archaeologists may have heeded the cautious message of the London symposium, there were a number of them who expressed a growing committment to the idea of Tertiary Man. Geikie, in particular, was convinced that eventually the remains of "Preglacial Man" would be found in England and "at such elevations as will cause the hairs of cautious archaeologists to rise on end".[39]

EOS AT IGHTHAM

Since his conversion in 1859, Prestwich had harboured the growing conviction that an English Abbeville would eventually be discovered in the clay pits and brickfields of either Kent or Sussex. It seems to have been largely this prospect which led him to the decision to build a villa that overlooked the River Darent at Shoreham in Kent. In 1872, he retired (from the family wine business in London) to Shoreham fully expecting to devote the remaining years of his life to gardening and to his scientific pursuits. This plan was shattered soon thereafter when, on the death of John Phillips (1800–74), he was offered the chair of geology at Oxford. Finding himself unable to refuse the appointment, he came out of retirement and on 11 November 1874 was duly installed at Oxford, where he apparently threw himself vigorously into his new duties and the cause of scientific education. As a direct result, little time was left during the next decade to devote serious attention to the subject of human antiquity. By 1887 however, with his health failing, he finally decided to step down and retire a second time to Shoreham, where he began to take a more active and lively interest in the work of the palaeolithic hunter, Benjamin Harrison (1837–1921), who owned a grocery shop in the small village of Ightham, situated some seven miles east of Shoreham.

Standing some 300ft above sea-level on the southern slope of the North Downs, Ightham overlooks the Weald of Kent and Sussex. To the north, the chalk Downs rise steadily to a height of 750ft, forming the northern rim of the Chalk Plateau that overlooks the Thames estuary and the marshes of Essex and Suffolk. Running from east to west the chalk phalanx of the North Downs traverses the length of the county and at its western end is punctuated by several rivers, such as the Darent and the

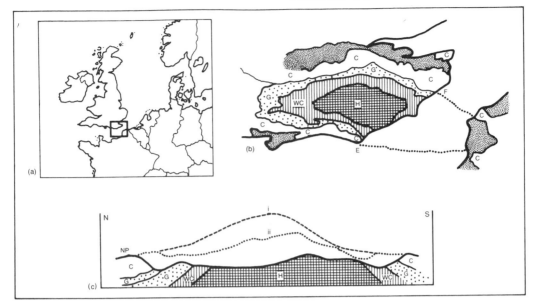

The geology of the Weald and adjacent regions. (a) General map showing relationship between south-east England and north-west Europe. (b) Geological map of the Weald and adjacent formations in south-east England and north-west France. The dotted line indicates the former extension of the boundaries of the Weald to France: F, Folkestone (Kent), E, Eastbourne, Beachy Head (Sussex). (c) Diagrammatic representation of the "Dome" hypothesis; i, represents the ancient Wealden elevation; ii, intermediate stage of erosion; C, chalk; G, Greensand and gault; WC, Wealden clay; H, Hastings beds; NP, plateau of North Downs. (Based on the British Museum's Guide to the antiquities of the Stone Age, *1902*

Medway, which drain north into the Thames estuary.[40] It was largely on this Chalk Plateau, north of Ightham, and around Oldbury Hill to the west, that Harrison had made his principal discoveries.

Although Harrison's interest in archaeology preceded his first meeting with Prestwich at Shoreham in 1879,[41] the meeting seems to have been the turning-point in his studies. It was then that Harrison had apparently asked Prestwich about the correspondence between the implement-bearing gravels of the Somme valley and the gravel-beds of south-east England. Responding to this question, Prestwich is said to have pointed out of his study window overlooking the Darent river valley, saying: "If we take the Darent to be the Somme, the implement-bearing gravels would lie at about the level of the railway station".[42] Harrison could hardly believe his ears, because many of the stone artifacts then spread upon Prestwich's desk had been found at levels even higher than that of Shoreham railway station. As Harrison well knew, it was widely accepted in geological circles that the entire southern portion of England and north-west France had originally been covered by a dome of chalk. Deposited during the Cretaceous, this dome had been eroded away during the immense interval of time separating the Cretaceous and Recent epochs, leaving only the bordering rims of the North and South Downs in England, while the remnants of its eastern rim could be found across the English Channel. According to this hypothesis, the stone implements he had found on the Chalk Plateau were much older than those of the Somme, since lower elevations represented more recent levels

Examples of Prestwich's "hill-drift" implements. (From Prestwich, 1889)

of erosion in the original chalk dome. Although he did not share these thoughts with Prestwich at the time, the inference seemed unavoidable to Harrison, and it was evidently at this time that he began, in earnest, a search for stone implements in the high gravels of the Chalk Plateau and by 1887 had amassed a collection of 405 stone artifacts.

The fact that many of Harrison's stone artifacts had been found at such high elevations, however, had not been lost on Prestwich. But while intrigued by this collection, it was not until January 1888 that Prestwich finally turned his attention to Harrison's case:

> I have now finished the second volume of Geology, which will, I hope, be out about the end of the month. I shall, therefore, be ready to engage in some other work, and if you are still of the same mind I will take in hand and describe your "finds" of palaeolithic flint implements round Ightham; and see, if possible, whether any further conclusion can be drawn from them . . .
>
> Finding them in such extraordinary numbers and at such various levels is certainly a very novel feature.
>
> To do this will involve a good deal of work on your part, and some on mine. So we should have to take time about it, and if you will let me have the particulars I require in the course of two or three months, it will do very well.[43]

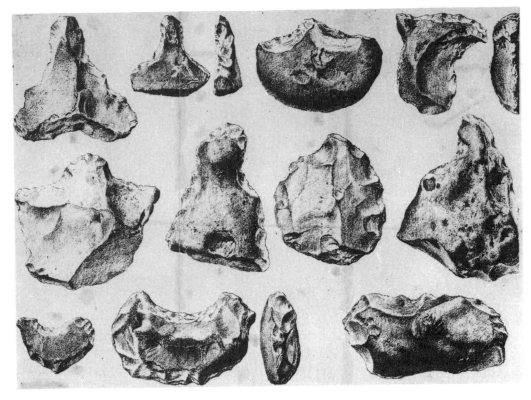

Examples of the Prestwich-Harrison Plateau implements. (From Prestwich, 1892)

Prestwich wanted Harrison to characterize each implement in his collection and to indicate, on a contour map of the district, precisely where they had been found. By mid-summer Harrison had completed this phase of the work. Of the 405 implements in his collection, 22 had been found at an elevation of 500ft, 199 between 400 and 500ft, and 184 below 400ft.[44]

Among the 500ft group was a crudely chipped specimen, labelled No.464, which Harrison thought resembled the primitive stone tools described by Mortillet. He had in fact found a similar implement in the Darent valley gravels in 1881, but had consigned it temporarily to the waste heap of his collection largely because John Evans had unceremoniously rejected it.[45] Like Mortillet, Harrison was convinced the industrial sequence of the Palaeolithic had been preceded by what he called the "pot hooks and hangers" of human culture, and that this formative cultural stage had had its roots in pre-glacial times. Unsure of where Prestwich stood on this issue, Harrison decided to include the putative eolithic specimen No.464 "as a fly to see whether he would rise", and much to his surprise and satisfaction, Prestwich took the bait. By return of post came the message from Shoreham: "If you have anymore stones like No.464, send them at once".[46]

Although this signalled to Harrison that "the day of the rude implements — eoliths — had dawned", the ever cautious Prestwich was quick to point out that "it will not do to found a theory on a single specimen". Indeed as he later told Harrison, "It has always been my practice not to hurry any question, or to express a hasty opinion. This has no doubt, led in many instances to my being forestalled, but it has landed me on safer ground."[47] His plan was first to establish a reliable chronological framework of the Wealden gravels, and then to tackle the question of the eoliths, or, as he preferred, "rude implements".[48]

On the evening of 6 February 1889, Prestwich delivered to the Geological Society of London a preliminary report on the distribution and probable age of the flint implements found in the neighbourhood of Ightham. With characteristic caution and care Prestwich led his audience through a maze of charts and contour maps summarizing the geology and topography of the district. This region, he said, was "somewhat exceptional" in that it provided some important clues to the natural history of the Weald. In particular he claimed the region bore the marks of glacial action and was convinced this had been a factor in its denudation.[49] Although such a proposition ran counter to the view that the glaciers had not penetrated into southern England, Prestwich concluded from this perspective that the drifts found in this region below the 300ft level belonged to the Late Glacial and early Postglacial and as such, were in many ways analagous to river-valley terraces; whereas those found above the 400ft mark, and particularly those associated with the Chalk Plateau, could be attributed either to early glacial or Tertiary origin. Into this broad sequence Prestwich then introduced the various flint implements that Harrison had recovered. As he went on to demonstrate, this flint collection was separated into two heterogenous groups: namely the "high-hill drift implements", a mixture of polished (Neolithic) and unpolished (Palaeolithic) artifacts; and the "High Plateau implements" characterized by "their general brown and ochreous colour, rude shape, and worn appearance".[50] To Prestwich the implication of all this was unavoidable:

> [The] physiographical changes [alluded to above] and the great height of the old chalk plateau, with its "red clay flints" and "southern drift" high above the valleys containing Postglacial deposits, point to the great antiquity — possibly Preglacial — of the palaeolithic implements found in association with these summit drifts.[51]

Although some of the specimens in the "High Plateau" group looked doubtful, the argument over whether they were natural or artificial objects was academic, John Evans believed, until the general validity of Prestwich's chronology was established[52]; and on this point there was considerable disagreement. The geologist William Whitaker (1836–1925) noted that "great caution was needed in attempting to correlate the drifts of southern England with those of other areas"; and he further reminded his geological colleagues that "there was no evidence of the existence of Glacial Drift south of the Thames, though such "finds" occurred immediately to the north of it".[53] Prestwich, however, was unmoved by Whitaker's argument.

After this meeting Prestwich, as planned, set about the task of establishing the validity of his proposed chronology. To this end the veteran geologist, aided by Harrison, spent several months in the summer of 1890 surveying and examining sites in the Darent valley and on the neighbouring Chalk Plateau. The results of this work, presented to the Geological Society on 21 January 1891, convinced Prestwich of the "great antiquity of the Chalk Plateau drift and implements":

> [I]f we are to assume [Prestwich noted on this occasion], as there is every reason to suppose, that the great denudation of the valleys has been the work of Glacial [and Postgalcial] times, then these implements [of the High Plateau] may probably be assigned, as I before suggested, to a pre-Glacial or early Glacial period.[54]

On this occasion Prestwich's glacial scenario was severely criticized by the mining geologist Clement Le Neve Foster (1841–1904) and Archibald Geikie (1835–1924), then

Director-General of the Geological Survey. To them the proposition that the Chalk escarpment had been sculptured by drifting ice was unfounded.[55] To this criticism, Prestwich replied that he had not meant to imply that the great northern ice-sheet had extended over south-east England, but rather that "a southern central ice-area may then have existed in the Wealden highlands, and [that] ice and snow in the [associated valleys, such as at Darent] had been local".[56] Although Prestwich's geological friend, William Topley (1841–94) admitted that there was some evidence of ice-action in the Darent valley, he confessed that he was not willing to follow his old friend in "attributing the escarpment to glacial action". He also observed that while the great age of the Plateau gravels was "beyond question", the antiquity of the implements (some of which he said "might reasonably excite suspicion") would remain in doubt until they were actually found *in situ*.[57]

In the absence of a more compelling counter-argument,[58] Prestwich moved into the final phase of his plan. "We can now make arrangements for bringing the subject [of the rude Plateau implements] before the Anthropological Institute", he informed Harrison,[59] who was asked to assemble an exhibit of his best finds. He instructed that "They should be grouped and the most typical ones selected for illustration and slightly sketched [along with] some general account of your finds and of geological considerations".[60] Prestwich planned to append Harrison's notes to his own paper, which was to be entitled: "On the Primitive Characters of the Flint Implements of the Chalk Plateau of Kent".[61]

On the evening of 23 June 1891, Prestwich and Harrison placed their case for a British eolithic industry before the membership of the Anthropological Institute in Hanover Square, London. The meeting was well attended and included such luminaries as Edward Burnett Tylor (1832–1917), who presided over the session, General Pitt-Rivers [Augustus Lane Fox] (1827–1900), John Allen Brown (1831–1903), John Evans and William Boyd Dawkins. Its reception was decidedly mixed. Predictably Dawkins reacted strongly against the evidence, noting as Topley had earlier, that all of the implements to date had been surface finds.[62] Evans concurred, and recommended "extreme caution" before accepting the exhibited evidence. In his opinion they represented two different sets of materials: those that were genuine artifacts and seen to be indistinguishable from regular palaeoliths; and a series of stones whose chipped edges could be attributed to the "agency of Nature rather than of man".[63] Pitt-Rivers on the other hand, while agreeing with much of what Evans and Dawkins had said, was anxious not to discount a matter that had yet to be thoroughly worked out; and as he reminded his colleagues, in 1859 Prestwich himself did not accept:

> ... the antiquity of the implements of the drift period until he and others had found them embedded in the gravels of the Somme ... These are the precedents upon which our existing beliefs have been formed, and we certainly ought not to be satisfied with less conclusive evidence for the antiquity of implements of a still earlier date.[64]

Allen Brown, an enthusiastic palaeolithic hunter himself, was similarly inclined though not so demanding. Having found similar forms in the Thames valley (in a drift near Farnham, 360ft O.D.), he felt there was good reason to suppose that these implements might well represent an earlier industrial stage. Though acknowledging that it would "be desirable that some of the implements should be found *in situ*", Brown said he was prepared in the meantime to adopt Prestwich's opinion that "[Man] may have lived ... before or during the incoming colder condition of climate in Great Britain".[65]

A MAN OF THE ONE HUNDRED FOOT TERRACE

With few exceptions, the human remains that had been discovered in Britain thus far were shown to be either Neolithic or of a more recent age. On the few rare occasions when they had been found under circumstances indicative of a greater antiquity, their fragmentary nature had rendered them essentially useless in establishing the physical identity of the skeleton to which they belonged. In 1895, however, a human skeleton that had been found on the northern rim of the Chalk Plateau at Galley Hill in Kent was presented to the Geological Society of London by the palaeontologist, Edwin Tulley Newton (1840–1930), as a possible representative of the British Palaeolithic.

Edwin Tulley Newton, provided the first description and evaluation of the controversial Galley Hill remains in 1895.

The Galley Hill skull was discovered in the autumn of 1888 by an amateur fossil collector Robert Elliott (1839–1909), at a chalk pit overlooking the River Thames, near Northfleet in West Kent. The remains comprised a near complete braincase (minus facial bones), the right portion of the lower mandible and an assortment of postcranial bones, all of which were apparently in a poor state of preservation and evidently had been extracted with great difficulty from what appeared to be an undisturbed gravel deposit situated near the crown of the pit.

Although acknowledging that he had initially been prepared to dismiss the Galley Hill skeleton as a Neolithic burial, Newton reported that this diagnosis did not stand up to subsequent scientific scrutiny. To begin with, despite the fact that no experienced geologist had been on hand when the discovery was made and that the exact site had since been destroyed, the geologists, William Topley and Clement Reid (1853–1916), had examined the pit at Newton's request and both were of the opinion that the gravel terrace had originally been in an "indisturbed condition". Topley also confirmed the suspicion that the terrace formed part of the "high-level terrace-gravel of the Thames valley".[66]

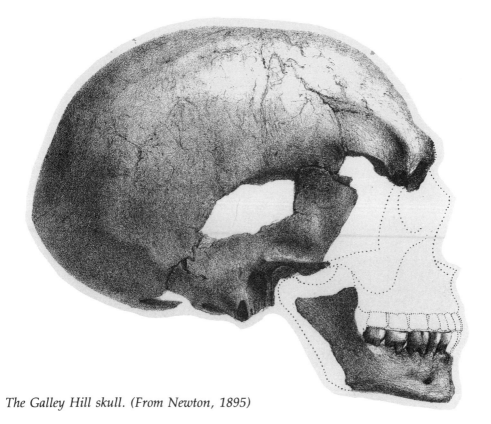

The Galley Hill skull. (From Newton, 1895)

Newton's enthusiasm for this skeleton was reinforced by a collection of palaeolithic implements which Elliott had found in the same stratum as the human bones. While many of these looked like regular palaeoliths, several were "deeply-stained primitive forms", similar to Harrison's "brownies" from the High Plateau near Ightham, and whose human authorship, Newton noted, might well have been doubted, had they been found alone.[67]

As for the skeletal remains, Newton's attention was directed to the skull. What impressed him particularly was its "extreme length ... in proportion to its width", but unlike other dolichocephalic crania he had examined, the Galley Hill cranium was further marked by its general thickness, prominent eyebrow ridges and moderately receding forehead. While many of these individual characters could be found in British Neolithic and Bronze Age crania, the closest resemblance to the Galley Hill skull Newton could find was the skull that had been discovered on the banks of the River Nore at Borris, Ireland. Like Galley Hill, the Borris skull had prominent superciliary ridges and a retreating forehead. When Huxley had described this skull, in 1865, he had attributed it to what he called the "river-bed type", a cranial form that subsequently became synonymous with the Long-Barrow skulls of the early Neolithic in Britain. These latter crania, while overtly dolichocephalic, did not manifest strongly developed eyebrow ridges.[68]

Cognisant of Huxley's earlier allusion to the similarity of the Long-Barrow crania to aboriginal Australian skulls, and to those found in Scandinavian burial mounds (which in turn had been likened to the Eskimo type), Newton extended his comparisons to include these various forms. The closest approximation to the Galley Hill configuration was found among the crania of Eskimos and Fijians. In the case of the former the major difference was seen to be the "entire absence of thickened superciliary ridges"; whereas the latter, while manifesting "strongly developed superciliary ridges" had, in sharp contrast to the Galley Hill skull, a "fuller" and more prominent forehead.

In light of these results and the apparent geological antiquity of the skull, Newton moved his comparisons to the Palaeolithic crania from the Continent. As he pointed out, the best documented evidence of Palaeolithic Man was the two "remarkable human skeletons" which had been found at Spy, in Belgium, a decade earlier. From this comparison Newton found there were both striking similarities and differences between the Galley Hill and the Spy crania. With regard to the differences, he stressed not only the greater development of their eyebrow ridges, but also the presence of a post-orbital stricture which, along with a broad and inflated parietal region, gave these crania a distinctly bulging appearance unlike the Galley Hill specimen. A similar dichotomy was also revealed in the comparison of the jaws. Although in both appearance and dimensions their dentitions were "very nearly the same", the general structure of the Spy jaw diverged dramatically from that of Galley Hill: where the latter is comparatively small and has a projecting chin, the Spy jaw is "remarkable for the depth of the horizontal ramus and for its vertical, or slightly receding chin". However, except on a few minor points of anatomy, Newton found that the limb bones of the Spy skeleton did not diverge radically from those of Galley Hill.

In his subsequent discussion of these findings Newton seriously questioned whether the Galley Hill skull could be regarded simply as an English counterpart of the Borris skull, which Huxley had diagnosed as "the most ancient race known in Ireland and an extreme form of the Long Barrow type of England". Rather, it seemed that the Galley Hill and Borris skulls might represent a much earlier type of humanity, one that hailed not from the Neolithic but the Palaeolithic. If this was the case, was the Borris-Galley Hill race a derivative of the Continental race of Neanderthals, or an independent lineage? Newton seemed to favour the former idea:

> Hitherto we have not known of any physical characteristics of the race which made the Palaeolithic implements found in Britain. It has been supposed by some writer that there is no real break between the Palaeolithic and Neolithic races, but that a gradual change in type of implements may be traced, indicating a gradual development of the race that made them. If this be the case, then it might be that the Neolithic people descended from a Palaeolithic race, represented by Galley Hill and Borris skulls; having in the meantime developed higher crania, a fuller frontal, and rounder occipitals, at the same time losing the strong superciliary ridges.[69]

As Newton went on to acknowledge, there was in Britain, as in Continental circles, general support for the idea that the human species had originated and evolved somewhere outside of Europe, most probably in Central Asia. According to this viewpoint, the European fossil and archaeological record was interpreted as a discontinuous series — a succession of invasions throughout the Palaeolithic and Neolithic. Among the most ardent supporters of this race-succession paradigm in Britain was William Boyd Dawkins. In his version of this paradigm the European Neanderthals had been replaced during the Aurignacian by a palaeo-Eskimo type, who in turn had been succeeded in the Neolithic, first by an Iberian people (represented by the Basques), who were followed by a series of "Aryan" invasions.

These Neolithic invaders were, Dawkins argued, "immeasurably superior" to the aboriginal Eskimos of western Europe, but while they were completely driven out of Europe, leaving only their bones and artifacts, the Neolithic Iberians and Aryans were believed to have left the imprint of their physical type on modern European populations. As this scenario suggests, Dawkins believed there was a biocultural break between the Palaeolithic and Neolithic.[70]

Addressing this issue, Newton suggested that if Dawkins was correct in his assumption that the Europeans were Palaeolithic rather than Neolithic, and if, as he believed, the Galley Hill skeleton represented a Palaeolithic race, then it could be argued that the Eskimos were a derivative form who had lost their "strong superciliary ridges and developed their characteristically broad and anteriorly directed malar bones".[71]

Dawkins, who was in Newton's audience at Burlington House, chose not to debate this point. Instead he joined forces with John Evans, who strongly doubted the provenance of the Galley Hill skull.

Significantly, however, this opinion was not shared by a number of eolithophiles who were present. Allen Brown for one, said that as a "believer" in the biocultural continuity between the Palaeolithic and Neolithic, it was not surprising to him to find:

> a skull in the drift which showed affinities with some of the Palaeolithic skulls and those of the early Neolithic as in the specimen before them.[72]

This opinion was endorsed by the craniologist John G Garson and William Johnson Sollas (1849–1936), a former student of Huxley and professor of Geology and Zoology at Trinity College, Dublin.

In spite of this seemingly favourable reception the question of the skull's provenance prevailed, and ultimately this doubt, compounded with the uncertainties that still surrounded the evolutionary significance of the European Neanderthals, led to the Galley Hill skull and Newton's provocative hypothesis being placed, as Dawkins and Evans had recommended, in a "suspense account".

THE IGHTHAM CIRCLE

In the meantime, as Prestwich's views gathered support, Harrison's fame began to spread, and to attract to Ightham a steady flow of the curious and the devoted, who spent their weekends tramping across the North Downs in search of the remains of Plateau Man.

Among the earliest and most dedicated members of the developing Ightham Circle had been William J Lewis Abbott (1863–1933), a London jeweller and amateur geologist, and the Latin scholar, naturalist and geologist Alexander [James] Montgomery Bell. But despite their energetic efforts to tip the balance of opinion after Prestwich's delivery at the Anthropological Institute in 1891,[73] it was not until the British Association meeting held at Oxford in August 1894, that a significant advance in the eolithic debate was finally made. Here, the geologist and eolithophile Thomas Rupert Jones (1811–1911) presented a sympathetic synopsis of Prestwich's work on the Ightham "rudes", or, as he preferred "brownies", which led directly to the appointment of a committee to oversee an excavation of the west Plateau drifts to determine whether or not eoliths were to be found in these desposits.

The British Association "Eolith" Committee included Evans (chairman), Prestwich, Harrison and Harry Govier Seeley (1839–1909), professor of geology and palaeontology at King's College, London. Since Prestwich (who died in 1896) was ill at the time,

Three leading figures in the Ightham Circle during the 1890s: (left) Benjamin Harrison; (centre) Thomas Rupert Jones; (right) William J. Lewis Abbott. (Photograph of Abbott, courtesy of the Geological Society, London)

Harrison was left to supervise the operations and was directed to inform his colleagues of the progress of the work, which began early in October 1894. By the beginning of November, Harrison's labourer had opened two sections, one of which produced a few "worked" objects at a depth of 8ft, while the other yielded a number of Plateau palaeoliths and "rudes" below a depth of 5ft.[74] While Prestwich was heartened by Harrison's "convincers",[75] Evans remained unimpressed:

> The flints of which you send rough sketches [Evans wrote] have more the appearance of having been intentionally shaped than the two I have here. Has the absolute uselessness of such flints as tools never struck you, nor the fact that if the edge of a flint is chipped by hand it may just as well be made to present an acute as a right angle?[76]

Seeley on the other hand, while inclined to Evans' viewpoint, preferred at this juncture to suspend judgement.[77]

Although failing to unite the committee, the results of Harrison's excavations had, at least in the minds of some, established the geological provenance of the Plateau "rudes" which, as the eolithophile Alfred Russel Wallace (1823–1913) predicted, brought forth "more converts".[78] Among these new converts had been Edwin Tulley Newton and William Cunnington (1813–1906), a fossil collector from Devizes; but whereas Newton retained the conviction that the "Plateau rudes" had "been done intentionally",[79] the Devizes collector rapidly recanted his allegiance.

From his initial study of Harrison's collection, Cunnington had accepted the Plateau eoliths as artificial, since as he later confessed, "I knew of no natural flints of the same shape and character".[80] A subsequent and more detailed study of the specimens, however, led Cunnington to the conclusion that the chipped flints from the West Kent Plateau were not pre-Palaeolithic implements but natural objects.[81] This conclusion was based on the observation that "eolithic" chipping had occured on

Paleolithic implements from the Kent Plateau gravels, long after the tool had been manufactured.

Cunnington's case was presented to the Anthropological Institute on 6 April 1898 and, contrary to his expectations, he did not carry the day. Although several of those present, such as the geologists Frederick William Rudler (1840–1915) and Aubrey Strahan (1852–1928), supported Harry Seeley, who continued to suspend judgement,[82] the pervading opinion was pro-eolithic. The leading proponents were Henry Woodward (1832–1921), then Keeper of Geology at the British Museum (Natural History), and Rupert Jones — both of whom threw their weight behind the contention that Plateau "brownies" were of pre-Pleistocene age and not natural accidents "but of intentional origin";[83] — an opinion that was endorsed by A E Salter, the Revd Robert Ashington Bullen (1850–1912) and the fledgling amateur palaeontologist and geologist, Alfred Santer Kennard (1870–1948), who at the time was working in collaboration with Lewis Abbott on the excavation of a fossiliferous fissure at Basted, near Ightham.[84] Like his mentor,[85] Kennard vigorously objected to Cunnington's attribution of the Plateau "brownies" to natural causes "when no attempt had been made to show what those causes were, and how and when they operated"[86]. Replying to this criticism the geologist John W Gregory (1864–1932) noted that until now no attempt had been made to show that the implements in question had in fact been fashioned by either natural or artificial forces. Furthermore he stressed that Cunnington's evidence was based not on a single specimen as Kennard had claimed, but on a series from Harrison's collection, which, he contended, strongly supported the opinion that the Plateau eoliths were of natural origin[87].

Shortly thereafter, the Belgian geologist, Aimé Louis Rutot (1847–1933), of the Museé Royal d'Histoire Naturelle de Belgique in Brussels, began finding artifacts similar to those found in Kent. From the materials recovered from a number of sites in Flanders and elsewhere in France, Rutot claimed to have found several separate eolithic industries documenting the genesis of human culture in the Pliocene through to the emergence of the Chellean in the basal deposits of the Quaternary. This sequence comprised three distinct industrial types: the Reutelian, Mafflian and Mesvinian, the latter being considered to correspond with the eoliths of the West Kent Plateau.[88]

Buttressed by Rutot's work, the opening years of the new century saw significant gains for the eolithic movement both at home and abroad. Indeed, there was now hardly a meeting where the subject was not aired in one form or another.[89] But perhaps more revealing than anything else was the decision in 1902, by the authorities at the British Museum (Natural History) which hitherto had resisted placing eoliths on display, to formally recognize their existence and accord them a place in an exhibit called "Antiquities of the Stone Age".[90] Likewise, on the Continent, Rutot's energetic campaign for eoliths led to a number of significant conversions, the most notable being that of the prehistoric archaeologist, Louis Capitan (1854–1928), at the Ecole d'Anthropologie in Paris,[91] and the Breslau anatomist, Hermann Klaatsch (1863–1916).[92]

Responding to these events, John Evans, the ever-faithful watchdog of British archaeological interests, visited Brussels in 1903 to examine Rutot's collections first-hand. Excitedly the Belgian savant wrote to Harrison saying that he believed he had "succeeded in making Evans understand the eoliths and that he [was] very near adopting them".[93] Rutot, however, had misread the intransigent Englishman's mild manner, for on returning to England, Evans calmly informed Harrison that his opinion was unchanged.[94]

This viewpoint was shared by Marcellin Boule (1861–1942), at the Muséum National d'Histoire Naturelle in Paris. From the outset Boule had regarded both the eoliths and Rutot with suspicion. He once likened him to "an apostle with faith only in his own renovating genius".[95] Like Cunnington before him, Boule was convinced that most, if not all, of the eoliths were natural objects produced by a variety of geological forces, such as the torrential action of glacial rivers or the compression of deposits. The problem was how to demonstrate this experimentally. In 1905, Boule's attention was drawn to the cement works near Mantes (Seine-et-Oise), west of Paris, where in the huge mixing vats clay, chalk and water were churned "at the speed of the Rhone in flood". Here, among the flints that had inadvertently been subjected to this action, Boule found forms resembling those designated by Rutot and others as eoliths.[96]

Although some of the British eolithophiles were willing to concede that many of the Ightham "brownies" were nothing more than débris, they were not, as Edwin Ray Lankester (1847–1929), then Director of the British Museum (Natural History), indicated in his presidential address to the British Association at York in 1906, willing to "throw the baby out with the bathwater". To justify this position, several members of the Ightham circle such as Francis J Bennett (b. 1845), tried to demonstrate that while the machine-made eoliths produced by Boule resembled the real thing, they were actually quite different.[97]

Although the years immediately following Boule's attack were, as Abbott later confessed to Rutot,[98] bleak ones, the eolith case received a not entirely unexpected boost in 1909 from East Anglia.

THE EAST ANGLIA PUSH

The coastal cliffs near the town of Cromer in Suffolk provide important clues to the natural history of this region. Here the uppermost strata, composed of varying thicknesses of gravel drift, sit directly upon a thick deposit of "chalky boulder clay", which extends over the greater part of East Anglia. Lying between these upper layers and a basal mantle of chalk are the so-called Cromerian beds, whose constituent strata mark the transition from the Upper Pliocene to the Lower (Red Crag deposits) and Middle Pleistocene (Cromer Forest bed series). During the early 1860s, Charles Lyell had made a study of these East Anglian formations and had predicted that one day the Cromerian beds would yield ancient human remains. In fact before the century was out, Lewis Abbott reported the discovery of flints showing "unmistakable" signs of human workmanship in the "elephant" stratum of the Cromerian deposits.[99] After the turn of the century there were repeated reports of similar findings, many of which prompted anxious visits from the ever-vigilant, but now aged Evans.

In 1909, a year after Evans' death, James Reid Moir (1879–1944), who then assisted his father in managing a tailor's shop in Ipswich, began finding chipped implements in deposits beneath the Red Crag formations. Evidently Moir's natural impulse was to rush into print, but he was warned against doing so by his friend, Percy George Hamnall Boswell (1886–1960), who later became Professor of Geology at Imperial College, London. Reminding Moir of the uncertainties that still surrounded the geology of the Red Crag deposits, Boswell also drew his attention to the prevailing anti-eolithic sentiment.[100] Although initially heeding Boswell's advice, Moir was none the less convinced of the significance of his finds. He decided to take his case to Lankester, whom he knew to be favourably disposed to eolithic theory, as well as being an expert on East Anglian geology and palaeontology. On receiving samples from Moir's finds, Lankester wrote back: "You are certainly right in holding that early man must have worked in such a rougher way as this before he arrived at the high art of the perfect leaf-shaped and almond-shaped palaeoliths."[101] Evidently it was largely

Lankester's interest and promise of support that finally prompted Moir to throw all caution to the wind and announce in 1910 the arrival of preglacial man in East Anglia.[102] Not unexpectedly, Moir's discovery received the immediate endorsement of Abbott and other members of the Ightham circle, and in particular Frank Corner (1862–1939), a London physician and enthusiatic collector, who immediately relayed the news to his leader:

> Mr. Moir, Ipswich, has found implements of ancient types, under "glacial" and Crag deposits. Position and implements not open to doubt. I have seen twenty feet of undisturbed Crag . . . Pre-Crag Man.[103]

Harrison came quickly to the conclusion that Moir's specimens were, in form and character, less primitive than the High Plateau eoliths, and more closely analagous to the implements that he regarded as representing the transition from the Eolithic to the Palaeolithic.

However, as Boswell had predicted, Moir's claims were immediately challenged. Among these early critics was Fred N Haward (1871–1953), a London engineer with a passion for archaeology, and Samuel Hazzledine Warren (1872–1958), an amateur geologist who earned his living as a wholesale merchant in Whitechapel. In the case of Warren, his anti-eolithic views were already on record. When Boule had published his observations made at the Mantes cement works, Warren had released the results of his own investigations using a screw press to simulate natural geophysical forces.[104] From these studies, Warren believed that Rutot's eoliths, as well as those of Kent Plateau, could be explained by subsurface pressures that accompany foundering geological strata. The East Anglian specimens, as he immediately informed Moir, appeared to him to be of natural origin also.[105] Haward, following Warren's earlier example endeavoured to account for Moir's specimens in much the same way.[106] In an effort to intercept this anticipated attack, Moir published the results of his own extensive experiments in which he claimed all efforts to reproduce the sub-Crag froms by subjecting flints to chance forces of many kinds had repeatedly failed; whereas, he noted, he had managed to reproduce fair copies of them by deliberate knapping.[107]

At this point Lankester entered the fray with his communication to the Royal Society on 16 November 1911, entitled: "The discovery of a novel type of flint implements, proving the existence of skilled workers of flint in the Pliocene age."[108] To describe the most distinctive form of Moir's sub-Crag flints, which were shaped like the beak of an eagle, Lankester introduced the term "rostro-carinate" and referred them to what he called the "Icenian" (the Roman name for East Anglia) industry. Although many critics regarded this as nothing more than tactical camouflage, Lankester was convinced that Moir's East Anglian forms originated in the Pliocene and were prototypes of the early Palaeolithic industries.

With the renewed enthusiasm engendered by the discoveries in East Anglia, the search for the author of the sub-Crag "eagle beaks" and the Plateau "brownies" accelerated. In the closing months of 1911, a near complete, but anatomically modern human skeleton was discovered in the same brickfield where Moir had found the sub-Crag rostro-carinate tools some two years earlier. Here, the so-called Red Crag deposit sit directly upon the extensive London Clay beds. Between these Red Crag beds and the surface are two major strata: the Middle Glacial Sands and the Chalky Boulder Clay. According to Moir the Ipswich skeleton had been found at the junction between the boulder clay and the underlying sand and gravel stratum, and he was convinced that he had found the artificer of the rostro-carinate industry. The geologists, William Whitaker and John E Marr (1857–1933), whom Moir had called in to examine the site, however, were sceptical. While they could find no evidence to suggest that it had been an intrusive burial, both were seemingly reluctant to commit themselves to the idea of an essentially modern skeleton being contemporaneous with the basal boulder clay. Whitaker was clearly at a loss to explain the occurrence. "I fail to understand", he wrote in his report, "how man could have lived at the time of the commencement of the boulder clay".[109] Marr, on the other hand, while admitting that the stratum lying over the skeleton represented boulder clay, thought it a possibility that "the clay may have moved from another place" after its primary deposition.[110] Moir had no such reservations. He was convinced that the skeleton was contemporaneous with the chalky boulder clay. The skeleton was later described by Arthur Keith (1866–1955), Conservator of the Hunterian Museum at the Royal College of Surgeons, London.[111] Although Keith shared Moir's enthusiasm for this skeleton, there were many, including Lankester, who did not. At this time the idea of the great antiquity of the modern human form was still regarded by many as an evolutionary heresy, and Lankester worried that Moir's endorsement of the Ipswich skeleton might seriously jeopardize advancement of the case for the rostro-carinate industry. Indeed, within months of this discovery becoming known, it was apparent to Lankester that discussions of the Ipswich skeleton were becoming muddled up with the rostro-carinates, "with which he has no more to do than has the Emperor of China ...", Lankester angrily commented to Moir. Much to Lankester's obvious relief the Ipswich controversy was soon overshadowed by an even more remarkable discovery made in the Weald of East Sussex, at a place called Piltdown, during the summer of 1912. As his confidential report to Moir indicates, he found the Piltdown remains a much more attractive proposition:

> ... I have today seen the new fossil man and heard all about it. It is simply splendid ... It was found in a gravel of a very peculiar kind — a thin layer, containing very rough Chellian [sic] flints and some like sub-Crag things — others like Ightham. The glaze and appearance of these flints is quite peculiar, more like Ightham than anything else. Bits of teeth of Elephas meridionalis, of Hippopotamus, and some others — fragments — all in a condition resembling sub-Crag — occur...
>
> It seems quite possible that it is our Pliocene Man — the maker of rostro-carinate flints! at any rate if they say to us, "you say we call in vague – unknown agencies – such as torrents, and pressure to produce these flints by natural fracture, but you are in the same position of calling in a hypothetical man. You have no other evidence that such a man was there!" Now we can say, "Here he is."[112]

2   Piltdown: a *prima facie* case

There was a general idea that the missing link would be a beast with beetling brows and low forehead. These, however, were mere excrescences like the horns of the cow, and they would be nearer the truth in looking for an animal with a rounded head and steep brows.[1]

THE DELIVERY

The Weald — the Andredeswealde of the Saxons, the Anderida Forest of the Romans — is that tract of land enclosed by the chalk formations of the North and South Downs. In the north the chalk Downs traverse the entire length of Kent. At Guildford, these formations turn south towards Portsmouth and the Isle of Wight in the west; while in the east they run from Petersfield through Steyning to Lewes. At Lewes, the county town of East Sussex, where Gideon Mantell (1790–1852) had once delighted the imagination of early Victorians with the mysterious footprints of Wealden iguanodons and other *Wonders of Geology*,[2] the chalk phalanx of the South Downs is deflected southwards to Beachy Head, where they erupt as a long and dramatic skirt of white cliffs.

Built on the steep western slope of the Ouse river valley, the old picturesque town of Lewes has a commanding view of the Sussex Weald and the rich lowland plain which stretches south-east towards Pevensey. From Lewes, the Ouse flows south through the Downs to Newhaven on the coast, while to the north it snakes its way through gentle and green, undulating country from its source in the central Weald. After flowing eastwards past Sheffield Park, situated some miles west of the small market town of Uckfield, the Ouse turns south towards Lewes. It is at this bend, on the north bank, about a mile from the river and a little more than a mile or two from Uckfield, on a small plateau near Piltdown Common in the parish of Fletching, that Charles Dawson (1864–1916), an amateur geologist and a solicitor with chambers in Uckfield, found an old gravel bed that had yielded the remarkable finds seen by Lankester.

While later described as a pit, it was in reality a shallow trench that had been dug into a gravel bed situated on the north-west side of a tree-lined drive leading to Barkham Manor where Dawson was Steward. Over the years this deposit had been exploited as road metal, resulting in a small trench extending north-eastwards, parallel to the drive. At Piltdown this gravel bed forms an irregular band that varies anywhere from 6 inches to 3 feet in thickness, and rests on the undulating surface of the Hastings Beds, a complex series of sedimentary rocks that dominate the underlying structure of the central Weald. Although composed largely of sandstone and sand, with subordinate beds of clay, limestone and ironstone seams are not an uncommon feature, as indicated by the characteristic chocolate colour of the Barkham Manor gravels. Also, "brown" flints are occasionally encountered. What had initially led Dawson to this gravel bed at Piltdown, as he later recalled, had been the observation of such "peculiar brown flints" being used to mend a farm road close to Piltdown Common.[3] While flint deposits were not unknown in the central Weald they were generally of the "tabular" variety, rather than of the "nodular" form more

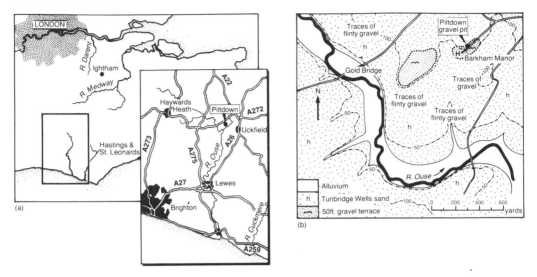

The Piltdown site: (a) general map showing part of south-east counties of Kent and Sussex, with inset showing general location of Piltdown; (b) more detailed geographical map of the district surrounding Barkham Manor. (Based on Edmunds in Weiner et al., 1955:274)

commonly found in the Chalk formations of the North and South Downs. On making further enquiries, Dawson was apparently "astonished" to learn that these brown nodular flints had come from the local gravel bed at Barkham Manor; no such flint deposits had ever before been recorded this far north. Indeed, the limit of flint-bearing gravels in the Ouse valley was at that time placed some 4 to 5 miles to the south, midway between Piltdown and Lewes. The distribution of these flints was generally thought to represent the residue of the Wealden chalk dome, and it was supposed that during its slow erosion, its resident nodular flints had either been crushed or swept to the rim of the evolving bowl of the Kent and Sussex Weald.

Exactly when Dawson first became interested in the Barkham gravel bed is not clear, but whenever it was, it appears that he did not follow through with an immediate study of its geological significance. However, recognizing that the bed might well be fossiliferous he apparently did take the precaution of asking the farm hands at Barkham to keep a sharp look-out for any bones or fossils they might uncover. Since this gravel bed was only intermittently worked for a few weeks a year, depending on the condition of the farm's roads, several years apparently passed before the reported "coconut" incident occurred, which, as Dawson later claimed, served to heighten his interest in this site still further.

Evidently, sometime in 1908, while working the gravel bed at Barkham Manor, an object resembling a "coconut" was accidently shattered by a labourer's pickaxe. A fragment of this "coconut" was retrieved and later handed to Dawson who identified it as a portion of a thick human cranium (left parietal). Galvanized by this discovery, Dawson made an immediate but unsuccessful search for the other fragments. Assisted by Samuel Allinson Woodhead (1862–1943), a close friend and chemistry instructor at Uckfield Agricultural College, he spent a whole day in a fruitless effort to recover the smashed remains. According to Dawson's recollection of this venture, they found only "pieces of dark brown ironstone closely resembling the piece of skull". He also recalled that the search was hampered by "the season being wet, [which made fossils] ... difficult to see".[4]

While there was every reason to suppose that the missing fragments had been removed with the gravel to be used as road metal or crushed beyond recognition by farm traffic, Dawson evidently could not bring himself to abandon the site: "I still paid occasional visits to the pit", he remembered, "but it was not until several years later that, when having a look over the rain-washed spoil heaps, I lighted on a larger piece of the same skull which included a portion of the left supra-orbital border".[5] And not long after, during another visit to Barkham Manor, he reportedly found a piece of a hippopotamus tooth. These latter finds were it seems made sometime in the autumn of 1911.[6]

It was, however, some months before Dawson got around to reporting these finds to his "old friend", Arthur Smith Woodward (1864–1944), the Keeper of Geology at the British Museum (Natural History) in South Kensington. His reason for bringing these finds to Woodward's attention was not just a matter of friendship, but rather because since 1884 he had been an honorary collector for the Museum. "I have come across a very old Pleistocene (?) bed", he wrote to Woodward, early in February 1912:

> overlying the Hastings Bed between Uckfield and Crowborough which I think is going to be interesting. It has a lot of iron-stained flints in it, so I suppose it is the oldest known flint gravel in the Weald.

He also noted, unceremoniously, that he had discovered a "portion of a human (?) skull", which he likened in "solidity" to the human jaw that had been found near Heidelberg some years earlier.[7]

By return of post, Woodward expressed an interest in Dawson's finds and indicated his desire to examine the site. However, frustrated first by the weather,[8] and then a trip to Berlin in April to examine the remains of the colossal Cretaceous dinosaurs which had been discovered by recent German expeditions in East Africa,[9] it was not until late May[10] that Woodward was finally able to examine Dawson's Piltdown collection. A week later, on Saturday, 2 June, Woodward made the long awaited visit to Piltdown.

The details of this excursion have been preserved in a letter written by the Jesuit priest and budding palaeontologist Pierre Teilhard de Chardin (1881–1955), whom Dawson had known since 1909, when they had met, quite by accident, in a quarry near Hastings. Sharing a common interest in Wealden fossils, these two men had, since that first encounter, developed a friendly scientific alliance which had led, among other things, to the assembly of a valuable collection of Wealden fossil plants that Dawson had duly relayed to the British Museum (Natural History), where it was subsequently described by the Cambridge botanist Albert C Seward (1863–1941). Although Dawson is known to have shown Teilhard his finds some weeks earlier it appears that, like Woodward, this was his first visit to the Piltdown site. According to Teilhard's letter, the day began with a "hearty English breakfast" at Dawson's home in Lewes, followed by a short train ride to Uckfield where they met up with Woodward and from there, "armed with all the makings for a picnic", they all set off by car for Barkham Manor. Here, Teilhard's letter continues:

> [W]e were left off ... on a grassy strip 4–5 metres wide, which skirts a wooded path leading to a farm. Under this grass, there's a 50 centimetre layer of gravel which is gradually being removed to be used for roads. A man was there to help us dig; armed with picks and sieves, we worked for several hours and finally had success. Dawson discovered a new fragment of the famous skull ... and I myself put a hand on a fragment of an elephant's molar; this made me really worth something in Woodward's eyes. He jumped on the piece with the enthusiasm of a youth and all the fire that his apparent coldness covered came out...[11]

Workers at Piltdown circa 1912–13. (From left to right) Robert Kenward jnr. (standing), Charles Dawson (sitting), 'Venus' Hargreaves (centre), Arthur Smith Woodward and the goose 'Chipper'.

Teilhard's letter, however, made no mention of the triangular-shaped palaeolith he also found that afternoon.[12]

Woodward was impressed by what he saw and agreed with Dawson that the pit warranted further investigation. It was resolved that they would devote their summer weekends and occasional holidays to sifting through the spoil-heaps and to the careful excavation of neighbouring undisturbed patches of the site. Teilhard was apparently otherwise engaged.[13]

According to both Dawson's and Woodward's later accounts of their work at Piltdown during the summer of 1912, they were able to distinguish three distinct strata in the gravel bed. At the top there was a thin layer of top-soil that sat on a stratum of pale yellow sand and clay. Below this lay a thick seam of dark brown "ferruginous" gravel, which in the basal layers was cemented together into a hard mass by resident iron oxide, hence the frequent mention in their published reports of the use of pickaxes. Later, in 1913, excavations revealed a fourth layer, consisting of a thin band of yellow mud that served to partition the "ferruginous" gravel stratum from the Wealden bedrock below.[14]

The work was, as Woodward later reported, slow because of the stained condition of the bones which rendered them almost invisible against the dark coloured gravel.[15] He explained:

Arthur Smith Woodward and the Abbé Henri Breuil (circa 1913) at Piltdown.

> We could not employ more than one labourer to do the heavy work of digging because every spadeful had to be watched, and generally passed through a sieve. It was also necessary to crawl over the spoil heaps each time that the rain washed the particles of gravel and made them more easy to examine. We [thus] spread the gravel as much as possible, so that, if there were rain between our visits, it could be well washed in readiness for our return.[16]

Despite these difficulties, the first weeks at Piltdown appear to have been marked by several notable finds:

> In one heap of soft material rejected by the workman we found [Woodward recalled] three pieces of the right parietal bone of the human skull — one piece on each of three successive days. These fragments fitted together perfectly, and so had evidently not been disturbed since they were thrown away. After much inspection, which prevented my discarding it as a piece of iron-stone, I found in another heap an important fragment which fitted the broken edge of the occipital bone [which is presumed to have been the bone found by Dawson on June 2nd] and gave us the line to contact with the left parietal bone.[17]

In addition to these finds, Woodward and Dawson also recovered a handful of eoliths, the fossilized teeth of an elephant, mastodon and beaver; and in an adjacent field, "a piece of antler of a red deer and a tooth of a horse, both fossilized, which [they] supposed had been thrown over the hedge by the workmen".[18]

Because neither Woodward nor Dawson kept a record of their work at Piltdown it is not possible to say with any confidence when and by whom many of these various finds were made. However, from a comparison of their published recollections, it appears that the right parietal and occipital fragments were found shortly before the discovery of a broken lower jaw. This latter find was made by Dawson in the presence of Woodward sometime towards the end of June, after a reportedly "unproductive day's work". Recalling this incident, Woodward wrote many years later:

> Mr. Dawson was exploring some untouched remnants of the original gravel at the bottom of the pit, when we both saw the half of a human lower jaw fly out in front of the pick-shaped end of the hammer which he was using.[19]

On closer examination this specimen was found to be the right half of a remarkably apelike mandible. While the chin region was missing, the body of the mandible still retained two molars that looked decidedly more human than apelike. This, together with the fact that it had been recovered from a spot immediately adjacent to where Woodward had found a cranial fragment, led them to conclude that the jaw had belonged to the shattered skull. To have supposed otherwise, as several critics later did, was, in Woodward's opinion, unjustified. The likelihood of making such a find "in a single cubic yard of gravel", would not only be "startling", but also defied the laws of probability.[20] Indeed both were convinced that they had found the remains of entirely new form of humanity — a creature who had once roamed across the High Plateau of Kent and Sussex at the dawn of the British Palaeolithic.

THE SYNTHESIS

According to Boyd Dawkins' reconstructed map of Western Europe, at the commencement of the Pleistocene the River Ouse, like the Somme, had formerly been tributaries of an ancient river flowing westwards on the present site of the English Channel. The fact that the Piltdown site sat on a plateau which Dawson had estimated to be situated between 80 and 120ft above the present level of the River Ouse, naturally led him and Woodward to equate this bed with the 100ft Terrace of the Somme and similar river valley systems of north-west Europe.[21] It appeared to them that the gravel sheet covering the Piltdown plateau had been laid down sometime either during the Upper Pliocene or, at the latest, in the early Pleistocene.

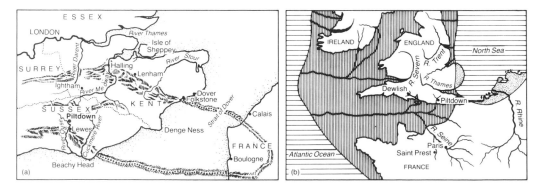

The geological relationship between the south-east of England and the north-west of France: (a) another version of the "Dome" hypothesis showing the Weald, the position of Piltdown, and the extension of the Wealden boundary to France (after Keith, 1915); (b) map of southern England and northern France, showing the course and tributaries of the ancient channel river. (After Boyd Dawkins in Keith, 1915)

The faunal remains that had been recovered were a mixture, and could be separated into two distinct groups. The first, represented by broken pieces of teeth, were of two species of elephants, namely *Mastodon arvernensis* and a primitive form of elephant (*Stegodon*) which resembled the early Proboscideans that Hugh Falconer had found in the Siwalik Hills of India; later this guess was verified by a number of workers who identified the molars as belonging to *Elephas planifrons*.[22] The remains in the second group consisted of portions of two teeth of *Hippopotamus amphibius*, two molars of *Castor fiber* (beaver) and a molar tooth from a modern horse *Equus caballus*, plus the remains of a red deer *Cervus elaphus*.[23]

The two species of elephants in the first group were Pliocene-Pleistocene forms, and rather exceptional finds. Although the remains of fossil elephants were not unknown in England, they had, until this time, tended to be of the southern mammoth, *Elephas meridionalis*, a type which had been found at Barcombe, a site situated some 7 miles south of Piltdown, by the geologist Robert Godwin-Austen (1808–84) in the mid 1850s,[24] as well as in the Red Crag deposits of East Anglia. The remains of *Mastodon arvernensis*, however, were unknown in England and, hitherto, had only been found on the Continent.[25] As for the "primitive" *Stegodon*, it appeared to be an entirely new form. At this time the species of elephant known to have successively inhabited the European Pleistocene, and which served as important chronological markers, were:

Lower Pleistocene	*Elephas meridionalis*
Middle Pleistocene	*Elephas antiquus*
Upper Pleistocene	*Elephas primigenius*

Thus, the Piltdown species could be attributed to either the Upper Pliocene or to the still vague hinterland of the boundary between the Tertiary and the Quaternary, the First Glaciation, which was, by this time, becoming more widely known as the Günz stage. In contrast, the fauna in the second group were more varied and unequivocally Lower Pleistocene; but depending on the interpretation, the assemblage could be attributed to either the First (Günz-Mindel) or Second (Mindel-Riss) Interglacial.

The condition of the remains in both groups was also mixed. In the first group, they were highly mineralized and showed varying degrees of having been "rolled" by water action; whereas the second group were seen to be in a better state of preservation. Besides being less mineralized, they also showed little or no signs of having been subjected to any violent rolling action.[26] A similar situation was reflected in the stone artifacts and the human cranial fragments. Some were worn, while others showed "no more wear and tear than they might have received *in situ*".[27] Taking this evidence into account, Dawson concluded that the gravel bed must have been reconstructed sometime during the early Pleistocene, and that the bed probably represented a flood deposit. Since all of the fossil remains had been found in a relatively small area of the gravel bed it seemed reasonable to suppose that the remains had been brought together in an eddy. But were the various components of this assemblage coeval, or were some of them adventitious? One possible scenario was that the worn dental remains *Stegodon* and *Mastodon arvernensis*, along with the rude and battered eoliths, had become inadvertently mixed in with the other remains when the bed was reconstructed at the commencement of the Pleistocene.

As the geological and archaeological expert, Dawson was undoubtedly guided by knowledge of the work done by the French archaeologist, Victor Commont (1866–1918), in the Somme river valley. Besides establishing the 100ft Terrace as being synonymous with the Lower Palaeolithic, Commont's study had also provided evidence to support the existence in the high gravel terraces of the Somme for a Pre-Chellean industry. By this time it was generally accepted by most workers that the Chellean represented the crudest form of the Lower Palaeolithic core tool industries, while the finer and more symmetrical forms of these core tools, characterized by Boucher de Perthes' "haches" or "coup de poing", represented a refinement of the technique which many workers now identified as belonging to the Acheulean tradition. The crudely retouched flints of the Pre-Chellean were considered by Commont to be the prototypes of the Chellean-Acheulean "coup de poing". Not everyone agreed with this viewpoint, but there were many who did, and not surprisingly the eolithophiles among them were quick to note the similarity between their assemblages and those of Commont's.

Although there was at this time still considerable uncertainty surrounding the correlation of the industries of the Lower Palaeolithic with the glacial-interglacial cycles, the Chellean was generally viewed as the commencement of the Palaeolithic which seemed to coincide with Geikie's Second Interglacial (or using the nomenclature of Penck & Brückner, the Mindel-Riss); whereas the Acheulean appeared to straddle the next glacial advance (Riss) and interglacial period (Riss-Würm), where it overlapped with the Mousterian.

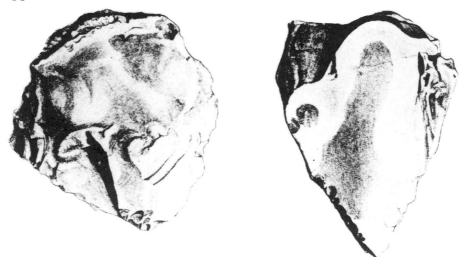

Examples of Piltdown palaeoliths.

Unlike Dawson, who seems not to have had any strong views on the subject of eoliths,[28] Woodward had been an early convert to the opinions of Prestwich and Harrison.[29] Recognizing that this was still a controversial issue, Woodward prudently chose not to promote this viewpoint, a decision which Lewis Abbott later condemned as "dishonourable" and "disgraceful to science".[30] In Abbott's opinion, the authorship of the crude artifacts from Piltdown was beyond question, and he had, on being shown some of them by Dawson at the beginning of July, issued the authoritative diagnosis: "Man — Man all over".[31] But Dawson was troubled by this blanket diagnosis: some of the Piltdown eoliths were hardly worn at all, while others had a battered appearance — several of which were highly reminiscent of Harrison's Plateau "brownies". Among these Dawson noted that they were of the "awl and hollow scraper" variety. Furthermore, as he later noted:

> The true "bulb of percussion" hardly ever shows itself on these supposed implements,
> except on a very small scale, as the prismatic fracture of the flint does not admit of it,
> and their form and chipping, whether natural or artificial, were largely governed by
> this species of fracture.[32]

While Dawson clearly harboured some reservations on a number of the eolithic forms in the Piltdown assemblage, there were others whose rude workmanship he likened to those of the Chellean or Pre-Chellean industries. These implements were characterized by being worked on one face only, as well as by their "massive", and slightly worn appearance. Furthermore, they had been found in a "very slightly higher stratum" where the remains of the human skull had been found; and "among the spoil-heaps were found others of a similar, though perhaps earlier stage".[33] Through these carefully chosen words Dawson appeared to be implying that the Piltdown artifacts might well represent a definite cultural sequence.

The reconstruction of the skull was also not without its difficulties. Indeed there appear to have been several attempts made at assembling its pieces before settling on the version that was finally unveiled on 18 December at the Geological Society. From the nine cranial fragments it was possible to reconstruct four larger pieces of the original brain case, representing nearly the whole of the left side, and a considerable portion of the parietal region of the right side which articulated with a large fragment of the occiput. But, since the upper margins of the left and right parietals (with the accompanying sagittal suture) were missing, it was not immediately clear how they should be articulated. This was critical since their relative position ultimately determined the size of the cranial vault. Although the small occipital fragment Woodward had found enabled the larger occipital fragment to be articulated with the right parietal region, the problem was lining up its median line with the left side of the cranium. Convinced that he was dealing with a primitive form of humanity it was Woodward's expectation that the cranial volume would be smaller than that of either a modern or Neanderthal cranium. Evidence for the true position of the middle line of the left side, Woodward contended, could be found in the frontal portion of the brain-case. This fragment, the largest continuous piece of bone in the collection, comprised portions of both the frontal and parietal regions. Here, near the lambdoid suture of the parietal, Woodward said:

> The position of the middle line is indicated by the impression of the longitudinal sinus
> on the cerebral [inner] face of the bone at both these points, and by a slight
> longitudinal ridge along the outer face at the hinder end of the parietal region.[34]

Using these anatomical landmarks he was thereby able to orientate the two incomplete halves of the shattered skull into what he believed to be their correct positions. The result was a skull measuring 150 millimetres across its widest part, and just short of 190 millimetres in length.

Since a small portion of the eyebrow ridge remained on the left frontal bone, it was possible to determine that the skull did not possess inflated eyebrow ridges that characterized Neanderthal crania. Indeed, aside from the general thickness of the cranial bones, the emerging conformation of the cranium was decidedly modern in appearance. The endocranial surface of this skull proved to be most revealing; the whole pattern of the middle meningeal veins and arteries of the brain which formerly filled the internal cavity looked most primitive, and served to reinforce the conviction that the associated ape-like mandible belonged with the skull.

In both size and appearance Woodward believed the mandibular fragment corresponded well with the cranium, but there were several problems. Firstly, the

The main cranial fragments of Piltdown I.

fragment representing the right half of the jaw was missing its articular condyle and secondly, its articular socket — the glenoid cavity — was not represented on this side of the cranium. This problem was overcome, however, by reversing the right half of the mandible to take the place of the left half, where the glenoid cavity was well-preserved in the left temporal fragment. Since this cavity and surrounding region was in all respects anatomically modern, Woodward presumed that the missing

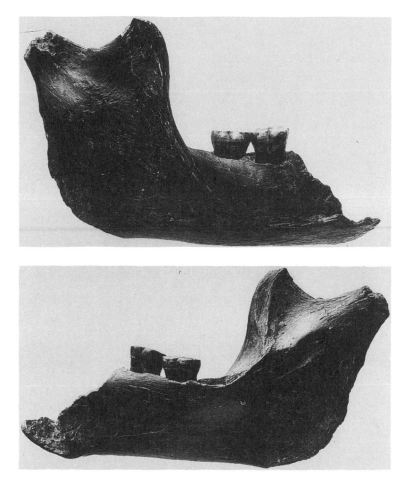

The Piltdown right mandibular ramus: (above) external view; (below) internal view.

mandibular condyle had a corresponding morphology — a decision that was grounded in other anatomical features of this curious jaw.

In a number of details the Piltdown mandible was found to have some human and some anthropoid ape characteristics. Compared with chimpanzee and other anthropoid apes, the jaw had a decidedly gracile appearance. Its sigmoid notch was shallower than normally encountered in the rami of ape mandibles; a fact which led Woodward to infer that the articular condyle must have been short as in fossil and modern human mandibulae. But perhaps more than any other feature, the one that had clearly drawn Woodward's attention from the outset, was the flat crowns and nonaligned occlusal surfaces of the two *in situ* molars, a condition clearly indicative of a wear-pattern common among Australian aborigines and other modern "primitive" races, and never encountered in ape dentition. There were, however, some major differences that served to underscore not only its ape affinities but also to separate it from all other known human jaws.

The chief differences were to be found in the mandibular body. Aside from being a vehicle for a lower set of teeth, the mandible also serves as an anchor for the muscles of mastication, as well as the origin of the muscles of the tongue and the floor of the mouth. The chewing or masseter muscles are attached to the outer surface of the mandibular body, whose insertion in modern human jaws leave only a vague impression on the bone surface. In the Piltdown jaw, however, this region has a deep hollow for the insertion of a seemingly powerful masseter muscle. More striking is the condition of its interior surface. In human and ape jaws, the inner aspect of the mandibular ramus is marked by an opening (foramen) for the dental nerve, whose anterior margin carries a small projecting spine. Originating directly below this foramen, and running obliquely down the remaining length of the ramus is a groove which carries blood vessels and nerves to the mylohyoid muscle. In the Piltdown jaw this so-called mylohyoid groove is not markedly expressed, in fact, as Woodward noted only a "slight impress" of this groove was detectable. Another feature is the flange of bone known as the mylohyoid ridge, to which the muscular floor of the mouth is attached. In human jaws, and to a lesser extent in apes, this ridge is conspicuous, but in the Piltdown mandible this region of the body is remarkably smooth.

Commenting on some of its more overt apelike characters, Woodard said that in addition to its ramus being wide and stout, as in apes:

> It is ... very interesting to note that as the ramus curves [and slopes down] to the symphysis, its lower margin exhibits an increasingly wider flattening, which begins the second molar, [and then] slopes upwards and outwards, and ends in front in a strongly retreating chin.[35]

In the ape jaw the muscle attachments for the tongue (the genio-glossal) and larynx (genio-hyoid) are located in a deep pit situated above a bony flange, sometimes known as the simian shelf, which serves to anchor the digastric muscles. In modern humans this genial pit and simian shelf are absent. Since the upper part of the symphysis was absent in the Piltdown mandible, and the fractured end provided no visible information on the original structure of this region, Woodward speculated that these muscles had in all probability been attached in much the same way as modern apes. Thus, in reconstructing this area, Woodward decided to compromise, and restore it as an intermediary form between that of an ape (namely chimpanzee) and that of the most primitive of human jaws — those of the fossil Neanderthalers. In making this decision Woodward was undoubtedly aware of the Darwinian prediction that the early progenitors of the human family had in all probability been equipped with "great canine teeth",[36] and as such provided the Piltdown jaw with moderately large, but totally hypothetical canine teeth. "If this restoration prove[s] to be correct", he later commented:

> the length of the alveolar border in front of the molars is 60 mm, instead of 30 to 40 mm, as in all known human jaws [fossil and otherwise]; and it seems difficult to fill this space without assuming that a relatively large canine was present.

But, taking other factors into consideration, Woodward reasoned:

> [T]he canine in any case cannot have been very prominent ... [given] the remarkable flatness of the worn surface of the molar teeth. [Their] Enamel and dentine have been equally worn down by very free movements in mastication, and such a marked regular flattening has never been observed among apes, though it is occasionally met with in low types of men.[37]

Accordingly a large canine tooth was modelled, whose dimensions were equal to those of a male chimpanzee and far beyond those of the largest known human canines. As for the rest of the teeth in the dental arcade, Woodward inferred that the width and shape of the incisors would also be more ape-like.

Some other interesting features of the Piltdown dentition were revealed by X-ray pictures which served to underscore further in Woodward's mind the transitional status of the Sussex mandible. While the roots of the Piltdown molars were divergent and not fused, as they are in Neanderthals, their form and spacing was much more reminiscent of "primitive" modern human races than those of apes. The restored Piltdown dentition was a mixture. In front the teeth were decidedly simian, while in the rear they were essentially human. In light of all these findings, Woodward made the muzzle and front teeth of the restored Piltdown mandible wider and more massive than that of chimpanzee. To harmonize with this he gave the symphysial and chin region a markedly backward sloping appearance, again comparable to that of a chimpanzee; while the entire dental arcade he presented as a parabolic arrangement (similar to that found in the human condition), rather than the characteristic parallel pattern found in the anthropoid apes.

On reaching this stage, under Woodward's watchful direction, the skull and mandible were restored and fitted by Frank Barlow (1880–1951), a senior preparator at the British Museum (Natural History). The resulting form was quite remarkable — a curious blend of ape and human features. The assembled braincase, although distinguished by its low capacity (estimated to be 1070 cc), its overall globular appearance and more particularly its steep smooth-browed forehead was, as Woodward confessed, surprisingly modern and scarcely a basis for removing it from the human genus. But when the jaw was added and the face restored, the Piltdown skull underwent a remarkable transformation to a form of humanity quite distinct from that of any of the known ancient and modern forms of *Homo*.

THE INTERPRETATION

In 1895, several months after Edwin Tulley Newton had paraded the Galley Hill skull before the Geological Society, the Dutch anatomist, Eugène Dubois (1858–1941), had descended upon London armed with the remains of what he believed was the long awaited missing link, the transitional form between man and ape which Ernst Haeckel (1834–1919), his former mentor at the University of Jena, had predicted back in the late 1860s.[38] These remains consisted of a single upper molar tooth, a heavily mineralized skullcap and a thigh-bone, which he had found while digging in a fossiliferous gravel terrace situated along the Bengawan (Solo) River, near Trinil in Central Java during 1891 and 1892. While incomplete, enough of the skullcap remained to appreciate the existence of a heavy, overhanging eyebrow ridge that was somewhat reminiscent of the Neanderthals. Beyond this bony ledge, the forehead slopes back at a dramatically low angle, and at the rear, the occipital bone is bent sharply down and forward, resulting in a cranial profile that also crudely mimicked that of Neanderthal crania. Unlike Neanderthals, the Trinil skull was found to have a much smaller cranial capacity, estimated to be in the region of 850 cubic centimetres. The thigh-bone, which was found some 50 ft away, but in the same stratum as the skullcap, was essentially modern in appearance. While this, and the seemingly bizarre marriage of a decidedly ape-like skullcap to a modern femur, led many workers to dispute the association, Dubois was convinced they belonged together and that he had found Haeckel's hypothetical construct *Pithecanthropus*.[39] In recognition of this he dubbed his fossil *Pithecanthropus erectus*.

From the mammalian fauna found in association with these bones, Dubois had assigned the Trinil fossil to the Lower Quaternary, but he wondered if it might even be earlier. The difficulty was, as Dubois himself had acknowledged,[40] distinguishing between Tertiary and Quaternary faunas in a region that had been unaffected by glaciations. Be this as it may, Dubois was persuaded that his specimen was pivotal — connecting the human fossils of the Middle and Upper Pleistocene with those of the anthropomorphous apes of the Pliocene and Miocene. He viewed Lartet's *Dryopithecus*, the Miocene ape from France, as an evolutionary cul-de-sac, and believed that the Miocene-Pliocene fossil ape, *Palaeopithecus sivalensis*, which had been found in the Siwalik Hills of north India,[41] marked the point where the anthropomorphous apes diverged from the human stem.

Although there was a sizeable number of both British and Continental workers who endorsed Dubois' general thesis, this movement was neatly counterbalanced by non-believers,[42] many of whom supported the German anatomist, Rudolf Virchow (1821–1902), who had argued that the skullcap belonged to an extinct giant gibbon and dismissed the human femur as a fortuitous association.

During the next decade Dubois' *Pithecanthropus* and its inferred relationship to the European Neanderthals was subjected to a careful and protracted study by the Strasbourg anatomist Gustav Schwalbe (1844–1916). From this study Schwalbe was able to confirm Fraipont's earlier assessment of the Spy material, that the Neanderthals did indeed represent the remnants of a distinct group that had occupied Europe during the Middle Palaeolithic. But unlike Fraipont, and Huxley before him, Schwalbe believed that the Neanderthalers were so far removed from all existing varieties of humanity as to warrant the rank of a distinct species: *Homo primigenius*. This claim for a new taxon was, Schwalbe believed, justified by the numerous "pithecoid" (apelike) features resident in Neanderthal crania.

In elevating the Neanderthals to the status of a separate species, it was not Schwalbe's intention to exclude them from human evolution as many of his contemporaries thought. On the contrary, he was merely following normal zoological practice which enabled a species to be defined on strictly morphological grounds; and as an adherent to transmutational theory, he was fully aware of the presumed fact that an ancient species could undergo progressive change and thereby be ancestral to related extant forms. Furthermore, viewing the fossil record this way served to underscore the case for the European Neanderthals being structural intermediates between the *Pithecanthropus* in the Lower Pleistocene and the human fossils of the Upper Pleistocene, who in turn were seen to bridge the structural chasm which he saw between *Homo primigenius* and the Australian aborigines, then considered to be the most primitive of extant human beings. Although favourably disposed to this linear arrangement, it was, Schwalbe recognized, also possible to portray both the Neanderthals and *Pithecanthropus* as specialized off-shoots from the main line of human evolution. But as he pointed out, such an arrangement still did not eliminate either the Neanderthals or *Pithecanthropus* as representative stages in the development of modern *Homo sapiens*: "For in the latter case also, the ancestors must have looked similar to the preserved remains of *Pithecanthropus* and *Homo primigenius*".[43]

The general acceptance of Schwalbe's Neanderthal hypothesis was then seriously undermined by new evidence. Throughout the nineteenth century there had been scattered reports of anatomically modern human skeletons being found in ancient strata, but by and large these discoveries had been conveniently dismissed by evolutionists as either chance associations or simply the results of uncritical assessments and control of stratigraphic techniques. However, during the closing years of the first decade of the twentieth century, evidence surfaced at the rock

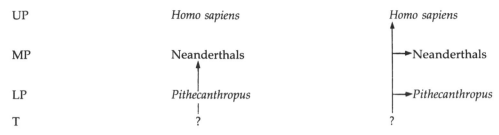

A schematic representation of Schwalbe's views on the possible phylogenetic relationship of Neanderthals and *Pithecanthropus* to modern humans (1906). UP: Upper Pleistocene; MP: Middle Pleistocene; LP: Lower Pleistocene; Tertiary epoch.

shelters of La Ferrassie and Combe Capelle in the Dordogne region of south-west France, which narrowed the temporal separation of the Mousterian Neanderthalers from the anatomically modern human skeletons of the Aurignacian.[44] This evidence, compounded with the results of new comparative anatomical studies (which confirmed Schwalbe's earlier findings that the Neanderthal skeleton was peppered with structural peculiarities) prompted a number of workers to reject the Neanderthalers as the evolutionary precursor of modern *Homo sapiens*.[45]

Among the various workers at this time who were vigorously promoting this antagonistic view had been Marcellin Boule at the Muséum National d'Histoire Naturelle in Paris. Boule became convinced of the enormous structural hiatus between Neanderthals and modern humans, largely as the result of a meticulous study of the near complete Neanderthaler skeleton found at La Chapelle-aux-Saints, near Corrèze, France, in 1908. These findings, compounded with evidence of what seemed to Boule to be a quantum leap in human culture at the boundary of the Mousterian and the Aurignacian,[46] led him to conclude that the Neanderthalers could no longer be regarded as a reasonable antecedant of modern humanity.

These views were announced, three months before the official unveiling of the Piltdown discoveries, at the 14th International Congress of Anthropology & Prehistoric Archaeology held in Geneva during September 1912. Here Boule proclaimed that the European Neanderthalers were an archaic and extinct species and that as a consequence should be immediately dropped from the human family tree. At the same time he also condemned Dubois' fossil, declaring it to be nothing more than a giant gibbon![47] But if Mousterian Man had not been the progenitor of modern man, who was? In the absence of a suitable precursor of modern humans, Boule was obliged, for the moment at least, to leave this question in abeyance. However, when details of the Piltdown discovery became known, Boule was provided with both a plausible precursor of the *Homo sapiens* lineage and justification for the opinion that there had not been one, but two "races of men" living in the Lower Palaeolithic.[48]

As Boule's provocative report at Geneva clearly indicates, the evolutionary significance of Dubois' fossil had, by 1912, come to be invested with considerable uncertainty — a situation that had been aggravated by the disappointing results of the 1907-8 Selenka expedition to Java which were published in 1911.[49] Besides being unable to resolve the question of the disputed femur, the German geologists in the Selenka team were unable to agree on the age of the bone-bearing stratum at Trinil. Opinions varied from the Middle to the Lower Pleistocene. While this lack of consensus had undoubtedly lent support to the continuing argument for the separation of the femur and skullcap, and for the latter being a fossil ape, it did not completely eradicate support for Dubois' monistic thesis. However, those who

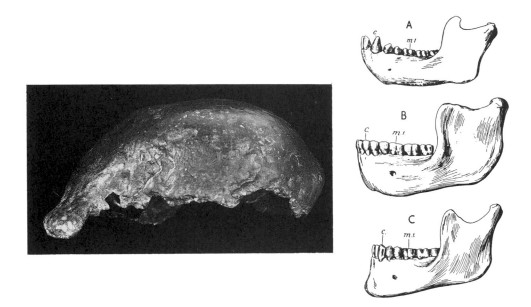

Fossil man: (left) The Trinil skullcap (Java); (right) mandibles of (A) chimpanzee, (B) Heidelberg man, (C) modern man. (From History of the Primates, *Fig. 30)*

continued to accept the humanity of these remains were now obliged to admit either that it was merely a representative of a specialized side-branch that had preserved its archetypic form into a later geological epoch, or, as was the case with Woodward, that it was an eastern counterpart of an early Neanderthaloid form. Like his French counterpart, Woodward was also predisposed to this catastrophic view of the Neanderthal lineage — a position that was subsequently endorsed by the Piltdown discovery.

While the configuration of the faunal and archaeological assemblages at Piltdown precluded the possibility of determining the precise age of the Sussex fossil, Woodward agreed with Dawson's assessment that it could not have been later than the early Pleistocene. This being the case, there were at this time only two other human fossils of seemingly comparable age, namely Dubois' Trinil fossils, and the so-called Heidelberg jaw.

In direct contrast to Dubois' fossil, the Heidelberg jaw had been found (in 1907) under circumstances that had left little doubt as to its geological age and, at least prior to the unveiling of the Piltdown skull, had served to provide an image of the hitherto ellusive form of Pre-Chellean Man. Although it had come to be popularly known as the Heidelberg jaw, it had in fact been found in a sand-quarry located on the banks of the Neckar, a tributary of the Rhine, near the village of Mauer, situated midway between Heidelberg and Mannheim.

At this quarry a complete cross-section of the ancient river terrace of the Neckar had been exposed. The upper stratum, about 20ft thick, represented recent loess and was equated with Prestwich's "low-level valley-gravels". Situated directly beneath this recent loess lay a deposit, about 20ft thick, of a more ancient loess which was considered by most German workers to represent the junction between the Third (Riss) and Last (Würm) Glaciation, a period when the Neanderthals and the associated Mousterian culture had predominated. Below this were stacked many alternate strata of sand and gravel, amounting collectively to a depth of over 50ft, known as the Mauer Sand Beds. It was in the deepest stratum of these beds, some 80ft from the present surface, along with the remains of several well-preserved fossil mammalian bones, that the massive human but distinctly ape-like mandible had been found. No cultural artifacts, however, had been recovered from the site.

On the basis of the associated fauna, Otto Schoettensack (1850–1912), a geologist from the University of Heidelberg, had determined that the Mauer sands corresponded with the "preglacial forest beds of Norfolk", which placed the horizon of the jaw, as Rutot and others later argued, at the commencement of the Pleistocene in the First (or Günz-Mindel) Interglacial. From his comparative study of the Heidelberg jaw, Schoetensack also concluded that it was more "pithecoid" than any human mandible yet found.[50] In contrast to the mandibles of the later Neanderthals of the Mousterian, the Heildelberg jaw is not only larger but also more more robustly built. The body is thick and deep, particularly in the region of the premolars. Also, where the jaws of the Neanderthalers possess in many instances a vestigial chin, this feature is completely absent in the Heidelberg specimen. Although the mental symphysis is buttressed on the inside, there is no evidence of a simian shelf. Indeed the inner aspect of this jaw possesses all the hallmarks of its human status which include a well-marked mylohyoid ridge on either side, a prominent mandibular foramen on both rami, as well as a particularly conspicuous groove for the mylohyoid nerve and vessels on the left side. Likewise the dental arcade is parabolic, and all of the teeth are essentially modern in form, and the dimensions were seen to fall within the then known range for Neanderthal dentition.

Faunal type	Sites	
	Piltdown	Heidelberg
Plio-Pleistocene		
Mastodon arvernensis	+	−
Elephas antiquus	−	+
Elephas meridionalis	+	−
Dicerorhinus etruscus	−	+
Hippopotamus sp.	+	−
PLEISTOCENE		
Equus spp	+	+
Cervus elaphus	+	+
Castor fiber	+	+
Capreolus capreolus	−	+
Ursus sp.	−	+

Comparison of the palaeontological assemblages at Piltdown and Heidelberg (Mauer Pit), based on Dawson & Woodward (1913) and Schoetensack (1908).

Whether viewed separately or collectively, it was quite evident to Woodward that anatomically both the Heidelberg and Trinil fossils differed dramatically from that of

Piltdown. Furthermore, compared with the Neanderthaloid skulls of the Mousterian, it did not possess their characteristic anterior flattening and inflated supraorbital ridges, which had long been regarded as hallmarks of primitive and Palaeolithic Man. While recognizing that the absence of large eyebrow ridges in the Piltdown skull could be attributed to the fact that the specimen was a female (which was supported by the general "weakness of the mandible"), Woodward felt it was unlikely that "a full-grown male of the same race" would have developed a supraorbital prominence approaching either that of the Mousterian Neanderthalers or *Pithecanthropus*. Also it was evident from a comparison of the Javan and Piltdown crania that the capacity of the latter was much greater, but as Woodward knew well, such a finding was precisely in accord with current expectations and ideas on the evolution of the human brain. In fact when the renowned neuroanatomist Grafton Elliot Smith (1871–1937), who held the chair of anatomy at Manchester University, was invited to examine the endocranial cast of the Piltdown skull, he saw it immediately as a realization of his prophecies on the pre-eminence of the brain in human evolution and the resident claim for the high antiquity of the modern human species.[51] Taking all of this into account, and the fact that both the Javan and German fossils were "almost (if not absolutely) of the same geological age", this could only mean", Woodward finally concluded, "that by the close of the Pliocene the human lineage had "already differentiated into [two] widely divergent groups".[52]

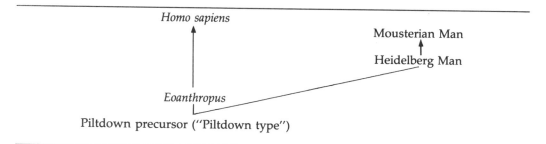

A schematic representation of Woodward's interpretation of the Piltdown hominid (Dawson & Woodward 1913).

To explain the specific configuration of the Piltdown skull, and its evolutionary significance, Woodward subsequently drew on the established zoological principle that the descendants of a common ancestral stock in the course of ontogenic development pass through structural stages reminiscent of the adult ancestor. Accordingly, Woodward contended that where the human cranium had essentially retained its archaic rounded form, the anthropoid apes "during the lapse of Upper Tertiary time" had "gradually undergone changes which are more or less exactly recapitulated in the life-history of each individual recent ape". This being the case,

> [I]t seems reasonable to interpret the Piltdown skull as exibiting a closer resemblance to the skulls of the truly ancestral mid-Tertiary apes than any fossil human skull hitherto found ... [And that this] Piltdown type has gradually become modified into the later Mousterian type,[53] by a series of changes similar to those passed through by the early apes as they evolved into the typical modern apes, and corresponding with the stages in the development of the skull in an existing ape-individual. It tends to support the theory that Mousterian man was a degenerate offshoot of early man, and probably became extinct; while surviving man may have arisen directly from the primitive source of which the Piltdown skull provides the first discovered evidence.[54]

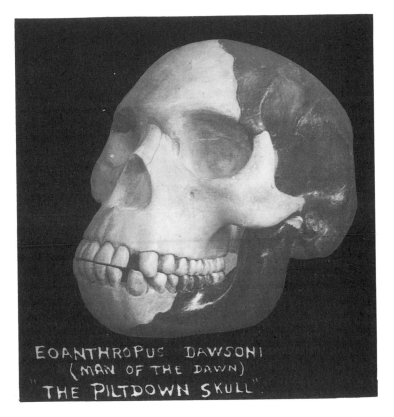

Piltdown skull reconstruction by Arthur Smith Woodward.

THE LEAK

Despite efforts to keep it a secret, news of the remarkable human skull found at Piltdown was leaked by an anonymous informant to the *Manchester Guardian*, which printed the story on Thursday, 21 November 1912. While divulging no information on where in Sussex and by whom the discovery had been made, or that the relic was now in the care of the British Museum (Natural History), the *Guardian's* report did reveal that the skull was in fragments and that they had been found in association with animal bones dating from the beginning of Pleistocene. "There seems to be no doubt whatever of its genuineness, and more than a possibility of its being the oldest remnant of a human frame yet discovered on this planet", the *Guardian* claimed. To which it was added:

> We shall probably have to wait for a little while longer before the full details of the discovery and the considered verdict upon it of our highest geological and anthropological authorities are formally laid before the scientific world, but enough is already known to warrant the announcement which we make today ... It will be extremely interesting to learn how far it bridges the gap between the skulls of the most man-like ape and the most ape-like man so far known to science, but the fact that it has been unhesitatingly recognised as human and not simian would appear to indicate that more than half of the difference must still remain.[55]

Meeting room, Geological Society of London, Burlington House, Picadilly, London. The 'parliamentary' layout of the room, chosen when the Society was founded in 1808 and occupied rooms in Somerset House, was retained on relocation to Burlington House in 1874 and was remodelled in 1972.

Within hours of this story breaking, a few enterprising news reporters found themselves being ushered through the steepled galleries of the British Museum (Natural History) and into Woodward's presence. Woodward later divulged, to his former mentor Boyd Dawkins, that he was both surprised and annoyed by this leak, but he gave no hint of these emotions in the interview he granted.[56] Besides confirming the substance of the *Guardian* story, Woodward went on to tell the reporters that the find had been made in a quite accidental manner:

> Workmen were engaged in digging a gravel pit on the site of an old river bed. They turned over some broken bones, which in all probability would have been lost forever had it not been for the presence of a gentleman — a solicitor by profession — who is well versed in such matters, and who at once realised the importance of the discovery ... [and had] ... collected the fragments...[57]

Because his investigations were still far from complete, and evidently fearing that if the "finders" identity became known it would lead to the discovery of the site and the possibility of it becoming "haunted" by enthusiasts "filled with the hope of digging up still further relics", Woodward declined to elaborate further. "I can only advise you", he told the assembled reporters, "to be patient. We are pursuing our investigations, and the result will be made known at a meeting of the Geological Society in December." However, when pressed to comment on the *Guardian's* claim that the skull was "the oldest remnant of a human frame yet discovered on this planet", Woodward replied without hesitation: "Yes, it is the earliest that has ever been found, except the one in Java... and", he added, "it might possibly be found to supply a link between the ape and man."

THE UNVEILING

During the next three weeks speculation in the press stirred the smouldering embers of scientific and public interest into an excited flame of anticipation. Though only a week before Christmas, and in spite of the notice reminding Fellows that seating was limited, the turnout for the meeting of the Geological Society of London in Burlington House on the night of Wednesday, 18 December 1912, was unprecedented. The Society's meeting room was filled to capacity and, as one anonymous eyewitness reported, the scene "wore the air of expectancy which characterizes the House of Commons on the eve of a revolutionary budget".[58]

Shortly after eight o'clock, the crowded meeting was called to order by the Society's president, Aubrey Strahan, who after first attending to regular business, introduced the authors of the much awaited communication. Woodward's well-versed solicitor was the first to speak. Referring to the remains that lay upon the table in front of him, Dawson revealed that they had been recovered from a flint-bearing gravel bed located in a field near Piltdown Common in East Sussex and went on briefly to explain how these discoveries had been made. Following this introduction, and with the aid of several lantern slides, Dawson described the distribution of the flint-bearing gravels in the central Weald, which, as he stressed, had neither been mapped nor previously recorded. He went on to deal with the question of the chronological age of the gravels and whether the resident bones were all of the same age. With regard to the human bones, Dawson concluded that they were in all probability contemporaneous with the the Lower Pleistocene fauna represented in the assemblage, while the other animal remains (represented by several varieties of extinct elephants) were likely to be older. The latter, he conjectured, had probably been introduced into the gravels from a neighbouring site, when the Ouse gravel terrace was being formed at the beginning of the Pleistocene epoch. This conclusion, he said, corresponded well with both the stratified nature of the gravel bed and the archaeological picture which consisted of a mixture of palaeoliths and eoliths. The former he noted were patently of human manufacture, and reminiscent of "Pre-Chellean" tools, which were, in both style and technique, in accordance with the supposed geological date of the human remains. As for the eolithic forms that had been recovered, Dawson astutely side-stepped this controversial issue by simply noting in conclusion that whether artificial or natural, many of them closely resembled those found in the High Plateau gravels at Ightham.

Picking up where Dawson had stopped, Woodward shifted quickly to a detailed consideration of the hominid remains. Methodically he reviewed each of the nine cranial pieces that had been found along with the fragment of the lower jaw, and explained why and how they had been fitted together to give the model which he then unveiled to his riveted audience. As he pointed out, the cranial fragments were "sufficiently well-preserved to exhibit the shape and natural relations of the frontal, parietal, occipital and temporal bones, and to justify the reconstruction of some other elements [namely the jaw] by inference". While acknowledging the pithecoid nature of the mandible, there were, he told his audience, compelling reasons for not treating this as an unrelated fossil form. Aside from various anatomical clues, the fact that it had been found so close to the skull, plus the similarity between these bones in colour and condition, he believed, endorsed a monistic interpretation. This being the case, it was abundantly clear, he went on to say, that the Sussex fossil represented an annectant type, which raised the question of its taxonomic status. In this regard, Woodward confessed:

> The brain-case alone, though specifically distinguished from all known human crania of equally low brain-capacity, by the characters of its supraorbital border, and the upward extension of its temporal muscles, could scarcely be removed from the genus *Homo*; the bone of the mandible so far as preserved, however, is so completely distinct from that of *Homo* in the shape of the symphysis and the parallelism of the pre-molar series on the two sides, that the facial parts of the skull almost certainly differed in fundamental characters from those of any typically human skull. I therefore propose that the Piltdown specimen be regarded as the type of a new genus of the family Hominidae, to be named *Eoanthropus* and defined by its ape-like mandibular symphysis, parallel molar-premolar series, and narrow lower molars which do not decrease in size backwards; to which diagnostic characters may be probably added the steep frontal eminence and slight development of brow-ridges. The species of which the skull and mandible have now been described in detail may be named *Eoanthropus dawsoni*, in honour of its discoverer.[59]

As for its evolutionary significance, Woodward said it clearly argued in favour of the view that by the end of the Pliocene Epoch the human lineage had already separated into two divergent stocks, one of which evolved into the "degenerate offshoot" of the Neanderthalers, and the other, represented by the Piltdown skull, which gave rise to modern *Homo sapiens*.

To round off the presentation, Woodward then invited Elliot Smith to comment briefly on his preliminary study of the neurocranial endocast. Speaking extemporaneously, Smith summarized the salient features of the Piltdown brain. Superficially, he said, it was comparable to several well-known palaeolithic brain-casts, but was distinguished by a suite of unusual characters, such as the "singularly primitive arrangement of sulci". Taking all of these features into account, Smith said, he had no compunction in regarding the Sussex specimen as "the most primitive and most simian human brain so far recorded; one, moreover, such as might reasonably have been expected to be associated in one and the same individual with the mandible which so definitely indicates the zoological rank of its original possessor". As for the apparent paradox of an ape's jaw welded to a human brain, Smith said this should not come as a complete surprise to anyone who had kept abreast of developments in human palaeontology. "In the process of evolving the brain of man from the ape", he explained:

> the superficial area of the cerebral cortex must necessarily be tripled; and this expansion was not like the mere growth of a muscle with exercise, but the gradual building-up of the most complex mechanism in existence. The growth of the brain preceded the refinement of the features and of the somatic characters in general.[60]

In the discussion that followed it soon became apparent that opinion was divided on two major issues: the age of the skull, and the validity of Woodward's reconstruction.[61]

Addressing both of these issues Lankester said that he had been privileged to examine both the specimens and the site some weeks earlier.[62] Although privately, he later admitted to harbouring some reservations on the association of the mandible and skull,[63] he gave no indication of this in his commentary.[64] Rather, at this time his attention was focussed on Woodward's chimpanzee-like reconstruction of the jaw's symphysial region, which, as he had told Woodward earlier, he seriously questioned if the jaw had been "of the chinless type" like the Neanderthals.[65] But while hailing Woodward's decision as a "very bold step", he nevertheless considered it was fully justified, given the jaw's overt simian form and its obvious divergence from that of the Heidelberg mandible.[66] As for the question of the specimen's age, Lankester agreed that the evidence was equivocal — though he wondered if the human bones might not be earlier than had been supposed.[67] Regarding Dawson's cursory treatment of the eolithic component in the archaeological assemblage, Lankester registered strong objections to the employment of the terms "Eolith" and "Chellean". Since the 1900s when he had become involved in the eolithic controversy, Lankester had developed a violent dislike of the word "Eolith", particularly after Boule's attack in 1905. Since that time the term had been freely applied to both primitive edge-trimmed flints and all sorts and conditions of naturally broken specimens. Likewise, his objections to the use of the term "Chellean" were grounded in the fact that there was still some disagreement about what constituted the basal Chellean industry. Hence he recommended that for the time being it was perhaps better to describe the Piltdown implements, without reference to names "which had no authorized and accepted meaning".[68] These objections were dismissed later in the evening by Reginald Smith (1874–1940), an antiquarian from the British Museum, who felt that Dawson's adoption of the French classification was, in the circumstances, fully justified. In his opinion, "it was idle to decry or ignore the types and terminology that made European archaeologists mutually intelligible. ."[69]

The next to comment was the anatomist and Conservator of the Hunterian Museum of the Royal College of Surgeons, Arthur Keith. Like Lankester, Keith said that he was troubled by Woodward's restoration of the jaw, which he said "approached too nearly the characters of the chimpanzee". He went on to say that the very simian characters of sub-symphysial region of the mandible, compounded with the large anterior teeth and primitive features of the brain seemed to him "altogether incompatible with the Chellean age assigned by the Authors". In his opinion the skull belonged with the earliest and not the latest faunal remains. Keith said he was convinced that the authors were unaware of the greatness of their discovery. They had, in his opinion, discovered the elusive Tertiary Man. This conclusion, he said, was clearly supported by the mandible's overall simian character,[70] and the attendant eoliths. To suppose that it was later rather than earlier simply ignored the evidence, Keith protested. Developing this proposition Keith drew attention to Elliot Smith's statement that there was every indication from the configuration of the endocranial cast that the Piltdown brain stood on the threshold of having the "power of spontaneous elaboration of speech", yet evidently was precluded from doing so by the conformation of its jaw. Convinced that the enterprise of tool-making was grounded in the faculty of speech, Keith went on to argue that if this primitive form of humanity was, as he suspected, the artificer of the crude Piltdown implements, there was good reason to suppose that the jaw was not as apelike as Woodward had depicted it.[71]

Not surprisingly this movement to upgrade the antiquity of the Piltdown specimen brought William Boyd Dawkins to his feet. Unlike Keith, who was an advocate of both eolithic theory and the idea that the cornerstone of human evolution was rooted in the

Reconstructed from a part of the jaw and a portion of the skull: the most ancient known inhabitant of England – the newly discovered man of Sussex. Supplement to the Illustrated London News, *December 28, 1912.*

Tertiary, Dawkins saw the crucial stages in the evolution of the human species unfolding in the Pleistocene, hence the urgency of his attack. According to him it was indisputable that the human remains, as well as the associated implements, all belonged to the Pleistocene. The Pliocene fauna were, he contended, "merely adventitious". Indeed, all of the evidence, he believed, pointed to the discovery of the long-awaited missing link between man and the higher apes and confirmed precisely what he had been saying for the last forty years, namely that human evolution had been restricted essentially to the Pleistocene age. As for Keith's argument of an intrinsic relationship between the skill to work flints and the capacity to speak, Dawkins replied that "examples in the political world show that power of speech and actual capacity to act in the practical things of life were unrelated".[72]

Contrary to expectations, this attack on Keith and his advocacy of Tertiary Man did not draw fire from Keith's close friend, Wynfrid L H Duckworth (1870–1956), the eolithophile-anatomist from Jesus College, Cambridge. Duckworth did note however, that while he endorsed Woodward's restoration which had realized the anticipations of students of human evolution, it was evident that if they were to be completely fulfilled, the problem of the precise antiquity of the skull required solution.[73]

At this point the geologist Clement Reid disputed Dawson's estimated age of the Piltdown "drift". While acknowledging that there had been no "detailed drift survey" of the Wealden basin, he noted that some work had been done on coastal formations and that these had been shown to be of a much later date, belonging at the most to the Middle Pleistocene. It therefore seemed highly probable, Reid contended, that the Piltdown deposit and the low plateau on which it rested belonged to a base-level plain that had seemingly been formed during the same time period. Had it been earlier, he said, the Wealden lowlands would be covered by marine deposits, as was the case on the coastal plains. But whatever their precise age might be, Reid was convinced the Piltdown deposit was neither pre-Glacial nor early Pleistocene. Rather, he said:

> [T]hey belong to an epoch long after the first cold period had passed away . . .
> [occurring] at the very base of the great-implement bearing succession of Palaeolithic
> deposits in the South-East of England.[74]

This viewpoint was subsequently challenged, but not before David Waterston (1871–1942), an anatomist from King's College, London, lodged his dissatisfaction with Woodward's monistic interpretation of the Piltdown skull. Waterston confessed that he found it hard to conceive of a functional association between a jaw that was so palpably simian and a cranium that was in all its essential features human. It was therefore difficult to believe that the two specimens came from the same individual. In particular what most concerned Waterston was, as Woodward had pointed out, the close resemblance to the modern morphology of the glenoid fossa in the left temporal bone. This being the case, Waterston said:

> It must be borne in mind that the configuration of the glenoid fossae in man was such
> as to adapt them for articulation with a human jaw, and not with the mandible as
> found in chimpanzee; and, if the jaw had formed part of the skull, it was precisely in
> the temporal bone that one would have anticipated some variation in structure from
> the present-day condition.[75]

The next speaker was Alfred Kennard, who brought the discussion back to the question of the site's age. It was Kennard's opinion that the Piltdown gravel bed should be correlated with the 100ft Terrace of the Thames Valley.[76] They were of similar elevation and the archaeological assemblages were identical. He also noted that the high-level terraces in the Thames Valley had yielded remains of several Pliocene mammals. Thus while agreeing with Reid that the true succession of the Pleistocene in the Weald had yet to be worked out, he was convinced this would have to be based on palaeontological evidence — an opinion that was endorsed by the next speaker, Edwin Tulley Newton. Not surprisingly, Newton supported Keith's reading of the evidence. Both the colour and condition of the bones, he said, seemed to point in the direction of the Pliocene rather than the Pleistocene.[77]

Strahan then closed the discussion and invited Dawson and Woodward to respond to the various points that had been raised. Dawson spoke first and confined himself to the dating issue. From a strictly anthropological point of view, Dawson said, he was quite prepared to accept an earlier date for the origin of the human remains, and confessed that perhaps he and Woodward had "erred on the side of caution in placing the date as early Pleistocene". However, given the fact that some of the remains had been found in different strata, and the variation in the "rolled" condition of the various remains, this had indicated to them "a difference as to age, but not to the extent of excluding the possibility of their being coeval".[78] Following this up, Woodward said that despite the marked differences between the Piltdown and Heidelberg mandibles he was convinced this did not imply a difference in geological age. He also acknowledged that this led to the provocative conclusion of the coexistence of two divergent forms of humanity at the beginning of the Pleistocene. As for the particular configuration of *Eoanthropus*, he said that it was quite possible that it may represent the remnants of an earlier form that had survived into the early Pleistocene. He also admitted that the restoration of the mandible was, "a bold experiment", but added that he "failed at present to conceive of any other interpretation of the fossil".[79] And as everyone present fully appreciated, until the hypothetical canine was found, this particular issue would have to remain a point of contention. In conclusion Woodward said that it was his intention to carry the search forward, but that he was reminded of the recent failure of the Selenka excavations in Java, and "did not anticipate certain success in future work at Piltdown".

THE SITUATION

Commenting on what had transpired at Burlington House the night before, Aubrey Strahan told the *Manchester Guardian* that he was convinced of the "extreme antiquity" of the Piltdown site, stating that he had examined it firsthand.[80] The geology of the Piltdown gravels, he said, were complex, and not wholly synonymous with the situation found in the Thames river valley, as had been suggested during the discussion period. He also stated that not only had there been no general geological survey of the region for many years, it was also likely that there would not be one for some time; a fact that must have disturbed him, since the controversy of the skull's antiquity turned on the question of whether it was "buried originally in the stratum in which it was found or whether it had been washed out of some still earlier geological formation into that stratum". If the former supposition was true, Strahan continued, then the remains must be of Pleistocene age, as Dawson and Woodward had supposed. But in the latter case — that is, if the skull was already fossilized long before it came to its final resting place at Piltdown — then it might well be a relic of the Pliocene or of an even earlier age. At this point, Strahan was asked how a "derived" fossil might be detected. He replied that a derived fossil would be extremely difficult to determine but that one possible avenue of investigation might be the tests employed by mineralogists to estimate degrees of fossilization.[81] The chief argument in support of the contemporaneity of the braincase and jaw was, Strahan continued, grounded in the fact that they had been found within a few feet of one another. "If they had been disturbed in the way necessary to the other theory it was reasonable to suppose that they would have been more widely separated." As for Waterston's theory that the remains belonged to two different creatures, Strahan declined to comment.

As the Strahan interview indicates, in spite of all its imperfections, the case Dawson and Woodward had laid before the Geological Society was a compelling one. Indeed there appears to have been very few who were not willing to endorse the opinion expressed by Keith at Burlington House, that these remains constituted "the most important [find] ever made in England, and of equal, if not of greater importance than any other yet made, either at home or abroad".[82] During the next four years further discoveries were made at Piltdown which served to consolidate this point of view.

3 Bones, stones & egos I: the Piltdown debates: 1913

False facts are highly injurious to the progress of science, for they often endure long; but false views, if supported by some evidence, do little harm, for every one takes salutary pleasure proving their falseness.[1]

AN ALTERNATIVE ARRANGEMENT

The first consignment of the Piltdown casts made to order by the Damon Company of Weymouth was distributed sometime towards the end of April 1913, which coincided with the publication of the Dawson & Woodward description of the finds. For nine pounds and seventeen shillings, an interested buyer received copies of the cranial fragments, the jaw, the endocranial cast, and a model of the restored skull; for an additional investment of two pounds and ten shillings, plaster facsimiles of 3 palaeoliths and 3 eoliths were also available.

Among the first to receive a complete set of the Piltdown casts was Arthur Keith,[2] who set to work immediately on studying Woodward's reconstruction. Aside from a number of anatomical points that had nagged Keith since first viewing the remains,[3] there was the simple fact that the restored skull in its present form clashed completely with his theoretical expectations. He was convinced Woodward had made an error not only in the restoration of the jaw, but also the braincase. In his estimation the present overall configuration of Woodward's model was far too ape-like.

Until recently, Keith had been an ardent follower of the so-called linear concept of human evolution which embodied the notion that the human species had reached its modern estate by an orderly and progressive series of metamorphic steps away from its natal simian form. Indeed, in 1895, when Dubois brought his Javan fossil to London, Keith had chided his reticent colleagues for not accepting the Dutchman's evidence. The curious amalgam of a modern human femur and a brutal pithecoid skull did not, in his opinion, violate Darwinian principles. "It seems to me highly probabl[e]", he wrote at the time, "that the frame of man reached its perfection for [bi]pedal progression long before his brain attained its present complex structure".[4] Moreover, this transition had occurred in the Pliocene, since which time, Keith contended:

[H]uman structural progress has lain in an increase of brain, and a dimunition in the masticatory and alimentary systems. In these features [based on the available evidence] we may suppose that early Quaternary man approached the primate ancestors of the race; in these features he certainly comes nearer to the present simian type. But, for the purpose of giving us a clue to the human line of descent, the fossil remains at present known assist us not one single jot. Their configuration is quite conformable to the theory of a common descent; they bear out the truth of that theory. They also show us that man since the Tertiary period has changed structurally very little. There is nothing remarkable in this, for allied primate forms (*Palaeopithecus sivalensis* and *Dryopithecus*) demonstrate to us that since the Miocene period, the anthropoid type has changed but slightly. We need not then be surprised at being obliged to seek deep within the Tertiary formations the evidences of human descent.[5]

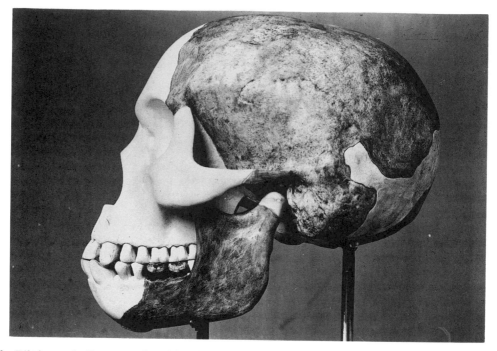

The Piltdown skull cast produced by the R.F. Damon Company, Weymouth, England, based on the reconstruction by Woodward et al. in 1912. The dark areas represent the original bone fragments, the restored areas are white. Note the large projecting (reconstructed) canine in the lower jaw. This expectation was later satisfied in 1913.

Consequently, Keith had envisioned Dubois' *Pithecanthropus* and the Neanderthals in much the same way as Sollas had at the Royal Society in 1907: "as the piers of a ruined bridge which once continuously connected the kingdom of man with the rest of the animal world".[6]

Although by 1910 there were already a number of European workers who were inclined to the opinion that the Neanderthals were simply the terminal twigs of a dead branch of man's ancestral tree, Keith had resisted this movement. While cognisant of the fact that the evidence from La Ferrassie and Combe Capelle provided considerable support for the notion of the Neanderthals having been abruptly replaced by anatomically modern humans, the evidence still did not rule out completely the possibility of a regular transition from one to the other — though he admitted it must have occurred at a much faster rate than he had originally supposed. In an effort to explain this, Keith had conjectured in his 1911 Hunterian Lecture, that the swift transition from the Neanderthaloid to the modern humanoid form might well be linked in some inexplicable way to a change in pituitary function; for as he noted: "When this gland becomes enlarged, as it occasionally does in the disease known as acromegaly, the Neanderthal characters are developed in the subjects of the disease in an exaggerated and bizarre form".[7] Keith was also temporarily consoled by the fact that no Neanderthaloid remains had yet "been found in a stratum which lies over or is more recent than the one containing a representative of a modern race".[8] Indeed, when Reid Moir had sent him the Ipswich skeleton which had been found beneath the chalky boulder clay of East Anglia, Keith had fully expected to encounter

Arthur Keith at work in his laboratory at the Royal College of Surgeons, circa 1912. (Library of the Royal College of Surgeons, London)

the remains of Neanderthaler. Instead it bore an uncanny resemblance to that of the palpably modern human skeleton found at Galley Hill in Kent.[9] Although, according to Keith, he had been "grievously disappointed" by Moir's delivery, it appears that once the initial shock had worn off it suddenly occurred to him that the Ipswich skeleton provided a key not only to the Neanderthal problem but also to that of Galley Hill.[10]

When Keith first examined the Galley Hill skeleton in 1909[11] it had thrown him into a quandary, for contrary to Newton's earlier claims, he could find no significant anatomical evidence which served to demarcate the specimen from the modern form. And yet according to Newton the specimen had been found buried in the 100ft Terrace. Was then the modern human skeleton a very ancient type? And if so, how ancient? And how did this equate with the traditional view of the beetle-browed Neanderthals having been the precursor of the modern human form?

A subsequent visit to the Galley Hill chalk pit, followed by discussions with Newton placed "any doubts as to the date and authenticity of skeleton absolutely out of court", Keith later claimed.[12] Based on current knowledge of the Thames river valley, the 100ft Terrace at Galley Hill was thought to correspond with the "last of the temperate intervals which lie within the Glacial Age" — which, using the nomenclature of Penck & Brückner then coming into vogue, was another way of saying the Riss-Würm Inter-glacial. Translated roughly into years, Keith estimated that the age of the Galley Hill skeleton was somewhere in the region of 170 000 years.[13] According to Penck's estimates, the duration of the Glacial Epoch had been in the order of 800 000 years.[14] Keith, however, favoured Sollas' more conservative figure of

Louis Rutot, Belgian geologist and advocate of eolithic theory. (Institut Royal des Sciences Naturelles de Belgique, Brussels)

400 000.[15] Thus, correlating the age of Galley Hill with what was then known of Neanderthal chronology, it appeared to him that the first 200 000 years of the Pleistocene had witnessed the gradual emergence and refinement of the Neanderthalers from their Tertiary precursor, and that the remaining 200 000 years documented the subsequent evolution and distribution of the modern human races.[16] At this stage there still seemed ample time separating the Galley Hill skeleton from the Neanderthals for them to have been the former's progenitor, and furthermore he was still confident that remains would eventually be found in British soil furnishing evidence of this transition. But this expectation was subsequently dashed by the Ipswich skeleton, whose discovery was, as Keith so aptly put it, akin to finding a "modern aeroplane in a church crypt which had been bricked up since the days of Queen Elizabeth"[17]

In his report on the Ipswich skeleton to the Prehistoric Society of East Anglia on 21 February 1912, Keith said:

> If Mr. Moir and I are right in assigning the remains here described to a man who lived in Suffolk before the formations of the boulder clay, then there can be no doubt we are dealing with one of the earliest representations of man yet discovered. The only other remains which are certainly older are the Heidelberg jaw and the fossil man of Java.[18]

Armed with this evidence and that of the Galley Hill remains, Keith moved with amazing speed in organizing his retreat from orthodoxy to heterodoxy. Using his annual Hunterian Lecture as a platform, Keith boldly announced early in the spring of 1912 that there had not been one, but two parallel forms of humanity during the

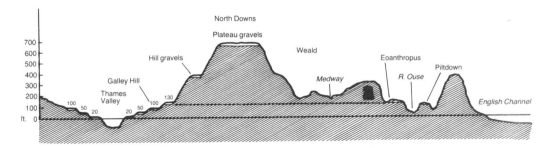

A diagrammatic section across the Thames Valley and Weald of Sussex: (a) represents central anticlinal axis running through Weald. Note that Galley Hill is placed at 100 ft level and Piltdown at 130 ft.

Pleistocene, and that in Britain at least, there was now every reason to suggest that long before the Mousterian age in France, modern man had made his appearance.[19]

While the reaction to this proclamation by orthodox hardliners such as Boyd Dawkins was predictable,[20], Keith's general message was echoed in Duckworth's book *Prehistoric Men*, which appeared in January 1912. Here Duckworth agreed that the simplistic linear "story of evolution" was incorrect, and that it was more than probable that "men of [the] Galley Hill type [had] preceded in point of time men of the lower Neanderthal type".[21] Shortly thereafter, this opinion was confirmed by the discoveries at Piltdown.

While the revelations at Piltdown had seemingly dealt a death blow to the linear theory of human evolution, they did not lead to an automatic acceptance of either the Ipswich or Galley Hill specimens as evidence for the high antiquity of the human species — hence Keith's particular concern with Woodward's interpretation of the Piltdown skull.

In approaching the Piltdown cranial jigsaw puzzle, Keith was guided by Rutot's conviction that the age of the Piltdown gravel bed was not early Pleistocene as Messrs Dawson & Woodward had claimed, but Pliocene. Keith had made a special visit to Brussels earlier in March to discuss this matter with Rutot, whom he considered to be the leading authority on the Plio-Pleistocene geology of Western Europe.[22] According to Keith, the Belgian professor, on hearing that the elevation of the Piltdown gravels was 120ft above sea-level, had declared: "That deposit is Pliocene in date; it is nearly of the same as the deposits at St Prest, on the Eure, near Chartres".[23] As Keith well knew it was here at St Prest that Desnoyers had discovered fifty years earlier the first evidence claimed to be the handiwork of Tertiary man. Furthermore, as Rutot went on to explain, the deposits at Piltdown and St Prest lie within a common watershed. During late Pliocene times the Ouse and the Eure had once been tributaries of the same ancient river that had drained westwards into the Atlantic. Rutot also told Keith that the "worked flints" he had discovered at St Prest were much later than those found either at Ightham or Piltdown. In his opinion the Piltdown fauna confirmed this. He also reminded Keith of the eolithic forms that had been found west of Piltdown near Dewlish in Dorset. Aside from the eoliths, which were said to resemble those of the High Plateau in Kent, Rutot also drew attention to the deep trench that had been found there by the Reverend Osmond Fisher (1817–1914). This trench, approximately 100 feet long and almost 12 feet deep had been deliberately cut into the Dewlish chalk, and among the gravel and sand filling this pit had been found the remains of elephants similar to the kind that had been recovered at St Prest and Cromer — *Elephas meridionalis*. Fisher had been convinced the trench had been a prehistoric elephant trap.[24] Rutot agreed.

Taking all of this evidence into account, Keith had returned to London completely convinced that Woodward's *Eoanthropus* was representative of a far more advanced hominid and that this form belonged to the Pliocene — a conclusion he had no problem in harmonizing with his earlier position on Galley Hill and Ipswich. The apparent geological connection but anatomical differences between these latter skeletons and that of Piltdown, Keith felt, could be readily explained. In the case of Galley Hill, these remains had been found at the 100ft level, whereas, at Piltdown the human remains clearly belonged to a higher and thereby older terrace. From all indications when the 100ft Terrace of the Thames was being formed, humankind had entered a transitional cultural stage, which Rutot called the Strepyan. The middle and lower (later) portions of this terrace embraced the development of the Chellean and the resultant Acheulean, whose geological age was thought to correspond with the mid-Pleistocene. Below, at the 50ft level, the Achulean merged with the Mousterian culture which sat on the boundary between the Middle and Upper Pleistocene. This being the case, it was, in Keith's opinion, the Chellean flints and Pleistocene fauna that were the trespassers at Piltdown, and not the elephants and eoliths as Dawson and Woodward had contended. Viewed in this way it is easier to appreciate why Keith had pursued a morphology of *Eoanthropus* that would stand much closer to Galley Hill and Ipswich than to the anthropoid apes.

According to Keith, he had imagined that the problem with Woodward's model resided in his reconstruction of the jaw, but after some days of poring over the cranial fragments and comparing them with an Australian aboriginal skull he had selected from the Hunterian collections, he discovered that there were also problems with the reconstructed braincase. Initially he was drawn to the similarity in the size of their respective parietal bones, which was not expected since the skull he had selected had an estimated brain capacity of 1450 cc (considered to be the average norm for modern humans), compared to the 1070 cc of Piltdown. This surprise was further increased by a comparison of their temporal bones, particularly the squamal region, which extends upwards to connect with the lower border of the parietal to form the vertical wall of the skull. A large temporal squama or plate is highly indicative of a large enclosed brain. Although the Piltdown temporal squama was broken, enough of it remained for its original size to be estimated with some exactitude. Keith found it to be slightly larger than that of the Australian specimen! Yet the estimated capacity of the Sussex cranium had been determined to be nearly 400 cc smaller than that of the Australian skull. It was while searching for an explanation for this discrepancy, Keith later reported, that he discovered what was believed to be a fundamental error in the restored braincase.

In piecing the skull fragments together it appeared that Woodward, in endeavouring to equate the stark modernity of the braincase with the ape-like jaw, had made a number of significant concessions to the imagination. At the same time as giving it a lower cranial capacity, he had also endowed the cranium with an asymmetrical configuration, by contrast to the symmetrical nature of lower mammalian crania — in the modern human cranium the right and left halves are not of equal size. This asymmetry was thought to reflect increased hemispherical specialization resulting from the acquisition and refinement of speech and related functions. The extent of this asymmetry in Woodward's model, however, surprised Keith, who expected to find a much higher degree of symmetry in such a primitive cranium. The cause of the marked asymmetry in Woodward's model was, he contended, grounded in the

James Leon Williams who assisted Keith in his reconstruction of the Piltdown remains (1913). For further details see Chapter 8, and in particular endnote No 62. (From Clapp's biography, published in the Dental Digest, *1925)*

erroneous identification of the skull's middle-line. Woodward had identified this middle-line of the cranial roof at "the hinder end" of the left parietal fragment. Keith, on the other hand, placed this critical reference point further to the right, namely at the tip of the triangular wedge of this same fragment. This "tip", according to Keith, coincided with the anatomical land-mark known as "lambda", the point where the sagittal suture (that knits the left and right parietals together at the top of the skull) and the lambdoid sutures (that weld the parietals to the occiput) converge. In lining up this new reference point with the undisputed median point of the occipital (attached to the right section), the entire left section of the Piltdown cranium had to be moved dramatically. The resulting configuration was "revolutionary". Keith later wrote:

> The height of the brain chamber is increased by nearly half an inch. The width and fullness of the top parts are enlarged. The brain capacity is augmented; the shape of the brain is changed. The anomalous conformation of the occipital bone, the extreme asymmetry of the lambdoidal suture, almost disappear, and all the points we are familiar with in human skulls ... leap to the eye.[25]

Keith's view of the jaw was also the antithesis of Woodward's. Among the various points which led him to this conclusion was the essentially modern appearance of the glenoid fossa and the molar teeth. In Keith's mind these characteristics, along

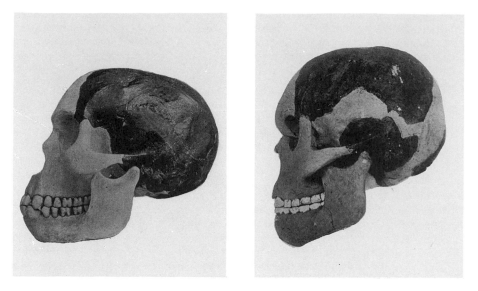

Piltdown gets a face-lift (1913): (left) Woodward's reconstruction; (right) Keith's reconstruction, note the absence of the large projecting canine.

with the refined attachments for the temporal muscles, argued strongly against Woodward's case for a chimpanzoid mandible with large prominent canines. Keith believed that the reconstructed symphysial region could be adequately filled with teeth which were modern in form but of larger dimension — similar to that of Heidelberg. Such a mandible he believed was more consistent with the anatomical realities of the braincase. Thus, while he busied himself with the restoration of the braincase, J Leon Williams (1852–1932), an American dentist living in Hampstead, with whom he had recently become associated, attended to the task of making a model of the Piltdown jaw according to Keith's new specifications.[26]

By the end of June Keith was ready to make his move. The first to see the product of his labours was Grafton Elliot Smith, who was clearly rattled by what he saw and heard. Relaying the broad details of this meeting to Woodward, Smith wrote:

> ... Keith ... showed me his restoration of the Piltdown skull, at which he has been working ever since the Piltdown casts were acquired by the R.C.S. Museum a month ago. As the matter of putting together of the fragments vitally affects my part of the work I carefully examined all the points raised by him; and as a result I am quite convinced that we shall have to modify the restoration in some respects. I was never quite happy about the right parietal and occipital regions ... Since I have received the models of the bone fragments I have not had time to investigate the matter for myself; but in the light of Keith's work I see quite clearly what has happened. The brain (both cerebral and cerebellar hemispheres) is markedly asymmetrical and the ridges of separation of the cerebral and cerebellar depression on the occipital bone are *not* in the mesial plane, the positions of which is shown by the crest on the inferior surface of the occipital. This means that the occipital in your reconstruction must be rotated to the right. This will throw out the right parietal and broaden the skull.
>
> I have not yet had time to go into the examination of the temporal region, but according to K[eith]. the temporal bone has been inclined at an angle with the parietal. His third point is that the mandibular fragment includes the symphysial region; so that normal sized human teeth will completely fill up the space allowed by the alveolar

process [the space to accommodate the maxillary canine]. I have convinced myself that the occipital and right parietal regions in your reconstruction need some modification: into the other two points I have not gone in detail yet, but there seems a strong prima facie case for a reexamination of them also.

I think as the casts are now in the hands of a good many people (who no doubt will ultimately be led to such conclusions) that some statement should be made as soon as possible with regard to the matter. Perhaps you would look into the evidence Keith has collected and see what you think? Or would you prefer me to reexamine the whole matter at issue and send a note to "Nature"? What I fear may happen is that Schwalbe or some other continental authority may arrive at these conclusions before any British statement has been made . . .[27]

Shortly after receiving this letter, Woodward contacted Keith and a meeting was arranged for the afternoon of Thursday, 10 July. While the details of this meeting are not known it appears that Woodward did not go alone to the Royal College of Surgeons, but was accompanied by Barlow and a team of consultants, namely Lankester, Arthur Swayne Underwood (1854–1916), a Harley Street dentist and professor of dental surgery at King's College, and William Plane Pycraft (1868–1942), a colleague from the British Museum (Natural History).[28] (Pycraft's particular forté was osteology). Elliot Smith had another engagement and was unable to attend this meeting. According to Keith's telegraphic entry in his diary for 10 July, he was under the impression that his presentation had "convinced" Lankester, but that Woodward had been "upset". He was right on both counts.

As for Lankester, there was no doubt, he told Moir, that Keith was "to a large extent right" and that Woodward was wrong. But he went on to say that he had told both Keith and Woodward that:

The form of the symphysis of the lower jaw is totally unlike that of any known human jaw and is very close to that of the same part in a chimpanzee. There is no guess or fancy about this and if all you fellows would stick to the solid thing on the table and not wrangle about fancies, all would be well. (X [Elliot Smith] made a fool of himself, as I guessed at the Geological that night [18 December 1912], jawing away about the wonderful character of the braincase . . . We don't need him to tell us that it is all out of proportion and centering. That was not what he said at the Geological! but it is as obvious a pike-staff). The wide flattened piece of the jaw near the symphysis, makes the owner of Piltdown more ape-like than the owner of the Heidelberg jaw. I don't care tuppence whether the braincase was possibly this, that, or the other . . . It is sufficient for any sober scientific statement that here we have a lower jaw with two flat human-like molars, and a chimpanzee-like symphysial region. A very interesting fact because in the course of time when new discoveries are made, it may lead to further definite knowledge as to early man and man-like creatures. As to arguing from it to anything about flint chipping, or power of articulate speech, it is a waste of words and imagination — at present.[29]

Although there can be little doubt that Woodward had left the Royal College under a cloud, it is also evident that he was not entirely persuaded by Keith's anatomical acrobatics. Indeed, there is every reason to suppose that he had seen this move in much the same light as Dawson, who felt that Keith was juggling the bones in an effort to fit Piltdown into his scheme of things.[30] It was not a secret that Woodward regarded Keith's views on the great antiquity of *Homo sapiens* as an "amusing heresy";[31] in fact, earlier in April during his lecture series on "Recent Discoveries of Early Man" at the Royal Institution he had attacked the concept and disdainfully dismissed the Ipswich and Galley Hill skeletons as "merely late burials".[32] Although he was willing to concede that some of Keith's points on the braincase were reasonable, the same could not be said for his views on the jaw. Until he had an opportunity to look into the matter fully, Woodward was not going to allow himself to be railroaded by either Keith's tactics or Elliot Smith's apprehensions.

By the beginning of August, Smith's anxiety over Woodward's seeming intransigence was heightened further by reports that a group of German anthropologists at the Nuremburg meeting of the Deutsche Anthropologische Gesellschaft had openly censured the Piltdown reconstruction.[33] He fully expected that this might become an issue at the scheduled meetings of the Anatomical Section of the International Congress of Medicine in London;[34] for as Smith knew, it had been arranged for Woodward to demonstrate the Piltdown remains to the Congress on 11 August. But unbeknown to Smith, Keith was also aware of this development and had arranged with the Oxford anatomist Arthur Thomson (1861–1933), the designated chairman of the Anatomical Section, to place a "second demonstration" on the programme. Evidently it was Keith's plan to use this opportunity to not only forestall an anticipated attack from the German camp, but also to force a show-down with Woodward.[35]

From all accounts Woodward's scheduled demonstration of the original specimens at the British Museum (Natural History) passed without incident. Following a review of the salient features of the Piltdown cranium and mandible, he then apparently recapitulated the rationale for his reconstruction. Although admitting that it was possible that there had been some error in the articulation of the bones, a "malposition which might diminish the actual size of the brain", Woodward said that he still stood by his reconstruction of the mandible. There was no doubt in his mind as to the simian nature of the mandibular symphysis, and this alone justified the decision to assign the Piltdown remains to a new genus. The assembly then adjourned to the lecture amphitheatre at the Royal College in Lincoln's Inn Fields, where Keith exhibited his reconstruction and gave his reasons for augmenting the cranial volume by 400 cc. The difference between his model and that of Woodward's, he declared, was not "simply a matter of opinion, but a principle of the most elementary fact". Seizing Woodward's model and holding it up to his audience, Keith is reported to have said with "infinite scorn", that such an individual would have been prevented not only from eating but also breathing! "If a student had brought up a skull like this one, he would have been rejected for a couple of years", he added mockingly.[36] The impossibility of Woodward's model, he continued, rested essentially on an erroneous conception of the jaw. All of the evidence argued against a big canine tooth. There was no room for an anthropoid eye-tooth. Not only was the chief muscle of mastication smaller than that found among modern Australian aborigines, but the joint of the lower jaw was exactly as in modern humans. It was abundantly clear that the mechanism of that joint was simply incompatible with the idea of there having been a large projecting canine. Keith said that, bearing all this in mind, it was evident that Woodward's model was fundamentally wrong and that revisions along the lines he had suggested were warranted.

In the discussion that followed, Elliot Smith said that urgency of business had prevented him from giving the matter at hand the attention its importance clearly demanded. Thus while not in a position to provide an informed opinion on the true merits of Keith's case, he admitted that there was little question that the braincase as moulded by Woodward did require some alteration. He also said that he was not surprised by the cranial volume of Keith's reconstruction, since he had long maintained the preeminence of the brain in human evolution. Neither was he disturbed, as Keith evidently was, by the association of a primitive human brain with a simian jaw. Such a situation was seen to be in accordance with the view that the perfection of the human brain must have preceded the refinement of the human face and jaw. Raoul Anthony (1874–1941), a neuroanatomist from the National Museum of Natural History in Paris, concurred, but added that while Woodward's model stood in need of certain alterations, he was not prepared to accept Keith's bold propositions in all their details.[37] Duckworth, however, was less reserved, saying that he had come independently to the same conclusion: a mistake had been made in the restoration of the skull. In his opinion, Keith was right; the brain capacity was nearly 1 500 cc. Responding to this, Thomson remarked that had he been handed the jaw without the other fragments, his reaction would have been: "Here is a simian fossil; we must give him a simian setting".

In reply to these views, Keith said he did not think his audience quite realized the importance of the Piltdown skull. It brought home the incontrovertible fact that at the commencement of the Pleistocene, or perhaps more accurately at the end of the Pliocene, the human brain had reached its full size. This fact, he said, opened up a new insight into our the past — "a vista of human cultures coming struggling to us over perhaps a million of years".

Although the impression conveyed in the newspapers was that Keith had carried the day, it was clearly a qualified victory. He had perhaps won a battle, but certainly not the war. There were some observers, such as Boyd Dawkins, who were not even prepared to grant this much. In his estimation, Keith had not only exaggerated, but had also grievously distorted the facts — particularly as they related to the age of the specimens. "So far as I know", Dawkins wrote in a letter to the Editor of the *Daily Express*:

> no traces of modern types of mankind have as yet been found in any undisturbed deposit of [either Pliocene or early Pleistocene] age in any part of the world. Those relied upon by Dr. Keith are certainly proved in the case of Ipswich to have been an internment that may be of any age, from the Neolithic times down to to-day, and in the other cases [e.g. Galley Hill] are not of clearly defined geological age.[38]

Besides challenging Dawkins' contention that the Piltdown gravels were unequivocally Pleistocene, Reid Moir begged to know what "justification" Dawkins had for saying that the case against the Ipswich skeleton had been "proved". Dawkins did not respond either to this or to Lewis Abbott's letter which appeared in the *Express* several days later. Abbott, like Moir, did not mince his words. The evidence, in his opinion, all pointed in the direction Keith had indicated, and he bemoaned the fact that since his youth Dawkins had emulated "the historic Mussulman who closed the Koran and declared that any book that supported it was unnecessary and should be destroyed, and any that differed from it should be similarly treated"![39]

In the meantime, on another front, Francis Bather (1864–1934), who was Assistant Keeper in Woodward's department at the British Museum (Natural History) in South Kensington, attacked Keith's arrogant disregard for the International Rules of Zoological Nomenclature. Specifically, Bather had objected to Keith's labelling of the Piltdown casts in a public exhibit at the Royal College as "Homo piltdownensis". In defence of this action, Keith wrote:

> The generic name of *Homo* cannot be withheld from an individual in whom the brain and skull are human in every essential feature save one — the chin ... We are concerned, therefore, with only the specific part of the designation ... Mr. Dawson's name should certainly be associated with the most important discovery ever made of our predecessors. But for him the skull bones of *Homo dawsoni* ...would have been

ground to dust on a country road by the wheels of carts lumbering to market. While Bather is strictly in the right, I should like to urge the feasibility of breaking the law and naming this extinct human race *Homo piltdownensis* . . . [because] . . . we have been in the habit — these past 50 years past — of naming fossil men according to the place in which their remains were first found . . . If, however, this method of naming new human species [after the discoverer] is followed, matters will become very complex for our descendants. From what has happened in the last 40 years in Europe we may safely expect that there must be scores of extinct species and genera of men — of which at present we know nothing. Now, if we are to attach the name of the discoverer to each new species of fossil man . . . — descendants will, I think, regret that the laws of nomenclature are so inflexible.[40]

Dawson's reaction to this was surprisingly lighthearted. Replying anonymously in the *Daily Express*, he wrote:

I am told that Dr. Arthur Keith and Dr. Bather are disputing in the "Times" as to what is my right name. Permit me to say that I have not the slightest objection to Dr. Keith naming his plaster reconstruction Homo Keithii, if he will only leave me at rest, but I do not think it right he should discuss a lady's age.[41]

There were many, however, who were not amused by Keith's antics. William Sollas for example was "astonished" by Keith's behaviour. "Even supposing you did get the bones out of the middle line", he told Woodward, "what of it? We all make mistakes. But that is no reason why the first man who thinks he has found one out should spread his wings and crow in this shameless fashion". It appeared to him that the whole affair was a storm in a teacup:

It doesn't seem to me to matter two straws whether the cranial capacity is close on 1100 c.c. or 1500 c.c. Your point is the combination of a human brain and an ape's jaw and the more human the former the more interesting the combination becomes. Both 1100 and 1500 c.c. are actual human capacities at the present day; so why all the fuss? And now like a child crying for the moon he wants to be allowed to name your fossil! . . .[42]

THE VINDICATION OF WOODWARD

Early in June, Dawson and Woodward resumed their diggings at Piltdown. Apart from the excursion of the Geologists' Association to Barkham Manor early in July,[43] the summer at Piltdown appears to have been uneventful until the weekend of 8–10 August, when Dawson discovered the left and right nasal bones (along with splintered fragments of the turbinals) of their now celebrated skull.[44] While the turbinals were reportedly too fragmentary to be of much use, the nasal bones were intact and found to fit "perfectly" beneath the median suture of the restored skull; but as they both recognized, this discovery neither confirmed nor invalidated the facial configuration of Woodward's model. However, in light of the garbled reports from Nuremburg and Keith's pending attack, the find was encouraging and clearly gave Dawson reason to denounce recent speculations on the skull's exact conformation as premature. "When we have done with the pick and shovel", he told a reporter from the *Sussex Daily News*, "it will be quite time enough to call in the doctors".[45]

From the outset of the season they had directed their efforts to recovering the missing teeth of the lower jaw, but these efforts went unrewarded until the afternoon of Saturday, 30 August, when the all important canine tooth was discovered. The find, however, was not made either by Dawson or Woodward, but by Father Pierre Teilhard de Chardin, who had returned to England earlier in August to take his spiritual retreat at Ore Place in Hastings, and was spending a few days with Dawson before making his way back to France. The circumstances surrounding this fortuitous discovery were later recalled by Woodward:

> We were then excavating a rather deep and hot trench in which Father Teilhard, in black clothing, was especially energetic; and, as we thought he seemed a little exhausted, we suggested that he should leave us to do the hard labour for a time while he had comparative rest in searching the rain-washed spread gravel. Very soon he exclaimed that he had picked up the missing canine tooth, but we were incredulous, and told him we had already seen several bits of ironstone, which looked like teeth, on the spot where he stood. He insisted, however, that he was not deceived, so we both left our digging to go and verify his discovery. There could be no doubt about it, and we all spent the rest of the day until dusk crawling over the gravel in the vain quest for more.[46]

Subsequent study of the tooth revealed that it was indeed the missing right lower canine. Furthermore, in both size and shape, it closely resembled the one Woodward had prophesied in his controversial model. Understandably Woodward was ecstatic — for it not only vindicated his restoration, but also administered a fatal blow to Keith's contentious thesis.

Originally Woodward had planned to wait and announce this sensational news at the British Association meetings in Birmingham later in September, but much to his annoyance he was robbed of this melodrama by a leak to the *Daily Express* which ran the story on Tuesday, 2 September. Aware of how much this plan had meant to his colleague, Dawson was naturally shocked by the disclosure. "The worst is that I have no doubt it was done by someone here who ought to have known better", Dawson wrote apologetically. "It is a great pity and undermines things in more ways than one and I am very annoyed about it."[47] Although Dawson did not venture to suggest the identity of the culprit, the inference was that it had been one of his clerks who had tipped off the *Express*.

During the next two weeks Woodward, with the assistance of Pycraft and Barlow, made a detailed study of the canine tooth. The preliminary results confirmed his earlier prognostications. In fact, as he subsequently revealed to the delegates of the British Association that gathered in Central Hall, Birmingham, to hear him speak on the evening of 16 September, there was now definite proof that the anterior teeth of the Piltdown mandible resembled those of an ape, which more than amply justified its recognition as a genus distinct from *Homo*. Furthermore, Woodward said that while his recent studies of the braincase convinced him that an alteration was necessary to remedy a defect in the position of the parietal bones, the envisioned change was minimal and did not, contrary to what Keith had proposed, significantly change the volume of the cranium. In this regard Woodward said, it appeared that Keith's results had been based on a failure to recognize the mark of the superior longitudinal sinus on the interior surface of the frontal region and by unduly widening the parietal region. This conclusion, he said, had been confirmed by Elliot Smith who was in the midst of preparing a detailed study of the braincase which he planned to present shortly to the Royal Society.[48]

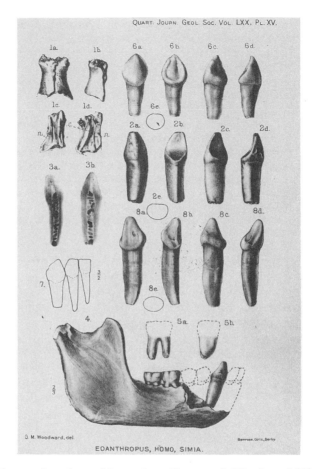

QUART. JOURN. GEOL. SOC. VOL. LXX. PL. XV.

G. M. Woodward. del.   Bemrose, Colle., Derby

EOANTHROPUS, HOMO, SIMIA.

The Piltdown canine tooth and nasal bones from Dawson & Woodward (1914). 2a–2d Various views of the canine tooth attributed to Eoanthropus. *3a–3b X-ray of canine to show sand grains. 6a–6d, Human canine tooth, similarly compared. 8a–8d,* Simia satyrus *(chimpanzee) canine tooth, included for comparison. 4. Piltdown canine tooth inserted in mandible. 1a–1b, Nasal bones: 1a.: front view. 1b.: left side view.*

A STRUGGLE IN *NATURE*

While it may have appeared that Woodward's address in Birmingham had "neatly laid out" Keith, this was in fact far from the truth. Reid Moir, for one, did not think Woodward had carried off all the laurels, and was clearly disturbed by Pycraft's flamboyant piece in *The Illustrated London News* which had made light of Keith's recent efforts to modify Woodward's model. "There is no doubt but that Professor Keith was in error in his reconstruction of the lower jaw in regard to the canine teeth, but has his reconstruction of the skull been seriously challenged", Moir questioned:

> If it has been I have been singularly unfortunate in seeing no account of such a criticism. Mr Pycraft attempts, in an indefinite manner, to accuse Professor Keith of twisting his facts to suit his theory; and while I am confident no man who knows

Professor Keith will do other than scout such a suggestion, I am more than surprised to find such an accusation emanating from those who have endeavoured to prove from this Piltdown discovery that the antiquity of man does not go back beyond the Pleistocene period.[49]

But if Keith had been wrong about the jaw, was it not possible that he had also been mistaken in his arguments for the braincase? And if not how did he propose to reconcile these two seemingly divergent anatomies?

As Keith saw the situation at the time, there were three possible explanations of the evidence. First, there was the possibility that David Waterston had been correct and that the skull and mandible were in fact parts of different kinds of beings. The attraction of this argument was offset by the essentially human appearance of the molar teeth. Second, it was possible that Woodward's monistic synthesis was, in spite of its inherent problems, correct. A third possibility was that neither Woodward's nor his own reconstruction was correct, but rather that the real configuration of the Piltdown skull lay somewhere between the two.

Originally he had lodged four major objections against Woodward's reconstruction of the Piltdown jaw, all of which in his estimation precluded the possibility of a large and projecting canine: (1) the modern conformation of the glenoid cavity; (2) the apparent side-to-side wear pattern of the molar teeth; (3) the relatively small size of the temporal muscle which rises from the side of the skull and acts on the jaw; and (4) the appearance of the mastoid region which determines the way the skull is hafted to the neck. In anthropoid apes the mastoid processes are splayed out as wide bony flanges in order to provide adequate room for the insertion of powerful neck muscles, whereas in the Piltdown skull these processes form downward projecting knobs as found in modern human crania. Although there was no denying that the canine had greatly strengthened Woodward's case, there were nevertheless several features of this tooth which troubled Keith and led him to initially question whether or not it belonged to the Piltdown mandible. To begin with, the crown of the tooth was deeply worn, but evidently not by attrition against the upper projecting canine, but by the upper lateral incisor — a wear pattern not unusual in anthropoid canine teeth. Then there was its colour and condition. It was a much darker shade than the two *in situ* molar teeth; and in marked contrast to these teeth, it showed signs of excessive wear and tear. This latter finding Keith found difficult to equate with Arthur Underwood's recently published X-ray pictures of the mandible,[50] which showed that the third molar, or wisdom tooth, (indicated by the socket) had not fully erupted at the time of death. This was remarkable because in anthropoid apes the canine and third molar are known to erupt at the same time. Given the markedly simian nature of the Piltdown mandible, it was Keith's expectation that these should have erupted about the same time also. This being the case, it seemed strange to Keith to find an excessively worn tooth (a condition more indicative of a mature individual) and an nonerupted third molar (synonymous with a more immature individual) in the same individual. But while harbouring some reservations about whether or not this canine tooth belonged to the Piltdown mandible, Keith, in accepting that the mandible represented a very primitive form, supposed that it must have belonged to one of the same kind — though he was at a loss to adequately explain the existence of a projecting canine tooth with a palpably modern glenoid cavity and what seemed to him to be an essentially modern braincase.

In an effort to justify this peculiar state of affairs, Keith postulated that the Piltdown specimen was not the ancestral form of modern humans as Woodward had conjectured. It appeared to him that, like the Neanderthals, it had been one of several forms that had arisen and subsequently been swept to the evolutionary sidelines by the emergence of *Homo sapiens*:

> We must presume, then, to account for certain facts, that the common ancestor of human races possessed simian eyebrow ridges and a simian chin-plate. From that common ancestry springs one form, in which the eyebrow ridges were dominant and persisted, but the chin-plate was recessive and disappeared, the combination found in Neanderthal man. In another form, the eyebrow ridges were recessive, but the chin-plate was dominant, the combination found in Piltdown man. We may presume, independently of corroborative facts — the discoveries of remains of the modern type of man, at Castenedolo (Italian Pliocene), at Olmo (Italian early Pleistocene),[51] at Galley Hill (mid-Pleistocene) — that there was a third form evolved at the same time as the other two, one in which both eyebrow ridges and chin-plate were recessive. This third form would give us the ancestry of modern human races of men. Far from proving, as Dr. Smith Woodward evidently thought, that the modern type of man could not have existed at the time the 100-foot terrace of the Thames valley was deposited, the discovery at Piltdown has furnished us with the strongest evidence in favour of his early, probably Pliocene, evolution.[52]

While Keith was coming to these conclusions, Elliot Smith found himself engulfed by a sea of malicious gossip, which among other things portrayed him as a fair-weather man. Although this criticism had perhaps been unduly harsh, Smith had certainly not assisted his own case. In fact, as he admitted to Woodward, it was not until after the discovery of the canine had been announced, followed by the arrival of Woodward's new restoration, that he put his mind to work on the problem:

> For the first time since the casts of the bone fragments came into my possession [April] I had time yesterday [9 September] to sit down for an hour and puzzle them out, so that when your restoration came today I was able to telegraph at once. Keith has been led astray by opposing the "articular" surface of the temporal squama to that of the parietal and everything in that region depends upon the true fit which the real specimens in your possession give. I think your reconstruction [is] a close approximation to the truth ... I [have] put the right parietal further back than you have done so as to bring it almost to touch the small fragment linking it to the occipital. I think your right parietal boss is further forward than the left ... I also made the median line cut the frontal tongue of bone about 4 to 5 mm. further to the right than you have done. None of these things however materially affect my published statement ...[53]

Thus, in an effort to correct his public image, or as he explained it to Woodward:

> To put myself right with local people and the anatomists generally — some of whom are only too ready to make reckless statements concerning me — I have sent a note to "Nature," which I think you will approve. Without treading on anyone's toes I have made quite clear my own opinions; and I hope it may have some influence in checking the malicious gossip now current.[54]

In his note to *Nature*, Smith said:

> ... Recent events have made it difficult for those who have relied wholly upon what has appeared in print to form any accurate conception of the meaning and importance of the Piltdown skull- fragments. It is quite certain that they afford the first evidence we have obtained of a hitherto unknown group of the Hominidae, so fundamentally distinct from all the early fossil men found in Europe as to be worthy of generic

distinction — a "dawn-man" of a very primitive and generalised type . . . [The] curious association of features is not paradoxical, as some people pretend. The small and archaic brain and thick skull are undoubtedly human in character, but the mandible, in spite of the human molars it bears, is more simian than human. So far from being an impossible combination of characters, this association . . . is precisely what I anticipated in my address to the British Association at Dundee (Nature, September 26, 1912, p.125), some months before I knew of the existence of the Piltdown skull . . . That the ape-like conformation of the chin region signifies the inability to speak is surely a patent fallacy. Articulate speech must have come while the jaws were still simian in character . . . A great source of misunderstanding will be got rid of if these obvious facts and the considerations based upon them be admitted. In conclusion, I may answer many questioners by affirming that I still hold to every word of my preliminary note published in the Quarterly Journal of the Geological Society . . .[55]

Smith's communiqué seemed to have the desired effect and undoubtedly contributed to the illusion that an end to the controversy was near at hand. In fact shortly after Smith's letter was published, the newspapers were claiming that the "gulf" which had divided Woodward and Keith had now been "practically bridged over". (But this was not the case. Not only was Waterston making waves,[56] but Keith was readying himself for a blistering counter attack.) During the course of a lecture which Keith had delivered to the Faculty of Medicine at Birmingham University on 7 October, he reportedly confessed to being a "wiser man", saying that the basis of his argument had been wrong and Woodward had been right. Mesmerized by this gallant and seemingly conciliatory gesture, the press completely missed the significance of Keith's subsequent arguments for the great antiquity of the modern human form, and his charge that the evidence supporting such a viewpoint had been sentenced without a trial.[57] As his letter to Nature (published on 16 October) revealed, the case had not been closed:

> In my opinion [Keith wrote], Dr. Smith Woodward has made a grave mistake in his restoration of the occipital region, and therefore the brain cast which he obtained from his reconstruction — the basis of Prof. Elliot Smith's preliminary note to the Geological Society — does not give an accurate representation of either the size or general form of the brain of Piltdown Man.[58]

In addition to sending a signal to the Woodward camp regarding his continuing dissatisfaction with the configuration of the Piltdown braincase, Keith's letter to Nature was, as the above passage indicates, deliberately designed to confront Smith. This decision to confront him publicly was not undertaken lightly. They had been friends since 1898 when they first met in Duckworth's rooms at Jesus College while attending the International Zoological Congress. But as Keith saw it, Smith had not been completely honest in his Piltdown dealings, and the time had now come for him to decide whether he was to run with the fox or with the hounds. Thus began a protracted, and an increasingly acrimonious struggle in the pages of Nature that was to lead ultimately to the end of their long friendship.

Responding to Keith's letter of 16 October, Smith said, "Now that my friend Prof. Keith has explained so lucidly his reasons for making a big brain-case of the Piltdown fragments it is possible to define precisely the point at issue between us."[59] He went on to say that the crux of the problem was the criteria used for determining the middle line in the posterior parietal region, and charged that Keith's "error" could be attributed to his ignorance of the original specimens. "Anyone who examines the left parietal and temporal bones cannot fail to recognize that there is no room for any doubt as to the relative position of these bones the one to the other, which is not that claimed for them by Prof. Keith."[60] The inference that Keith had placed too much reliance on what could be deduced from the plaster casts was not kindly received. Keith was furious, and replied that Smith had done both Woodward and Barlow a grave injustice by his suggestion that the casts were untrustworthy. To which he added:

> Anatomists have had no difficulty in gaining the freest access to the actual specimens; even those, who like myself, regard the original reconstruction of the skull and brain cast as fundamentally erroneous, have had the privilege granted them on repeated visits to see the Piltdown fragments in Dr. Smith Woodward's keeping. [61]

He then went on to note that Barlow's casts were highly accurate and completely trustworthy. He also admitted that his symmetrical reconstruction was at variance with Woodward's, which as he again stressed, was not based on opinion but the rules of anatomy, and as such, he had merely placed the fragments in their correct anatomical positions. To which he sarcastically added:

> It is clear, from his letter (*Nature*, October 30, p.267) that Prof. Elliot Smith knows of another method, one which fulfils the same conditions, but gives a much smaller brain capacity. All that is necessary to convince me that he is right and I am wrong is a drawing of that reconstruction ... I have articulated the fragments in the manner suggested in his letter, and find that the degree of asymmetry in his suggested reconstruction is as great as in the original. It is possible that I have misinterpreted some of the indications given in his letter. Any error of this kind would be cleared up by a drawing.[62]

Despite the professed pacific intention of the latter sentences, Keith's letter of 16 October contributed nothing to this end. Smith not only resented the twisted interpretation that had been placed on his remarks concerning Barlow's casts, which he endeavoured to correct, but also failed to understand why an anatomist of Keith's calibre had managed to misplace the true position of the median line. Not only was its position confirmed by the impression of the median longitudinal sinus, but there were also, Smith pointed out in his next letter to *Nature*:

> [T]hree other features of the bone in the neighbourhood of the [median] line ... namely the supralambdoid flattening, the arrangements and medial relations of the meningeal grooves, and the median groove in the frontal region...[63]

Using these reference points, and employing a diagram as Keith had demanded, Smith then showed that the two halves of the skull were not, and could not be, brought into symmetrical positions — as Keith contended they should. Furthermore, he claimed that there was considerable peripheral evidence to support the asymmetrical nature of the Piltdown skull. In particular he noted how much thinner the cranial wall was on the right side in comparison to that of the left. And with this he returned the ball to Keith's court.

Although acknowledging the eloquence of Smith's argument, Keith conceded nothing. While throwing further criticism on the methods Smith had employed, Keith also reminded Smith of his own work in defence of his identification of the the middle-line:

> Seven years ago, Prof. Elliot Smith published a short paper (*Anat. Anz.* 1907, vol xxx., p.574), which is justly regarded as authoritative. He directed attention to the preponderance of the left occipital pole of the brain, and attributed that

preponderance to the specialisaton of the right hand; only the slightest degree of asymmetry is observable in anthropoid apes. Indeed, at that time Prof. Elliot Smith definitely stated that he regarded symmetry of the occipital poles — in my opinion an absolutely just deduction — as a simian character. He will, therefore, if he retains the present reconstruction, have to modify to some extent the opinion he has expressed of the brain of Piltdown man — that it is "the most primitive and simian brain yet recorded." As regards the asymmetry of the occipital lobes, it is my opinion, ultra-modern.[64]

Smith was denied an opportunity to respond to this in the pages of *Nature*.[65] Evidently it was thought that this was enough,[66] but as Smith later confided to Alfred Cort Haddon (1855–1940), the Cambridge physical anthropologist, he believed Keith had managed to persuade the Editor of *Nature* not to publish his rebuttal.[67] In spite of this the debate continued with Keith maintaining that his construction was the correct one and Smith vigorously denying it.

In an effort to resolve this stalemate, one of Keith's anatomy colleagues, Frederick Gymer Parsons (1863–1943) of St Thomas' Hospital, proposed that he and some of his fellow anatomists select a skull which they would break into fragments like those found at Piltdown and submit them to him for reconstruction. Keith accepted the challenge, but insisted that if the fragments were to be a close imitation of the Piltdown problem it was essential that the middle line should be in no way be apparent on the fragments. A skull was prepared accordingly and delivered to Keith on 6 January 1914 by a former associate of Smith's, Douglas Derry (b 1874) of University College.[68] A little more than a week later, Keith presented Derry with his reconstruction which was subsequently shown to match the cast of the original within just a few cubic centimetres. As might be expected, Keith used the exercise to his full advantage. Parading his sensational feat before the Royal Anthropological Institute on 20 January 1914, Keith said that it proved beyond question that the restoration of the human skull was not an art, but a science:

> [T]he skull is framed according to definite principles; that all its parts are correlated, and that it is possible from a part — if our knowledge is accurate and full — to reconstruct the whole. If this is not true, then our hope of obtaining a knowledge of extinct forms is well-nigh hopeless, for we cannot expect to find complete fossil skulls. If the history of early man is to be built at all, it must be built out of fragments.[69]

Shortly thereafter, with the smell of blood still in the air, Smith made his long awaited presentation to the Royal Society, and, not surprisingly, the scheduled event drew a large and expectant crowd, which included Keith. From all accounts it was not a disappointing afternoon. Smith had apparently come to London determined to put Keith in his place and to restore the battered image of Woodward's *Eoanthropus*.[70] Accordingly, as he later told Alfred Haddon, he made no effort to disguise his contempt for Keith's recent behaviour:

> I had to speak straight because so many British anatomists have been content to dance to Keith's rag-time, without attempting to think for themselves; and foreign anthropologists think therefore that all the anatomists are supporting him ... For years I have stood up for Keith, at times at the peril of my own reputation [and] sanity, in the hope of restraining him from too wild excesses.[71]

Although the inference of this letter suggests that Smith had had a field day at the Royal Society, it seems that Keith thought otherwise. Recalling this event some years later, he wrote:

... [I]n the discussion which followed I did not mince my words in pointing out the glaring errors in the reconstructed brain-cast he exhibited to the meeting ... and so it happened that he and I filed out side by side. I shall never forget the angry look he gave me. Such was the end of a long friendship. He must have felt I was right, for he never published the paper he read to the Royal Society, and when, at a later date, he ... [finally made and published] ... a reconstruction of the Piltdown skull, [the] result did not differ materially from mine ...[72]

THE VIEW FROM SOUTH KENSINGTON

During the weeks following the British Association meetings in Birmingham it appears that Woodward was increasingly bombarded by Keith's reported arguments against the canine tooth. In addition to dismissing Woodward's opinion that the canine wear pattern was attributable to a large projecting upper canine, Keith also relayed through Dawson (who made several visits to the Royal College at this time to examine the Hunterian Museum's extensive primate collections) his concern for the apparent differences in the condition of the canine and third molar. "He points out that the 3rd molar so far as he can judge from [Underwood's] skiagrams [X-rays] was not quite up", Woodward was informed by Dawson:

> And therefore the animal was young (as the sutures also show). Then, that the canine and 3rd molar in Anthropoids always grow their permanent 3rd molars and the canines at the same time. Ergo. As the canine is so worn it could not have belonged to the same individual. I reminded him that supposing that this was the rule with the apes, we were dealing with an intermediate form and as the times for appearance of the 3rd molars in the human jaw were most variable and quite unconnected with the growth of the canines — that his new theory was not a very safe one. I also reminded him that the 3rd molars have already showed rudimentary characters both in the human jaws as well as certain of the anthropoids. The 3rd molar is often placed at such an angle as to look inward and is almost useless for mastication and the fangs are often not fully developed. <u>Besides all this we have two molar teeth worn quite as much as the canine!</u> We both remained unconvinced it seems! ... However, he still believes the mandible belongs to the skull and evidently does not think Waterson [sic] counts at all ...[73]

Woodward remained essentially unconvinced by these and related points, and believed that the canine had interlocked with the opposing upper canine tooth in much the same way he had conceived in his original restoration. He also felt there was no evidence to support the view that the canine had been affected by the position of the upper incisors; and dismissed Keith's reservations about the lack of concordance between the condition of the canine and the evidence for a nonerupted third molar:

> The degree of wear of this newly-discovered canine tooth is of especial interest, when considered in connexion with the worn condition of the first and second molars in the mandible to which it apparently belongs. As already described, both these molars are flattened by mastication down to the level of the middle area of their crown, while the third molar (known only by its socket) must have been fully in place. The permanent canine should therefore be completely extruded and in use, whether the order of appearance of the teeth corresponded with that in Man or with that in the Apes. As, however, the enamel of its inner face is not merely worn, but entirely removed by mastication, the tooth must have been well used for a considerable period. It probably, therefore, came into place before the second and third molars, as in Man — not after one or both of these teeth, as in the Apes.[74]

Charles Dawson (left) and Arthur Smith Woodward (right) pondering on their reconstruction of the Piltdown skull. This photograph was taken in the basement of the British Museum (Natural History) circa 1913. (Courtesy of Mrs Margaret Hodgson)

Evidently Underwood had convinced Woodward that the socket of the third molar was that of a fully erupted tooth. Had they been otherwise, Underwood contended, "the roots could not have been on a plane with those of the other molars".[75]

Woodward was further assured of the correctness of his position by the results of a comparative study he had conducted, which revealed that:

> ... [A]mong known Upper Tertiary and Recent Anthropoids, the permanent lower canine of *Eoanthropus* agrees more closely in shape with the milk-canine both of Man and of the Apes than with the corresponding permanent tooth in either of these groups. It is also obvious that the resemblance is greater between *Eoanthropus* and *Homo* than between the former and any known genus of Apes. In other words, the permanent tooth of the extinct *Eoanthropus* is almost identical in shape with the temporary milk-tooth of the existing *Homo*. Hence it forms another illustration of the well-known law in mammalian palaeontology, that the permanent teeth of an ancestral race agree more closely in pattern with the milk-teeth than the permanent teeth of its modified descendants.[76]

Similarly, Woodward could see no reason to change his mind about the overall configuration of the braincase — in spite of all the fuss in *Nature*. He was convinced that Smith was right and Keith was wrong. This being the case, his model needed only a slight readjustment of the "occipital and right parietal bones" in order to bring them into line with Smith's "exact determination of the median plane" of the skull —

the result of which did not alter "essentially any of the conclusions already reached".[77]

THE REAL QUESTION

By autumn's end, it was quite evident to Boyd Dawkins that not only was Keith not chastened by the discovery of the canine tooth, but that he was still intent on pushing *Eoanthropus* into the Pliocene, in spite of evidence to the contrary. But while Dawkins had viewed Keith's public manoeuvres with increasing alarm, it was not until the evening of 17 December, 1913, that he was presented with an opportunity to take the Hunterian Professor to task on what he considered to be a flagrant abuse of the facts.

In addition to hearing Woodward's account of the fortuitous canine and Smith's complex argument for the "exact determination of the median line", the crowded meeting of the Geological Society on that evening also heard Dawson announce that some progress had been made in distinguishing the relative ages of the fossiliferous strata in the Piltdown pit — it was the resulting discussion of this latter report which gave Dawkins the opportunity he had been seeking.

According to Dawson, it now appeared that the Piltdown gravel-bed consisted of four well-defined strata, the first being a thin layer of surface-soil beneath which lay a bed of light-coloured, undisturbed gravel of varying thickness. It was from this second stratum that Woodward had apparently plucked a triangular shaped palaeolithic implement in the summer of 1912. The third bed, which also varied considerably in thickness, was marked by its "dark ferruginous" appearance. It had been from this stratum that the mandible and cranium had been recovered. This stratum had been found to rest unevenly on a fourth bed, situated directly above the Hastings Beds, composed of pale yellow sand and clay, which, Dawson noted, had so far proved to be unfossiliferous.

The recovery of the fossil remains of a beaver (*Castor fiber*)[78] from this third bed, Dawson said, appeared to confirm his earlier hypothesis that this "dark-ferruginous" bed, composed largely of Pliocene drift, had been reconstructed in the early Pleistocene. Also, it appeared to him that there was a "marking-off of the third or dark-bed from the second or lighter-bed", that had yielded several examples of Chellean-like stone tools.[79]

Commenting on these findings, Keith said he was "glad" to hear that the particular stratum in which the remains of the skull had been found was being distinguished from the "more superficial stratum" in which the flints of the Chellean type had been found. For, as he went on to say, it was quite evident that the human remains had hailed from the Pliocene rather than the Pleistocene. Had human remains not been discovered in the *Eoanthropic* stratum, he said, no one would have hesitated in regarding the deposit as of Pliocene age. This brought not only Dawkins to his feet, but also William Sollas, who spoke first. Sollas said that he strongly objected to the inference of Keith's remarks. In his opinion Dawson had acted correctly and was merely following standard geological procedure in dating a deposit by the most recent fossils in it, which in this case was, he added (and no doubt with some relish), unquestionably Pleistocene. Concurring with this Dawkins went on to point out the fallacy of Keith's argument. The Pliocene fauna at Piltdown was, as Dawson had suggested, clearly derived from the destruction of a neighbouring Pliocene deposit. Therefore, they offered no information on the age of the gravel bed, except that the gravels of which they formed a part were accumulated at a much later date. Furthermore, he continued, Pliocene mammalian assemblages recovered on the Continent had been found to be composed exclusively of extinct forms; whereas at

Geologists' Association party visiting the pit at Piltdown on 12 July 1913.

Piltdown they were seen to be a mixture of extinct and living forms. The presence of an antler of a red deer (*Cervus elaphus*) was particularly instructive he thought, because it was completely unknown in the Pliocene of Europe, but abundant in the Pleistocene and later strata. He also noted the comparatively "unrolled" condition of this specimen, as well as that of the human bones and their associated palaeolithic tools. This evidence alone, he felt, was sufficient proof of their Pleistocene age.[80]

The following day a provocative summary of this meeting appeared in *The Morning Post*, which clearly defined the current status of the debate. According to the *Post*:

The real question that is being fought out is this: Did man reach his modern estate in mind and body during the Pleistocene period — some one or two hundred thousand years ago, or is the antiquity of self-conscious circumstance adopting man of much greater antiquity? Did he appear a million or two years ago — early in the Pliocene? It is really over that question the fight is being waged. Dr. Smith Woodward supported the Pleistocene age of man's origin; Professor Keith saw man's beginning in the more ancient Pliocene period. If the first-named is right, our human history is a short tale with a few missing chapters; if Professor Keith is right, there are missing volumes — volumes whose former existence we are only now beginning to suspect. If we lay our trust on worked flints as evidence of man's existence — such flints as are supposed to bear the impress of man's hand — then, indeed, man's story must begin at even an earlier date than the Pliocene. If the *Eoanthropus* of Dr. Smith Woodward represents the stage of evolution reached by man early in the Pleistocene period, then it is clear that we have passed from a semi-human to a truly human estate at a rapid rate. If the *Eanthropus* of Professor Keith is Pliocene and representative of the men of that epoch, then the progress to our present estate is a long and tedious progress. The fight last night was apparently over a few fossil fragments of a human skull — in reality, it was a battle between "Pleistoceners" and "Plioceners" — it was a fight over the antiquity of man.[81]

Responding to this, Dawkins praised the insights of the *Post* reporter, but complained that the article had failed to inform the paper's readers of whether the "fight was fought to a finish, or whether one of the principals was knocked-out". And as Dawkins went on to reveal, it was his conviction that the "fight" between Keith and Woodward at Burlington House had ended with a knock-out which, he himself, had delivered. In reviewing the case against Keith, he wrote:

He says that the fragments of the skull have been wrongly put together . . . He especially denied the presence of ape-like upstanding canines . . . All these points were discussed last Wednesday, and it was conclusively proved that Dr. Smith Woodward's restoration is substantially accurate, although the nose is shown, by the recently found nasal bones, to be slightly smaller than it is there represented. [And] According to Professor Elliot Smith, Dr. Keith's restoration is impossible. The lower canine, also recently discovered . . . places beyond question the fact that the restoration of the lower jaw is also accurate, although the tooth is slightly smaller and relatively broader than it was supposed to be. To this statement of the case Dr. Keith made no adequate answer. It may therefore be accepted by the public as a carefully reasoned verdict of the scientific experts, most competent to give a judicial decision.

Nor can it be maintained that *Eoanthropus* is of Pliocene age, although the Pliocene mammalia occur in the gravels. Their bones and teeth are all in condition of pebbles and have obviously been derived from the destruction of Pliocene deposits like the Norfolk crag, then existing in the district. They offer, therefore, no information as to the age, except that the gravels of which they form a part, were accumulated later than those strata . . . With few exceptions all the Pliocene mammalia, belong to extinct species. All those assigned by Dr. Smith Woodward to the Piltdown gravel period belong to living forms, and the red deer made its first appearance in Europe in the early Pleistocene. The palaeolithic implements also found with *Eoanthropus*, are identical with those of the older Pleistocene gravels of the Thames valley, and point to the same age . . . the early Pleistocene.[82]

Be this as it may, the fact remained that neither Keith nor his various supporters were persuaded by these arguments, and thus much to Dawkins' growing frustration, the "battle" between the "Plioceners" and "Pleistoceners" did not fade, but continued to gather momentum.

4   Bones, stones & egos II: the Piltdown debates 1914–1917

If you open ... Pandora's Box you never know what Trojan 'orses will jump out.[1]

STONES OF CONTENTION

Lewis Abbott was one of several who took exception to Boyd Dawkins' attempt to exclude Tertiary man from the Piltdown discussions. With characteristic bombast and immodesty, Abbott had assailed the "oracular pronouncements" of the Manchester geologist, claiming them to be full of contradiction, and describing them as a patent misrepresentation of the known facts.[2] Indeed his assault just stopped short of charging Dawkins with scientific incompetency. Abbott had been particularly irritated by the way Dawkins had side-stepped the eolithic issue by attempting to pass off the Piltdown implements as "characteristic" palaeolithic forms. "I am prepared to challenge the Professor", Abbott announced in his strident letter to the *Morning Post*:

> to bring forward a sample drawer of Thames gravel implements identical with those found at Piltdown. I think I may lay claim to have worked as hard on classification of types as many people, and have collected with my own hands hundreds of thousands of specimens, and I challenge the Professor to enumerate six, nay, one single, characteristic of these flints which fixes their age as Chellean. Of all the mystifying libels that have been circulated in connection with Piltdown man, and the one that is calculated to prevent his true age and nature being understood, it is the one which makes him of Chellean age.[3]

And, if, as Dawkins admitted, these implements had been made by *Eoanthropus*, whom he had assigned to the 80 ft terrace, Abbott questioned:

> what sort of creature was it that produced the beautiful specimens of the 100-ft terrace and still greater altitudes of the Thames Valley? ... [And] If the changes which have taken place in the transformation of *Eoanthropus* to *Homo* were affected while something altogether much less tha[n] 80ft. has been excavated, what changes must there have been between *Eoanthropus* and the implement-making creature so far back as even the 400ft-level?

In venting his anger on Dawkins, Abbott was also tangentially chastizing Woodward for not standing up to his old mentor and supporting his long-held belief in the Plateau "brownies". His "distortion" of the Piltdown artifacts "into Chellian [sic]" was, Abbott believed, "as dishonourable as it [was] preposterous", and furthermore, a disgrace to science.[4]

Although Abbott was under the impression that his letter had given Boyd Dawkins his "eternal quietus",[5] it had, in fact, achieved nothing of the sort. Not only had Dawkins ignored Abbott's challenge, he had also made no attempt to respond to any of the other criticisms levelled at him. To Dawkins, the vicious outburst merely served to confirm his contempt for the scientific activities of the Sussex jeweller. Apart from harbouring a generally low opinion of Abbott, it was Dawkins' sincere conviction that

James Reid Moir (circa 1920), Ipswich businessman and avid eolithophile. (From the Keith papers, Library of the Royal College of Surgeons, London)

the business of the eoliths was no longer a scientific issue — a fact which he believed had been more than ably demonstrated by the geologist W H Sutcliffe a year earlier at the Manchester Literary and Philosophical Society.[6] Besides discounting the Piltdown eoliths, Sutcliffe had also dispensed with Reid Moir's rostro-carinate industry, claiming that, along with all the other so-called eolithic implements recovered from the Kent Plateau and elsewhere, these were nothing more than natural débris.

Like Abbott, Reid Moir had also been alarmed by Dawkins' letter to the *Morning Post* (23 November, 1913), for, as he immediately recognized, this movement to downgrade the Piltdown artifacts directly affected the controversy that still surrounded his sub-Crag eagle-beak implements. Hence, Moir had rushed off a rebuttal in the

January issue of *Antiquary*, declaring that Dawkins' statements did not stand up to scientific scrutiny:

> The early Pleistocene period was occupied by the phenomena of the Great Ice Age, during which masses of glacial clays and gravel were laid down over the face of the country. These deposits, of the Contorted Drift of Cromer, the Middle Glacial Gravel and Chalky Boulder Clay, are so well known and do not contain any true palaeolithic implements, and are generally recognised to be pre-palaeolithic in age. Thus, if this gravel at Piltdown is contemporaneous with definite "palaeolithic" implements, then it must, I think, be assigned to the Middle Pleistocene.
>
> It is evident the discoverers of the human remains [at Piltdown] felt that the view based upon geological grounds as to the age of the deposit was supported by the fact that what they consider as definite palaeolithic implements have been found in the gravel bed. These implements have been described by Mr. Charles Dawson as similar in workmanship to those of the "Chellean or pre-Chellean stage," but it is somewhat difficult to grasp exactly what this means. The flints which owing to the kindness of Dr. Smith-Woodward, I have seen and handled do not certainly correspond to the Chellean type as I understand it, and "pre-Chellean" may mean that they belong to any human period earlier than that of Chelles.
>
> In my opinion, these Piltdown "palaeoliths" approximate very closely to the humanly struck flints which occur in the Chalky Boulder Clay of Suffolk, and it seems that the gravel which contains them may possibly be of pre-glacial age. But these particular implements were found in the upper layers of the Piltdown gravel, while the human bones occurred in the lower most stratum associated with a much older and more primitive type of worked flints.

To Moir the eolithic problem was not just a matter of stratigraphy but also psychology. Many workers simply could not get beyond the fact that eoliths, whether they be Harrison's Plateau "brownies" or his sub-Crag eagle beaks, looked more like natural objects. Although in the wake of Lankester's endorsement of his pre-Crag flints in 1911, he had secured the unswerving loyalty of several important heavyweights in London and provincial antiquarian circles, including Arthur Keith, Arthur Evans (1851–1941) [the son of Sir John Evans], the physician-archaeologist William Allen Sturge (1850–1919)[7] and Charles Hercules Read (1857–1929), Keeper of the Ethnological Department at the British Museum (in Bloomsbury), he had also picked up along the way (in addition to Dawkins) several formidable opponents, the most notable being the Oxford geologist William Sollas.

As Sollas made quite clear in his book *Ancient Hunters*, which appeared early in the spring of 1912, he was not predisposed to eolithic theory, and his unsympathetic account of the Plateau implements had provoked a retaliatory attack from Lankester, who in his review of Sollas' book wrote:

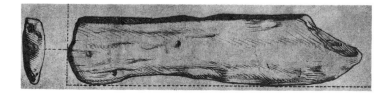

An example of Moir's sub-crag bone implements. Moir believed the implement shown had been used for 'boring'. It was recovered from the detritus-bed underlying the Red Crag at The Nursery, Martlesham, near Woolbridge. (From Plate XXVII Moir, 1915a: 122)

Marcelin Boule, French palaeontologist and opponent of eolithic theory. Early critic of Woodward's interpretation of the Piltdown remains.

The Professor is I regret to note, one of those who enjoy this "sham" fight. It would have been better for his readers had they been informed that there is really no "Eolith" controversy at all, but that some archaeologists have called very early and roughly broken flints by the name "Eolith" in order to mock at the archaeologists who first made use of the word. It should be discussed whether certain broken flints A found in beds of gravel unconnected with the present valley at a given locality X are of human workmanship or not. It should also be quite independently discussed whether other equally or more ancient broken flints B from locality Y are of human workmanship, and so on with regard to several other independent sets of flints from widely separate localities and of various geological antiquity. Obviously the only sensible thing to do is to examine each case on its merits. But an ingenious muddle-maker had the Mephistophelian inspiration to speak of them all as "Eoliths," whereupon another declared that he could make eoliths in a road with a cartwheel, and a respected palaeontologist [Marcellin Boule] produced broken flints from a chalk-mill and said they, too, were "eoliths". . .[8]

To make matters worse, shortly after this review was published, Lankester and Sollas clashed publicly in Oxford, where the former had come to promote Moir's case for the East Anglian rostro-carinate industry. While the details of this confrontation have not been preserved, the essence of what transpired is captured in a satirical verse ("Oratio capitalis pro-Rostris") written by the Oxford anthropologist Robert Marett (1866–1943) and published in the pages of *The Oxford Magazine* on 9 May, 1912:

Well, it happened rather late that the Knight to Oxford came
With his Family Paladium which had brought him so much fame;
. . . And another famous Science Man, who was strong on
"Ancient Hunters."
But when the latter saw the [Rostro-carinate] Flint, said he,
"Your man is mythic.
I consign him and his weapons to the Plusquam-Eolithic!"
Then the Knight replied, "Allow me! I proceed to demonstrate
That no implement is handier than the Rostro-carinate."
Of the professorial Cranium there is very little left;
It is sprung in all its Sutures, and the Basion is cleft.
Yet mark it well, O Visitor! For it proves to any fool
That the Sub-Crag Rostro-carinate was a Prehistoric Tool.[9]

Samuel Hazzledine Warren, London wholesale merchant and leading antagoinst of the British eolithic movement. (Photograph by K. Absolon in Essex Naturalist, **30**, 1959)

Later that summer, Sollas discovered, at a coastal site near Selsey Bill (situated midway between Portsmouth in the west and Bognor Regis in the east), a series of flints that closely resembled the controversial eagle-beaks of East Anglia, which, as he later argued at the British Association meetings in Birmingham the following year, had been produced by wave-action.[10] While Lankester and Moir both agreed that the Selsey Bill flints bore a superficial resemblance in general outline to the rostro-carinates, they contended that a close examination of Selsey Bill flake–scars showed them to be fundamentally different.[11] Where the East Anglian flints were said to display a deliberate pattern of flaking that was consistent with that found in palaeolithic tools, the fractures of the Selsey Bill specimens were thought to be otherwise.

In the meantime, while Sollas was busy on the beach at Selsey Bill, Marcellin Boule had visited Moir in the company of Henri Breuil (1877–1961) and evidently they had not been impressed by what they saw at Ipswich.[12] Although it was not until 1915 that Boule finally got around to publishing an account of this visit, his derogatory opinions had apparently been widely known, which undoubtedly had given further impulse to the renewed attacks from Moir's arch enemy Samuel Hazzledine Warren.

"For my part", Warren told a meeting of the Royal Anthropological Institute early in 1914:

> as I go backwards and forwards from the Prestwich collection of eoliths at South Kensington, to the collection of sub-Crag flints deposited by Sir Ray Lankester at Bloomsbury, I can only say that whichever series I examine the last always appears to me, from the point of view of being human implements, as the more incredible![13]

Drawing on both his own work and that of his colleague Fred Haward, Warren presented the results of a series of experiments he had performed to test Moir's diagnostic attributes of artificial artifacts. But his array of tables and scattergrams were as confusing as they were impressive. Besides demonstrating that the absence of a bulb of percussion did not imply the absence of human manufacture, it also appeared that other attributes commonly associated with the manufacture of flint implements, such as facet angles, could also be reproduced in naturally fractured stones. While Warren freely admitted that his investigations did not invalidate the proposition that Harrison's Plateau eoliths and Moir's sub-Crag materials were tools, there was nevertheless, he concluded, still every reason to suggest that they could well have been produced by natural agencies.

Warren was appreciative of the eolithophiles' argument that the palaeoliths could not have been the first human implements, and that they must have been on *a priori* grounds preceded by a more primitive — "eolithic" stage of culture. But as the work of Baldwin Spencer (1860–1929), and others had demonstrated from the description of the lithic tools used by the Australian aborigines, the most primitive stone implement was the simple unretouched pebble, which they used as a hammer. Furthermore, it was also apparent from such studies that tools were not exclusively made from stone, but involved an array of both perishable and durable materials, such as wood, shells, bone, teeth and claws of wild animals. Thus it was quite possible, he conjectured, that the cultural sequences of the Palaeolithic had been preceded by an "Age of Wood", a level of cultural attainment that had employed natural and essentially unrefined objects, including stones. This being the case, Warren felt that the eolithic forms put forward by Harrison and Moir did not meet this expectation:

> I do not understand why the earliest group of stone implements should be incapable of cutting. I am not forgetting that large numbers of eoliths — supposing them to be human implements — belong to the scraping group of cutting tools. But even scrapers require a definite edge, which is often not very apparent on the eoliths. [Furthermore, he noted] . . . If the eoliths are scrapers, the group is not primitive, but highly specialized. It hardly seems credible that such high specialisation of form (and presumably of function) should be reached with implements that, viewed as practical tools, are less efficient than naturally broken stones which may be picked up ready made . . . [But where edge-chipping is found, Warren continued] it is my experience that the[se characters] . . . is dependent partly upon the character of the raw material which is locally available and partly upon the geological forces which have acted upon that material. [Thus] . . . If the eoliths were human implements it appears to me that we should expect that their characteristics would be independent of associated geological forces, but would be dependent upon the relative ages of the deposits containing them. As a matter of fact we do not find that earlier deposits consistently contain more primitive eoliths and later deposits more advanced eoliths. In a broad view of the evidences, the characteristics of eolithic groups bear no discoverable relation to the age of the deposits containing them . . .[14]

Shortly after these views were published, sometime toward the end of June, Woodward and Dawson found a curious bone "implement" at Piltdown. Recalling the circumstances of this discovery many years later, Woodward said that he and Dawson had been watching their labourer, Venus Hargreaves, wielding his broad pick-axe:

> when I saw some small splinters of bone scattered by a blow. I stopped his work, and searching the spot with my hands, pulled out a heavy blade of bone of which he had damaged the end. It was much covered up with very sticky yellow clay, and was so large as to excite our curiosity. We therefore washed it at once, and were surprised to find that the damaged end had been shaped . . . we also noticed that the other end had been broken across, and we thought it must have been cracked by the weight of the gravel under which it was originally buried. Mr. Dawson accordingly grubbed with his fingers in the earth around the spot where the broken end had lain, and soon pulled out the rest of the bone, which was still more surprising. This piece was also covered with sticky yellow clay, but when we had washed it we found that it had been trimmed by sharp cuts to a wedge-shaped point.[15]

In Barlow's capable hands the specimen was subsequently mended and made ready for study. The object was a stout and almost straight blade of bone, measuring 41 cm long and varying from 9 to 10 cm in width. The thicker end had been shaved into a point, while the other had been rounded like the base of a cricket bat. It was a strange-looking object, the like of which they had never seen before. The modelling was, as far as Dawson and Woodward were concerned, unquestionably intentional,[16] but they wondered how Warren and Haward would react to it. Judging from the letter Haward wrote soon after viewing the specimen, both he and Warren were guarded in their reactions. It appears both were troubled by a number of niggling queries:

> Could the cut portion have been done in late Palaeolithic times, on an old Pliocene bone? [Also such cuts (or rather "hacking')] must have required sharp implements of serviceable design, and if done at a time of the skull surely one tool [of this kind] would have been found. Warren and I were discussing the so-called implements found. I am by no means sure that I believe them to be humanly chipped. I want to examine them all again. I think Warren is of similar opinion, but neither of us likes to be definite, for I don't think enough is yet known. . .[17]

A quite different reaction was elicited from Moir who was invited to examine the specimen in November. By this time, it seems that Dawson and Woodward had come to the conclusion that the object was an implement which had been fashioned from the upper part of a third trochanter of an extinct elephant and that it had probably been a "digging stick" used for grubbing up roots for food. Moir agreed. He also felt the available evidence justified the suggestion that bone implement and the Piltdown skull were of the same age, namely Pliocene![18] For, in addition to the bone implement, several other finds had been made during the summer of 1914 which served, he believed, to reinforce this argument. The rolled fragments of teeth of *Rhinoceros etruscus* and *Mastodon arvernensis* were found, the former by Davidson Black (1884–1934), a Canadian anatomist on sabbatical leave from Western Reserve University in Cleveland, Ohio, who had spent part of his summer working in Elliot Smith's department at Manchester. Moir also informed Woodward that he too had recently found similar bone objects at Ipswich, and was convinced they were analogous to the Piltdown implement both in form and age. But prudently, he added:

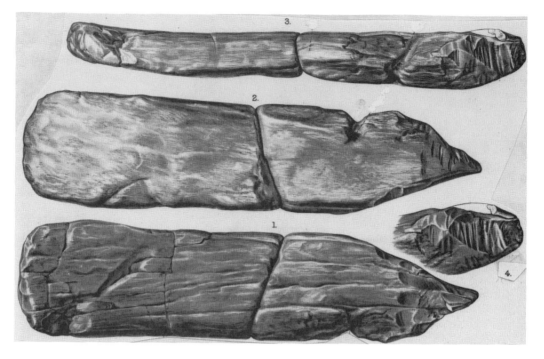

Piltdown bone implement. 1. Outer surface of bone. 2. Inner (medullary) surface of the bone. 3. Outer edge of bone. 4. Detail of cut facets on the outer edge of bone. (From Plate XIV, Dawson & Woodward, 1915)

> [I]t is [probably] wise to be on the safe side and you are in my opinion, perfectly justified in leaning towards a Pleistocene date. Surely no one will dispute the age of that [the Piltdown] worked bone. The material in its crevices satisfied me as to its antiquity. Also its condition precludes a modern date.[19]

The reaction at Burlington House on the evening of 2 December 1914 was mixed, with the discussion focussing largely on its possible function and manufacture. The Bloomsbury antiquarian Reginald Smith said that it was evident from the discussion that there was at least one point on which all were agreed, namely that human work was exhibited on the bone. Furthermore, judging from its condition and stratigraphical location in the pit, Smith said there was no question that they were dealing with "the oldest undoubted work of man in bone" — though he could not imagine any use for an implement that looked like part of a cricket-bat! But, he continued:

> The possibility of the bone having been found and whittled in recent times must be considered; and, if it were not shaped in its fossil state, it had evidently never been used for any purpose such as grubbing for roots, as the cuts were unscratched, and must have been made with an even-edged chopper. Experiment might prove whether a similar surface could be produced by cutting, as opposed to fracture...[20]

The apparent differences in the cut and natural surfaces of the bone suggested to Alfred Kennard that the bone had not been in a fresh state when it had been carved; and he agreed with Smith that comparative experiments with fresh and fossil bone might throw some light on the question as to how the implement had been made.

Warren endorsed this view and then went on to say that it had always appeared to him "that wood and bone must have been used before flint," and that the evidence from Piltdown seemed to confirm this.[21]

Responding to these various remarks, Woodward said that while no such experiments had been carried out, both he and Dawson were convinced the bone was fresh when it had been cut, though the fact that these cut marks bore no markings of battering and scratching was, he admitted, a curious problem. No mention, however, was made of Reid Moir's discoveries, or their relevance to the issue of the age of the Piltdown skull.[22]

Woodward's failure to advertise Moir's finds did not surprise the East Anglian archaeologist. In his estimation Woodward and Dawson had become lackeys to Dawkins,[23] and this was clearly borne out, he felt, by Dawson's attempt to jettison the Piltdown and Ipswich eoliths at the joint meeting of the Prehistoric Society of East Anglia and the Royal Anthropological Institute held in the latter's apartments in Great Russell Street, London, the following February.

Evidently Dawson had been persuaded by recent arguments that the eoliths recovered from Piltdown, as well as those from Ipswich, were natural objects, or as he called them: "tricks that Nature sometimes plays on *Homo sapiens*". Leaning heavily upon the work of Warren and Haward, the Sussex solicitor opened with the statement:

> A great deal of error may be created regarding supposed implements of human workmanship from early gravels and horizons, by the adoption of unscientific methods of collection and exhibition on an occasion like this. Let me give an example: Bulbs of percussion once looked upon as infallible signs of human workmanship are now known to occur upon flaked surfaces of nodular flint, by reason of perfectly natural causes. Again, flaking and edge chipping indistinguishable from human workmanship also frequently occurs from natural or accidental causes. (It has been the practice too much, to study edge-chipping and flaking, only in association with flint forms regarded as of human workmanship). It is well within the bounds of possibility that a bulb of percussion formed by accident, and natural flaking (which is humanlike), may occur in the same specimen, and the general form should more or less resemble an implement of human workmanship . . . [Hence] if the collector should then proceed further and perhaps after much search and selection among thousands of flints should occasionally find other such fortuitous examples, and should finally group all these selected specimens into one assemblage, the exhibition of it without other explanations, would probably be taken to afford overwhelming proof that man was coeval with the particular early deposit from which the specimens had been derived. The collector would thus not exhibit a CHARACTERISTIC series, but a collection of EXCEPTIONS, and he would accidentally gain his point by a sort of unconscious *suppressio veri*. In reality, his victory would be a PSYCHOLOGICAL one, and not a scientific one.[24]

Dawson then claimed that breakages of such flints were entirely analagous to the natural fractures which could be induced in a prismatic material such as starch. To illustrate his point he gave a telling and novel demonstration. By shaking or sitting on a bag of starch, he revealed how easy it was to reproduce all of the "well-known" eolithic shapes.[25] During this delivery he also apparently made a number of snide remarks about the rostro-carinates,[26] which naturally provoked Moir. Although Lankester was not present, Moir relayed the shocking news to him, and he replied:

> I am glad you pitched into him. He has never ventured to expound these suggestions to me, and I think it is not quite decent of him to hide up his notions to me, and to

expound them when I am not there. Of course prismatic flints has nothing to do with rostro-carinates. I observe too that he used the silly word "Eolith" which is always done for the purpose of making confusion and false suggestion.[27]

While it is difficult to gauge from this what the general response to Dawson's ingenious paper had been at the Institute, it is evident that neither Moir nor Lankester viewed it as a major set-back. In fact, a week later, Moir delivered his paper on the bone implements he had found below the Suffolk sub-Crag, which he believed would soften the opposition.[28] Besides providing evidence testifying to the "existence of a race of intelligent beings prior to the deposition of the Pliocene strata of East Anglia", Moir believed these worked bones would also confirm the true age and nature of the curious bone implement from Piltdown. For as his paper revealed, he had conducted a number of experiments on fossilized bone using flint implements and found that such material was extremely difficult to work. Likewise, fortuitous percussion produced irregular breaks in such bone. Using fresh bone however, it was possible, with practice, to control the process of fracturing and to achieve a desired form that could then be further modified with stone implements.

Much to Moir's obvious chagrin, the impact of his "bone" paper was completely overshadowed by the appearance of Marcellin Boule's devastating critique of the British eolithic movement.[29] After a detailed consideration of the evidence that had been recently proferred to support the existence of Tertiary Man in England, Boule concluded that the so-called flint implements were of a purely physical and natural origin. As for the recent debates over the Piltdown remains, Boule indicated that he was inclined to Woodward's case rather than Keith's, and was, in particular, convinced that the former's attribution of the remains to the lower Pleistocene was fully justified. But he also registered some reservations about Woodward's arguments for the association of the mandible.[30]

Brushing this latter opinion to one side, Boyd Dawkins saw his opportunity to strike back, and sallied forth in the pages of the *Geological Magazine* with a blistering attack on Moir and Lankester, claiming that Boule's "masterly essay", simply proved what he, Sollas, Warren, Haward and others had been saying all along: the rostro-carinates were nothing more than natural débris.[31]

While Dawkins' tactical communication plainly caused Moir some irritation, the article by Boule frustrated and incensed him, as shown by his bitter letter also published in the *Geological Magazine*:

> ..." La paléontologie humaine en Angleterre" ... is the most extraordinarily biased statement it has ever been my ill-fortune to read... In this note I propose to emulate M. Boule's "severity," and to speak out plainly as he has done. But I do not intend to make any reply to the threadbare and foolish arguments he uses to support his case, arguments to which I have replied to a great number of times, and which I do not intend to discuss any further ... [It is my] opinion that both M. Boule and M. Breuil are hopelessly biased in favour of the view that the human race is not more ancient than the early Chellean period, and I hold this view for the following reasons. It has come to my knowledge from an unimpeachable source that many weeks before either of these gentlemen visited Suffolk or had seen a single one of my specimens, they had expressed their disbelief in the value of my discoveries. I also know from personal observation, that when they were here they showed very plainly and unmistakably that they did not intend to examine carefully and scientifically the sub-Crag flints or the beds from which they were derived, nor did they spend more than a few minutes in examining the section in the pit where the Ipswich skeleton was found. Their attitude to all the things they saw was careless and almost petulant, and in my opinion quite unscientific. Regarding the capabilities of MM. Boule and Breuil of judging

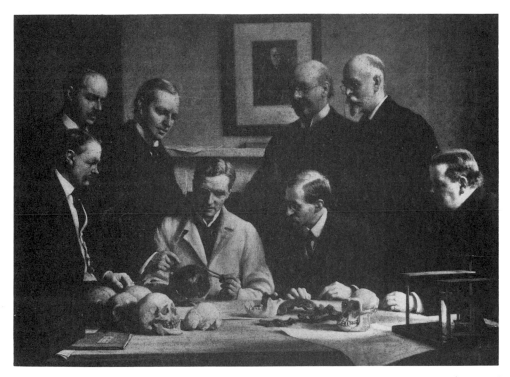

The John Cooke painting of the 'Piltdown gang'. Centre (wearing a laboratory coat) Arthur Keith, to his left (seated) Pycraft and Lankester, to his right, Underwood. Behind (left to right) Barlow, Elliot Smith, Dawson & Woodward. (Courtesy of the Geological Society, London)

> whether a flint has been flaked by nature or by man, I am of the opinion that neither of them is capable of such a judgement... These [and other related observations] are the facts, and no references to the curious remarks of Professor Boyd Dawkins, or the worthless flints collected by Professor Sollas on the beach at Selsey Bill, will alter them...[32]

Although that year Keith's pro-eolithic book *The Antiquity of Man*[33] did much to dismantle the obstacle erected by Boule and his British counterparts, it was some years before Moir finally achieved a significant shift in attitude towards his sub-Crag material — a movement which was largely underwritten by events that were inextricably entwined with the Piltdown case.

A SOURING STALEMATE

As the summer of 1915 melted into autumn, the forces of the British Empire had ground to a halt in far-away Gallipoli, and on the Western Front the struggle had become a war of trenches, barbed wire and machine guns in which military advantage was now measured in terms of yards gained and casualties inflicted. A year earlier everyone had expected the war with Germany to be a short and decisive conflict, but it was now quite obvious that it was going to be a long and bloody affair — the worst of which was yet to come. Against the back-drop of this unfolding drama, the issue of the Piltdown skull paled in the minds of the British public before the spectre of German dirigibles gliding across the rooftops of London and the lengthening lists of the dead, missing and mutilated. While newspaper editors were turning their minds to these more pressing matters, the unveiling of John Cooke's oil painting at the annual May exhibition of the Royal Academy for 1915 added to the public illusion that the Piltdown controversy was at an end and that a consensus had been reached.

The Cooke painting had created quite a stir and was, as indicated by the *Illustrated London News*, the highlight of the exhibition. As the London periodical explained, the painting was based loosely on the much publicized meeting at the Royal College of Surgeons in August 1913. Rather than using this formal setting, Cooke had chosen to place his subjects in what could well have been the front parlour of Keith's home in Highbury.[34] The effect was cosy. In the background, above the mantlepiece strewn with papers, Cooke had hung the portrait of Charles Darwin who stared ominously down at the group gathered about a table littered with bones and scientific paraphenalia. Seated at the centre of this table is Keith (wearing a white laboratory coat), examining the Piltdown skull. To his left, also seated, are Pycraft and Lankester, while to his right stands the diminuitive figure of Underwood. Standing behind Keith, and looking on (from left to right), are Barlow, Smith, Dawson and Woodward.

To the innocent bystander the painting was perhaps little more than a celebration of the induction of the "earliest Englishman"[35] into the annals of British science, but to anyone who was familiar with what had gone on since the unveiling in 1912, Cooke's subtle composition had neatly captured the underlying geometry of the Piltdown controversy: Dawson and Woodward standing united, erect and dignified, while their chief protagonist Elliot Smith is seen to be instructing Keith on some anatomical feature of the Piltdown cranium. To his side Barlow looks on with calm confidence, as Underwood hovers protectively, ready to assist Smith in his efforts. Likewise, to the left of Keith, Pycraft, with his former mentor at his side, appears poised, equally ready to interject and show Keith precisely what Smith means. But while this had undoubtedly been the situation in 1913, it would have been apparent to an informed onlooker in 1915 that the scenario depicted in Cooke's painting had since evolved into something far more labyrinthine. Indeed, the situation was now not unlike that in which the Entente found itself in the closing months of 1915.

To begin with, Dawson and Woodward now seemed to be at logger-heads over the significance of the Piltdown eoliths. Where Dawson was evidently set on dismissing them as natural débris, Woodward, in his recently published *Guide to the Fossil Remains of Man in the Department of Geology & Palaeontology of the British Museum (Natural History)* made it clear that he thought otherwise.[36] Then, in the midst of all this, the American palaeontologist Henry Fairfield Osborn (1857–1935) and his group at the American Museum in New York City had taken issue with the canine, charging that it belonged in the upper and not the lower jaw, and, adding insult to injury, they had proceeded to issue a new reconstruction of the skull.[37] While Woodward still continued to defend his restoration of the skull, it was quite plain from the paper he had read before the Geological Society a year earlier that he was not entirely without his own doubts. His paper had dealt with a recently discovered lower jaw of a Miocene dryopithecoid ape from Lérida, Spain. Comparing this jaw with other fossil primate material and the Piltdown jaw, Woodward noted that while the Lérida jaw closely approximated that of Lartet's *Dryopithecus* and appeared to fit the gradational series from *Mesopithecus* (a fossil macaque) to *Dryopithecus* to Heidelberg, there not only appeared to be "no place for a stage resembling that of any adult existing Ape", but it was also "difficult" to derive the Sussex skull from this series.[38]

Elliot Smith, however, had no such reservations. In fact, while attending the British Association meetings held in Australia during the summer of 1914 he was provided with what he considered to be "complimentary evidence" supporting Woodward's restoration of the Piltdown skull.[39] This corroborative evidence was a human skull that had been languishing in the collections of the Queensland Museum since the late 1880s when it had been found by a boundary-rider on the Talgai station, not far from Warwick on the Darling Downs of Queensland. Evidently impressed by the skull's large molars and rugged appearance, and the fact that it had been recovered from a river bed containing the remains of *Diprotodon* and other fossil marsupials, the Australian geologist, Tannatt W Edgeworth David (1858–1934) had ventured to present the skull to the British Association meetings in Sydney as evidence to support the claim that human beings had ferried across the Wallace line and entered Australia long before the great marsupials had become extinct — in a nutshell, David believed the Talgai skull was quite probably of Pleistocene age.[40] Smith concurred but what drew his attention most was the remarkable similarity between the dentition of the Talgai and the Piltdown crania. He was convinced Talgai not only confirmed Woodward's reconstruction but also provided important insights into the way the maxillary-mandibular canines in the Piltdown specimen had interlocked, and, on returning to England, Smith had quickly gone to work on bringing the Talgai evidence to bear on the Piltdown case.[41]

In sharp contrast to Smith,[42] Lankester was clearly baffled and undecided on several issues, as he made quite clear in his popular book *Diversions of a Naturalist*, which was published in September 1915. Unlike Moir, he was not convinced by the idea that *Eoanthropus* had been the artificer of either the flint tools or the bone implement that had been recovered from the pit. "I see no reason for supposing", he wrote:

> whatever may be the age which we may have to attribute to Eoanthropus, that that creature was capable of flaking flints to a desired shape or of making fire or had developed the use of articulate speech. Nor is there any evidence to show that the humanly cut elephant-bone recently found at Piltdown by Mr. Dawson was cut by Eoanthropus. It is more probable that this was done by a more highly developed creature of the genus Homo.

In fact, he went on:

> [T]he only ground which at present justifies the association of Eoanthropus with the Hominidae or human series rather than with the Simiidae or ape series — derived from a common ancestry — is the man-like rather than ape-like size of the brain, which we must attribute to Eoanthropus on the assumption, which is at present a reasonable one, that the half-jaw and the incomplete skull found near each other at Piltdown are parts of the same individual.[43]

Keith, on the other hand, was not surprised by the elephant bone implement, and agreed with Moir that the Piltdown eoliths were implements and belonged, along with the skull, to the Pliocene. In spite of his continuing objections to the reconstruction of the brain-case he was now, it seemed, resigned to Woodward's interpretation of the jaw, and unlike Lankester, he was also fully prepared to admit that the remains constituted a single individual — though he was still at a loss to adequately explain the fit between so apelike a jaw with so human a skull.[44]

During the closing months of 1915, while German strategists were putting the final touches to a plan to break the stalemate on the Western Front, W. Courtney Lyne, a Birmingham dentist, completed a study on the Piltdown canine which he also believed would tip the balance of opinion and lead to a revised and perhaps more plausible restoration of the Sussex remains. But like the German offensive at Verdun, Lyne's bold attack failed — mired in a murky sea of criticism.

Essentially, Lyne's paper, which was presented to the Royal Society of Medicine on 24 January 1916,[45] examined some of Keith's earlier thoughts on the Piltdown canine. But where Keith had conjectured that the tooth's condition was indicative of it belonging to a mature individual, Lyne thought otherwise. As he went on to explain, the size of the pulp cavities in mammalian teeth tended to diminish with increasing age, and in the Piltdown canine it was evident from Underwood's X-ray pictures that this tooth had possessed considerable pulp. Yet, he noted, the sagittal suture of the cranium had closed, and it was generally agreed by most workers at this time that this event occurred post-puberty, somewhere in the early twenties. "Have we found some ancient Canute who forbade the waves of time to surge around his canine?" Lyne marvelled. He suspected not, but rather that the canine did not belong with the jaw. Having made his case for the Piltdown canine being a deciduous (milk) tooth, whose pulp cavity, he noted, bore "an extraordinary likeness" to that of a young orangutan, Lyne extrapolated that the permanent canine in all probability far exceeded the dimensions given it by Woodward. Taking this into account, and the particular configuration of mandible and its *in situ* molars, Lyne believed there was "indubitable evidence" that the Piltdown canine was "incongruous", and that "no power on earth can alter the fact that 'the canine' has yet to be found, and is as yet hypothetical".[46] "If, then", Lyne mused:

> we accept this canine as deciduous and cannot correlate it satisfactorily with Piltdown man, all we can do at this stage is to theorize, and to me the following way out of the maze of doubts is to postulate, in late Pliocene times, a large anthropoid showing humanoid tendencies, and with moderately raised canines (? *Pithecanthropus erectus*); and branching off from this we have one type still maintaining fairly large deciduous canines, such as that found at Piltdown, belonging to a humanoid anthropoid, but probably not the property of an Eoanthropus, and the other type retaining smaller (human) deciduous canines, with the ancestral pattern maintained, and coincidently passing on to the eruption of non-raised permanent canines. Then we could see how the canine found at Piltdown and the modern deciduous human canine are somewhat alike in shape, since both would be descendants of one common near related ancestor. He would be a bold man who asserted that all anthropoid types in early Pleistocene or late Pliocene times had yet been revealed . . . [I admit however that this] . . . is only one more hypothesis . . . But the anatomical evidence regarding the other facts will, I trust, at least impel cautious anatomists to assume a *sub judice* attitude pending further discoveries, concerning the caninism [sic] of the Piltdown man. The loom of Time may yet weave for us the sure features of this creature.[47]

Woodward's response to this was tempered by the recent arrival of what he called the "lastest ROT from the U.S.A.",[48] a paper written by the American mammalogist Gerrit Smith Miller (1869–1956), on the Piltdown mandible which had struck at the very heart of Woodward's monistic restoration. It was Miller's opinion that the Piltdown jaw was not human but rather that of a fossil ape! Hence on hearing Lyne's proposition, Woodward's patience was sorely tested. At the same time as Miller was laying claim to the jaw as a "new species of chimpanzee", Lyne was now attempting to discount the canine. "It seems to me most improbable — almost incredible", he declared, that "a unique Primate skull" would be found in same place as "an absolutely new Primate jaw", along with an "entirely new Primate tooth".[49]

Keith also registered his dismay at such a proposal. Although acknowledging that the canine pulp cavity was large, and admitting that there was a problem of harmonizing the canine with the jaw, and the jaw with the skull, Keith said:

When I considered the type of wear upon the Piltdown canine — which I presume is a lower right canine tooth, although there is now a school in America which places it as an upper canine tooth on grounds which I do not understand[50] — I was forced, as it were, to the conclusion that, with such a type of wear, side-to-side movements would be possible and that Dr. Smith Woodward was probably right in assigning it to the human being he had named *Eoanthropus*. I may say I would not readily forsake a position I had taken up if I found it represented the nearest possible approach to the truth. One wishes to state our inferences so that they will hold true when we are all dead and gone.[51] I concluded, with all the evidence in front of me, that the probability was that Dr. Smith Woodward was absolutely right: that he had found the missing lower canine of the right side, and that my law was evidently wrong — that is to say, the law which I postulated concerning the form of the glenoid cavity. I had supposed that our glenoid cavity had assumed its present shape as the projecting canine disappeared and assumed a position flush with the surface of the other teeth. Our knowledge of the movements of the jaw is not by any means final. My present difficulty relates to the manner in which the upper canine tooth of Eoanthropus articulated with the teeth of the lower jaw ... [and as yet I have not obtained] a satisfactory solution of this difficulty ... [As for Lyne's arguments on the molar and canine pulp cavities, Keith went on to say] I do not think [they] absolutely eliminate the tooth from belonging to the jaw; and I take practically the same view as Dr. Smith Woodward, who approaches it from a different standpoint. I am of the opinion, at the present time, that the mass of evidence is in favour of the three portions [i.e. canine, mandible, and skull] going together as parts of the same individual.[52]

Underwood felt Keith had pretty much summed up what he had intended to say, but nevertheless went on to highlight his objections to Lyne's thesis that the canine was a deciduous tooth. The age of the tooth was, Underwood insisted, clearly evident from its excessively worn appearance. In fact, he said, "It has gone so far as partially to invade the pulp cavity itself". And he added:

By looking with the microscope at the surface, you can see the portion of pulp where the secondary dentine has been formed to resist that invasion. I do not think one can build too much upon the calcification of the pulp: I think it is asking a well-known law to bear too severe a superstructure. The wear and tear question, I think, entirely proves that the age of that tooth is a great deal more than the age which has been assigned to it [by Lyne] ...[53]

While confessing that teeth were not his area of speciality, Elliot Smith could not resist observing Keith's apparent change of heart. Previously, as he wryly noted, Keith had claimed that the canine was "too old to belong to the same individual as the molars"; And now Lyne was attempting to play the same game, except he claimed that the tooth was not too old but "too young". He also reminded Lyne's audience that "we are considering a type of creature which hitherto was entirely unknown", and therefore:

It is rash ... to argue from speculations as to what ought to be found in claiming discrepancies in the features which actually are found. When one considers the fact that many writers are now claiming that the mandible did not belong to the same individual — or even the same genus or family — as the skull, and that Mr.Lyne suggests that the canine was not a part of either, we have to consider the possibility that three hitherto unknown man-like apes, or ape-like men, died side by side; but while one of them left a fragment of his cranium without jaw or teeth, another part of the mandible, without any of the cranium, and a third his canine without any fragment of jaw or skull, I claim that the balance of probability — and, as Dr. Smith Woodward has said, it is a question of probabilities that we have to deal with — against this hypothesis of three different unknown creatures leaving complementary fragments is simply colossal.[54]

Furthermore, Smith noted that Lyne and his fellow heretics had, in their exuberance, overlooked the fact that the anthropoid apes had disappeared from Europe by the middle Pliocene. Hence, he said:

> To bring a hitherto unknown ape into England in the Pleistocene Period involves an upheaval of palaeontological teaching, and on the present occasion adds an element of improbability to Mr. Lyne's contentions which is even greater than that which I have already indicated.[55]

Just as his critics had been *suaviter in modo, fortiter in re*, Lyne replied that he had also done what needed to be done, and said that the arguments presented against his thesis, and particularly those of Keith, had not moved him:

> In his [Keith] reconstruction I think the wear is supposed to have been produced by the upper lateral incisor, mainly, at any rate. I suppose every one of us in this room is aware that we can protrude the lower jaw, and that animals can and do protrude it in that way when trying to attack or bite another. I have tried to get the forward bite of his reconstruction within the last twenty-four hours, and find that the tips of the canines, when that is attempted, simply impinge on the first premolars, and will not allow the mouth to shut at all. This also seems to happen with Dr. Smith Woodward's reconstruction at South Kensington . . .[56]

With regard to the suggestion that three individuals may have been present in the Piltdown assemblage, Lyne replied that he was "not responsible for this view", and admitted that the "mandible goes with the skull". As far as he was concerned the issue was whether the canine belonged with the jaw.[57]

Although Lyne is said to have remained resolute in his convictions about the canine,[58] nothing more was heard from him on the issue. But while Lyne had been silenced, the same could not be said of Gerrit Miller in Washington, who continued to promote the view that the Sussex mandible was not human, but rather the jaw of a fossil ape.

DUELLING WITH A DUALIST

Since 1912, the American physical anthropologist Aleš Hrdlička (1869–1943), based at the Smithsonian Institution in Washington DC, had viewed developments in England with increasing anxiety. Having spent the last couple of years dealing with the heresies of the Argentinian palaeontologist Florentino Ameghino (1859–1911) and his followers who had claimed that Argentina had been the "cradle" of the human genus,[59] Hrdlička was distressed to find his Anglo-Saxon colleagues headed in the same direction.

Because the commercial casts of the skull had yet to be distributed, Hrdlička's initial report (written in the summer of 1913) was, by necessity, a summary of the available literature; but in spite of this it is abundantly clear that he was far from comfortable about the association of the jaw with the cranium. Indeed, as his later efforts reveal,

Two American dualists: (left) Aleš Hrdlička (circa 1912); (right) Gerrit S. Miller, portrait taken 1897. (Smithsonian Institution Archives, Washington D.C.)

he was convinced that the jaw belonged to an entirely separate being. If this could be proved, it would be much easier to dismiss the cranial bones as a modern intrusive burial, for, as he had stated in his preliminary report, the geological circumstances in which the remains had been found were far from satisfactory. In fact, he said, the entire history of the Piltdown specimen illustrated the "usefulness and need, especially in the Old World, of scientific supervision of excavations", and had concluded his report by saying that while "It represents doubtless one of the most interesting finds relating to man's antiquity ... the last word has not yet been said to its date and especially as to the physical characteristics of the being it stands for".[60] Hrdlička was prevented at that time, by work relating to the preparation of an ambitious exhibit for the 1915 Panama-California Exposition in San Diego, from pursuing the matter any further.

While it is not possible to prove conclusively that it had been Hrdlička who had prompted Miller to undertake his critical study of the Piltdown jaw, it is known that as the debate gathered momentum between 1913 and 1915, Miller frequently consulted with Hrdlička on related issues,[61] and from their correspondence it is plain that Hrdlička was at this juncture more than satisfied to leave the task of dismantling Woodward's "improbable monster" to his colleague in the Department of Mammals.

Evidently following Hrdlička's suggestion,[62] Miller began his study of the Piltdown jaw with a comparison of the jaws of *Pongidae* and a series of (modern and fossil) human crania. From this study he concluded that:

[T]he characters of the mandible and lower molars throughout the order Anthropoidea are much more diagnostic of groups than has hitherto been realized. [And that this had convinced him], . . . on the basis of the evidence furnished by the Piltdown fossils and by the characters of all the men, apes, and monkeys now known, a single individual cannot be supposed to have carried this jaw and skull.[63]

As for the jaw, Miller reported that in its general characters it was readily distinguishable from those of the Asian orangutans (*Pongo*) and the African gorillas (*Gorilla*), but when compared with those of chimpanzees (*Pan*) these discrepancies dissolved, — or nearly so. Indeed he found two specimens in the Smithsonian collections which closely matched the Sussex specimen in both size and shape. These specimens were subsequently "mutilated in as nearly as possible the same manner" as that of Piltdown and used to support his case that: "[T]he main peculiarities of the fossil, apart from the large teeth and robust horizontal shaft, l[a]y within the limits of variation" for the genus *Pan*. The size and configuration of the Piltdown molars were attributed to a species difference. The canine, however, was found to compare favourably in all respects (save its size) with the left upper canine of an adult female chimpanzee.[64]

Miller agreed, therefore, with his colleagues at the American Museum that the Piltdown canine was, irrespective of its taxonomic status, an upper and not a lower canine tooth.

To further support his case for removing the Piltdown jaw from Woodward's reconstruction, Miller's attention was drawn, as Waterston's and Keith's had been, to the glenoid region of the braincase, the point of contact between the jaw and skull:

> The facts are [Miller reported] that the Piltdown skull presents extreme human characteristics in the glenoid region calling for correspondingly extreme human conditions of narrow and strongly convex articular surface in the mandible which hinged on it. But this entire mandible, from symphysis to base of condyle, is like that of a chimpanzee . . .In order to fit its articulating surface to that of the skull it would be necessary to imagine an abrupt change of plan in the few millimeters of condyle that have been lost . . .[65]

Another incongruity was noted in the area where the temporal muscle originates on the skull and the point where it is inserted in the mandible:

> In general features the area of origin for the whole muscle is strictly human, . . . [though he admitted] its extent is considerably less than in many of the human skulls [examined] . . . [However,] [t]he area of insertion of the muscle on the Piltdown mandible has not only all the more important general characters peculiar to this region in *Pan*; it has also the individual features which in living members of that genus are connected with the greatest extension of the area of origin of the muscle on the skull . . . [Thus] [i]n order to associate this jaw with the braincase it would therefore be necessary to assume the existence of an animal related to both *Homo* and *Pan* but with a temporal muscle working on a different mechanical scheme from either; that is, moderate in size and strength at the region of origin on the skull and excessively heavy at the mandibular end. That such an animal may have lived cannot be denied; but nothing so contrary to the facts which are now known need be believed without the evidence of a jaw found in place . . .[66]

Miller considered the conformation of the nasal bones and basicranial region also supported the general incompatibility of the Piltdown jaw with the patently human

Another American dualist: William King Gregory. (American Museum of Natural History, New York)

braincase. In the case of the former they demonstrated that the nasal floor was anteriorly shortened — a configuration not found in either monkeys or the extant great apes, while the anatomy of the latter revealed that this "fundamental part of the skull was completely adjusted to the task of supporting a human brain in the upright position".[67]

In arriving at the inevitable conclusion, Miller recognized that his dualistic thesis brought forth two difficulties: first, the statistical probability of finding such remains within a few feet of each other, and second, the question of the supposed absence of chimpanzees from the European Pleistocene. He answered these questions in the following way:

> Concerning the first nothing can be said, except that those local conditions which caused the deposition of one specimen near a given spot might be expected to act in about the same way with another. The second is at least partly met by the fact that a tooth ... not certainly distinguishable from the first lower molar of a chimpanzee has been found in the [P]leistocene of Germany. Until the discovery of further material it seems proper to treat the case as a purely zoological problem by referring each set of fragments to the genus which its characters demand.[68]

Accordingly he moved that the taxon *Eoanthropus* be discarded, and the Sussex braincase be reassigned to the genus *Homo*, while the jaw and its attending canine be considered as the type specimens of a new species of chimpanzee: *Pan vetus*.

There were a number of American workers who, besides Hrdlička, found Miller's argument compelling — and several of them had previously gone on record as supporters of Woodward's monistic interpretation of the Sussex remains. Most notable among these new apostates was George Grant MacCurdy (1863–1949) from the Yale Peabody Museum and William King Gregory (1876–1970) who worked under Henry Fairfield Osborn at the American Museum of Natural History in New York. In the February 1915 issue of *Science*, MacCurdy recanted his enthusiasm for the Piltdown skull. "The prehistoric archaeologist sometimes uncovers strange bedfellows", he wrote:

> no other discovery is quite so remarkable in this respect as the assemblage from the now famous gravel pit at Piltdown Common ... Nature has set many a trap for the scientist; but here at Piltdown she outdid herself in the concatenation of pitfalls left behind.[69]

From the perspective of Miller's iconoclastic study, and evidently also from Marcellin Boule's recently declared reservations about the jaw ("elle sonne faux"), MacCurdy said that it was now evident to him that Woodward's model would never "ring true" — because, however much the parts were adjusted, they were clearly never intended for each other. As for Woodward's argument on the close proximity of the specimens, MacCurdy agreed with Miller:

> Association can never be made to take the place of articulation; and so far as Piltdown is concerned, nothing short of actual articulation of the mandible with the skull should have sufficed to outweigh the lack of harmony existing between these parts.[70]

In MacCurdy's opinion this had been ably demonstrated by Miller, and the conclusion was inescapable: there were two individuals at Piltdown! However, such a revision, he felt, did not minimize the importance of the Piltdown finds:

> [They] contribute to our knowledge of the fossil fauna of the period ... by the addition of the chimpanzees to the list. [And] As for the Man of Piltdown, he still exists and is quite as ancient as he was before the revision, which is saying a good deal; even if he is robbed of a muzzle that ill became him. The only thing missing is *Eoanthropus*, and since he was never there anyway, the loss is small ...[71]

Two years earlier, Gregory had published a detailed account of the Sussex finds which he had examined first-hand while in London in September 1913.[72] Although registering some concern in this article about the association of the jaw and skull,

Gregory had ultimately concurred with Woodward's restoration of the remains and the view that *Eoanthropus* was "indeed some sort of man in the making ...", a decision he had grounded in the apparent plausibility of the attendant assemblage.[73] Gregory's underlying doubts were encouraged by Miller's paper. In his note to the *American Anthropologist*, Gregory announced that he too was now prepared to argue in favour of a "generic identity" between the Piltdown jaw and that of a chimpanzee.[74] He also inferred that this opinion was shared by a number of his colleagues at the American Museum, which, as was made clear later, included Osborn.[75]

The public reaction in England to Miller's paper was mixed. Albert G Thacker of the Public Museum in Gloucester, for example, wrote in *Science Progress* that he thought the case Miller had brought forth "could hardly be better stated"; whereas the geographer Harry Hamilton Johnston (1858–1927) considered it absurd.[76] As for the principals in the debate, Lankester chose not to address the matter in his *Daily Telegraph* column, though he had privately informed Miller that he had had his doubts from the outset, and was "glad" to see that his original disinclination to "admit the identity of the jaw — has been justified by your important discussion and comparisons".[77] Keith, on the other hand, was a little more direct, though his reaction was delayed. Using his review of Osborn's *Men of the Old Stone Age* as a platform, Keith showed his displeasure with Miller's thesis, claiming that not only was Osborn (and by inference his followers) "all at sea as regards the discovery of Piltdown", but that the Piltdown dentition was "as unlike chimpanzee teeth as teeth can be".[78] Smith also chose to address Miller through his review of Osborn's book, though in his case the attack was more immediate. In addition to taking issue with Osborn and his group's treatment of the Piltdown canine, Smith also took the opportunity to repeat his argument against the dualistic interpretation of the Piltdown remains: "[This] would involve", Smith repeated:

> the supposition that a hitherto unknown and extremely primitive apelike man, and an equally unknown manlike ape, died on the same spot, and that one of them left his skull without the jaw and the other his jaw without the skull. Not only so, it would involve also the admission that an anthropoid ape was living in England in middle Pleistocene times ...[79]

Shortly after this review appeared in May 1916, Smith reiterated his views at the Manchester Literary & Philosophical Society,[80] but during the summer the thrust of his campaign against Miller was deflected by a rather curious review of Keith's recently published book in *Man*, written by the British anatomist-anthropologist William Wright (1874–1937). What disturbed Smith in this review was not so much Wright's inclination towards Miller's view, or his apparent support of Keith's thesis on the "priority of *Homo sapiens*", but rather the comment:

> It is unfortunate that Professor Symington's criticism of Professor Elliot Smith's interpretation of the endocranial cast was not published in time to be incorporated in the volume ...., for only in a less degree than Professor Keith's criticism does it succeed in finally disposing of the ill-fated first essay at reconstruction and many of his opinions based thereon.[81]

Johnson Symington (1851–1924) held the chair of anatomy at Queen's University of Belfast, and as Wright well knew, he and Smith had, in recent years, become bitter enemies. While the extent of their friendship prior to the British Association meetings in Australia is unclear, what there was of it had evidently dissolved with Symington's impassioned attack on Smith's account of the Piltdown endocranial cast in

Melbourne.[82] Specifically, Symington believed Smith had gone beyond the limits of rational science when he had proclaimed the Sussex cast to be "more primitive ...than any known human brain or cranial cast"; for, as he later repeated in his Struthers Lecture in February 1915, it was a fallacy to think that the form of the brain was accurately mirrored in the cranial cavity. The truth was, Symington believed, that these casts revealed very little, and he thought it would have been more prudent of Smith to have admitted "frankly the limitations" of such material rather than to weave fanciful stories "on such slender data".[83] Smith vigorously denied this and had proceeded with his presentation to the Royal Society which led Symington to deliver another attack in the pages of the *Journal of Anatomy and Physiology* in which he again denounced Smith's work as "highly speculative and fallacious".[84]

While Smith was settling things with Symington and Wright,[85] the American dualists were clearly puzzled by the British response to Miller's thesis or rather lack of it. Hrdlička for one was anxious to know what was going on, and had written to Symington asking for inside information. Symington replied that as far as he could tell from a recent visit to South Kensington, Woodward and Pycraft were adamant that Miller was wrong. Furthermore he told Hrdlička:

> I believe that most of the anatomists in this country agree that there has been too much rash speculation regarding the significance of the Piltdown fragments. [And] [a]s you are aware, I have endeavoured to correct this tendency so far as the brain estimates are concerned.[86]

Similarly Miller had learned through his connections at South Kensington that opinions there, at least outside Woodward's department, were divided over the association issue. He also gathered from one of his informants, Martin A C Hinton (1883–1961), then a volunteer worker in the Zoology Department at the British Museum (Natural History), that Woodward was "not inclined to reply" to his paper, and if he did, Hinton conjectured: "I think the only reply will be on the 'improbability' score".[87] No specific reasons were offered to account for this reported reticence. One possible reason, and one that must have undoubtedly crossed Miller's mind, was the knowledge that another skull had been found at or near Piltdown in 1915. Miller had learned of this discovery in December 1915 through Lankester, who had told him that:

> Dawson has recovered (and shown to me) portions of another skull — similar to that from Piltdown — in the same gravel at a distance of three miles or so from Piltdown ... Mr. Dawson has not yet, I believe, published this discovery. What he showed me were fragments of the roofing bones — one part of the frontal with supra-orbital ridge. They were in the same mineral state as the original skull, and as briefly seen by me appeared to resemble the bones of the original skull ...[88]

This, however, was not privileged information, for Lankester had announced it in a footnote of his 1915 book *Diversions of a Naturalist*.[89] But since then there had been no mention or discussion of this discovery in the literature. While resisting the temptation to directly question Woodward, Miller followed Hrdlička's suggestion and did the next best thing by writing to Pycraft, for according to Symington, he was "busy studying skulls of the chimpanzee and hoping to prove that the mandible at Piltdown is human...".[90] In establishing contact with Pycraft, Miller magnanimously offered his British colleague access to the casts he had used in his study. While volunteering no information on Dawson's recent finds, Pycraft accepted Miller's offer, and went on to say:

I am just off for a much needed holiday so I cannot comment at length on your paper. I can only say this, that it amazes me. I have taken your objections and contentions, one by one, and I venture to say you haven't a leg to stand on ... I have had the advantage of closely studying at least three times as many (chimpanzee skulls) as you seem to have had, and a vastly larger collection of human skulls: with which, by the way, you do not seem to have either a large acquaintance, or a large collection to draw upon. Finally, you have laboured under the disadvantage of never having seen the actual Piltdown remains. But all these reasons should have saved you from dogmatism — but they didn't. However, my reply will reach you soon.[91]

Whatever Miller's reaction to this letter may have been, it certainly could not have matched his anger when he saw Pycraft's article early in February 1917. Pycraft had not pulled his punches. "A very brief study of his [Miller's] arguments will show", Pycraft said:

that they are based on assumptions such as would never have been made had he not committed the initial mistake of overlooking the fact that these remains — which, by the way, he has never seen — are of extreme antiquity, and hence are to be measured by standards of the palaeontologist rather than the anthropologist. This unfortunate lack of the right perspective has caused him to overlook some of the most significant features of these remains, and has absolutely warped his judgement in regard to the relative values of the likeness between these fragments and the skulls of the chimpanzee which he has so woefully misread.[92]

Then, as he had promised, he took each one of Miller's objections and contentions, and endeavoured to reveal either their inherent weakness or falseness. For example, on the question of the molars, Pycraft wrote:

Mr. Miller tells us that he has found teeth in the jaw of a chimpanzee worn in a precisely similar manner, and he gives a photograph purporting to bear out this statement. Yet no impartial critic will agree that this photograph in the least supports his statement. Of all the teeth which I have examined, and these represent at least twice as many as Mr. Miller has examined, I have failed to find one which can in any way be compared to these teeth of Piltdown ... It is idle indeed to pretend that the molars of the chimpanzee are indistinguishable from those of the Piltdown jaw. Prof. Keith has already remarked, radiographs of the Piltdown jaw show that they are of the typical "taurodont" type, therein differing conspicuously from the molars not only of the chimpanzee but all of the great apes ... [And] [n]o less characteristic is the condition of the grinding surface of the crowns of worn molars of the chimpanzee. Contrary to Mr. Miller I have in no single instance yet found these teeth with the surface worn to a perfectly level table at right angles to the vertical axis of the tooth. This is a common feature of human teeth, and is most conspicuous in those of the molars of the Piltdown man ... [And so on].[93]

And in conclusion he suggested that:

[Miller had] endeavoured, throughout, to confirm a preconceived theory; a course of action which has unfortunately warped his judgement and sense of proportion ...[94]

Hrdlička was astonished by the tone and innuendo present in Pycraft's article. In his estimation the entire argument was based purely on the assumption that the "Piltdown geology" was beyond reproach, which, he said was "clearly not the case". He was also incensed by Pycraft's insinuation that Miller's study had been flawed by the inadequacies of the National Museum's collections.[95] Gregory was also disgusted

Woodward's "hatchet-man": William P. Pycraft, osteologist in the Department of Zoology at the British Museum (Natural History).

by what he called Pycraft's "hectoring, lawyer-like" tactics, and as he later told both Hrdlička and Miller, he remained unconvinced by the counter-arguments. He also urged Miller to respond, as did Hrdlička. Both were convinced that nothing was to be gained by waiting for the details of Woodward's new evidence. For as Gregory had commented in one of several letters he wrote to Miller at the time:

> I feel doubtful whether Smith Woodward's new evidence will be adequate to prove the original association. The new molar will have to be absolutely identical with one of the old molars and the new piece of occiput will have to be beyond question the same as the old occiput and unless they have a large piece this will be difficult to prove.[96]

In fact it was a full year before Woodward's paper finally made it into print, and in the meantime Miller was obliged to prepare his reply to Pycraft without the benefit of the new evidence.[97]

Although on close examination Pycraft's article left much to be desired in its handling of the scientific arguments, the general thrust of the paper and its timing resulted in a political triumph. And this, it is conjectured, is precisely what it had been intended to be. At the same time as giving the Americans something to think about, the article also served to weaken the opposition at home and to prepare the way for Woodward's dramatic announcement of the confirmatory find made by Dawson in 1915, of a second *Eoanthropus* in the Piltdown gravels.

THE MOVE TO CHECKMATE

Following the recovery of the bone implement in the summer of 1914 it looked as if the pit had yielded all of its treasures.[98] Several new trenches had been dug but they had yielded nothing, and during that autumn Dawson widened the search to neighbouring fields.[99] It was not until the beginning of January 1915 that Dawson's search finally turned up trumps. "I believe we are in luck again!" he had written to Woodward excitedly:

> I have got a fragment of the left side of a frontal bone with portion of the orbit and root of nose. Its outline is nearly the same as your original restoration and being another individual the difference is very slight.
>   There is no sura [sic] orbital foramen and hardly any superciliary ridge. The orbital border ends abruptly in the centre with a sort of tubercle, and between it and the nose is a groove or depression $\frac{3}{4}$ inch in length. The section is just like Pycraft's model section and there are indications of a frontal suture. The wall of the left sinus shows a shallow depression in the [?] section. The tables are thin and the diploe very thick. The general thickness seems to me to correspond to the right parietal of *Eoanthropus* ... The outer surface is very rough, but the general colour and condition much the same as *Eoanthropus*. The forehead is quite angelic![100]

Later that same year Dawson recovered several more fragments of this skull, namely the middle portion of the occipital bone and a human molar tooth.[101] And subsequently, Woodward later reported, a fragment of a rhinoceros molar, which provided an index for dating the remains, was found at the site by a "friend" of Dawson's.[102]

While there is no tangible evidence of there being a plan to bring these finds forward at the December 1915 meetings of the Geological Society, there is considerable evidence to justify the abandonment of such a plan, had it existed. Dawson was apparently ailing from an "anaemic condition" which, during the closing months of 1915, got steadily worse causing him to seek medical help,[103] and his situation did not improve. On 10 August 1916 he died. This developing situation was confounded further when Woodward's son, Cyril, became dangerously ill in October 1915 with appendicitis, which was complicated by post-operative thrombosis.[104] But whether by design or accident there is little question that in delaying this report Woodward scored a tactical victory in the debate with Miller and the American dualists.

Presenting these remains to the Geological Society on the evening of 28 February, 1917, Woodward claimed:

> From the new facts now described it seems reasonable to conclude that *Eoanthropus dawsoni* will eventually prove to be as definite and distinct a form of early Man as was at first supposed; for the occurrence of the same type of frontal bone with the same type of lower molar in two separate localities adds to the probability that they belonged to one and the same species.[105]

Elliot Smith who reported on his examination of the cranial remains of Piltdown II, said:

[The new finds] afford[ed] further corroboration of the opinion that I expressed with reference to the endocranial cast of the Piltdown [I] skull; namely that it presents features which are more distinctly primitive and ape-like than those of any other member of the human family at present available for examination.[106]

In the discussion that followed, Pycraft reiterated the arguments against Miller's thesis and concluded that Piltdown II formed a link in a chain of evidence that, in his mind, completely demolished the dualistic thesis. Keith concurred saying that they established "beyond any doubt that *Eoanthropus* was a very clearly-differentiated type of being", and that he fully agreed with Pycraft and Woodward that the lower molar of Piltdown II and the original mandible and teeth must be ascribed to *Eoanthropus* and "constituted the characteristic features of the type". Although Lankester said he had some lingering doubts about the provenance of Piltdown II, he went on to agree with Woodward and the other commentators that Dawson's new finds made it "impossible to regard Piltdown man as an isolated abnormal individual".[107]

With the war then at its height this news spread rather slowly, and it was not until several years after the war was over that the full impact of Woodward's announcement on the scientific community was felt.[108]

5 Steps to the scaffold: the Piltdown controversy 1918–1950

... [T]his business of human phylogeny is becoming highly complex. We seem to be getting so many dead ends hanging about — phyla that lead nowhere — and all over the world at that. The South African series must be a blind-side line, and now ... Piltdown and Swanscombe off the mainline– where are we to look for the real ancestral line?[1] ...

CONVERTS, SCEPTICS, AND THE FAITHFUL

Although during the next decade it became increasingly apparent that Woodward's dramatic announcement of Piltdown II at Burlington House in 1917 had failed to precipitate a scientific consensus, it did serve to check further advances on the dualistic front. In fact it even led to a number of significant conversions in Gerrit Miller's camp.

Among the first of Miller's casualties was the Canadian, William Diller Matthew (1871–1930), who was then Curator of Vertebrate Palaeontology at the American Museum of Natural History in New York City. Matthew apparently viewed the celebrated remains at the British Museum (Natural History) early in 1921. Soon thereafter, James H McGregor (1872–1954), another palaeontologist from the American Museum, made a visit and reported back to Henry Fairfield Osborn that he too was "forced to admit that ... the pro-*Eoanthropus* party has a pretty strong case". Any reservations that Osborn may still have harboured in this regard were quickly dispelled by his own pilgrimage to South Kensington on 24 July 1921. Recalling this visit in the pages of the American Museum magazine *Natural History*, he wrote:

> ... Dr. Woodward [gave me] full and free opportunity. . . for the closest comparison and study [of all the remains]. At the end of two hours, in which also worked flints and a large implement of cut *Mastodon* thigh bone were examined, the writer was reminded of an opening prayer of college days, attributed to his professor of logic in Princeton University: "Paradoxical as it may appear, O Lord, it is nevertheless true . . ." So the writer felt. Paradoxical as it appears to the comparative anatomists, the chinless Piltdown jaw, shaped exactly like that of a chimpanzee and with its relatively long, narrow teeth, does belong with the Piltdown skull, with its relatively flat, well formed forehead and relatively capacious brain case![2]

As for the "three minute fragments" of Piltdown II, Osborn said:

> [They are] exactly those which we would have selected to confirm the comparison with the original type . . . Placed side by side with the corresponding fossils of the first Piltdown Man they agree precisely; there is not a shadow of difference.[3]

With unbridled admiration, Osborn then went on to praise Woodward for not only establishing "beyond question the authenticity of the Dawn Man of Piltdown", but also for not yielding to the temptation of writing: "I told you so"; a comment which, he felt, might well have appeared "from a less patient and dignified pen". Chastened, Osborn concluded his recantation with the warning:

		Age	Status
MONISTIC VIEW			
1. Skull + Jaw	[A]	Pliocene	Eolithic
2. Skull + Jaw	[B]	Lower Pleistocene	Lower Palaeolithic
DUALISTIC VIEW			
1. Skull	[C]	Lower Pleistocene	Lower Palaeolithic
Jaw	[D]	Plio-Pleistocene	Anthropoid ape
2. Skull	[E]	Pleistocene-Holocene	Palaeolithic-Neolithic
Jaw	[F]	Plio-Pleistocene	Hominoid-hominid form

A summary of the status of the monistic-dualistic debate between 1917 and 1930. [A] Moir (1918b), Keith (1925a), Osborn (1921b); [B] Woodward (1917), Broom (1918), Burkitt (1921b), Churchward (1922), Kleinschmidt (1922), Sollas (1924), Smith (1924, 1931), Curwen (1929); [C] Boule (1923); [D] Giuffrida-Ruggeri (1918, 1919), Miller (1918), Ramström (1919,1921), Teilhard de Chardin (1920), Boule (1923), Mollinson (1921, 1924), Frassetto (1927), [E] Hrdlička (1922, 1930); [F] Hrdlička (1922, 1923a, 1923b), Gregory & Hellman (1926), Pilgrim (1927).

An American convert: Henry Fairfield Osborn with Woodward (right) at Barkham Manor in 1921; (right) Osborn in 1933 just prior to his death. (American Museum of Natural History, New York)

> Nature is full of paradoxes and . . . the universe is not the human order: that we should always expect the unexpected and be prepared to discover new paradoxes . . .[4]

At the same time as abandoning Miller, Osborn not only embraced Woodward's *Eoanthropus* but also the Piltdown eoliths. Up until this time the American had been rather guarded in his views on eolithic theory. Although evidently impressed by what he saw at South Kensington, it appears a subsequent visit to Reid Moir in Ipswich finally pushed him over the edge and confirmed his belief in the eoliths.[5]

While intrigued by Moir's rostro-carinate flints, what took Osborn's attention, besides the Piltdownian bone implements, was a collection of sub-Crag implements Reid Moir had recently gathered from a site near Foxhall, a small village located a few miles east of Ipswich.

Moir's interest in the Foxhall site had been aroused by Keith's reference to it in his book *The Antiquity of Man*. As Keith had noted, it was here, earlier in the last century, that a human lower jaw had been found and demonstrated to the Ethnological Society of London in the mid 1860s by the American phrenologist Robert Harnham Collyer. Coinciding with a similar discovery made at the Moulin Quignon gravel pit near Abbeville in France, the Foxhall jaw had attracted some attention. The two jaws were not dissimilar in either shape or condition, and both had been found in circumstances which initially supported their claim to great antiquity. In the case of the Moulin Quignon jaw, however, it had been found in association with stone implements which were later shown by Prestwich and Evans to be forgeries.[6] As a result, the validity of the Moulin Quignon jaw was thrown into doubt and ultimately dismissed as a recent specimen. Following the Moulin Quignon affair, Collyer's attempt to establish the great antiquity of the Foxhall jaw was greeted with considerable caution.[7] Huxley, for one, had been plainly sceptical:

> [I]t has some peculiar characters, but they do not appear to me in themselves adequate to lead me to ascribe the bone to an extinct or aberrant race of mankind, and the condition of the bone is not such as I should expect a crag fossil to be.[8]

In fact, according to an evaluation issued at the time by the anatomist George Busk (1807–86), the jaw, while infiltrated with iron, was found to have retained a portion of its gelatine; from which Busk concluded:

> On the whole, therefore, though not of the portentous antiquity it would have claimed had it been contemporary of *Elephas meridionalis*, the "coprolite jaw" fairly claims a considerable age . . .[9]

After this Collyer and the Foxhall jaw slipped into obscurity.

Keith's particular interest in the lost Foxhall jaw stemmed from the fact that its anatomical profile (determined from a drawing Collyer had published of the specimen), closely matched not only that of Moulin Quignon but also of Galley Hill He was convinced this was not an accident, but that they represented a "pre-Mousterian" race that bridged the gap between modern *Homo sapiens* and the earlier precursorial form: the Ipswich skeleton. The fact that both the Foxhall and Moulin Quignon jaws were said to retain "animal matter", did not, he contended, invalidate them as genuine Pleistocene specimens.[10] When Keith made these pronouncements, however, his "presapiens" scheme had pivoted largely on the acceptance of not only his particular interpretation of the Piltdown remains but also the equally contentious Ipswich skeleton. But in 1916, following further excavations at the Ipswich site, Moir was forced to accept John Marr's earlier suspicion, that the boulder clay stratum beneath which the Ipswich skeleton had been found was not undisturbed as originally believed, but had been reconructed in "post-chalky boulder clay times". As such Moir reluctantly announced that the skeleton was in all probability "referable to a late Palaeolithic epoch".[11] It was in this context that Moir had turned his attention to investigating the old Foxhall site.

Working from Collyer's 1867 publication, Moir relocated the now disused "coprolite pit" at Foxhall and set to work on its excavation. By 1920 he was able to report the discovery of two clearly delineated strata bearing the traces of man in the form of flint implements. One of these "floors" was situated at a depth of sixteen feet (which was the level at which Collyer reported the jaw had been found) at the centre of the Red Crag formation; the second was located at the base of the Red Crag, in what Moir referred to as the "Lower Detritus-Bed." This latter horizon stood on the boundary of the Quaternary Red Crag formations and the Tertiary Coralline Crags. The flint material recovered from the two implement-bearing strata were thought to demonstrate the evolution of the sub-Crag rostro-carinate industry.[12]

It would perhaps be misleading to give all of the credit to Piltdown II for softening attitudes towards Moir's sub-Crag materials, but there is little question that in Osborn's case it had been a major factor. Evidently the same may also be said for Sollas who noted, after his visit to Foxhall in 1920, that the Piltdown Man might well have been the maker of these artifacts.[13] Furthermore, it appears that this evidence was sufficiently compelling to persuade the Oxford don to write in the third edition of his *Ancient Hunters*, that the Foxhall discoveries had relieved him of "all doubts" as regard the sub-Crag rostro-carinates.[14] Another unexpected convert had been the Abbé Henri Breuil, who visited Moir in 1921, but in his case it seems that his conversion had been quite unrelated to the recent events at Piltdown.[15] His countryman Boule, however, was not impressed and continued, just as Warren did in England, to argue against eolithic theory.[16]

Like Sollas, Osborn was quick to recognize the analogies between the Foxhall and Piltdown artifacts, for as he noted in his 1921 (December) article:

> [B]y placing the implements side by side, may enable us to settle one of the remaining points of doubt about the "dawn man," namely his geologic antiquity. Anatomists now agree that *Eoanthropus* is of a very ancient type, altogether such as we should expect to find at the very beginning of the Quaternary age of man or even in the Tertiary . . . In 1914 [referring to when he was writing his book *Men of the Old Stone Age*] . . . [i]t seem[ed] reasonable . . . to interpret the Piltdown skull as exhibiting a closer resemblance to the skulls of our human ancestors in mid-Tertiary times than any fossil skull hitherto found." It was only the Piltdown flints, at that time mistakenly compared with those of pre-Chellean time, which led the writer to believe that the Piltdown man belonged in the Middle Quaternary, an opinion which he is now prepared to abandon.[17]

While Gerrit Miller's reaction to these events is not known, Aleš Hrdlička was flabbergasted and had immediately dispatched a confidential note to Gregory asking him for his opinion on the matter. Unlike Osborn, who was rather inclined to be impetuous, Gregory was, Hrdlička believed, a much more level-headed fellow. But much to his astonishment, Gregory replied that he too was favourably inclined to Osborn's views.[18] Although Gregory's reply did not go into detail, it appears, Gregory told Elliot Smith in an earlier letter, that his conversion had been based on the stereoscopic photographs of the Piltdown I and II molars McGregor had brought back from London. Having carefully studied these photographs, Gregory informed Smith:

> I gladly admit that they look very much alike and afford convincing evidence for the association of the jaw and skull. I have had to "eat crow" several times. It is not always pleasant but it is probably like the scroll of the prophet: bitter in the mouth but sweet in the belly.

Aleš Hrdlička (circa 1930). (National Anthropological Archives, U.S. National Museum of Natural History, Smithsonian Institution, Washington D.C.)

To which he added:

> I have the greatest respect for your work and for Dr. Smith Woodward's, and I hope neither of you feel that I have been led away by talking with Miller and Hrdlicka. It was never a personal matter with me and the only thing I ever resented was Pycraft's remarks about Miller, which were most unfortunate... It was "some nerve" to say that Dr. Gregory "accepts Miller's arguments without investigating the matter himself". If he only knew how much time I have wasted on the blessed business.[19]

To add insult to injury Hrdlička learned soon thereafter that MacCurdy had also had a change of heart.[20] But besides revising his views on Piltdown, MacCurdy went on to endorse Moir's Foxhall sub-Crag, claiming that they demonstrated the existence of a Tertiary hominid.[21]

As a designated member of the American delegation to the XXth International Congress of Americanists that was held in Rio de Janiero during August 1922, Hrdlička persuaded his superiors at the Smithsonian of the economic advantages of combining these duties with a brief excursion to Europe. Thus during the autumn of 1922 Hrdlička was also provided with an opportunity to review the celebrated Piltdown remains.[22]

By contrast to Osborn's "two hours", Hrdlička reportedly spent the better part of "two days" poring over the remains. From the very beginning, Hrdlička later wrote in his report published in the 1922 December issue of the *American Journal of Physical*

Anthropology, "there was a strong feeling of incongruity and lack of relationship [between the jaw and skull], and this feeling only grew on further study". Invariably there exists a marked correlation between a skull and its jaw, he said, "a finely chiseled mandible of medium or sub-medium strength belongs as a rule to a skull that is characterized in the same way, and vice versa".[23] But in the case of the Piltdown remains no such harmony existed. He noted his amazement at how closely the molars of Piltdown I and II approximated one another, not only in their dimensions and morphology, but also in the "degree and kind of wear". Since the probability of such a duplication in two supposedly distinct individuals was remote, if not "almost impossible", Hrdlička rightly wondered if there had not been some mistake and that the Piltdown II molar actually belonged with the original jaw.[24] Woodward insisted that there had not been a mix-up and that Dawson had found the Piltdown II molar with the cranial fragments at another site situated some miles from the Piltdown I site. This question continued to trouble Hrdlička, and several years later, in 1926, (by which time Woodward had retired from the Museum), Hrdlička approached Woodward's successor, Francis A Bather (1863–1934) on this issue:

> Among the Piltdown [II] remains there is a loose molar which looks as if it were a counterpart from the other side . . . of the Piltdown jaw. This tooth I was told by someone — or I read it somewhere, I cannot clearly recollect — was found after Mr. Dawson's death with some other objects among his possessions, but without any data as to the circumstances of its discovery. Possibly you or your good assistant could tell me just what is what from the records in your possession or other knowledge.[25]

While directing Hrdlička's attention to Woodard's 1917 paper, Bather also alerted Woodward to the American's inquiry. Woodward replied:

> [T]he fragments of the second Piltdown skull and tooth were not "found" among Mr. Dawson's property after his death. I knew they were there because he had told me of them at the same time of his discovery; he also told me that he found them on the Sheffield Park Estate, but he would not tell me the exact place — I can only infer from other information that I have . . .[26]

While Hrdlička remained sceptical about the precise attribution of the Piltdown II molar,[27] he was convinced that the Piltdown crania were essentially modern and that the jaw did not belong with the Piltdown I braincase. In fact the closer he studied the jaw, the more convinced he became that it represented a genuine fossil. But a fossil of what: an anthropoid ape as his colleague Miller had claimed? While agreeing with Miller that in a number of respects the jaw approximated that of a chimpanzee, Hrdlička noted in his report that there were at the same time a "whole series of features" (not all apparent in the casts Miller had studied) which served, it seemed to him, to demarcate it from *Pan*. But of all the noted characters, it appears that what really impressed him more than any other were the teeth. In addition to possessing a cusp pattern similar to that of human molars, Hrdlička also noted the height of the enamel which was much higher than that usually encountered in chimpanzee teeth. Also the crown height was much higher than that normally found in pongid teeth and closely matched that of human teeth. The dimensions of the Piltdown teeth also closely approximated those of the Heidelberg jaw. As for the much disputed canine, there was no denying that it bore a strong resemblance to that of an ape, but there was, he contended, every reason to suppose it belonged with the jaw. He also concurred with Woodward's diagnosis that it was a right lower canine, and not a maxillary tooth as Osborn and his followers had presumed. While the wear pattern on the canine was "somewhat peculiar", he did not think it "incompatible" with this opinion. In spite of all this, it is clear that Hrdlička could have quite easily argued in favour of Miller's thesis had he chosen to do so, but for reasons linked to his commitment to the Neanderthal hypothesis and the notion that Europe had been the "cradle of humanity", the idea of the jaw representing an early hominid precursor, possibly an advanced dryopithecine ape, was a far more attractive proposition. This idea was not an entirely novel one, for in 1917 the Italian anatomist, Gioacchino Leo Sera (1878–1960), had suggested that the Piltdown teeth were "perhaps better compared with those of a primitive *Dryopithecus* than with those of a chimpanzee".[28] Convinced that this was indeed the case, Hrdlička set about the task of establishing the jaw's "true" identity.[29] Although he later admitted that a paucity of suitable material prevented a definite conclusion, the hypothesis was clearly too attractive to be discarded and thus he ventured:

> The close relation of the Piltdown molars to some of the late Miocene or early Pliocene human-like teeth of the Bohernz,[30] as well as those of the Ehringsdorf jaws,[31] while not conclusive alone, raises legitimately the query as to whether man may not have evolved altogether in Western Europe.[32]

Having made a case for the liberation of the jaw from its modern-looking braincase, Hrdlička was then free to attack the argument of the skulls reputed antiquity:

> There are several points of weakness in this connection. The first is the circumstances of the find. The discovery and removal of the first [and second] skull was not supervised by scientific men; there is no [precise] information as to exactly how [they] lay and whether or not there was any noticeable disturbance in the gravel. No amount of trust and benevolence can quite fill these defects of the evidence . . .[33]

He also noted that none of the skull fragments found showed any sign of wear and tear. Here, he said, "is an enigma which needs, it seems, some further discussion". Of course this same argument could also have been applied to the jaw, but for obvious reasons, Hrdlička was evidently prepared, in this instance, to overlook the shortcomings of the jaw's geological provenance in favour of its morphological attributes. Accordingly, Hrdlička said:

> . . .it must be plain that any far-fetched deductions from the Piltdown materials [namely the skull fragments] are not justified. This applies particularly to the superficially attractive conclusions that the Piltdown remains demonstrate the existence in the early Pleistocene, long before the Neanderthals and even the Heidelberg forms of men with practically modern-sized and modern-formed skulls and brains and directly ancestral to *Homo sapiens*.[34]

However, very few workers at this time were willing to follow Hrdlička's movement to evict the incubus of the great antiquity of the modern human form from the evolutionary scenario. His argument relating to the taxonomic status of the jaw also failed to gather significant support. The allusion to the dryopithecoid affinities of the Piltdown molars was not a compelling argument for disassociation, in fact if anything, the presence of such features could just as easily be orchestrated to reinforce the transitional status of the fossil. Thus while the Piltdown union of an ape-like jaw and human skull continued to be an "improbable monster" to some, there were just as many who were not offended by the marriage; for as Sollas repeated in the 1924

Gerrit S. Miller (1937): American mammalogist who, in 1915, endeavoured to demonstrate that Woodward's reconstruction of the Piltdown skull was erroneous. He claimed that the jaw was that of a fossil chimpanzee. (Smithsonian Institution Archives, Washington, D.C.)

edition of his *Ancient Hunters*, it was "a combination which had ... long been previously anticipated as an almost necessary stage in the course of human development".[35]

FOREIGN SIGNPOSTS

As Gerrit Miller reiterated in his 1929 review of the controversy:

Deliberate malice could hardly have been more successful than the hazards of deposition and recovery in so breaking the Piltdown fossils and losing the most

Raymond Dart and the Taung skull. (Barlow Rand Archives)

essential parts of the original skull as to allow free scope to individual judgement in fitting the pieces together ... According to the different reconstructions the form of the cranium may be completely human in striking contrast to the apelike jaw, or it may have partially simian features which cause this contrast to become less.[36]

But as he went on to note, an even greater impediment was the prevailing confusion in palaeoanthropological circles regarding the question of the human pedigree. While it was generally agreed that the modern human species represented the product of a "long and gradual process of development away from nonhuman ancestors", opinions diverged dramatically on the details of how this was achieved. There were those who claimed that the development of the brain had been a primary factor, while others considered the emergence of an upright gait to have been a more critical event in the hominisation process. Accordingly, the human fossil record, what there was of it, could be shuffled and reshuffled to fit a particular theoretical position and seemingly still not be in violation of evolutionary principles. While Miller was not overly impressed by the activities of the palaeoanthropologists, he had to agree that these divergent viewpoints were not mutually exclusive, though he was not so sure it would be possible to bring about a reconcilation of the warring parties in the absence of new and compelling evidence. He concluded, somewhat pessimistically, that until such evidence was found, the debates, particularly as they pertained to the Piltdown fossil, would continue to be circular and unproductive.[37]

Although the kind of evidence Miller was looking for began to surface during the years between the two World Wars, both the rate of discovery and the dissemination of this new information was both slow and episodic. With or without the jaw, and whether on or off the mainline of human evolution, the Piltdown fossil continued to demand the attention of workers who had made human evolutionary history their business.

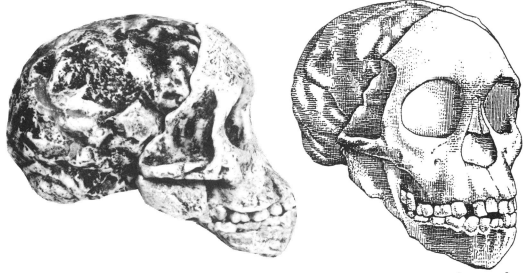

The Taung skull: (left) lateral view of a replica of the Taung skull; (right) drawing of a plaster cast of the face and endocranial cast viewed from the right side. Drawn by T.L. Poulton, in Smith (1927).

Among this new evidence was the Taung skull found in 1924 at the Buxton Limeworks, situated some eighty miles north of Kimberley in the northern Cape Province of South Africa. Believing the fossil to be that of an ape and that it might be of interest, it was saved and subsequently delivered into the hands of Raymond Dart (1893–1988), who held the chair of anatomy at the University of the Witwatersrand in Johannesburg. Communicating the results of his preliminary study of the fossil to *Nature* in February 1925, Dart reported that his fossil ape was remarkable in that it displayed a suite of characters that were decidedly more *"humanoid"* than *"anthropoid"*. He was convinced the skull was that of a juvenile representing an "extinct race of apes intermediate between living anthropoids and man".[38] In marked contrast to living and fossil apes, the position of the *foramen magnum*, the hole in the base of the skull where the spinal column enters the brain, was much farther forward — though not as much as in modern human crania. From this Dart concluded that the Taung ape had stood erect. The general conformation of the cranium was also seen to depart from that of any known ape. The forehead, while not as vertical as in the Piltdown specimen, did not recede quite as dramatically as it did in either the apes or the fossil hominids such as in the Javan *Pithecanthropus* and the European *Neanderthals*. In a number of other respects, however, particularly in the anatomy of the jaw and dentition, it diverged radically from the Sussex fossil. The Taung's milk canines were much smaller, for example, and there was no indication of a diastema between the premolars and the canines on either side of the lower jaw. Where in apes (and hinted at in the Piltdown specimen) the interior aspect of the symphysial region was characterized by the presence of a wedge of bone — a simian shelf — in the Taung specimen there was no such structure, in fact, the entire region of the mandible was, as Dart noted, far more reminiscent of the Heidelberg jaw.[39] Along with the molars and the parabolic configuration of the dental arcade, the jaw was in every essential detail comparable with the human rather than ape situation. Another remarkable feature that continued to puzzle workers for several years to come, was the size of the brain cavity. Even taking into account its juvenile status, it was extrapolated that in the adult form, this humanoid ape probably possessed a cranial capacity not far removed from that of the gorilla. An examination of the endocranial cast, however, left little doubt in Dart's mind that the Taung brain had been an "instrument of greater intelligence" than that of either gorilla or any other living anthropoid.[40] Summarizing the find, he wrote:

> Unlike *Pithecanthropus*, it does not represent an ape-like man, a caricature of precocious hominid failure, but a creature well advanced beyond modern anthropoids in just those characters, facial and cerebral, which are to be anticipated in an extinct link between man and his simian ancestor. At the same time, it is equally evident that a creature with anthropoid brain capacity and lacking distinctive, localised temporal expansions which appear to be concomitant with and necessary to articulate man, is no true man. It is therefore logically regarded as a man-like ape. I propose tentatively, then, that a new family of *Homo-simiadae* be created for the reception of the group of individuals which it represents, and that the first known species of the group be designated *Australopithecus africanus*, in commemoration, first of the extreme southern and unexpected horizon of its discovery, and secondly, of the continent in which so many new and important discoveries connected with the early history of man have recently been made, thus vindicating the Darwinian claim that Africa would prove to be the cradle of mankind . . .[41]

Acceptance of these claims was impeded by several technical difficulties. First there was the juvenile status of the fossil. Given the well-known fact that the immature cranial form in anthropoid apes tended to assume the "foetal hominid" form, there were very few workers who were willing to adopt Dart's far-reaching conclusions based on such evidence, no matter how suggestive it might be.[42] The general feeling was that Dart had found an interesting but probably aberrant form of ape. Second, the provenance of the skull was far from certain. It had apparently been "blasted" out of a limestone formation at "a vertical depth of 50 feet", but how this computed with the European Tertiary and Quaternary was not at all clear.[43]

Although the subsequent discovery by the anatomist Robert Broom, (1866–1951), during the late 1930s of adult australopithecines at a number of other South African sites confirmed the essential details of Dart's initial claims, it was not until after World War II that the tide of scientific opinion began to turn in favour of the South African australopithecines being "in or near the line which culminated in the human form".[44]

In the meantime, Dart's announcement in *Nature* had appeared to be little more than an interesting side-show. Keith felt that the young South African anatomist had laid too much emphasis on what was clearly a "foetal form" — though he had to agree it was a very remarkable one:

It may be [Keith went on to note] that *Australopithecus* does turn out to be "intermediate between living anthropoids and man", but on the evidence now produced one is inclined to place *Australopithecus* in the same group or sub-family as the chimpanzee and gorilla. It is an allied genus . . . The geological evidence will help to settle its relationships.[45]

Elliot Smith, on the other hand, felt Dart was justified in creating a new species and even a new genus for his interesting fossil, and furthermore was not unduly troubled by the juvenile status of the fossil. "The size of the brain", he commented:

affords very definite evidence that the fossil in an anthropoid on much the same plane as the gorilla and the chimpanzee . . . But the fossil is an imperfectly developed child, whose brain would probably have increased in volume to the extent of a fifth had it attained the adult status. Hence it is probable the brain would have exceeded in bulk the biggest recorded cranial capacity for an anthropoid ape, about 650 c.c. As the most ancient and primitive human brain case, that of Pithecanthropus, is at least 900 c.c. in capacity, one might regard even a small advance on 650 c.c. as a definite approach to the human status. The most suggestive feature . . . is the position of the sulcus lunatus and the extent of the parietal expansion that has pushed asunder the lunate and parallel sulci — a very characteristic human feature.[46]

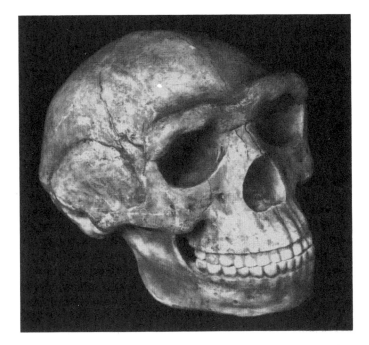

Peking Man: Sinanthropus pekinensis. *Left oblique view of a cast of an adult "female" cranium (restored by Franz Weidenreich) found near Zhoukoudian (Choukoutien), stituated some 25 miles south-west of Beijing, China.*

Woodward's views tended more in the direction of Keith than Smith. He too considered the fossil's age status prevented an accurate assessment of the skull, and believed the absence of a simian shelf was one of several characters that could probably be accounted for by the specimen's immaturity. As for Dart's inference that

Peking investigators: (left) Davidson Black; (centre) Franz Weidenreich; (right) Abbé Henri Breuil and Pere Teilhard de Chardin. (American Museum of Natural History, New York)

his fossil had secured the Darwinian prophecy that Africa had been the cradle land of humanity, Woodward said that while it was probably "premature to express any opinion as to whether the direct ancestors of man are to be sought in Asia or in Africa", he was certain that whatever the case turned out to be, "[t]he new fossil from South Africa [would be seen to have] little bearing on the question".[47]

Woodward, amongst others, did not share at this time Dart's enthusiasm for an African genesis. Since the late eighteenth century when the philologist William Jones (1746–94) opened the door to the hypothetical existence of a prototypic "Aryan" language with his demonstration that Sanskrit belonged to the Indo-European linguistic stock, the idea that the biocultural roots of Europe lay buried in Central Asia had ebbed and flowed in popularity. In the 1920s, the Asiatic hypothesis was enjoying a renaissance and at the forefront of this movement was Henry Fairfield Osborn, who since the beginning of century had been advocating Asia as the "paleontologic Garden of Eden", and proposed that it had been here on the high central plateau of Mongolia that the Darwinian "struggle for existence [had been most] severe and [had] evoked all the inventive and resourceful faculties of . . . the Dawn Men . . . while the anthropoid apes were luxuriating in the forested lowlands of Africa and Europe".[48] Indeed, it had been precisely this expectation that had led him in the early 1920s to mistakenly assign a Nebraskan peccary molar to a new primate genus — *Hesperopithecus* which he claimed displayed definite hominid affinities.[49] But while Osborn's personal ambitions in central Mongolia were never realized,[50] he at least had the satisfaction of knowing that his promotion of the Asiatic hypothesis had indirectly contributed to the impulse that led Davidson Black to the discoveries near Peking (now Beijing) in the late 1920s and early 1930s.

Had Davidson Black followed the advice of Hrdlička, when he arrived at the Peking Union Medical College in 1919, it is not inconceivable that subsequent events in China may have been quite different. Although supportive of Black's quest for early man in China, Hrdlička was highly critical of the Canadian's insistence on the "strategic importance of Asia".[51] It was Hrdlička's conviction that the crucial events in the human evolutionary drama had taken place not in the eastern sector of the Old World, but in the west. He considered Black's decision in 1927 to erect a new hominid genus, *Sinanthropus pekinensis*, based on two human molar teeth found in 1921 at a site near Choukoutien (now Zhoukoudian), a small town located some thirty miles south-west of Peking, to be "rash".[52] It was, however, largely on the basis of the interest generated from this seemingly "rash" report that Black secured the necessary funds to initiate a systematic excavation of the Choukoutien site — the product of which was a series of spectacular finds made between 1929–32 — which transformed Peking from a scientific backwater into a thriving international centre for palaeoanthropological research, attracting among others, the French workers Pierre Teilhard de Chardin and Henri Breuil.

While prepared to acknowledge that there were morphological similarities between the Peking remains and the Javan skull-cap found by Dubois, Black insisted that they were in essence quite distinct. He was convinced his sinanthropine fossils warranted ancestral status. The geology of the site seemed to point to the early Pleistocene, thus making it a contemporary of the Dawn Man of Sussex. Reviewing this evidence in 1935, Woodward suggested that perhaps *Sinanthropus* and *Eoanthropus* were contemporaries and as such represented "east and west" varieties of Dawn Man.[53] Given his earlier rejection of Dubois' Javan fossil, Boule, not unexpectedly, rejected such a notion and along with it Davidson Black's suggestion that his fossils were ancestral forms.[54] In Boule's opinion *Sinanthropus* was a pre-hominid, possibly related to *Pithecanthropus*, and accordingly urged Black to rename his fossil to bring it into line with this diagnosis.[55] Although Elliot Smith countered this move by claiming that there were significant differences between the Chinese and Javan endocrania to justify their generic separation, in the final analysis he too denied *Sinanthropus* ancestral status.[56] Hrdlička likewise endeavoured to demote the Peking material, insisting that it was essentially a Neanderthaloid form.[57] Keith also believed that he could see Neanderthal features in Black's fossils and argued that morphologically the Chinese sinanthropines stood midway between Dubois' fossil and the Neanderthals, and thus could not be regarded as a progenitor of *Homo sapiens*.[58]

In the meantime Hrdlička had endeavoured to repatriate the exiled European Neanderthals. Using the 1927 Huxley Memorial Lecture as his platform, Hrdlička argued eloquently for their ancestral status.[59] Although immediately countered by Elliot Smith,[60] the offensive was not a complete failure. Shortly thereafter, the German anatomist and physical anthropologist Franz Weidenreich (1873–1948), who had begun his career under the tutelage of Schwalbe at Strasbourg University, joined Hrdlička in his advocacy of a "Neanderthal phase" in human evolution.[61] In the mid 1930s, following Davidson Black's sudden death, Weidenreich was chosen to succeed him at the Peking Union Medical College, providing him with a unique opportunity to study and compare the Asian fossil hominids with those from Europe.

Like Hrdlička, Weidenreich was highly critical of Woodward's monistic interpreta-tion of the Piltdown remains. He did not, however, favour Hrdlička's contention that the Piltdown jaw was a fossil dryopithecoid ape, but was more inclined to the opinion expressed in 1932 by the German anatomist Heinz Friedrichs, who had concluded from his study of the Piltdown remains, that the jaw stood in close proximity to that of an orang-utan and proposed it be reclassified as *Boreopithecus dawsoni*.[62] Although at a loss to account for the eoanthropine canine, Weidenreich was convinced it had "no relationship whatever to the mandible and still less to the fragments of the brain case".[63] As for the other teeth, he wrote:

[N]ot one of the teeth of the Piltdown remains represents a primitive hominid type like *Sinanthropus*. The two right molars in situ belong to an orang-like anthropoid . . . and the left isolated one is a recent human type . . .[64]

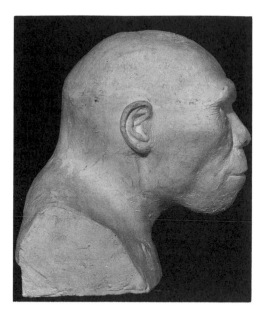 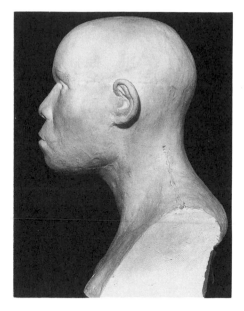

Maurice Wilson's reconstructions of (left) Peking Man and (right) Piltdown Man.

Accordingly, Weidenreich completely rejected Woodward's suggestion that *Eoanthropus* and *Sinanthropus* were regional variants of "Dawn Man". To him there was no justifiable reason to believe that the European Neanderthalers could not have advanced to modern *Homo sapiens* — though unlike his American counterpart at the Smithsonian, he was inclined to think that this evolutionary transition had occurred outside Europe — probably somewhere in western Asia.[65]

To some extent, this latter proposition was supported by the Neanderthaloid skeletons that had been recovered by the joint Expedition of the British School of Archaeology in Jerusalem and the American School of Prehistoric Research, under the general direction of the British archaeologist Dorothy A E Garrod (1892–1968),[66] between 1929 and 1934 at Mount Carmel, near Haifa. These skeletons were quite remarkable. Some were unmistakably Neanderthalers, while others were a curious blend of ancient and modern characters. To both Weidenreich and Hrdlička the inference of this evidence was quite apparent: it was a population in transition. Convinced of this, Hrdlička had hoped that the task of describing the Mount Carmel skeletons would fall into the hands of the Americans, his own in particular, but instead it went to Keith and Theodore D McCown (1908–69), then a graduate student from the University of California, Berkeley, attached to the American School of Prehistoric Research.[67] Although McCown was predisposed to the view that the Mount Carmel skeletons formed a single population that was in the throes of evolutionary change, Keith leaned heavily in the direction that two distinct populations were represented (one Neanderthaloid and the other presapient) which had interbred, forming a new and hybrid population.[68] The point was debatable, but as things stood in the 1930s, Keith believed the latter position was more tenable than the former — as shown by evidence recovered from both Europe and Africa.

The evidence for an African presapiens population had been recovered by the Kenyan anthropologist and palaeontologist Louis S B Leakey (1903–72), one of Keith's many devoted followers.[69] In 1932 Leakey had boldly announced in *Nature* that he

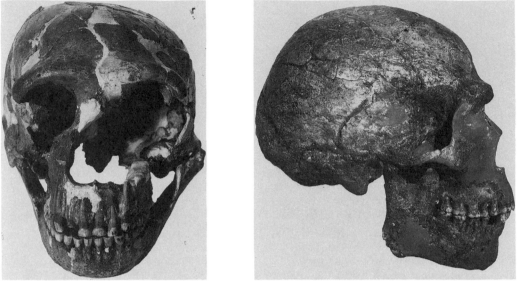

The Mount Carmel (Palestine) remains: (left) the Tabūn cranium, frontal view; (right) lateral view of the skhūl V cranium.

had discovered what he believed to be the first "well-authenticated" remains of the true ancestor of modern man in Africa.[70] This evidence consisted of a fragment of a human jaw found at a site called Kanam, in Kenya, and a handful of cranial fragments collected at nearby Kanjera.[71] According to Leakey's estimates the Kanam-Kanjera material was more or less contemporary with that of Piltdown, and had concluded therefore that the Sussex fossil could not be ancestral to *Homo sapiens* — though he did admit it was probably more related than any other known fossil to the human lineage.[72] Although this proclamation caused quite a stir at the time, the validity of Leakey's case was soon undermined by a devastating attack from Reid Moir's old geologist friend, Percy Boswell at the Imperial College, London. From the outset Boswell had been suspicious of the geological provenance of Leakey's materials, and after visiting Kenya Colony in January 1935 he was even more convinced that Leakey had been impetuous in claiming the Kanam jaw as a contemporary of Piltdown. On returning to England in 1935, Boswell criticised Leakey's work at Kanam and Kanjera in *Nature*, claiming not only that it was impossible "to find the exact site of either discovery [i.e., Kanam and Kanjera] since the earlier expedition neither marked the localities on the ground nor recorded the sites on a map", but:

> Moreover, the photograph of the site where the mandible was found, exhibited with the jaw fragment at the Royal College of Surgeons, was, through some error, that of a different locality; and the deposits (said to be clays) are in fact of entirely different rock (volcanic agglomerate).[73]

Leakey, however, refused to back down and remained committed to the importance of his finds which he contended in his 1935 book *The Stone Age Races of Kenya* could not only be dated "geologically, palaeontologically and archaeologically", but that they represented "the oldest known human fragment yet found in the African continent", if not the "most ancient fragment of true *Homo* yet discovered anywhere in the world".[74]

Alvan T. Marston, a London dentist and archaeologist who discovered a Middle Pleistocene hominid cranium at Swanscombe which set in motion a new phase in the Piltdown controversy. (Picture Post, *19 November 1953. Courtesy of Hulton-Deutsch)*

While Leakey's advance on the presapiens front in Africa had been temporarily checked by Boswell's scathing critique, in Europe the presapiens position received an unexpected boost from the discoveries made first at Steinheim, Germany in 1933, and then at Swanscombe, England, in 1935. Although both the Steinheim and Swanscombe cranial remains were incomplete, their morphology and geology were complimentary to presapiens theory. Associated faunal remains at both sites were indicative of their belonging to the Lower Pleistocene. But where to many the German fossil looked decidedly Neanderthaloid, the British specimen was seen to be eminently sapiens-like. Not unexpectedly this evidence brought Keith out of his shell; the Swanscombe find provided him with new grist for his mill, and also opened a new chapter in the Piltdown controversy.

THE SWANSCOMBE CATALYST

Keith and Woodward were among the first to view the fossil human occipital bone which the Clapham dentist Alvan T Marston (1889–1971) had found in the 100ft

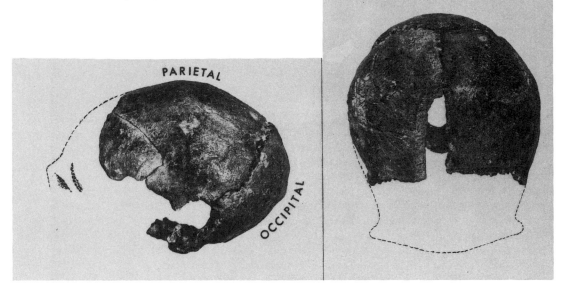

Reconstruction of the Swanscombe skull.

terrace of the Thames river valley at Swanscombe in Kent on 29 June 1935, in association with a series of unbraded flint implements of the Acheulean type (synonymous with the Lower Palaeolithic). From the bones and teeth of several extinct mammals found in the same horizon it appeared that Marston's human fossil had lived sometime in the Middle Acheulean, which, in geological terms, was somewhere between the Mindel-Riss and Riss-Würm interglacials (synonymous with the Lower-Middle Pleistocene).[75]

Keith's initial verdict on seeing the Swanscombe occiput was that it belonged unquestionably to *Homo sapiens*, closely resembling Piltdown, but of a later form and in the direct line of succession to *Eoanthropus*.[76] Woodward, on the other hand, hinted at it being either an early Neanderthaler or yet "another form of human skull in the Lower Pleistocene". While clearly not overly impressed by Marston's find, Woodward nevertheless urged the dentist to show the fossil at the forthcoming meetings of the British Association at Norwich, noting:

> I am doubtful if he can speak to be heard, and whether he is capable of writing a scientific paper ... [and I see] very little hope of finding more of the skull, but ... we must wait and see.[77]

He was, however, wrong on both counts. Marston proved to be a most energetic and competent communicator, and the following March he found the left parietal bone, thus providing a more complete picture of the Swanscombe cranium.[78] Meanwhile, whilst preparing for his Norwich presentation, Marston approached Elliot Smith in the hope that he would offer an opinion on the fossil. Smith agreed and shortly thereafter Marston sent him casts for examination. From his study of the endocranial casts, Smith concluded:

> The exceptional size and form of the visual territories upon the two hemispheres ... are definitely simian and point to a much more primitive stage than *Eoanthropus*.

The new Kent skull although suggestive of the Piltdown skull is definitely more primitive . . .[79]

In the light of the earlier opinions of Keith and Woodward, this diagnosis came as some surprise to Marston. Searching for a possible explanation of these seemingly contradictory statements, Marston toyed with the idea that perhaps his fossil was either, as Woodward suggested, a Neanderthaler, or that perhaps the Swanscombe find belonged not with Piltdown Man as Keith had proposed, but with its apparent contemporary, Heidelberg Man. For as he later told his audience at Norwich:

> It is very difficult to believe that Piltdown . . . should have anything at all to do with the Pliocene eoliths. I would much rather think of Piltdown as being related to the Chelles-Acheulean culture phase, as the 100-ft terrace suggests, and of course we know that the new fossil had nothing to do with the Pliocene. It is Middle Pleistocene. I do not think that the new fossil can be much later than Piltdown. I am prepared to believe that it may be earlier than Piltdown, and, with the reservation made at the beginning that Heidelberg may not be Neanderthaloid, I am prepared to say that the new fossil may not be Heidelberg — but it is certainly not Neanderthal.[80]

As this indicates Marston was at this time labouring under the misconception, as indeed was everyone else, that the Swanscombe and Piltdown sites were of equivalent age. He was stunned when Kenneth P Oakley (1911–81), a palaeontologist and geologist from Woodward's old department at South Kensington, corrected his attribution of the Piltdown gravels to the 100ft terrace. Earlier in his presentation Marston had quoted Sollas' estimates, saying that the "height of the gravels above the Ouse is 25 metres" and therefore could be "referred to the 30 metre terrace". But as Oakley pointed out, the recent investigations by Francis H Edmunds (1893–1960), of the Geological Survey, had determined that the Piltdown deposits corresponded to the "50-ft terrace with derivatives from higher levels".[81] What the reaction of the Norwich audience was is not known, but clearly it had a profound impact on Marston — though prudently he did not share his immediate thoughts with either Oakley or the rest of his audience at Norwich.

The implication of Oakley's statement was that Piltdown was later than Swanscombe: but how reliable was Edmunds' study and what length of time actually separated the two horizons? Although the faunal assemblage at Swanscombe was indicative of the Middle Pleistocene it was not by any means certain whether it was early or late. Another and more pressing problem was equating the two cranial forms represented at Swanscombe and Piltdown. From a strictly morphological viewpoint the idea of Swanscombe being ancestral to Piltdown harmonized completely with the omparative assessment of the two endocrania by Smith — but this hypothesis only made sense if the Piltdown skull was considered without its apelike jaw.

During the winter of 1935–6, Marston immersed himself in the Piltdown literature and apparently made a number of visits to the British Museum (Natural History) to view the public display of the Sussex materials. By the early spring of 1936 Marston found himself a zealous dualist. The canine tooth belonged to an ape, he decided. His reasons for believing this were grounded in the shape of its root: where the root of the human canine is straight, in the Piltdown specimen it is curved. The observation was not a new one, but what made his argument more compelling, he believed, was the fact that unlike his predecessors he had the benefit of the sinanthropine material from Choukoutien. Without exception the canine roots of these early hominids were straight. Furthermore, the crown of the Piltdown canine was deflected, as it is among anthropoid apes, outwards laterally towards the cheek, instead of giving an edge-to-edge bite. The excessive wear pattern of the tooth was also considered to be indicative of the "function and diet" of an ape. As for Hrdlička's proposition that the jaw belonged to a dryopithecine ape, Marston rejected this in favour of Miller's original chimpanzee argument. But he felt that Miller and other dualists had been led astray by their approach to the evolution of human dentition:

> The conclusion to be drawn from the study of the morphological characters of the teeth as affecting the problem of Man's evolution is that Man has not evolved through any of the existing anthropoid apes, but in parallel with them. According to Hrdlička the primitive feature of the shovel-shaped incisors,[82] lingual rim and fossa formation seen in recent man and characterising the upper incisors of [fossil hominids such as] Sinanthropus . . . caused Hrdlička to draw the conclusion that the real ancestral line of man had not been discovered, and that the direct line of human ancestry ought to show a more human-like keilomorphy (rim formation) as well as koilomorphy (hollowing out of the lingual surface of the front teeth). The discovery of Sinanthropus some years later confirmed this prediction, and I would use this argument to emphasise that the teeth of the type of Man represented by the Piltdown cranial fragments should be teeth which are more human in type even than those of Sinanthropus, human in type and in function and not teeth which are definitely chimpanzee-like in type and function.[83]

Naturally Marston was anxious to claim priority for his fossil, but he was not insensitive to Woodward's position. The situation was delicate. The British Museum (Natural History) was in the process of evaluating his materials and he realized his proposal to resuscitate the old dualist controversy might place this work in jeopardy, particularly if Woodward was to turn against him. Hence in an effort to keep matters straight, it is believed that Marston initially discussed his dilemma with Martin Hinton who was working on the identification of the Swanscombe fauna,[84] and that it was through Hinton, (directly or indirectly), that Woodward learned of Marston's stance. In answer to an inquiry from Woodward, Marston informed him that:

> [T]here can be little doubt that the status of the Piltdown will have to be revised. Since I feel that I have established a case for the rejection of the canine, and the matter will have to be thrashed out, I will let you see my evidence to the point when you come, because I feel that it would be better for the change of view which is bound to come, to come rather as a matter of concurrence of opinion based on the new knowledge which the new discovery has offered to the elucidation of which after all, not a great deal of certainty existed before — than as a matter of controversy. Piltdown cannot be earlier than Swanscombe, nor earlier than the Middle gravels of the 100 foot terrace. My opinion is that Piltdown is later, and certainly that it if Swanscombe had been found first, Piltdown would have been accepted without question as an advanced type. Do not think I am speaking boastfully, because I know that any fresh discovery may necessitate the re-orientation of previously accepted views, and moreover, because I know the re-orientation although it may be suggested by me will not be effected except by the judgement of science in general.[85]

While there is every reason to suppose that Woodward accepted Marston's invitation to visit him at his home in Clapham Common to discuss this issue early in April 1936, nothing is known of what transpired there. Also, in the absence of any correspondence from either party or any of their known associates, it is not possible to provide an accurate interpretation of the subsequent evolution of Marston's attitude during the next year. However, this much is clear: in June 1936 the *British Dental Journal* published his arguments against the association of the jaw. This was then followed by a presentation at the Royal Society of Medicine on 23 November in which he reiterated the argument for the "excision of the mandible" from the Piltdown skull.[86] Shortly thereafter the *Journal of the Royal Anthropological Institute* published a 67 page article in which Marston not only provided a detailed account of the finds made at Swanscombe, but also repeated his critical views on the status of the Piltdown mandible. He then requested the Institute to appoint a "research committee" to investigate his various claims for the Swanscombe skull and the associated finds.[87]

Although the "Research Committee" of the Royal Anthropological Institute endorsed the view that the Swanscombe skull was indeed "an indigenous fossil of the 100-ft terrace", belonging (probably) to the Middle Pleistocene, it was unable to arrive at a definite conclusion regarding the fossil's taxonomic status. As Wilfrid Le Gros Clark (1895–1971), professor of anatomy at Oxford, noted in his report, the broad and massive Swanscombe occiput, while bearing a number of features that could be "readily matched in modern skulls", there were others such as "the great thickness of the bone along the occipito-temporal suture (at the lateral margin of cerebellar fossa)", which served to make it a rather "exceptional" specimen.[88] But unlike Smith, the Oxford anatomist could find nothing in the endocranial cast which departed significantly from that of modern human crania. Geoffrey Morant (1899–1964) of the Galton Laboratory, University College, London, concurred and felt the skull could represent either a group in the direct line of descent of *Homo sapiens*, or if not in the direct line at least closer to it than the European Neanderthals.[89] The report, however, made no mention of Marston's controversial views on the relationship between Swanscombe and Piltdown, but did note that the remains had been presented by Marston to the Trustees of the British Museum.

Coinciding with the publication of this report was Keith's article in the *Journal of Anatomy* in which he endeavoured to counter Marston's destructive thesis by claiming that Piltdown was the earlier form, while Swanscombe was, at most, late Achulean, and that they were chronological variants of the same type. This article also provided Keith with an opportunity to rectify an error in his earlier attempts to reconstruct the Piltdown skull. Where he had supposed that the two halves of the Sussex skull had been symmetrical and of equal size, it was now evident to him from the evidence afforded by the Swanscombe occiput that these British crania were characterized, as Smith had originally contended, by an extreme degree of asymmetry. Accordingly Keith presented a new reconstruction of the Piltdown skull reflecting these findings, which, as a consequence, reduced the cranial capacity by a little more than a 100 cc.[90] Unfortunately, by this time Smith was not able to appreciate this move, for when Keith's article appeared he had been dead for well over a year.[91]

With war clouds once more gathering over Europe, attention was again diverted away from the past and focussed on an uncertain future, and it was not until after the war, in 1947 that Marston launched the first of a series of forays into the monistic camp.

In his initial strike, made at a meeting of the Geologists' Association in London during June 1947, Marston drew heavily on Edmunds' 1925 reassessment of the height of the Piltdown terrace to support his argument for the separation of the Piltdown jaw from the braincase, which he continued to claim, was more recent than the Swanscombe skull.[92] To further support his case for the comparative modernity of the Piltdown cranial fragments, Marston claimed that their deep chocolate colour was misleading because they (unlike the mandible) had been treated with a bichromate preservative solution. Their original colour, he contended, had been grey — the general colour of most animal bones found in the Wealden region.[93] Marston had evidently gleaned this information from the 1935 study, published by Arthur T Hopwood (1897–1969), on the Piltdown fauna, in which it was noted that Dawson had apparently soaked his initial finds in "solution of bichromate of potash to harden them".[94] As Hopwood noted in his monograph, the latter fragments, and in particular the occipital fragment found *in situ* by Woodward during the summer of 1912, had not been treated in this manner. Hence, given the fact that its colour (though visibly lighter) matched that of the earlier as well as later fragments, this argued strongly against Marston's thesis. But while this aspect of Marston's offensive collapsed, his account of the anatomical and geological problems that still continued to surround the Sussex remains prompted Kenneth Oakley to remark, in the discussion that followed Marston's presentation, that perhaps some of the difficulties alluded to might be resolved by the application of a test developed by Adolphe Carnot, a French mineralogist, at the close of the nineteenth century. According to Carnot the fluorine content of fossil bone increased with geological age, and Oakley felt that perhaps the fluorine analysis of the respective bones might throw some light on the controverted issue of their association.[95]

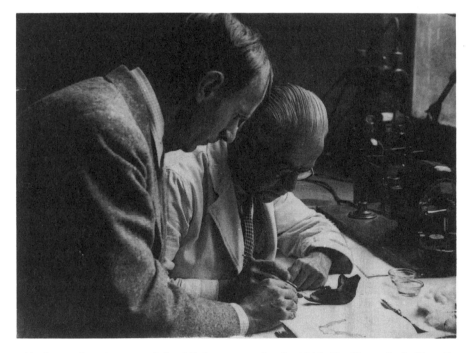

The preliminary flourine test of the Piltdown remains in 1949: Dr Kenneth Oakley discussing with Mr. L.E. Parsons (right) where the mandible of Piltdown man could be sampled with the least risk of damage.

Although, as claimed by several contemporary observers,[96] Oakley's subsequent work on Piltdown had been largely the product of Marston's agitations, it is also clear that his idea of using the fluorine technique as a possible indicator of association and relative dating had preceded Marston's delivery at the June meeting of the Geologists' Association. In fact the idea had been growing in his mind for some time, but it was not until January 1947, while attending the first Pan-African Congress on Prehistory held in Nairobi, that he apparently saw an opportunity to test the potential of Carnot's methodology. On hearing Leakey's continuing arguments regarding the antiquity of his Kanam-Kanjera materials, Oakley had volunteered to submit these contentious bones and associated fauna to the Home Office Forensic Science Laboratory in London for fluorine analysis in the hope that they might shed some light on their relative antiquity. Unfortunately because of excessive amounts of background fluorine in the Kenyan material, Oakley was unable to resolve Leakey's problem. However, as he later reported to the Dundee meetings of the British Association in August 1947, these disappointing results did not invalidate the method.[97]

Early in 1948, in a further attempt to test the validity of the fluorine methodology, Oakley chose to compare the much disputed Galley Hill remains with those of Swanscombe, both of which had been found in the same vicinity in Kent. The results were stunning and showed quite conclusively that indigenous bones in the Middle Pleistocene gravels at the Swanscombe site contained around 2.0 per cent fluorine, whereas those from Upper Pleistocene gravels were found to have levels of fluorine hovering around the 1.0 per cent mark, while post-Pleistocene bones were found to contain even less. By contrast, the reputed Middle Pleistocene remains from Galley Hill, proved to contain only small amounts of fluorine — the figures hovering, without exception, in the region of 0.2 to 0.4 per cent! Presenting these results to the British Association meeting in Brighton in September 1948,[98] Oakley said the conclusions were unavoidable: the Galley Hill skeleton was not indigenous to the 100ft terrace, but an intrusive burial, and estimated that it probably dated, at the earliest, from the end of the Pleistocene.

The results of Oakley's investigations did not take Keith completely by surprise, for as he had noted in his 1938 paper, it was already apparent to him that something was amiss with his concept of presapiens theory. And on reviewing this new situation, Keith admitted that he had been wrong, admitting that as early as 1931 it had become evident that events had overtaken him:

> By 1936 the evidence ... convinced me that it was easier to believe that there was a flaw in the geological evidence of the antiquity of Galley Hill man than that a race or type of mankind could continue for 100,000 years without undergoing evolutionary change. And so I have had to abandon the claims of the "modern type of man" to a high antiquity, the very thesis which I set out to prove so long ago.[99]

He also admitted that he was now more favourably inclined to the idea of the South African australopithecines representing an important stage in human evolution, and that perhaps too much emphasis had been placed on the significance of the Piltdown fragments.[100]

Armed with the Galley Hill-Swanscombe results, Oakley secured permission from the Museum authorities during the closing months of 1948, to extend his investigations to the Piltdown materials. The results of the tests performed under the direction of Randall Hoskins in the Government Laboratory, London, became available during the summer of 1949 — a summary of which Oakley delivered to the British Association meetings in Newcastle early in September, followed by a more detailed communication to *Nature* the following spring.[101]

In contrast to the Lower Pleistocene Piltdown fauna, which was found to have a fairly high fluorine content (ranging from 1.9 to 3.1 per cent), the remaining components of the faunal assemblage, including the various remains of *Eoanthropus* I and II were found to have a considerably lower fluorine content (ranging from 0.1 to 1.5 per cent). These latter results, Oakley felt, were consistent with Dawson's original interpretation of the Piltdown gravel terrace, namely that it had been reconstructed

The 1949–50 results of the fluorine analysis conducted on the Piltdown assemblage.

Specimen	Cat No	% Fluorine content
Eoanthropus I		
Left parieto-frontal	(E 590)	0.1
Left temporal	(E 591)	0.4
Right parietal	(E 592)	0.3
Occipital	(E 593)	0.2
Right mandibular ramus	(E 594)	0.2
Right first molar	(E 594)	<0.1
Canine	(E 611)	<0.1
Eoanthropus II		
Right frontal	(E 646)	0.1
Occipital	(E 647)	0.1
Left first molar	(E 648)	0.1
PILTDOWN FAUNA		
Lower Pleistocene		
Mastodon arvernensis molar	(E 595)	1.9
Mastodon arvernensis molar	(E 622)	2.3
Elephas sp molar	(E 596)	2.7
Elephas sp molar	(E 620)	3.1
Rhinoceros sp premolar	(E 623)	2.0
Middle Upper Pleistocene		
Hippopotamus sp molar	(E 598)	0.1
Hippopotamus sp premolar	(E 599)	1.1
Cervus elephas antler	(E 600)	1.5
Castor fiber molar	(E 603)	0.4
Castor fiber mandible	(E 619)	0.3
Holocene		
Indet. bone (subfossil)	(E 1387)	0.1
Fragment of fresh bone	(P 33)	<0.1
Bos taurus phalange	(P 1389)	0.3

N.B. The faunal list is not complete, for full-details, see Oakley & Hoskins (1950:381)

on several occasions and that during these episodes various "new" remains had been introduced. Based on the composition of this assemblage, he confessed that it was impossible to determine whether the "final settlement" of the deposit had taken place in the Middle or Upper Pleistocene — though it seemed most likely that it had coincided with the introduction of the *Castor* remains. But while the timing of this event had, by necessity, to remain a matter of conjecture, the results, Oakley felt, precluded all possibility of it having been earlier than the Middle Pleistocene. Furthermore, he noted that the results seemed to favour the conclusion that:

> All the specimens of *Eoanthropus*, including the remains of the second skull found two miles away, are contemporaneous ... The question of the precise geological age of the Piltdown gravel is open to further inquiry, but taking the balance of available evidence, *Eoanthropus* may be provisionally referred to the last warm interglacial period (Riss-Würm interglacial; that is, early Upper Pleistocene, although here it should be noted that some authorities count Riss-Würm as Middle Pleistocene).[102]

Marston, however, was not satisfied. He believed Oakley had been far too generous in attributing Piltdown to a Pleistocene horizon. In his opinion the specimen belonged in the Holocene along with the Galley Hill skeleton. The fluorine estimations in both cases were almost identical, but as Oakley later pointed out, such a conclusion was a fallacy based on ignorance of the method:

> To assess the [relative age] of a specimen [based on local bio-stratigraphy], one first makes a comparison between its fluorine content and that of specimens in the same bed or at the same locality whose [relative regional and general stratigraphical age] are known. When this was done for the Piltdown material, it was found that the specimens were certainly not Villafranchian [Plio-Pleistocene] but that, judging on this basis alone, they could not belong either to the youngest group of the Pleistocene fossils in the bed or to the Holocene group. Since the mandible, canine, and part of the occiput were found in situ at the base of the gravel in association with the remains of beaver, which showed the same fluorine content, there can be no reason to doubt that Eoanthropus is Pleistocene. The presence of beaver in the gravel is proof that it was laid down by the river. The Ouse has not flowed at this level, 50 feet above its present bed, since the early Upper Pleistocene times;[103] so that the minimum age of Eoanthropus is assured on that score alone. Fluorine has evidently been less abundant in the ground water at Piltdown than at Swanscombe, or at any rate it has been less available . . . since Lower Pleistocene times. This fact, however, does not invalidate the primary interpretation of the uniformly low fluorine content of all the widely scattered fragments of Eoanthropus. It merely makes it difficult to be sure on this evidence alone whether Eoanthropus is Middle Pleistocene or early Upper Pleistocene.[104]

The London dentist remained unmoved. While the results of Oakley's tests had been pretty much what he had expected, particularly as they pertained to the cranial fragments, it is evident that Marston was clearly taken aback by the fact that the mandible and canine tooth shared "with the cranium the same low fluorine content",[105] and for the moment at least, his campaign against Piltdown stalled.

Oakley's results did not guarantee the association of the parts, but as was noted by the Los Angeles physical anthropologist Joseph Birdsell (b. 1908) shortly after the Oakley & Hoskin paper appeared, they certainly increased the probability. Furthermore, Birdsell felt that the late date now affixed to the remains made it "increasingly awkward" to attribute the mandible, as the dualists had claimed, to some unknown ape. "Considerations of time, climate, and ecological competition", all conspired, he felt, to make it "increasingly improbable that the mandible can be in this fashion disassociated from the vault".[106] But Birdsell was also acutely aware of the dramatic changes that were currently underway in palaeoanthropology. Indeed the conference at which he had made these statments, the 15th Symposium on Quantitative Biology held at Cold Spring Harbor, Long Island, New York, in the summer of 1950, clearly mirrored the new direction in which human evolutionary theory was now headed. Where previously the connections between morphology and genetics, and taxonomy and morphology had been tenuous, workers were now earnestly searching for a rapprochement of genetic theory and palaeoanthropological data. While some years were to pass before the full impact of the Cold Spring Harbour Symposium on the "Origin and Evolution of Man" was generally felt, it is clear from the published proceedings of this ground-breaking conference that many of the ideas that had served to nurture both Piltdown and the presapiens paradigm had been abandoned and that a more benevolent attitude had surfaced, not only with regard to the australopithecines but also to the pithecanthropines and Neanderthals. Even if Oakley's results had placed the Piltdown remains at an earlier rather than a later date, they would have been just as difficult to explain in the context of this change in focus. In fact, as Birdsell confessed at Cold Spring Harbor, the Piltdown skull, particularly as it was now dated, presented a "more embarrassing problem than it did in its pre-fluorine chronology". The problem was now how to resolve this new dilemma Oakley had created.

6 Scotoanthropus fraudator

Sola Philistaeos asini maxilla necavit, Nunc doctos uno Simia dente fugat.[1]

A FRUSTRATED SUPPORTER

Following the publication of his collaborative study with Randall Hoskins in 1950, Kenneth Oakley endeavoured to consolidate the case for the unity of the Piltdown remains by using the new technology of electron microscopy.[2] The Piltdown teeth were once again carefully scrutinized and compared with a series of non-human primate teeth. These elaborate investigations failed to prove or disprove Woodward's original thesis.

In continuing his defence for the integrity of the Piltdown skull, Oakley was neither blind nor insensitive to the anatomical demands of the dualists, but as many of these critics freely admitted, save perhaps Marston, the Piltdown chimera was much more acceptable with its jaw than without. The arguments favouring the monistic view were certainly no less compelling. For example, Keith had suggested that perhaps the anatomical peculiarities of Piltdown jaw had been the product of genetic isolation.[3] Oakley thought the idea not unreasonable:

> I think [Oakley wrote to Keith] Britain was quite possibly isolated during the great interglacial [presumably referring to the Riss-Würm] when the sea-level was relatively high. The straits of Dover may have been cut during the intense erosion accompanying a low sea-level at the time of the second glaciation [?] It is not generally realized that the last link between Britain and the Continent, the link which existed during the Submerged Forest Period, was formed by the Dogger Bank lowlands. The Dover-Calais ridge had been breached at a much earlier date...[4]

Furthermore, Oakley recognized that it was possible to turn Keith's former argument on the relationship between Piltdown and Swanscombe around and still not be in violation of either facts or theory. The jaw and its attendant idiosyncracies may have been acquired independently, as Keith had suggested, while the skull essentially reflected a general evolutionary refinement of the Swanscombe type. Support for his latter idea could be found in the Fontéchevade skullcap which had been recovered near Charente (France) in 1947.[5] As with Piltdown and Swanscombe, this French skullcap was remarkably thick, but in all other respects the form of its braincase was essentially modern. The accompanying cultural and faunal assemblage was not markedly different from that of Piltdown, and was characterized by as many ambiguities. Viewed from a cultural perspective, the Fontéchevade implements had been identified as Clactonian, a Mousterian-like industry dating from the Riss-Würm interglacial. The fauna from this site was, however, a mixture. Some of the mammalian bones were considered to be early (i.e Mindel-Riss), while others were thought to be much later (Riss-Würm). The fact that the composition of this mixed faunal assemblage departed radically from those associated with the Acheulean-Mousterian sites in the Dordogne region, could suggest that the Fontéchevade site was perhaps much earlier, dating from the Mindel-Riss.[6] This idea was soon dispatched by Oakley's fluorine analysis of the remains in 1951.[7] In presenting these results to the Wenner-Gren Foundation Symposium on Anthropology held in New York in June 1952, Oakley reported that the material was more recent — in fact he said it compared most favourably with Piltdown.[8]

While this coupling of Fontéchevade with Piltdown did not explain the anatomical enigma of the Sussex remains, it undoubtedly served to support Oakley's continuing commitment to the monistic view. Yet it is also evident that his enthusiasm was, by this time, waning, because a point had been reached where he saw little hope of pursuing a productive line of research that would settle the issue once and for all. In fact, as he told his colleagues in New York, this matter would in all probability remain unsolved "until another mandible of the same type is found in association with its cranium".[9] Oakley therefore turned his attention away from Piltdown to the more exciting challenge of applying his dating techniques to the fossil hominids that were being discovered at an astonishing rate in Africa.

In the autumn of 1952 Oakley submitted a proposal to the Wenner-Gren Foundation for Anthropological Research in New York for funds to stage an international conference in London, aimed at organizing "Research on Fossil Hominidae in Africa". The idea was attractive to the Foundation since it would provide valuable information on which to base the future dispensation of its funds in this rapidly expanding area of anthropological research. Accordingly Oakley was immediately awarded a grant of $1000 to cover his anticipated expenses.[10]

Oakley's conference, held in 1953 at Burlington House during the last five days of July, was an unqualified success, as his report to the Wenner-Gren Foundation indicates. While it laid the foundations for future research in sub-Saharan Africa,[11] it also unexpectedly triggered a new and startling inquiry into the status of the Piltdown remains.

THE WEINER HYPOTHESIS

On Thursday, 30 July 1953, the Wenner-Gren conference on "Early Man in Africa" shifted its venue from the meeting room of the Geological Society in the West End to the British Museum (Natural History), where Oakley had organized a program of events that included, among other things, a demonstration by Arthur Hopwood of the original skull of *Proconsul* and other Miocene Hominoidea that had been collected in East Africa prior to World War II.[12] Later in the day the delegates were taken on a tour of the Geology Department where they viewed, among other things, the celebrated Piltdown remains. Since many of those present had never seen or handled the originals this experience caused quite a stir. Evidently, opinions were as divided then as they had been in the past.[13]

Among those who saw the specimens for the first time was the South African physical anthropologist Joseph Weiner (1915–82), who had received his training under Dart in Johannesburg and now worked in Le Gros Clark's department at Oxford. Disinclined to the monistic interpretation, and finding himself that night seated at dinner together with Oakley and Sherwood Washburn (b. 1911) from Chicago University (another sceptic),[14] it was not surprising that the conversation was eventually brought around to the subject of Piltdown and the reasons why the Museum had not mounted a systematic excavation of the site where the crucial Piltdown II remains had been found. Was it not, after all, the key to the entire debate? Oakley agreed with his earnest colleagues, but remarked that while they knew the general place where Dawson had found these specimens — Sheffield Park — they did

Joseph S. Weiner, Oxford University: South African-born anthropologist who, with Oakley and Le Gros Clark, proved that the Piltdown remains were forgeries. (Courtesy Prof. G. Ainsworth Harrison)

not know the exact spot. All that was known about this second site was a postcard Dawson had sent Woodward in July 1915.[15] But why had he failed to record so important a fact? Had Dawson perhaps relayed this information verbally to Woodward? If he did, why had Woodward also neglected to preserve information on the whereabouts of this all important site? Had his notes been mislaid?

While the precise facts of this three-way conversation have long since faded from memory, it is evident from Oakley's subsequent correspondence with Weiner that even if these questions had been asked, his responses would have been based largely on conjecture. The extent of his knowledge at this time was simply that there was no known record of the site's location. But whatever else may have been said that night, the simple fact that the site of Piltdown II could not be located and that it had quite possibly been known only to Dawson was a "curious piece of information", which, compounded with the memory of seeing the actual remains, set Weiner's mind thinking on the "larger Piltdown conundrum".[16]

Returning to Oxford that night Weiner found himself unable to calm his thoughts and sleep. Recalling that troubled night, he later wrote:

> Thinking it all over again I realized with astonishment that while there were in fact only two possible "natural" theories, i.e. that Piltdown man was in fact the composite man-ape of Woodward's interpretation, or that two distinct creatures, fossil man and fossil ape, had been found side by side, neither of the "natural" explanations was at all satisfactory. [But] . . . what other possible explanation could there be? . . . If the jaw and cranium had not come together by nature or blind accident then could they have got there by human agency? This would mean that someone by chance or error had dropped the jaw in the pit (perhaps used as a rubbish dump) dug in gravel which happened to contain other fossil remnants. [But, was it reasonable to suppose that this had] been repeated at the second site? Perhaps site II was after all of exaggerated significance or had been mistakenly interpreted [as Hrdlička and others had been saying all along]. Or could [Piltdown II be disposed of] by supposing that the bits had actually come from the Barkham Manor site two miles away, in gravel brought across for some reason or other[?] [But] [e]ven if one were prepared to accept them, this elaboration of ancillary hypotheses still avoided the main issue. For even if the jaw had been thrown on to the gravel, to meet with the cranium, it was still a fossil jaw . . . [or was it?] . . . [C]ould the jaw possibly be modern? . . . To say the jaw was modern [however] implied that the fluorine analysis had been inaccurate or that the published results must be in some way compatible with modern bone recently buried. In effect this would imply that the most reasonable interpretation of the results had been in error . . . [But then again there was the problem of the teeth. They] . . . were almost unanimously acknowledged to possess features quite unprecedented in modern apes — the flat wear of the molars and the curious type of wear of the canine had never been matched in an ape's mandible. [But if the jaw was indeed modern . . . how could these facts be explained away? Was it possible that they were "deliberately ground-down teeth"?] . . . Even as a mere hypothesis this inference could at once dispose of two of the most intransigent Piltdown posers: how the jaw and teeth had ever got there and how the teeth had come by their remarkable wear. But the hypothesis of a deliberate "salting" of the Piltdown gravels clearly carried much wider implications, and the idea was repellent indeed. . .[17]

It has been suggested that Weiner came to his forgery hypothesis through Marston's recent experiments.[18] To support his thesis that the Piltdown jaw had no business with the braincase, Marston had taken plaster casts of orangutan molars and filed down their occlusal surfaces to match the same condition as the Piltdown molars. Likewise to "demonstrate" the canine's true identity he had inserted a plaster model of it into the socket of a female orangutan jaw, and reiterated his claim that it was an immature tooth "belonging to a young adult ape", and that even though Oakley's fluorine tests had shown that the jaw and canine were of the same age, they were incompatible with the braincase which he continued to believe was modern.[19] But unlike Weiner, Marston did not suspect foul play. As far as he was concerned the association of the Piltdown parts was purely accidental. In fact when it was finally announced on Saturday, 21 November 1953 that the mandible and canine were forgeries, Marston refused to accept the evidence.[20]

To say the least it was a startling proposition, and Weiner, during the first days of August, carefully reconsidered the pros and cons of his hypothesis. The distinctly human appearance of the molars of both Piltdown I and II had been a major impediment to the advancement of the dualistic theory throughout the entire history of the Piltdown controversy. On examining a cast of the jaw, he was immediately

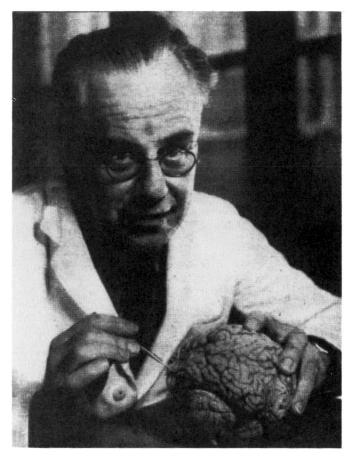

Professor Wilfrid Edward Le Gros Clark, Oxford University: British anatomist and enthusiastic supporter of Dart's views on the significance of the South African Australopithecines. With Weiner and Oakley proved that the Piltdown remains were forgeries.

struck not only by the flatness of the wear pattern but also an unexpected "lack of continuity" of the biting surface" between the first and second molars. Such a situation he felt was highly indicative of their having been tampered with.[21] To test this hypothesis the occlusal surfaces of a series of chimpanzee molars were filed down in an effort to duplicate the condition of the Piltdown molars. Much to his surprise this was quite easy to do, and the resulting appearance of these molars was astonishingly similar to those of Piltdown. To further enhance the similarity Weiner stained these teeth with a solution of potassium permanganate. But was this enough to establish a forgery? If the intention had been to pass off the jaw of a modern ape as a fossil, and to withstand the scrutiny of scientific experts, it would be necessary not only to abrade the teeth but it would also be imperative to remove other tell-tale features. In the Piltdown jaw as well as the flattened molars, two critical diagnostic features were absent: the entire chin region and the mandibular condyle. Without these it was impossible to determine the bicondylar width and thereby confirm the association of the braincase with the jaw, and, in the absence of an intact condyle, the argument for the jaw's ape affinities was lacking definite proof. Weiner was also sure the peculiar characters of the canine could be explained by "deliberate tampering". But did all these points add up to a prima facie case; and if so, how could he bring this case to Oakley's attention and secure access to the originals to test his hypothesis, without precipitating a scandal? He was not at all sure how Oakley would react. In 1949, when Oakley had presented his results to the Oxford University Anthropological Society,[22] Weiner broached the idea of the mandible being much younger than had been supposed; and contrary to expectations, Oakley had not been at all receptive to his anatomical arguments against the unity of the Piltdown specimens. Oakley believed that it was unlikely that a modern specimen could have such a high level of fluorine. Yet, Weiner believed, this objection could be countered, for as indicated in the 1950 Oakley & Hoskins paper, the probable experimental error of the method of estimation was ± 0.2 per cent. Thus although the published fluorine content of the jaw was 0.3 per cent, it might well be less than 0.1 per cent — a figure more in line with that of recent bone.[23] Weiner believed that this argument was further sustained by an observation Oakley had made while drilling for a sample of dentine, namely that: "Below the extremely thin ferruginous surface stain the dentine was pure white, apparently no more altered than the dentine of recent teeth from the soil".[24]

Having spent the better part of a week mulling over his thesis, Weiner finally decided to place his case before his professor, Le Gros Clark and see what he thought. He was persuaded by both the experimental evidence and the supporting arguments. Weiner then revealed his anxieties concerning Oakley and suggested a possible course of action, which Le Gros Clark agreed to. Given the sensitive nature of Weiner's hypothesis, it was agreed that Oakley should be contacted by telephone rather than letter. According to Weiner, Clark's call to Oakley stressed:

> One . . . that the first fluorine dates must be incorrect and that [the] fluorine tests would have to be redone . . . [Second] . . . that . . . the material had been stained, probably superficially. [Third] . . . [that] Oakley look at the surfaces of the molars and also of the canine, to see whether it was at all obvious that artificial abrasion had been applied . . . [And finally] . . . the general point [was made] to Oakley . . . that we should regard the allegation of a forgery as a hypothesis to be refuted or validated by as many tests as we could apply, and that unless we obtained really cast-iron results then the idea of a forgery would have to be given up. . .[25]

As might be expected, Oakley was taken aback by the call from Oxford, but evidently Le Gros Clark had stated the case well because Oakley said he would review the materials and call back. Exactly how long this took is not known, but later that same day Oakley returned the call as promised saying, Weiner remembered, "that he was utterly convinced that artificial abrasion had been applied. [And that] [i]t was certainly obvious on the canine". Oakley also agreed that the British Museum should be actively involved in the "exposure", but that in the interim the entire matter should be kept secret.[26]

THE JAW AND CANINE DISMISSED

Microscopic examination of the Piltdown dentition revealed the presence of fine scratch marks on both the molars and canine which suggested the application of an abrasive. While this could not be conclusively proved, the possibility was strengthened by other circumstantial evidence. In the case of the Piltdown I mandibular molars, the borders of the flat occlusal surfaces were sharp-edged and showed no signs of the bevelling which is usually produced by natural wear. There was also an

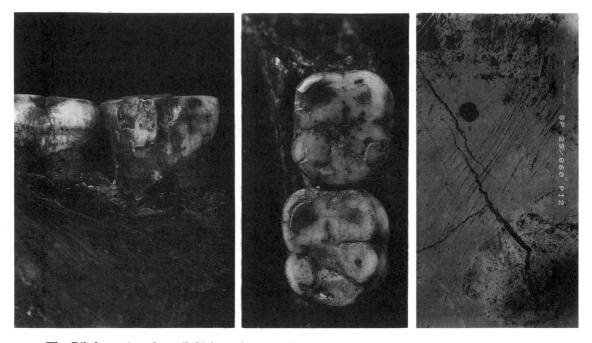

The Piltdown 1 molars: (left) lateral external view; (centre) view from above; (right) scanning electron microscope view of molar surface showing scratch marks.

unevenness in the amount of dentine exposed on the antero-internal and antero-external cusps. In the Piltdown molars more dentine had been exposed in the former than the latter. Normally, the lateral cusps are worn more rapidly than the medial ones. Similarly, not only was the extent of the flatness of these surfaces considered inconsistent with normal wear patterns, but the degree of wear in the two molars was seen to be almost identical. This was considered most odd, since usually the first molar is more worn than the second.

A closer examination of the controversial canine tooth also revealed a number of inconsistencies. Le Gros Clark agreed wholeheartedly with Weiner's objections to the mode of wear of this particular tooth — it was quite unlike that of any known ape or human. Furthermore the tooth's degree of wear was quite out of keeping with the new X-ray pictures, which strongly supported Courtney Lyne's earlier argument for the immaturity of the tooth: the pulp cavity was open and wide. Microscopic examination of the surface of the tooth's crown revealed fine vertical scratch marks which Clark considered "quite consistent with the surmise that [this tooth had been] abraded by artificial means".[27]

Using an improved methodology it was possible to estimate much smaller amounts of fluorine than had been possible when first applied to the Piltdown remains in 1949. These new estimations revealed a marked difference in content between the cranium and the jaw and its supposedly associated canine. The inference was that the mandible and canine (and the isolated Piltdown II molar) were essentially modern, whereas the cranium was that much older.

How much older was impossible to say, though Oakley conjectured that it might well be Upper Pleistocene as he had originally claimed in 1950.[28] These findings were

A simplified and composite table of results reported in Weiner et al (1953:143–144).

Remains	% Fluorine	% Nitrogen
Controls		
Fresh bone	0.1	4.1
Upper Pleistocene bone	0.1	0.7
Molar (modern chimpanzee)	<0.06	3.2
Piltdown I		
Cranium	0.1	1.4
Mandible	<0.03	3.9
Molar (dentine)	<0.04	4.3
Canine (dentine)	<0.03	5.1
Piltdown II		
Frontal	0.1	1.1
Occipital	0.03	0.6
Isolated molar (dentine)	<0.01	4.2

found to harmonize completely with the organic content of the respective bones. Although as noted earlier, it had long been recognized that the organic content of fossil bone was an unreliable measure of antiquity, significant advances had been made since the late 1940s using nitrogen as a relative indicator of organic age.[29] Whereas a fluorine assay reflects the gradual accumulation in bone of an exogenous element, the nitrogen content indicates the progressive loss of organic matter from the bone itself. Accordingly, in fresh or recent bone the nitrogen content is very high while its fluorine content is very low; but with the passage of time this situation is reversed.

In the light of these results Weiner's suggestion that perhaps these remains had been superficially stained was investigated. As was already well-known, the first cranial fragments found by Dawson had been dipped in a solution of potassium bichromate, but according to later accounts, subsequent finds had not been treated in this fashion. Yet the cranial fragments and mandible found by Dawson and Woodward during the summer of 1912 closely matched the colour of the original finds. The dark chocolate colour of these bones was thought to be due to the presence of iron in the Piltdown gravels. A trial drilling, deeper into the body of the mandible, revealed the superficiality of this external colour; whereas the cranial fragments appeared to be more deeply stained thoughout their thickness. Subsequent chemical analysis of the mandible and the cranial fragments confirmed Weiner's suspicions. The jaw contained chromate, while the cranial fragments reportedly found during the summer of 1912 were evidently free of this element. The remains of Piltdown II were also examined and found to contain only small amounts of chromate. There was also a detectable difference in the amount of iron staining between the mandible and cranial fragments of Piltdown I. Where the latter fragments were found to have an iron content approaching 8 per cent, the mandible was found to have surface content of 7 per cent, while on a sample from its interior only 2-3 per cent of iron was found. Taking all of these findings into account it was difficult to avoid the obvious conclusion. Iron and chromate staining had been deliberately applied to the mandible in order to match it with the cranial fragments. Piltdown II appeared to belong with Piltdown I.[30] Both in colour and in fluorine and nitrogen content (as well as anatomical characters) there was a striking concordance between these two supposedly independent crania. As for the canine, its "ferruginous" coat was found

Osbert Lancaster's cartoon in the Daily Express, *London, 24 November 1953. (Courtesy of* Express Newspapers)

to be a soft non-metallic, paint-like substance.[31] Like the mandible, it too had been stained to match the general colour of the Piltdown assemblage.

While these results had opened up new avenues of investigation, it was thought that a fairly substantial case had been made against the mandible and canine to warrant the release of a preliminary report. This was duly prepared in the closing weeks of October by Weiner, Oakley and Clark and published on 21 November, 1953. "From the evidence which we have obtained", their report concluded:

it is now clear that the distinguished palaeontologists and archaeologists who took part in the excavations at Piltdown were the victims of a most elaborate and carefully prepared hoax. Let it be said, however, in exoneration of those who have assumed the Piltdown fragments to belong to a single individual, or who, having examined the original specimens, either regarded the mandible and canine as those of a fossil ape or else assumed (tacitly or explicitly) that the problem was not capable of solution on the available evidence, that the faking of the mandible and canine is so extraordinarily skilful, and the perpetration of the hoax appears to have been so entirely unscrupulous and inexplicable, as to find no parallel in the history of palaeontological discovery. . .[32]

While registering some shock, the international scientific community was, on the whole, relieved by this appalling news. For as Weiner and his co-investigators had noted:

"Piltdown Man" (*Eoanthropus*) was actually a most awkward and perplexing element in the fossil record. . . being entirely out of conformity both in its strange mixture of morphological characters and its time sequence with all the palaeontological evidence of human evolution available from other parts of the world.[33]

THE FULL EXTENT OF THE FORGERY

When Weiner first presented his hypothesis to Le Gros Clark he had imagined that the forgery was limited only to the incongruous jaw and controversial canine. Suspecting that Dawson must have been in some way involved in this escapade, Weiner decided to go to Lewes, Dawson's home town,[34] to see what he could dig up, and it was through his enquiries there that Weiner was led to A P Pollard, Assistant Surveyor of the Sussex County Council. Pollard had been the executor of the estate of Harry Morris, a well-known local amateur archaeologist and passionate eolithophile. Although Pollard had ensured that a major portion of Morris' flint collections found an appropriate home in local museums, he had retained a large cabinet, which in addition to some notes written by Morris, also contained a collection of eoliths and the stone implement which had reportedly been recovered from the Piltdown gravels by Dawson. Pollard informed Weiner that Morris was under the impression that some deception had been carried out at Piltdown and was convinced that the flint tool, which had supposedly come from there was a forgery. Furthermore, Morris had apparently recorded these suspicions in his notes. Weiner was intrigued by this new intelligence and asked if he might have access to Morris' cabinet, but much to his horror, Pollard admitted that not having any particular interest in archaeology, he had, some years earlier, swapped the cabinet with a Frederick Wood of Ditchling for a collection of bird's eggs![35] Pollard also said that Wood had since died and that he had no idea of what had happened to Morris' cabinet.

A week later, in the company of Geoffrey Ainsworth Harrison (Professor of Physical Anthropology at Oxford), Weiner went in search of Morris' missing cabinet.[36] Contrary to his worst fears, Weiner and Harrison found that Wood's widow was still living in Ditchling, a village situated a few miles west of Lewes, and that she was still in possession of Morris' cabinet. The cabinet, Weiner later recalled:

[Consisted of] twelve drawers, nearly all filled with flints of various kinds, though mostly of Harry Morris's easily recognizable eoliths, everything neatly labelled. We started with the top drawer and worked our way down, our anxiety increasing as we proceeded. In the twelfth and last drawer of all was the "Piltdown" flint, and with it two documents. . .[37]

The Morris flint implement was similar both in shape, patina, and colouring to the "pre-Chellean" Piltdown flints. On the flint, in Morris' hand, was written the faded

The Morris Flint. It should be noted that Morris' writing has faded over the years and that this photograph was taken using an infra-red technique.

note: "Stained by C. Dawson with the intent to defraud (all). — H.M." On an accompanying card, Morris had written: "Stained with permanganate of potash and exchanged by D. for my most valued specimen! — H.M." In addition several other cryptic messages were found in this drawer:

> *Dawson's Farce:*
> Let not light see my black and deep desires.
> The eye wink at the hand; yet let that be
> Which the Eye fear when it is done — to see![38]

And another read:

> Judging from an overheard conversation there is every reason to suppose that the canine tooth found at P'Down was imported from France! [And yet another reads]... I challenge the S.K. Museum authorities to test the implements of the same portions as this stone which Dawson says were "excavated from the Pit!" They will be found to be white if hydrochlorate [sic] acid be applied. H.M. Truth will out.[39]

The allegations proved correct. The three palaeoliths found at Piltdown as well as the implement from Morris' cabinet did not pass the acid test. When dilute hydrochloric acid was applied to these implements their characteristic orange-brown stain dissolved, revealing a pale yellow-grey surface of patina below. Subsequent experiments carried out by Alfred Allinson Moss, a British Museum mineralogist, demonstrated that the colouring of these flints could be reproduced by dipping a patinated flint in a solution of ferric chloride and then exposing its wet surface to ammonia fumes — the resulting chemical interaction produced an orange-brown coat of ferric oxide. While it is impossible to know if this had been the same method employed by the forger, it was evident that the natural state of these flint implements had been deliberately camouflaged to compliment the color of the Piltdown "Brownies".

Using an X-ray spectographic method of analysis developed by E T Hall of the Clarendon Laboratory at Oxford, the Piltdown flints were subjected to further scrutiny. As expected, Hall's analyses showed that all the Piltdown flints were ferruginous. But much to everyone's surprise the implement (No E 606) discovered by Teilhard de Chardin on the afternoon of 2 June, 1912, contained appreciable traces of chromium. No trace of chromium could be found in any of the soil samples, or in any of the naturally occurring stones and flints collected at Piltdown. Why this particular specimen had been singled out for this special treatment is not immediately apparent, but as Weiner later suggested, it may well have had something to do with the fact that it was regarded at the time as a critical find — in that unlike the other palaeoliths that had been recovered from the site, E 606 had been found in situ, in a stratum lying directly above the horizon where both the occipital fragment and mandible were later found.[40]

From these findings the validity of the so-called bone implement was seriously questioned. As was noted when the specimen was first presented to the Geological Society in 1915 the various facets on the bone's surface were devoid of scratch marks. Much later, Breuil had questioned whether the object had been a tool, suggesting instead that perhaps it was a natural object which had been chewed on by a beaver.[41] Oakley too had viewed this object with some reservation in his 1949 book Man the Toolmaker.[42] While finding no evidence to support Breuil's thesis, Oakley's attempt to whittle either fresh or recently dried bone convinced him that the bone must have been shaped with an even-edged metal blade. The detection of iron stain on the facets of the cut surfaces confirmed Oakley's suspicion that this object was also a forgery.

With the collapse of the archaeological assemblage, attention shifted to the associated mammalian bones. These elements had been crucial in determining the case for the antiquity of the human remains. Had they too been carefully selected and planted with a view to establishing the authenticity of the Sussex skull and its associated eolithic industry?

As indicated by the results of the earlier fluorine tests (which were repeated),[43] the Piltdown fauna separated into two groups, as had been previously determined by regular palaeontological dating. All of the unquestioned Pliocene material (i.e. Elephas, Mastodon, and Rhinoceros) was seen to have a very high fluorine content (ranging from 1.9–3.1 per cent), whereas in the post-Pliocene group the fluorine levels were not only much less but also highly variable. Levels ranged anywhere from 0.1 to 1.5 per cent. Spectrographic analysis of the remains from these two groups yielded some provocative insights. Given Dawson's earlier penchant for bichromate, the discovery of chromium in some of these specimens was not unexpected, but the detection of gypsum (calcium sulphate) was a surprise. Soil analysis had indicated that the concentration of sulphate ions is unusually low in the Piltdown gravels, hence it is not possible to attribute the presence of gypsum in these specimens to a normal mineralization process. It therefore seemed that in addition to being dipped in bichromate, some of the Piltdown fauna had also been artificially treated, probably with a solution of acidic iron sulphate which, it was conjectured, had interacted with calcium phosphate still present in the bones — forming the gypsum deposits.[44] In addition to the hippopotamus molar reportedly found by Dawson in the spring of 1912, this compound was also detected in the beaver remains (a mandible and incisor) found in 1913 by Dawson and Woodhead. In the case of these specimens subsequent investigations left little doubt that they too were forgeries. Attached to one of the beaver molars was material believed to have been the residue of its original matrix: further examination of this material showed it to be composed of a "gummy" substance that had evidently been employed as an adherent for an exterior coat of gravel debris. While hippopotamus remains in Britain were not unknown, they were more often found in caves than open sites. The unexpectedly low fluorine content of the Piltdown hippopotamus molar was more in keeping with a limestone deposit, in which fluorination of bones and teeth is usually at a minimum. This was confirmed by the results obtained on specimens from the Ghar Dalam Cave in Malta. Using one of these Maltese molars it was shown that by first soaking the specimen in a solution of ferrous sulphate and then treating it with tannic acid, it was possible to reproduce the appearance and condition of the Piltdown hippopotamus tooth.[45]

As these results emerged it became apparent from soil analyses that the geochemical conditions at Piltdown were at variance with the enormous array of fossils found there. The distinct possibility that the Piltdown gravels were in reality unfossiliferous was borne out by Woodward's own failure to recover anything of interest after Dawson's death in 1916,[46] and further by the excavation at the site in 1950.[47] Combining these facts it now seemed highly probable that the entire mammalian assemblage had been imported. While it was impossible to identify with any degree of certainty the original source of these faunal remains, it was palpably clear it had not been Piltdown. In the case of the "Pleistocene" elements there was little doubt that they had been derived from local sites in either Kent or Sussex, but in the case of the "Pliocene" components there was good reason to suppose that they might have come from further afield: either East Anglia or quite possibly from abroad.

As will be recalled, one of the primitive elephant molars found at Piltdown had been assigned by Woodward to *Stegodon*, rather than to the Upper Pliocene form *Elephas meridionalis*. He believed this Piltdown elephant to be a new type which closely resembled those found in the Siwalik Hills by Falconer — a comparison later confirmed by a number of workers, including Hopwood, who assigned these Piltdown elephant molars to *Elephas planifrons*. In England, the only comparable set of elephant teeth known came from the Red Crag deposits of Suffolk, but while they resembled the Piltdown specimens in their reddish-brown colour, from a anatomical viewpoint the were not thought to be as primitive. This problem was soon resolved by radiometric analyses.

Simplified table of faunal analyses, based on Weiner *et al* (1955:262–265).

Material	F	N	G	I	C	U
Piltdown fauna						
Mastodon arvernensis molar	1.9	—	0	5	0	32
Elephas [Stegodon] molar	2.5	—	0	1	<0.05	203
Hippopotamus molar	<0.05	0.06	++	3	1.0	2
Cervus antler	1.5	—	0	3	0	4
Equus molar	0.67	1.2	+	4	0	<1
Rhinoceros premolar	2.0	—	0	6	0	32
Castor incisor	0.1	—	+	10	0	<1
Castor mandible	0.28	1.8	++	6	0	<1
Worked bone "implement"	1.3	—	0	2	0	<3

Material		F	N	G	I	C	U
Comparative fauna							
Bovine rib (Swanscombe)	[1]	2.0	<0.01	–	1	–	10
Rhinoceros (Somme)	[2]	1.2	–	–	<0.5	–	10
Hippopotamus (Malta)	[3]	0.1	0	–	<0.1	–	3
Elephas (Tunisia)	[4]	1.0	<0.01	–	0.15	–	194
Mastodon (Suffolk)	[5]	1.89	0.07	–	9	–	15
Elephas (Siwalik)	[6]	0.78	–	–	<0.1	–	49

Key: (F) fluorine, (N) nitrogen, (G) gypsum [calcium sulphate], (I) iron, (C) chromium. Note that these estimations are reported as percentages. (U) Uranium content, results expressed in counts per minute. [1] Middle Pleistocene, from the Barnfield pit where Marston made his discoveries; [2] Upper Pleistocene specimen from Menchecourt sand pit, near Abbeville, Somme river valley, France; [3] Lower Pleistocene specimen from Ghar Dalam Cave, Malta; [4] Lower Pleistocene site at Ichkeul, Tunisia; [5] Lower Pleistocene specimen from Red Crag, Suffolk; [6] Lower Pleistocene specimen, Siwalik Beds, NW India (see Table X, Weiner *et al* (1955:279–282).

For some years there had been a growing interest in the geo-chemical distribution of radioactive elements and their possible utilization as chronological indicators.[48] In developing this line of enquiry C F Davidson of the Geological Survey in London had been investigating the possibilities of employing uranium since there was evidence suggesting that it was widely distributed and that, under favourable conditions, this radioactive element accumulated in bone and other phosphatic material.[49] Convinced of its possible utility, Davidson had, on reading the 1953 Weiner, Oakley, and Le Gros Clark report, approached Oakley, suggesting that uranium measurements might yield additional information on the relative ages of the fossils.

Although "there were too many variables governing the absorption of uranium" to provide a reliable means of dating, the results Davidson and his workers obtained complimented those obtained using fluorine and nitrogen. But besides this, the uranium studies also provided incontrovertible evidence for the foreign origin of the Piltdown "planifrons" molars. The uranium content of these molar fragments was found to be extraordinarily high (in the region of 200 counts per minute), and far in excess of the counts obtained from any of the six specimens analysed from East Anglia. The average count obtained on these specimens was fifteen. Similarly, fossils tested from a dozen European and Indian Lower Pleistocene sites all failed to show a radioactivity in excess of 28 counts per minute. However, on extending the comparison to North Africa, a near perfect match was achieved with a molar tooth which had been recovered from fossiliferous site at Ichkeul, near Bizerta, Tunisia, and donated by the French palaeontologist Camille Arambourg (1885–1969).[50] Not only did this Tunisian specimen compare closely in its uranium content to that of Piltdown, but there was also close agreement in their respective fluorine contents.

Although the molars of *Mastodon* and *Rhinoceros* from Piltdown showed no evidence of artificial staining, it was inferred from their colour, degree of mineralization, and uranium content that they were, in all probability, imported from the Red Crag of East Anglia.[51]

These discoveries now led Weiner and Oakley to question the authenticity of the Piltdown braincase. Initially, since the fluorine and nitrogen content of the cranial fragments seemed consistent with their antiquity, it had been supposed that the hoax had been organized around a genuine discovery, and that the flint implements and various animal bones had been subsequently planted to develop a case for the great antiquity of these remains. Further investigation, using an X-ray crystallographic

Simplified table of the analyses of Piltdown hominoid bones, based on Weiner et al (1955:262,279).

Specimen	F	N	G	I	C	U
Piltdown I						
Parietal (left)	0.15	1.9	+	6	1.5	0.9
Frontal (left)	0.15	0.3	+	6	1.5	0.9
Temporal (left)	0.18	0.2	++	8	1.0	0.4
Parietal (right)	0.15	1.4	++	5	0	0.1
Occipital	0.14	0.3	+	6	0	0.8
Nasal bones	0.21	3.8	++	10	0	<0.1
Mandible	<0.10	3.9	0	3	0.30	<0.1
Piltdown II						
Frontal	0.11	1.1	++	10	0.05	<0.1
Occipital	<0.10	0.6	++	9	0.04	<0.1

Key: (F) fluorine; (N) Nitrogen; (G) gypsum (calcium sulphate); (I) iron; (C) chromium; (U) uranium. With the exception of the latter which is reported in counts per minute, all other results are reported as percentages.

The full extent of the forgery. Photograph of meeting at the Geological Society of London at Burlington House on 30 June 1954.

method, showed that the main mineral constituent of these bones, hydroxy-apatite, had been partially replaced by gypsum! Like some of the animal bones, these fragments had also been artificially stained to match the colour of the Piltdown gravels. The cranial fragments of Piltdown II were found to have undergone a similar treatment. In the light of these findings, and since the formerly associated "Upper Pleistocene" fauna had now been shown to be fraudulent, Oakley felt that the low fluorine content of the cranial fragments was more consistent with it being a post-Pleistocene specimen.

An earlier argument for the antiquity of the skull had been its "remarkable" thickness. In downgrading the age of the Piltdown skull further, Oakley was obliged to account for this feature in a modern cranium. While admitting that this was a comparatively rare feature in modern crania (and more often than not a pathological condition),[52] Oakley was able, without too much difficulty, to point to several crania in the collections of the British Museum (Natural History) whose general thickness closely matched that of Piltdown.[53]

On 30 June, 1954, the full extent of the Piltdown forgery was made public.[54] The Piltdown mandible was almost certainly that of a recent hominoid ape, most probably an orang-utan.[55] The canine tooth which had been reshaped and deliberately stained was also unquestionably that of an ape. The so-called turbinal bones were not identifiable as such, and in all probability were merely bone slivers from a non-human limb bone. The human cranial fragments along with several of the attendant animal bones had been treated with an iron solution to produce a colour matching that of the Piltdown gravels, as had the associated flint implements. The bone implement had been shaped by a steel knife and had also been stained. On the basis of radiometric, fluorimetric and other chemical and physical studies it was possible to dismiss all of the associated fauna at Piltdown as "plants", some of which were clearly of foreign origin. In fact there did not appear to be a single specimen in the entire collection that could be said to have genuinely originated from Piltdown.

THE MISSING LINK

Running parallel with the scientific investigations had been an inquiry aimed at identifying the mastermind behind this elaborate forgery. Weiner's inquiries in Lewes during mid August 1953 had led him to Morris' cabinet and his accusatory notes.

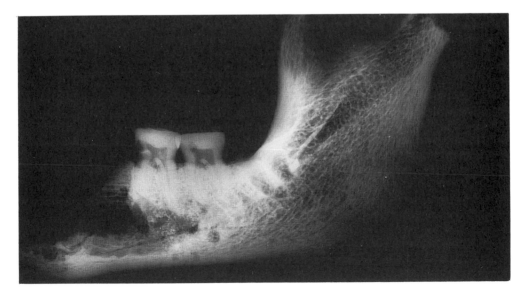

Fragmentary mandibular ramus reported as discovered in ferriginous river gravel at Piltdown in June 1912, linked with fragments of an exceptionally thick human cranium discovered in the same gravel and described as a "missing link". The radiograph exhibited here shows that the bone is unmineralised and that the roots of the molars are long as in all modern apes.

Weiner had also acquired copies of Dawson's correspondence with Woodward in an effort to gain a more complete picture of what transpired at Piltdown. Unfortunately Woodward did not make copies of his outgoing letters, and unable to locate any of these letters in Dawson's papers, Weiner had to make do with Dawson's surviving letters to Woodward, which while not uninformative, did not provide a complete picture of either Dawson's or Woodward's activities during the Piltdown period. In fact, Weiner was amazed to find how little was really known about the finds. The official publications were decidedly vague when it came to such details as to when, where, and by whom a particular discovery was made. Woodward's posthumous book on Piltdown, *The Earliest Englishman*, was found to be equally obscure on these critical details. Weiner was also surprised to learn that there was no official log or field notes to draw on; and neither Dawson nor Woodward, it appeared, had kept diaries that could be used to fill in missing pieces of information. But what he lacked in primary documentation was made up for by an abundance of informants, many of whom had been former associates of Dawson.

Contrary to Weiner's expectations, Dawson's correspondence made no mention of Morris. However, in a letter written to Woodward early in 1913 Dawson mentioned that not only were "two men in Lewes" very excited by the Piltdown eoliths and were busily making large collections of them, but also that he had become "a little disliked for venturing an opinion as to the possibilities of some of them".[56] It is conjectured that this might well be an indirect reference to Morris and his associate [Major] Reginald Adams Marriott (1857–1930), who at that time was Governor of Lewes Jail. For as Weiner later learned from Keith,[57] both Morris and Marriott were avid eolithophiles and, in 1913, Morris was indeed "turning sour because of scepticism", which could be interpreted to mean Dawson's criticism. According to Keith's recollections, Morris had been a bank clerk in Lewes where he lived in "two rooms — crammed to overflowing with eoliths and palaeoliths", and he could remember helping both Morris and Marriott in their eolithic cause. Given the apparent animus between Morris and Dawson, Weiner was quite naturally intrigued as to how the Lewes bank clerk had managed to persuade Dawson to part with the Piltdown palaeolith. The possibility that Morris had falsified his flint to incriminate Dawson was ruled out by the fact that the staining method employed on Morris' artifact matched that of the Piltdown palaeoliths. Furthermore Morris was under the impression that potassium permanganate had been used to colour the flints, but chemical analysis had failed to detect the presence of manganese on any of these artifacts, including Morris'. But just as intriguing was his "portentous accusation" that the Piltdown canine was also a forgery, namely that it had been "imported from France". Where did this suspicion originate? Was it mere conjecture? Morris' cryptic note suggested that he had gathered this from an over-heard conversation. But when and where did he hear this conversation? Morris' notes were undated. Was it possible that Morris' suspicions had been aroused by Marriott?

Weiner's investigations revealed some interesting connections. He soon discovered that Marriott had been a Major in the Royal Marine Artillery and had done a tour of duty in the Middle East. In addition to seeing action in Tunis during the Arabi Pasha's rebellion (for which he was subsequently decorated by Queen Victoria), Marriott was also responsible for organizing and commanding the Egyptian Camel Corps in the Nile expedition of 1885–86. Following his retirement, and prior to his appointment as Governor of Lewes Jail, Marriott had worked at the Admiralty in the Naval Intelligence Department. Besides being a staunch supporter of Morris' eoliths, he was also a keen amateur geologist with rather definite and somewhat unorthodox views, which among other things embraced the rejection of the Wealden dome hypothesis.[58]

Weiner also learned that Marriott had been closely associated with Martin Hinton, who had long harboured a rather jaundice view of the Piltdown remains. Another of Mariott's associates had been Alfred Kennard, who had also previously voiced his suspicions about the Sussex relics.

In the case of Kennard, his scepticism was confirmed by Samuel Hazzeldine Warren whose antagonistic views on the eoliths were well known. In 1946, two years after Woodward's death, Kennard had written to Warren saying:

> I have always thought it was a great pity that someone didn't speak out about Piltdown and the unsatisfactory nature of the evidence. But ASW [Arthur Smith Woodward] was an authority and who were you or I to challenge his conclusions, backed as they would be by the Nat. Hist. Officials. I know Hinton was not satisfied but he had his job to think over...[59]

Since Kennard was no longer around to be questioned, Weiner was unable to pursue the Marriott connection with him. Hinton, however, was living in retirement near Bristol. In fact when the forgery was first announced in November 1953, Hinton had rushed off a letter to *The Times* which led to an interesting exchange between him and Le Gros Clark. In his letter he claimed that:

> Had the investigators been permitted to handle the actual specimens, I think the spurious nature of the jaw would have been detected long ago. Apart from the time when the actual specimens were exhibited in a showcase in the Geological Gallery I got within handling distance only on one occasion, and then I did not handle them. *Eoanthropus* is a result of departing from one of the great principles of palaeontology; each specimen or fragment must be regarded as a separate document and have its characters read. Here that principle was abandoned... In 1912 I was a volunteer in the Geological and Zoological Departments. I did not see the Piltdown material until the reading of Smith Woodward's paper at the Geological Society. As soon as I saw the jaw, and later the canine tooth, I knew that had they come into my hands for description they would have been referred without hesitation to the chimpanzee which was already known to occur in some of the Pleistocene deposits of Europe. I later found that my future chief, Oldfield Thomas... was of the same opinion.[60]

Le Gros Clark, took exception to both the tone and implication of this letter, and wrote to Hinton accordingly. As he informed the grumpy mammalogist, Woodward had allowed free access to the originals. In fact he had himself viewed the specimens in 1916 when he was a postgraduate student at St Thomas' Hospital in London.[61] Although Le Gros Clark's letter did not change Hinton's view of Woodward, it did bring forth some additional information which reinforced Weiner's conviction that Kennard had, in all probability, been privy to Marriott's views on the subject:

> Of course [Hinton replied], I had not the slightest intention of attributing any personal reluctance to Smith Woodward, I have no doubt he would show the specimens to anyone interested quite freely... [But he added]... It is a pity that S.W. was so secretive before his paper was read. Had he talked to Old Thomas or even to me I do not think Eoanthropus would have been invented. With regard to the faker of the jaw and canine tooth I do not know who he was; but suspect he was a local man who thought it very amusing to pull Dawson's leg. Kennard (who died a little time ago) always said he knew who had done it. But he never mentioned names. The thing or rather 2 things I am quite certain of is that neither Dawson or Kennard were guilty. Neither possessed the inclination to do such a thing or the necessary knowledge.[62]

Shortly after this exchange, Weiner's theory regarding the Marriott-Kennard connection, was challenged by the testimony of a Captain Guy St Barbe who was brought to Weiner's attention by Wilfred Edwards (1890–1956), then Keeper of Geology at the British Museum (Natural History). "By an extraordinary coincidence", Edwards wrote to Weiner, "a housekeeper-companion who lives with us at home was visiting friends near St Albans and met there a Capt. G. St Barbe who once lived in Sussex [and who reportedly]. . . knew a lot about [the Piltdown affair]. . . and would like to unburden himself to somebody!" St Barbe unburdened himself to Weiner and Geoffrey Harrison.

Prior to moving to Hertfordshire, St Barbe had lived at Coombe Place in Uckfield and knew Dawson quite well — they were members of the same country club and often had a round of golf together. He was, however, more friendly with Marriott than Dawson and knew nothing of Morris. According to St. Barbe he had become suspicious of Dawson when, one day (circa 1913) he found the solicitor in his chambers surrounded by dishes and chemicals. Dawson was staining bones.[63] He later discussed this with Marriott and they came to the conclusion that Dawson was "salting the mine". But, "for the sake of Dawson's wife" they decided to say nothing and "agreed to keep the thing to themselves". Later, after Dawson's death, St Barbe confessed he had confided his story to Hinton with whom he was very friendly. He was apparently also on friendly terms with Kennard, but reportedly told him nothing. While acknowledging that Hinton may have told Kennard, St Barbe felt that he was more likely to remain quiet, particularly as he had been asked to keep the story private, and he thought Hinton was the sort of man to do so.[64] St Barbe also told Weiner and Harrison that he was convinced Dawson was being blackmailed. But by whom? St Barbe did not elaborate. Was it possible Dawson had been found out by another whose silence was being bought? It was an unexpected twist, but one that was for the time being grounded only in gossip.

During the course of Weiner's subsequent interview with Hinton early in 1954, it became increasingly apparent that while the former Keeper of Zoology may have learned of Dawson's experiments from St Barbe (though this was never confirmed), it was clear that besides thinking Dawson incapable of perpetrating the fraud, he was also convinced that the Piltdown materials were phoney and had been imported — probably from Montpellier. This proposition was of particular interest to Weiner for two reasons. First, the full extent of the forgery was only now becoming apparent and nothing was known publicly of these findings. And second, in pointing to France as a possible source, Hinton appeared to be echoing Morris' original claim. Had perhaps Morris overheard Hinton? Or had Morris' "overheard conversation" been his way of referring to the Marriott-St Barbe theory? Was there a common thread linking Hinton with Morris? Hinton was not forthcoming. He later claimed that his suggestion to Weiner that Montpellier might be the source was "a pure spur of the moment guess".[65]

The possibility of a French connection at Piltdown was further enhanced by information volunteered by Robert Essex, a biology schoolmaster who had taught at Uckfield Grammar School during the Piltdown period. Nearly stone deaf and wearing an inefficient hearing-aid, Essex had surfaced at the British Museum (Natural History) early in January 1954 anxious to tell his story. The interview was conducted by Oakley and Edwards. "It was a difficult and not a very satisfactory [one]", Edwards later informed Weiner:

> Most of his supposed evidence was elaborate surmise; he was pretty hopeless on dates and it was not clear whether he had worked out his theories since the Piltdown exposure of last November or how much he had suspected forty years ago. Briefly he is convinced that Teilhard de Chardin was the hoaxer and he did not think anyone else was involved.[66]

Essex believed Dawson had been an innocent victim, duped by a conniving French cleric. While the details of Essex's seemingly preposterous story did not hold together, Weiner did not dismiss completely the possibility of Teilhard's involvement. The *Stegodon* molar, the E 606 palaeolith, and the canine tooth, all found by him, had been shown to be forgeries! It was, of course, quite possible that he, like Dawson, had been an innocent victim. But everyone concerned with these investigations, including Weiner, was puzzled by Teilhard's attitude. In spite of repeated attempts by Oakley to get answers to specific questions, the Frenchman's replies had been evasive as well as contradictory on a number of details. Indeed at one point he even denied being a close friend of Dawson.[67] Was he simply embarrassed by the whole affair? It was possible, Le Gros Clark thought, but:

> If he knows something about the perpetrator (but was not himself implicated) surely he could say so — or at any rate make clear that he is not able to divulge matters which he regards as confidential? To say that he only knew Dawson slightly when he had so many contacts with him — helped him in his excavations — stopped in his house, seems rather ridiculous. On the other hand, I cannot imagine him ultimately planning the forgery. . .[68]

Unable to advance the case against Teilhard, Weiner's attention shifted back to Marriott and Morris. Was it possible that Marriott had been involved? Weiner's investigations along this line led nowhere. While it was possible that Marriott may have been the source of the radioactive elephant molars, Weiner could find no evidence to corroborate this nor could he prove that Marriott had had the necessary skills to fabricate the elaborate forgery at Piltdown. The same went for Morris, and St Barbe's unsolicited testimony seemed to vindicate both, while providing, it seemed, the probable source of Morris' charges against Dawson. Had St Barbe told Marriott who had taken Morris into his confidence, and who, in turn, had made it his business to check the story by securing one of Dawson's spurious flint implements? Whether it had been obtained directly from Dawson, as Morris' note seems to suggest, or whether he had secured it from some other source, such as Lankester or one Dawson's other colleagues, Weiner was unable to determine; but whatever the source had been, the undeniable fact was that the Piltdown flints were forgeries and that there now seemed to be every reason to suppose that they had been concocted by Dawson.

Since beginning his inquiries, Weiner had accumulated a wealth of information on the Sussex solicitor, a good deal of it damaging. Some of it was no more than malicious gossip, but there were other stories which held up to closer scrutiny and cast Dawson in a somewhat different light than his obituaries had portrayed him. There were two stories in particular which attracted Weiner's attention. The first was the "Castle Lodge incident". Apparently in 1903, the Sussex Archaeological Society received word that the "Lodge", which they had used since 1885, located in the ground's of Lewes Castle, had been sold and they were told that they would have to find new quarters. This took the Society's Council completely by surprise, since it had been understood that if and when the property was ever offered for sale they would have the first option on it. To make matters worse it was learned that the Lodge had been acquired by a Society member, namely, Dawson. Evidently, Dawson had made his bid for Castle Lodge on the Society's stationery and the vendor, assuming that the solicitor was acting in their interest, had proceeded with the transaction. While Dawson's defenders dispute the claim that he had deliberately set out to mislead the vendor and "hoodwink" the Society, it appears that Weiner was persuaded otherwise. Equally disturbing to Weiner was the criticism levelled at Dawson's two-volume work, the *History of Hastings Castle*. Published in 1910, this imposing work was received with mixed reviews. Some believed it was destined to become the standard work, while others were less than complimentary. There were some, in fact, in particular Louis F Salzman (1878–1971), a medieval historian and Council member of the Sussex Archaeological Society, who, Weiner reported, considered the work to be "less a product of genuine scholarship than of extensive plagiarism".[69] Salzman's estimation of Dawson's *History* was later endorsed by J Mainwaring Baines who, in 1954, was Curator of the Hastings Museum. In Baines' opinion, well over half of Dawson's text had been "copied unblushingly" from an old manuscript written by the antiquarian William Herbert who had carried out excavations at Hastings Castle in 1824.[70] While later acknowledging that these and similar stories both distorted and obscured Dawson's stature as a collector and amateur scientist, Weiner was cognisant that they also lent credibility to the developing case against the Sussex solicitor.

But what kind of man was Dawson? Was he an underhanded scoundrel as these stories suggested? Although enjoying the status and privileges that went with being a successful country solicitor, what sustained him and gave motive to his daily journey from his home in Lewes to his chambers in Uckfield was not a skillfully worded codicil but rather an unremitting passion he had nurtured since childhood for palaeontology and geology. As a schoolboy at the Royal Academy in Gosport, his free hours had been spent studying the Hampshire countryside, and when at home he could be found scouring the Chalk formations for fossils around St Leonards, near Hastings, where his father, a barrister had an elegant house in Warrior Square. But to look upon Dawson as a mere dilettante, whose later eminence had been nothing more than a stroke of good fortune, is far from the truth. Through an early relationship with Samuel Beckles F.R.S. (d.1896), a distinguished geologist who had been a neighbour, Dawson had served an informal apprenticeship in Wealden geology. It had been under Beckles' critical and watchful eye that the young Dawson had assembled and catalogued a sizeable and valuable collection of fossil reptiles which was eventually, in 1884, donated to the British Museum (Natural History). In recognition of his acumen, the Museum installed him as an honorary collector, and shortly thereafter he was made a fellow of the Geological Society.

Between this time and the years immediately preceding the events at Piltdown, Dawson continued to add specimens to his cabinet at the Museum, including three new species of iguanodon, one of which the palaeontologist Richard Lydekker (1849–1915) named after him. He had also been responsible for finding, in 1891, after a long and persistent search, the minute teeth of two hitherto unknown Wealden mammals, namely *Plagiaulax* and *Dipriodon* (later described by Woodward).[71] Prior to this, these primitive Mesozoic mammals had only been found in North America, where they had first been described by the Othniel Charles Marsh (1831–99). Given the extent of the Cretaceous formations in south-east England, Dawson had correctly anticipated their presence in these geological strata near Hastings. All of this work received high praise, and not only from Woodward.

In light of his early attraction to geology and palaeontology it is surprising that Dawson did not go onto university to finish his education as his two brothers did.[72] Instead, on leaving school in 1880, for reasons which are no longer known, he followed his father into the legal profession, and was articled to F A Langhams, a firm of solicitors in Hastings. Following the completion of his legal training in 1890, Dawson moved to the small rural town of Uckfield, some eight miles north of Lewes, where he applied himself to the task of building his professional career. In addition to a deepening involvement in local civic affairs, which eventually led to his appointment as Town Clerk, he had also managed by the end of the decade, to land the lucrative Stewardships of several large estates (including Barkham Manor) in the surrounding district. In spite of his increasing public and professional responsibilities, Dawson appears to have remained loyal to his scientific interests. Yet it was not until 1905, the year that he went into partnership with Ernest Hart, and of his marriage to Hélène Postlethwaite (1859-1917), a widow (with two grown children) from Lewes, that Dawson finally found himself in a position to rearrange his priorities and to devote a greater part of his time and energies to the pursuit of his interests and the continuing expansion of his cabinet at the Museum.

It was difficult to imagine Dawson as the forger, but try as he may, Weiner was unable to disentangle Dawson from the suspicious series of events that had transpired at Piltdown. From beginning to end, Dawson had been a pivotal figure. To suppose that he had been an innocent dupe simply did not tie in with the available evidence. Such a scenario required that his activities coincide simultaneously with those of an unknown perpetrator. Had Dawson's activities been confined merely to the Barkham Manor site then such a proposition, while stretching the imagination, was not inconceivable; but to suppose that this had been repeated at Sheffield Park, where the remains of Piltdown II had been reportedly recovered, was difficult to accept. This problem was further complicated by the cranial fragments Dawson had supposedly found in July 1913 at Barcombe Mills, a site located a few miles south of Piltdown. Although Dawson reported this discovery to Woodward, claiming that the skull might well be "a descendant of Eoanthropus",[73] for some inexplicable reason, the material was ignored. Later, after Dawson's death it was retrieved and formally taken into the collections of the British Museum (Natural History), where it continued to languish in obscurity until 1949, when it was examined by the South African palaeontologist Robert Broom (1866–1951).[74] Broom thought that Dawson's hunch had been correct.[75] Later, however, the anatomist – anthropologist Ashley Montagu (then affiliated with Rutgers University, New Jersey), who had assisted Oakley in downgrading Galley Hill, came to quite a different conclusion. He felt the remains represented more than one individual and that they were of a "neanthropic type" – though he did agree with the idea that they might be of "Upper Pleistocene age".[76] The Barcombe Mills material worked against the idea of Dawson having been an innocent victim; all of these fragments had been treated in the same fashion as the material from Barkham Manor and Sheffield Park. For Weiner this was just too much of a coincidence to ignore.

Simplified table of the analyses of the Barcombe Mills material, based on Table III and X, in Weiner et al (1955: 262 and 279).

Specimen	F	N	G	I	C	U
BARCOMBE MILLS MATERIAL						
Frontal	0.07	2.4	++	11	0	0.3
Parietal	0.10	0.3	+	−	0	0.7
Zygoma	0.04	1.8	++	−	0	−

Key: (F) fluorine, (N) nitrogen, (G) gypsum (calcium sulphate), (I) iron, (C) chromium, and (U) uranium. With the exception of the latter which is reported in counts per minute, the remainder are percentages.

There was, of course, the distinct possibility that Dawson had been an unwilling accessory to the crime, but Weiner could find no trail, "except conjecture, leading to a possible blackmailer".[77] There was also a possibility that the forgery had been conceived by another individual and that Dawson had been a willing co-conspirator. Although Weiner flirted briefly with this idea, it was ultimately rejected in the

Kenneth Oakley. (From an article in Picture Post, *28 February 1953. Courtesy of Hulton-Deutsch)*

absence of any supporting evidence. Was it possible that Woodward had been involved? Weiner had considered the prospect, but as he soon discovered, what evidence there was pointed to his innocence rather than his guilt.[78] The fact that Woodward kept no copies of his letters to Dawson was not particularly significant since this does not seem to have been a regular practice of his. With few exceptions, it was his custom to simply record on a received letter the date of his reply, which he occasionally embellished with a note indicating his reponse to a specific question.[79] Furthermore, he does not seem to have kept a personal diary or log of his daily activities at the Museum, but again this was not unusual. Weiner, did however, find it rather strange that Woodward had left no record of his activities at Piltdown. Whether these had been removed at the time of his retirement and then lost, he was unable to determine. Was this significant? Although in retrospect this all seemed to support the view of some of Weiner's informants, such as Martin Hinton, that Woodward was secretive (particularly about Piltdown), this charge did not stand up to investigation. In Hinton's case there is no question that he had not been consulted, but this is hardly surprising considering his junior status at the Museum in 1912. Also, while there is little question that following the discovery of the jaw in the summer of 1912, Woodward went to some lengths to keep things as quiet as possible, this action was justifiable. In addition to wishing to protect the site from possible vandalism, it appears that Woodward was also anxious to avoid a premature disclosure and to contain speculation until he had time to consider the significance of the finds and to consult with his own circle of trusted colleagues. Following the unveiling, however, it is abundantly clear that Woodward was far more open, and had allowed free access to the originals, contrary to Hinton's later charge.[80]

Weiner continued to be troubled by the palpable lack of detail in any of the published reports about when and how many of the discoveries were made. But how much importance should be attached to this? Is it possible to construe from this a deliberate attempt to hide or obscure facts? Superficially it might appear so, but overall this opinion is difficult to defend. Take for instance the case of the earlier finds made by Dawson prior to the summer of 1912. While in retrospect their precise history is admittedly vague, at the time Dawson's account of them was deemed more than adequate — in fact, if anything he was praised for his tenacity. In recounting his story to the Geological Society, Dawson indicated how he first became interested in the gravel bed at Barkham Manor, followed by the discovery of the human skull (which was shattered by a labourer's pick axe) some four years earlier, and his subsequent attempts to recover these fragments which culminated in the discovery of a second fragment in the autumn of 1911. This chronology can hardly be considered an attempt to bury the finds in obscurity. There have been many discoveries before and since Piltdown, that are just as vague in the reporting of such details. Thus, while the reports of Dawson and Woodward leave much to be desired, their imprecision is considered to be neither exceptional nor overtly misleading.

Similarly Weiner found the manner in which the gravel bed was investigated after Woodward became involved disconcerting. While it is evident from the report of the work conducted at the site during the summer of 1913 (and after), that it had been performed in systematic fashion, the method employed, though guaranteeing the screening of all the excavated material, was clearly not designed with a view to reconstructing an accurate picture of the site and the spatial distribution of finds. As a consequence it is impossible to know from the available records, what the original location of any of the finds (made during the summer of 1913 on) had been. The relevance of this apparent lack of sophistication is open to debate. While it is possible to find reports of excavations from the same period that are seemingly more methodical in their approach, there are just as many that are far worse. Thus, in spite of all its shortcomings, it is not possible to say with any conviction that this excavation contravened acceptable practices of the time. But in recognizing this, it is also apparent that the methods employed at Piltdown undoubtedly enhanced the implementation of the forgery, and there is no escaping the fact that Woodward, if not responsible, at least condoned the method of excavation at Piltdown. Was there still a possibility that he had been a party to this deception?

It was quite evident from Dawson's correspondence that Woodward first learned of the Sussex skull in February 1912 and that it was not until late May that he finally had an opportunity to examine the finds. A week or so later he is known to have made his first visit to the site. Had Woodward had prior knowledge of either the skull or the site, there would have been no reason for these letters. But how reliable are these letters as evidence? It is possible that if Woodward and Dawson were in league together these letters were a mere subterfuge, contrived to supply Woodward with an alibi. But this is highly unlikely. In the first place why go to such elaborate lengths to establish an alibi that could quite easily have been achieved by laying a paper trail at the Museum? And secondly, while these letters might provide substance to Woodward's lack of involvement until June 1912, they do little to assist Dawson's case. Had they been co-conspirators, surely these letters would not have existed. While it is well nigh impossible (using this evidence) to construe Woodward's prior involvement, there is also no evidence to support the notion that he might have been persuaded to join in after 2 June 1912. In fact Dawson's letters, if admitted as evidence, absolve Woodward completely from any responsibility in the forgery, as does the "evidence" of the chromate issue. Dawson had dipped the cranial fragments

"Piltdown Man", the Piltdown village pub. After the forgery was exposed the landlord considered re-using its former name, "The Lamb".

he had recovered from the pit before 1912 in a bichromate solution to "harden" them, and later, this practice ceased (though not completely as the results of chemical analysis indicate). It is suggested that this apparent switch in technique might well reflect Woodward's disapproval of bichromate treatment, for as is evident from his later writings on the subject, he thought that Dawson had abandoned this practice. The fact that the colour of the earlier specimens approximated those found after Dawson had dispensed with his "hardening" technique was presumably enough to convince him that the matter did not warrant mentioning in the first report. Had Woodward been involved, what reason would there have been to change or modify this procedure? Furthermore, why would he later divulge this important piece of information about Dawson's early use of bichromate, unless he believed it was of little or no significance. Then there is Woodward's continuing obsession with the Piltdown gravels, long after the pit became sterile in 1915. Why would he continue this search so extensively if he knew the truth of the matter?

Presuming that Dawson had been the instigator, what grounds, if any, were there for supposing that Woodward could have been persuaded to join forces with the solicitor in the perpetration of this forgery after 2 June 1912? In responding to this question it is necessary first to consider Woodward's professional standing at the time and then to weigh this against the possible benefits and risks involved. There is little question that Woodward was at the peak of his career. In the preceding thirty years at the Museum he had produced a mountain of work which ranged over a wide area of palaeontology — though his international reputation was grounded largely in his work on Palaeozoic and Mesozoic fish. Besides his Keepership at the Museum, he had received significant outside recognition for his contributions to science that included the prestigous Wollaston Fund (1889) and Lyell Medal (1896) of the Geological Society, honorary doctorates from the University of Glasgow (1900) and St Andrews (1911), and a Fellowship of the Royal Society (1901). Precisely where his future ambitions lay in 1912 are difficult to determine. There does, however, appear to be some truth in the rumour that he hoped one day to be Director of the British Museum (Natural History).[81] Could such an ambition have provided sufficient motive to pursue such a dangerous course of action? The advantages of being associated with an important discovery are just as obvious as are the disadvantages of being linked with a forgery, and it seems more realistic to suggest that the risks attached to the latter venture would have been simply too great to have made it worthwhile for him. The former possibility is a completely different matter altogether. Being intimately associated with a major discovery, even one that was as controversial as that of Piltdown, has clear advantages. This type of opportunity was rare and was one that Woodward would undoubtedly have had great difficulty in ignoring. It is easy to see how Woodward's ambitions might have clouded his judgement and cause him to compromise his standards of thoroughness for which he had hitherto been renowned.[82]

Thus, while there is much in Woodward's subsequent actions at Piltdown which cast him in an unfavourable light, these shadows of suspicion are seen to evaporate on closer scrutiny. If he is guilty of anything it is of negligence; had he insisted on the jaw being analysed along with the cranial fragments, the entire affair may never have seen the light of day.

In bringing forward his case against Dawson, Weiner was also acutely aware of the fact that the weight of the circumstantial evidence he had mustered was insufficient to "prove beyond all reasonable doubt" that the Sussex solicitor had been solely responsible for the deception perpetrated at Piltdown. Weiner had to confess that, remote as it seemed, it was not inconceivable that Dawson "might have been implicated in a joke, perhaps not even of his own, which went too far".[83]

During the next thirty years both Weiner and Oakley watched, with undiminished interest, attempts by others to resolve the issue of the forger's identity. Although rumour has it that both Weiner and Oakley solved the mystery and decided to take it with them to the grave, this is not borne out by their surviving papers. It is evident that both had seen some of the evidence to be presented here, but had either failed to recognize its significance, or had decided against pursuing it.[84] But before this evidence can be presented it is necessary to first examine other known competing theories.

7 Black knights and arrant knaves

"If there's no meaning in it", said the King, "that saves a world of trouble, you know, as we needn't try to find any. And yet I don't know," he went on ... "I seem to see some meaning in them, after all."[1]

THE PIT AND THE PENDULUM

Although Joseph Weiner's investigations had cast a deepening shadow of suspicion over Charles Dawson, they did not, as he acknowledged, completely erase the possibility that Dawson had been duped by an unscrupulous individual. The idea was not without its attractions, but was it feasible? And perhaps more important, could such a proposition be defended? Weiner had his doubts.

While it was possible to identify among Dawson's (as well as Woodward's) associates several individuals who had both the necessary skills and resources required to perpetrate the forgery, on closer scrutiny, most, if not all of them, fell short of fitting the bill when it came to demonstrating an early and continuing association with the solicitor. This latter point is crucial, and one that time and again has been either overlooked or played down by many Piltdownian sleuths, for as Weiner correctly notes, the entire fabric of the forgery hinged on Dawson's discovery and growing committment to the potential importance of the gravel bed at Barkham Manor. Hence, to support the proposition that Dawson had been the victim of an "unknown manipulator", requires, Weiner argues, that this individual should not only to have an intimate and detailed knowledge of the solicitor's interests and affairs (plus a complete grasp of the potentialities of both the Piltdown sites), but also an uncanny "acquaintance" with his movements and inquiries.[2] But presuming that such an individual did exist, is it reasonable to suppose that this shadowy figure, however well-informed he may have been, would have been capable of implementing this elaborate and protracted forgery without inside assistance?

CHRONOLOGICAL SUMMARY OF EVENTS

Prior to May 1912

1899 (?) Dawson discovered gravel pit. Circa 1908 "coconut" incident. Coinciding with this was Dawson's first meeting with Teilhard de Chardin. Between 1908 and May 1912 (assisted on occasions by Woodhead) Dawson reportedly recovered from the Piltdown pit several pieces of a shattered human cranium, plus molar fragments of ancient hippopotamus and elephants; and a number of palaeoliths and eoliths.

Summer 1912

2 June: Dawson found "cranial fragment" while Teilhard reportedly found Palaeolith E 606 and (fragment) elephant molar.
June–August: Sometime, probably in late June, the important jaw was found. During this period and on into August several more cranial fragments were recovered by Dawson and Woodward, along with a variety of mammalian bones, plus an additional assembly of archaeological materials.

Summer–Autumn 1913

3 July: Dawson found human frontal bone at (?) Barcombe Mills. Early in August (circa 10th), the nasal bones and turbinals were found at Piltdown site. Teilhard recovered the canine tooth on 30 August. In mid October Dawson and Woodhead found lower jaw of beaver and associated fragments. In addition to the above, several other finds were made which included more flint implements and molar fragments of several mammalian fossils.

Summer 1914

Sometime during July Davidson Black found a rhinoceros molar. This was followed by Woodward's discovery of a mastodon molar. A bone implement (in two pieces) was recovered by Dawson and Woodward.

1915–1917

On 9 January 1915: Dawson informed Woodward that he had found an eoanthropine frontal bone at (?) Sheffield Park site. Later, on 30 July 1915, Dawson reported the discovery of a molar tooth belonging to the same "new" eoanthropine series. On 10 August 1916 Dawson's death announced. Woodward later presented the Sheffield Park material to the Geological Society (February 1917) as evidence for a second *Eoanthropus*.

The Barkham Manor (Piltdown I) site: a view of the Barkham estate (circa 1912) from vantage point located due east of the manor house (visible in the distance).

Today the Piltdown gravel pit is nothing more than a shallow depression in the ground. The area where most of the remains were found is marked by a weathered monolith of Yorkshire stone which stands in a narrow strip of ground running parallel to the drive and a thick hedge, some several hundred yards from the Tudor style Victorian Manor House.[3] Apart from the absence of the tall fir trees lining the drive to Barkham Manor (and a low discontinuous hedge on its eastern side), all is much as it was when Dawson and Woodward worked there. Now, as then, the Manor House

The "Piltdown" gravel pit. This photograph is believed to have been taken during the winter of 1913. Note proximity to the manor house and associated farm cottage in the background.

has an uninterrupted view of the site. To gain access to it without being seen either a relatively exposed easterly approach must be taken (across open ploughed fields), visible only from the east wing of the Manor, or the approach from the north-west, where the view is obscured by a tall continuous hedge and trees. Of the two, the latter is clearly the most satisfactory. Having gained access to the pit by either of these routes, the chances of our shadowy figure going undetected, particularly during the day, are remote; and at night, while the risk of detection would be diminished, there would be other obvious difficulties. Besides this, as in any small rural community, strangers are quickly spotted and treated with suspicion. Piltdown is no exception. Indeed, when Woodward and Teilhard de Chardin visited Barkham Manor with Dawson on Saturday, 2 June, 1912, they did not go unnoticed. This unfamiliar entourage, armed with picks and shovels, set tongues wagging, and had mobilized the local constabulary, as Woodward recalled:

> [A]nd on the following Monday morning the local constable appeared at Mr. Dawson's office in Uckfield (where he was Clerk to the Magistrates), stating that he had a report to make. Mr. Dawson, as usual in such cases, admitted the constable, and was surprised to learn from him that "three toffs, two of them from London, had been digging like mad in the gravel at Barkham, and nobody could make out what they were up to". Mr. Dawson's embarrassment may be imagined, but he remained calm and quietly explained to the constable that there were flints in the neighbourhood, and perhaps the men he reported were merely harmless seekers of these flints. He then showed some of the flints to the constable, explained their interest, and asked him to look out and report on any that he might find in certain parts of his beat.[4]

A view looking down the drive (circa 1912–13). Note hedges on both sides of the drive. The individuals depicted in this photograph (left to right): "Venus" Hargreaves, Arthur Smith Woodward (with the goose "Chipper"), Charles Dawson, and Robert Kenward Snr. (tenant of Barkham Manor) – the dog has not been identified!

Another view looking down Barkham Manor drive, circa 1930, with Woodward in the foreground. This photograph is believed to have been taken by Lady Woodward or her daughter Mrs Margaret Hodgson.

Working at the pit. This photograph (circa 1913), besides revealing a general impression of the site, also provides some information on apparatus used, note wheelbarrow in the background and pickaxe in right foreground. In addition to the goose "Chipper", the individuals depicted (from left to right) are: Hargreaves, Woodward and Dawson.

Furthermore, it is evident, particularly after the summer of 1912, that the task of making an unauthorised visit to the pit would have been frustrated by the watchful eyes of the Manor's tenant Robert Kenward, who as Dawson reported to Woodward early in 1913, was dutifully standing guard and "hoofing off enthusiasts from his farm". His daughter Mabel Kenward (1885–1978) was, Dawson added, "especially pugnacious against intruders".[5]

The defence for the idea that the forger had been an "outsider", is further complicated by other factors. This individual would, as already mentioned, have had to have been privy to Dawson's initial movements at Piltdown, which would have to have been carefully synchronized with the normal activities surrounding this pit prior to it be taken over as a "protected" archaeological site. Without such knowledge, planted material could have been unwittingly removed along with the gravel that was being exploited as road metal. Later this knowledge would need to be extended to encompass Woodward's activities at the pit; with his subsequent involvement the timing of the plants and discoveries would have become even more critical. In order not to arouse his suspicions and to safeguard his continuing interest it was imperative that Woodward should at least witness some of the discoveries. To have him make a number of discoveries would have enhanced this cause. Thus, in addition to the need

This particular photograph shows Dawson and Woodward busily sieving excavated material, while Hargreaves looks on. Photograph evidently taken by Leon Williams (see text) during the summer of 1913. It appears from Dawson's shirt that it was not taken on the same day as the photograph opposite.

of having advance information as to when Dawson and Woodward would be together at the site, it would be necessary to know precisely where at the site they intended to focus their attention. For without such intelligence it would be very easy to plant material incorrectly in a soil heap that had already been examined.

The general strategy employed at these diggings involved the removal of an assigned section of gravel (usually several days in advance of a scheduled visit) by a hired labourer, who then spread out the removed earth to be "washed and dried", before subsequent sieving operations. While these preliminary preparations would undoubtedly have made it much easier to plant material, there would still have been the problem of identifying the correct patch of earth in which to leave the plant — without being detected. While many of the items found at the site had been recovered by sieving "fresh" gravel treated in the manner described, it appears that a number of critical finds, such as the jaw, had been found *in situ*, and contrary to popular belief, to plant such a find and have it appear genuine, is not an easy task — particularly when dealing with seasoned field workers.[6] This would seem to indicate that either the circumstances of these *in situ* finds had been so plausible and so well disguised that they would pass scientific scrutiny, or that the finds had not been honestly reported . . .

Left: William Ruskin Butterfield, from 1909 to mid 1930s, Librarian of Hastings Public Museum and Library, familiar, in this capacity, with Charles Dawson and Lewis Abbott. Right: Arthur Conan Doyle – "The Crowborough Kid". A postcard of Conan Doyle's portrait sent to Keith (along with an invitation to dinner) following their brief battle over spiritualism in the columns of the Morning Post *in 1925. On the rear of the postcard Conan Doyle had written "Great 3rd round exhibition contest between the Crowborough Kid and Battling Arty of Lincolns Inn Fields. Admission 2d. Referee and Time Keeper H.G. Gwynne". (Library, Royal College of Surgeons, London)*

Putting aside the question of Dawson's complicity in the affair and the technical problems attending the planting of the materials, is it still possible to identify among Dawson's many associates anyone who might not only have been privy to the solicitor's activities at Piltdown, but who besides being well-equipped and motivated was also sufficiently disengaged from Dawson to have acted independently in the manner proposed? There are a several who warrant consideration as suspects. Most of them, but not all, were investigated by Weiner. Although many of them were ultimately cleared of suspicion following further inquiry (and there is no new evidence to justify their resurrection), two continued to attract Weiner's suspicions, but, in spite of his continuing efforts he was unable to build a substantial case against either of them. They were William James Lewis Abbott and Pierre Teilhard de Chardin. Besides these individuals, several additional suspects were suggested by other workers: William Ruskin Butterfield (1872–1935), [Sir] Arthur Conan Doyle (1859–1930), Martin Hinton, [Sir] Grafton Elliot Smith, William J Sollas, and Samuel Allinson Woodhead. While enjoying some popularity at the time of their announcement, few of these cases have stood up to scrutiny. Some are little more than embroidered gossip, but others go beyond mere rumour. All, however, are seen to share a common theme, that the forgery was an exercise in malice, aimed either at Woodward or Dawson.

BUTTERFIELD AND DOYLE

In Guy van Esbroeck's book *Pleine Lumière sur l'Imposture de Piltdown* published in 1972, it was charged that William Ruskin Butterfield, Curator of the Hastings Museum, had been the infamous forger. According to Esbroeck, the hoax had been engineered by Butterfield to spite Dawson, and that this act of revenge hinged on events surrounding the discovery of an almost complete iguanodon skeleton at Old Roar Quarry (Silverhill) near Hastings in 1909.

Precisely how Dawson learned of this discovery is no longer clear, but as a known collector with long standing connections with the British Museum he must undoubtedly have had an extensive network of informants — though there is no evidence to indicate that he had learned of the discovery via Butterfield. In fact the apparent rapidity with which Dawson negotiated the capture of the iguanodon remains, strongly suggests that he might have had prior dealings with the men at Roar Quarry. Whatever the source of his information, it appears that Dawson wasted no time in investigating the reported find, and on 4 April 1909, he excitedly informed Woodward:

> We have got on the track of a Dinosaur (at Hastings), rather an extensive series of bones ... At present we seem to be upon the pelvic region and I arrived in time to superintend getting out the sacrum but the mud was so awful that I could hardly see them well enough to judge what we had got, but I believe it is of the Iguanodon type ...[7]

During the next month Dawson spent considerable time at the Roar Quarry supervising the removal and crating of this ancient reptile for shipment to Woodward in London. This is of particular interest (as well as being relevant to Esbroeck's thesis) since it was during this time that Dawson first met Pierre Teilhard de Chardin who was stationed at Ore House in Hastings and was in the midst of completing his training as a Jesuit priest.[8] Like Dawson, the Jesuit was an avid fossil hunter. Whether he too had been lured there by news of the discovery, or whether his rambles had brought him to Roar Quarry simply by chance is no longer clear, but whatever the circumstances, it occasioned his first meeting with Dawson.[9]

Some months later Teilhard made a visit to the Hastings Museum (in the company of another Jesuit priest, ? Félix Pelletier) where Butterfield was Curator.[10] Much to Teilhard's amazement and obvious embarrassment, Butterfield knew nothing of the Roar Quarry iguanodon and was not only distressed to hear that the find had gone to London, but was, Teilhard later told his father, visibly upset to learn that Dawson had not bothered to inform him of his intentions. After all Dawson was a member of the Hastings Museum Association: where was the man's loyalty? As Teilhard recalled, Butterfield "change[d] colour", for evidently it was one of his "dreams" to have an iguanodon in his collection and to have one taken out "almost from under his very nose" was just too much to bear. Recognizing that he had blundered, Teilhard wrote to Dawson to warn him of his indiscretion. Dawson is said to have replied:

> with a very friendly letter, but still smacking of someone who smells gold and the halls of the British Museum behind him, and who lets his scorn for Hastings and its

museum break through. He declares that the people of Hastings would only ruin the
skeletons if they tried to keep them, and I think he's right.[11]

Esbroeck's interpretation of all this was that Butterfield was so angered by Dawson's
actions that he decided to take revenge on his colleague by concocting the elaborate
hoax at Piltdown. It is presumed that Butterfield knew of both the existence of the
gravel deposits at Piltdown and their significance (which is unsubstantiated).
However, having alerted the solicitor's attention to the potential of the gravel beds in
the neighbourhood of Piltdown, Butterfield then began his fiendish scheme of fakery
— selecting fossils primarily from the Hastings Museum's collections. His access to
the Piltdown pit was Venus Hargreaves, the Uckfield labourer used by Dawson and
Woodward. Through this "unique complice", Butterfield was assured that Dawson
had no chance of avoiding finding fossils. With this accomplished, Butterfield is said
to have persuaded the eolithophile, Harry Morris, to secure one of Dawson's fake
flints — evidently believing Morris's experienced eye would ultimately reveal the
truth![12]

According to Esbroeck, the curator intended to implicate Teilhard as well as
Dawson. Not only were some of the remains of continental origin, but the Jesuit
palaeontologist had made several of the finds. In particular, he had been chosen to
discover the vital canine, which, so Esbroeck contended, had been dropped at
Teilhard's feet by Hargreaves. But if Dawson had been Butterfield's primary target
why did he confuse matters by involving the young priest? What did Butterfield have
against Teilhard? Had Hargreaves made a mistake, or had Morris gone farther than
Butterfield intended?

Besides these questions there are a number of other problems with Esbroeck's
ingenious thesis. First, there is the problem of establishing the reality of the
Butterfield–Dawson animus. We have only Teilhard's report of Butterfield's (?
momentary) anger and absolutely no evidence of any long-standing emnity between
the curator and the solicitor. Is Esbroeck's interpretation of Teilhard's report of this
incident a reasonable one? It is possible that what Teilhard witnessed was simply
embarrassment, followed, perhaps, by anger, but directed not so much at Dawson
but at himself for having to plead ignorance about events happening on his own
territory. But even if Butterfield's anger had been directed at Dawson, is it reasonable
to suppose that it would have been enough to precipitate and sustain the protracted
and far-reaching drama enacted at Piltdown? From all accounts Butterfield was a
rather placid and retiring fellow, completely devoid of "pose and push",[13] who seems
to have enjoyed the privileges and freedom that came with his position at the Brassey
Insitute in Hastings. This alone makes it difficult to imagine him risking all of this over
the fate of one iguanodon skeleton, which in all probability could not have been
suitably accommodated by the Museum anyway. Then there is the question of
whether Butterfield had the necessary skills required to fabricate the Piltdown
forgeries. Although as a curator of a local museum his interests had to cover a wide
range of subjects, it appears his particular forté had been ornithology, an interest
nurtured since his childhood days in Yorkshire; much later he branched out into
entomology. It seems most improbable that he directed the Piltdown scenario. But
supposing he had, having carefully prepared his string of specimens, why would he
risk everything by relying on a farm labourer? To say the least this would have been a
precarious link, with few guarantees that in the event of a premature discovery of the
forgery, Hargreaves would not have revealed the name of his mentor. Furthermore,
while Hargreaves might well have been a dependable navvie, how reliable was he has
a prestidigitator? Esbroeck seems to think "Old Venus" could have carried out the

required manoeuvres, but whether Butterfield would have thought so is another matter altogether. Finally, in using the iguanodon incident as the prime motive, Esbroeck has presumed that the date of the first plant at Piltdown, the finding of the "coconut", occurred shortly after Teilhard's meeting with the disgruntled Butterfield; but while it is acknowledged that this date has yet to be firmly established, there is every reason to suppose that it preceded the events at Roar Quarry, implying that by the summer of 1909 the seeds of the forgery had already been sown.

Not having examined Dawson's surviving correspondence, Esbroeck was not aware of Butterfield's marathon bicycle ride from Hastings to Crowborough in May 1911 to view what Arthur Conan Doyle had mistakenly identified as the footprint of a Wealden iguanodon.[14] This incident, while adding fuel to the Curator's claimed interest, in this direction, also serves to introduce the proposition made in 1983 by a "retired" American archaeologist John H Winslow,[15] that Sherlock Holmes' creator had masterminded the forgery.

"If it were true", one critic later commented, "Winslow's hypothesis would constitute an historical nicety of the first magnitude".[16] Unfortunately the case he brings against Conan Doyle is grounded almost entirely in supposition. Although Winslow is correct in pointing to a relationship between Dawson and Doyle, it appears that this connection was not made until sometime after the summer of 1909,[17] which immediately casts some doubts on Doyle's culpability in the Piltdown affair. However, while it is difficult to document both the evolution and extent of Dawson's relationship with the famed writer, it is evident that by the autumn of 1911 their association had reached a sufficient stage of familiarity to warrant an invitation for the Dawsons to lunch at Crowborough.[18] Furthermore, among the few individuals (other than Dawson) who may have known of the Piltdown site prior to 1912, none have been shown to have had any direct links with the Crowborough author. From the available evidence it appears that Doyle first learned of the site's existence in the autumn of 1912, by which time Piltdown was an "open secret". According to Dawson, late in November (1912) he received an enthusiastic note from Doyle in Crowborough (situated some six miles east of Uckfield) offering to drive him anywhere he wanted to go.[19] If nothing else, this tells us that Doyle had not learned of the Piltdown skull from Dawson, and also that Doyle could not have visited the site "openly" and before this date. For had he in fact been privy to the events that transpired at Piltdown during the summer of 1912, why would he now suddenly write to the solicitor exhibiting excitement about the skull?

John Winslow's case is further frustrated by the absence of an explanation for not only the plants at Barkham Manor, but also those at Sheffield Park and Barcombe Mills. Then there is the highly debatable question of motive. It is contended that the primary target of the forgery had not been Dawson but rather Ray Lankester. The root of the struggle between Doyle and Lankester was over spiritualism.[20] Doyle was a supporter, while Lankester considered the entire movement a sham. During the closing decades of the nineteenth century, Lankester had exposed the fraudulent activities of the American medium Henry Slade[21] and, as Winslow documents, he continued during the Piltdown era, to heap contempt on advocates of the movement. The Piltdown forgery was therefore, Winslow believes, conceived to trap the materialist Lankester. Precisely when Doyle hatched his plot is not made very clear, but Winslow appears to place emphasis on the presentation Lankester made to the Royal Society in 1911 (where he strongly defended Reid Moir's thesis for Pliocene man in East Anglia), and seems to imply that this had been what set Doyle in motion.[22] If this is what Winslow means to imply, it does not harmonize very well with some of the known facts. Lankester did not address the Royal Society until

16 November 1911, which left Doyle with precious little time to put the wheels in motion. Secondly such a possibility does not tie up with Dawson's statement made to the Geological Society on 18 December 1912, when he reported that he had recovered a *second* cranial fragment "in the autumn of 1911". Also (and in the absence of the preceding objections), Winslow fails to muster evidence to support the opinion that Doyle had the necessary expertise to manufacture the forgery, beyond his statement that "[Holmes was] a forensic genius", whose exploits were to become "required reading for the police forces of several nations". Presuming that Doyle did indeed have the ability, why did he not spring the trap he is supposed to have so carefully set for Lankester? It is submitted that the reason was because the trap was not set in the first place.

SOLLAS AND SMITH

The case against William J Sollas is founded on an accusation made by James Archibald Douglas (1884–1978), former Professor of Geology at Oxford (1937–50), just prior to his death, in a tape recording entitled: "The Piltdown Skull".[23]

Evidently what had set Douglas off on his pursuit of Sollas was Ronald Millar's book *The Piltdown Men* published in 1972. Although Millar had accused Grafton Elliot Smith, the case was not a compelling one, and Douglas was intrigued by the fact that Sollas had not figured prominently in the Piltdown debates. Why? He also learned that Sollas had not been present at Burlington House on the evening of 18 December 1912.[24] Then he remembered Sollas' purchase of potassium bichromate, and that he had borrowed ape teeth from Oxford's Department of Anatomy. Although Kenneth Oakley tried to dissuade Douglas from making public this kind of evidence, the aged don persisted.[25]

It was Douglas' contention that Sollas had a "bitter dislike" for Woodward and that he had concocted the forgery with a view to discrediting his enemy! But before examining the alleged motive it is necessary first to look at the substance of Douglas' claim, that Sollas had been the perpetrator:

> I know that Sollas knew Dawson and had visited him, but on how many occasions I cannot say for I was abroad at the time. Dawson, a Sussex solicitor, would be unlikely to have most of the items which were included in the fake, whereas Sollas had easy access to anything like that (in the) through the Museum at Oxford ... Some of the fragments of the skull were stained with potassium bichromate and I consider this most significant. I can remember as it was yesterday a small packet arriving at the Museum which [C J] Bayzand, the assistant, and I unpacked and found to contain potassium bichromate. We both said "What on earth's the professor ordered this for?" ... [Bayzand] knew that Sollas would never have used [the substance] in the department for [photographic purposes [since he did all of Sollas's photography] ... Then I remember Sollas borrowing apes' teeth from the Department of Human Anatomy at Oxford, but where would Dawson have got such things except from a colleague? ... When the skull was proved to be fraudulent it would appear obvious that Dawson must have had an accomplice. The bones did not originate there ... They must have been provided from an outside source by someone who had higher scientific attainments than Dawson and it is possible that the thing started as a joke and then got out of hand. I am not suggesting that Dawson knew Sollas and Smith Woodward were bitter enemies, but it may have been put to Dawson that to make a fool of a man of the standing of Sir Arthur Smith Woodward would be very, very difficult and if successful, would be, so to speak, the highlight of his [Dawson's] many fakeries ....[26]

William Johnson Sollas.

What can be made of the inference that Sollas knew Dawson prior to the unveiling at Burlington House in December 1912? Both were members of the Geological Society, and shared a common associate in Woodward. It is not unreasonable to suppose that Sollas might have known of Dawson prior to 1912, though it is difficult to find a reason for Sollas to visit Dawson prior to 1912, unless of course they were in league together. Supporters of Douglas' hypothesis will be disappointed to learn that Dawson's surviving correspondence from this period makes no mention of the Oxford geologist. Unfortunately, since Douglas was abroad, exploring in the Andes, from 1910 through to the beginning of 1913, he is far from being a reliable source of information on Sollas' movements during this critical period.[27]

Although Douglas clearly underrated Dawson's abilities, it is debatable whether he would have had all the resources and skills required to pull off the entire forgery single-handed. But examined closely the Dawson–Sollas scenario conjured up by Douglas makes no real sense. There is not a hint of public scandal surrounding the Uckfield solicitor during the Piltdown period exept the innuendo buried in Salzman's 1910 review of Dawson's *History of Hastings Castle* . To suggest that Sollas selected Dawson as his connection because of his credentials as a faker, is absurd. Similarly, his vague reference to potassium bichromate and the acquisition of ape teeth are meaningless as evidence unless tied to specific events.[28] The inference however, that

Sollas had the necessary expertise to have been the mastermind behind the forgery does make sense. Not only was he an established authority in comparative anatomy and palaeontology, but also an accomplished geochemist, much of his earlier career in geology had been devoted to the investigation of the processes of fossilization in sponges[29] and the formation of flint, all of which provided him with specialized knowledge, as well as the technical skills that would have served him well in the Piltdown enterprise, had he been so inclined — which raises the issue of motive.

The motive attributed to Sollas is a deep and bitter hatred of Woodward. If this is true then he hid it completely from view. His letters to Woodward (written during the period 1912 to 1923) suggest a relationship quite different to the one conveyed by Douglas.[30] As in the case of Conan Doyle, there is the problem of equating the motive with historical events. To the claim that Sollas contrived the forgery to hurt Woodward, the obvious rejoinder must be that it did just the contrary. Presuming that Sollas had been the forger, he was given an excellent opportunity to spring the trap in 1913, when Keith and others unleashed their criticisms against Woodward's reconstruction. Instead, Sollas had nothing but praise for Woodward and sarcasm for Keith.[31]

In an effort to question Sollas' integrity and presumably provide substance to his thesis, Douglas revived the issue of the Sherborne Horse's Head. This matter concerned the discovery, made circa 1911 by two schoolboys from Sherborne School in Dorset, of a bone fragment bearing the engraved head of a horse. The find was subsequently transmitted to Woodward, who in April 1914, brought it to the attention of the Geological Society.[32] His description of the specimen was cautious, as suggested by his paper's title: "On an apparently Palaeolithic engraving on a bone from Sherborne (Dorset)". Later, in the autumn of 1925, Sollas announced in a new edition of his popular book *Ancient Hunters* that the Sherborne artifact was a forgery.[33] How did Sollas come by this information? According to Douglas the source was his laboratory assistant Charles Bayzand. Evidently, Bayzand had been at Sherborne when the engraved bone was found; he had been helping R Elliot Steel, the school's science master, in organizing his geological collections, Douglas recalls:

> Two boys brought to him [Bayzand] a semi-fossil bone on which was scratched a horse's head. This was purely done as a trick to fool their science master. Bayzand accused them of this which they first denied and then, when he found on a table in the library a book by Boyd Dawkins open at the picture of a horse's head which had been discovered somewhere up north, I forget where . . . then they confessed . . . and it was the laughing stock of the whole school and they had given it to their science master who had sent it up to . . . Woodward . . . Now Sollas knew this to be true and never made any attempt to tell Smith Woodward, to warn him or to stop him reading a paper on the subject. Then, ten years later, in 1924, in the third edition of his Ancient Hunters, Sollas for the first time made it public . . . thus belittling Sir Arthur Smith Woodward's work, and . . . I maintain that a man who could do this once was perfectly capable of doing it a second time.[34]

Besides being a somewhat distorted account, it is also open to another and quite different interpretation. When Woodward countered this accusation in *Nature*, January 1926, he noted that one of the schoolboys, Arnaldo Cortesi, confirmed the "genuineness of the find", and that this testimony was backed by Elliot Steel. Woodward also called attention to his visit to the site in 1923, in the company of Elliot Steel, noting that while they had not found any additional specimens, both he and Steel were totally convinced that the engraved bone had been contemporary with the Mammoth teeth and other Pleistocene remains that had been collected from the

Grafton Elliot Smith (circa 1915). (Library, Royal College of Surgeons, London)

neighbourhood and were on display in the Sherborne School Museum.[35] Responding to this, Sollas admitted that his accusation was based on information given him by Bayzand, but refused to accept Woodward's argument, pointing out that the correspondence between the Sherborne artifact and the one found at Creswell, Derbyshire, was simply too great to ignore. Appended to Sollas' published letter was a note from Bayzand, who reiterated his claim that the whole affair "was a trick played solely for the benefit of the science master [Steel] without any idea that it would go any further". To which he added: "Its success was a source of much merriment at the school, particularly amongst those boys who were under this master, and I was even invited by some to inspect the fake". Bayzand confessed that he could not remember precisely when this happened, either 1912 or 1913 he thought, but he claimed to have dismissed the matter from his mind until:

> I learnt, not without surprise, that Sir Arthur Smith Woodward had communicated the "discovery" to the Geological Society. When later I read his account I at once informed Prof. Sollas of all that I knew, and so am directly responsible for the statement made by him in the third edition of "Ancient Hunters".[36]

Although the results of later investigations strongly favour the view of the Sherborne Horse being a genuine artifact,[37] what is important is how this affair was perceived in 1926. Douglas seems to think Sollas' announcement hurt Woodward, but this seems not to be the case. Shortly after the exchange between Woodward and Sollas (and

Bayzand), Elliot Steel issued a strong rebuttal to Bayzand's version of the Sherborne affair which was also printed in *Nature* .[38] Neither Sollas nor Woodward, it would seem, pursued the matter further. Given what is known of Sollas' temperament it is unlikely that he would have left this issue unresolved, unless he thought he might be wrong.[39] Which raises the question of the relationship between Bayzand and Sollas, and Douglas' place in the scheme of things. The nature of the relationship between Douglas and Sollas is not known, but it looks as if it was not Sollas but Douglas who was settling a grudge. Because of Sollas' longevity (he died at 87 without vacating his Chair at Oxford) Douglas was obliged to wait many years before finally assuming the Professorial mantle.

The case brought by Ronald Millar against Grafton Elliot Smith is also flimsy, a fact Millar himself acknowledged. The coincidence of Smith's "tumultuous appearance in England" and the remarkable "turn of events in Sussex", Millar felt could not be ignored. Smith had all the necessary qualifications, "both esoteric and professional",[40] and the "discoveries" at Piltdown served to underscore the validity of his theoretical predictions regarding the pre-eminence of the brain in human evolution.

Not unexpectedly Millar's case was quickly discounted in British scientific circles,[41] but in Australia the proposition that Elliot Smith instigated the hoax was viewed somewhat differently by the historian, Ian Langham (1942–84). He felt this hypothesis did much to "illuminate" the puzzling set of circumstances surrounding the Talgai skull and Smith's involvement therein.[42] But, although as Langham showed, there were surprising links between the Talgai affair and Smith, and the position he had taken with regard to the Sussex skull, when it came to demonstrating a direct link between Smith and the Piltdown episode he could do no more than Millar. As his subsequent investigations revealed, while it is possible to forge a tentative (pre-1912) link between Smith and Woodward, through Boyd Dawkins, it is not possible to extend this to Dawson. Furthermore, it is abundantly clear from the existing archival evidence that both Dawkins and Smith were not privy to the events at Piltdown until after the summer of 1912, and contrary to popular belief, Smith is not known to have participated in the work at Piltdown until after 1915. In fact the first recorded visit by Smith is in July 1916, when he and Woodward spent two weeks excavating at Barkham Manor.[43] It could be argued, of course, that this was a critical move. Dawson was dying in his bed at Lewes and Piltdown II had yet to see the light of day. Had Smith agreed to assist Woodward in order to persuade him of the validity of Dawson's second eoanthropine material? It is possible, but unlikely. For if Smith had known that Piltdown was bogus he would hardly have been inclined to invest valuable time searching for material he knew did not exist, and more important, had he wanted to convince Woodward of the validity of Dawson's second series he could have achieved this without spending two fruitless weeks at Barkham Manor. Also, and contrary to Millar's opinion, it is contended that while Smith might have had the requisite technical qualifications, both his temperament and behaviour argue strongly against his possible involvement. As his former Australian colleague John Wilson noted, he was prone to phases of "intense concentrated effort" punctuated with intervals of "apparent inertia".[44] In this regard it is worth noting that Smith's publications on Piltdown-related matters are not as impressive as some would have us believe, and certainly do not, by any stretch of the imagination, represent a significant investment of time.[45] His most energetic and productive period was in the autumn of 1913 when he clashed with Keith over the reconstruction issue — but at stake here was not so much Woodward's model as Smith's ego. Furthermore, it is also apparent that from 1909 to 1915, Smith was very much preoccupied with the task of furthering his position at Manchester University, which would have left him little time for extramural activities in Sussex.[46]

ABBOTT AND HINTON

Among the galaxy of names that surfaced during the course of Weiner's investigations in 1953, Lewis Abbott's name was among the few he retained on his short list of possible culprits. Weiner's suspicions were grounded in a number of facts which collectively enhanced the possibility of his involvement.

It could be demonstrated that Abbott knew both Woodward and Dawson long before the events at Piltdown. Exactly when Abbott first met Woodward is unclear, but it must have been before 1894, since Woodward purchased a number of items of jewellery from Abbott in 1893 that included an engagement ring.[47] At this time Woodward was courting Harry Govier Seeley's eldest daughter, Maude, whom he married in 1894. Seeley was Woodward's former Professor of Geology at King's College. Also Abbott's early and intimate association with the Woodwards and Seeleys is further supported by the fact that in the mid 1890s Abbott took over the tenancy of Seeley's house in Sevenoaks (near Tunbridge Wells) in order to be nearer to Ightham where he was working with Kennard and Harrison.[48] Later, in 1898, he moved further south to Hastings, where he opened a jeweller's shop on the Parade at St Leonards. It was here, at Hastings, that Abbott and Dawson evidently first met, but again precisely when this happened is uncertain. The first piece of documentary evidence concerning this association is dated 1905, when the Hastings Museum was formally taken over by the Municipal Council, but it is thought that their relationship precedes this event by some years.[49] However, from this date on it is possible to document, until 1915, their joint presence on a number of committees serving the Museum and its Curator, William R Butterfield.

As Weiner was repeatedly told by many of his informants, Abbott had the resources, the skills, and knowledge to have manufactured the forgery.[50] His personal collections were known to have been enormous, many of the items representing the product of his labours throughout the Home Counties (including Sussex).[51] Was it possible that some of the materials recovered from Piltdown actually came from Abbott's collections? The fact that the radioactivity of the Piltdown rhinoceros and mastodon teeth strongly matched similar material from the Suffolk Red Crag, where Abbott was known to have worked on and off during the two decades immediately preceding the events at Piltdown, served to reinforce Weiner's suspicions. As Weiner recognized, what Abbott did not have, could quite easily have been obtained either through other private collectors or purchased from commercial dealers such as Gerrard's in Camden Town (London),[52] or perhaps other less reputable sources such as James Smith, a well-known rag and bone merchant in Whitechapel.[53] While this might have been the case, was it reasonable to suppose, as many of Weiner's informants did, that Abbott had the ability to conceive and execute the forgery? Although willing to acknowledge that Abbott's experience in geology and palaeontology did not preclude him from having conceived the faunal and archaeological assemblages at Piltdown, Weiner was not at all convinced of his abilities in the areas of human and comparative anatomy.[54]

There are also a number of other reasons for eliminating Abbott as a possible suspect. To begin with there is his personality. Abbott *appears* to have had the respect of not only Woodward, but also Keith and several other notable members of the scientific establishment.[55] However, as Keith later confessed to Weiner, the Sussex jeweller was "pushy and self-opinionated".[56] In fact, as Weiner subsequently learned from his other informants, as well as from Abbott's own correspondence, Keith had been more than generous in his characterization of this little, dark, bearded man. In addition to his blatant immodesty (which seems to have grown with age),[57] it also appears that Abbott never mastered the gentle art of diplomacy. Consumed by his own sense of importance, Abbott conducted his life under the arrogant illusion that he was surrounded by fools and that he was an ignored genius. Compounding this with Abbott's unquestioned intellectual commitment to the theoretical implications of the Piltdown scenario, complicates the issue of motive. For while it is possible to credit Abbott with an intellectual reason for fabricating evidence to support the existence of "Plateau Man" — the artificer of the much maligned eolithic industries of south-east England — it is difficult to see why Abbott would have chosen Dawson to be the midwife of his dreams. Why not be completely responsible himself? But even supposing that on this occasion he had managed to check his ego, it is still difficult to understand why, as the presumed mastermind behind the forgery, he would have excluded himself so completely from the events that unfolded at Piltdown. Is it possible that he had initially been involved, and that Dawson had cut him out? This is unlikely and is not supported by the available facts. As far as can be determined, Abbott was oblivious of the existence of the gravel bed at Barkham Manor prior to 1912. Although he later claimed credit for having caused Dawson to look out for early gravel formations in the Weald,[58] this should not be misconstrued as evidence for his prior knowledge of the Piltdown pit. Furthermore, to suppose that Dawson and Abbott where initially in league together and that the solicitor had, for some reason, decided to cut the jeweller out, presents a number of problems. Besides placing the entire escapade at risk, this action would have undoubtedly strained the Dawson-Abbott relationship to breaking point. Yet, in the summer of 1912, Dawson is known to have consulted with Abbott on the status of some of the Piltdown eoliths.[59] It is submitted that even given Abbott's passionate enthusiasm for Plateau Man, he would not have sat idly by awaiting Dawson's inevitable ascent to fame, but would have seen to it that the mission was aborted. As for the idea that he acted independently of Dawson, while technically feasible, it runs counter to the personality argument and is no more compelling than any other scenario. Unless backed by real incriminating evidence, such theories are ultimately little more than idle speculation.

A much more reasonable reading of the available facts is that Abbott saw himself as Dawson's mentor and confidant. Not only did he put Dawson on the road that led to Piltdown, but he also confirmed the "superlative importance" of the solicitor's initial finds — urging him to bring them to Woodward's attention. In the ensuing excitement, Dawson apparently neglected to acknowledge Abbott's input, hence the jeweller's frustrated remarks to Rutot:

> Dawson behaved very badly to me over the whole affair, for as my principal assistant said when he saw no reference to me in the report: "[I]t is very certain no Lewis Abbott, no Piltdown man".[60]

In an article, published in the *Hastings & St Leonards Observer*, on 1 February 1913, Abbott revealed:

> [O]ur former townsman [and] my colleague on the Museum Committee, Mr. Charles Dawson [found a number of Wealden gravels some thirteen years before] . . . producing spoils which he brought on to me from time to time . . . Seeing some [flints] on a road near Uckfield, he lost no time in making enquiries about the place whence [they] had been obtained, and he was directed to the pit he already knew, but the importance of which he had not recognized until now. Upon asking the men if they

had ever found any bones, he was informed that a long while before the men had found a "cokernut," which they had broken up and thrown upon the heap. In that "cokernut" the sagacity of Mr. Dawson saw a prize, and after a great deal of searching he recovered a fragment of a skull, which he brought on to show me. Its enormous thickness and manner of fossilisation immediately impressed me with its superlative importance . . . Subsequently he took it to Dr. Smith Woodward . . . and the two gentlemen agreed to exert every effort [to find the remaining fragments]; and the fates rewarded their zeal . . . Amongst [the rewards] . . . were many flints, better worked than those Mr. Dawson had brought to me [earlier]. Then there are bones . . . of fauna . . . pointing unmistakably to a Pliocene age. [Following a description of these finds and the cranial fragments, Abbott then got to the subject of the jaw, which he noted was] essentially chimpanzoid, and no doubt had it been unaccompanied by the skull, which is a mixture of human, the gorilloid, and the chimpanzoid, it would have been considered to have been a highly specialized form of chimpanzee . . .

Although Abbott describes the skull and jaw in considerable detail, giving the impression that he is quite familiar with the specimens, it is evident that this knowledge is actually quite unexceptional and not based on privileged information. Much of it could have been gleaned quite easily from accounts written in the many newspaper and magazine articles that appeared between Christmas 1912 and the New Year,[61] and perhaps embellished by additional information supplied either by Dawson or any of his colleagues (such as Kennard) who attended the meeting at Burlington House.[62] Of greater interest, however, is his account of Dawson's discovery of the Uckfield gravel bed and subsequent events. Firstly, he notes that Dawson had known of the gravels in the Uckfield district since the turn of the century, a point which Dawson later verified. Secondly, Abbott makes no mention of having seen the site. Was he being coy or honest? In light of other claims made in the article, if he had known of this site and visited it (prior to 1912) he would surely have mentioned it. Rather it seems far more reasonable to suppose that Abbott had not been privy to Dawson's earlier activities at Piltdown. The fact that Dawson kept the site's location a secret from Abbott is hardly surprising. Most collectors are instinctively guarded about such information, a fact Abbott would have understood and appreciated. For Dawson to have released such information before the site had been evaluated would have opened up the risk of his "rights" being infringed and the site being plundered. Thirdly, and just as revealing, is Abbott's account of the "cokernut" incident. This incident is a key event, and it is evident from Abbott's version that he was not as well-informed as he would have us believe.

In the final analysis, while Abbott fulfils the requirements expected of the forger, there is little in the way of evidence to support either his direct or indirect involvement in the affair.

Why Weiner retained him on his list of suspects is not at all clear. Was it because he still had lingering doubts or simply that he forgot to strike his name from the list? His surviving notes on Abbott contain no new leads and what little information he collected over the years since 1953 did little to advance a case against him.

Equally unsatisfactory is the case against Martin Hinton. There are several versions circulating that implicate him either as the central figure or part of a general conspiracy aimed at bringing down Woodward.[63] Both Weiner's and Oakley's files are filled with notes and correspondence relating to Hinton and the charge that he and some of his Ightham associates conspired to fabricate the Piltdown forgery. While much of this material makes stimulating reading it too must ultimately be seen as gossip.

According to various sources Woodward was not a popular figure at the British

Museum (Natural History). He was, reportedly, a martinet, possessive both of his authority and the materials in his charge. Emerging from the gossip relayed to Weiner and Oakley, there is a rumour of a rivalry between Woodward and Michael Rogers Oldfield Thomas (1858–1921). But whether this was true and what the basis of the rivalry had been is no longer clear. Thomas was a mammalogist in the Department of Zoology, whereas Woodward was a palaeontologist, working from the Department of Geology. Unlike Woodward who rose quickly through the ranks to the position of Keeper, Thomas did not.[64] Having married well, Thomas was relieved of financial pressures that otherwise might have driven him to aspire to higher administrative appointments; instead he devoted himself to his work and his recreational interest, croquet. Aside from an interest in mammalogy there appears to have been little common ground between these two men. In temperament Thomas was the antithesis of Woodward; where the latter enjoyed his own company, Thomas is said to have had an aversion to solitude. While it is not inconceivable that there may have been bad blood between the two men, it is also possible that Thomas and Woodward simply did not communicate with each other and that Hinton read more into this than there really was. Given the marked differences in the style and manner of these two men, it is hardly surprising that Hinton would have found the relaxed and sociable Thomas a more conducive colleague.

Hinton began working at the British Museum (Natural History) at the turn of the century as a "volunteer" in zoology and it was not until after World War I, in 1921, that he finally secured a full-time appointment. In 1927 he became Deputy Keeper of Zoology and in 1936 he succeeded William Calman (1871–1962) as Keeper, a position he held until his retirement in 1945. In the meantime he earned his living as a legal clerk at Inns of Court in The Temple, London, while pursuing an interest in geology and mammalology. One of his earliest and most enduring friendships had been with Alfred Kennard, Lewis Abbott's protégé. During the first decade of the century, Hinton and Kennard collaborated on a number of projects intimately connected with the Pleistocene geology of the Thames river valley,[65] as well as work on faunal remains from Ightham and the Red Crag of Suffolk.[66] Both shared a healthy allegiance to eolithic theory, but neither of them, it seems, had any direct dealings with Dawson. As for Woodward, Hinton and Kennard had little or no outside contact with him, aside from periodic encounters at the Museum.

As Weiner's investigations revealed, there was a distinct possibility that Hinton (and Kennard) may have been privy to the Marriott–St Barbe hypothesis that Dawson was "salting the mine".[67] It is therefore possible that Hinton might well have been the source of the rumour William King Gregory heard during his visit to the Museum in the summer of 1913. According to Gregory he had heard that it was "suspected by some that [the Piltdown remains] . . . are not old at all; [but] that they . . . represent a deliberate hoax, a negro or Australian skull and a broken ape jaw, artificially fossilized and planted in the gravel-bed to fool the scientists".[68] If Hinton was responsible for transmitting this rumour this allows other possibilities, but it must be stressed that it is by no means certain that he was the source.[69] To suppose that Hinton had Gregory's ear infers that he was sufficiently close to the American to trust him not to reveal the source of his information, and there is no evidence to suggest that this was the case.[70] Also, as Hinton's position at the Museum was still tenuous, it seems highly improbable that he would have risked both his reputation and prospects at the Museum by such an action. The same might also be said of the much more serious allegation that he and Kennard, or another of his Ightham Circle followers, had engineered the forgery with a view to making a fool of Woodward. The fact that such a plan also risked delivering a devastating blow to the credibility of the Ightham Circle and its fabled "Plateau Man", should not be overlooked.

Martin Alister Campbell Hinton.

While Hinton may have been a latent dualist, there is no evidence to support the view that he seriously suspected the authenticity of the finds until he was reportedly told by St Barbe about Dawson's activities in his office at Uckfield in 1913. But while it remains uncertain when he first heard the St Barbe story, it is probable that it was not until after 1926;[71] in that year Hinton published a paper on British Pleistocene mammalia in which he openly endorsed the Piltdown remains:

> At Piltdown, in my opinion, we see dim indications of what the fauna of the South of England was in the earliest part of the High Terrace stage . . . Eoanthropus himself is surely as primitive a mammal as one could wish to find in a post-glacial deposit; too primitive to be associated with Chellean implements, but possibly responsible for the Eoliths.[72]

Had Hinton suspected the validity of the finds at this time then he would surely not have issued this endorsement, but would have avoided the subject altogether. After this time (until 1953) Hinton appears to have remained silent on the subject of Piltdown. To say the least, knowledge of the St Barbe story placed him in a rather awkward position. He now occupied a position of authority at the Museum and the Piltdown remains were among the Museum's most treasured possessions. But was the St Barbe story true? And if so, what, if anything could he do about it? Then, unexpectedly, Marston began agitating against Piltdown. Contrary to expectations, Hinton did little to publicly support Marston's cause; instead he seems to have adopted the opposite view. Or did he? Marston later claimed that Hinton advised Frank Corner (a close friend of Marston), by letter, not to "pay too much attention to the [Piltdown] finds".[73] Was Hinton indirectly assisting Marston through Corner?[74] Possibly, but Hinton neither denied nor confirmed Marston's story; to have admitted to the existence of this letter would have made him an accessory after the fact.

Having been privy to the hitherto unfounded allegation that the Piltdown finds were fraudulent it is not unreasonable to suppose that Hinton considered the possible identity of the forger. In his opinion it might well been someone from the Ightham Circle:

> The temptation to invent such a "discovery" of an ape-like man associated with late Pliocene Mammals in a Wealden gravel might well have proved irresistible to some unbalanced member of old Ben Harrison's circle at Ightham. He and his friends (of whom I was one) were always talking of the possibility of finding a late Pliocene deposit in the Weald . . . I spent the long vacation of 1902 and the Easter and part of the long vacation of 1906 in searching the water partings in the Weald near Ightham . . . But I was not successful . . . Old Ben and I had many a walk to likely spots . . .[73]

Shortly after making this statement Hinton told a friend (John Irving, a BBC producer) living in Bristol, that he believed the perpetrator had been working at the British Museum at the time of the hoax, and that he was unable to reveal his name because he was still alive.[76] To some this amounted to a confession, others believed his reference to the forger being alive at the time of the unmasking was a red herring, and that he was really pointing, indirectly, to Woodward.

WOODHEAD

In 1898, after receiving his bachelor's degree in chemistry from Durham University, Samuel Allinson Woodhead moved to Uckfield where he became an instructor at the local Agricultural College. Later, while at the Uckfield College, he completed a Master's thesis and ultimately his doctorate. Woodhead was Public Analyst and Official Agricultural Analyst for the counties of East and West Sussex, while also aspiring to becoming the Principal of the Uckfield Agricultural College. With the outbreak of war in 1914, the college was closed and Woodhead was relocated to Lewes where he resumed his duties as Public Analyst while opening a private practice as a consulting analyst and bacteriologist.[77] Given Woodhead's extensive background in chemistry and his known collaboration with Dawson at the gravel bed at Barkham Manor prior to 1912, it is not surprising that he should have been a primary suspect. Following this line of investigation Oakley made contact with Woodhead's eldest son Leslie (1907–69) early in 1954, who provided him with what, at first, seemed to be some very revealing insights. In particular Oakley was informed that:

> Charles Dawson brought the skull to Dad as soon as he found it and realised it was something out of the ordinary. They went back together to look for missing parts and Dad was actually there when the jaw was found and Dad HIMSELF found the eye tooth which was on the path by the side of the digging . . .[78]

About a week later, in an effort to assist Oakley's inquiries, Leslie Woodhead volunteered another interesting fragment of information:

[T]here are no [surviving] letters or documents of Dad's [relating to his analysis of the Piltdown bones] and all I can go on is memory which is of course rather vague after all this time . . . [but I do recall that] He [Dad] was always very definite about the fact that it was not long after Dawson brought the skull to show him that he and Dawson went back and found the jaw — a matter of days at the most NOT months. Again the tooth was found within a day or so of the jaw — on a Saturday as a matter of fact.[79]

Naturally both Oakley and Weiner were intrigued. Were the jaw and canine in Leslie Woodhead's story and the celebrated jaw and canine of *Eoanthropus* the same? Weiner took up the investigation and asked Leslie if he could be more definite about the timing of the events he had described. Woodhead's son replied:

It is quite easy for me to remember that the first find was made early in 1908 because Dad used to say it would always be easy for me to know the age of the Piltdown skull as it was found within a very short time of my birth . . . I was born on Dec. 13th 1907 . . . [T]alking it over with Mother . . . She agrees with me that the jaw was found very soon after the first part of skull and that was before Dr. Smith Woodward came into the picture . . . I have always been of the opinion that it was the eye tooth that Dad found . . . It was only after Dr. Oakley wrote that the Father Chardin claimed to have found the eye tooth that I wondered if I had been wrong but the more I think of it the more certain I am that it was the eye tooth that Dad said he found . . . Mother said he had some vague idea that TWO jaws had been found and that there was something wrong about the finding of the second tooth that is the one found in Aug. 1913 . . . [Also] Mother is quite certain that Dad was much less friendly with Dawson after the skull was found than before but she had always put it down to another reason.[80]

It appeared to both Weiner and Oakley there were two possible ways of reading this new information. The first was that the Piltdown jaw and canine had been found prior to 1912 and reburied to be "rediscovered", or, that over the years, the events described and their chronology had become confused. A subsequent review of the official account of what transpired at Piltdown and Dawson's correspondence

Samuel Allison Woodhead. (Courtesy of Lionel Woodhead)

revealed that during the autumn of 1913, two months after Teilhard discovered the controversial canine tooth, Woodhead and Dawson recovered from the site the mandible and canine of a beaver. Furthermore, it was possible from a letter written by Dawson to Woodward, to date the recovery of this find: 4 October 1913, which happened to fall on a Saturday. Was this the solution to the confusion? Weiner and Oakley believed it was, despite the obvious attractions of having Woodhead involved.

In 1985, Peter Costello, a literary historian living in Dublin, reviewed this evidence and concluded otherwise; not only was Woodhead involved, but he had contrived the entire scheme and Dawson had been his innocent victim. In developing this case, Costello had evidently been impressed by a letter shown to him by the Cambridge archaeologist [and editor of the journal *Antiquity*] Glyn Daniel (1914–86) from Woodhead's youngest son, Lionel (b. 1911). In this letter, Lionel Woodhead writes:

> ... Sometime in the 1930s my mother gave me the facts which are as follows. Mr. Dawson asked my father how one would treat bones to make them appear older than they were and my father told him how it could be done. I would point out that my mother was present at this meeting. A few weeks later Dawson "found" some of the bones and my father accompanied him on trips to Piltdown and even "found" some bones himself. Unknown to Dawson my father took some back to his lab where he became very suspicious. Before he could ask Dawson what he was trying to do the "find" had been publicized. Unfortunately for what happened later my father was an extremely loyal friend and did not give the secret away. However, the friendship cooled after this since obviously my father felt he had been used without his consent ...[81]

Comparing this testimony with that of Lionel's elder brother, Leslie, it is immediately apparent that not only does it go much further in implicating Dawson, but also provides substance to the earlier inference made by Leslie Woodhead that the Dawson–Woodhead relationship had "cooled". But how reliable was this letter? Was Lionel Woodhead now divulging information originally held back by his elder brother? Or was it mere supposition — a well meaning (but misguided) attempt to account for the oral tradition that there had been a rift between Dawson and Woodhead, while at the same time removing all doubt of the latter's complicity in the affair? If this had been Lionel Woodhead's intention, it failed miserably[82] — in fact it backfired.

In Costello's opinion (while not completely dismissing the possibility of Dawson being in league with Woodhead) it looked as if the whole business had been engineered by the chemist rather than the solictor. "There certainly was a break of some kind between Dawson and Woodhead", he claimed, "but it did not come about as his son suggests. If Woodhead knew it was a hoax yet continued to help Dawson, there is, I am afraid, only one conclusion to be drawn: that Samuel Allinson Woodhead was responsible".[83] To say the least, this was a precipitous argument, based solely on a single letter whose reliability (as admissable evidence) had yet to be established. What other evidence does this worker provide to support his case against Woodhead? Very little. Earlier in the article, and to support the case that Dawson was, in all probability, duped, Costello endeavours to validate the "coconut" incident, claiming that it was a genuine find. Costello suggested that it may have been the skull of a plague victim![84] But why only the head had been buried there is left unexplained. Having established a case for this episode (but ignoring the possible counter-argument that it too, like the rest that was to follow, could have been planted), Costello then examines Dawson's discovery of the second skull fragment in the "spring" (Dawson said it was in the autumn) of 1911. It was at this point, Costello contends, that Woodhead conceived his plan. Although Costello is correct in stating that Woodhead had analysed some of these bones, it has not been firmly established when this analysis was actually performed. Although making a superficial attempt to account for how Woodhead might have come by the jaw, he makes no attempt to address the problem of remaining elements found there, and more particularly the crucial issue of whether Woodhead had the necessary background to create the subtle archaeological and palaeontological scenario implied by the total assemblage. While Woodhead's credentials in chemistry are beyond question, can the same be said of his expertise in palaeontology, archaeology and comparative anatomy? Not on the available evidence. Thus, while he might have had the opportunity (in fact he is the one person of all the suspects considered who had relatively free access to the pit), it is not possible to defend Costello's case simply on "opportunity" and "chemical skills". What, too, was his motive?

Shortly after the publication of Costello's hypothesis, new "evidence" surfaced which provided him with a motive. It was announced by Glyn Daniel in the pages of *Antiquity* that John T Hewitt (1868–1954), former Professor of Chemistry at Queen Mary College, London University, had confessed to a neighbour that "he and a friend had made the Piltdown Man as a joke".[85] According to Daniel's informant, Hewitt's confession had taken place somewhere around 1952–3. It remains uncertain, however, whether this "confession" had occurred before or after the revelations of November 1953. Why Hewitt, having made his "confession," made no effort to leave a formal statement of his exploits in his papers, remains a mystery — or does it? Daniel seemed to think the confession was novel, but there are several such confessions on file in the archives at the British Museum (Natural History),[86] and all have been shown to be groundless. The possibility that Hewitt's claim was mere bravado was, it seems, never entertained. However, following this lead, Costello discovered that Hewitt and Dawson had, during the late 1890s, been involved in an issue over a natural gas deposit which Dawson had evidently discovered near Heathfield railway station in 1897. Hewitt was apparently hired by the railway company to examine the site and evaluate its commercial potential since Dawson's communication to *Nature* had suggested that the gas might well have illuminative properties. Hewitt's analysis revealed that the gas was composed mainly of methane, with no detectable traces of oxygen.[87] Dawson was not convinced. Shortly thereafter, as Costello relates: "Dawson, together with his friend Sam Woodhead, returned to the site . . . Woodhead sampled the gas and ran further tests. He found oxygen was present".[88] The results of these new tests were communicated by Dawson to the Geological Society later in 1898.[89] Soon thereafter the gas was used to light Heathfield railway station.[90]

Costello makes much of this, claiming that Dawson's new study impugned Hewitt's scientific integrity — "no professional academic cares to be set right by a mere amateur dabbler, especially in the cocky manner of Charles Dawson".[91] Not only does this reference to Dawson's amateur status fail to grasp the nature of the British scientific community at that time, but it is also an exaggerated interpretation of Dawson's paper to the Geological Society. The language of Dawson's paper is neither strident nor accusative. It is, however, combative in that it directly challenges the results of Hewitt's study. But is this not the very essence of the scientific enterprise? Thus to suppose that Hewitt had taken umbrage and then spent the next decade waiting for an opportunity to take revenge on the "cocky" Dawson does not make much sense. Also it is important to remember the fact that the entire issue hinged on the analysis of the gas which was performed by Woodhead not Dawson. Nevertheless Costello contends that this "clash" was "the genesis of the Piltdown hoax".

Later, in 1905, Hewitt joined the Society of Public Analysts (of which Woodhead was already a member), and in 1911, both sat as members of the Society's governing Council. Costello claims that it was at this time that Hewitt heard, through Woodhead, of Dawson's activities at Piltdown, and saw his opportunity. But instead of working alone, it is suggested that Hewitt persuaded Woodhead, Dawson's "friend", to act as "the man on the spot". Why Woodhead would agree to such a proposition Costello doesn't say. Yet the mere fact that they belonged to the same society and served on a committee together is hardly a basis for what he calls: "the Hewitt–Woodhead nexus".

Costello's hypothesis is further complicated by an attempt to equate his original case against Woodhead with knowledge gleaned from Hewitt's neighbour, who reported that "[Hewitt] had the help of at least two other people, one of whom withdrew [!], to be replaced by the second after a few months ... [and it is surmised] that these people were fellow academics".[92] Rather than simply opting for Woodhead as the second academic, Costello, knowing of past speculation that Martin Hinton (and perhaps others) at the South Kensington Museum might have been involved, suggests a possible connection between Hewitt and Hinton, noting that both shared a friendship in common with the chemist Raphael Meldola (1849–1915) at the Imperial College. Hinton and Meldola are even reported to have been members of the Essex Field Club. For good measure, it is also suggested that perhaps Woodhead did not secure the Piltdown jaw from Hastings, as he had originally supposed, but that perhaps Hewitt did, with the aid of someone at "Imperial College, or at Cambridge ... which he and Woodhead then broke and treated".[93] By mentioning Cambridge, Costello embraced the rumour (evidently relayed by Daniel) that W H L Duckworth might have also been involved. In putting forward these ideas (as "possible lines of further inquiry"), Costello argues that Hewitt and Woodhead did not "intend the hoax to last". Which makes it all the more incredible that it managed to go undetected for almost forty years with so many people involved!

TEILHARD DE CHARDIN

On 19 November 1953, Kenneth Oakley wrote to Pierre Teilhard de Chardin in New York telling him:

> By the time this reaches you, probably you will have heard about the dramatic revelation that you and Woodward were "hoodwinked" at Piltdown [note the absence of Dawson's name]. The enclosed notes will give you the main facts. A copy of the full report will be sent to you almost immediately. We should greatly appreciate it if you would send some comments on these findings. We would particularly like to be able to file in our archives any recollections of yours which might throw light on this inexplicable hoax.
>
> We have found that some of the flints which were reported as being from the site have been artificially stained![94]

In reply Teilhard wrote:

> I congratulate you ... in spite of the fact that, sentimentally speaking, it spoils one of my brightest and earliest palaeontological memories ... But now the pyschological riddle remains.
> Of course nobody will even think of suspecting Sir Arthur Smith-Woodward. But to a lesser degree this holds for Dawson too. I knew pretty well Dawson, since I worked with him and sir [sic] Arthur three or four times [inserted in margin: Teilhard has

written "at Piltdown"] (after a chance meeting in a stone quarry near Hastings in 1911). He [ie Dawson] was a methodical and enthusiastic character ... And, in addition, his deep friendship with Sir Arthur makes it almost unthinkable that he should have systematically deceived his associates for several years. When we were in the field I never noticed anything suspicious in his behaviour. The only thing which puzzled me, one day, was when I saw him picking up two large fragments of the skull out of a sort of rubble in a corner of the pit (these fragments had probably been rejected by the workmen the year before). I was not in Piltdown when the jaw was found. But, a year later when I found the canine, it was so inconspicuous amid at [sic] the gravels which had been spread on the ground for sifting that it seems to me quite unlikely that the tooth could have been planted. I can even remember Sir Arthur congratulating me on the sharpness of my eyesight ... As far as the fragments of Piltdown Locality 2, are concerned, it must be observed that Dawson never tried to emphasize them particularly, although (if I am correct) these specimens were announced after the finds in Locality 1 were complete. He just brought me to the site of Locality 2 and explained [to] me that he had found the isolated molar and the small pieces of skull in the heaps of rubble and pebbles raked at the surface of the field ...[95]

During the next couple of months further letters were exchanged, in which Teilhard became increasingly defensive, at least so it seemed to both Oakley and Weiner. What particularly intrigued them was Teilhard's admission that he had both seen the remains of Piltdown II and the site where they had been reportedly recovered. Dawson did not report these finds to Woodward until 1915, by which time Teilhard was serving as stretcher-bearer in France Had he made a mistake? Oakley pursued this further. Teilhard replied:

Concerning the point of "history" you ask me, my "souvenirs" are a little vague. Yet, by elimination (and since Dawson died _during_ the first war, if I am correct) my visit with Dawson to the second site (where two small fragments of skull and the isolated molar were supposedly found in the rubbish) must have been late July 1913. I cannot remember whether Smith-Woodward was with Dawson and me, this particular day. But the possibility is not excluded.[96] [To which he added in a handwritten postscript]: When I visited the site N° 2 (in 1913?) the two small fragments of skull and the tooth had already been found, I believe. But your very question makes me doubtful! Yes, I think definitely they had been already found, and that is the reason why Dawson pointed to me the little heap of raked pebbles as the place of the "discovery".

Bearing in mind this and the fact that Teilhard had been so closely involved with Dawson and the events at Piltdown only served to increase Oakley and Weiner's suspicions. Had he been Dawson's accomplice? Or had he duped Dawson? While both were possibilities there was not much to go on. Later, during the summer of 1954, Teilhard visited England, which provided Weiner and Oakley with an opportunity to pursue their inquiries further. But contrary to expectations their meetings with Teilhard were unrewarding. The Frenchman now seemed most reluctant to discuss the matter — as is shown in Oakley's memorandum to Weiner regarding Teilhard's interrogation at the British Museum (Natural History) on the morning of 9 August 1954:

... He spoke only of African work, but I slipped in your question about writing to him. He said "Yes by all means". Then [the Keeper Wilfred Norman] Edwards came into the room. Again he spoke only of Africa, and of joint interest there. E[dwards] said, "Ah ha. Yes I'm trying to wean Oakley from Piltdown too. I expect _that_ amused _you_ quite a lot" (clapping hand on T. de C.'s arm with jovial chuckle)? "Well not really, you see, it was a souvenir of my youth and so to me it was rather sad". "Indeed", said

Pere Pierre Teilhard de Chardin "on the beach at Hastings" circa 1911. (Helicon Press, Baltimore)

E., "I can well imagine your feelings" (in rather harsh sarcastic tone). [With this T. de C. reportedly shifted the conversation to recent discoveries in human palaeontology, and shortly thereafter Edwards suggested that Oakley take Teilhard to see the Museum's Director, Gavin de Beer] ... I did [this and] left them alone for 10 minutes while I sought [Arthur T.] Hopwood. On returning to de Beer's room, I found T. de C. and the Director in animated conversation (in French); the former busy disclaiming much knowledge of Dawson and rapidly getting onto the subject of the disappearance of the Pekin skulls.[97] He terminated the Piltdown conversation saying: "They have done great work in clearing it up". Having deposited T. de C. with Hopwood I found Edwards, placed your manuscript [of *The Piltdown Forgery*] in his hands and suggested that he should try to see T. de C. again with this as an excuse. A clerk took a message to Hopwood's room, that the Keeper would like to see T. de C. for a moment before he left. [Shortly thereafter Hopwood delivered Teilhard to Edwards] ... [H]e came into E's room accompanied by H., saying "I have only a moment ... an appointment at 12.30, you know". [Evidently in an attempt to draw the Frenchman out] E. then said "Weiner has completed the MS of a book on P[iltdown forgery] and concludes that D[awson] was wholly responsible for the fraud. Do you think that is wise, is it perhaps going too far". I gather that T. de C. then spent 15 minutes telling E. what he told us, that he scarcely knew D[awson], "as a man, not at all", so he could not express an opinion about his character, but "didn't it seem more likely that the pit had been a rubbish hole and that the fossils etc. had been thrown there? ... Edwards [then] tried to pull him back to the point ... T. de C. [responded by] saying: "Yes, Weiner told me about the book Saturday, he spent about an hour, with his questions, he seemed quite *worked up* about this business — yes, and Oakley too!" [To which] Hopwood [added patronizingly]: "Yes, I have told Oakley, it is not worth *bothering* too much about it". "Well, well, I told Weiner", said T. de C., "if he *likes* I will look at the proof of his book, but I really must go now . . ."[98]

Although Teilhard subsequently corrected a number of his earlier mistakes in chronology, he was either unwilling or unable to add anything more regarding his activities with Dawson in the summer of 1913. Seven months later (on Easter Sunday, 1955), he suffered a fatal heart attack in New York.[99] In what appears to have been his last communication with Weiner, he wrote:

> . . . I have very little to add to what I could tell you, in the course of conversation with Oakley. Except that, for the dates. I think you must rely on the Dawson letters. "A la réflexion", it is quite possible that the first meeting in the Hastings quarry (in which, I *think*, I heard of the Piltdown skull fragments for the first time) should have happened as early as 1909 (?) . . . In 1913, my staying overnight [at Dawson's home] in Lewes (and the trip to Piltdown) was *pre-arranged*. But I can absolutely not remember whether the "initiative" came from me or from Dawson. In fact the occasion . . . was so "naturelle" for a meeting (after a year I had spent in Paris, with Boule) that it could not have been missed. I have never kept a single letter from Dawson. Too bad . . .[100]

During the next three decades several attempts were made to pin the forgery on Teilhard, the most recent being the case brought forward by the Harvard palaeontologist, Stephen J Gould.[101] As this investigator correctly notes his suspect was present at all the critical times. From 1908 to 1912 it is possible to document his increasing involvement with Dawson, culminating in the visit to Barkham Manor in June 1912 (shortly before his departure for Paris). The following year, in August, Teilhard returned to England. It was during this brief visit he found the crucial canine tooth. And in 1914, Teilhard made yet another visit to England, though on this occasion, so it seems, he stayed in Canterbury for the whole time. According to Teilhards's published correspondence he left Paris for Folkestone on 25 September 1914 and proceeded to Canterbury to begin his tertianship.[102] Three months later he was conscripted into the army, and began service in the medical corps on 22 January 1915.[103]

All of this unquestionably makes Teilhard a highly attractive candidate. But while it acknowledges the existence of opportunity it is by no means clear what chance the young priest would have had to prepare his materials at the seminary. He could of course have had outside help — but who? Was it possible that he had been Dawson's accomplice? While clearly undecided (in the absence of strong supporting *evidence*) where to ultimately place the blame, Gould was convinced of Teilhard's culpability in the episode. As he saw it, Teilhard's probable motive for assisting Dawson (whom he implicates largely by default) was a curious mixture of nationalistic spite and the "irresistible" desire to test the gullibility of the scientific establishment.[104] But in spite of Gould's authoritative style and his claim to have "read all the official documents",[105] his case ultimately boils down to little more than an informed opinion which pivots precariously on Teilhard's garbled testimony and his admission that he had been shown both the site and remains of Piltdown II some two years before Dawson declared these "findings" to Woodward.

It seems unlikely that Teilhard, had he been involved in the trickery at Piltdown, would have made such an important admission, particularly in a letter. Had he been either the prime mover or Dawson's accomplice it is conjectured that a more probable course of action would have been to say nothing and to await further questions — for at the time he had no idea how much Weiner and Oakley really knew. Also, it was dangerous for the Frenchman to seek to secure his own innocence by incriminating Dawson since, as Weiner's subsequent correspondence reveals, it invited suspicion of a possible collusion between the two — a fact that must have become clear to him as inquiries continued.

The crux of the case against Teilhard rests on the assumption that in 1913 he had been shown both the site and remains of Piltdown II. But had he? It is conjectured that what Dawson had shown Teilhard was not the Piltdown II site but rather that of Barcombe Mills. As it will be recalled, it was at this latter site Dawson reportedly found some cranial fragments and an isolated human molar. Whereas the Piltdown II site is thought to be located in Sheffield Park, an estate situated some miles west of Barkham Manor, Barcombe Mills lies to the south — on the west bank of the Ouse, midway between Lewes and Uckfield. Although Teilhard provides no information by which to distinguish between these two sites, the fact that he called it "Locality 2" was purely supposition. The probability that he had been taken to Barcombe Mills rather than to Sheffield Park is enhanced by the fact that on 3 July 1913, Dawson informed Woodward:

> I have picked up the frontal part of a skull this evening on a plough field covered with flint gravel. It [sic] a new place, a long way from Piltdown . . . [situated] about 40 to 50 feet above the present river Ouse. It is not a thick skull but it may be a descendant of Eoanthropus . . .[106]

For reasons that are no longer clear these remains were not handed over to Woodward at this time. Later, in 1917, when they were accessioned into the collections of the British Museum (Natural History), they consisted of the frontal bone described above, plus three other cranial fragments and a single molar tooth.[107] Although Dawson's surviving correspondence provides no clues as to when the molar tooth and other cranial fragments were added, his description of the Barcombe Mills frontal bone clearly separates it from a similar fragment later attributed to Piltdown II.

A month after Dawson announced the Barcombe Mills find to Woodward, Teilhard arrived in England. In a letter to his parents, dated 27 July 1913, he outlined his planned itinerary:

> I leave Paris on August 1. Friday night I'll be in Canterbury . . . where I think I'll be until the 8th and from there I go on to Hastings. I will make my retreat at Ore Place from the 15th to the 24th; in the beginning of September I'll be going to Jersey to do a little excavating [with ? Félix Pelletier]. I'll be back at Vieux-Colombier [Paris] by the 1st of October.[108]

Prior to making his spiritual retreat in Hastings, it appears that Teilhard had arranged to spend a few days with Dawson at Lewes, which also included a three-day excursion to Piltdown:

> . . . *Most of the time* [my emphasis] we spent digging in Uckfield in the gravel pits of Piltdown; I went on Friday [8 August], all day Saturday [9 August], and Sunday afternoon [10 August] . . .[109]

It is contended that it was during this period that Teilhard was shown not "Locality 2" (i.e. the Piltdown II site in Sheffield Park) but Barcombe Mills. Given the superficial similarity between the Barcombe Mills and Piltdown II materials it is conceivable that Teilhard subsequently came to believe that he had been shown the latter rather than the former and that this confusion had not dawned on him until after Oakley and Weiner began their inquires — and with it the realization that he had inadvertently cast suspicion not only upon his old friend Dawson but also himself. This being the case, why had he not explained this confusion to Weiner and Oakley? Would they have understood? Perhaps. But it was evident from his experience at the British Museum (Natural History) that his British colleagues were patently suspicious of him and his relationship with Dawson (whom they clearly regarded as the most likely candidate). Thus, given the distinct possibility that his motives for suddenly changing his story would have been misinterpreted, Teilhard evidently decided that the most expedient (as well as the most honourable) course of action was to say nothing.

8 Beyond a reasonable doubt?

. . . [T]he faker must have known more about primate anatomy than all the highly distinguished anatomists he deluded. He knew enough to take them in not once but repeatedly . . . If he knew as much as this why did he not satisfy his ego more simply by becoming the foremost physical anthropologist of his day . . .?[1]

THE LANGHAM BRIEF

On Saturday, 21 December 1912, an anonymous article was published in the *British Medical Journal* describing the now famous proceedings at Burlington House which took place three days earlier. To the casual reader this article may have seemed little more than a summary, but in fact it contained some rather specific information that was not generally known at the time. For example, it stated that:

> . . . The scene of this "find" lies some nine miles north of Lewes, in the valley of the Sussex Ouse, which, rising in the Weald, breaks through the South Downs at Lewes, and enters the sea at Newhaven. After flowing eastwards past Sheffield Park the Ouse bends southward. On the north bank, at the bend, about a mile from the river on a flat field near Piltdown Common, in the parish of Fletching, situated 80ft. above the level of the river, this bed of gravel that the fossil bones were found . . . Four years ago farm labourers were digging or deepening a duck pond on the gravel bed; they dug out a "thing like a cocoa-nut" and threw the splinters on the rubbish heap near by. It was from this rubbish heap that Mr. Dawson recovered the greater part of the skull, but the lower jaw was dug out of the undisturbed stratum at a later date by the authors of the communication at the Geological Society . . .[2]

Arthur Smith Woodward quite naturally wondered who the author had been and how he had come by this privileged intelligence. Was it possible that the piece had been written by Arthur Swayne Underwood, his Piltdown dental consultant? The Harley Street surgeon denied it,[3] and, distracted by other more pressing matters, it seems that Woodward did not pursue the matter further.

While rummaging through the archives of the Royal College of Surgeons in London, Ian Langham discovered, quite by accident, the answer to Woodward's earlier inquiry. The anonymous article had been written by Arthur Keith. In his weekly diary for 1912 (December), Keith had written:

> I write for BMJ [British Medical Journal] on the meeting Monday night (16th); on Wednesday [18th] wrote acct. for Morning Post (got home at 12) dined with Reid Moir. On Thursday long interview with Manchester Guardian: thus keeping things as straight as I could during the week and thrusting a quiet and fairly effective spoke in the Boyd Dawkins and Smith Woodward wheel. I expect it will be war to the death between the R.C.S. [Royal College of Surgeons] and S.K. [South Kensington Museum].[4]

Langham was, to say the least, fascinated by this extraordinary entry. What particularly attracted the Australian's attention was Keith's admission that he had

Arthur Keith, 1912.

written the article on December 16th, two days before the event actually occurred!

On re-reading the anonymous article it became clear to Langham why Woodward had been disturbed. There was no doubt that the author had been privy to explicit knowledge about the location of the site. Had he been to Piltdown? Or was he simply relaying second-hand information? But it was not just a matter of knowing the exact location; there were other specific details, such as the reference to the discovery in 1908 of the "cocoa-nut", which had been accidentally broken by farm labourers digging in the gravel bed, and how Charles Dawson had diligently applied himself to the task of recovering the remains of the shattered skull.

From his knowledge of the events preceding the unveiling at Burlington House, Langham knew that Keith had not been allowed to view the original specimens until 2 December. Furthermore, it was patently clear, not only from Keith's diary entry, but other sources, that the Hunterian Professor was not a member of Woodward's inner circle of friends. If Keith had not received this information directly from Woodward, who else could have informed him? Or was there a more sinister explanation? While

Langham's suspicions were aroused, it appears that he checked this impulse until he had more to go on.

As Langham discovered, Keith was a very methodical worker. Unlike Woodward he kept a meticulous log of both his Museum and extramural activites. He maintained two diaries: a daily (office) and weekly (home) summary.[5] In the former the entries are brief, often simply amounting to the name of a visitor, while the latter contains more substantive and personal reflections. Langham discovered in the weekly diary that Keith (accompanied by his wife) had visited Piltdown on 4 January 1913:

> Yesterday Celia and I got up at 7. Caught the Uckfield train L[ondon] Bridge at 9.7. Uckfield in hollow of tributary valley of Sussex Ooze [sic] — at 11.20. Lunch at Maiden's Head [located in Uckfield High Street]. Head westward on foot across another tributary valley and by one-30 were on the Piltdown Common — heath form of land. Hastings sand bed coming to the surface. Common used as golf course. Chas. Dawson agent for Bracknor [sic] estate gives notice that turf etc. not to be removed. Through village of Piltdown leaving Fletching on our right, crossed the slow valley of the Ooze [sic] and up to the village of Newick on other side. Found circular route could not be carried out owing to the state of paths came back by Piltdown — boys told us where Sussex skull found: fir avenue leading to farm — white gate: on delta plateau above the Ooze [sic]. didn't see the gravel bed anywhere. Back at the Maidens Head 4.15. Tea and warmth. Left Uckfield 4.17 [sic] Lewes 6.12. Victoria at 7.45. Dinner there and home having walked upwards of 12 miles and tired.[6]

In light of his article in the *British Medical Journal* (BMJ), it is not surprising that Keith found his way to Piltdown. But what is puzzling, and further aroused Langham's suspicions, is why Keith, having come so far, abruptly terminated his search at the gate to the Barkham Manor House. If, as his diary would have us believe, the objective of his visit had been to view the celebrated gravel bed, why did he not walk the extra couple of hundred yards to the Manor House and complete his mission?

Two weeks after Keith's visit to Piltdown, *The Sphere*, a London periodical, published an anonymous article on Piltdown, describing where "the most ancient skull in the world was found":

> A few days ago, writes a correspondent, I set out for Piltdown Common . . . I had never heard of this Sussex common until the discovery of the skull, although the heath can boast a golf course. The easiest way to reach it is by main-line train to Lewes, and thence by motor train to the little hillside town of Uckfield . . . The road to Piltdown pitches up and down due west from the town . . . and about two miles away one plunges down to the stream level and rises again some 80 ft to the common . . . I kept on the left-hand road until I approached a spot marked "Barkham" on the ordnance map and then struck across the common towards an avenue of firs. At the side of this avenue was a ferruginous-looking cutting or excavation, simple enough in appearance, but indeed the shrine for which I was making. Closer examination of the gravel showed that it was promising-looking ground — the kind to arouse the expectations and curiosities of the anthropologist and prehistorian. It was strange as one stood at the side of this little trench to think of the interest this spot has created in scientific circles . . ."[7]

From the notes written by Langham on his copy of this short article, there is little question that he believed Keith had been the author. Unfortunately this is not verified by Keith's diary. Langham's reasons for crediting Keith with the article are based, in part, on the timing of publication, the general similarity between it and Keith's own account of his excursion to Piltdown on 4 January, and the fact that Keith is known to have had connections with *The Sphere*[8].

Assuming for the moment that Keith was indeed the author,[9] why would he omit reference to this fact in his diary? How reliable are his diaries in this regard? While they are littered with many such references, it is quite evident that not all of his publications are mentioned. It could be argued therefore that it was either innocently overlooked or deliberately omitted. The inference drawn from Langham's notes is that it was the latter, and that his motive for not claiming authorship was grounded in the intention that lay behind the piece. He was convinced that Keith had visited Piltdown before 4 January and that during this earlier visit he had been seen but not identified.[10] Evidently the point that Langham would have gone on to make was that if Keith had written the *Sphere* article, which explicitly states that he had stood at the edge of the pit, he clearly did not do this on 4 January. Furthermore, as Keith's diary makes clear, from the 5th until the 18th his scheduled commitments would have prevented another trip to Sussex. If indeed he had been to the "edge of the pit", and it was not on the 4th, then he must have visited the pit before. From this it can be inferred that the 4 January entry is, as Langham's notes contend, "deliberately misleading", implying that this was his first visit and that he did not know the exact location. Thus it is presumed that the 4 January visit had been undertaken to establish the fact that he (and his wife) had been to Piltdown but did not know where the pit was located; while the subsequent article in *The Sphere* was evidently aimed at creating a stampede of visitors to the "shrine" — thereby diverting attention away from his earlier, clandestine visit. But even if the *Sphere* evidence is unconvincing in support of the case for an earlier visit, it does not invalidate the interpretation placed on the 4 January visit, — that it had been intended to create the illusion that he was unaware of the pit's exact location.

Considered together with the anonymous *BMJ* article, there now seemed little question in Langham's mind that Keith was in some way involved in the Piltdown affair. But how? Was he simply using the situation to his own advantage or was he more directly involved? As Langham well knew rumours about the Sussex find began circulating sometime before the story was printed in the *Manchester Guardian* on 21 November 1912. In fact Keith had written to Woodward as early as 2 November requesting an opportunity to view the specimens,[11] but it was another month before he finally saw the treasure.[12] As Keith later noted in his diary, the visit was a relatively short one:

> Went down — on way to Zool[ogical Society] tea — to Nat. Hist. Museum to see Smith Woodward's remains — early Pleistocene: of which so many rumours have reached me of late days: Got dark when I worked in Hall: lights being turned out. Taken first into his room where he unlocked from his drawers (cabinet) small box with fragments. . .[13]

As Keith goes on to indicate, the purpose of his visit was to examine carefully the actual remains and to view Woodward's reconstruction. Exactly how long he remained at the Museum, studying the pieces, is not known, it was probably not more than an hour at the most. Is it possible that during that time Woodward divulged the information that later appeared in Keith's *BMJ* article? This is unlikely because there is good reason to suggest that Woodward suspected Keith of being responsible for leaking the story to the *Manchester Guardian*. (see later). Who else in the South Kensington clique might have been willing to confide in him? The possibilities are limited. By the end of November 1912 Woodward's inner-circle is known to have included (besides Dawson): the Museum preparator, Frank Barlow, Dawkins, Lankester, Pycraft, Moir, Edgar Willett (a close friend of Lankester's),[14] and

Underwood. As Woodward's letter to Underwood suggests he had been privy to all the facts, but exactly how much the others knew is not clear. It is known that Lankester and Willett had seen both the remains and had visited the site on 9 November 1912.[15] This is of particular importance since Lankester was a close associate of Moir's, and of all the men in Woodward's group, the one most likely to have confided in Keith was Moir. But while Moir had been allowed to examine the remains at South Kensington early in November, it seems he had not been privy to all of the details concerning the exact location of the site and the circumstances that led to this sensational find. While it remains possible that Lankester may have divulged details of the site's location to Moir, there is no evidence to support this. Also, it is by no means certain that Lankester himself was, at this point in possession of all the facts relating to the prehistory of these finds. Aside from Woodward (and possibly Underwood) the only other person who had detailed knowledge was Dawson. Had Dawson been Keith's source?[16]

A search of Keith's diaries failed to establish any direct association between he and Dawson until 20 January 1913, when he noted in his daily diary: "Chas. Dawson, Piltdown here". While in his weekly diary, he entered: "Today the above [referring to his 5 January entry which recounted the details of his visit to Piltdown] Chas. Dawson came into see me at College. A clever level headed man . . ." Recalling this visit in his memoirs, published in 1950, Keith wrote of this same visit:

> One morning early in 1913, when I entered my office at College, I found a gentleman waiting for me. He introduced himself as Mr. Charles Dawson. We had a pleasant hour together. His open, honest nature and his wide knowledge endeared him to me. He quite appreciated the attention I was giving to his special child — Piltdown man! . . .[17]

The inference drawn here is that this had been their first meeting. Langham, however, was not convinced. His reasons for doubting this testimony rested largely on a recent reading of Joseph Weiner's transcript of the visit (with Kenneth Oakley) to Keith at his home at Downe, Kent, on the afternoon of 21 November 1953. The purpose of this visit was two-fold. First, it was to soften the blow of the recent revelations, and second, to record Keith's reactions and memories of the Piltdown episode. He had, after all, been actively engaged in the controversy, and with the exception of Teilhard, represented a direct and intimate link with the events of 1912. During the course of this meeting, Keith was asked about his relationship with Dawson:

> [Keith said] that he was "an open, honest chap", [and] that he had talked to him often. "When did you first see him?" we asked. Keith said, "The first time was when he came to see me to apologise for not being in a position to give me the material because I was the only man with any real experience, and he appreciated that but because of his long association with Smith Woodward he felt it was not possible." When was this occasion? Keith thought and said, "Before the famous meeting of 1912", and then suddenly he said, "No, it was in fact afterwards, at the time when I was on bad terms with Smith Woodward". He seemed to me [Weiner] puzzled that in fact it had been after the meeting (and Oakley and I did tell him that we knew that Dawson had written to Smith Woodward in May 1912, about his pleasure of having discovered the twelfth [sic: should be thirteenth] dorsal vertebra and photographed it under the very nose of Keith) . . . [Neither Weiner's nor Oakley's reports of this meeting record if, and how, Keith responded to this latter information] . . . [Weiner] then asked him how he had obtained the 1908 date [for the initial discovery of the skull, namely the "coconut" incident, which Keith mentioned specifically in his *Antiquity of Man* (1925, II:491]. He

was surprised at this ... He said he was fairly sure that Dawson must have told him this date.[18]

The next day Keith wrote to Weiner:

> It was passing kind of you and Oakley to make the journey to Downe and to explain so convinvingly [sic] the treachery of my old friend Charles Dawson. I'm glad Smith Woodward will never know of it but if you have any means of getting in touch with Dawson do rub it into him that after 40 years you have found him out. After you left I went searching amongst my papers and found a sort of manual I made entries in from time to time in my earlier years at the College of Surgeons from 1908 on. I have a full acct. of my first sight of the Piltdown material a week before the famous meeting on December 18, then one of my visit my wife and I paid to Piltdown a week after the meeting, and then the first relevant note under the date January 28 [sic], 1913 ... so that must have been my first personal meeting with him.[19]

While Weiner's reaction to this (and Oakley's come to that) went unrecorded, it is evident that these documents served to reinforce Langham's suspicions that Keith was not being entirely honest in his account of his relationship with the Sussex solicitor.

As Langham recognized, the "twelfth dorsal vertebra" incident referred to by Weiner, though suggestive of a prior interaction, did not in itself prove they had met before the time Keith insisted they had. Although both Weiner and Oakley had

Ian Langham at Piltdown 1984. (Courtesy of Rev Dr Robin Harvey)

initially been puzzled by this curious incident, they had ultimately pushed it aside — unable to make anything of it. Langham realized that if he could demonstrate an even earlier connection between Keith and Dawson it would obviously strengthen his explanation of the so-called "twelfth dorsal vertebra" incident. The problem was where in the haystack to look to find the needle. Since Keith had destroyed all of his Dawson correspondence,[20] it was unlikely that any clues remained in existence among his papers at the Royal College of Surgeons. And there was nothing in Dawson's correspondence in the archives of the BM(NH) which gave the slightest hint of an earlier connection. In narrowing the search it dawned on Langham that one thing that might connect the two was their respective association with museums. In Dawson's case he was a member of the Hastings Museum Association. Had Keith had any past dealings with this institution? Keith's diaries supplied the answer. In his weekly diary (1911), under July 15th, Keith noted: "On Thursday went to Brighton Museum Association [meeting] . . ."[21] And as Langham discovered, this Association ran an excursion to Hastings hosted by Ruskin Butterfield, Charles Dawson, Lewis Abbott, and other members of the Hastings & St Leonards Natural History Society and Hastings Museum Committee. According to the *Hastings & St Leonards Weekly Mail & Times* (15 July 1911)[22] the guests of honour included Francis Bather from Woodward's department at the British Museum (Natural History), Reginald Smith from the British Museum (Bloomsbury branch) and "Mr. Arthur Keith, Royal College of Surgeons, Lincoln's Inn Fields . . ." Evidently during this visit Dawson and Abbott gave a guided tour of the archaeological sites around Hastings and later in the day Dawson lectured on the "History of Hastings Castle". If they had not met before, there could be no question that they met that day.[23]

This piece of information cast a somewhat different light on Dawson's reported activites at the Royal College of Surgeons in May 1912. As will be remembered, three months earlier Dawson had told Woodward of his initial findings at Piltdown, but it seems that circumstances conspired against Woodward making the necessary journey down to Lewes to review the evidence at that time. In March, when Woodward was ready, Dawson indicated that his home was being "turned up-side down" by painters and builders, and then there was the weather, "At present the roads leading to it [the site] are impassable and excavation is out of the question", he told Woodward.[24] Shortly thereafter, and no doubt to secure his colleague's continuing interest, Dawson sent him, for identification, a hippopotamus molar he had recovered from Piltdown. Woodward confirmed the diagnosis and cautioned Dawson about letting anyone else know about his recent acquisitions until he had time to fully evaluate them. Dawson replied:

> I will of course take care that no one sees the pieces of skull who has knowledge of the subject, and leave all to you. On second thoughts I have decided to wait until you and I can go over by ourselves to look at the bed of gravel. It is not far to walk from Uckfield and it will do us good![25]

In April the prospects were further complicated by Woodward's departure for Berlin to study dinosaur remains collected by a recent German expedition in East Africa. The London Chapter of the German Colonial Society had invited him to lecture on this subject, and hence his visit to Berlin. Dawson's next communication with Woodward was on 12 May, when he wrote:

> Since I saw you I have been writing on the subject of "the 13th Dorsal Vertebra", in certain human skeletons, which I believe is a new subject. I send you the result and if

you think well enough of it I should be very much obliged if you would introduce the paper for me at the Royal Society. I am very anxious to get it placed at once because I have had to work the photographs under the nose of Keith and his assistant. I gather from the latter that Keith is rather puzzled as to what to make of it all, and I want to secure the priority to which I am entitled . . .[26]

Essentially the subject of Dawson's short paper (8 typewritten [double-spaced] pages) dealt with the occurrence of a thirteenth thoracic vertebra in the human skeleton.[27] The normal number is twelve; whereas apes have thirteen. The loss of a vertebra in the human spinal column was thought to have had something to do with the acquisition of an upright posture. Although Dawson was correct in noting that there was very little in the literature on this subject, earlier that year A-F Le Double (1848–1913), a French anatomist from Tours, had published an extensive study *Variations de la colonne vertbbrale de l'homme, et leur signification au point de vue de l'anthropologie zoologique.''*[28] Keith had been asked by the Royal Anthropological Institute to review the book, and, even more interesting, he did nothing about it for a while. When he finally did get around to submitting his extremely short review of Le Double's work in 1915, he simply noted that: "The late appearance of a notice of this really valuable work is wholly due to an oversight on the part of the reviewer".[29] Why had Keith taken so long to write a ten-line (!) review of such a "valuable work"? Was there a connection between Le Double's book and Dawson's paper? Had Dawson really expected to communicate this paper to the Royal Society and had he really hoped that Woodward might use his authority to push the paper through? Or was the paper merely a camouflage? But to hide what? Langham believed that some time between July 1911 and the beginning of 1912, Dawson and Keith had conceived the plan to fabricate the long awaited missing link. Between January and May 1912 the final details, and in particular the problems surrounding the selection and preparation of the jaw, were settled. Although Dawson's legal work took him occasionaily to Lincoln's Inn Fields and the associated law courts, he would have had little or no reason for repeated visits to the Royal College of Surgeons. The "13th Dorsal Vertebra" paper provided him with an alibi — supplied by Keith. Since the paper would never be read it is conjectured that Keith directed Dawson's attention to five specific skeletons exhibiting supernumerary vertebra on display in the Hunterian, and to further assist the solicitor, loaned him Le Double's book. Dawson was proficient in French. Precisely when Dawson took the photographs he used to illustrate his paper is not known, but it is further conjectured that it was done, most probably during the first week of May when Keith was in Jersey examining the La Cotte de St Brelade site which had yielded human Pleistocene remains.[30] This allowed Dawson to establish his story with Keith's assistant (Richard H Burne), who reportedly told Dawson that his boss was "puzzled as what to make of it all", and which lent further weight to the subsequent story he relayed to Woodward.

Precisely how Langham proposed to harmonize this emerging scenario with what was known about Dawson's earlier activities at Piltdown is not immediately apparent from his notes. But one thing is clear and that is his acknowledgement of Dawson's account of the so-called "coconut" incident.

What is known about this incident? In the official account of the discoveries made at Piltdown in 1912, Dawson presents only a vague chronology of events. Having established that his interest in the Piltdown pit had been aroused by the "peculiar" flints found there, Dawson then noted:

> Upon one of my subsequent visits to the pit, one of the men [farm labourers] handed me a small portion of an unusually thick human parietal bone. I immediately made a

search, but could find nothing more . . . It was not until some years later, in the autumn of 1911, on a visit to the spot, that I picked up, among the rain-washed spoil heaps . . . another and larger piece belonging to the frontal region of the same skull . . .[31]

There are, however, some discrepancies between this account and that which Dawson is reported to have given at Burlington House on the evening of 18 December 1912. According to various newspaper reports Dawson is quoted as having said that he was first handed a fragment of a human cranium "four years ago", that this and subsequent fragments constituted the remains of a skull which had been accidentally broken and then discarded by labourers working the gravel bed because to them it looked like a "cocoa-nut". The original notes used by Dawson at the Geological Society on 18 December, confirm this story. Under the heading, "Brief Story of Discovery", he wrote:

Human skull found and broken by workmen. Hence subsequent digging both in spoil-material and in bottom layer of gravel left untouched by them.[32]

Why this part of the story was omitted from the official report is not at all clear, but whatever the reasons, it elicited no inquiries at the time.

As Steward of the Manors of Barkham, Netherall and Tarring Camois, Dawson had many occasions to visit Barkham Manor and he associated his discoveries with his duties as president of the periodic Court Barons of these estates. Their meetings were held at approximately four year intervals (generally at Barkham Manor House). According to existing records, a Court was convened shortly after Dawson received the Stewardship of Barkham Manor on 27 July 1899, followed by Courts held on 3 October 1904, 10 May 1907, and 4 August 1911.

Later, in 1913, Dawson published in the *Hastings & East Sussex Naturalist* another account of how he first became interested in the Piltdown gravel bed:

Many years ago, I think just at the end of the last century, business led me to Piltdown. It was a Court Baron at which I was president, and when business was over and the customary dinner to the tenants of the Manor was awaited, I went for a stroll on the road outside the Manor House. My attention was soon attracted by some iron-stained flints not usual in the district . . . Being curious as to the use of the gravel in so remote a spot, I enquired at dinner . . . where he obtained it . . . I was informed that the flint gravel was dug on the farm and that some men were then actually digging it to put on the farm roads . . . I was glad to get the dinner over and visit the gravel pit, where, sure enough, two farm hands were at work digging in a shallow pit three or four feet deep close to the house. . . . As I surmised that any fossils found in the gravel would probably be interesting and might lead to fixing the date of the deposit, I specially charged the men to keep a look out . . . Subsequently I made occasional visits . . . On one of my visits, one of the labourers handed me a small piece of bone . . . a portion of a human cranium . . . I at once made a long search, but could find nothing more . . . and soon afterwards made a whole day's search in the company of Mr. Allinson Woodhead MSc, but the bed appeared to be unfossiliferous . . . [I]t was not until several years later, I lighted on a larger piece of the same skull . . . [and] afterwards I found a piece of a hippopotamus tooth . . .[33]

Aside from Dawson's somewhat misleading description of the pit's location (which he would have had to pass in order to get to the Manor House), this account provides a more definite chronology in which to place other known information, and thereby narrow down the possibilities regarding the date of the "coconut" episode. It is quite possible, bearing in mind Abbott's insistence that he alerted Dawson to the importance of Wealden gravels at the beginning of the century, that Dawson's initial interest in the Piltdown gravel bed dates from either the first Court Baron he attended in 1899, or the second in 1904. As for the proposition that Dawson received the first piece of the human cranium at the time of his third Court in 1907, there is some doubt. While Samuel Woodhead's son, Leslie, suggested that the first find had been made "early in 1908",[34] this was later disputed by Mabel Kenward's testimony.[35] Although confirming the "coconut" story, she was convinced the event had been much later:

> Since seeing you [she wrote to Oakley] I have been trying to trace the years — so long ago — I now am quite sure the "coconut" was found in the autumn of 1910 or the spring of 1911. The gravel-pit was flooded always in the winter and so no digging could be done. How I remember it so well is because it was a very wet winter — I was in Paris at the time of the big flood in France — the whole of the Seine valley — and a great part of Paris was under water... So I have every reason to remember 1910-1911. In Francis Vere's book "Piltdown Fantasy" [1955] — he says the skull was found in 1911.[36] This was when the digging [of the gravel by the farm labourers] resumed.[37]

This much is certain: a skull, or at least part of one, was uncovered and accidentally shattered by farm labourers while working the gravel bed at Barkham Manor, sometime between the spring of 1907 and the autumn of 1911. The latter date is highly questionable, and does not tie in with Dawson's declaration that it had been earlier. It seems most unlikely that he would have made such statement knowing that it could be contested. But if it was not 1911, when was it? It is contended that Dawson's own statement at Burlington House on 18 December 1912, was probably closer to the truth, namely that it was "four years earlier". Whether it was 1908, or even 1909, actually makes little difference. The important point was to establish a case for the archaeological potential of the site, and to fix in popular memory the incident, which later Dawson vaguely linked to the periodic Court Barons.

It is far from certain whether Langham's annotations represent his final position on this matter, but as they stand it would seem that he envisioned the following chain of events. Sometime between 1905, when Dawson's personal and business arrangements changed, and 1910 when his relationship with Woodward is seen to intensify, the solicitor entertained the idea of transforming the Piltdown gravel bed into a major archaeological site. And it is clear from Dawson's correspondence at this time that he had been on the look out for a big find, something worthy of Woodward's attention.[38] Next a suitable skull was procured, an unusually thick one, perhaps an Australian aboriginal skull, which he then placed in the gravel bed and awaited its discovery. Whether he had intended for it to be shattered, or whether he had deliberately modified the skull prior to its planting, Langham does not speculate, but whatever Dawson's intentions may have been in this regard, the next couple of years were spent recovering the fragments in preparation for their subsequent (?) treatment[39] and replanting.

Sometime shortly after the Museum Association meeting at Hastings in July 1911, Langham conjectures, Dawson visited Keith in London to show him a fragment of the skull he had found at Piltdown. It is surmised that it had been the memory of this meeting which flashed into Keith's mind on that November afternoon when Weiner and Oakley came to visit:

> ...The first time was when he came to see me to apologise for not being in a position to give me the material because I was the only man with any real experience, and he appreciated that but because of his long association with Smith Woodward he felt it was not possible ...

Langham believed that when Dawson brought this skull fragment to Keith, the discussion naturally turned to the kind of jaw that would be associated with such a thick and apparently very ancient cranium — and it was from this "crucible" that the forgery emerged in its final form.

Given the particular configuration of the cranial fragments and the fact that they had been broken in such a way as to preclude an accurate reconstruction, is it reasonable to suppose that their shape was the result of a fortuitous blow of labourer's pickaxe, or had they in fact been deliberately tailored? It is presumed that it had been the latter. Whether Langham ever considered the possibility that the skull Dawson brought Keith was not the one finally employed, and that there had been a substitution, is not known. This "switch" hypothesis is not an entirely novel one. In fact Weiner had hinted at a such a possibility in his 1955 book *The Piltdown Forgery*, he where reprints a report from the *Sussex Express* of January 1954 which states that in 1906 Dawson came into possession of an "unusual" human skull:

> Mrs Florence Padgham, now of Cross-in-Hand, remembers that in 1906, aged thirteen, when living at Victoria Cottage, Nutley, her father gave Charles Dawson a skull, brown with age, no lower jaw bone, and only one tooth in the upper jaw, with a mark resembling a bruise on the forehead. Dawson is supposed to have said, "You'll hear more about this, Mr Burley".[40]

Exactly what "unusual" entailed neither Weiner nor the article says. Whether Dawson had used this skull or one similar, is of course pure speculation, but the proposition is not an unreasonable one. Besides providing an alternative explanation for the particular configuration of the cranial parts, it might account for the existence of the Barcombe Mills material — though it can be just as easily argued that this material was procured later. If indeed Dawson had brought Keith the latter material, this would further reinforce the necessity for the switch, and perhaps also explain why he went to Keith in the first place, rather than Woodward. The point being that this skull (i.e. the Barcombe Mills fragments), while of interest, was not compelling and certainly not one that would have captured Woodward's imagination; whereas, given Keith's convictions on the great antiquity of the modern human form, it is not difficult to imagine why Dawson might have approached him with such material. But whether this is the case or not, there can be little question that the cranial fragments in both instances would have required modification, and that this would have been done by Keith and not Dawson.

Furthermore, it is important not to loose sight of the fact that the selected orangutan jaw was rather unusual. The dimensions of the jaw indicate that it was on the lower range of variation for orang females and as such was a rather rare specimen, and its attraction lay in the fact that many of the usual diagnostic features were poorly expressed. The exact source of the specimen remains uncertain, but there are several possibilities, all of which, as Langham well appreciated, Keith would have had knowledge of and access to.[41] Thus, whatever Langham's stance on the "switch" hypothesis, might have been, his notes leave no doubt — he saw the jaw as the "master-stroke", which he attributed exclusively to Keith. In the meantime, while Keith was preparing this specimen during the spring of 1912, Dawson was busy setting the stage by discretely showing a sample of the Piltdown I cranium to a few of his Sussex cronies.[42] The object of this exercise was evidently to "test the waters", while at the same time providing substance to his subsequent story of how the discovery at Piltdown was made.

THE QUESTION OF MOTIVES

In entertaining the proposition that Dawson and Keith had been co-conspirators it is necessary to consider what possible motives had driven them in this extraordinary enterprise.

It is conjectured that in Dawson's case his motive was tied primarily to his ambition to become a Fellow of the Royal Society, an honour that marked the pinnacle of scientific achievement. Achieving this accolade was not an easy matter, but it is evident from his later correspondence that he had seen Piltdown as a possible route. Indeed, in 1914, he secured a certificate of candidacy, which was renewed every year until his death in 1916;[43] and there is every reason to suppose that, had he lived, he would have been duly elected — an eventuality that would have been based almost entirely on his achievements at Piltdown.

But would Dawson have risked his scientific reputation, not to mention his standing in the legal profession, for such an ambition? Given the argument that this forgery had been designed to withstand scientific scrutiny, it is contended that the advantages far out-weighed the risks involved. Although the chances of detection would remain a constant threat, once the discovery had been successfully launched into the scientific arena, the impact of such a disclosure, if, and whenever it came, would be minimized by the argument that he had been "hoodwinked" as had his eminent colleagues. While disclosure was an embarrassing prospect, it is one that a professional solicitor might have lived with far more easily than perhaps a professional scientist, such as Woodward, who had been largely responsible for its promotion — which raises the issue of the Dawson-Woodward connection. In light of Woodward's apparent innocence and Charles Dawson's long-standing relationship with him, is it reasonable to suppose that Dawson had played Jekyll and Hyde with him?

To guarantee the success of a venture such as this required the endorsement of a reputable scientist, one with credentials beyond reproach, who could carry it with conviction into the scientific arena. Woodward was an ideal vehicle, but is it reasonable to suppose that Dawson was capable of behaving in such a cold and calculated manner, and more especially with someone with whom he had long been associated? This is a debatable point, and one that hinges on the fact that it has previously been supposed that they were "close" friends. There is no question that their association was long-standing, dating from the early 1890s, but it is far from clear how close they had been. Based strictly on the surviving correspondence, it would seem that Dawson's association with Woodward prior to 1909 had been rather episodic, whereas, after this time, there is a demonstrable change. Furthermore it needs to be stressed that these letters provide very little in the way of evidence on which to base an accurate assessment of their relationship. The odd reference here and there to Woodward's son, and his passion for cigarette cards (Dawson evidently collected them for "Cyril"), and the occasional invitation not to "forget to look us up when this way", while indicative of a greater familiarity than one would expect from a purely professional relationship fails to substantiate the proposition that they were intimate friends. It is therefore contended that any qualms Dawson may have had in this regard were offset by his own ambitions, and the fact that Woodward actually stood to gain considerably by his involvement in the affair. Even considering the awful prospect of the Piltdown remains being dismantled sometime in the future, his position would be no more awkward than Dawson's, or any of the others who later endorsed the scheduled discoveries at Piltdown.

As with Dawson, it is possible to assemble evidence of a dark side to Keith's persona, and Langham had assembled a long list of his personality traits (extracted from his autobiography). While much of this does little more than advance the fact that Keith was a complex individual, whose life, like so many other human beings, is seen to be filled with contradictory twists and turns, it must also be admitted that there is nothing here which could be used to eliminate him from such a venture. Like Dawson, Keith was highly social, and seemed to thrive on controversy and combat. And it is patently clear from both his autobiography (as well as his private correspondence) that he was both ambitious and willing to take whatever risks might be necessary to promote his career.

Having in 1894 successfully defended his M.D. thesis on the "Myology of the Catarrhini", based on fieldwork in Siam (1888–92), Keith had set his heart on becoming a professional anatomist which would have enabled him to legitimately pursue his first love: anthropology. This, however, was easier said than done and like others before him he was appalled by the lack of opportunities. In the autumn of 1895, Keith finally secured a position, as a demonstrator in anatomy, at the London Hospital in Whitechapel. Within months of beginning his formal career in 1897 he published a series of heavily documented articles on the anatomy of the anthropoid apes in the monthly scientific journal *Natural Science* in 1897. From this base, Keith planned his magnum opus, a book on the evolution of man, and in the same year a contract was negotiated with the publisher John Murray. During the next three years he devoted his spare time to this project and in October 1900 the completed manuscript was transmitted to his publisher. The work, entitled "Man and Ape: A Statement of the Evidence of their Common Origin as it Stands Today", was divided into 22 chapters, made up of 405 pages of typescript, and included 78 original drawings. Three months later Keith's manuscript was returned with a letter extolling the scientific merits of the work, but warning of its limited public appeal. Murray refused to go on with it, despite the contract. Recalling this moment, Keith wrote: "Murray's reception of that book was my bitterest disappointment in my struggle for place and reputation among my fellow anatomists".[44] Although as he noted, the "old Adam, in me was not quite dead",[45] it was plain to him that anthropology, for the time being, would have to take second place to the business of his future in anatomy — and he arranged his research priorities accordingly. It was a sensible move, since the work produced during the next eight years, which he later called "The Waiting Years", unquestionably secured his appointment at the Royal College in 1908. Among this body of work are his researches into the causes of cardiac arrhythmia, and his collaborative work with Martin Flack (1882–1931) on the sinoauricular node of the heart and its role in the initiation and control of normal rhythmic contraction of the heart.[46]

In successfully triumphing over the competition for the Hunterian Conservatorship, Keith at last found himself in a position to revive his anthropological interests. It is apparent from his autobiography that on assuming this prestigious position, he saw as one of his main goals the restoration of the Museum to its former glory. In the twenty one years prior to his appointment, the position had been held by Charles Stewart (1840–1907), who evidently did little to build upon the work of his immediate predecessors: Richard Owen (1804–92) and William Flower (1831–99), both of whom had promoted anthropology. In reviewing their respective contributions to the Hunterian collections, Keith was particularly drawn to Flower's section on the prehistoric inhabitants of Britain. From this was to emerge his ambitious resolution to expand the collection, and make it the basis of an anthropological history of the British peoples which would provide him with a focus for his future Hunterian Lectures and promote his mission to transform the Museum into a "Mecca" for anthropologists and students of human evolution.[47] By 1911 these plans were well underway.

This brief survey of Keith's career prior to 1912 would seem to detract from his involvement in the Piltdown affair. Had he not after all secured one of the most prestigious positions in anatomy? Could he not have achieved all of his declared ambitions without Piltdown? Probably, but it is debatable whether his reputation in anthropological circles would have been so well-established had he not had Piltdown around which to organize his work and ideas. Furthermore, there seems little doubt that had it not been for Piltdown, the evidence on which he had based his particular argument for the antiquity of the modern human form, namely the Galley Hill skeleton, and later the Ipswich skeleton, would have collapsed long before it actually did.

As implied in Chapter 3, Keith's obsession with the Galley Hill skeleton was (probably) closely interwoven with his personal and professional ambitions, and in choosing to promote this specimen to support his provocative thesis on the antiquity of *Homo sapiens*, he was left with few supporters. It is clear that he had kept his options open until 1911, as indicated by his continuing though clearly weakening support for the European Neanderthalers. Although this latter situation was not unique to Keith, the particular stance that he had taken was. The Piltdown remains provided him with the empirical evidence needed to justify the interpretation he had placed on Galley Hill, and it could be argued that had Piltdown not been hovering in the wings, Keith would not have burned all of his bridges in March 1912 when he endorsed the Ipswich skeleton and pruned the Neanderthal twig from the human evolutionary tree.

There appears to be more to Keith's conception of the Piltdown skull than just the mere anticipation of nature. It also seems he had envisioned it as a heuristic device: a means by which he could instruct and advertise his anatomical prowess. It also provided the infrastructure for his prospective history of the British while a copy served as the centre-piece of his anthropological exhibit at the Museum. Hope became reality and, after 1913 the attendance figures for Keith's Hunterian lectures rocketed to an all-time high.[48] Keith had become a celebrity, and he had not discovered a thing — except Woodward's mistakes!

If these had been Keith's motives, he would not necessarily have gained by being more intimately connected with the discovery and description of the remains; he would, in fact, have been obliged to adopt a defensive posture rather than an offensive one — and it is much easier (as well as safer) to attack than it is to defend. Since it was impossible to predict precisely how these remains would be received, it made much more sense to launch an attack, which, if handled correctly, would allow him to collect kudos with the minumum of risk.

Seen from Keith's viewpoint his partnership with Dawson was an attractive one. Since Dawson appeared to have no intellectual axe to grind, he offered neither a threat nor an impediment to Keith's intellectual and institutional ambitions. Dawson's aims were simple: fame and a Fellowship of the Royal Society. Although perhaps more subtle, Keith's motives were, in the final analysis, not much different from those of Dawson. They were self-serving. While there were risks involved, provided they remained calm there was everything to gain and nothing to lose. Indeed, once the skull was "launched" neither Keith nor Dawson would be greatly injured by its demolition. But again, provided they played their cards with care, there was every reason to suppose that this would never happen. The only real problem was securing Woodward's committment to the finds without arousing his suspicions; it was critical that he should not have the slightest inkling of Dawson's relationship with Keith. Hence the need to secure an alibi for Dawson's visits to the Royal College in the early spring of 1912. After this time Dawson could have had no direct and traceable contact with Keith until after the official unveiling. Thereafter there would have been legitimate reasons to meet, though the real purpose would had to have been camouflaged. They each had their separate roles to play. Dawson was the man on the spot: responsible for delivering a predetermined schedule of finds and monitoring events within Woodward's inner circle. Keith's role was to publicly promote the finds and to nurture the debate. The greater the debate, the greater the rewards.

THE DELIVERY REVISITED

To secure Woodward's interest it was critical that his initial experience at the pit be a compelling one. Once he was hooked, the all important jaw could be delivered at the appropriate moment. Although Woodward had specifically requested that no one else be involved, especially anyone "who has any knowledge of the subject", Dawson was undoubtedly aware of the obvious advantages of having a witness on hand — particularly a witness whose credentials were beyond reproach. Teilhard de Chardin was perfect. Who would doubt the integrity of a priest? Woodward had not met Teilhard, but he knew of him through the important collection of fossil Wealden plants he had transmitted, through Dawson, to the British Museum (Natural History).[49] The difficulty here was not so much the task of engaging the priest's interest, but rather the problem of synchronizing his schedule with that of Woodward's. But perhaps he thought that showing Teilhard some of the material might render him more flexible.

According to Teilhard, the solicitor visited him at Ore House, Hastings, on Saturday, 20 April:

> He brought [to show] me some prehistoric remains (silex [flint tools], elephant and hippopotamus [teeth], and especially, a thick, well-preserved human skull) which he had found in the alluvian deposits not far from here; he did this in order to stir me up to some similar expeditions; but I hardly have the time for that anymore.[50]

By mid May, however, it appears that Teilhard was beginning to have second thoughts — as he revealed in a letter to his confrère Félix Pelletier then stationed in Jersey:

> I forgot to tell you that when Dawson came along last time he appeared with a large carefully wrapped box from which he excitedly drew one third of the skull of "Homo Lewensis" found by him during these last years in some alluvia ... near Uckfield. The skull is certainly very curious, of deep chocolate colour and especially of a stupefying thickness ... Dawson [also] brought along a sample of the alluvium ... and species of what is found there: teeth of hippopotamus, elephant (fragments) and one or two very beautiful silex, which were covered with a compact patina. I would like to work there for an hour or two, perhaps that can be arranged ...[51]

Sometime between May 23rd and 27th Woodward viewed these same remains and arrangements were made for him to visit Piltdown on June 2nd, along with Teilhard de Chardin.

In addition to witnessing Dawson's recovery of another fragment of the "coconut", Woodward saw Teilhard find a fragment of an elephant molar. "He jumped on the piece with the enthusiasm of a youth and all the fire that his apparent coldness covered came out", Teilhard recalled the next day in a letter to his parents.[52] Woodward was hooked, and during the next month additional finds were made, along with the jaw.

The ensuing debate and the opportunities it might create all hinged on Woodward's reaction. It was Keith's expectation that Woodward, under Boyd Dawkins' influence, would attempt a compromise reconstruction but it was most unlikely that he would endeavour to reconstruct the jaw along the lines of Heidelberg. There was also the remote possibility that he might reject it.

Although Woodward had from the outset connected the jaw with the cranium, there is every reason to suppose that he had had mixed feelings about the association once he began the difficult task of reconstruction. Three versions were produced before finally selecting the one presented at Burlington House on 18 December. Evidently it had been these difficulties which prompted Keith to request "a glimpse" of Woodward's "wonderful find"[53] early in November; but at this stage (and for obvious reasons) it seems Woodward had been reluctant to expose his diffidence to Keith. In light of this and the looming threat that Woodward might suddenly give up and dispatch the jaw, it is suspected that either Keith or Dawson leaked the story to the *Manchester Guardian*. The piece has a definite Keithian ring to it, and it appears that Woodward may have thought so too. "I suspect I can identify the thief", he told Boyd Dawkins, "and shall treat him cautiously in the future. If I am right, the man has not seen the specimens — has only asked me questions." But whichever of the two was responsible, the article had the desired effect: it brought Woodward out into the open and committed him to the mission he had been chosen for.

On 29 November Keith approached Woodward again.[54] He was getting anxious. In order to gain a tactical advantage in the debate he needed to have seen the originals. Without this his plans for writing the *BMJ* leader were thwarted, and he was prevented from counselling Grafton Elliot Smith who had been invited to report on the endocranial cast.[55] Was Keith angling to get Smith in his corner, or did he have some other motive in mind? While they were reportedly friends, Langham suspected that Keith was secretly jealous of Smith, and that it may have been his intention to bring the Manchester anatomist down a peg or two. After an anxious weekend, Keith finally received permission from South Kensington, and late on Monday afternoon, December 2nd, he was allowed to view the originals. He diligently recorded the visit in his weekly diary:

> Biggest fragment an almost complete left parietal: 2/3 of right. Left rather beyond sagittal sut[ure] which is closed. Bone 10 mm thick. Uniform. 120 long: 90 from zyg[oma] to temp[oral] ridge. 60 to midline: Cor[onal] sut[ure] of modern pattern. Left parietal up to ear angular. Temp[oral] ridge strong in frontal but ext[ernal] ang[ular process] not prom[inent] although thick and strong: forehead evidently not slanting: but only eminence present: Greater part of left temp[oral] mastoid of modern form: so is meatus and glenoid: so is [? articular] emin[ence] and zygoma except latter is strong. Squam[ous] not expanded. 3rd frontal well seen wide open gyrus ridge — vestib[ular] hiatus big. Petrous rather small. Meningeal came through outer end of petro-sphenoid sinous. Large mastoid [?word].
>
> Part of Occipit[al] from for[amen] mag[num] back said to have lambdoid sut[ure]: certainly on parietal but seems much lower than right. No torus: usual modern occip[ital] markings. [?word] impression small.
>
> Total length 190. Total width= 150. Intermast[?oid distance] 150/ Bifrontal 130. Think they have artic[ulation of] occip[ital] and mastoid all wrong. Lower jaw [body] rather long and ramus narrow. Shallow body and symphy[sis] anthropoid. Teeth about 12-13 [words missing due to crumbled edge of page] . . . Heidel[berg] best . . . [remainder of text missing due to crumbled condition of diary pages].[56]

On July 22 1938 Sir Arthur Keith unveiled a monolith memorial in the grounds of Barkham Manor, Piltdown, to mark the site of the discovery of the Piltdown skull by Mr Charles Dawson.

He omitted to mention, however, his letter to Smith:

> I took [in] S[outh]. K[ensington Museum] on my way to the Zoological Tea tonight and saw the Sussex man, or woman rather, for the size of the teeth and small size of the temporal muscles and occipital markings best fit with that idea.
> The Mastoid, ear and temporo-maxillary joint and zygoma are absolutely of the modern type; the wear on the teeth, the temporal muscle — the form of the joint are incompatible with a big canine. I think they [Woodward] are construing the symphysis region wrongly in supposing they have left ½ as far as the middle line. I'm sure there is 8–10 mm missing — even if it were ultra anthropoid that would be the case. The occipital region: the manner in which the head is hafted to the neck is of the modern form. But the thickness of the bone, the flattening and width of the cranial cavity are neanderthaloid — except La Quina was a thin-walled skull.
> I think the c[ranial]. c[apacity]. will turn out to be about 1200 cc — not a small brain is it? I found Barlow trying to reconstruct — 2nd attempt. In the present attempt they have the petrous bones directed almost horizontally inwards with the apices 2½ inches apart an absolutely impossible distance unless the basilar plate were twice the width of that of the gorilla. At present they are making the skull 150 mm wide. I think the real width should be less but not until they get the occip[ital] bone in its right place. Of course I couldn't keep quiet and probably gave more advice than was welcome. But it is a great find: a revelation and a verification all combined.[57]

Smith's reaction to Keith's communication is not known, and it is not entirely certain that he ever replied. But whatever Keith's intentions may have been,[58] he was now in a position to proceed.

On 6 December, Woodward wrote to Keith:

> The 3rd edition of the lady is now ready and the base now fits the mandible beautifully. I have made a fine theory which I think will please you.[59]

Woodward had played directly into his hands!

Two weeks later on 16 December, two days before the official unveiling of the Piltdown remains, Keith prepared his draft of the *BMJ* leader. In keeping things "straight", while "thrusting a quiet and fairly effective spoke in the Boyd Dawkins and Smith Woodward wheel", Keith wrote:

> . . . [T]he date at present assigned to the Galley Hill man [is Middle Pleistocene].[60] This opinion, however, was combated; their critics claimed the same age for the human bones as that ascribed to the animal bones found with the human skull. There was thus a sharp divergence of opinion as to the antiquity of the human remains; in the opinion of the finders and their supporters they are Middle Pleistocene; in the opinion of some of their critics they are Pliocene. However that may be, the characters of this very ancient individual are of a more primitive type than any yet found in Europe.[61]

AND SUBSEQUENT EVENTS

During the next three years several more recoveries were made from the Barkham gravel bed which served to nurture and direct the Piltdown debate. It was Keith's primary intention to reconstruct the Piltdown skull to meet his own requirements,[62] and to use this as a *prima facie* case to support his thesis on the great antiquity of the modern skeletal form. This plan, however, did not unfold as neatly as expected. Contrary to Keith's expectations, Woodward remained committed to his own model of the Piltdown skull — despite energetic attempts, at the Royal College on Thursday,

10 July 1913, to persuade him otherwise Then, to complicate matters, word arrived that the Germans had also taken exception to Woodward's reconstruction. Keith was now left with no option but to publicly demolish Woodward's thesis and promote his own restoration. In an attempt to offset the impact of this step (and evidently to back Woodward up) Dawson told the newspapers that he felt the whole dispute had been grossly exaggerated and that: "It is only after we have finished with the pick and shovel that it will be appropriate to call in the doctors".

Next came the discovery of the "fortuitous canine" tooth, which is believed to have been arranged in a spirit of crisis management, but it is not at all clear who the "Manager" was. Langham's notes seem to favour the idea that it was Dawson acting without Keith's approval. His reasons for supposing this seems partly based on the "inferior" nature of this particular forgery, and Keith's attitude during the August debates — and, in particular on Keith's apparent attempt to rename the Piltdown skull. In a nutshell, Langham believed Keith and Dawson were in the middle of a "blue". Without doubt the tooth incident left much to be desired, but despite its many, now obvious shortcomings, the fact remains that it was generally accepted as a genuine find until 1953. Whilst Keith's labelling of his reconstruction "Homo piltdownensis" might have been an ill-considered swipe at Dawson, the solicitor seems to have viewed the matter differently. He was, like Keith, quite aware that such a move was contrary to the International Rules of Zoological Nomenclature. Keith had perhaps done this simply to underline the position he had been forced into at the International Congress of Medicine in London, but in taking this course of action he also knew that he had seriously weakened Woodward's position. The canine served to correct this.

Despite the complications caused by this new find, it actually did little to deter Keith from his original goal. Indeed his unexpected clash with Elliot Smith during the autumn of 1913 allowed him to regain some of the ground he had lost, while at the same time drawing attention away from David Waterston's letter to *Nature* on November 13th. Since Keith and Waterston regularly played golf together, he probably knew well in advance that this attack was coming. It is therefore conjectured that Keith deliberately goaded Smith in order to create this diversion.

Following the anatomical battle of 1913, it was Keith who was responsible for shifting the focus of the debate to the Pliocene-Pleistocene issue.[63] The so-called "cricket bat," the bone implement recovered in the summer of 1914, was evidently designed to support not only this move, but also to reinforce Reid Moir's case for similar objects found in East Anglia. This in turn assisted in shoring up Keith's highly contentious views on the Ipswich skeleton. Furthermore, in making this move Keith was able to circumvent further public discussion of specific anatomical problems posed by the discovery of the canine tooth.

Of all the finds made after 1913, the most crucial had been those of Piltdown II. Although it is by no means certain if this had been part of the original plan, or something that was put in place later, there is every indication that it was not constructed as Oakley had suggested from the residue of Piltdown I [see fn 30, Chapter 6]. Dawson's allusion to the Barcombe Mills material as a possible representative of an evolutionary sequence in the Weald, compounded with Piltdown I (and II), has a definite Keithian ring, and provides some support to the suggestion that unlike the canine, it had not been the product of crisis management. But whether they had been conceived originally or later, there can be little question these remains had been ready well before the winter of 1915 to counter any attempts that might be made to sever the jaw from the skull. In addition to Woodward, whose loyalty to the earliest Englishman seemed to be wavering in the closing months of 1914, there was

Arthur Keith (circa 1953) in his study at Downe, Farnborough, Kent. (Library, Royal College of Surgeons, London)

also Courtney Lyne, who suddenly appeared on the horizon. While there does not appear to be a direct link between Lyne's developing interest in the Piltdown debate and Woodward's temporary lapse into uncertainty, there is every indication that Lyne's appearance on stage had played a role in the timing of Piltdown II's "discovery". From all appearances, Lyne's first visit to the British Museum (Natural History) was in December 1913, followed by another in December 1914.[64] And on 9 January 1915, Dawson wrote to Woodward saying:

> I believe we are in luck again! I have got a fragment of the left side of a frontal parietal ... [whose] general thickness seems to me to correspond to the right parietal of Eoanthropus."[65]

Several months later, on 17 May, Keith noted in his daily diary: "Lyne here with wild theories". Two months later Dawson reported that he had found a "molar tooth" to go with the earlier cranial fragment. Whether Woodward took possession of these finds at the time or later, is not at all clear. The surviving correspondence seems to suggest that it was after rather than before Dawson's death. It seems that Woodward had also neglected to gather information on precisely where in Sheffield Park Dawson had found the crucial Piltdown II remains. By the time the significance and utility of this material was realized, Dawson lay dying in his bed in Lewes. In light of Woodward's apparent disinterest, and evidently to ensure that these finds would see the light of day, Dawson took the precaution of reporting his discovery to Lankester, who was in the process of completing his book *Diversions of a Naturalist,* and Dawson knew, would not resist the temptation to note this. But it seems, ironically, that it was not Lankester but the dualist Gerrit Miller who saved the day.

With Piltdown II (and the Barcombe Mills material) in place, the evolutionary significance of the original finds at Barkham Manor were essentially secured. No further plants were necessary. In the meantime, while awaiting the eventual disclosure of the Sheffield Park finds, Dawson and Keith attended to their respective public images. To underscore his detachment from Keith and impartiality in the entire affair, Dawson assumed a distinctly antieolithic posture. Although his paper to the Royal Anthropological Institute in February 1915, antagonized specific members of the Ightham Circle, particularly Lewis Abbott and Harry Morris, and not to mention Moir and Lankester[66] this move did much to enhance his image as an objective scientist, which also did not hurt his still unrealized ambition of receiving a Royal Society Fellowship. Although in this regard Dawson's correspondence registers a continuing impatience with the Royal Society as well as some disappointment in not receiving any formal recognition from the Geological Society for his momentous discovery, it appears that by the summer of 1915 he had resigned himself to waiting for the inevitable. As for Keith, he became less combative, evidently preparing himself for the anticipated moment when he would be called upon to defend Woodward against Lyne's ill-conceived attack. And when it came, his acrobatics did not go unnoticed either by his fellow eolithophiles or Elliot Smith. But as the Hunterian professor explained to Kennard:

> ... You may be sure that if I had a leg to stand on that I would fight: but when you fight you keep an eye not on your contemporaries but on the men that come after you and me — I would rather be right with them than with my contemporaries and you ... [in] spite of many boyish blunders Smith Woodward's general conclusions will hold true...[67]

Keith's prognostications, however, proved incorrect, and during the next two decades his brainchild slipped progressively and irrevocably from grace. Yet in spite of these unexpected developments, the ever resourceful Keith was careful to prepare the way for the inevitable day of reckoning...

Notes and References

1 THE SEARCH FOR TERTIARY MAN

[1] Huxley (1863:159).
[2] Buckland (1836, I:104–106).
[3] For a detailed review of the history of this revolutionary shift in scientific opinion, see Grayson (1983). See also the communications of Prestwich (1859, 1860, 1861), Evans (1859), and Lyell (1860).
[4] Although the publication of Charles Darwin's evolutionary synthesis coincided with the acceptance of human antiquity (at least in British scientific circles), these two events were not directly related, see Gruber (1965), Grayson (1983), and Stocking (1987).
[5] Darwin (1871:3).
[6] Prestwich (1861:309).
[7] Prestwich (1861:309).
[8] See Agassiz (1840a, 1840b). While Agassiz generally receives all the credit for this hypothesis, it is evident that others had contributed to its formulation, such as Johann von Charpentier (1786–1855). For further details, see North (1943).
[9] Murchison (1839).
[10] Prestwich actually made two presentations on 27 March and 19 June 1862. These two papers were subsequently published together (Prestwich 1863). For details of his subsequent extension of this study, see Prestwich (1866).
[11] Prestwich (1863:301–2). It is interesting to note that during the early 1870's Prestwich had worked on the geological problems related to the construction of a Channel tunnel, see Prestwich (1874).
[12] Geikie (1871:545–53), cited in Geikie (1877:127).
[13] Geikie (1877:531–2). With regard to the earlier work, see Wood & Rome (1868), Tiddeman (1872), Dakyns (1872), Goodchild (1875), and Aitken (1876). For further insights into scientific thinking on the Glacial period prior to the mid 1870's, see Drayson (1873).
[14] Geikie (1877:531–532).
[15] Garrigou, cited in Daniel (1950:100)
[16] Evans, a paper manufacturer from Hemel Hempstead who had accompanied Prestwich on his historic visit to the Somme river valley in April 1859. Like Prestwich he too had greeted the question of the contemporaneity of human beings with extinct mammalia with incredulity, see Evans (1943:100–103). His paper, confirming Prestwich's observations, was presented to the Antiquarian Society on 2 June 1859.
[17] Letter from Evans to Prestwich, 25 May 1859, in Prestwich (1861:311–12).
[18] Lubbock (1865:1–2). It is interesting to note that Lubbock also used the term "Archaeolithic" for Palaeolithic, which seems, for a while, to have been favoured by many French workers (see Hamy 1870:7).
[19] For details on Mortillet's anthropology, see Hammond (1980)
[20] Since Classical times the sequence of periods in which stone, bronze and iron had been used as the chief material for toolmaking had been recognized. During the 1830s and early 1840s, the Scandinavian antiquarians Jens J A Worsaae (1821–85) and Christian Thomsen (1788–1865) formalized this so-called "three-age system" to organize their museum collections.
[21].This fossil ape, the first European dyropithecine to be found, had been recovered by the naturalist Alfred Fontan and subsequently described by Lartet. The specimen consisted of two fragments of a mandible with some teeth, and an associated piece of the symphysis. Because oak leaves had been found in other sites in the region, Lartet named the specimen after the dryads, or oak nymphs of Greek mythology, see Lartet (1856).
[22] Fraipont & Lohest (1887). For further details on the site, see the reports made by the geologists Marcel de Puydt and Max Lohest (1886, 1887) who were responsible for making the discovery.
[23] Huxley (1863:157).
[24] Lyell (1863:510–13).
[25] Lyell (1863:515).
[26] See Bourgeois (1868), and Hamy (1870:57–60).
[27] Bourgeois (1868:70).
[28] See Mortillet (1868, 1873). It should be noted, however, that Mortillet did not accept all of the specimens in Bourgeois' collection as human artifacts.

[29] Lubbock (1865), see Hamy (1870:39–42).

[30] Mortillet (1883).

[31] For details on the French materials, see Rames (1884) and Mortillet (1883). The Portugese material had been collected by the geologist Carlos Ribeiro (1813–82) whose findings were presented to the International Congress at Brussels in 1872 and Lisbon in 1880 (see Ribeiro 1873, 1884).

[32] Contrary to the suggestion made by Albert Gaudry (1827–1908) that this specimen might represent a common ancestor of the modern ape and human lineages, in the 1860s and 1870s the perception of this fossil had been more modest. At this stage the remains served simply to demonstrate that the divergence of the "higher apes" from the "lower apes" had occurred in the Upper Miocene, and that the apes had been widely spread throughout the Old World (even in Europe); an apparent fact that undoubtedly help nurture the expectation that hominid bones and artifacts of at least Pliocene age were a very real possibility. For further insights on the perception of this fossil during the early 1870s, see Darwin (1871 [1979]:138).

[33] Mortillet (1883:301–2). Regarding his rejection of Gaudry's proposal, see p 125. See also Mortillet & Mortillet (1881). As indicated by the 1903 edition of Le Préhistorique, Mortillet supported the idea of the Neanderthals representing an intermediate link between modern humans and Pithecanthropus. For further details on this latter fossil, see Chapter 2.

[34] Evans (1878:149). This meeting was held on 22 May 1877. The programme consisted of 3 papers delivered by Boyd Dawkins, McKenny Hughes, and Tiddeman. For further details, see text.

[35] Evans (1878:150–1).

[36] Falconer had played a catalytic role in the establishment of the human antiquity paradigm. It was largely through his urging that Prestwich had gone to Abbeville in April 1859 to investigate Boucher de Perthes' claims. For further information on this episode, see Prestwich (1899:111–36), as well as Gruber (1965) and Grayson (1983:179–85). In addition to his earlier pioneering excavations in the Siwalik Hills of north-west India, Falconer was also an established authority on Indian flora. For background information on his palaeontological researches, see Murchison (1867).

[37] This uncertainty is clearly reflected in the papers presented at the London symposium, see particularly the contrast between Hughes (1878:162–5) and Tiddeman (1878:165–73).

[38] Dawkins (1880:90–2).

[39] Letter from Geikie to the botanist and palaeolith hunter Worthington G Smith [1835–1917], dated 2 May 1881, in Harrison (1928:91).

[40] Running through the central Weald there is an east-west anticlinal (uplifting) axis. As a consequence rivers emanating in the Weald drain either to the north into the Thames or south into the English Channel. For further details on the geology of the Weald, see Edmunds (1935).

[41] According to Harrison's biographer, by the late 1860s his early interests in natural history had passed the "wild flowers stage" and had moved increasingly toward the "archaeological" and "geological" (Harrison 1928:44), and he was already a regular correspondant with such men as "Good old Rupert" Jones, Henry Woodward and John Lubbock.

[42] Harrison (1928:84).

[43] Letter dated 4 January 1888, in Harrison (1928:128).

[44] This was later refined into 5 groups, consisting of 46 specimens found at or above the 500ft level; 211 found between the 400 and 500ft level; 139 found between 300 and 400ft; 12 from the 200 and 300ft level; and 3 found between 100 and 200ft, see Prestwich (1889:281–2).

[45] See Harrison (1928:131–2).

[46] (Harrison 1928:133). Later, in a letter to Fred N Haward (see later section in this chapter), Harrison wrote that Prestwich had said: "Where did you get this, and have you any more?" (see Harrison 1928, fn, p.133).

[47] Letter dated 9 November 1890, in Harrison (1928:157).

[48] Apparently wishing to avoid any confusion between the Plateau artifacts and those of Mortillet, Prestwich continued to use this term rather than "eoliths" until 1895.

[49] Prestwich did not address this subject, instead he deferred to the authority of William Topley (1875).

[50] Prestwich (1889:285–6).

[51] Prestwich (1889:292).

[52] Evans, in Prestwich (1889:295–6).

[53] Whitaker, in Prestwich (1889:296).

[54] Prestwich (1891:129).

[55] Le Neve Foster (p 161) and Geikie (p 162), in Prestwich (1891).

[56] Prestwich (1891:163). In fact, Prestwich believed that this dome had originally risen to an elevation of some 2800 feet. For further details on Prestwich's views on the subject of Wealden denudation, see Prestwich (1887, 1899:68–72, 91–5, 377–9).

[57] Topley, in Prestwich (1891:161).

[58] As noted by Whitaker, and later by Allen Brown (in Prestwich 1892:296–7), the denudation of the Weald could be explained by subaerial erosion — an idea subsequently championed by Lewis Abbott and others.

[59] Letter dated 13 February 1891, in Harrison (1928:160).
[60] See letters dated 5 and 13 February 1891, in Harrison (1928:160–2).
[61] Prestwich (1892).
[62] Dawkins, in Prestwich (1892:273–4). With regard to Dawkins' comments, Prestwich said he failed to "see the drift" of his argument, "except the expression of a general disbelief". They seemed to him to be "irrelevant, and not directed to the real issue" (Prestwich 1892:276).
[63] Evans in Prestwich (1892:271). It should be noted that Prestwich's general argument against this had been that the "rude" flints were stained much the same colour as the unbroken flints from the same drifts — even on their chipped edges.
[64] Pitt-Rivers, in Prestwich (1891:273).
[65] Allen Brown, in Prestwich (1892:274).
[66] Newton (1895:520–1). Here Newton cites Whitaker's memoir on the *Geology of London* (1889).
[67] Newton (1895:521).
[68] Newton (1895:512). For Huxley's views, see his notes appended to Samuel Laing's book on *Prehistoric Remains from Caithness*, London (1866).
[69] Newton (1895:517).
[70] Dawkins (1874, 1880).
[71] Newton (1895:517).
[72] Brown, in Newton (1895:527). Another eolithophile present was Lewis Abbott who is mentioned in the next section.
[73] For example, on 11 November 1892, Bell presented a paper supporting Prestwich's theory to the Anthropological Institute. This paper was primarily directed against the criticisms of Boyd Dawkins. Later, in 1893, Lewis Abbott exhibited and described a series of eoliths to the Geologists' Association, followed by an excursion to Ightham (Abbott 1893). See also Abbott's paper on "Plateau Man in Kent" published in *Natural Science* (1894) in which he noted: "It is greatly regretted that the necessary funds are not forthcoming to carry out a thorough system of excavations upon the plateau, and to trace the relations of this drift to the undoubted Pliocene beds of the neighbourhood, which we are quite sure would confirm Mr Harrison's discoveries" (1894:266).
[74] See Harrison's report (1895:349–51).
[75] See letters from Prestwich dated 30 October and 28 December 1894, in Harrison (1928:194–5).
[76] Letter to Harrison, dated 13 November 1894, in Harrison (1928:195).
[77] See Seeley, in Cunnington (1898:297).
[78] Letter from Wallace to Harrison, dated 11 August 1893, in Harrison (1928:189). Wallace was, as he told Harrison earlier, astonished that his colleagues continued to resist "any possible extension of the evidence as to a greater antiquity than the palaeolithic gravels" (letter dated 20 January 1888, in Harrison 1928:130). For further details on Wallace's public posture on this issue, see Wallace (1887).
[79] Newton to Harrison, dated 24 December 1895, in Harrison (1928:202).
[80] Cunnington (1898:293). Cunnington first visited Harrison in March 1896, in Harrison (1928:205).
[81] Cunnington's initial pro-eolithic stance can be seen from the article he wrote for the November issue of *Natural Science* (1897); while his recapitulation appeared later in the *Journal of the Anthropological Institute* (1898).
[82] See Rudler, Strahan and Seeley, in Cunnington (1898:298, 297 respectively).
[83] Woodward and Jones, in Cunnington (1898:297).
[84] See Abbott, in Bennett (1907: Appendix I), and Newton (1894:188). It is also interesing to note that Kennard was at this time attending Abbott's lectures on "gemmology" at the London Polytechnic. Abbott later quit teaching in 1898 when he moved to St Leonard's, near Hastings, Sussex, where he opened a jewellers shop.
[85] See Abbott (1898:111–6).
[86] Kennard, in Cunnington (1898:299).
[87] Gregory, in Cunnington (1898:300).
[88] See Rutot (1899, 1900). In addition to these categories, Rutot also described an industry identified as the "Strépyan" which he regarded as a prototype of the Chellean. Later, his "Mesvinian" industry was identified as being synonymous with the Clactonian industry later described by Hazzledine Warren (1926). Much of the pre-Chellean and Chellean industries were later reclassified as phases of the Acheulean.
[89] For example at the 1902 British Association meeting in Belfast there was a heated exchange (reported in the *Geological Magazine*) between the eolithophile Francis J Bennett of the Geological Survey and Boyd Dawkins over a paper presented by W J Knowles (1902:757) on the discovery and status of eoliths found in Irish preglacial gravels (see Coffey 1901). Knowles, incidentally, was convinced these materials were artifacts.
[90] See Harrison (1928:256).
[91] See Anonymous (1903) and Capitan (1904). Initially Capitan had held the view that natural forces, such as wave action and strata compression could produce eolithoid objects, see Mahoudeau & Capitan (1901:149–53).

[92] Klaatsch (1903).

[93] Letter dated 19 October 1903, in Harrison Papers (Rochester Museum Archives, Kent, England).

[94] Letter dated 23 January 1903, in Harrison Papers (Rochester Museum Archives, Kent, England).

[95] Boule (1903:704).

[96] Boule (1905:261–2).

[97] See Bennett (1906) and Abbott (1906).

[98] The extent of this can be gauged from a letter Lewis Abbott sent Rutot, in which he complained bitterly about the anti-eolithic "prejudice" that had surfaced soon after Boule's attack: as evidenced by the growing reluctance of *Nature* and other scientific journals to carry pro-eolithic articles. His letter is dated 1 November 1905, in Rutot papers (Archives of the Royal Institute of Natural Sciences in Brussels, Belgium).

[99] Abbott (1897:89).

[100] Boswell (1945:67).

[101] Letter dated 30 May 1910, in Moir (1935:20).

[102] See Moir's letter to the London *The Times*, 17 October 1910, reprinted in Lankester (1912:284). This was followed by a lengthy study of the implements, presented to the Prehistoric Society of East Anglia on 12 December 1910 (Moir 1911).

[103] Corner's letter was dated 10 October 1910, in Harrison (1928:293).

[104] Warren (1905).

[105] See Moir (1911).

[106] Haward (1912).

[107] See Moir (1912a, 1912b).

[108] Lankester (1912). According to Keith (1944:737) this communication was "received by the Royal Society with an extreme degree of scepticism [but that] Lankester slaughtered the opponent's of Moir's thesis". Unfortunately because Lankester's paper was not accompanied by discussion notes it is not possible to confirm Keith's report; also this apparent confrontation was not reported in the press (at least not in *The Times* nor the *Manchester Guardian*).

[109] Whitaker, in Moir (1912c:2–3).

[110] Marr, in Moir (1912c:3).

[111] Keith, in Moir (1912c:10–16).

[112] In Moir (1935:108–9). This undated letter appears to have been written around the 27 October 1912, when Lankester is known to have viewed the Piltdown specimens at the British Museum (Natural History) in South Kensington (see Spencer 1990:1.2.15).

2   A PRIMA FACIE CASE

[1] From an editorial comment on Arthur Smith Woodward's Royal Institution lectures in April 1913, in *Morning Post*, 2 April 1913.

[2] Mantell lived in Lewes at Castle Place, where in addition to being a practising physician, he was also an avid geological collector and lecturer. His *Wonders of Geology* (1839) was among one of the most successful of the popular books on geology and palaeontology written at the time.

[3] Dawson, in Dawson & Woodward (1913:117–8).

[4] Dawson (1913:76).

[5] Dawson (1913:76).

[6] Dawson & Woodward (1913:117–8).

[7] Dawson, dated 14 February 1912, in Spencer (1990:1.2.1). It is presumed that Dawson had intended to write either "I have a thick" or "I think I have [a] . . ." and that it had been found at the same site.

[8] See Dawson to Woodward, 24 March 1912, in Spencer (1990: 1.2.2). Here Dawson notes: "At present the roads leading to it are impassable and excavation is out of the question . . . I will have a look at the place, if the weather improves, and see if things are possible, but I feel sure nothing short of four fine days would set matters straight enough to even see the gravel." In the same letter he also notes that there was a rail strike.

[9] This trip was evidently in preparation for a lecture, on dinosaurs of East Africa. Woodward had been invited to deliver to the London Chapter of the German Colonial Society.

[10] See Dawson to Woodward, 23 May 1912, in Spencer (1990:1.2.8).

[11] Letter addressed to his parents and dated 3 June 1912, see Letter No 67, Teilhard (1965) 1968: 195, 197–8.

[12] See fn 1: p 122 and Plate XVI, figure 2, in Dawson & Woodward (1913).

[13] In July 1912, Teilhard returned to France, see Teilhard's letter to Dawson, 10 July 1912 in Spencer (1990:1.2.12).

[14] Dawson, in Dawson & Woodward (1914:82–3).

[15] See Woodward (1948:8), and Dawson (1913:77).

[16] Woodward (1948:8-9).

[17] Woodward (1948); see also Dawson (1913).

[18] Woodward (1948:11); see also Dawson & Woodward (1913:121).

[19] In Woodward's account he infers that this event occurred after the discovery of the parietal and occipital fragments (see text), noting: "Finally, on a warm evening after an afternoon's vain search . . . " Woodward (1948:10–11). Likewise, Dawson in recounting these events. writes: "It was not until we had been busy on and off for some weeks that after a hard and unproductive day's work I struck part of the lowest stratum of the gravel with my pick, and out flew a portion of the lower jaw from the iron-bound gravel" (1913:77). It is also interesting to note that in a letter to Woodward, dated 30 June 1912, Dawson briefly discusses a human mandible found at Cheddar Cave in the Mendip Hills, near Bristol, see Spencer (1990:1.2.11). As Weiner (1955:89) notes, the allusion to the Cheddar mandible, which like the Piltdown specimen has a missing chin region, is highly supportive of the latter having been found in late June. For further details on the Cheddar specimen, see Davies (1904) and Seligman & Parsons (1914).

[20] Woodward (1948:65).

[21] According to Dawson, the gravel bed was situated "above the 100-foot contour line, averaging about 120 feet at Piltdown, and lies about 80 feet above the level of the main stream of the Ouse. The river has cut through the plateau, both with its mainstream and its principle branch, which is called the Uckfield River" Dawson, in Dawson & Woodward (1913:119).

[22] This initial identification was made by Freudenberg (1915) and Matsumoto (1918), and later confirmed by the work of Hopwood (1935), and Osborn (1942).

[23] In addition to the antler fragment (found in the field adjacent to the gravel bed), the proximal end of a metatarsal (split longitudinally) had been found in one of the spoil heaps, see Dawson & Woodward (1913:121,142).

[24] See Dixon (1878:110).

[25] In Dawson & Woodward (1913:142), Woodward noted that a "Proboscidean tooth near as primitive" as that found at Piltdown had been found in a Pliocene deposit in Austria. On the Continent the remains of *Mastodon arvernensis* had generally been found in association with the small *Rhinoceros etruscus*. Later, in 1914, such an association was made at Piltdown by the discovery of a molar fragment. For further information on what was then known about extinct species of elephants and their distribution, see Flower & Lydekker (1891:427–35) and Osborn (1915).

[26] Dawson & Woodward (1913:123).

[27] Dawson & Woodward (1913:123).

[28] See Dawson (1913).

[29] This is evident from Woodward's statements in his textbook, *Outlines of Vertebrate Palaeontology* (1898), see also his pro-eolithic remarks to Benjamin Harrison in the company of the American biologist from Brown University, Alpheus Spring Packard (1839–1905) in 1900, in Harrison (1928:237). In contrast to Packard who was not an eolithophile, Woodward had, on this occasion, unhesitatingly endorsed Harrison's attribution of an eolithic specimen to the pliocene.

[30] Abbott to Rutot, 4 January 1914, in Spencer (1990:3.1.1).

[31] Dawson to Woodward, 30 June 1912, in Spencer (1990:1.2.11).

[32] Dawson (1913:82). See also a similar statement made at the unveiling on 18 December 1912 at Burlington House. In the published version of this presentation, Dawson wrote: "Whether natural or artificial, the fractures appear to have been largely governed by the prismatic structure of the flint. Both the rolled and unrolled "Eoliths" are deeply stained and patinated, but the former to a much greater extent than the latter" (Dawson & Woodward 1913:123).

[33] Dawson & Woodward (1913:123).

[34] Woodward, in Dawson & Woodward (1913:125).

[35] Woodward, in Dawson & Woodward (1913:131).

[36] Darwin ([1871] 1979:143).

[37] Woodward, in Dawson & Woodward (1913:132).

[38] For a synopsis of Dubois' London visit, see Keith's article in *Pall Mall Gazette* (1895). For further details of Dubois, see Theunissen (1989).

[39] In 1866 and then more specifically in 1868, Haeckel had predicted that the first human beings ("*Homo primigenius*") had evolved from a non-European preglacial member of the anthropomorphous apes, in either "Lemuria" (a landmass that was thought to have sunk beneath the Indian Ocean) or Africa. "Considering the extraordinary resemblance between the lowest woolly-haired men, and the highest man-like apes," Haeckel said, "it requires but a slight imagination to conceive an intermediate form connecting the two . . . The form of their skull was probably very long, with slanting teeth; their hair woolly; the colour of their skin dark; of brownish tint. The hair covering the whole body was probably thicker than that of the still living human species; their arms comparatively longer and stronger; their legs, on the other hand, knock-kneed, shorter and thinner, with entirely under-developed calves; their walk but half-erect" (Haeckel 1868, in McCown & Kennedy 1972:143).

[40] Dubois (1908).

[41] This Asian dryopithecoid form was first described and named by Richard Lydekker, see his notice of (1878) and catalogue (1887).

[42] Among the protagonists were Brinton (1895); *Cunningham (1895a, 1895b); Dames (1896); Haeckel (1895, 1899); Houzé (1895); Keith (1895); Manouvrier (1895, 1896); Marsh (1896); Martin (1895); Nehring (1895); Neviani (1896); Sollas (1895); Topinard (1895); von Luschan (1895); Verneau (1895); while the antagonists included Branco (1898); Kolbe (1895); Kollmann (1895); Krause (1896); Lydekker (1895); Pettit (1895); Rosenberg (1896); *Turner (1895); Virchow (1895); Volz (1897); Waldeyer (1895). The two asterisked workers are of particular interest because of their influential positions in British anatomical circles. In the case of Daniel J Cunningham (1850–1909), then professor of anatomy at Dublin, he had been willing to acknowledge that the skullcap resembled that of a gibbon, but felt Dubois' fossil was an ancestral form — though not a direct "link between man and the anthropoid apes" (1895a). William Turner (1832–1916), who was professor of anatomy at Edinburgh University, on the other hand, although admitting the humanity of the parts, he rejected their claimed association.

[43] Schwalbe (1906:14). For a more detailed account of Schwalbe's views, see Smith (1987).

[44] This synthetic conclusion was first reached by Klaatsch and Rutot, see Giuffrida-Ruggeri (1910), and later Keith (1912). The two sites were excavated by independent groups. The Ferrassie rock shelter was excavated by Dennis Peyrony (1869–1954) in collaboration with Louis Capitan; while at Combe Capelle the work was done by a German team led by the Swiss antiquarian Otto Hauser. These sites are located in the Dordogne region of France: La Ferrassie in the Vézere valley, while Combe Capelle is situated about 20 miles to the south in the Couze river valley, a tributary of the Dordogne. The two sites were later found to overlap. At La Ferrassie the archaeological deposits began in the Acheulean and ended in the Aurignacian, whereas at Combe Capelle they commenced with the Mousterian and terminated in the Solutrean. In addition to their respective cultural and faunal assemblages, both sites yielded human remains. At La Ferrassie human remains were recovered in the Mousterian horizon (later described by Capitan as a Neanderthaloid skeleton), while at the other site an anatomically modern human skeleton was found in the Aurignacian level. The contrast between these two skeletons, linked to the fact that the Aurignacian followed immediately after the Mousterian, led workers such as Rutot and Keith to question the Neanderthal hypothesis and consider modern humans as descendants of an independent lineage.

[45] For example Boule (1909–12); Giuffrida-Ruggeri (1910); Klaatsch (1910); Sera (1910a, 1910b); Rutot (1910).

[46] In 1901 the Grotte des Enfants (in the Grimaldi caves), near Mentone on the French Riviera, yielded two anatomically modern human skeletons (thought to have Negroid characters). These skeletons were situated at the interface between an Aurignacian and a Mousterian level. Although subsequently attributed to an Auriginacian horizon, Boule was convinced they belonged to the lower (older) level. It has been argued that his willingness to adopt this viewpoint was grounded in his overt hostility to Mortillet's posture not only in the sphere of human palaeontology but also in his particular brand of politics, see Hammond (1980).

[47] For a summary of Boule's presentation at Geneva, see report (anonymous) in Nature 90:290–1 (1912); and Boule (1913:662–664), as well as Boule (1910–13).

[48] "Of these two races", Boule said, "the Piltdown race seems to us the probable ancestor in the direct line of recent species of man, Homo sapiens; while the Heidelberg race [see next section of text] may be considered, until we have further knowledge, as a possible forerunner of Homo neanderthalensis (Boule 1913: 245–6).

[49] This German expedition had been mounted by Lenore Selenka, the widow of the renowned palaeontologist Emile Selenka (1842–1902). For full details on this expedition, see Selenka & Blanckenhorn (1911).

[50] See Schoetensack (1908). For a more accessible summary of this find, see Hrdlička (1930:90–98). Currently this fossil is regarded by most workers as a western variant of Homo erectus [syn. Dubois' Pithecanthropus]. See Kraatz (1985:268–271) for a review of recent research on the Heidelberg fossil and site.

[51] See Grafton Elliot Smith's presidential address to Section H (Anthropology) of the British Association in Dundee on 8 September 1912: Smith (1912).

[52] Woodward, in Dawson & Woodward (1913:137–8).

[53] Woodward referred specifically to the Neanderthal Man found in 1907 at La Chapelle-aux-Saints, citing Boule's published description of this skeleton, see Woodward, in Dawson & Woodward (1913:141, fig 9).

[54] Woodward, in Dawson & Woodward (1913:139).

[55] The Manchester Guardian, 21 November 1912: Anonymous two-column article (945 words) entitled: "THE EARLIEST MAN? Remarkable Discovery in Sussex." The story was filed in London, Wednesday 20 November 1912. An abbreviated version of this story was printed in the London Evening News on 21 November. This account differs only in as much that it noted that the cranial bones were "very much thicker" than those of modern human crania, and that the "finder", a "scientist living in Sussex", was scheduled to lecture on the skull before the Geological Society of London on 18 December 1912.

[56] Woodward to Dawkins, 25 November 1912, in Spencer (1990:1.2.25). Prior to his appointment at the South Kensington Museum in 1882, Woodward had studied geology under Dawkins at the [Victoria]

University of Manchester (1880–1882). Since that time he had maintained a cordial relationship with his former professor.

[57] From report in London *Daily Sketch* 22 November 1912.

[58] Anonymous leader in the *British Medical Journal*, dated Saturday, 21 December 1912, see Chapter 8 for further details.

[59] Woodward, in Dawson & Woodward (1913:135–7).

[60] Smith, in Dawson & Woodward (1913:147).

[61] It should be noted that the following narrative is (except where otherwise indicated) based largely on the "official" transcript of the discussion appended to the published version of the Dawson & Woodward (1913) paper.

[62] Lankester visited Piltdown on 9 November 1912, see Spencer (1990:1.2.19), following a preview of the specimens in London sometime towards the end of October, see Woodward's annotation of Lankester's undated letter, in Spencer (1990:1.2.15).

[63] See Chapter Four, and in particular Lankester's exchange with the American zoologist Gerrit S Miller.

[64] Although noting that it was by no means "certain that the lower jaw and skull belonged to the same individual", it appears that Lankester was not doubting the validity of Woodward's monistic thesis but rather pointing to the possibility of more than one individual of the same type being represented in the assemblage.

[65] Letter from Lankester to Woodward, 11 December 1912, in Spencer (1990:1.2.29).

[66] Notwithstanding his verbal fencing, Lankester's subsequent message to the reader's of his column "Science From an Easy Chair" in *The Daily Telegraph* was full of praise and adulation for the Sussex find. "In spite of their imperfection", Lankester wrote, "they are of extreme importance, and constitute a new step in the acquirement of solid, tangible knowledge as to the development of man from ape-like ancestors ... It comes nearer to the realisation of the missing link than anything yet discovered" (6 January 1913).

[67] This ties in with the opinion Lankester had relayed to Dawson when he visited the Piltdown site early in November: "Lancaster [sic] came to the gravel pit today ... and seemed very satisfied with it all, and thinks as you do that the age of the human remains are probably late Pliocene or early Pleistocene" Dawson to Woodward, 9 November 1912, in Spencer (1990:1.2.19).

[68] Lankester, in Dawson & Woodward (1913:147–8).

[69] Smith, in Dawson & Woodward (1913:150–1).

[70] Keith, in Dawson & Woodward (1913:148).

[71] From the various newspaper reports of this meeting it appears that the discussion period did not proceed in quite the orderly fashion the "official" report would seem to indicate. In fact this facet of the discussion and the subsequent exchange with Boyd Dawkins is based on a report appearing in the *Manchester Evening Chronicle*, 19 December 1912; and an interview Keith gave the next day to the *Manchester Guardian*, 20 December 1912.

[72] From report filed in the *Manchester Evening Chronicle* 19 December 1912.

[73] Duckworth, in Dawson & Woodward (1913:149). It is also of interest to note that Duckworth pointed out that the mylohyoid ridge character was not "so constant" as Woodward had suggested, see also his letter (5 June 1913) to Woodward on this subject, Spencer (1990:2.3.17).

[74] Reid, in Dawson & Woodward (1913:149–150). A similar argument was made by the Irish geophysicist John Joly (1857–1933) when Woodward exhibited the remains to the Royal Dublin Society on 28 January 1913. For further details of this meeting, see Spencer (1990: notes appended to Letter 2.3.4)."

[75] Waterson, Dawson & Woodward (1913:150). Later, in 1913, Waterston made another unsuccessful attempt to persuade his colleageus against Woodward's monistic interpretation.

[76] Kennard, in Dawson & Woodward (1913:150). It should be noted that Kennard's authority in this regard was founded on his recent study of the implement-bearing terraces of the Thames valley with the amateur mammalogist Martin A C Hinton, see Hinton & Kennard (1905). For further details on Hinton, see Chapter Four.

[77] Newton, in Dawson & Woodward (1913:151).

[78] Dawson, in Dawson & Woodward (1913:151).

[79] Woodward, in Dawson & Woodward (1913:151).

[80] Strahan visited Piltdown in the company of Dawson on 10 December, see Spencer (1990: 1.2.28).

[81] This suggestion is of interest since in the published version of Dawson & Woodward (1913), the results of a rudimentary chemical analysis of one of the cranial fragments is reported. The fact that Strahan makes no mention of this in his interview, could be taken to infer that this analysis was undertaken after the unveiling but before the publication of the paper in April 1913. Also it should be noted that Strahan was not the only one to suggest this line of investigation. Indeed Lankester had recommended a comparative chemical analysis of some of the bones to Woodward on 13 November 1912, see Spencer (1990: 1.2.22).

[82] Keith, in Dawson & Woodward (1913:148).

3 BONES, STONES & EGOS I

[1] Darwin (1871 [1979]:315).

[2] According to Keith's 1913 Diary (Library, Royal College of Surgeons), he received the complete set of Piltdown casts on 14 May, as indicated by his mention of the price paid in his 3 June entry: "£12.7.0. casts of Piltdown."

[3] Keith was among the few who were privileged to view the specimens prior to the unveiling. Keith's examination took place on 2 December 1912, see Spencer (1990:1.2.27); and 15 December: "Been at South Kensington again to see Sussex skull. Puzzled about jaw," in Weekly Diary 1912, Library Royal College of Surgeons.

[4] Keith (1895a)

[5] Keith (1895b:368–369).

[6]Sollas (1908:337). Sollas' paper on the European Neanderthals was presented to the Royal Society on 14 November 1907. At this time Sollas was professor of geology at Oxford, a position he had held since 1898. Unlike Keith, Sollas remained faithful to the Neanderthal hypothesis until after the arrival of Piltdown.

[7] Keith (1911a:723), see also Keith (1911b:119–20).

[8] Keith (1911b:119).

[9] Keith, in Moir (1912).

[10]Keith (1912a:734).

[11]See Keith (1911a). From all accounts Keith's attention had been drawn to this specimen by Frank Corner, who a year earlier had purchased the remains from Robert Elliot, in whose care they had languished since 1895. Believing the skeleton to be of great importance, Corner had evidently taken the remains to Paris the following year in the hope of making a profit. But while some members of the Parisian Société d' Anthropologie had expressed an interest, it appears that Corner's plans were thwarted by Boule who is reported to have dismissed the Galley Hill remains as mere "bric-à-brac". Meanwhile, Keith who had recently been installed as the new Conservator of the Hunterian Museum at the Royal College of Surgeons, was in the process of resuscitating his earlier interest in anthropology, and with the approval of the College's governors, had launched an ambitious scheme to assemble a comprehensive exhibit of the prehistoric inhabitants of Britain. On hearing of this, Corner had apparently made post-haste for the Royal College, fully expecting to negotiate a financial transaction. Instead, it seems Keith had pressed Corner to make it a gift to the Museum. Although Corner declined to do so, he did however agree to loan the specimen to Keith so that he might examine it at his leisure. According to Keith's diaries it appears that in September 1909 arrangements were made for Frank Barlow at the BM (NH) to make casts of the remains, and that after this time the originals appear to have been moved back and forth between the Royal College of Surgeons and South Kensington until February 1912 when the latter institution acquired them.

[12] Keith (1912c:307; 1911a, and 1911b).

[13] Keith calculated this in the following way: "The river has not only worn its estuarine valley down 90 to 100 feet owing to an elevation of the land, but in the opinion of experts has also eroded and filled up a channel from 40 to 50 feet below its present level. Measured at its lowest estimate the Thames-bed has been lowered and raised at least 170 feet . . . Seeing how little the level and aspect of the valley have altered since the Roman period, and that there is no reason to presume that changes in level and climate occurred at a faster rate in past times than in the present, one may safely allow a period of 1000 years for every foot which the river has worn away or laid down. On this basis of computation the antiquity of the Galley Hill remains may be estimated at 170,000 years — probably an under-estimate" (Keith 1911a:722).

[14] Penck (1909, III:1153–76).

[15] Sollas (1900).

[16] Keith (1911a:722–4).

[17] Keith (1911b:143).

[18] Keith, in Moir (1912:16).

[19] Keith (1912a).

[20]Dawkins' resistance to Keith's thesis can be gauged by his comments at the meeting of Section H (Anthropology) of the British Association in Dundee in September 1912, see report in *The Times*, Monday, 9 September 1912, page 3.

[21] Duckworth (1912:132).

[22] According to Keith's 1913 Diary (Library, Royal College of Surgeons), he arrived in Brussels at 5.30 pm on Friday 14 March 1913, and returned to London Monday 17 March. This visit to Rutot is briefly mentioned in his autobiography, Keith (1950:368).

[23] Keith (1914b:442).

[24] See Fisher (1888:819), and his communication to *Nature* in September 1913 (p.6). For information on the Dawlish eoliths, see Grist (1910).

[25] Keith (1915a:345). For complete details of Keith's approach to the reconstruction of Woodward's model, see Keith (1915a:337–55).

[26] Shortly after this Williams was inducted as a Fellow into the Royal Anthropological Institute. His reconstruction of the jaw was featured in an article published in the *Illustrated London News* 16 August 1913. Later that year, however, Williams abruptly returned to America, settling in New York, where he gave several lectures on Piltdown (e.g. presentation to the New York Academy of Sciences in January 1914), see Spencer (1990:3.1.5), as well as publishing an article in the December (1913) issue of *Scientific American* For further details on Williams, see Chapter 8.

[27] Letter dated 4 July 1913, in Spencer (1990:2.3.22). According to Smith his meeting with Keith had been the day before, following his attendance at a Royal Society Council meeting. Keith's diary, however, indicates that this meeting had been on 26 June and that Leon Williams had been there also.

[28] According to Stearn (1981:190), from 1892 to 1898 Pycraft had served as Lankester's assistant at Oxford. During that time Lankester had been the Linacre Professor of Comparative Anatomy. When Lankester was appointed Director of the British Museum (Natural History), Pycraft was brought along as his "private helper" and after Lankester's departure in 1907, he was retained "to take charge of osteology". Pycraft, Lankester and Underwood so it seems had all had some input into Woodward's restoration.

[29] Lankester to Moir, circa 10 July 1913, in Moir (1935:112–113).

[30] In this regard Dawson, on hearing of Smith's communique from Woodward, had replied: "I suppose Keith's idea is to try and make out that the [cranial] capacity was normal to fit in with some of his former determinations such as in the case of the Ipswich skeleton?" Dawson to Woodward, 9 July 1913, in Spencer (1990:2.3.24).

[31] See Keith (1950:324).

[32] The texts of Woodward's two Royal Institution lectures were not published. Summaries, however, can be found in various newspaper reports. Lecture 1, see for example *Morning Post* 2 April 1913 and *Globe* 2 April 1913; Lecture 2, see *Daily Telegraph* 9 April 1913 and *Morning Post* 9 April 1913. Woodward's derogatory comments on the Ipswich and Galley Hill skeletons were made in the second lecture.

[33] According to a note in the *Blatt der Deutschen Gesellscahft für Anthropologie, Ethnologie und Urgeschichte* (1913) XLIV, delegates at the Deutsche Anthropologie Gesellschaft meeting (3–10 August) in Nuremburg the British were openly censured for giving their "approval to the manner in which the Piltdown skull had been reconstructed". See F Birkner: "Die Funde von menschlichen Knochenreston bei Piltdown der Sussex". *Archiv für Anthropologie* **XLIV**:102–103, 1913. Several reports of this censure appeared in the British press, see *Pall Mall Gazette* 11 August 1913; London *Evening Standard* 11 August 1913, and Dawson's interview in *Sussex Daily News* 11 August 1913.

[34] Elliot Smith to Woodward, 8 August 1913, in Spencer (1990: 2.3.31).

[35] See article in *The Times* 11 August 1913, which draws attention to these arrangements: "There are two items in the programme of the Anatomical Section of the International Congress of Medicine for to-day. The items are entered on the programme merely as visits (1) to the Department of Geology of the British Museum at South Kensington; (2) to the Museum of the Royal College of Surgeons in Lincoln's Inn Fields; in reality the visits are made to settle certain questions which have arisen over the oldest human remains yet discovered in Europe ..." It appears from Keith's 1913 Diary that he had written this piece in *The Times*, see entry for 17 August: "Last week has been eventful owing to Piltdown coming up as informal matter at Congress and the mistakes having been discovered by Germans thought it better to compel discussion and hence saw Editor of Times on Sat (9th) and had article out on Monday — day of visits to Museum[s]."

[36] "The Battle of the Skull", in *The Times* 12 August 1913.

[37] Later, in September, Anthony published his thoughts on the controversy in the Parisian *Revue Anthropologie*. Here he reiterated his support for Keith's arguments, and noted his general preference for the idea of placing the Sussex specimen in the human genus (Anthony 1913:293–306).

[38] Letter to Editor, dated 15 August, *Daily Express* 16 August 1913.

[39] Letter to Editor, undated, in *Daily Express* [?20] August 1913.

[40] Bather's letter to the Editor of *The Times* was dated 12, August, and was printed the following day. Keith's letter (undated) appeared in the *The Times* on 14 August.

[41] Letter (dated 13 August and signed "EOANTHROPUS dAWSONI [sic]"), *Daily Express* 15 August 1913. Dawson's authorship has been determined from a letter he wrote to Woodward dated 13 August 1913, in Spencer (1990:2.3.32).

[42] Sollas to Woodward, 14 August 1913, in Spencer (1990:2.3.33).

[43] This excursion was arranged earlier in March, see Abbott to Woodward 5 March 1913, in Spencer (1990:2.3.7). Details of this outing can be gleaned from two newspaper reports: (i) Anonymous, "Geologists in Sussex", *Sussex Daily News* 14 July 1913; and H. Kidner's piece, "A Field Day in Sussex", in *The Christian World* 17 July 1913.

[44] See Dawson & Woodward (1914:85, 86–7).

[45] Interview with Dawson, entitled: "The Piltdown Skull: Explanation of the Present Situation: Statement by Mr. Dawson", in *Sussex Daily News*, 11 August 1913.

[46] Woodward (1948:11–12).

[47] Letter dated, 2 September 1913, in Spencer (1990:2.3.35).

[48] See Woodward's summary of his British Association lecture in *Nature* , 25 September 1913, pp 110–11.

[49] Moir, letter to editor, *The Illustrated London News*, 27 September 1913.

[50] Underwood (1913).

[51] These are European counterparts of the Galley Hill skeleton. The Olmo skeleton was discovered near Arrezo in Tuscany in 1863; while the Casteneldolo skeleton had been found near Savona in Liguria. This latter skeleton had been described Arturo Issel (1842–1922) in 1867; while the former had been described by Karl Vogt (1821–1902). These skeletons were later endorsed by the Italian anthropologist Guiseppe Sergi (1841–1936) in 1916. However, it appears from a letter written to Keith in 1912 that Sergi was already favourably disposed to these specimens. This letter is of passing interest because of his bold statements on the Neanderthal issue: "... I think the Man of Neanderthal is not the forefather of Man of Galley Hill; the two men were living together in Quaternary times; but the Palaeoanthropus (as I call the Neander type) is extinct; the Galley Hill man is still living ... I also believe the Neanderthal man has not been in America — only an inhabitant of Central Europe ... In Italy the Man of Castenedolo has not been accepted, but I am canvassing ..." (KP/RCS BOX N-Z: Sergi 16 February 1912.)

[52] Keith (1914b:452–3); see also Keith's paper in the *Lancet* (1913a).

[53] Smith, 10 September 1913, in Spencer (1990:2.3.40).

[54] Smith, 26 September 1913, in Spencer (1990:2.3.45). Smith's note was published on 2 October 1913, see Smith (1913).

[55] Smith (1913a:131).

[56] See Waterston's communication to *Nature* (13 November 1913). The impact of Waterston's note was, however, deflected by the ongong Keith–Smith exchange.

[57] See "Piltdown Skull Controversy — Identity dispute settled" *Birmingham Gazette* 8 October 1913.

[58] Keith (1913b:107).

[59] Smith (1913b:267). The letter is undated, but was published in the 30 October issue of *Nature*.

[60] Smith (1913b:267). It is interesting to note that Smith had not, since viewing the originals early in December 1912, seen them again until this time, when he apparently viewed them on two occasions. The first was on Wednesday, 8 October (in the company of Woodward), and second on Friday, 31 October in the company of the John T Wilson (1863–1945), an anatomist from Sydney University. According to Keith's Royal College diaries, he made 4 visits to the British Museum (Natural History) during this period to view the Piltdown remains, and to examine the "new" restoration made by Woodward, Pycraft and Barlow.

[61] Keith (1913b:292). This letter appeared in the 6 November issue of *Nature*.

[62] Keith (1913b:292).

[63] Smith (1913b:318). The letter is dated 30 October 1913, and was published in the 13 November issue of *Nature*.

[64] Keith (1913b:345).

[65] Smith was, however, able to reply (indirectly) in a Piltdown related article published by *Nature* in December; see Smith (1913c). Subsequently Smith reviewed the entire affair (as he saw it) in an article published in the April 1914 issue of *Bedrock*. As he notes in his preface, the primary objective of the article was to undertake a "frank examination and criticism of the expression of opinion which have excited such a distracting and befogging influence" (Smith 1914b:2).

[66] According to *Nature's* records the Keith–Smith exchange had been handled by "G", which is thought to be [Sir] Richard Arman Gregory (1864–1952), who later became Editor of *Nature* (1919–39) in Langham Papers.

[67] Smith to Haddon, 8 April 1914, in Spencer (1990:3.1.13).

[68] Derry had worked with Smith in Egypt where he succeeded the latter in 1909 as Professor of Anatomy at the Medical School in Cairo. Smith had held this position since 1900. For further details on Derry and his relationship with Smith during this Egyptian interlude, see Dawson (1938).

[69] Keith (1914a:31). This paper was delivered as Keith's presidential address to the Annual General Meeting of the Royal Anthropological Institute, and entitled: "The reconstruction of fossil human skulls".

[70] While the text of this paper was never published, Smith's attitude to Keith and *Eoanthropus* at this juncture are neatly summarized in his *Bedrock* article, published in April 1914.

[71] Elliot Smith to A C Haddon, 8 April 1914, in Spencer (1990:3.1.13).

[72] Keith (1950:326).

[73] Dawson to Woodward, 26 November 1913 (underlining in original), in Spencer (1990:2.3.66).

[74] Woodward, in Dawson & Woodward (1914:90).

[75] Underwood (1913), and Underwood, in Dawson & Woodward (1914:99).

[76] Woodward, in Dawson & Woodward (1914:91).

[77] Woodward, in Dawson & Woodward (1913:86). See also Elliot Smith's appended note: "On the exact determination of the median plane of the Piltdown skull" (*Ibid*, 93–7).

[78] This find was apparently made by Dawson and Samuel Woodhead in October 1913, see Dawson to Woodward 5 October 1913, in Spencer (1990:2.3.49).

[79] Dawson, in Dawson & Woodward (1913:85–6).
[80] Dawkins, in Dawson & Woodward (1914:98).
[81] Anonymous article, *Morning Post* 18 December 1913. For further details, see Chapter 8.
[82] Dawkins's letter is dated 22 December, published in the *Morning Post* 23 December 1913.

4 BONES, STONES & EGOS II

[1] Ernest Bevin (1881–1951) cited in Barclay (1975:67).
[2] Abbott's letter is dated 1 January 1914, and was published in the *Morning Post* [2] January 1914.
[3] Abbott, in the *Morning Post* [2] January 1914.
[4] As noted in Chapter 2, Woodward had been an eolithophile since the early 1890s. Abbott's opinions on Woodward's apparent retreat are revealed in a letter he wrote to Rutot in which he notes: "The way Boyd Dawkins has hypnotized his old student Smith Woodward is quite a psychological study. That distortion of the age [of the Piltdown artifacts] into Chellian [sic] is a dishonorouable as it is preposterous and disgraceful to science" Abbott to Rutot [4] January 1914, in Spencer (1990:3.1.1).
[5] See Abbott to Rutot [4] January 1914, in Spencer (1990:3.1.1).
[6] Sutcliffe's paper was read to the Manchester Society on 18 March 1913. The paper was strongly anti-eolithic, and both Dawkins and Elliot Smith repeatedly drew on this summary in their respective public denunciations of the Piltdown eolithic artifacts, see for example Smith's presentation to the Manchester Literary & Philosophical Society on Tuesday 18 November 1913 reported in *Manchester City News* 22 November 1913; and Dawkins' public lecture at the Manchester University Museum early in January 1914, see report in the *Manchester Guardian* 12 January 1914.
[7] It is interesting to note that like Moir, Sturge had also been a victim of Dawkins and they were mortal enemies. According to one of Weiner's informants, Dawkins had "stuck his knife into poor old Sturge with his usual ferocity [precisely when this incident had taken place is unknown], which so upset him that it brought on one of his heart attacks from which he [apparently] suffered" (MSS WEI 3.16 B Seligman 31 March 1955).
[8] Lankester's review of Sollas' book appeared in the *Saturday Review* 16 March 1912. By contrast, see Warren's (1912) review in *Man*.
[9] For a copy of the complete text of Marett's poem, see Moir (1935:33–5).
[10] Sollas (1913a:788–90).
[11] See Lankester (1914, 1921a, 1921b) and Moir (1913a, 1913b, 1914, 1916b, 1918a, 1919, 1920).
[12] See Sollas (1913b:329).
[13] Warren (1914a:430).
[14] Warren (1914b:549–50).
[15] Woodward (1948:44).
[16] Like Warren and Haward, a number of workers subsequently wondered if this bone had been accidently modelled by the gnawing of rodents and the like. For example, the Swedish palaeobotanist Alfred Nathorst (1850–1921) suggested to Woodward that perhaps the Piltdown bone had been sculpted by the beaver whose bones they had found in the pit, see Nathorst to Woodward 6 October 1915, in Spencer (1990:4.1.24).
[17] Haward to Woodward 1 July 1914, in Spencer (1990:3.1.23).
[18] Moir to Woodward 22 November 1914, in Spencer (1990:3.1.36).
[19] Moir to Woodward 28 November 1914, in Spencer (1990:3.1.37). For further details on Moir's bone implements, see Moir (1915a).
[20] Smith, in Dawson & Woodward (1915:148).
[21] Warren, in Dawson & Woodward (1915:149).
[22] Woodward, in Dawson & Woodward (1915:149).
[23] Some insight into Moir's developing attitude can be gleaned from his exchange with Woodward in November 1914 regarding a meeting at the Geological Society in 1913 devoted to the eolith controversy, see Spencer (1990:3.1.35). Specifically, Moir believed he had been unfairly treated at this meeting — and it is evident that he felt Dawkins and his followers had been given a greater opportunity to express their opinions than the pro-eolithic participants, see *Proc Geol Soc Lond* 70:ii–xiii for further details of this meeting. It is also interesting to note that during 1914, Moir's position was further exacerbated by an attack from the Cambridge geologist T McKenny Hughes, an old ally of Boyd Dawkins. See his pro-Sollas article [in the *Cambridge Antiquarian Society's Communications* (1914-15) Vol XVIII:64] on a specimen in the Sedgwick Museum (Cambridge) that was reported to be identical to Moir's sub-Crag flints. The specimen, Hughes noted had been found on a beach! For Moir's response, see *Geol Mag* Vol 2 (n.s):191.
[24] Dawson, "Notes from Piltdown Lecture 23 Feby. 1915" pages 2–6. These unpublished notes were made in a "Kingsway" bound exercise book (pages unnumbered), located in the Piltdown Collection, Palaeontology Library, British Museum (Natural History): DF 116/16. These notes have been extensively edited, in Dawson's hand. The "original" text is written in black ink, and subsequent "corrections" have

been made with a lead pencil, a blue pencil, and red ink — which suggests they had been done at different times. The extract presented here is largely free of these editorial corrections.

[25] According to the *Journal of the Royal Anthropological Institute* (1915) Vol 45:364, Dawson's paper, entitled: "Sussex Ouse Valley Cultures", was illustrated by lantern slides, and subsequently discussed by Moir, Warren, Grist and Barnes. Also, as implied in fn 24, Dawson's paper was not published.

[26] It should be noted that in Dawson's lecture notes the rostro-carinates appear simply as a heading without appended notes, see DF 116/16, p 21. However, on p 19, under notes to lantern slide 16, Dawson made reference to an "Ouze [sic] valley prismatic" flint which he likened to a rostro-carinate form, and in parenthesis he has written: "READ LANCASTER [sic] — Attempt to place [word unclear] the skeleton of Rostro-carinate series on prismatic lines." It is conjectured that it may have been these comments to which Lankester alludes in his letter to Moir, see fn 27.

[27] Lankester to Moir (undated letter), in Moir (1935:114).

[28] Moir (1915a). This paper was delivered to The Prehistoric Society of East Anglia on 3 March 1915.

[29] Boule (1915). This article appeared in the January–April issue of *L'Anthropologie* (Paris), under the title: "La Paléontologie Humaine en Angleterre".

[30] Boule (1915:60–2). As this suggests, Boule, while supportive of the Dawkins–Woodward view that human evolution had been confined essentially to the Pleistocene, he did not embrace their vision of how this had been achieved. In this regard his opinions are closer to those of Keith. The only problem with Keith's scheme was that it demanded a more expansive time framework, which Boule was not prepared to accept.

[31] Dawkins (1915:470–1).

[32] Moir (1915b:476–8).

[33] Keith (1915a). This book was published by Williams & Norgate on Friday, 8 October 1915.

[34] The picture was painted at Cooke's studio in Chelsea, see Spencer (1990:4.1.17) during the autumn of 1914, and from all accounts each individual portrayed sat separately by appointment, see Spencer (1990:3.1.32).

[35] This description was first used by Alfred Cort Haddon at the British Association meeting in Birmingham in 1913, see report in the *Birmingham Gazette* 17 September 1913.

[36] Woodward (1915:9).

[37] See Osborn to Woodward 5 April 1915, in Spencer (1990:4.1.16).

[38] Woodward (1914:320).

[39] Smith left England for Australia towards the end of May 1914, see Spencer (1990:3.1.15) and returned early in November, Ibid (1990:3.1.32). For contemporary reports of his sojourn in Australia, see particularly the interview printed in the *Sydney Morning Herald* 3 July 1914.

[40] David & Wilson (1914). For further details on this specimen, see Oakley et al (1975:203–4) and Smith's involvement, see Langham (1978).

[41] In addition to a lantern slide presentation to the Manchester Literary & Philosophical Society in February 1915 (Millar 1974:149), he also appears to have supplied Woodward with copies of his slides and full account of the skull, see Spencer (1990:4.1.34), and Dawson had duly brought the relevance of the Talgai skull home to his readers, see Dawson (1915:183) and Langham papers.

[42] See Smith's (1915) review of Woodward's *Guide* in the *Geological Magazine*.

[43] Lankester (1915:291).

[44] Keith (1915a:302, 477–8).

[45] Apparently because Lyne was not a Fellow of the Society, he was not permitted to communicate the paper himself — though he was allowed to be present and to reply to the discussion that followed. His paper was read by a dental colleague, Montagu F Hopson, whom is believed to have been associated with Guy's Hospital.

[46] Lyne (1916:48, 43, 47).

[47] Lyne (1916:50).

[48] See Woodward to Dawson 20 December 1915, in Spencer (1990:4.1.37).

[49] Woodward, in Lyne (1916:52).

[50] Keith is referring to the recent opinions published by the American palaeontologist Henry Fairfield Osborn and his co-workers at the American Museum, see Osborn's letter to Woodward 5 April 1915, in Spencer (1990:4.1.16) and Osborn (1915:144).

[51] This viewpoint was reiterated in a letter Keith wrote to Alfred Kennard the following day. Evidently Kennard was puzzled by Keith's attitude, particularly with regard to Woodward. On this subject, Keith said: "That the jaw goes with the skull I have not the least shadow of doubt — but that the tooth goes with the jaw there is good room for doubt but very little room for doubt that if not this individual that it is of the same kind or species. You may be quite sure that if I had a leg to stand on that I would fight: but when you fight you keep an eye not on your contemporaries but on the men that come after you and me — I would rather be right with them than with my contemporaries and you will find — that [in] spite of many boyish blunders Smith Woodward's general conclusions will hold true." Keith to Kennard 25 January 1916, in Spencer (1990:4.2.5).

[52] Keith, in Lyne (1916:52–55).

[53] Underwood, in Lyne (1916:56). Commenting later, on the apparent disharmony between a young (large) pulp cavity and an old worn tooth, Dawson made the following suggestion to Woodward: "The pulp cavity . . . is certainly large. It does not seem to have occurred to anyone that as one end is open [which according to Underwood had been pierced by wear] the walls of the cavity may have been the subject of post-mortem decay, and that bacteria may have cleaned away the comparatively soft walls during a prolonged soakage in water and sand", in letter to Woodward, dated 6 February 1916, in Spencer (1990:4.2.8).

[54] Smith, in Lyne (1916:57–58).

[55] Smith, in Lyne (1916:58).

[56] Lyne (1916:61).

[57] Lyne (1916:62).

[58] See MSS WEI 3.18 M R Bielby (née Lyne) to J S Weiner 5 October 1955, Weiner Piltdown Files, Palaeontology Library, British Museum (Natural History). As this letter indicates, after 1916, Lyne maintained an intermittent correspondence with Keith. Although this is supported by a number of letters present in Keith's papers at the Royal College of Surgeons, they are on matters quite unrelated to Piltdown matters, see KP/RCS BOX XXX: Lyne Material. Also it should be noted that when the discovery of Piltdown II was announced, Lyne was among the first to endorse these finds — despite his continuing reservations about the canine, see Lyne to Woodward 22 May 1918, in Spencer (1990:5.1.3).

[59] Specifically, Ameghino had proposed that the Hominidae had evolved *in situ* from an indigenous fossil primate form he called *Homunculus*, and that this evolution was represented in the South American fossil record by a series of transitional forms which had made their appearance during the early Miocene. The earliest of these hominid precursors was the so-called *Tetraprothomo* represented solely by an atlas vertebra and femur. As this appellation indicates, Ameghino envisioned four discrete evolutionary stages connecting his *Homunculus* with the genus *Homo*: *Tetraprothomo*, *Diprothomo*, *Prothomo*, and finally *Homo*. As Ameghino's series indicates, he completely by-passed *Pithecanthropus* and the European Neanderthals. Furthermore, as this scheme suggests, Ameghino was a supporter of the greater antiquity of the modern human skeletal form; a fact which had led Keith to endorse Ameghino's case (see Keith 1911b). Hrdlička, on the other hand, was a Neanderthal supporter. For further details on Ameghino and Hrdlička's counter-efforts, see Hrdlička (1912) and Spencer (1979, I:330–75).

[60] Hrdlička (1914:501, 509).

[61] It is interesting to note that Woodard and Pycraft were quite sure Hrdlička was behind Miller's attack, and this is made quite clear in Pycraft's paper "A Reply to Mr Gerrit S. Miller" in *Science Progress* (1917:389). Here Pycraft notes: "Some time ago Mr. Gerrit S. Miller of the Smithsonian Institute [sic], Washington, was *requested* by Dr. Aleš Hrdlička, of the United State National Museum, to compare a set of casts of the skull of the Piltdown man, supplied by the British Museum, with the skulls of anthropoid apes . . ." (my emphasis).

[62] See Miller (1915:2).

[63] Miller (1915:2).

[64] Miller (1915:13).

[65] Miller (1915:14–15).

[66] Miller (1915:15–16).

[67] Miller (1915:16–17).

[68] Miller (1915:18–19). This is a reference to a molar found at Taubach near Weimar, Germany, in 1892, which had been described by Alfred Nehring (1845–1925) in 1895. Nehring (1895b) was of the opinion that the tooth was chimpanzee-like. This diagnosis, however, was later disputed. For example, Schwalbe (1904) had attributed it to a Neanderthaler; while others remained uncertain, see for example Duckworth (1912:23). Miller's view, however, was subsequently endorsed by Gregory (1916a), but disputed by Boule (1923:146) who leaned toward Schwalbe's view, which in turn was contested by Hrdlička (1923a, 1923b) who was of the opinion it was a dryopithecine molar.

[69] MacCurdy 1916:228).

[70] MacCurdy (1916:229).

[71] MacCurdy (1916:230–231).

[72] The duration of Gregory's London visit is not known. However, it is clear that he had been there during late August and that he had departed sometime during mid September. This is verified by a postcard he sent Woodward on his return to New York (see Spencer 1990:2.2.47) and Teilhard's mention (Letter No 32, 10 September, in Teilhard (1965) 1967:104–105) of meeting "a certain Gregory (from the New York Museum)" shortly after the discovery of the canine tooth (see Spencer 1990:2.3.35).

[73] Gregory (1914:200).

[74] Gregory (1916b:384). This article was published in the July–September issue of the *American Anthropologist*, and essentially reiterates an earlier statement made in the June issue of the American Museum *Bulletin*. See Gregory 1916b:315–316 and fn 75 (below).

[75] Osborn's conversion was made clear in the 2nd edition of his *Men of the Old Stone Age* [published in February, 1916], where he noted that he accepted the reference of the Piltdown jaw to the genus *Pan*, p 512.

In addition to Osborn, there was also William Diller Matthew (1871–1973), who went on record as supporting Miller by stating that his thesis was "irrefutable," see Matthew et al (1916) [published January 1916].

[76] Thacker (1916:648) and Johnston (1916:349–350).

[77] Lankester to Miller 23 December 1915, in Spencer (1990:4.1.39).

[78] Keith (1917:82–85). This review was published in May. For a more immediate but private reaction to Miller's paper, see his letter to Kennard, dated 25 January 1916. Here Keith wrote: "I do not think he [Miller] shows at all an intimate knowledge of the anthropological world ... In every one of [Miller's objections] I could cite for you in [t]he gorilla, chimpanzee, orang — just the same kind of incompatabilities as we are puzzling over in Piltdown ..."

[79]Smith (1916a:321–322).

[80] Smith (1916b). This paper was delivered on 25 May 1916. "In considering the possibility of more than one hitherto unknown ape-like man or man-like ape expired in Britain side by side in the Pleistocene period, and left complementary parts ... the element of improbability is so enormous as to be set aside except for the most definite and positive anatomical reasons. [But as Smith went on to argue] ... [T]he skull revealed certain features of a more primitive nature than any other known representatives of the human family" (p.xxix).

[81] Wright (1916:126).

[82] See Smith to Woodward 11 November 1914, in Spencer (1990:3.1.32).

[83] Symington (1915:99–100). The Sir John Struthers (1823–1899) Memorial Lecture was established in 1911 when Keith gave the inaugural address.

[84] Symington (1916:130). This paper was published in the January 1916 issue of the *Journal*.

[85] Smith (1916c). See also Smith's (1917) review of Pycraft (1917).

[86] Symington to Hrdlička 12 June 1916, in Spencer (1990:4.2.15).

[87] Hinton to Miller 11 January 1916, in Spencer (1990:4.2.2).

[88] Lankester to Miller 23 December 1915, in Spencer (1990:4.1.39).

[89] See Lankester (1915:284). Here Lankester noted in relation to his discussion of the association problem: "The recent discovery by Mr. Dawson of fragments of a second skull of the same character as the first and at the same spot justifies a certain amount of hesitation in concluding that the lower jaw and the fragments of the first found skull belong to one individual". As Lankester, later noted in his letter to Miller (see fn.88): "I say 'at the same spot' but it appears that it was 3 miles distant".

[90] Symington to Hrdlička 12 June 1916, in Spencer (1990:4.2.15).

[91] Pycraft to Miller 22 August 1916, in Spencer (1990:4.2.18).

[92] Pycraft (1917:390–1).

[93] Pycraft (1917:401,402–3).

[94] Pycraft (1917:409).

[95] Hrdlička to Miller 28 April 1917, in Hrdlička Papers, National Anthropological Archives, U.S. National Museum of Natural History, Smithsonian Institution, Washington DC.

[96] Gregory to Miller 30 March 1917, in Spencer (1990:4.2.26).

[97] It is interesting to note that during this interim period (1916–17) Miller was in communication with both Woodward and Pycraft, but neither, so it seems, offered any information on the new evidence, see Letters 4.2.23, 4.2.25, 4.2.27, 4.2.28, 4.2.29, 4.2.30, in Spencer (1990). Miller's rebuttal was subsequently published in the first (January–March issue) issue of Hrdlička's *American Journal of Physical Anthropology* which appeared in July 1918; whereas Woodward's article in the *Quarterly Journal of the Geological Society*, describing Piltdown II, was released several months earlier, see Lyne to Woodward 22 May 1918, in Spencer (1990:5.1.3).

[98] Indeed during the summer of 1916, Woodward, assisted by Elliot Smith and Henry H Godwin-Austen (1834–1923) worked at Piltdown without apparent success, see Spencer (1990:4.2.13; 4.2.17).

[99] Dawson to Woodward 21 November 1914, in Spencer (1990:3.1.34).

[100] Letter dated 9 January 1915, in Spencer (1990:4.1.1). The symbol [?] indicates an unclear word and the underlining is by Dawson.

[101] Although in the case of the Piltdown II occipital fragment there is no record of when and precisely where it was found, it appears that the molar was recovered sometime late in July, see Dawson to Woodward 30 July 1915, in Spencer (1990:4.1.21). Here Dawson noted: " ... I have got a new molar tooth (Eoanthropus) with the new series. But it is just the same as the others as to wear. It is a first or second right m[olar]. The roots are broken ...". It is inferred from Dawson's mention of "new series" that the occipital had already been found. Had this not been the case it is suggested that he would have simply referred to the frontal fragment he had found earlier in January.

[102] Woodward (1917:3).

[103] See Woodward to Dawson 20 December 1915, in Spencer (1990: 4.1.37). According to the death certificate [HB 081703] issued in Lewes, on 10 August 1916, Dawson had been suffering from "pyorrhoea alveolaris" for five months, "anaemia" for nine months, and "septicaemia" for forty-two days [see Spencer

(1990: Section 4.2)]. It has been suggested by Millar ([1972] 1974) that Dawson had been suffering from pernicious anaemia. This appears to have been based on Dawson's mention in a letter to Woodward, dated February 1916 [see Spencer (1990:4.2.8)] that he was receiving "serum therapy". If by this Millar means to imply that Dawson was being treated with liver extract, it should be noted that this form of treatment for pernicious anaemia was not introduced until 1926. It is possible, however, that Dawson may have been suffering from some form of aplastic anaemia. In such conditions an accompanying infection and the ulceration of the mouth are not uncommon. Another possibility, but one that is highly debatable is that he was suffering from syphilis and was being treated with either arsenic or mercurial compounds, both of which are capable of producing an agranulocytosis. It should be noted that mercury compounds can also cause "pyrrhoea" but this developing condition is generally accompanied by other symptoms that are not reported in Dawson's case. On presenting this "syphilis hypothesis" to a practicing pathologist, Dr Stanley S Raphael, he noted: ". . . [A]lthough Dawson may have had syphilis it was not a diagnosis that a doctor in a small country town would have cheerfully put on the death certificate and it is a disease that may well have been non-apparent to casual acquaintances . . . There is [also] a general impression that syphilis was more common in Edwardian times, but the statistics are not very reliable" (Personal communication dated 10 September 1987).

[104] See Dawson to Woodward 15 October 1915, in Spencer (1990:41.26). According to Mrs Margaret Hodgson, Woodward's daughter, her brother Cyril had been suffering from appendicitis, that had been further complicated by post-operative thrombosis (personal communication).

[105] Woodward (1917:6).

[106] Smith, in Woodward (1917:8).

[107] For the source of these various opinions, see Pycraft (p 9), Keith (p 10) and Lankester (p 10), respectively in Woodward (1917).

[108] What visible support there was for Miller's dualistic thesis in Britain prior to 1917 was, so it apperars, quickly lost, see for example O'Donoghue (1918:102–107). This particular individual was a zoologist affiliated to University College, London.

5 STEPS TO THE SCAFFOLD

[1] Letter from the anatomist Frederic Wood Jones to Arthur Keith 11 February 1939, in Spencer (1990:5.1.57).

[2] Osborn (1921a:582).

[3] Osborn (1921a:581).

[4] Osborn (1921a:590).

[5] Osborn (1921b).

[6] In April 1863, Boucher de Perthes announced the discovery of the right half of a human mandible in association with a detached molar and several palaeoliths at Moulin Quignon, situated a few miles east of Abbeville. This discovery, so the zoologist William B Carpenter (1813–85) noted in the Athanaeum had been found in "[a] gravel bed [situated] about 100-ft. above the present level of the river, and therefore corresponds in position with the upper gravels of St Acheul . . . so that if we accept the conclusions of Mr. Prestwich as to the relative ages of these gravels, this human jaw was buried in the deepest, and therefore the oldest portion of the earliest fluvialtile deposits" (Carpenter 1863:523). The subsequent investigations of Prestwich and Evans, however, led to the discovery that some of the Moulin Quignon artifacts were forgeries. This prompted Falconer, who had been among the first to visit the site and endorse the finds, to reconsider his position. The detached molar, which Boucher de Perthes had given him as a gift was sectioned and examined by George Busk and John Tomes (1815–95). The cut surface of this tooth appeared "white, glistening, full of gelatine, and fresh looking" (Falconer, in Prestwich 1899:179). In the meantime the French had become generally committed to the finds, and were confused by the vacillations of their British confrères. On 9 May 1863 a conference was held in Paris to consider the matter. The jaw was sawn in half and the interior looked much like the detached molar. But while this confirmed the suspicions of the British, the French remained unconvinced. For a detailed account of the proceedings in Paris, see Delesse (1863); Falconer, in Murchison (1868,I:601–25); and Cohen & Hublin (1989:201–21). After three days of deliberation, the conference moved to Abbeville to examine the site first-hand. Opinions remained divided. Subsequently, Evans provided evidence supporting the view that "a regular system of imposition ha[d] been carried on by the gravel-diggers of [Moulin Quignon]" (Evans 1863:19–20). In the light of this evidence, support for the jaw rapidly dwindled. It was widely believed that the jaw had been recovered from a Neolithic burial site (not uncommon in the region) and planted with the spurious artifacts to arouse Boucher de Perthes' interest. For further information on this, see Appendix to the 3rd edition of Lyell's Antiquity of Man(1863).

[7] See Collyer (1867). According to Collyer's paper the jaw was found in 1855 by farm labourers excavating a "bed of coprolites" near Ipswich, Suffolk. The specimen was then purchased from the finder by "J. Taylor" a local chemist (pharmacist), who in turn brought it to the attention of a "Sir Thomas Beaver" who passed it

along to Collyer. The jaw was said to have been found 16 feet below the surface of the pit. As indicated by Huxley's reaction the jaw was anatomically modern in form. After 1867, Collyer slipped from view. He is believed to have returned to America, taking the Foxhall jaw with him. The present whereabouts of the specimen is unknown.

[8] Letter (undated) from Huxley to Collyer, cited in Hrdlička (1930:25).

[9] Busk, cited in Hrdlička (1930:25–26).

[10] Keith (1915a:198).

[11] Moir (1916a:109).

[12] See Moir (1920, 1921, 1922). See also Moir's eolithic synthesis published in *Natural History* in 1924.

[13] Sollas (1920).

[14] Sollas (1924:104).

[15] Breuil (1922:228). From all accounts Breuil had been persuaded not only by Sollas' conversion but also by the enthusiastic report sent to him by the Cambridge archaeologist, Miles Crawford Burkitt (1890–1971). For details on Burkitt's pro-Tertiary Man stance, see Burkitt (1921a, 1921b).

[16] See Boule (1923) and Warren (1921, 1922, 1923). As this suggests, the eoliths still confronted considerable opposition. And despite Moir's apparent gains in the 1920s, by the end of the 1930s it is evident that Moir was once again isolated. This progressive shift is reflected in the work of Moir's one-time ally A S Barnes, who during the late 1930s produced a string of papers denouncing the artificiality of the eoliths (see Barnes 1938, 1939a, 1939b).

[17] Osborn (1921a:590).

[18] Gregory to Hrdlička n.d. 1921, in Gregory Papers, Library of the American Museum of Natural History, New York City. See also Gregory's statement in his 1922 book on ... *Human Dentition*: "The two molar teeth, although greatly worn, show the primitive Dryopithecus pattern which is disguised in all the hominidae; the molars appear to agree generically with those of the very old Chimpanzees figures by Miller. They differ from all human molars that I have seen in being relatively long and narrow, and in having the posterior moiety less widened transversely." As indicated in the text, Hrdlička was convinced the Piltdown jaw was a dryopithecoid form, and it is interesting to note that Gregory was annoyed that Hrdlička had not given him due credit for his work on the dryopithecine pattern in human dentition. See fn 28.

[19] Gregory to Smith 12 May 1921, Spencer (1990:5.1.12).

[20] From all accounts MacCurdy viewed the Piltdown remains sometime during the summer of 1922. For further details on his changed opinions on *Eoanthropus*, see MacCurdy (1924).

[21] MacCurdy, in Capitan (1923:67). These views were expressed in concert with Charles Fraipont and Capitan who formed a "commission" of the "International Institute of Anthropology" to investigate Moir's claims.

[22] Evidently Hrdlička was able to justify this trip on the grounds that he needed to make "on-site" arrangements for the 1923 summer program of the American School in France for Prehistoric Studies (later renamed the American School for Prehistoric Research) which had been founded in 1921, of which he was Director for 1923. In addition to his visit to England, Hrdlička spent several weeks touring sites in France, Belgium, Germany, Austria and Czechoslavakia.

[23] Hrdlička (1922:337).

[24] Hrdlička (1922:346–347).

[25] Hrdlička to Bather 6 October 1926, Spencer (1990:5.1.23). Woodward retired from the Museum in 1924, whereupon Bather became Keeper of Geology, a position he held until his death in 1934.

[26] Woodward to Hrdlička 26 October 1926, Spencer (1990:5.1.25).

[27] See Hrdlička (1930:87, 88–89).

[28] Sera (1917). Unlike Hrdlička, this Italian anatomist supported the monistic intrepretation of the Piltdown remains. His 1917 paper is also of interest since it reflects an initial attempt to equate the recently discovered dryopithecoid fossils in the Siwaliks by Pilgrim (1915). In this regard it is important not to loose sight of the work of the German palaeontologist Max Schlosser (1903) and Gregory's paper on primate dentition and phylogeny (1916a). Indeed it had been on the basis of this latter work that Gregory subsequently supported Guy Pilgrim's (1915) thesis that the European and Indian Miocene dryopithecoid apes stood "very close, if not actually in the line of human descent" (Gregory 1916:384–387; see also Gregory's note to *Science* in 1915). Also it is interesting to note that in both of Hrdlička's papers on this possible connection no mention is made of Gregory's work, which did not help their already strained relationship.

[29] Hrdlička (1923a, 1923b, 1924).

[30] These are dryopithecoid teeth attributed to *Dryopithecus rhenanus* which had been found during the 1850s near Tübingen, Germany, in the so-called "Bohnerz deposits", that had been identified as belonging to the lower Pliocene. Casts of these teeth were in the collections of the American Museum in New York, which Gregory made available to Hrdlička.

[31] The Ehringsdorf jaws were recovered from a limestone quarry in the Ilm valley, near Weimar, Germany, between 1914 and 1916. They were initially described by Schwalbe (1916) who attributed them to "Homo

primigenius" (syn. *Homo neanderthalensis*). See also the report by MacCurdy (1915) who was of much the same opinion. For further details on these remains and the skull found at this site in 1925, see Hrdlička (1930:229–241).

[32] Hrdlička (1923a:216).

[33] Hrdlička (1930:88–89).

[34] Hrdlička (1930:89–90).

[35] Sollas (1924, and 1915:54).

[36] Miller (1929:441). The first sentence of this quote is identical to the statement made in his original paper, see Miller (1915:1).

[37] As reported by Oakley & Groves (1970), there is some evidence that after 1929 Miller had entertained the idea of the Piltdown molars having been artificially shaped. Apparently, in 1930, he had asked A Remington Kellogg (later director of the US National Museum of Natural History [1948–1962]) "to seek an opportunity to look at the original Piltdown teeth ... because he had come to the conclusion that their shape had been artificially modified". Later, in 1966, according to Ted McCown, Miller had told him that he had been "persuaded by his colleagues not to publish his suspicions on the grounds that without positive proof this would be too serious an allegation ..." (Oakley & Groves 1970:789). But whatever Miller's reasons may have been for not pursuing this line of inquiry (particularly after the Second World War), and whether in fact he had been really committed to this opinion, there is, as Oakley & Groves (1970) stress, little question that prior to 1929 he had been committed to the idea of the Piltdown jaw being a genuine fossil.

[38] Dart (1925:195). For details on discovery, see Tobias (1984).

[39] Dart (1925:196–197).

[40] Dart (1925:197).

[41] Dart (1925:198).

[42] This is clearly reflected in the reactions of Hrdlička (1925), Woodward (1925), Keith (1925b), Smith (1925), Underwood (1925), and Sollas (1925).

[43] Dart (1925:195,199). This concern for the lack of geological data on the Taung specimen can be seen from the comments solicited by *Nature* on the discovery, see particularly those of Keith (1925b:234) and Smith (1925:235).

[44] Keith (1947), in Le Gros Clark (1967:38).

[45] Keith (1925b:234).

[46] Smith (1925a:235).

[47] Woodward (1925:235–6).

[48] Osborn (1926a:vii; 1926b:266–7). For references to Osborn's earlier commitment to this idea (particularly with regard to primates etc), see Osborn (1900, 1918). Another advocate of the Asiatic hypothesis had been W D Matthew who in 1914 had formally advanced the theory that northern Asia had been the centre of dispersal for mammals — the impulse being changing climatic conditions during the Tertiary period, culminating with the onset of Pleistocene (characterised by increasing fluctuations in temperature).

[49] See Osborn (1922). Subsequently, the Nebraskan molar tooth was shown to be an extinct species of pig! For further details and general reaction to this spurious find, see Spencer (1990:5.1.13–5.1.16).

[50] During the 1920s a series of five expeditions were sent to Central Asia, for further details of these expeditions see Roy Chapman Andrews' chronicle: *On the Trail of Ancient Man* (1926). The Foreword to this work was written by Osborn. For a summary of the work achieved, see *Science* (1930) LXI:481–2, and for specific details on Osborn's committment to the Asiatic hypothesis, see Osborn (1924, 1926, 1927).

[51] See Black to Hrdlička, 31 March 1926, Hrdlička Papers, National Anthropological Archives, National Museum of Natural History, Smithsonian Institution, Washington DC; see also Black (1925:238–183).

[52] Hrdlička to Gregory 22 June 1927, in Gregory Papers, American Museum of Natural History, New York.

[53] Woodward (1935:137).

[54] Boule (1937).

[55] Boule (1929).

[56] Smith (1931a:43, 46). As indicated by Smith's phylogenetic chart, *Eoanthropus* and *Sinanthropus* were thought to have shared a common ancestor. The latter was considered to have branched off from the sapiens line much earlier (Pliocene), whereas the former had departed much later (early Pleistocene). It should be noted, however, that Smith considered Black's fossil to represent a late survivor of the sinanthropine lineage into the Lower Pleistocene.

[57] Hrdlička (1930:365–368).

[58] Keith (1931:275–294).

[59] It is interesting to note that Hrdlička was the first American to receive the coveted Huxley Medal since 1908 when William Z Ripley of Harvard was accorded the honour. Hrdlička delivered the Huxley Lecture on 8 November 1927, which was published later that year in the *Journal of the Royal Anthropological Institute* (Hrdlička 1927).

[60] See Smith's communication in *Nature* (1928a) [January] and in *Scientific American* (1928b) [August]. In

Nature he wrote: "In his recent Huxley lecture . . . Dr. Aleš Hrdlička has questioned the validity of the specific distinction of Neanderthal man, an issue which most anatomists imagined to have been definitely settled by the investigation of Schwalbe in 1899, and the corroboration afforded by the work of Boule . . . The only justification for re-opening the problem of the status of Neanderthal man would be afforded by new evidence or new views, either of a destructive or constructive nature. I do not think Dr. Hrdlička has given any valid reasons for rejecting the view that *Homo neanderthalensis* is a species distinct from *Homo sapiens*.

[61] Weidenreich (1928).

[62] Friedrichs (1932). It is interesting to note that Franz Weidenreich contributed a six-page "foreword" (pp 199–204) to this long and detailed article.

[63] Weidenreich (1937:149). See also Weidenreich's sceptical remarks on the "chimaera" in his 1943 paper and again in his 1946 work *Apes, Giants and Man*. Here he wrote: "All that has been known of early man since the discovery of the Piltdown fossils proves that man cannot have had an ancestor with a lower jaw of a completely simian character". A similar view was expressed by Herman Sicher (1933), another German anatomist.

[64] Weidenreich (1937:149).

[65] Weidenreich (1943, 1949).

[66] This activity had been prompted by the discovery of the so called Galilee skull found in 1925 in a cave known as Mugharet-el-Zuttiyeh, near Lake Kinneret. The skull was later described by its discoverer Francis A J Turville-Petre (1927) as possessing definite Neanderthaloid characters. For details on this find, see Hrdlička (1930:303–310).

[67] See Hrdlička to MacCurdy September (n.d.) 1932, in Hrdlička Papers, National Anthropological Archives, US National Museum of Natural History, Smithsonian Institution. In this letter Hrdlička suggested to MacCurdy that the Mount Carmel material be divided between himself and Keith. MacCurdy, although sympathetic to his colleagues motives, thought it might be "unfair" to McCown who, after all, had been intimately involved in the discoveries from the start, see MacCurdy's report, dated 15 September 1932. Hrdlička agreed (?reluctantly). McCown later returned to Berkeley where he went on to become a faculty member of the Department of Anthropology.

[68] McCown & Keith (1939). It should be noted that the reason for the apparent delay in publication of this work was because the skeletal material had to be first removed from the breccia in which it was encased. This cleaning process was a long and tedious job, done largely by McCown and his assistants. Although Hrdlička had hoped to be involved in the description of this material, Keith did keep him apprised of developments: "As we uncover the anatomy of the Carmelites", Keith wrote, "the more distinctive their anatomy becomes. We have 13 individuals, more or less, and each one might represent a separate race, for so great is the individual variation. Many have Neanderthal characteristics, while others are more modern. The Neanderthal peculiarities, however, are in the ascendency. I suspect we have a mongrel population" (Keith to Hrdlička 13 February 1936, in Hrdlička Papers, NAA, US National Museum of Natural History, Smithsonian Institution). Replying to this Hrdlička countered that he was sure the population represented one in the process of transition: "an intermediate stage in the gradual evolution of man to his present form" (Hrdlička to Keith 6 March 1936, Hrdlička Papers, NAA, US National Museum of Natural History, Smithsonian Institution).

[69] See Cole (1975:61) and Keith (1950:501–2).

[70] Leakey (1933).

[71] This was not Leakey's first attempt to establish the antiquity of the modern human form in Africa. Some years earlier, in collaboration with the German explorer Hans Reck (1886–1937), he had ventured forth in support of the antiquity of an anatomically modern "Oldoway" skeleton which Reck had found at Olduvai Gorge in 1913, see Leakey 1928 and Leakey (1931) *et al* (1928).

[72] Leakey (1934:221).

[73] Boswell (1935:371). For further details on the Leakey-Boswell affair, see Cole (1975:86–104).

[74] Leakey (1935a:9; see also 1935b). It should be noted here that when the Kanam and Kanjera specimens were later submitted to radiometric analysis in 1962 the results were highly indicative of an Upper rather than a Lower Pleistocene age, see Oakley (1974, 1975). But again contrary to expectations Leakey clung doggedly to his version of the presapiens theory.

[75] See Marston (1937:403). For further details on the Swanscombe skull, see Day (1986:19–25). Marston demonstrated his finds to Woodward and Keith (accompanied by McCown) at the Royal College of Surgeons on 28 August 1935, see Spencer (1990:5.1.45).

[76] Keith, in Marston (1937:403), see also fn 75.

[77] From letter to Dorothea M A Bate dated 29 August 1935, Spencer (1990:5.1.45).

[78] Marston (1936a).

[79] Smith, in Marston (1937:374, and repeated on p. 401).

[80] Marston (1937:404).

[81] Oakley, in Marston (1937:394). For details of this survey, see Edmunds (Fig 10), in White (1926).

[82] Although this ubiquitous dental character had been noted in the earlier literature, it was not until Hrdlička stumbled on the character in modern and fossil hominid crania that it was finally subjected to a thorough investigation. Hrdlička believed it had an evolutionary significance and used it support his Neanderthal hypothesis and related scheme for the peopling of the New World, see Hrdlička (1920, 1921).

[83] Marston (1936b:218).

[84] Although as indicated by Hinton's letter to Marston (dated 24 March 1936), Spencer (1990:5.1.50), he did begin by working on the Swanscombe fauna, it appears from the Swanscombe Committee Report of the Royal Anthropological Institute that this task was later taken over by Oakley, see Hinton et al (1938:28).

[85] Marston to Woodward 1 April 1936, in Spencer (1990:5.1.51).

[86] See Marston's humorous "Notice of Operation" advertising his Royal Society presentation, Spencer (1990:5.1.52). See also his summary of "The Case for the Piltdown Jaw" published in the January issue of Discovery, (1937b).

[87] See introduction to the Swanscombe Committee Report, in Hinton et al (1938:18). This committee consisted of Hinton, Oakley, W E Le Gros Clark (Professor of Anatomy, Oxford), Frank Corner, Aylwin Cotton (Institute of Archaeology, London University), H G Dines (Geological Survey), C F C Hawkes (British Museum), W B R King (Geology Department, University College), G M Morant (Galton Laboratory, University College), and S Hazzledine Warren.

[88] Clark, in Hinton et al (1938:58).

[89] Morant, in Hinton et al(1938:97).

[90] Keith (1938). See also Keith's correspondence with Hrdlička on this topic, Spencer (1990:5.1.53;5.1.54); and Keith (1950:643–5). It should be noted here that Keith had used a similar, though less powerful argument for the so-called "London skull" or as it was referred to by others, the "Lloyds" skull found in 1925. The skull was originally described by Elliot Smith (1925b). In Smith's estimation the skull had neanderthaloid affinities — "a stray representative" that had survived in Aurignacian times in Britain. In 1931 Keith rejected this view claiming that it closely resembled the Piltdown skull and that the London skull was a direct descendant. Smith retaliated in his review of Keith's 1931 book, dismissing this notion and Keith's continuing efforts to "exaggerate the size of braincase and brain" of the Piltdown skull. "There is no justification for such misleading statements", Smith contended. "I showed that the Piltdown skull and jaw are not disharmonious, that the general architecture of the braincase is no less simian in character than the jaw" (Smith 1931b:965).

[91] Shortly after preparing his preliminary report on the Swanscombe endocranium, Smith's health began to rapidly deteriorate and he died on New Year's Day 1937. Thus, where Marston had originally hoped to secure Smith's future assistance in preparing his materials for publication, this idea had to be abandoned.

[92] Following the 1947 Geologists' Association meeting, Marston also delivered an attack in June 1949 at the Royal Anthropological Institute in which he examined the flourine results on Galley Hill and Swanscombe, while apparently calling on Oakley to apply the test to Piltdown, see Marston (1950:299).

[93] See Marston (1950:294–5).

[94] Hopwood (1935:48). Potassium bichromate (or dichromate) is a well-known histological–fixative. It is also commonly employed as lead intensifier in photographic processing. This latter fact is not without interest since Dawson is known to have dabbled in photography, see Spencer (1990:2.3.5). Hopwood was a palaeontologist and a member of the Geology Department at the British Museum (Natural History). It should be noted that the Piltdown fauna was not the primary focus of this work. As indicated by Osborn's reference to the same issue in his posthumous monograph on The Proboscidea (1942:966), this information was well-known.

[95] From all accounts Oakley had chanced upon reference to Carnot's work during the war when he had been temporarily seconded to the Geological Survey to investigate sources of phosphates for use as a fertilizer. Later (1964:122) he acknowledged that he had not been the only one to recognize the potential application of Carnot's work in palaeoanthropology. In 1932, the French archaeologist Vayson de Pradenne had noted the utility of the test as indicated by comparative flourine analyses of fossil animal bones and the supposedly ancient Calaveras skull found in a Californian mine shaft in the mid 1860s.

[96] Marston's campaign against the Piltdown mandible and Oakley's fluorine work were clearly linked in the public mind, as seen by the comments of the anatomist Lawrence Wells (1908–1980) in the Daily Mail 15 June 1949. Commenting on Oakley's recent revelations, Wells said: "I think he [Marston] has made a case that has got to be answered. It is difficult in the light of what we know of early types of man to give a satisfactory place in anthropological sequence to this Piltdown jaw". Indeed the extent to which this link between Marston and Oakley had been fixed can be seen in Oakley's request to William T Stearn to modify his statements on Marston in the manuscript of his book The Natural History Museum at South Kensington (1981), noting that "it would be an irony if Marston went down in history as having initiated the fluorine testing that led to the Piltdown exposure" (Oakley to Stearn 22 June 1981, in P.MSS KPO: Piltdown File, BMNH). Although in Stearn's published text Marston is credited with having requested Oakley to apply the fluorine test to the Piltdown remains, this is qualified by the note that: Oakley had "already, before 1943, contemplated application of the [fluorine] test to the Piltdown remains . . ." (Stearn 1981:245).

[97] Oakley (1948:336–337).

[98] Oakley (1948). These results were later formally presented in a definitive study (in collaboration with Ashley Montagu) of the Galley Hill skeleton which was published by the British Museum (Natural History) in 1949.

[99] Keith (1948:265).

[100] Keith (1948:229).

[101] Oakley's *Nature* article (co-authored with Hoskin) was published on 11 March 1950.

[102] Oakley & Hoskins (1950:381,382).

[103] Edmunds (1950).

[104] Oakley (1953:47). It should be noted that this article was written in 1952 as part of an international symposium on anthropology organized by Louis Kroeber and Sherwood L Washburn under the auspices of the Wenner-Gren Foundation held 9–20 June 1952 in New York.

[105] Marston to Oakley 1 May 1950, Spencer (1990:5.2.17), and Marston (1950:299).

[106] Birdsell, in Stewart (1951:107).

6 SCOTOANTHROPUS FRAUDATOR

[1] Anonymous note entitled: "Scotoanthropus fraudator" on British Museum (Natural History) stationery, in DF 116/17: Piltdown Miscellanea and Weiner Papers, MSS WEI: Box 1/ Piltdown File. Translation: "A single ass' jawbone the Philistines dismay'd, but learned reputations an ape's sole tooth has flayed".

[2] This work was carried out in collaboration with David Scott at the National Institute of Dental Research, Bethesda, Maryland, see Spencer (1990:5-2-20-2) for further details. In addition to these electron microscope studies, it also appears that Oakley had asked Professor J T Randall, then Director of the Medical Research Council's Biophysics Research Unit at King's College, London, to make a comparative examination of the collagen content of the various Piltdown remains. According to Oakley (*in* Weiner *et al*, 1955:255) this request was made in March 1952, and that the results were "inconclusive."

[3] Keith to Oakley 4 January 1950, Spencer (1990:5.2.13).

[4] Oakley to Keith 10 January 1950, Spencer (1990:5.2.15).

[5] For details on this skull, see Henri-Martin (1947).

[6] Wiegers (1952:61–4).

[7] Oakley, Hoskins, Henri-Martin (1951).

[8] This conference was organized by the Berkeley anthropologist Alfred Kroeber, see Wenner-Gren 45th Anniversary Report, p 20. One of the products of this symposium was Kroeber's edited volume *Anthropology Today: An Encyclopedic Inventory* (1953). Oakley's contribution to this volume was on "Dating fossil human remains", see Oakley (1953:45–6).

[9] Oakley (1953:46).

[10] See Wenner-Gren Grant Number 753 (awarded 9 December 1952): "To aid expenses of conference and travel for research on Early Man in Africa".

[11] K P Oakley (1953) "Early Man in Africa" File, Wenner Gren Foundation, New York. The five-day program consisted of an afternoon session at Burlington House on Monday, 27 July, and a full day on the 28th. On Wednesday, the day was split between a morning session at Burlington House and an afternoon visit to the Royal College of Surgeons (hosted by Frederic Wood Jones, then Curator of the Hunterian Museum). The following day (Thursday) the conference convened at the South Kensington Museum (see next section of this chapter). The last day, Friday, 31 July, was spent visiting the Powell-Cotton Museum at Birchington-on-sea to examine their primate collections. According to Oakley the major recommendations emerging from the discussions that took place in the Board Room of the British Museum (Natural History) on the afternoon of 30 July, were: " 1) Further research on the distribution and character of breccias in dolomite and limestone belts of southern Africa correlated with the study of micro-faunas; 2) study of Quaternary climatic changes with techniques of soil chemistry and faunal studies; 3) study of chronological and geographical distribution and character of pebble tool industries; and 4) dating of Middle and Later Stone Age cultures by means of radio-carbon. The region recommended to receive highest priority, following several lines of research and using all applicable techniques, was that of Northern and Southern Rhodesia, Nyasaland, and the Belgian Congo south of Katanga (reported dated 19 July 1954)." These proposals were made by a panel which included Oakley, Camille Arambourg (1883–1969) [Muséum National d'Histoire Naturelle, Paris], Le Gros Clark [Oxford University], Arthur T Hopwood (1897–1969) [British Museum (Natural History)], Clark Howell (b.1925) [Chicago University], G H R von Koenigswald (1902–82) [Utrecht University], G Mortelmans [Brussels University], Hallam Movius (b.1907) [Harvard University], J C Trevor (1908–67) [Cambridge University], Sherwood L Washburn (b.1911) [Chicago University], and Lawrence H Wells (1908–80) [Edinburgh University].

[12] In addition Oakley had also arranged several special exhibits which included recent secured casts of all the South African australopithecine materials, Leakey's Kanam and Kanjera materials, the original

[Neanderthaloid] Rhodesian skull (which Woodward and Pycraft had both studied when it was first found in the early 1920s), and the Singa skull (found in the Sudan). For further details on these two latter skulls, see Day (1986:267–73) and Stringer (1979) respectively.

[13] Weiner ([1955] 1980:26). Washburn to Spencer, 3 April 1987 (personal communication).

[14] This dinner was held at the Rembrandt Hotel in Thurloe Place, which is situated a short distance from the Museum in South Kensington. It was at this hotel that most of the delegates stayed while attending the Wenner-Gren conference.

[15] See Dawson to Woodward 30 July 1915, see Spencer (1990:4.1.21) and appended notes for further details.

[16] Weiner ([1955] 1980:27). Washburn's curiosity had also been aroused. In his case he was "intrigued" by the condition of the mandible, and on returning to Chicago had written to Oakley requesting a set of photographs of the jaw showing the pattern of surface cracking. "Oddly enough", he commented, "none of the other fossil jaws seem to be split in that way. Very comparable splitting appears in modern jaws which are a little decalcified and dry. I think I will try a few experiments in duplicating the condition. . ." Washburn to Oakley 16 August 1953, Spencer (1990:6.1.3).

[17] Weiner ([1955] 1980:27–30). As Weiner noted his "cogitations" on the Piltdown conundrum had occupied his thoughts into "the small hours on my return to Oxford after the Wenner-Gren dinner" (Weiner [1955] 1980:30).

[18] See Millar ([1972] 1974:200–1). There is no direct evidence linking Weiner's hypothesis with that of Marston's earlier experiments. While it is evident from a later publication (see Weiner, in Weiner et al 1955:233) that Weiner was aware of Marston's 1952 experiments, it is not known if he had seen this publication before August 1953; and even if he had, it seems clear from the chronology of events that it did not have the impact Millar has suggested. From all of the available evidence there is no reason to doubt Weiner's account of the evolution of his forgery hypothesis.

[19] Marston (1952:1–4,10–12).

[20] In addition to his various antagonistic statements reported in the press, he also made several direct attacks on Weiner, Oakley and Le Gros Clark. For example, on Wednesday, 25 November 1953 at an evening meeting of the Geological Society, Oakley and Weiner presented a summary of their initial results on the Piltdown jaw and canine. Marston was present and used the occasion to publicly criticize the results. While the newspaper reports of this meeting are somewhat confused — all indicate that the meeting had been upset by outbursts from Marston. For further information on Marston's continuing dissatisfaction see Section 6.3, Spencer (1990). Also his declining opinions on Weiner, Oakley, and Le Gros Clark can be gauged from a letter he wrote on 17 May 1955 to a colleague (A Gunner): ". . .Get it into your noodle that there was no Piltdown forgery . . . With de Beer [and Oakley] as the mouth-piece. . . Le Gros Clark the wind-bag and Weiner as the garbage collector . . . I have got them "holed" and am biding my time. . ." (DF 116/39 Piltdown Letters 1955–1961).

[21] Weiner ([1955] 1980:32).

[22] Oakley's talk was given on Wednesday, 2 November 1949, see Weiner, in Harrison (1983).

[23] Weiner ([1955] 1980:30–1).

[24] Oakley & Hoskins (1950:379), see also Weiner ([1955] 1980:33). It should be noted that Oakley himself drew attention to this shortly after receiving word of Weiner's hypothesis, see Oakley to Le Gros Clark 12 August 1953, in Spencer (1990:6.1.1).

[25] Weiner memorandum, dated April 1982, reprinted with editorial correction in Harrison (1983). According to Oakley's surviving notes, Le Gros Clark's telephone call was made on the afternoon of Thursday, 6 August 1953, and this is not at variance with the chronology revealed in the available correspondence from this period, see Spencer (1990).

[26] Weiner, in Harrison (1983:47). This posthumously published note by Weiner is of interest since it reflects an attempt to correct the popular misconception that Oakley had been the prime mover in the investigations that led to the discovery of the forgery. As Weiner goes on to note: ". . . not to put too fine a point on it, Dr. Oakley's role, though very enthusiastic, assiduous, unremittant and careful, was, in the nature of the event, supportive and collaborative. It was only after that phone call, when there were strong grounds for suspecting the forgery and the arguments had been put by Le Gros Clark and myself, that he saw how important the issue was, not merely for the British Museum, but most decidedly for the scientific assessment of the Piltdown remains."

[27] Clark, in Weiner et al (1955:240).

[28] Oakley, in Weiner et al (1953:143).

[29] See Cook & Heizer (1952). Since the late 1940s these two American workers at the University of California (Berkeley) had been investigating the nitrogen test as a possible means of determining the relative age of organic remains, see Cook & Heizer (1947).

[30] Recent comparative radiometric studies of the Piltdown I and II cranial fragments [see Spencer & Stringer, in Hedges et al (1989:210)] throws some doubt on this hypothesis. A sample of the Piltdown II cranium was recently submitted to the Oxford Radiocarbon Accelerator Unit, along with a resampling of the orang (Piltdown) mandibular fragment to assess whether the former could belong to Piltdown I. Earlier

radiometric studies by Vries & Oakley (1959) and Vogel & Waterbolk (1964) indicated that the mandible and Piltdown I cranial fragments were of similar age: 500 ± 100 and 620 ± 100 respectively. The new Oxford AMS results obtained on Piltdown II [OxA–1394] were 970 ± 140 yrs, while the age of the mandible [OxA–1395] was estimated to be 90 ± 120 yrs. While the latter date is not inconsistent with Oakley's (1959) view that it might represent a comparatively recent (i.e. nineteenth century) specimen, the same cannot be said for the Piltdown I and II cranial remains. The present results sugest that they might well belong to two quite *distinct* individuals.

[31] This was material was later identified as a bituminous compound, such as Cassel earth (Vandyke brown), see report by Werner & Plesters, in Weiner *et al* (1955:271–2).

[32] Weiner *et al* (1953:145).

[33] Weiner *et al* (1953:146). For further details on the immediate reaction to this news, see Section 6.2, Spencer (1990).

[34] The date of this visit to Lewes is uncertain, but seems to have been shortly after 6 August.

[35] According to Weiner ([1955] 1980:155) this exchange had taken place in 1948.

[36] This second outing to Sussex seems to have occurred sometime around the middle of August, see Weiner to Le Gros Clark 17 August 1953, Spencer (1990:6.3.1).

[37] Weiner ([1955] 1980:156).

[38] From Shakespeare's Macbeth, Act 1, scene 3.

[39] These documents are now preserved in the Piltdown collections of the British Museum (Natural History), DF 116/17.

[40] Weiner ([1955] 1980:58).

[41] Breuil (1938:56–7).

[42] Oakley (1949:98).

[43] See Weiner *et al* (1955). The results obtained were not significantly different from those published by Oakley & Hoskins (1950), see tables in text.

[44] This work was carried out by Claringbull and Hey, in Weiner *et al* (1955:252).

[45] Oakley, in Weiner *et al* (1955:251). For further details on this site see Despott (1918), Keith & Sinclair (1924) and Keith (1925a, I:345–7).

[46] In his book, published posthumously, Woodward wrote: "After Mr. Dawson's death in 1916, I was able to open a series of pits along the other side of the hedge in a field adjacent to the original pit. There I was helped by Professor Elliot Smith. . . and others. We began close to the spot where the skull was found and worked in both directions from that place. . . Our efforts, however, were all in vain. We found nothing of interest in the gravel. . ." (1948:13).

[47] See Toombs report published in 1950.

[48] See for example Frank W. Libby's (b 1908) work on the application of Carbon-14, see Libby *et al* (1949). This particular technique became increasingly popular, and depends on the presence of a constant amount of radiocarbon in all living animals and plants. At death, this isotope begins to decay at a known rate (half-life of 5730 years). Thus by measuring the amount of Carbon-14 remaining in a specimen it is possible to calculate the length of time that has elapsed since an organism's death. The method, however, is not, for obvious reasons, capable of dating events in excess of 70,000 years. As indicated in fn 30, the Piltdown I cranium and mandible were submitted for radiocarbon analysis, see Vries & Oakley (1959).

[49] Davidson & Atkin (1953).

[50] For details of this North African site, see Arambourg & Arnould (1950).

[51] Oakley, in Weiner *et al* (1955:250).

[52] In 1913 (at the International Medical Congress in London), the anatomist Samuel George Shattock (1852–1924) presented a report on the Piltdown skull. In particular he considered the possibility that its thickness may have been caused by disease. However, after reviewing a number of morbid conditions, Shattock ultimately rejected them all. In spite of this Shattock's report is ambiguous. Later Oakley reviewed this but came to no definite conclusions. For a while the author had considered that this skull might be one of the acromegalic skulls procured by Frank Corner for the Royal College of Surgeons, see Spencer (1984:21,fn 3). A subsequent examination of the specimen and available radiographs failed to support this line of enquiry.

[53] In particular, Oakley cited the example of the skull of an Ona Indian from Tierra del Fuego (No 1938.8.10.2), Oakley, in Weiner *et al* (1955:258–259).

[54] For details on this particular session, see report in *Nature* 10 July 1954, p.81.

[55] In the early 1980s Professor S L Washburn (University of California, Berkeley) suggested to Oakley that recent developments in palaeo-immunological studies might provide a means of identifying the Piltdown jaw (and canine). Subsequently, a small sample of the jaw and canine tooth were sent to Dr Jerold M Lowenstein (University of California School of Medicine) for immunological studies. Extracts from this jaw and canine were compared to collagen samples from humans, chimpanzees, orangutans, and rhesus monkeys. The results obtained confirmed that the jaw and tooth had belonged to an orangutan, see Lowenstein *et al* (1982).

[56] Dawson to Woodward 31 January 1913, Spencer (1990:2.3.4).

[57] Keith to Weiner 22 November 1953, Spencer (1990:6.3.6).

[58] Marriott (1918). Marriott was also a disciple of the astronomer-geophysicist Alfred W Drayson (1827–1901) who had postulated a "secondary rotation of the earth" (see Drayson (1888), and Marriott (1914)). Based on this phenomenon, Drayson had hypothesized that the last glacial advance [i.e. the Würm] reached its maximum about 30,000 years ago. For further details on Drayson and his work, see also his 1878 book.

[59] Kennard to Warren 17 May 1946, Spencer (1990:5.2.1).

[60] Hinton's letter is dated 29 November 1953, and was published in *The Times* on 4 December 1953 under the title: "Piltdown Man Forgery: Investigators' Access to Fragments."

[61] See Letter from Frederick G Parsons to Woodward 21 September 1916, Spencer (1990:4.2.19). During the early 1920s Le Gros Clark had assisted Woodward in his excavations at Piltdown.

[62] Hinton to Clark 29 December 1953, Spencer (1990:6.3.18). For further insights into Hinton and his earlier connection with the Piltdown controversy, see next chapter. Some of Hinton's former colleagues were not impressed by his letter to *The Times*. For example, William D Lang (a specialist in sponges and former assistant to Bather) wrote to Errol I White (an expert in fossil fish who had also worked under Bather's administration) commenting: "I saw Hinton's letter and it read as if he thought that had he had the material handed to him, he would have detected the fraud. But perhaps he didn't mean that. In any case, I think S. Woodward was right in letting only anthropological specialists . . . see the stuff for detailed handling, and Hinton was not one to be included for all his eminent work on Voles! I should say that his letter cuts very little ice. . ." (see Weiner Papers (Library of Palaeontology, British Museum (Natural History), MSS WEI 3.17 Lang 14 December 1953, Spencer, 1990:NOTE C:6.3.18).

[63] On 3 July 1913 Dawson wrote to Woodward about the discovery of a human frontal bone (at ? Barcombe Mills). According to Dawson the "base of the nose is rotten". He then goes on to state: ". . . Will you get Barlow to give us the recipe for gelatinizing, as the bone looks in a bad way and may go wrong in drying. I have got a saucepan and gas stove at Uckfield" (see Letter 2.3.21, Spencer 1990). Also earlier in the year, in another letter to Woodward, Dawson wrote: "Many thanks for the casts. . . I have been trying an experiment with it by duplicating the parts of the skull and jaw on each side in slightly different shade of brown. I have done this in water-colour which rubs off easily" (letter dated 23 April 1913, Spencer 1990:2.3.14). Either of these events could explain St Barbe's experience. On the other hand, it could be argued that what St Barbe saw was something quite different and that Dawson's references to his various experiments were to provide a plausible cover-story — recognizing that St Barbe might mention it to his contacts at the Museum and that it might eventually come to Woodward's attention.

[64] Weiner memorandum to Oakley 5 January 1953, Spencer (1990: 6.3.22).

[65] Hinton to Gavin de Beer 17 March 1954, Spencer (1990: 6.3.49).

[66] Edwards to Weiner 7 January 1954, Spencer (1990:6.3.23). In 1955, Essex went public with this theory. A reprint of his article is in Bowden (1978).

[67] See Oakley Memorandum 9 August 1954, Spencer (1990: 6.3.61). ". . . I gather that T de C then spent 15 minutes telling E[dwards] what he told us, that he scarcely knew D[awson], "as a man, not at all", so he could could not express an opinion about his character. . ."

[68] Clark to Weiner 9 August 1954, Spencer (1990:6.3.62).

[69] Weiner (1955:176). Salzman, in *Sussex Archaeol Coll* (1910) 53:282. For further details, see Salzman in Spencer (1990: [Note E] 6.3.1 and [Note I] 6.3.30).

[70] Having examined both Dawson's text and that of Herbert's it is considered quite inaccurate to say that Dawson had "plundered" [read: plagiarised] Herbert's original work. Dawson acknowledges in his Preface that he used this manuscript, and whilst there are long passages in various chapters in which he either quotes or paraphrases Herbert, there are also references to his original source, for example "Description of the Military Site and Architecture (Volume II, Part V, Chapter IV, pp 513–515–520–548). In the Preface, Dawson notes in that arranging his materials it was "thought unnecessary to elaborate unduly the index, which has been left in the able hands of Mr George Clinch, F.G.S.". The index contains no reference to Herbert. Langham had made a similar survey and reached the same conclusions.

[71] Woodward (1892).

[72] While Dawson appears to have been the eldest, this has not been confirmed. One, Sir [Arthur] Trevor Dawson (1866–1931) was educated at the Royal Naval College, Greenwich where he became a specialist in ordnance. Later, he became Director of Vickers Armstrong Ltd. Dawson's other brother was a "parson" in Bath. Where the Rev. H L Dawson studied theology is not known.

[73] Dawson to Woodward 3 July 1913, Spencer (1990:2.3.21).

[74] The remains were catalogued by Woodward, who recorded that they had been recovered from "Pleistocene gravel in field on top of hill above Barcombe Mills railway station." The remains consist of: (i) a fragment of frontal bone (E 644a), (ii) fragment of right parietal (E 644b), (iii) pair of zygomatic bones, left (E 644c) and right (E 644d), and (iv) a lower right second molar tooth. This latter specimen, Woodward noted was "probably" from the same site, though it was "not certain".

[75] See Broom (1950), and Broom undated [?September] report, in Spencer (1990:5.2.10).

[76] Montagu (1951b:424).

[77] Weiner ([1955] 1980:200).

[78] The only known case on record implicating Woodward in the forgery is that made by "Jack" C. Trevor (1908–67) of the Duckworth Laboratory, University of Cambridge. Trevor's case (such as it is) can be found in a confidential letter [and rough draft of a communication he evidently planned to publish in *Nature*] to Oakley dated 13 February 1967 [Piltdown Archive, BMNH, DF 116/26]. Neither Oakley nor Weiner took Trevor's case seriously. Specifically he believed that Woodward and Dawson were co-conspirators. From all indications Trevor's views in this regard had taken shape as a result of several interviews he had had with Robert Essex. Like Essex, Trevor's chronology and mastery of details relating to the movement of various key players (particularly Woodward) are sadly lacking. Trevor's letter, however, contains a number of peripheral items which are of passing interest. First, he was convinced the Piltdown mandible was an orangutan — and suggested that it might well have originated from the collections of the Royal College of Surgeons — noting that it might well be a specimen of *Simia moro*, described by Richard Owen in 1836. What had led Trevor to this particular specimen and how Woodward had come by it, Trevor does not say. For further discussion of this proposition, see Chapter 8. Another interesting item is Trevor's reference to the rumour that Wynfrid L H Duckworth might also have been involved in the forgery — an idea he evidently vigorously opposed. He also said that he had a "bad conscience about Teilhard", noting that he ". . . may have guessed the secret or have been under the seal of confession, and [that] Dawson could have been blackmailed by the jeweller [Abbott]". Later, the Duckworth hypothesis surfaced in the work of Costello (1986), presumably via the Glyn Daniel conduit, see Chapter 7.

[79] See Spencer (1990).

[80] This is more than adequately documented in Spencer (1990). Furthermore the extent of his openness in this regard can be judged from the fact that in Janaury 1913 he was invited to present the skull to the Royal Dublin Society, and over Dawson's objections, Woodward had taken the originals to Ireland rather than the casts.

[81] According to Woodward's daughter (Mrs Margaret Hodgson) he was bitterly disappointed at being "passed over" in 1919. At this time Lazarus Fletcher (1854–1921) retired from the position, and Sidney F Harmer (1862–1950) was appointed. Three years later, Woodward retired and apparently never set foot in the institution again. As for his subsequent knighthood he is said to have regarded this as a "pay-off" for not having received the directorship. He held the Royal Medal of the Royal Society (1917) in higher esteem (Mrs Hodgson, personal communication).

[82] Contrary to popular opinion Woodward's other scientific work did not suffer as a result of his escalating involvement in the Piltdown controversy — as a review of his bibliography post 1912 clearly indicates, see Cooper (1945:104–112).

[83] Weiner ([1955] 1908:204).

[84] In July 1967 Weiner was contacted by contacted by Mr W R Le Fanu, Librarian of the Royal College of Surgeons to look at Sir Arthur Keith's private diaries. It is presumed Weiner acted on Le Fanu's communication. A week later, Le Fanu's assistant Jessie Dobson reported to Weiner that Keith had destroyed all of his notes and no Piltdown related letters had been located. (Between 1983–5 the author made a complete inventory and photographic record of Keith's papers [see Wenner Gren Foundation Award No 4422], and only a few minor Piltdown-related letters were found). As Weiner's subsequent exchange with Dobson indicates, he was far more interested in the Keith-Kennard connection; he does not seem to have investigated further the entries Keith made in his private diary between December 1912 and January 1913, See Weiner Papers MSS WEI, Library of Palaeontology, British Museum (Natural History).

7 BLACK KNIGHTS AND ARRANT KNAVES

[1] Chapter XII, "Alice's Evidence", in Lewis Carroll's *Alice's Adventures in Wonderland*.

[2] Weiner ([1955] 1980:200–201).

[3] This Victorian Manor House has a large hall, four reception rooms, six bedrooms, and three bathrooms, and stands in 35 acres of land. Directly associated are several other buildings, a four bedroomed oast house (standing on the west side of the drive and looking directly down on the gravel bed site) and a thatched barn.

[4] Woodward (1948:10).

[5] Dawson to Woodward 1 January 191[3], Spencer (1990:2.1.1).

[6] To reinforce this point it is pertinent to recall the notorious Moulin Quignon case. In proving the case of fraud at this site in 1863, Henry Keeping, a well-known collector and archaeologist from the Isle of Wight, was invited by John Evans and Joseph Prestwich to visit this French site and investigate the charge that there had been "a regular system of imposition . . . carried on by the gravel-diggers of Abbeville". Within a matter of days these suspicions were confirmed. For details, see Lyell (1863) and Evans (1863). Although

acknowledging that the circumstances at Moulin Quignon are quite different from that of Piltdown, it is contended that Dawson and Woodward were no less experienced than Keeping.

[7] Dawson to Woodward 4 April 1909, Spencer (1990:1.1.2).

[8] The training of priests in the Jesuit order is a rather lengthy process. In Teilhard's case he had entered the order in 1898 at Aix-en-Provence. From 1902 to 1905 he was stationed in Jersey (Channel Isles), followed by a period in Cairo, Egypt (1905–08). When he met Dawson he had just arrived in Hastings, where he remained until the summer of 1912. He was ordained at Hastings (on 24 August 1911).

[9] Teilhard's first encounter with Dawson is recorded in a letter to his parents dated 31 May 1909, Letter No 14, in Teilhard ([1965] 1968:47–8), the pertinent extract can be found in Spencer (1990: Note B 1.1.10).

[10] From all accounts this Museum was very modest and formed part of the Brassey Institute Library for which Butterfield became librarian in 1909, see Belt (1935:58).

[11] Teilhard to his Father, 1 July 1909, Letter No 16, in Teilhard ([1965] 1968:53).

[12] As indicated in Chapter 6 it is by no means certain when and how Morris came by the Piltdown implement. While there is every reason to suppose that it was procured directly from Dawson (as Morris' note implies) it seems that Morris' suspicions were not aroused until much later, around the time when Hinton was made privy to the St Barbe story, see Chap. 6.

[13] Belt (1935:60).

[14] Dawson to Woodward 13 May 1911, Spencer (1990:1.1.31).

[15] (Winslow & Meyer 1983:43).

[16] Lanhgam (1984:4).

[17] Dawson to Woodward 26 May 1909, Spencer (1990:1.1.3).

[18] Dawson to Woodward 30 November 1911, Spencer (1990:1.1.36).

[19] Dawson to Woodward [?28] November 1912, Spencer (1990: 1.2.26).

[20] Winslow & Meyer (1983:40–1). This aspect of the Winslow hypothesis was later attacked by Cox (1983:21–2) and Langham (1984). It is interesting to note that Doyle also crossed swords with Arthur Keith on this issue in the pages of the *Morning Post* in 1925. It appears that this exchange had been engineered by the newspaper's editor H E Gwynne (an old friend of Keith's), see Keith (1950:482–3). For further information on Keith's views on this issue, see Spencer (1979).

[21] Winslow & Meyer (1983:41)

[22] Specifically Winslow & Meyer state: "Lankester also predicted that other less crude man-modified rocks would shortly be found in pre-Pleistocene deposits. In 1911 he argued in a paper presented before the the the Royal Society that such rocks had indeed been discovered. He referred to some novelly-shaped flint implements, which he called rostro-carinate or eagle's beak, and some scrapers, hammers, and large one-sided picks recently found in Suffolk and Norfolk. He dated them from the Pliocene, or possibly earlier. Unwittingly, Sir Ray had set himself up. He provided a list of objects to be discovered or verified as being man-made, and the hoaxer obliged him on every count. The Piltdown flints included the eoliths he believed in ... and at least one of the unusual rostro-carinate type ... It was a case of self-fulfilling prophecy, with the hoaxer providing the wherewithal" (Winslow & Meyer 1983:42).

[23] This tape recording was played publicly for the first time at a symposium of Comparative Anatomy and Palaeontology held at Reading University in 1978. Later that year L B Halstead of the Reading Department of Geology communicated the details of Douglas' hypothesis to *Nature*.

[24] From all indications this is correct. Sollas' name does not appear in any of the lists recording the attendance of both members and visitors to Burlington House on the night of 18 December 1912 [Langham papers]. The reasons for Sollas' absence are not known.

[25] The evolution of Douglas' suspicions are documented in the following letters: Oakley to Douglas 3 October 1972; Douglas to Oakley 8 November 1972 and Douglas to Oakley 24 June 1973, in Douglas File, P.MSS KPO British Museum (Natural History).

[26] Transcribed directly from copy of Douglas tape in British Museum (Natural History) collections.

[27] According to Douglas's obituary in *Nature* (1978) 274: 196 (written by James M Edmunds), he had read geology and zoology at Oxford and took a First in Geology in 1905, when he began working under Sollas. In 1910 he and W E Balston went to South America, exploring in Peru and Bolivia, and returned in 1913. In August 1914 he was commissioned and served in France. He did not return to Oxford until 1919.

[28] See Oakley (1979:302). Here Oakley notes: "Only by special pleading could anyone argue that this chemical was ordered by Sollas for delivery to him in Oxford, after which (one would have to suppose) it was forwarded to Dawson in Lewes with instructions as to how it might be used. These are the thoughts of a Jabberwocky! Dawson would have had no difficulty in obtaining potassium bichromate from a pharmacy in Sussex ..."

[29] For example, see Sollas (1882a, 1882b, 1888, 1903).

[30] See for example Sollas to Woodward 14 August 1913, Spencer (1990:2.3.33). In addition to other letters in the collections of the British Museum (Natural History), I have two letters given to me by Woodward's daughter (Mrs M Hodgson) written by Sollas in 1921 and 1922 which confirm the opinion that there had been no visible change in the Sollas–Woodward relationship.

[31] Sollas to Woodward 14 August 1913, Spencer (1990:2.3.33).

[32] Woodward (1914c). This paper was delivered on 11 March 1914. A discussion of the paper is appended to the printed version in the *Quart J Geol Soc Lond* pp 101–103.

[33] Sollas (1924:529). Here in a footnote Sollas wrote: "There is a singular absence of an attempt at art in all the Palaeolithic stations of England. The horse figured here is, I am assured, a forgery introduced into the cave by a mischievous person; the horse described by Dr Smith Woodward is a forgery perpetrated by some schoolboys".

[34] Transcription (made by the author) from British Museum (Natural History) copy of the Douglas tape recording.

[35] Woodward's letter in *Nature* is undated. It is interesting to note Boyd Dawkins' involvement. According to Dawkins, he had seen the specimen (which incidentally had been returned to Sherborne School) and was convinced it was a genuine specimen. Evidently, not being an admirer of Sollas, he urged Woodward into battle: "It is a most highly prized specimen in the Museum of the School ... If you ask him [the Headmaster] to lend it, he would probably do so, and you could tell without difficulty whether it has been cut on a recent bone by an ingenious schoolboy as Sollas says it is in his usual insolent way. 'Go' for him! as I did ..." Dawkins' letter is dated 14 November 1925, and is bound in a copy of Dawkins' *Early Man in Britain* located in the Smith Woodward Collection, Library of University College, London.

[36] Bayzand (1926:233). Bayzand's letter is dated 21 January 1926, while that of Sollas' (printed directly above) is dated 22 January 1926.

[37] In 1979, R A H Farrar of the Royal Commission on Historical Monuments was invited to re-examine the Sherborne affair in the light of the controversy stirred up by Douglas' disclosures. His thorough and balanced report was published in the 1979 November issue of *Antiquity*. Later, in 1981 Farrar returned to this subject, along with Theya Molleson. These workers while cautious in their claims, concluded that the evidence seemed to weigh strongly in favour of the specimen being genuine.

[38] Steel (1926).

[39] Some insight to Sollas' character can be gleaned from the following anonymous obituary: "Sollas was a man of wide and varied interests. A good linguist, remarkably well read ... he delighted in discussion and controversy, in which his pleasant and occasionally sarcastic humour, his command of information, and the often unexpected turn of his attack, rendered him a doughty antagonist ... [Also] he was a somewhat impatient of routine work and of research which did not promise an adequate return of theory or principle, he was nevertheless unsparing in his demand for accuracy, and untiring in extracting, by experiment, observation, and hypothesis, the maximum yield from his facts ..." in *Obit Not Fellows of Roy Soc Lond* (1938) 2:273).

[40] Millar's case against Elliot Smith is revealed in the last pages of his book. My quotations are from page 231 (1974 Paladin edition).

[41] When Millar's work appeared, both Weiner and Oakley entertained the idea of publishing a joint rebuttal, see Weiner to Oakley 6 October 1972 [Miscellaneous Letters P.MSS.KPO] and Oakley to Weiner 8 October 1972 [Box 1 MSS WEI]. These initial plans coincided with a symposium organized by Professor Lord Solly Zuckerman marking the centenary of Smith's birth. This symposium was to be held at the Zoological Society of London on 9 and 10 November 1972. Weiner suggested that perhaps this might be a good opportunity to respond to Millar's charges. Oakley agreed but not being an admirer of Zuckerman he was reluctant to approach Zuckerman himself. Instead Weiner made the overtures on 11 October 1972 [Box 1 MSS WEI]. At this symposium Weiner (1973:20) and Zuckerman (1973:20) were sharply critical of Millar's thesis; see also Zuckerman's attack on Millar in *The Times Literary Supplement* on 27 October 1972.

[42] See Langham (1979:170). See also his article on the Talgai skull affair, published in 1978.

[43] See Woodward to Kenward 19 May 1916, Spencer (1990:4.2.13). According to this letter Woodward had arranged to spend the first two weeks of July at Barkham Manor with Elliot Smith, "as paying guests" of Robert Kenward.

[44] Wilson (1938:330).

[45] Between 1912, when Smith was invited to provide a report on the endocranial cast (2 pages), and 1917, he published 10 pieces on Piltdown related matters, most of them short reports and several simply restatements of earlier published arguments.

[46] Support for this view can be found in Dawson (1938) and Spencer (1990).

[47] See Edward's memorandum on an interview with Lady Woodward, dated 21 January 1954, Spencer (1990:6.3.30). In the early 1890s, prior to his move to Kent, Abbott had lived and worked in north London. During this same period he also ran a course on gemmology at the London Polytechnic; it is here that he first met Kennard.

[48] Kennard (1947:277).

[49] This event took place on 1 March 1905, and it is interesting to note that the guest speaker at this ceremony was Arthur Smith Woodward. Unfortunately records of prior activities of this Museum have not been located, so it is not possible to document whether Dawson and Abbott had met prior to this time —

though there is no reason to doubt that they had. Abbott's 1913 newspaper article (see later in text) seems to support this view.

[50] For example, the geologist Francis H Edmunds wrote to Oakley: "While I was in the district [circa 1924] I made the acquaintance of ... Abbott ... [who] told me that he had worked with Dawson on the Piltdown skull and the skull had been in his possession six months before Smith Woodward saw it; and I gathered from him that he had soaked it in bichromate to harden it ... It seems to me unlikely that Dawson, a solicitor, would have either the knowledge or the ability to make skilful forgeries ... Abbott certainly had the knowledge, skill, tools and opportunity to do so ..." Letter dated 24 November 1953, in Spencer (1990:6.3.7). In his 1986 survey of the Piltdown affair Charles Blinderman supported Abbott's possible involvement.

[51] Portions of Abbott's original collections can be found at the Wellcome Institute for the History of Medicine, London, and the Hastings Museum.

[52] Weiner ([1955] 1980:108).

[53] Kennard (1947:273).

[54] To back this argument Weiner drew attention to an exhibit Abbott had mounted at the Hastings Museum in 1909 to illustrate his work on "Prehistoric Races of Hastings". What attracted Weiner's attention as an anatomist was Abbott's exhibit No. 6 — prehistoric human teeth. In his description of this exhibit, Abbott wrote: "Human Teeth: Some worn down by gritty food, some jaws show abnormal dentition. In one case the last molar is more than twice the size of the first — an essentially pre-human character; another case shows shortening of the jaw at expense of the number of teeth. A normal jaw is shown for comparison."
Commenting on this Weiner wrote: "This molar "twice the size of the first" and its lodgement in the jaw would take any anatomists' immediate attention, for, I venture to say, it is unheard of in a normal adult jaw — unless Abbott was quite unable to distinguish between permanent and milk molars in a child's jaw!" ([1955] 1970:99).

[55] It is interesting to note that while Abbott seems to have enjoyed a much closer relationship with Woodward it was Keith rather than Woodward, who wrote his obituary (see The Times 12 August 1933).

[56] Keith to Weiner 25 November 1953, in Spencer (1990:6.3.8).

[57] See Abbott's correspondence with his close friend (and later executor) Edward Yates. Here Abbott is constantly referring to his own genius in making important discoveries. For example, in a letter dated 11 [?] March 19[?1]4, Abbott writes: "I have made a few more very important discoveries, new races and new things in flints. I wonder if the world will have to re-discover them," in Weiner Papers, MSS WEI Box I. Similarly, see Abbott to Woodward 26 January 1916 regarding the reception of his 1915 paper on Pliocene deposits in south-east England, he writes: "[This] will prove a blessing on the continent, where definitions appear about as muddled as they are here; they maintain that this is just what was wanted, and that it will put not only prehistoric archaeology on a new basis, but many other branches of science also." in File DF 100/40. For further extracts from this same letter, see Spencer (1990:4.2.6).

[58] Abbott to Woodward 24 November 1912, in Spencer (1990:1.2.24).

[59] Sometime in mid June 1912 Dawson visited Abbott and showed him some of the Piltdown eoliths. Reporting on this visit to Woodward, Dawson wrote: "He says they are "man — man all over". Certainly, one large one you have not seen, is a primitive hand-axe. Abbott says it is equal to Moir's best and of the same age — but!" Dawson to Woodward 30 June 1912, in Spencer (1990:1.2.11).

[60] Abbott to Rutot [4] January 1914, in Spencer (1990:3.1.1). It should be noted that the report mentioned here is evidently a reference either to the Abstract of the 18 December 1912 meeting published in the Proc Geol Soc Lond (1912–13) pp 20–7 (which seems unlikely) or to published accounts in the newspapers. Also it should be noted that while it is not known precisely what Dawson may have said on this occasion, it is clear that Abbott did not go unmentioned in the published version of the Dawson & Woodward (1913) communication.

[61] Among the many articles that appeared during this time, there are several that are particularly informative and could well have served as a source for Abbott's article which, incidentally falls far short of any of the following in detail: (i) anonymous in The Graphic 28 December 1912, and (ii) Pycraft's in The Illustrated London News 28 December 1912. Both of these are well illustrated. Another useful article appeared in Country Life, published on 4 January 1913. It needs to be stressed here that Abbott's mention of the missing canine is not significant, since this had been an issue discussed at the unveiling at Burlington House on 18 December 1912, which had been widely reported on.

[62] As with Sollas, Abbott was also absent from the unveiling at Burlington House in December 1912, but as he told Woodward, it was a busy time of the year for him and he could not spare the time to travel up to London, see Abbott to Woodward 15 December 1912, in Spencer (1990:12.30).

[63] See Halstead (1979); Bowden (1981), Matthews (1981).

[64] Thomas joined the Museum in 1878, four years prior to Woodward's arrival. When Thomas was assigned to the Zoology Department, William Henry Flower (1831–99) was Keeper, while at the same time as serving as Director of the Museum. Later, in 1898, Flower was succeeded by Ray Lankester, who like Flower was also Director. In 1907, when Lankester "retired" from the Museum, the Keepership of Zoology went to

Sidney Frederic Harmer (1862–1950), who held the position until 1921, when it was taken over by Charles Tate Regan (1878–1943).

[65] See for example Hinton, Kennard & Newton (1900), and Hinton & Kennard (1905, 1907, 1910).

[66] Hinton (1909, 1910, 1914).

[67] Although St Barbe was quite definite that he did not tell Hinton of his suspicions until after Dawson's death, this does not remove the possibility that Hinton may have learned of the story earlier through Marriott.

[68] Gregory (1914:190–191).

[69] It is suspected that this rumour had been communicated to Gregory and the New York group by Leon Williams who worked with Keith during the summer of 1913 on an alternative reconstruction of the Piltdown I parts, see next chapter for further details particularly fn 62.

[70] Had Hinton suspected foul play, which does not seem to have been the case at the time, it is far more likely that he would have confided in Miller rather than Gregory, as he had known Miller since 1909. But from all indications Hinton's first communication to Miller on the subject of Piltdown was in 1916, and then it was merely to confirm his conviction in the dualistic theory.

[71] During the next decade, as Weiner's papers document, there was growing speculation (particularly in Sussex archaeological circles) about the credibility of some of the Piltdown finds, see Spencer (1990:6.3.17, 6.3.52–54; 6.3.62). Although it is tempting to think of these rumours springing from a common source, this does not appear to have been the case. In a few instances it is conceivable that either Marriott or Morris might have been the source, but it is also possible that as Edmunds' re-evaluation of the elevation of the Piltdown gravel terrace became more widely known that this too had prompted speculation — particularly among certain members of the Sussex Archaeological Society. Indeed, Weiner had suspected there might well have been a link between these rumours and Rudyard Kipling's 1932 short story about a forged manuscript. But while it is quite possible that Kipling (an active member of the Sussex Archaeological Society) may have picked up on these rumours, his story, entitled "Dayspring Mishandled", in fact bears little or no resemblance to the events that transpired at Piltdown twenty years earlier.

[72] Hinton (1926:325–348).

[73] See Gavin de Beer to Hinton 22 March 1954, in Spencer (1990:6.3.50). Although as indicated in fn 74 there is some evidence to suggest that Hinton may have been indirectly assisting Marston's case, there is other evidence which throws a different light on Hinton's relationship with Marston. In addition to his apparent tardiness in dealing with the description of the Swanscombe faunal remains (a job later assumed by Oakley) [see Spencer 1990:5.1.50], Hinton's initial draft of the introduction to the 1938 RAI Swanscombe [skull] Committee report is clearly misleading with regard to Marston's role in the discovery of the cranial remains. Hinton claimed the initial find was made by a workman — thereby casting some doubt on the specimen's provenance. In the final printed version, however, this reference was dropped. See Spencer (1990:5.1.55) for further details. Precisely what Hinton's motives had been in this regard, and whether he acted alone or under pressure from within the Museum is far from clear.

[74] While Hinton's reported letter to Corner has never come to light, there seems to be little question that Corner was also dubious about Piltdown; but whether this suspicion had originated with Hinton, or from some other source has not been established. According to Dulcie H Pearson, who accompanied Corner to the unveiling ceremony of the commemorative monument at Barkham Manor on 23 July 1938 [see Spencer 1990:5.1.56, for further details], Corner is reported to have remarked: "They [the remains] could never have come out of that, derived or otherwise" (Pearson to Oakley 6 August 1957, MSS KPO Files).

[75] Hinton to Gavin de Beer 17 March 1954, in Spencer (1990: 6.3.49).

[76] See Oakley to Hinton's biographer R J C Hinton (Bristol University), 8 October 1975, MSS WEI Piltdown Files, Box 1.

[77] Based on information from Wright (1943:297).

[78] Leslie Woodhead to Oakley 10 January 1954, in Spencer (1990: 6.3.25).

[79] Leslie Woodhead to Oakley 16 January 1954, in Spencer (1990: 6.3.29).

[80] Leslie Woodhead to Weiner 6 February 1953, in Weiner papers, MSS WEI Box 3.

[81] Letter undated, in Costello (1985:171). As indicated by the introduction of this letter, this was not an unsolicited letter to Daniel, but was evidently written in response to a direct inquiry. At this time Daniel was retired Disney Professor of Archaeology at Cambridge and senior editor of *Antiquity*. Since the late 1960s, Daniel had taken a particular interest in the Piltdown affair and was in constant communication with Weiner and Oakley on the matter — particularly during the 1970s after the publication of Millar's book.

[82] While acknowledging the attraction of the Woodhead scenario, Daniel's decision to back it publicly with so little supporting evidence is, to say the least, extraordinary. As for Lionel Woodhead it still remains unclear whether he meant precisely what he had written. From personal communications with Mr Woodhead (1986) the inference is that he had intended merely to point to Dawson's suspicious behaviour. Furthermore it is unclear what the problem had been between his father and Dawson. While it is possible that it could have been prompted by his suspicion of Dawson, it could have been something quite unrelated to Piltdown matters, as his mother had suggested to his elder brother, Leslie. Also, it is quite possible that

Samuel Woodhead may have picked up on some of the rumours that evidently began circulating in Lewes during the 1930s, which may have influenced his attitude to Dawson and the recounting of events to his family. Furthermore, it is important not to underestimate his biographer's note that Woodhead was "a deeply religious man whose every action was governed by his Christian beliefs" (Wright 1943: 297). Costello has interpreted this to mean he was a religious fanatic (inferring that he might well have been a closet creationist), see taped BBC interview 22 November 1985.

[83] Costello (1985:172).

[84] Costello (1985:169). Here he notes that local archives make reference to several "medieval and late medieval . . . visitations of the plague, and that the bodies of the victims were buried on the common, that is at Piltdown . . . So of all places in the neighbourhood, Piltdown is the one where one would expect a stray medieval skull to turn up".

[85] Daniel (1986:59–60).

[86] For example, during the 1970s it was reported that the psychiatrist Frank Anthony Hampton (1888–1967) had confessed to a friend that he had concocted the Piltdown forgery. A subsequent investigation of Hampton by Dr H W Ball (former Keeper of the Department of Palaeontology) and Dr Ian Langham failed to substantiate the story. A review of this file, and subsequent evidence recovered from Kenneth Oakley's private papers relating to Hampton simply do not support Hampton's reported confession.

[87] Hewitt (1898).

[88] Costello (1986:145).

[89] See Dawson (1898a). In addition, as Costello notes, Dawson also presented the results to an earlier meeting of the South Eastern Union of Scientific Societies, see Dawson (1898b).

[90] In 1909, Dawson noted: "The Natural Gas site goes undiminished at Heathfield but no one has yet attempted to fathom its source and the company which took it up did it a bad turn and now, beyond the [railway] station lamps being lit by it, it is allowed to waste". In Dawson to Woodward 28 March 1909, Spencer (1990: 1.1.1).

[91] Costello (1986:145).

[92] Costello (1986:146).

[93] Costello (1986:146).

[94] Oakley to Teilhard 19 November 1953, in Piltdown Personal File (Teilhard de Chardin), DF 116/32 BMNH.

[95] Teilhard to Oakley 28 November 1953, in Spencer (1990: 6.2.15).

[96] Teilhard to Oakley 29 January 1954, in Spencer (1990:6.3.32).

[97] When the Japanese invaded China in 1941 the original fossil hominid material recovered from Choukoutien was crated and reportedly moved from the Peking Union Medical College to Camp Holcomb, the U.S. Marine base in Peking, for subsequent shipment to the American Museum in New York. In the ensuing chaos the collection was lost (probably destroyed). It should be noted, however, that prior to this event casts of all this material had been made and widely distributed. For further details on this episode, see Shapiro (1974).

[98] MSS WEI 4.19 Oakley 9 August 1954, in Spencer (1990:6.3.61).

[99] For further details, see Cuénot (1965:381–8).

[100] MSS WEI 3.17 Teilhard de Chardin 30 September 1954, in Spencer (1990:6.3.65).

[101] Gould's article appeared in the August issue of the American Museum (New York)'s publication *Natural History*. For earlier published (anti-Teilhard) attacks, see Essex (1955), Vere (1959), Leakey & Goodall (1969), and Bowden (1978).

[102] Letter to his mother (Paris) dated 24 September 1914, in Teilhard ([1965] 1967), Letter No. 58, page 156–7.

[103] Cuénot (1965:21–22), see also Marcellin Boule's letter to Woodward 6 March 1915, in Spencer (1990:4:1:10).

[104] Gould (1980:28).

[105] Gould (1980:14).

[106] Dawson to Woodward 3 July 1913, Spencer (1990:2.3.21).

[107] In the Museum register (completed by Woodward) the cranial remains (a fragment of a frontal bone and right parietal, plus a pair of incomplete zygomatics) are recorded as having been retrieved from a "Pleistocene gravel in field on top of hill above Barcombe Mills railway station". The single molar tooth is recorded as "probably from the same place (not certain)". Later, in 1949, the South African paleontologist-anatomist Robert Broom made a preliminary study of these remains, and concluded that they were the remains of an "Eoanthropic cranium", see Spencer (1990:5.2.10). This diagnosis was subsequently challenged by Ashley Montagu (1951).

8 BEYOND A REASONABLE DOUBT?

[1] Zuckerman (1972.:68–9). A similar observation was made at the time of the debunking by Ritchie Calder in his newspaper column (July 1955): ". . . [T]he ingenuity of Person X was fantastic. Not only was he a well-trained, though misguided ANTHROPOLOGIST, but he was a GEOLOGIST, who could reconstruct clues so that his colleagues were foxed. He was an ANATOMIST skilled in bones of man and animals; a DENTIST who could make modern teeth look like prehistoric teeth; and a CHEMIST who could take specimens and make them look genuinely ancient" in P.MSS KPO Newspaper Cutting File.

[2] *Brit Med J* 21 Dec 1912, p 1719.

[3] Underwood to Woodward 30 December 1912, Spencer (1990: 1.3.13).

[4] Keith's (private) Weekly Diary, Box D6/KP/RCS. It needs to be stressed here that Keith wrote another article for the *BMJ* which was published on 7 December. This paper was on "The Functional Nature of Caecum and Appendix." See *Brit Med J* 7 December 1912, pp 1599–1602. Early in 1913 several more articles were submitted and published but these can be accounted for in Keith's diaries and other sources.

[5] Comparing Langham's transcriptions from these diaries, covering the period December 1912 to February 1913, it is apparent that they reflect a quite different picture with regard to his Piltdown-related activities. The only mention of Piltdown in his "daily" diary is a reference to the 18 December meeting at Burlington House. Later, in January (1913) this particular diary notes Dawson's visit. Given the locations of these diaries it seems safe to assume that the "daily" diary was a more public document, whereas the "weekly" one was more private — whether he kept it secret from his wife is not known.

[6] Keith's Weekly Diary 1913, Box D6 KP/RCS.

[7] Anonymous article, *The Sphere* (1913) Vol 53:76.

[8] Shortly after the appearance of the anonymous January article, *The Sphere* published in its February issue a sizeable item on Keith's work about the death of Napoleon, within a section entitled: "A Literary Letter" compiled by "C.K.S.". In September 1913 Keith published an article in *The Sphere*, entitled "Our Most Ancient Relation". The article was published in his name, and he noted this publication in his daily diary (September 6th): "Sphere — Eo." Later, in January 1914, Keith wrote another article for this periodical on the skull and cast of Robert Burns.

[9] Determing authorship of anonymous articles is problematic. There are many statistical techniques that have been applied, and in the case of small articles, a statistical approach applied to the specific frequencies of words, word order and the like are clearly ineffective. For a recent discussion on this subject, see "Statistics and authorship" by M W A Smith in *The Times Literary Supplement*, 17 March 1989. This Letter to the Editor, provides a very useful bibliography.

[10] Langham's reasons for insisting on this clandestine visit were grounded largely in the confident manner in which Keith described the site in the *BMJ* article. As he knew it was a common practice of Keith's to visit all the sites he described whenever possible. Hence Langham's insistence that Keith had probably visited the Piltdown site before he wrote this article on 16 December. As Langham's papers indicate, he was also cognisant of the popular story Mabel Kenward liked to tell of how she had caught someone at the pit. For example, recounting a version of this story to Kenneth Oakley and Glyn Daniel in August 1973, she remembered: "One evening, early evening, I saw this tall man come up, not even up the drive, but across the fields — must have gotten over the hedges and ditches even to get there . . . and he walked to the pit and started scratching about . . . so I said excuse me are you an authorized searcher? . . . He didn't say one word. . . might have been a ghost. . . and off he went the same way he came across the fields. . . He was dressed in an ordinary grey suit but he had gum [wellington] boots on and he was very tall. . . a man in his forties" (see fn 35). Precisely when (and at what time of the year) this particular event took place is far from clear. Langham was convinced that this distant but vivid memory was of Keith's clandestine visit. Her general description of the mysterious interloper fitted Keith perfectly. Furthermore, it provided a possible explaination of why, when he visited Barkham Manor with his wife on 4 January 1913, he did not venture beyond the gate.

[11] Keith to Woodward 2 November 1912, Spencer (1990:1.2.17).

[12] Keith to Grafton Elliot Smith 2 December 1912, Spencer (1990:1.2.27).

[13] Keith Weekly Diary, Box D6 KP/RCS.

[14] Edgar William Willett (1856–1928). After gaining a first class degree in Natural Science in 1879, (New College) Oxford, Willett took his M.B. (1885) and M.D. (1904). His specialty was anaesthesia. According to various obituaries he "retired" from practice in 1906 (apparently he found surgery uncongenial) to devote himself to his hobbies: archaeology and croquet. For further details, see *Lancet* 21 April 1928, p 837. During the Piltdown period, Willett lived at "Farmleigh", Worth Park, Three Bridges, Sussex. Three Bridges is situated a couple of miles from Crawley. He seems to have been a close friend of Lankester, see Dawson to Woodward 24 March 1912 and 27 May 1912, Spencer (1990:1.2.2 and 1.2.9 respectively).

[15] Dawson to Woodward 9 November 1912, Spencer (1990:1.2.19).

[16] Prior to my work at the Royal College of Surgeons I had entertained a number of possible scenarios linking Keith with some of these individuals (other than Dawson who seemed the most likely candidate),

namely Moir, Pycraft and Barlow. The latter two, since they worked at the British Museum (Natural History) appeared particularly attractive. Although in Barlow's case it was possible to demonstrate a professional interaction with Keith dating from 1909, I could find nothing else to advance this case. The same applied to Pycraft. The problem here and elsewhere was the need to satisfy the problem of imposition. Given Keith's public prominence in the emerging debate it was unlikely that he would have risked repeated clandestine visits to Piltdown for this purpose. While Barlow could have fulfilled this role, it was evident that Pycraft, who was a cripple, would not have been able to perform this duty. As for the case against Moir there is none — other than that Piltdown clearly provided support for his work in East Anglia. But at the time Piltdown was unfolding, Moir was already heavily committed to dealing with the controversy that had erupted over the significance the rostro-carinate tools (and the Ipswich skeleton) he had found. Hence to suppose that he had attended to these issues at the same time as assisting Keith in the management of the Piltdown forgery seems most unlikely. Furthermore, such a proposition is not in keeping with what is known about his temperament. From all indications he was a highly strung individual, who suffered from insomnia and migraines. At the same time I also briefly considered the remote possibility that Lankester and Willett might have been involved — but again this did not stand up to scrutiny.

[17] Keith (1950:328).

[18] See Spencer (1990:6.3.5) for a comparison of the Weiner and Oakley versions of this interview.

[19] Keith to Weiner 22 November 1953, Spencer (1990:6.3.6).

[20] Reported in Weiner's transcript of the Keith interview, see Weiner 21 November 1953, in Spencer (1990:6.3.5).

[21] Keith's (private) Weekly Diary (1911), Box D6 KP/RCS.

[22] From Cuttings Book of W Ruskin Butterfield 1909–12, Hastings Museum in Langham papers.

[23] It should be noted that at this time Keith knew Abbott.

[24] Dawson to Woodward 24 March 1912, Spencer (1990: 1.2.2).

[25] Dawson to Woodward 28 March 1912, Spencer (1990:1.2.4).

[26] Dawson to Woodward 12 May 1912, Spencer (1990:1.2.7).

[27] A copy of this paper entitled: "On the Persistence of a 13th Dorsal Vertebra in Certain Human Races", is preserved in the Piltdown Collection (DF 116/16), Library of Palaeontology, British Museum (Natural History).

[28] Le Double (1912). It is interesting to note that Le Double had also published a similar treatise in 1903 on the human cranium, and the face (1906). For biographical details, see obituary in Brit Med J 8 November 1913, p. 1265.

[29] This short review appears in Man Vol 15, No 37.

[30] For details on this site, see Hrdlička (1930). In 1911 Keith worked on the human (Neanderthaloid) dentition recovered there, see Keith & Knowles (1911). Keith's visit to Jersey was from 2 May through to the 20th.

[31] Dawson, in Dawson & Woodward (1913:117–18).

[32] Dawson 1912 Notes, DF 116/16, Piltdown Archive, Library of Palaeontology, British Museum (Natural History).

[33] Dawson (1913:75–76).

[34] See Chapter Seven, section: "WOODHEAD" for details.

[35] Taped interview of Mabel Kenward at her home in Piltdown by Oakley (in the presence of Glyn Daniel and Mrs Robin Kenward) on 3 August 1973, in Piltdown Archives, Library of Palaeontology, British Museum (Natural History). According to Miss Kenward the so-called "coconut" had been shattered by Alfred Thorpe, who was one of the labourers working in the pit at the time. Her father, Robert Kenward, is said to have retrieved some of the fragments and brought them into the house. Later the remains were handed back to Thorpe with the suggestion that he give them to Dawson. Thorpe, however, is reported to have "thrown back all but one piece which he later handed to Dawson" (Costello 1985:169). Costello claims that his story was confirmed by Thorpe's daughter, Mrs Ernest Sergeant.

[36] It should be noted that the name Francis Vere is a pseudonym. Vere's real name is Bannister. Furthermore, he and his wife were lodging with Miss Kenward at the time of the debunking. Francis Vere, like Mabel Kenward, was convinced of Dawson's innocence.

[37] Kenward to Oakley 15 August 1973, in P.MSS OAKLEY, Piltdown File, Library of Palaeontology, British Museum (Natural History).

[38] See particularly Dawson to Woodward 30 November 1911, Spencer (1990:1.1.36).

[39] It is possible that Woodhead may have unwittingly assisted Dawson in supplying him with technical information regarding possible ways to stain bone. This information, however, could also have come from Keith. It is also not inconceivable that Dawson (unaided) devised the methods employed. While Keith's input in this matter is unclear it appears that he knew more than has been previously suspected. This is evident from his admission during his interview with Weiner and Oakley at his home in November 1953 that the Piltdown jaw had been stained with bichromate (see Spencer 1990: 6.3.5). How did he know this?

According to Keith, Dawson had told him. But why had Dawson elected to tell Keith and not Woodward? And perhaps more revealing, why had Keith remained silent on this crucial matter when Marston had raised the issue in 1936 and again after the War? Prior to 1953 it was generally believed that the jaw, along with all of the remains found after Woodward became involved had not been treated with bichromate. Viewed separately this piece of information is, of course, open to various interpretations, but when compounded with the other evidence presented in Chapter 8, it provides further support for the case against Keith.

[40] Cited in Weiner ([1955] 1980:194).

[41] While it is possible that the Piltdown jaw could have been obtained from a commercial or private source, it seems more likely that it had been procured from a known orang collection such as the one at the British Museum (Natural History) or the Royal College of Surgeons. Keith had a thorough knowledge of the collections of both institutions. At the South Kensington Museum the core of their orang collections (pre-1912) is derived from two major sources. The first is a series of some 20 or more crania and skeletons transferred from the Zoological Society of London, circa 1855 (much of which appears to have been collected by James Brooke (later Sir James Brooke, Rajah of Sarawak) in the 1840s.) The second is the Everett Collection, consisting of some 111 miscellaneous osteological specimens that included orangutan crania, recovered from Sarawak caves in Borneo during the third quarter of the nineteenth century, see Everett's catalogue communicated to the British Association meeting in Sheffield (1879), see *Brit Ass Adv Sci Report 1879* pp 149–55. The descriptions in this report are not entirely complete. For example in some instances a cranium refers to both skull and jaw, where in other cases it implies only the skull (minus the jaw). What makes this collection so interesting is that it was closely studied by Arthur Keith during the 1890s. In fact Keith had gone through it, identifying and labelling many of the specimens (which he initialled: "A.K"). There are a couple of crania (minus jaws) represented in this collection that in varying degrees match the Piltdown jaw, but in the absence of accurate records it is impossible to say whether these crania had jaws when Keith first examined them. As indicated by the records of the Hunterian Museum (Royal College of Surgeons) its orang collections had been extensive. In 1941, however, a large portion of this and other parts of the Museum's collections were destroyed during a German bombing raid. After this most of the surviving material was transferred to the BM(NH). Hence, it is impossible to check these records against specimens and to know what, if anything, had been "missing" prior to this event. As noted in Chapter 6, fn 78, Jack Trevor had suggested that the Piltdown jaw might be "*Simia moro*," belonging to a specimen described by Richard Owen (see *Trans Zool Soc* (1837) Vol II, Plate XXXIII). An effort was made to track down this specimen at both the Royal College and the South Kensington Museum, but without success. Whatever the fate of this particular specimen a comparison of Owen's illustration with that of the Piltdown jaw reveals some significant differences in anatomy. A much closer fit is the immature specimen shown in Plate XXX. However, it is considered most unlikely that the Piltdown jaw would have been procured from specimens such as these, which were well-documented.

[42] Among those (other than the Kenwards, Samuel Woodhead and Teilhard de Chardin), who are known to have seen some of Dawson's materials prior to 2 June 1912, is Ernest Victor Clark (1868–1954) of Lewes, see Weiner memorandum of Clark interview on 12 February 1954, Spencer (1990:6.3.41). Precisely when Clark saw the material is uncertain, but he was convinced it had been "before Woodward came into the picture". Another was Henry Sargent (1891–1983), former Curator of the Bexhill Museum (near Hastings), see transcript of Oakley's interview on 2 March 1954, in Spencer (1990:6.3.48). While Sargent was uncertain whether Dawson had shown him a cranial fragment in 1911 or 1912, he recalled that Dawson said "that he was going to take it to the BM (NH). . . " It is conjectured that this event was probably during the same time period that Dawson showed the material to Clark. Finally, there is every reason to suppose that Dawson did, as Abbott claimed in his *Hastings & St. Leonard's Observer* article on 1 February 1913, show him a fragment of the Piltdown cranium before it was shown to Woodward. In fact Abbott hinted at this in a letter to Woodward dated 24 November 1912, in Spencer (1990:1.2.24). Correlating this with what he reportedly told Francis Edmunds circa 1924, namely that "he had worked with Dawson on the Piltdown skull . . . [and that it been in his shop] six months before Smith Woodward saw it . . ." (see Edmunds to Oakley 24 November 1953, Spencer 1990:6.3.7), again correlates well with the other testimonies, and the inferred scenario.

[43] According to this certificate, Dawson's name was proposed by Henry Woodward, seconded by Lankester, and supported by the following Fellows: Smith Woodward, Edwin Tulley Newton, William Carruthers, Clement Reid, Lazarus Fletcher, George William Lamplugh, Horace B Woodward, William Whitaker, and Peter Chalmers.

[44] Keith (1950:233–234).

[45] Keith (1950:267).

[46] Keith & Flack (1906).

[47] Keith (1950:317). It should be noted here that among Keith's competitors for the Conservatorship had been Richard H Burne, who had worked under Charles Stewart since 1892. From all indications Burne never showed any resentment of the fact that he did not receive the postition, and evidently worked

harmoniously with Keith for the next 25 years. According to Keith, they had been friends prior to this event. They first met while Keith was working at the London Hospital in Whitechapel. Writing of their first meeting, Keith noted in his autobiography: "Burne was my own age. He had studied with Professor [G.B.] Howes [who held the chair of zoology at the Royal College of Science, South Kensington] . . . I stupidly supposed he was a hard-up student like myself. He invited me to dinner, giving an address in Gloucester Terrace, where I thought he lodged. I found him master of a West End establishment, married, and already with two children. It was a rich and cultured home, and I was entertained with a magnificence to which I was not accustomed" (Keith 1950:197). Later, in 1907, when Stewart stepped down at the Royal College, Keith and Burne apparently agreed to be "friendly rivals" in the competition for the post (see Keith 1950:285). All of this is mentioned, since it did occur to me at the commencement of the Piltdown project that perhaps Burne might have harboured some deep down resentment against Keith, and that perhaps he and Dawson had been in league together. But as in other cases mentioned, while the notion of Burne's being driven by professional jealousy is superficially attractive, it is a proposition that fails to withstand closer scrutiny.

[48] See for example "Statement of Attendance at Lectures, 1916, pasted at the front of Keith's daily diary, "Letts No.31 1915", in KP/RCS Box File D7:

Date	Lecturer	Lecture	No attending
Feb 4	J.B.Sutton	Hunterian	70
Feb 7	Z. Cope	Hunterian	40
Feb 9	J.F.Frazer	Hunterian	70
Feb 11	W.B.Bell	Hunterian	45
Feb 14	A. Keith	Hunterian	270
Feb 16	A. Keith	Hunterian	250
Feb 18	A. Keith	Hunterian	250
Feb 21	A. Keith	Hunterian	300
Feb 23	A. Keith	Hunterian	300
Feb 25	A. Keith	Hunterian	300
Mar 6	J.E.R.McDonagh	Hunterian	130
		S. Forrest Cowell (Sec)	
		9 March 1916	

[49] See Spencer (1990:1.1.30, 1.1.33, 1.2.1).

[50] Teilhard to his parents 26 April 1912, Letter No 65, in Teilhard (1965) 1968: 190–191.

[51] Teilhard to Pelletier 18 May 1912, in Schmitz-Moormann (1981:9).

[52] Teilhard to his parents 3 June 1912, Letter No 67, in Teilhard (1965) 1968:198).

[53] Keith to Woodward 2 November 1912, in Spencer (1990:1.2.17).

[54] Unfortunately a copy of this letter has not been located. Its existence is based on an entry in Keith's daily diary for 29 November: "Write Smith Woodward." Library, Royal College of Surgeons Box D6 KP/RCS.

[55] See Dawson (1938:59, fn 3). Here Dawson cites letter, dated 21 November 1912 from Smith to Raoul Anthony, which confirms this arrangement. It is not clear whether at this point he had seen either the originals or received the casts. His letter, dated 16 December, suggests that while he might well have seen the former, he had yet to study the latter. It should also be noted that on 30 November Smith had been an overnight guest at Keith's home in Highbury. Evidently Smith returned to Manchester the next day, see Keith's daily diary, entry for 30 November.

[56] Keith Weekly Diary, KP/RCS Box D6.

[57] Keith to Elliot Smith 2 December 1912, in Spencer (1990:1.2.27).

[58] Although Keith's account of what Eliot Smith is reported to have said at Burlington House two days later shows that he was familiar with the Piltdown parts, he was obviously either guessing at what Smith's inferences would be or deliberately misrepresenting him. The impression given by Keith's article is that Smith had been rather vague in his general conclusions, in that "little more than the general shape can be accurately made out". But as Smith revealed to his audience on the night of the 18th, he had come to a much more positive conclusion: the cerebral hemispheres were asymmetrical in the hind region, which was hardly surprising given the modernity of the cranial form. Yet, invoking a superior sensitivity in his fingertips, Smith declared that he had been able to trace the course of many of this brain's convolutions, and as such could confirm that it represented "the most primitive and most simian human brain so far recorded". Had Smith played into Keith's hand?

[59] See Note D appended to Letter 1.2.27, Spencer (1990). Later, the day before Keith wrote his *BMJ* article, he made another trip to South Kensington. This visit is noted in his weekly diary under Sunday, December 15th: "Been at South Kensington again seeing Sussex skull. Puzzled about jaw". Box D6 KP/RCS.

[60] In the published transcript of the discussions appended to the Dawson & Woodward (1913) communication, no mention is made of the Galley Hill skeleton. While it is possible that Keith's comments

on this had been edited out, it is also possible that he had forgotten to mention this on the night of December 18th.

[61] *Brit Med J* 21 December 1912, p 1719.

[62] Following the receipt of the Piltdown casts in mid May 1913, Keith immediately began working on his reconstruction. While he attended to the cranium, he seems to have secured the assistance of the American dentist J Leon Williams (then living in Hampstead) to prepare a reconstructed jaw according to his specifications. It is suspected that Williams was used to create the illusion that it was not just Keith who was dissatisfied with Woodward's restoration, see *Illustrated London News* 16 August 1913: "Man or Modern Man? The Two Piltdown Skull Reconstrusctions" in which was figured Williams' reconstruction of the jaw "approved by Keith". The origin of Williams' friendship with Keith is not known and appears to have been quite recent — despite the fact Wiliams had been in England since the late 1880s. According to his biographer George Clapp (1925:60), Williams delivered a paper "On the Formation of Dental Enamel" to the Royal Society in 1895 [later printed in *The Dental Cosmos* 1896], but after this little is known of his scientific activities until the Spring of 1913 when he was inducted as a Fellow into the Royal Anthropological Institute [see *J Roy Anthropol Inst* (1913) XLIII:724]. It is interesting to note in this regard that Keith was then the current president of the Institute. After the appearance of the Keith-Williams reconstruction in August 1913, sometime in November, Williams abruptly returned to New York. Whether this had been a sudden or planned move is not known. Furthermore, while it is tempting to suggest that Williams had suspected foul-play and had removed himself from the London scene to avoid involvement in a possible scandal, there is no evidence to support the idea that he had been in league with Keith. It is also suggested that Williams may have been the source of Gregory's (1914) reference to the rumour that the Piltdown remains were forgeries (see section on Hinton, Chapter 7).

[63] As will be recalled from Chapter 3, following Keith's battle with Elliot Smith, the focus of the Piltdown debate suddenly shifted. This is mirrored to some extent in the exchange between Keith and Boyd Dawkins at Burlington House on 17 December 1913, but more specifically in Dawkins' reaction to what he believed had been a distorted report of this encounter in the *Morning Post* the following day. This anonymous article was written by Keith. In his weekly diary, under the date 18 December he wrote the following entry: "On 17th a meeting at Geol over Piltdown again find I stand alone without a backer. — However got patient bearing and capt[ured] the Morning Post — which gave me over a col[umn] . . . " Box D6 KP/RCS. It also appears that Dawson knew that Keith was the author! This is known from a letter he wrote Woodward on 20 December 1913, see Spencer (1990:2.3.70). His information had come from the Editor of the *Post* who had asked for a rebuttal, but Dawson declined the invitation and told Woodward that he had asked Pycraft if he would care to respond to it. The question here is did Dawson learn the author's name from Editor of the *Post's* or had it come from Keith? If, as it is suspected, it came from the latter, why did Dawson tell Woodward? Was it a mistake or merely a manoeuvre to secure his reputation with Woodward? Either theory is quite reasonable, but it could also be argued that by telling Woodward who the author of this article had been, the intention was to secure a response from Dawkins. Whether Woodward did tell Dawkins has not been determined. Dawkins' letter to the *Post* is dated 22 December 1913. From all indications the strategy was to draw out Dawkins and thereby expose him to an anticipated attack from Keith's "Ightham Circle" allies — which is exactly what happened, see Chapter Four.

[65] See Spencer (1990:3.1.10, 3.1.11, 4.1.9).

[66] Dawson to Woodward 9 January 1915, in Spencer (1990:4.1.1).

[67] See Chapter 4 for further details. Abbott's displeasure with Dawson's paper is noted in a letter from Dawson to Woodward, dated 9 March 1915, in Spencer (1990:4.1.11) As for its impact on Harry Morris, this is largely inferred from Keith's subsequent behaviour. From all indications Keith went to some lengths to appease Morris, arranging among other things a demonstration of his materials at the Royal College and the Anthropological Institute; hence Keith's note to Major Marriott: "Morris must surely be a little "bucked" up with his growing conquest" (dated 16 October 1916, original in Weiner Papers, MSS WEI File 3). Keith's support of Morris continued into the 1920s. For further details, see Weiner ([1955] 1980:159–61) and Morris' article "A Suggestion as to the Border-land between Palaeoliths and Pre-palaeoliths," in *The East Sussex News* 17 April 1925. This latter article makes direct reference to Keith's support of his views and work. As to how Morris secured Dawson's Piltdown palaeolith remains a mystery. Finally, it is not inconceivable that Keith's continuing concern with Morris (and Abbott) might have been linked with an attempt to contain the St Barbe-Marriott story.

[68] Keith to Kennard 25 January 1916, in Spencer (1990:4.2.5). These comments were made in reference to Lyne's paper delivered the night before at the Royal Society of Medicine. Again the intent was to persuade his "Ightham Circle" allies — not to "rock the boat".

Literature cited

Abbott, W J L 1893. Excursion to Basted and Ightham. *Proc Geol Assoc* **13**: 157–163.

Abbott, W J L 1894. Plateau man in Kent. *Nat Sci* [London] **4**: 257–266.

Abbott, W J L 1897. Worked flints from the Cromer Forest Bed. *Nat Sci* **7**: 89–96.

Abbott, W J L 1905. Machine-made eoliths. *Man* **5**: 146–148.

Abbott, W J L 1913. Prehistoric man: The newly discovered link in his evolution. *Hastings & St Leonard's Observer* (Feb 1).

Abbott, W J L 1915. Pliocene deposits of the southeast of England. *Proc Prehist Soc E Anglia* **2**: 175–194.

Agassiz, L 1840a. *Etudes sur les glaciers.* Neuchatel.

Agassiz, L 1840b. On glaciers, and the evidence of their having once existed in Scotland, Ireland and England. *Proc Geol Soc Lond.* **54**: 1–28.

Aitkin, J 1876. On the unequal distribution of drift on opposite sides of the Pennine chain. *Quart G Geol Soc Lond* **32**: 184.

Alberti, F A von 1834. *Beitrag zu einer monographie des bunten sandsteins muschelkalks und keupers, und die Verbindung dieser gebilde zu einer formation.* Stuttgart.

Anthony, R 1913. Les restes humains fossiles de Piltdown (Sussex). *Rev Anthropol* (Paris) **23**: 293–306.

Anonymous 1841. Eleventh meeting of the British Association for the Advancement of Science. *Athenaeum*, pp. 612–630.

Anonymous 1903. Communications diverses. *Bull Soc d'anthropol de Bruxelles* **21**: lxxxiii.

Arambourg, C & M Arnould 1950. Note sur les fouilles paléontologiques executées en 1947–48 et 1949 dans le gisement. Villafranchian de la Garaet Ichkeul. *Bull Soc Sci Nat Tunisie* **II**: 149–157.

Arduino, G 1760. *Nuova raccolta d'opusculi scientifici e filologici.* Venice.

Aufrère, L 1936. Les premières découvertes préhistoriques dans la vallée de la Somme. *Bull Soc Prèhist Franç* **33**: 585–592.

Avebury, Lord, see Lubbock, J

Barclay, R 1975. *Ernest Bevin and the Foreign Office.* London.

Barnes, A S 1938. Les outils de l'homme tertiaire en Angleterre; Etude critique. *L'Anthropologie* **48**: 217–236

Barnes, A S 1939a. De la manière dont la nature imite le travail humain dans l'éclatement de silex. *Bull Soc Préhist Franç* **36**: 74–89.

Barnes, A S 1939b. The difference between natural and human flaking in prehistoric flint implements. *Amer Anthropol* **41**: 199–112.

Belt, A 1935. William Ruskin Butterfield (1872–1935). *Hastings & E. Sussex Nat* **5**: 57–61.

Bennett, F J 1901. The earliest traces of man. *Geol Mag* (London) **VIII**: 427.

Bennett, F J 1906. Machine-made implements. *Geol Mag* **3**: 69, 143.

Bennett, F J 1907. *The Story of Ightham.* London.

Beyrich, H E 1839. On the Goniatites found in the Transition formations of the Rhine. *Ann Nat Hist* **3**: 9–20, 155–165.

Bayzand, C J 1926. The Palaeolithic drawing of a horse from Sherborne, Dorset. *Nature* **117**: 233.

Black, D 1925. Asia and the dispersal of primates. *Bull Geol Soc China* **4**: 133–183.

Black, D 1927. Tertiary man in Asia: The Choukoutien discovery. *Nature* **118**: 733–734.

Blinderman, C 1986. *The Piltdown Inquest.* Buffalo, New York.

Boswell, P G H 1935. Human remains from Kanam and Kanjera, Kenya Colony. *Nature* **135**: 371.

Boucher de Perthes, J 1847. *Antiquités celtiques et ante diluviennes. Mémoire sur l'industrie primitive et les arts à leur origine.* Vol 1. Paris.

Boucher de Perthes, J 1857. *Antiquités celtiques et ante-diluviennes. Mémoire sur l'industrie primitive et les arts à leur origine.* Vol 2. Paris.

Boule, M 1903. [Review of Rutot's] Quelques découvertes paléontologiques nouvelles [Bull Soc Belge de géol 17: 188–197] *L'Anthropologie* (Paris) **14**: 702–704.

Boule, M 1905. L'Origine des éolithes. *L'Anthropologie* **16**: 702–704.

Boule, M 1911–13. L'Homme fossile de la Chapelle-aux-Saints. *Annales Paléontol* (Paris) 6: 111–172 (1911); 7: 21–56, 85–192 (1912); 8: 1–70 (1913).

Boule, M 1913. L'Homo néanderthalensis et sa place dans la nature, *C–R XIV Congr Intnl anthropol archéol préhist* (Geneve 1912). Tome II: 392–395.

Boule, M 1915. La paléontologie humaine en Angleterre. *L'Anthropologie* **26**: 1–67.

Boule, M 1921. *Les hommes fossiles* 1st ed. Paris.

Boule, M 1923. *Fossil Men* (translation of "Les hommes fossiles" [1921]). Edinburgh.

Boule, M 1929. Le Sinanthrope. *L'Anthropologie* **39**: 455.

Boule, M 1937. Le Sinanthrope. *L'Anthropologie* **47**: 1–22.

Bourgeois, L 1868. Etude sur des silex trouvés dans les depots tertiaires de la commune de Thenay, près Pontlevoy (Loir-et-Cher). *C–R Congr intnl d'Anthropol d'Archéol préhist* Paris (1867). pp 67–75.

Bourgeois, L 1873. Sur les silex considérées comme portant les marques d'un travail humain et découverts dans le terrain miocène de Thenay. *C–R intnl d'Anthropol d'Archéol préhist* Bruxelles (1872). pp 81–94.

Bowden, M 1978. *Ape-Men: Fact or Fallacy?* Bromley, Kent. (2nd ed: 1981).

Boyd Dawkins, W See Dawkins, W B

Branco, W 1898. Die menschenähnlichen Zähne aus dem Bohernz der schwäbischen. *Alb Jahr d Ver f Vaterland Naturk Würtemberg* **54**: 1–44.

Breuil, H 1922. Les industries pliocènes de la region d'Ipswich. *Rev anthropol* **32**: 226–229.

Breuil, H 1938. The use of bone implements in the Old Palaeolithic. *Antiquity* **12**: 56–67.

Broderick, A H 1963. *Father of Prehistory: The Abbé Henri Breuil: His Life and Times.* New York.

Brinton, G 1895. The *Pithecanthropus erectus. Science* II: 845.

Broom, R 1918. The evidence afforded by the Boskop skull of a new species of primitive man (*Homo capensis*). *Anthropol Papers Amer Mus Nat Hist* **23**: 67–79.

Buch, G von 1839. *Pétrification recueilles en Amérique par Alexandre de Humboldt.* Berlin: Royal Academy of Sciences.

Buckland, W 1820. *Vindicae geologicae; or, the connexion of geology with religion explained.* Oxford.

Buckland, W 1823, *Reliquiae diluvianae; or, observations on the organic remains contained in caves, fissures, and diluvial gravel, and or on other geological phenomena, attesting the action of an universal deluge.* London.

Burkitt, M C 1921a. Congress at Liège. *Proc Prehist Soc East Anglia* **3**: 453–457.

Burkitt, M C 1921b. *Prehistory: A study of early cultures in Europe and the Mediterranean basin.* Cambridge.

Busk, G 1861. On the crania of the most ancient races man. (Translation of Hermann Schaaffhausen's paper in Muller's Archiv 1858). *Nat Hist Rev* I: 155–175.

Capitan, L 1904. La question des éolithes. *Rev l'Ecole d'anthropol* **14**: 240–246.

Capitan, L 1923. **Rapport de Dr. Capitan.** *Rev anthropol* **33**: 58–67.

Carnot, A 1893. Recherches sur la composition générale et la teneur en fluor des os modernes et des os fossiles de différents ages. *Ann Min Paris* **3**: 155–195.

Carpenter, W B 1863. Discovery at Abbeville. *Athenaeum* **41**: 523.

Churchward, A 1922. *Origin and Evolution of the Human Race.* London.

Cave, A J E 1973. [Remarks on Piltdown forgery]. *In*: S Zuckerman (Ed), *The Concepts of Human Evolution.* London. p 26.

Clapp, G W 1925. *The Life and Work of James Leon Williams* New York.

Clark, J D 1976. Louis Seymour Bazett Leakey 1903–1972. *In*: G I Isaac & E R McCown (Eds), *Human Origins: Louis Leakey and the East African Evidence.* Menlo Park, California. pp 521–541.

Coffey, G 1901. Naturally chipped flints for comparison with certain forms of alleged artificial chipping. *Rep Brit Assoc Adv Soc* p 795.

Cohen, C & J-J Hublin 1989. *Boucher de Perthes 1788–1868. Les origines romantiques de la préhistoriques.* Paris.

Cole, S 1975. *Leakey's Luck: The life of Louis Seymour Bazett Leakey.* New York.

Collyer, R H 1867. The [Foxhall] fossil human jaw from Suffolk. *Anthropol Rev* (London) **V**: 331–339.

Conybeare, W D & W Phillips 1822. *Outline of the Geology of England and Wales.* Vol I. London.

Cook, S F & R F Heizer 1947. The quantitative investigations of aboriginal sites: Analysis of human bone. *Amer J Phys Anthropol* **5**: 201–220.

Cook, S F & R F Heizer. 1952. The fossilization of bone: Organic components and water. *Rep Univ Archaeol Surv (Berkeley)* **17**: 1–24.

Cooper, C F 1945. Arthur Smith Woodward, 1864–1944. *Obit Not Roy Soc Lond* **5**: 79–112.

Cope, Z 1959. *The History of the Royal College of Surgeons of England.* London.

Costello, P 1985. The Piltdown hoax reconsidered. *Antiquity* **LIX**: 167–171.

Costello, P 1986. The Piltdown hoax: Beyond the Hewitt connexion. *Antiquity* **LX**: 145–147.

Cox, D R 1983. [Comments on Winslow & Meyer (1983) hypothesis]. *Science 83* **4**: 21–22.

Cuénot, C 1965. *Teilhard de Chardin: a biographical study* Baltimore.

Cunningham, D J 1895a. Dr Dubois' so-called missing link. *Nature* **52**: 428–429.

Cunningham, D J 1895b. Dr Dubois' missing link. *Nature* **53**: 115–116.

Cunningham, W 1897. Authenticity of Plateau man. *Nat Sci* **8**: 327–333.

Cunnington, W 1898. On some palaeolithic implements from the Plateau gravels and their evidence concerning "Eolithic" man. *Quart J Geol Soc Lond* **54**: 291–300.

Curwen, E C 1929. *Prehistoric Sussex.* London.

Dakyns, J R 1872. The glacial phenomena of the Yorkshire uplands. *Quart J Geol Soc* **28**: 384.

Dames, W 1896. *Pithecanthropus,* ein Blindeglied zwischen Affe und Mensch. *Deutsche Runschau* **88**: 368–384

Daniel, G E 1950. *A Hundred Years of Archaeology.* London.

Daniel, G E 1985. [Editorial note to Costello (1985)]. *Antiquity* **LIX**: 167.

Daniel, G E 1986. Piltdown and Professor Hewitt. *Antiquity* **LX**: 59–60. [see Costello (1986)].

Dart, R 1925. *Australopithecus africanus:* The man-ape of South Africa. *Nature* **115**: 195–199.

Darwin, C 1871 (1979). *The Descent of Man, and Selection in Relation to Sex.* London. (Easton Press: Connecticut).

David, T W E & Wilson, J T 1914. Preliminary communication on an Australian cranium of probable Pleistocene age. *Rep Brit Ass Adv Sci (Australian meeting)* p 531.

Davidson, C F & O Atkin 1953. On the occurrence of uranium in phosphate rock. *C-R XIX Congr Géol Intnl* pp 182–184.

Davies, H N 1904. [The Cheddar skeleton]. *Quart J Geol Soc Lond* **LX**: 335.

Dawkins, W B 1874. *Cave-Hunting: Researches on the evidence of caves respecting the early inhabitants of Europe.* London.

Dawkins, W B 1880. *Early Man in Britain and His Place in the Tertiary Period.* London.

Dawkins, W B 1913. [Comments on Piltdown skull]. *In:* Dawson & Woodward (1913:000).

Dawkins, W B 1914. [Comments on Piltdown skull]. *In:* Dawson & Woodward (1914:000).

Dawkins, W B 1915. The geological evidence in Britain as to the antiquity of man. *Geol Mag* (n.s.) **2**: 464–466

Dawson, C 1897. Discovery of a large supply of natural gas at Waldron, Sussex. *Nature* **57**: 150–151.

Dawson, C 1898a. On the discovery of natural gas in east Sussex. *Quart J Geol Soc Lond* **54**: 564–571.

Dawson, C 1898b. Natural gas in Sussex. *Proc SE Union Sci Soc* pp 73–80.

Dawson, C 1898c. List of Wealden and Purbeck-Wealden fossils. *Brighton Nat Hist Soc Rep 1898* pp 31–37.

Dawson, C 1909 [1910]. *History of Hastings Castle* 2 vols. London.

Dawson, C 1913. The Piltdown skull. *Hastings & E Sussex Nat* **2**: 73–82.

Dawson, C 1915. The Piltdown skull. *Hastings & E Sussex Nat* **4**: 144–149.

Dawson, C & A S Woodward 1913. On the discovery of a Palaeolithic human skull and mandible in a flint-bearing gravel overlying the Wealden (Hastings Beds) at Piltdown, Fletching (Sussex). *Quart J Geol Soc Lond* **69**: 117–151.

Dawson, C & A S Woodward 1914. Supplementary note on the discovery of a Palaeolithic human skull and mandible at Piltdown (Sussex). *Quart J Geol Soc Lond* **70**: 82–90.

Dawson, C & A S Woodward 1915. On a bone implement from Piltdown (Sussex). *Quart J Geol Soc Lond* **71**: 144–149.

Dawson, W R 1938. *Sir Grafton Elliot Smith: A biographical record by his colleagues.* London.

Day, M H 1986. *Guide to Fossil Man.* Chicago.

Delesse, A 1863. La machoire humaine de Moulin de Quignon. *Mém Soc Anthropol Paris* **2**: 37–68.

Desnoyers, J 1829. [On Quaternary]. *Ann Sci nat* (Paris) **16**: 193.

Desnoyers, J 1863. Note sur des indices materiels de la coéxistence de l'homme avec l'Elephas meridionalis dans un terrain des environs de Chartres, plus anciens que les terrains de transport quaternaires des vallées de la Somme et de la Seine. *C-R Acad Sci* (Paris) **56**: 1073–1083.

Despott, G 1918. Excavations at Ghar Dalam [Malta]. *J Roy anthropol Inst* **XLVIII**: 215.

Dixon, F 1878. *The Geology of Sussex* [Rev. & augment. Ed T. Rupert Jones]. Brighton.

Drayson, A W 1973. *On the Cause, Date and Duration of the Last Glacial Epoch of Geology: and the Probable Antiquity of Man.* London.

Drayson, A W 1888. *Thirty Thousand Years of the Earth's Past History, Read by the Aid of the Discovery of the Second Rotation of the Earth.* London.

Dubois, E 1894. *Pithecanthropus erectus, eine menschenännliche Ubergangsform au Java.* Batavia.

Dubois, E 1896. On *Pithecanthropus erectus*: a transitional form between man and apes. *J Anthropol Inst* **25**: 240–255.

Dubois, E 1908. Das geologische Alter der Kendeng oder Trinilfauna. *Tijdschr K Ned Aard Genoot* (*Amsterdam*) **25**: 1235–1270.

Duckworth, W L H 1912. *Prehistoric Man* Cambridge.

Edmunds, F H 1925. see White (1925).

Edmunds, F H 1935. *The Wealden District* London.

Edmunds, F H 1950. Note on the gravel deposit from which the Piltdown skull was obtained. *Proc Geol Soc Lond* **106**: 133–134

Elliot Smith, G, see Smith, G E

Essex, R 1955. The Piltdown plot: A hoax that grew. *Kent & Sussex J* (July-Sept) pp 94–95.

Evans, J 1860. On the occurrence of flint implements in undisturbed beds of gravel, sands and clay. *Archaeologia* **38**: 280–307.

Evans, J 1863. The human remains at Abbeville. *Athenaeum* **42**: 19–20.

Evans, J 1878. Presidential address. *J Anthropol Inst* **7**: 149–151.

Evans, J 1943. *Time and Chance: The story of Arthur Evans and his forebearers.* London.

Everett, A H 1879. Second quarterly report on the Bornean cave exploration. *Rep Brit Assoc Adv Sci* (*Sheffield*) pp 149–155.

Falconer, H & P T Cautley 1846. *Fauna antiqua sivalensis, being the fossil zoology of the Siwalik Hills.* London.

Farrar, R A H 1979. The Sherbourne controversy. *Antiquity* **LIII**: 212–216.

Farrar, R A H & T I Molleson 1981. The Sherborne bone again. *Antiquity* **LV**: 44–46.

Fisher, O 1888. [On the Dewlish fissure]. *Quart J Geol Soc* **XLIV**: 819.

Flower, W H & R Lydekker 1891. *An Introduction to the Study of Mammmals Living and Extinct.* London.

Fraipont, J & M Lohest 1887. Recherches ethnographiques sur des ossements découverts dans les dépots quaternaires d'une grotte à Spy et détermination de leur age géologique. *Arch Biol* **7**: 587–757.

Frassetto, F 1927. New views on the "Dawn Man" of Piltdown (Sussex). *Man* **27**: 121–124.

Frere, J 1800. Account of flint weapons discovered at Hoxne in Suffolk. *Archaeologia* **13**: 203–205.

Friedrichs, H F 1932. Schaedel und Unterkiefer von Piltdown (Eoanthropus dawsoni Woodward) in neuer Unterschung. *Z Anat* Bd 98, pp 199–262.

Freudenberg, W 1915. *Die säugetiere des älteren quartars von Mitteleuropa.* Jena.

Geikie, J 1863. The phenomena of the glacial drift of Scotland. *Trans Geol Soc Glasgow* **1**: 2.

Geikie, J 1877. *The Great Ice Age and Its Relation to the Antiquity of Man*. 2nd ed. London.

Gervais, P [Postglacial deposits: Holocene] *Mém Acad Sci Montpellier* **1**: 413.

Giuffrida-Ruggeri V 1910. Nuove addizioni at tipo di Galley-Hill, e l'antichita della brachicefalia. *Arch Antropol Etnol* **XL**: 255–263.

Giuffrida-Ruggeri V 1918. Unicità del philum umano con pluralità dei centri specifici. *Rev Ital Paleontol (Perugia)* **24**: 1–15.

Giuffrida-Ruggeri, V 1919. La controversia sul fossile di Piltdown e l'origibe del philum umano. *Monitore Zoo Ital* **30**: 7–18.

Godwin-Austen R A See Austen, R A C.

Goodchild, J G 1875. The glacial phenomena of the Eden Valley and the western part of the Yorkshire Dale District. *Quart J Geol Soc Lond* **31**: 55.

Gould, S J 1980. The Piltdown conspiracy. *Nat Hist* **89**: 8–28.

Grayson, D K 1883. *The Establishment of Human Antiquity*. New York.

Gregory, W K 1914. The dawn-man of Piltdown, England. *Amer Mus J* **14**: 189–200.

Gregory, W K 1915. Is *Sivapithecus* an ancestor of man? *Science* **42**: 341–342.

Gregory, W K 1916a. Studies on the evolution of primates. *Bull Amer Mus Nat Hist*. **35**: 239–355.

Gregory, W K 1916b. Note on the molar teeth of the Piltdown mandible. *Amer Anthropol* **18**: 384–387.

Gregory, W K & M Hellman 1926. The crown patterns of fossil and recent human molar teeth and their meaning. *Nat Hist* **26**: 300-309.

Grist, C J 1910. Some eoliths from Dewlish, and the question of origin. *J Roy Anthropol Inst* **XL**: 192.

Gruber, J 1965. Brixham Cave and the antiquity of man. *In*: M E Spiro (Ed), *Context and Meaning in Cultural Anthropology*. New York. pp 373–402.

Haeckel, E 1895. *Systematische Phylogenie der Wirbelthiere*. Bonn. pp. 633–634

Halstead, L B 1978. New light on the Piltdown hoax. *Nature* **276**: 11–13.

Halstead, L B 1979. The Piltdown hoax: cui bono? *Nature* **277**: 596.

Hammond, M 1980. Anthropology as a weapon of social combat in late nineteenth century France. *J Hist Behav Sci* **16**: 118–32.

Hammond, M 1982. The expulsion of the Neanderthals from human ancestry: Marcellin Boule and the social context of scientific research. *Soc Stud Sci* **12**: 1–36.

Hamy, E-T 1870. *Précis de Paléontologie Humaine*. Paris.

Harrison, B 1895. High-level flint-drift of the Chalk: Report of the Committee, consisting of Sir John Evans (chairman), Mr B Harrison (secretary), Professor J Prestwich, and Professor H G Seeley. *Rept Brit Assoc Adv Sci* **65**: 349–351.

Harrison, E R 1928. *Harrison of Ightham* London.

Harrison, G A 1983. J S Weiner and the exposure of the Piltdown forgery. *Antiquity* **57**: 46–48.

Haward, F N 1912. The chipping of flints by natural agencies. *Proc prehist Soc E Anglia* **I** (2): 185–193.

Haward, F N 1912. The problem of eoliths. *Proc Prehist Soc E Anglia* **1** (4): 347–359.

Hedges, R E M, R A Housley, I A Law & C R Bronk. 1989. Radiocarbon dates from the Oxford AMS system: Archaeometry Datelist 9. *Archaeometry* **31**: 207–234.

Hewitt, J T 1898. Note on the natural gas at Heathfield station (Sussex). *Quart J Geol Soc Lond* **LIV**: 572–574.

Hinton, M A C 1909. On the fossil hare of the ossiferous fissures of Ightham, Kent, and on the recent hares of the Lepus variabilis group. *Sci Proc Roy Dublin Soc* **12**: 255–265.

Hinton, M A C 1910. A preliminary account of the British fossil voles and lemmings, with some remarks on the Pleistocene climate and geography. *Proc Geol Assoc* **21**: 489–507.

Hinton, M A C 1914. On some remains of rodents from the Red Crag of Suffolk and from the Norfolk Forest Bed. *Ann Mag Nat Hist* **13**: 186–195.

Hinton, M A C 1926. The Pleistocene Mammalia of the British Isles and their bearing upon the date of the Glacial period. *Proc Yorkshire Geol Soc* **20**: 325–348.

Hinton, M A C & A S Kennard 1905. The relative ages of the stone implements of the Lower Thames valley. *Proc Geol Assoc* **19**: 76–100.

Hinton, M A C & A S Kennard 1907. Contributions to the Pleistocene geology of the Thames valley. The Grays Thurrock area. Part II [for part I, see Hinton, Kennard & Newton 1900]. *Essex Nat* **15**: 56–88.

Hinton, M A C & A S Kennard 1910. Excursion to Grays Thurrock, Essex. *Proc Geol Assoc* **21**: 474–476.

Hinton, M A C, A S Kennard & E T Newton 1900. Contributions to the Pleistocene geology of the Thames valley. I: The Grays Thurrock area. *Essex Nat* **11**: 336–370.

Hinton, M A C et al. 1938. Report on the Swanscombe skull. *J Roy Anthropol Inst* **68**: 17–98.

Hood, D 1964. *Davidson Black: A Biography*. Toronto.

Hopwood, A T 1935. Fossil elephants and man. *Proc Geol Assoc Lond* **46**: 46–70.

Houzé, E 1896. Le Pithecanthropus erectus. *Bull Soc Anthropol Bruxelles* **15**: 18–55.

Hrdlička, A 1912. Early man in America. *Amer J Sci* **34**: 543–554.

Hrdlička, A et al. 1912. *Early Man in South America*. Bull Bureau Amer Ethnol, Smithsonian Inst.

Hrdlička, A 1914. The most ancient skeletal remains of man. *Ann Rep (1913) Smithsonian Inst* pp 491–552.

Hrdlička, A 1922. The Piltdown jaw. *Amer J Phys Anthropol* **5**: 337–347.

Hrdlička, A 1923a. Dimensions of the first and second molars, with their bearing on the Piltdown jaw and man's phylogeny. *Amer J Phys Anthropol* **6**: 195–216.

Hrdlička, A 1923b. Variation in the dimension of lower molars in man and anthropoid apes. *Amer J Phys Anthropol* **6**: 423–438.

Hrdlička, A 1924. New data on teeth of early man and certain fossil European apes. *Amer J Phys Anthropol* **7**: 109–132.

Hrdlička A 1925. The Taungs ape. *Amer J Phys Anthropol* **8**: 379–392.

Hrdlička, A 1927. The Neanderthal phase of man. *J Roy Anthropol Inst* **57**: 249–274.

Hrdlička, A 1930. *The Skeletal Remains of Early Man*. Smithsonian Misc Coll. No 83. Washington, D. C.

Hughes, T M 1878. On the evidence afforded by the gravels and brick-earth. *J Anthropol Inst* **7**: 162–165.

Huxley, T H 1863. *Evidence as to Man's Place in Nature*. London.

Issel, A 1867. Résume des recherches concernant l'ancienneté de l'homme en Ligurie. *C-R Congr Int Anthropol Archéol Préhist (Paris)*, p 67.

Johnston, H H 1916. [Review of H F Osborn's "Men of the Old Stone Age"]. *The Geographical J* **48**: 349–350.

Keith, A 1895a. One of a past generation. *Pall Mall Gazette* 12 December (evening edition), pp 1–2.

Keith, A 1895b. *Pithecanthropus erectus* — a brief review of human fossil remains. *Science Progress* **3**: 348–369.

Keith, A 1911a. The anthropology of ancient British races. *Lancet* (March), pp 722–724.

Keith, A 1911b. *Ancient Types of Men*. London.

Keith, A 1912a. Certain phases in the evolution of man (Abstracts Hunterian Lectures). *Lancet* (March 23, 30, April 6), pp 775–777, 734–736, 788–790.

Keith, A 1912b. Recent discoveries of ancient man. *Bedrock* I: 295–311.

Keith A 1912c. Modern problems relating to the antiquity of man. *Brit Med J* (September 21), pp 669–672.

Keith, A 1913a. The present problems relating to the origin of modern races. *Lancet* 2: 1050–1053.

Keith, A 1913b. The Piltdown skull and brain cast. *Nature* **92**: 107–109, 197–199, 292, 345–346.

Keith, A 1914a. The reconstruction of fossil human skulls. *J Roy Anthropol Inst* **44**: 12–31.

Keith, A 1914b. The significance of the discovery at Piltdown. *Bedrock* **2**: 435–453.

Keith, A 1915a.*The Antiquity of Man*. London.

Keith, A 1915b. [Review of Le Double's book "Variations de la colonne vertébrale de l'homme"]. *Man* **15**: [No 37] p 63.

Keith, A 1917. [Review of H F Osborn's "Men of the Old Stone Age"]. *Man* **17**: 82–85.

Keith, A 1925a. *The Antiquity of Man*. 2 vols. London.

Keith, A 1925b. The fossil anthropoid ape from Taungs. *Nature* **115**: 234.

Keith, A 1931. *New Discoveries Relating to the Antiquity of Man.* London.

Keith, A 1938–39. A re-survey of the anatomical features of the Piltdown skull with some observations on the recently discovered Swanscombe skull. *J Anat* **75**: 155–185 [Part I], 234–254 [Part II].

Keith, A 1948. *A New Theory of Human Evolution.* London.

Keith, A 1950. *Autobiography.* London.

Keith, A & G Sinclair 1924. Neanderthal man in Malta. *J Roy Anthropol Inst* **LIV**: 251–275.

Kennard, A S 1947. Fifty and one years of the Geologists' Association. *Proc Geol Assoc* **58**: 271–283.

Klaatsch, H 1910. Die Aurignac-Rasse und ihre Stellung im Stammbau der Menschheit. *Z Ethnol* **42**: 513–577.

Kleinschmidt, O 1922. Realgattung Homo sapiens (L). *Eine naturgesch Mongr des Menschen. Berajah, Zoogr infinita.*

Knowles, W J 1902. On objects of the Plateau kind from the interglacial gravels of Ireland. *Rep Brit Assoc Adv Sci* pp 756–757

Klobe, H 1895. Ueber den angeblichen Affenmenschen, *Pithecanthropus erectus* Dubois *Naturwiss Wochenschr* **10**: 70–72.

Kollman, J 1895. [Remarks on *Pithecanthropus*]. *Z Ethnol* **27**: 740–744.

Kraatz, R 1985. A review of recent research on Heidelberg man, *Homo erectus heidelbergensis*. In: E. Delson (Ed), *Ancestors: The hard evidence*, pp. 268–271. New York.

Kraatz, R & H Querner 1967. Die Entdeckung des *Homo heidelbergensis* durch Otto Schottensack von 60 Jahren. *Ruperto Carola, Heidelberg* **42**: 178–183.

Krause, W 1895. [Remarks on *Pithecanthropus*]. *Z Ethnol* **27**: 78–81.

Langham, I 1978. Talgai and Piltdown — The common context. *Artefact* **3**: 181–224.

Langham, I 1979. The Piltdown hoax. *Nature* **277**: 170.

Langham, I 1984. Sherlock Holmes, circumstantial evidence and Piltdown man. *PAN — Phys Anthropol News* **3**(1): 1–5.

Lankester, E R 1912. On the discovery of a novel type of flint implements below the base of the Red Crag of Suffolk, Proving the existence of skilled workers of flint in the Pliocene age. *Phil Trans Roy Soc* (London) **102** (B): 283–336.

Lankester, E R 1913. [Discussion of the Piltdown skull]. *In*: Dawson & Woodward 1913a: 147–148.

Lankester, E R 1914. Description of the test specimen of the rostro-carinate industry found beneath the Norwich Crag. *Roy Anthropol Inst Occ Papers*. No. 4.

Lankester, E R 1915. *Diversions of a Naturalist.* London.

Lankester, E R 1921a. A remarkable flint from Selsey Bill. *Proc Roy Soc Lond* **92**: 162–167.

Lankester, E R 1921b. A remarkable flint from Piltdown. *Man* **32**: 59–62.

Lapworth, C [1879] 1898. *Intermediate textbook of Geology.* Edinburgh.

Lartet, E 1856. Note sur un grand singe fossile qui rattache au groupe des singes supérieurs. *C-R Acad Sci* (Paris) **43**: 219–223.

Lartet, E 1861. Nouvelles recherches sur la coexistence de l'homme et des grands mammifrères caracteristiques de la dernière période géologique. II: Les grottes de Massat et la caverne de Savigne. *Ann Sci Nat* **15**: 177–253.

Lartet, E & H Christy 1875. [edited by T Rupert Jones]. *Reliquiae Aquitanicae: Being contributions to the archaeology and palaeontology of Périgord and the adjoining provinces of southern France.* London.

Leakey, L S B 1928. The Oldoway skeleton. *Nature* **121**: 499.

Leakey, L S B 1933. Die Menschenreste von Kanam und Kanjera, Kenya-Kolonie. *Anthropol Anz* **10**: 238–243.

Leakey, L S B 1934. *Adam's Ancestors.* London.

Leakey, L S B 1935a. *The Stone Age Races of Kenya.* Oxford.

Leakey, L S B 1935b. Fossil human remains from Kanam and Kanjera — a reply to Professor Boswell. *Nature* **138**: 643.

Leakey, L S B, A T Hopwood & H Reck. 1931. Age of the Oldoway Bone Beds, Tanganyika. *Nature* **128**: 724.

Leakey, L S B & A M Goodall 1969. *Unveiling Man's Origins.* London.

Ledieu, A 1885. *Boucher de Perthes. Sa vie, ses oeuvres, sa correspondence.* Abbeville.

Le Gros Clark, W E see Clark, W E Le Gros.

Libby, F W, E C Anderson & J R Arnold 1949. Age determination by radiocarbon content: Worldwide assay of natural radiocarbon. *Science* **109**: 227–228.

Lowenstein, J M, T I Molleson & S L Washburn 1982. Piltdown jaw confirmed as orang. *Nature* **299**: 294.

Lubbock, J 1865. *Prehistoric Times: As Illustrated by Ancient Remains and the Manners and Customs of Modern Savages.* London.

Lubbock, J 1913. *Prehistoric Times.* London. 7th ed.

Luschan, F von 1895. [Remarks on Pithecanthropus]. *Z Ethnol* **27**: 81.

Lydekker, R 1886. Note on Troglodytes sivalensis. *Palaeont indica* **4**: 2.

Lydekker, R 1895. Review of *"Pithecanthropus Erectus, eine Menschenähnliche Uebergansform aus Java"* by E. Dubious. *Nature* **51**: 291.

Lyell, C 1830–33. *Principles of Geology; being an attempt to explain the former changes of the earth's surface by reference to causes now in operation.* Vol 1 (1830), Vol 2 (1832), Vol 3 (1833). London.

Lyell, C 1839. *Elements de Géologie* Paris.

Lyell, C 1860. On the occurrence of works of human art in post-Pliocene deposits. *Rep 29th meeting Brit Ass Adv Sci. Notices & Abstracts*, pp 93–95.

Lyell, C 1863. *The Geological Evidences of the Antiquity of Man with Remarks on the Theories of the Origin of Species by Variation.* 3rd ed. London.

Lyne, W C 1916. The significance of the radiographs of the Piltdown teeth. *Roy Soc Med Proc* **9**: 33–62.

McCown, T D & A Keith *The Stone Age of Mount Carmel. II: The Fossil Human Remains from the Levalloiso-Mousterian.* Oxford.

McCown, T D & K A R Kennedy 1972. *Climbing Man's Family Tree: A collection of major writings on human phylogeny. 1699–1971.* New Jersey.

MacCurdy, G G 1914. Ancestor hunting: The significance of the Piltdown skull. *Amer Anthropol* **15**: 248–256.

MacCurdy, G G 1916. The revision of *Eoanthropus dawsoni. Science* **43**: 228–231.

MacCurdy, G G 1924. *Human Origins: A Manual of Prehistory.* New York.

McKenny Hughes, T, see Hughes, T M.

Mahoudeau, P G & L Capitan 1901. La question de l'homme tertiaire à Thenay. *Rev l'Ecole d'Anthropol* **11**: 129–153.

Manouvrier, L 1895. Discussion du *"Pithecanthropus erectus"* comme précurseur présumé de l'homme. *Bull Soc Anthropol Paris* **6** (sér 4): 12–47.

Mantell, G 1822. *Fossils of the South Downs.* London.

Mantell, G 1839. *The Wonders of Geology.* 2 vols. London.

Marriott, R A 1914. *The Change in the Climate & Its Cause.* London.

Marriott, R A 1918. The Downs and the escarpments of the Weald. *Sci Progr* **12**: 591–608.

Marsh, O C 1896. *Pithecanthropus erectus,* from the Tertiary of Java. *Amer J Sci* **49**: 475–482.

Marston, A T 1936a. Preliminary note on a new fossil human skull from Swanscombe, Kent. *Nature* **138**: 200–201.

Marston, A T 1936b. Chimpanzee or man? The Piltdown canine tooth and mandible versus the human specific characteristics of the straight canine and the fused alveolar-maxillo-premaxillary suture. *Brit Dental J*, pp 216–221.

Marston, A T 1937. The Swanscome skull. *J Roy Anthropol Inst* **67**: 339–406.

Marston, A T 1950. The relative ages of the Swanscombe and Piltdown skulls, with special reference to the results of the fluorine estimation tests. *Brit Dental J* **88**: 292–299.

Marston, A T 1952. Reasons why the Piltdown canine tooth and mandible could not belong to Piltdown man. *Brit Dental J* **93**: 1–14.

Martin, R 1896. Kritische Bedenken gegen den *Pithecanthropus erectus* Dubois. *Globus* **67**: 213–217.

Matsumoto, H 1922. Revision of *Palaeomastodon. American Mus Novit* **51**. [see also *Bull Amer Mus Nat Hist* (1924) **50**: 1–58].

Matthew, W D 1914. Climate and evolution. *Ann NY Acad Sci* **24**: 171–318.

Matthew, W D, C R Eastman & W K Gregory 1916. Recent progress in vertebrate paleontology. *Science* **43**: 103–110.

Matthews, L H 1981. Piltdown man: The missing links. *New Scientist* **90**: 280–282, 376, 515–516, 578–579, 647–648, 710–711, 785, 861–862; **91**: 26–28.

Millar, R 1974. *The Piltdown Men: A case of archaeological fraud.* London [Paladin edition. Originally published in 1972].

Miller, G S 1915. The jaw of Piltdown man. *Smithsonian Misc Coll* (November) Vol **65**, No 12.

Miller, G S 1918. The Piltdown jaw. *Amer J Phys Anthropol* **1**: 25–51.

Miller, G S 1929. The controversy over human "missing links." *Smithsonian Rept for 1928.* Washington DC pp 413–465.

Moir, J R 1911. The flint implements of sub-Crag man. *Proc Prehist Soc E Anglia* **I**: 17–43.

Moir, J R 1912a. The making of a rostro-carinate flint implement. *Nature* **90**: 334.

Moir, J R 1912b. The natural fracture of flint. *Nature* **90**: 461–463.

Moir, J R 1912c. On the occurrence of a human skeleton in a glacial deposit at Ipswich. *Proc Prehist Soc East Anglia* **I**(2): 1–16.

Moir, J R 1912d. An account of the discovery and characters of a human skeleton found beneath a stratum of chalky boulder clay near Ipswich. *Roy Anthropol Inst* **42**: 365–379.

Moir, J R 1913a. Problems of flint fracture. *Man* **13**: 54–56.

Moir, J R 1913b. The sub-Crag flints. *Geol Mag* **10**: 553–555.

Moir, J R 1914. A defence of the "humanity" of the pre-river valley implements of the Ipswich district. *Proc Prehist Soc East Anglia* **1**: 368–374.

Moir, J R 1915a. A series of mineralised bone implements of a primitive type from below the base of the Red and Coralline Crags of Suffolk. *Proc Prehist Soc East Anglia* **2**: 116–131.

Moir, J R 1915b. Human palaeontology in England. *Geol Mag* (n.s.) **2**: 476–477.

Moir, J R 1916a. Pre-Boulder Clay man. *Nature* **98**: 109.

Moir, J R 1916b. On the evolution of the earliest palaeoliths from the rostro-carinate implements. *J Roy Anthropol Inst* **46**: 197–220.

Moir, J R 1918a. Some flint implements of the rostro-carinate form from Egypt. *Man* **18**: 3–6.

Moir, J R 1918b. Pre-Palaeolithic man in England. *Sci Progr* **12**: 465–474.

Moir, J R 1919. A few notes on the sub-Crag flint implements. *Proc Prehist Soc East Anglia* **3**: 158–161.

Moir, J R 1920. The transition from Rostro-carinate flint implements to the tongue-shaped implements of river terrace gravels. *Philos Trans Roy Soc Lond* **209**: 329–350.

Moir, J R 1921. Further discoveries of humanly-fashioned flints in and beneath the Red Crag of Suffolk. *Proc Prehist Soc East Anglia* **3**: 389–430.

Moir, J R 1922. The Red Crag flints of Foxhall. *Man* No 61–62, pp 104–105.

Moir, J R 1924. Tertiary man in England [with a note by Sir E Ray Lankester]. *Nat Hist* (New York) **XXIV**: 636–654.

Moir, J R 1935. *Prehistoric Archaeology & Sir Ray Lankester.* Ipswich.

Mollison, T 1921. Die Abstammung des Menschen. *Die Naturwissenschaften* **9**: 128–140.

Mollison, T 1924. Neuere Funde und Untersuchungen fossiler Menschenaffen und Menschen. *Z Anat* **25**: 696–771.

Montagu, M F A 1951. The Barcombe Mills cranial remains. *Amer J Phys Anthropol* **9**: 417–426.

Morlot, A 1854. Notice sur le Quaternaire en Suisse *Bull Soc vaudoise, Sci nat* **4**: 41–45.

Mortillet, G de 1868. Homme tertiaire. *Matériaux pour l'histoire positive et philosophique de l'homme* **4**: 179–182.

Mortillet, G de 1873. Sur l'homme tertiaire. *Bull Soc d'anthropol* **8**: 671–684.

Mortillet, G de 1883. *Le Préhistorique.* Paris.

Mortillet, G de & A de Mortillet 1881. *Musée préhistorique.* Paris.

Murchison, C 1868. *Palaeontological Memoirs & Notes of the late Hugh Falconer, A M, M D, . . . with a biographical sketch of the author. Volume II: Mastodon, elephant, rhinoceros, ossiferous caves, primaeval man and his contempories.* London.

Murchison, R I 1835. On the Silurian system of rocks. *Phil Mag J Sci* **7**: 46–52.

Murchison, R I 1841. First sketch of some of the principal results of a second geological survey of Russia. *Phil Mag J Sci* **19**: 417–422.

Nehring, A 1895a. Menschenreste aus einen Sambaqui von Santos in Brasilien unter Vergleichung der Fossilreste des Pithecanthropus erectus Dubois. *Z Ethnol* **27**: 710–721.

Nehring, A 1895b. Ueber einen menschlichen Molar aus dem Diluvium von Taubach bei Weimar. *Z Ethnol* **27**: 573–577.

Neviani, A 1896. Pitecantropo o la seimmia-uomo e la teoria dell'evoluzione. *Rev sociol Roma* **3**: 205–233.

Newton, E T 1895. On a human skull and limb-bones found in the Palaeolithic terrace-gravel at Galley Hill, Kent. *Quart J Geol Soc Lond* **51**: 505–527.

North, F J 1943. Centenary of the Glacial theory. *Proc Geol Assoc Lond* **54**: 1–28.

Omalius d'Halloy, J-B de 1831. *Eléments de Géologie*. Paris.

Oakley, K P 1948. Fluorine and the relative dating of bones. *Adv Sci* **4** (16) 336–337.

Oakley, K P 1949. *Man the Toolmaker*. London.

Oakley, K P 1953. Dating fossil human remains. *In*: A L Kroeber (Ed), *Anthropology Today: An encyclopedic inventory*. Chicago. pp 43–56.

Oakley, K P 1964. The problem of man's antiquity. An historical survey. *Bull Br Mus Nat Hist* (Geol) **9**(5): 85–155.

Oakley, K P 1974. Revised dating of the Kanjera hominids. *J Human Evol* **3**: 257–258.

Oakley, K P 1975. A reconsideration of the date of the Kanam jaw. *J Archaeol Sci* **2**: 151–152.

Oakley, K P 1979. Piltdown stains. *Nature* **278**: 302.

Oakley, K P & M F A Montagu 1949. A reconsideration of the Galley Hill skeleton. *Bull Br Mus Nat Hist* (Geol) **1**(2): 25–48.

Oakley, K P & C R Hoskins 1950. New evidence on the antiquity of Piltdown man. *Nature* **165**: 379–382.

Oakley, K P C R Hoskins & G Henri-Martin 1951. Application du test de la fluorine aux cranes de Fontéchevade. *L'Anthropologie* **LV**: 239–242.

Oakley, K P & C P Groves 1970. Piltdown man: The realization of fraudulence. *Nature* **169**: 789.

Oakley, K P, B G Campbell & T I Molleson (Eds). 1975. *Catalogue of Fossil Hominids* Part III (Americas, Asia, Australia). London.

Osborn, H F 1915. *Men of the Old Stone Age: Their environment, life and art*. New York.

Osborn, H F 1921a. The Pliocene man of Foxhall in East Anglia. *Nat Hist* (New York) **21**: 565–576.

Osborn, H F 1921b. The Dawn man of Piltdown, Sussex. *Nat Hist* (New York) **21**: 577–590.

Osborn, H F 1922. *Hesperopithecus*, the anthropoid primate of western Nebraska. *Nature* **110**: 281–283.

Osborn, H F 1924. Where did man originate. *Asia* **24**: 427.

Osborn, H F 1926a. Introduction, R C Andrews' *On the Trail of Ancient Man*. New York.

Osborn, H F 1926b. Why Central Asia? *Nat Hist* **26**: 263–269.

Osborn, H F 1927. Recent discoveries relating to the origin and antiquity of man. *Science* **65**: 481–488.

Osborn, H F 1942. Achidiskodon planifrons of the Piltdown gravels. In: *The Proboscidea: A monograph of the discovery, evolution, migration and extinction of the mastodonts and elephants of the world*. Vol 2. New York. Vol **2**: 964–968.

Owen, R 1836. Osteological contributions to the natural history of the Orang Utans (Simia, Erxleben). *Trans Zool Soc Lond* **II**: 165–172.

Penck, A 1909. *Die Alpen im Eiszeitalter*. Leipzig.

Penck, A & E Brückner 1900. *Die Alpen im Eiszeitalter*. 3 vols. Leipzig.

Pettit, A 1895. Le *Pithecanthropus erectus*. *L'Anthropologie* **6**: 65–69.

Phillips, J 1838. Geology. *Penny Cyclopedia* **11**: 127–51.

Pilgrim, G E 1915. New Siwalik primates and their bearing on the evolution of man and the anthropoidea *Rec Geol Surv India* **45**: 1–74.

Pilgrim, G E 1927. A *Sivapithecus* palate and other primate fossils from India. *Palaeontol Indica* **14** (n.s.): 1–24.

Prestwich, J 1859. Sur la découverte d'instruments en silex associés à des restes de mammifrères d'espèces perdues dans des couches non remaniées d'une formation géologique récente. *C-R Acad Sci* (Paris) **49**: 634–636.

Prestwich, J 1860. On the occurrence of flint-implements, associated with the remains of extinct mammalia, in undisturbed beds of a late geological period. *Proc Roy Soc Lond* **10**: 50–59.

Prestwich, J 1861. On the occurrence of the flint implements associated with the remains of extinct mammalia, in undisturbed beds of a late geological period, in France at Amiens and Abbeville, and in England at Hoxne. *Phil Trans Roy Soc Lond* **150**: 277–317.

Prestwich, J 1863. Theoretical considerations on the conditions under which the drift deposits containing the remains of extinct mammalia and flint implements were accumulated; and their geological age. *Proc Roy Soc Lond* **12**: 38–52.

Prestwich, J 1866. On the Quaternary flint implements of Abbeville, Amiens, Hoxne etc., their geological position and history. *Proc Roy Inst Gr Brit* **4**: 213–222.

Prestwich, J 1874. On the geological conditions affecting the construction of a tunnel between England and France. *Proc Inst Civ Eng* **37**: 110–145.

Prestwich, J 1887. Considerations on the date, duration and conditions of the glacial period, with reference to the antiquity of man. *Quart J Geol Soc Lond* **43**: 393–410.

Prestwich, J 1889. On the occurrence of palaeolithic flint implements in the neighbourhood of Ightham, Kent: Their distribution and probable age. *Quart J Geol Soc Lond* **XLV**: 270–297

Prestwich, J 1891. On the age, formation and successive drift stages of the valley of Darent; with remarks on the palaeolithic implements of the district, and on the origin of its chalk escarpment. *Quart J Geol Soc Lond* **XLVII**: 126–163.

Prestwich, J 1892. On the primitive characters of the flint implements of the chalk plateau of Kent. With notes by B Harrison and de B Crawshay. *J Anthropol Inst* **21**: 246–276.

Prestwich, J 1895. The greater antiquity of man. *Nineteenth Century Mag* **37**: 617–628.

Prestwich, G A 1899. *Life and Letters of Sir Joseph Prestwich.* London.

Puydt, M de & M Lohest 1886. Exploration de la grotte de Spy. *Ann Soc Géol Belg. Liège.* **13**: 34–39

Puydt, M de & M Lohest 1887. *L'Homme contemporain du Mammoth à Spy, province de Namur (Belgique).* Bruxelles.

Pycraft, W P 1917. The jaw of the Piltdown man: A reply to Mr Gerrit S Miller. *Sci Progr* **11**: 389–409.

Rames, J-B 1884. Géologie de Puy Courny: Eclats de silex tortonien du bassin d'Aurillac (Cantal). *Matériaux pour l'histoire primitive et naturelle de l'homme* **18**: 385–406.

Ramström, M 1919. Der Piltdown-Fund. *Bull Geol Inst (Upsala)* **16**: 261–304.

Ramström, M 1921. Der Java-Trinil-Fund "*Pithecanthropus*" oder können die "*Eoanthropus*" und "*Pithecanthropus*" — Funde uns zuverlässige Aufschlüsse über die Anthropogenesis geben? *Upsala Läkareförenings Förhandl* **26**.

Reid Moir, J See Moir, J R.

Ribiero, C 1867. Note sur le terrain quaternaire du Portugal. *Bull Soc géol France* **24**: 692–717.

Ribiero, C 1873. Sur des silex taillés découvertes dans les terrains miocène et pliocène du Portugal. *C-R Congr intnl d'anthropol archéol préhist* (Bruxelles 1872). pp 95–100.

Ribiero, C 1884. L'Homme tertiaire en Portugal. *In C-R Cong Intntl d'anthropol archéol préhist* (Lisbon 1880). pp 81–118.

Rosenberg, E 1896. [Remarks on Pithecanthropus]. *C-R Congr Intnl Zool, Leiden (1895)*, p 272.

Rutot, A 1900. Les industries paléolithiques primitives. Note sur la découverte d'importants gisements de silex taillés dans les collines de la Flandre occidentale. Comparaison de ces silex avec ceux du Chalk-Plateau du Kent. *Bull Mém Soc Anthropol* [Bruxelles] **XVIII**. Mém No 1.

Rutot, A 1909. L'age probable du squelette de Galley-Hill. *Bull Soc Belge Geol* **XXIII**: 239.

Schaaffhausen, H 1858. See Busk.

Schimper, W P 1874. *Traité de Paléontologie végétale.* 3 vols. Paris.

Schlosser, M 1903. Anthropodis oder Neopithecus. *Zent Mineralog Geolog und Paleontol* **4**: 512–513.

Schlosser, M 1911. Beitrage zur Kenntnis der oligozänen Landsaugetiere aus dem Fayum. *Beitrage Pal Geol Oesterr* **24**: 153–167.

Schmitz-Moormann, K 1981. Teilhard and the Piltdown hoax. *Teilhard Rev* **16**: 7–15.

Schoetensack, O 1908. *Der Unterkeifer des Homo heildelbergensis aus den Sanden von Mauer bei Heidelberg.* Leipzig.

Schwalbe, G 1904. *Die Vorgeschichte des Menschen.* Braunschweig.

Schwalbe, G 1906. *Studien zur Vorgeschichte des Menschen.* Stuttgart.

Schwalbe, G 1914. Kristische Besprechung von Boule's Werk "L'Homme fossile de La Chapelle-aux-Saints." *Z Morphol und Anthropol* **16**: 227–610.

Sedgwick, A & R I Murchison 1842. On the distribution of the older or Palaeozoic deposits of the north of Germany and Belgium, and their comparison with formations of the same age in the British Isles. *Trans Geol Soc Lond* **6**: 221–301.

Selenka, L & M Blanckenhorn 1911. *Die Pithecanthropus-Schichten auf Java.* Leipzig.

Seligman, C G & F G Parsons 1914. [Cheddar man]. *J Roy Anthropol Inst* **XLIV**: 241.

Sera, G L 1910a. Nuove observazioni ed induzioni sul cranio di Gibraltar. *Arch Antropol Etnol* **39**: 151–212.

Sera, G L 1910b. Di alcuni caratteri importanti sinoria non rivelati ne cranio Gibralter. *Atti Soc Romana Antropol* **XV**: 197–208.

Sera, G L 1917. Un presto *Hominida* miocenico: *Sivapithecus indicus*. *Natura* **8**: 149–173.

Sergi, G 1914. La mandibola umana. *Rev Antropol, Roma* **19**: 119–168.

Sergi, G 1916. *Problemi di scienze contemporanea.* Torino.

Shapiro, H L 1974. *Peking Man: The discovery, disappearance and mystery of a priceless scientific treasure.* New York.

Shattock, S G 1913. *Morbid thickening of the calvaria; and the reconstruction of bone once abnormal; a pathological basis for the study of the thickening observed in certain Pleistocene crania.* Rep XVII Intnl Med Congr, pp 3–46.

Sicher, H 1937. Sur Phylogenese des Menschlichen Kiefergelenkes nebst Bemerkungen über den Schädelfund von Piltdown. *Z Stomatol* **35**: 269–275.

Smith, F H 1987. Gustav Schwalbe: Neandertal morphology and systematics 1899–1916. *Pan – Phys Anthropol News* **6** (1): 1–5.

Smith, F H & F Spencer (Eds) 1984. *The Origin of Modern Humans: A world survey of the fossil evidence.* New York.

Smith, G E 1912. Presidential Address (BAAS). *Nature* **92**: 118–126.

Smith, G E 1913a. The Piltdown skull. *Nature* **92**: 131.

Smith, G E 1913b. The Piltdown skull and brain cast. *Nature* **92**: 267–268, 318–319.

Smith, G E 1913c. The controversies concerning the interpretations and meaning of the remains of the Dawn-man found near Piltdown. *Nature* **92**: 468–469.

Smith, G E 1914a. On the exact determination of the median plane of the Piltdown skull. *In:* Dawson & Woodward (1914: 93–97).

Smith, G E 1914b. The significance of the discovery at Piltdown. *Bedrock* **3**: 1–17.

Smith, G E 1915. [Review of A S Woodward's "Guide to Fossil Man"] *Geol Mag* **2**: 129–132.

Smith, G E 1916a. [Review of H F Osborn's "Men of the Old Stone Age"] *Amer Mus Nat Hist J* **16**: 319–325.

Smith, G E 1916b. New phases of the controversies concerning the Piltdown skull. *Proc Manchester Lit & Philo Soc* **60**: xxviii–xxix.

Smith, G E 1916c. The cranial cast of the Piltdown skull. *Man* **16**: 131–132.

Smith, G E 1917. The problem of the Piltdown jaw: human or subhuman? *Eugenics Rev* **9**: 167.

Smith, G E 1924. *The Evolution of Man.* London.

Smith, G E 1925a. The fossil anthropoid ape from Taungs. *Nature* **115**: 235.

Smith, G E 1925b. The London skull. *Nature* **116**: 678–680, 819–820.

Smith, G E 1928a. Neanderthal man as a distinct species. *Nature* **121**: 141.

Smith, G E 1928b. Neanderthal Man not our ancestor. *Sci Amer* (August), pp 112–115.

Smith, G E 1931a. *The Search for Man's Ancestors.* London.

Smith, G E 1931b. Human palaeontology: A review of "New Discoveries Relating to the Antiquity of Man" by Sir Arthur Keith. *Nature* **127**: 963–967.

Smith, Woodward A, see Woodward, A S.

Sollas, W J 1881. Note on the occurrence of Sponge-spicules in Chert from the Carboniferous limestone of Ireland. *Ann Mag Nat Hist* **7**: 141–143.

Sollas, W J 1882a. The Sponge fauna of Norway. *Ann Mag Nat Hist* **9**: 141–165, 426–453.

Sollas, W J 1882b. On the formation of flint. *Rep Brit Assoc Adv Sci (Southampton)*, pp 549–550.

Sollas, W J 1888. Contributions to the history of flints. *Sci Proc Roy Dublin Soc* **6**: 1–5.

Sollas, W J 1895. Pithecanthropus erectus and the evolution of the human race. *Nature* **53**: 150–151.

Sollas, W J 1900. Evolutional geology (Presidential address, BAAS). *Rep Brit Ass Adv Sci (Bradford)*, pp 711–730.

Sollas, W J 1903. A method for the investigation of fossils by serial section. *Phil Trans Roy Soc Lond* **196**: 267–294.

Sollas, W J 1908. On the cranial and facial characters of the Neanderthal face. *Philo Trans Roy Soc Lond* **199**: 281–339.

Sollas, W J 1911. *Ancient Hunters and their Modern Representatives.* London.

Sollas, W J 1913a. The formation of rostro-carinate flints. *Brit Assoc Adv Sci* **83**: 788–790.

Sollas, W J 1913b. Paviland Cave: An Aurignacian Station in Wales. *J Roy Anthropol Inst* **43**: 325–373.

Sollas, W J 1920. A flaked flint from the Red Crag. *Proc Prehist Soc East Anglia* **3**: 261–267.

Sollas, W J 1924. *Ancient Hunters.* 3rd ed. London.

Sollas, W J 1925. The Taungs skull. *Nature* **115**: 908–909.

Sollas, W J 1926. The Palaeolithic drawing of a horse from Sherborne, Dorset. *Nature* **117**: 233.

Spencer, F 1979. *Aleš Hrdlička M.D. 1869–1943: A chronicle of the life and work of an American physical anthropologist.* 2 vols. Ann Arbor & London. Univ Mircofilms Intnl.

Spencer, F 1984. The Neandertals and their evolutionary significance. *In*: F H Smith & F Spencer: *The Origin of Modern Humans: A worldwide survey of the fossil evidence.* New York. pp 1–49.

Spencer, F 1990. *The Piltdown Papers.* London.

Spencer, F & C Stringer 1989. See Hedges *et al.* 1989.

Sperber, G H 1985. Comparative primate dental enamel thickness: a radiodontological study. *In*: P V Tobias (Ed.), *Hominid Evolution: Past, Present and Future.* New York. pp 443–454.

Stearn, W T 1981. *The Natural History Museum at South Kensington.* London.

Steel, R E 1926. The Palaeolithic drawing of a horse from Sherbourne *Nature* **117**: 341–342.

Stewart, T D 1951. The problem of the earliest claimed representatives of *Homo sapiens*. *In*: *Origin and Evolution of Man.* Cold Spring Harbor Symp Quant Biol **XV**: 97–107.

Stocking, G W 1987. *Victorian Anthropology.* New York.

Stringer, C B 1979. A re-evaluation of the fossil human calvaria from Singa, Sudan. *Bull Br Mus Nat Hist* (Geol) **32**: 77–83.

Symington, J 1915. On the relations of the inner surface of the cranium to the cranial aspect of the brain. *Edinburgh Med J* **14**: 85–100.

Symington, J 1916. Endocranial casts and brain form: a criticism of some recent speculations. *J Anat and Physiol* **50**: 111–130.

Teilhard de Chardin, P 1920. Le cas de l'homme de Piltdown. *Rev des questions scientifiques (Bruxelles)* **77**: 149–155.

Teilhard de Chardin, P 1953. The idea of fossil man. *In*: A L Kroeber (Ed), *Anthropology Today: An encyclopedic inventory.* Chicago. pp 93–100.

Teilhard de Chardin, P 1965. *Lettres d'Hastings et de Paris, 1908–1914.* Preface by H de Lubac, annotations by A Demoment & H de Lubac. Paris.

Teilhard de Chardin, P 1967. *Letters from Paris, 1912–14.* New York.

Teilhard de Chardin, P 1968. *Letters from Hastings, 1908–1912.* New York.

Thacker, A G 1916. The significance of the Piltdown controversy. *Sci Progr* **8**: 275–290.

Theunissen, B 1989. *The History of the First "Missing Link" and Its Discoverer.* Dordrecht.

Tiddeman, R H 1872. On the evidence for the ice-sheet in North Lancashire and adjacent parts of Yorkshire and Westmoreland. *Quart J Geol Soc Lond* **28**: 471–491.

Tiddeman, R H 1878. On the age of the Hyaena-bed at the Victoria Cave, Settle, and its bearing on the antiquity of man. *J Anthropol Inst* **7**: 165–174.

Toombs, H A 1952. A new section in the Piltdown gravel. *S East Nat* **57**: 31–33.

Tobias, P V 1984. *Dart, Taung and the Missing Link: An Essay on the Life and Work of Emeritus Professor Raymond Dart.* Johannesburg.

Topinard, P 1895. [Review of] Prof. Sir William Turner sur la description de M. Dubois des restes récemment trouvés à Java et attribués par lui à un *Pithecanthropus erectus. L'Anthropologie* **6**: 605–607.

Topley, W 1875. *Geology of the Weald.* London.

Turner, W On M Dubois' description of remains recently found in Java and named by him *Pithecanthropus erectus.* With remarks on the so-called transitional forms between apes and man. *J Anat Physiol* **9**: 421–445

Underwood, A S 1913. The Piltdown skull. *Brit Dental J* **56**: 650–652.

Underwood, A S 1925. The fossil anthropoid ape from Taungs. *Nature* **115**: 234–235.

Vayson de Pradenne, A 1932. *Les Fraudes en Archéologie Préhistorique.* Paris.

Vere, F 1955. *The Piltdown Fantasy.* London.

Vere, F 1959. *Lessons of Piltdown.* London.

Verneau, R 1895. Encore le *Pithecanthropus erectus L'Anthropologie* **6**: 725–726.

Virchow, R 1985 *Pithecanthropus erectus* Dubois. *Z Ethnol* **27**: 81–87, 336–337, 435–440, 648–656, 744–747, 787–793.

Vogt, K C 1866. Sur quelques cranes antiques trouvés en Italie. *Bull soc anthropol Paris* **1** (2 sér): 82–94.

Vogt, K C 1868. Sur le crane du vallée d'Arno. *Bull Soc Anthropol Paris* **III** (2 sér): 400–404.

Volz, W 1896. [On Dubois's *Pithecanthropus* Jahr-Berl schles Gesellsch vaterl **74**: 5–8.

Vries, de H & K P Oakley 1959. Radiocarbon dating of the Piltdown skull and jaw. *Nature* **184**: 224–225.

Waldeyer, W 1895. [Remarks on *Pithecanthropus*]. *Z Ethnol* **27**: 88.

Wallace, A R 1887. The antiquity of man in North America. *Nineteenth Century Mag* **22**: 667–679.

Warren, S H 1905. On the origin of "eolithic" flints by natural causes, especially by the foundering effects of drifts. *J Roy Anthropol Inst* **35**: 337–364.

Warren, S H 1912. [Review of Sollas' *Ancient Hunters*]. *Man* **12**: 203–206.

Warren, S H 1914a. The experimental investigation of flint fracture and its application to problems of human implements. *J Roy Anthropol Inst* **44**: 412–450.

Warren, S H 1914b. The eolithic controversy. *Geol Mag* (ns) **I**: 546–552.

Warren, S H 1921. A natural 'Eolith' factory beneath the Thanet Sand. *Quart soc Lond* **76**: 238–253.

Warren, S H 1922. The Red Crag flints of Foxhall. *Man No 22*, pp 87–89.

Warren, S H 1923. Sub-soil flint flaking. *Proc Geol Assoc London* **34**: 153–175.

Waterston, D 1913. The Piltdown mandible. *Nature* **92**: 319.

Weidenreich, F 1928. Entwicklungs und Wassentypen des Homo primigenius. *Natur und Mus* **58**: 1–13, 51–62.

Weidenreich, F 1937. Dentition of *Sinanthropus pekinensis*: a comparative odontography of the hominids. *Palaeontol Sinica* n s D No. 1.

Weidenreich, F 1943. Skull of *Sinanthropus pekinensis*: a comparative study of a primitive hominoid skull. *Palaeontol Sinica* n s D. No. 10.

Weidenreich, F 1946. *Apes, Giants and Man.* Chicago.

Weigers, F 1952. Das geologische Alter Schädels von Fontéchevade (Charente). *Naturwiss Rundschau* **2**: 61–64.

Weiner, J S (1955) 1980. *The Piltdown Forgery.* Chicago. [Originally published by Oxford University Press].

Weiner, J S 1973. Grafton Elliot Smith and Piltdown. *In*: S Zuckerman (Ed), *The Concepts of Human Evolution.* London. p 23.

Weiner, J S, K P Oakley & W E Le Gros Clark 1953. The solution to the Piltdown problem. *Bull Br Mus nat Hist* (Geol) **2**: 141–146.

Weiner, J S et al. 1955. Further contributions to the solution of the Piltdown problem. *Bull Br Mus nat Hist* (Geol) **2**(6): 225–287.

Whewell, W J 1832. [Review of 2nd volume of] "Principles of Geology" by Charles Lyell. *Quart Rev* **47**: 103–132.

White, H J O 1926. The Geology of the Country near Lewes. *Mem Geol Surv England & Wales.* Expl Sheet 319. London.

Winslow, J & A Meyer 1983. The perpetrator at Piltdown. *Science 83* **4**: 32–43.

Wilson, J T 1938. Sir Grafton Elliot Smith (1871–1937). *Obit Not Fellows Roy Soc Lond* **2**: 323–333.

Winlsow, J H & A Meyer 1983. The perpetrator at Piltdown. *Science* **83**: 32–43.

Wood, S V & J L Rome 1868. On the glacial and postglacial structure of Lincolnshire and southeast Yorkshire. *Quart J Geol Soc* **24**: 146–184.

Woodward, A S 1889–1901. *Catalogue of the Fossil Fishes in the British Museum (Natural History). Part I (1889), Part II (1891), Part III (1895), Part IV (1901). London.*

Woodward, A S 1890. [with C D Sherborn] *A Catalogue of British Fossil Vertebrata.* London.

Woodward, A S 1892. On a mammalian tooth from the Wealden Formation of Hastings. *Proc Zool Soc,* pp 585–586

Woodward, A S 1898. *Outlines of Vertebrate Palaeontology for Students of Zoology* Cambridge.

Woodward, A S 1911. On some mammalian teeth from the Wealden of Hastings. *Quart J Geol Soc Lond* **67**: 278–281.

Woodward, A S 1914a. [Note on Piltdown excavations in 1914]. *Nature* **94**: 5.

Woodward, A S 1914b. On the lower jaw of an anthropoid ape (*Dryopithecus*) from the Upper Miocene of Lérida (Spain). *Quart J Geol Soc Lond* **70**: 316–320.

Woodward, A S 1914c. On an apparently Palaeolithic engraving on a bone from Sherborne (Dorset). *Quart J Geol Soc Lond* **70**: 100–103.

Woodward, A S 1915. *A Guide to the Fossil Remains of Man in the Department of Geology and Palaeontology in the British Musuem (Natural History)* London.

Woodward, A S 1916. [Obituary] Charles Dawson F.S.A., F.G.S. *Geol Mag* **3** (6): 477–479

Woodward, A S 1917. Fourth note on the Piltdown gravel with evidence of a second skull of *Eoanthropus dawsoni. Quart J Geol Soc Lond* **73**: 1–10.

Woodward, A S 1925. The fossil ape from Taungs. *Nature* **115**: 235–236.

Woodward, A S 1926. The Palaeolithic drawing of a horse from Sherborne, Dorset. *Nature* **117**: 86.

Woodward, A S 1933. The Second Piltdown skull. *Nature* **131**: 242.

Woodward, A S 1935. Recent progress in the study of early man. *Rept Brit Ass Adv Sci* (Norwich), pp 129–142.

Woodward, A S 1948. *The Earliest Englishman.* London.

Wright, R F 1943. Samuel Allinson Woodhead. *The Analyst, J Soc Pub Analysts* **68**: 297.

Wright, W 1916a. [Review of A Keith's "Antiquity of Man"] *Man* **16**: 124–127.

Wright, W 1916b. The endocranial cast of the Piltdown skull. *Man* **16**: 158.

Zuckerman, S 1972. The Piltdown men. Letter in *Times Literary Supplement* (27 October), pp 1287.

Zuckerman, S 1973. Sir Grafton Elliot Smith 1871–1937. *In:* S. Zuckerman (Ed), *The Concepts of Human Evolution* London. pp 3–21 [see also *Symp zool Soc Lond* (1973) No. 33, 3–21].

Subject Index

Name Index

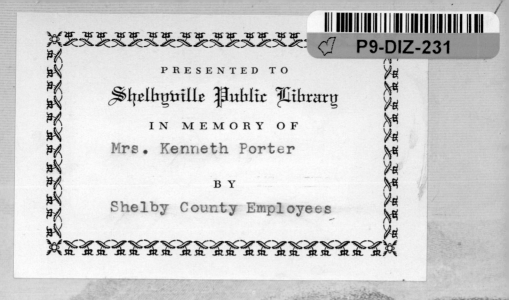

DISCARD

ROBERT BURNS

THE MAN AND THE POET

Robert Burns, 1795/6, Reid.
Courtesy Scottish National Portrait Gallery.

ROBERT BURNS

THE MAN AND THE POET

A Round, Unvarnished Account

Robert T. Fitzhugh

*Illustrated with Photographs
and Maps*

HOUGHTON MIFFLIN COMPANY BOSTON

1970

To

Dorothea

whose first present from the author
was a volume of Burns' poems

PREFACE

Deep in the general heart of men
His power survives.
WORDSWORTH

This book aims to deliver a round, unvarnished account of Robert Burns, one of the dozen major British poets, and a man of striking paradoxes. He has always fascinated both the parson and the profane, the Scot and the non-Scot, the bawdy and the sentimental, the patriot and the reformer, the Left and the Right, and those who relish song or satire. Of late he has attracted new-model analysts whose attentions would have probably pleased and certainly puzzled him. All of which is merely to say that Burns has always been an incandescent figure who moves readers according to their taste and interest. He flashed into popularity in 1786, and his fame endures around the world.

In his verse, Burns is ever a conscious and sophisticated craftsman, and in his famous vernacular poems he is a poet of superb gifts and grace, who adapted the popular forms and materials which he used as models, stamping his own work with brilliant originality. Given a marginal gloss, the vernacular poems are perfectly clear; in fact, much easier to read than Shakespeare. Burns is, moreover, one of the few literary figures who, like Dr. Johnson and Lord Byron, have a striking personality.

Burns is here presented mainly as he spoke for himself, and as those who knew him spoke of him. It is a sound principle to take him at his word unless there is specific reason to believe he may have been mistaken. At times, however, he was consciously vague, and occasionally he was given to syncopated statement. Within the limits of human fallibility, punctuation and spelling of quoted matter have been reproduced exactly.

Since there would be small reason for a life of Robert Burns had he not been a poet, the poetry is quoted extensively, both as prime biographical material and as a delight in itself. It should be noted, however, that Burns' poems and his songs are treated separately. Burns did not think of the songs as poems; they were always written for tunes, and were intended to be sung.

While avoiding dialogue with preceding biographers, this life attempts to deal straightforwardly with controversies, presenting the evidence, indicating probabilities, but not forcing conclusions. All readers who are familiar with the scholarship and criticism on Burns will recognize the many debts in this book, which are hereby acknowledged fully, freely, and happily. More detailed acknowledgment will appear in the Post Scripts to the various sections. A List of Major Sources, each with the abbreviation used for reference to it, will be found on page 445.

PERSONAL NOTE

This biographer's humility was quickened by his discovering that some cherished perceptions had been anticipated, and that even distinguished predecessors had erred. He can only hope that his own work will be a helpful addition and summary, and that any errors will be inconspicuous.

Writing a book is a lonely course with much comforting support along the way. Friends and colleagues are patiently curious about one's progress and often make helpful suggestions; strangers become wonderfully kind; and librarians graciously lighten one's burdens. To be particular: my colleague Bruce Park read and commented on an early and disorderly version of the manu-

script, and my fellow-Burnsian John Weston took time he could
ill afford to criticize the nearly completed text. Dr. Stanley Bardwell, my physician, interested himself in Burns' health record and
wrote a clinical analysis of the available data. Professors Raymond
Bentman, T. Crawford, David Daiches, Joel Egerer, James Kinsley, Ross Roy, and Robert Thornton answered questions and
argued points to my great advantage. Mr. H. J. R. Bankes made
available a photograph of Maria Riddell's portrait; Sir Thomas
Innes, Lord Lyon King of Arms, responded most courteously to
an inquiry; Mr. Charles P. Finlayson, Keeper of Manuscripts,
Edinburgh University Library, searched university records for the
date of Robert Riddell's honorary degree; Jinny and Wendy
Neefus and Bill Coons, of Hudson, New York, went far beyond
the call of duty in helping prepare illustrations; Mr. W. A.
Findlater of Dublin sent details of his ancestor, Alexander Findlater, Burns' Excise Supervisor, and the photostat of a letter from
Burns to him; Dr. Douglas Guthrie of Edinburgh supplied explanations of Eighteenth Century medical terms; Mr. Edward
McKiernan, Librarian of the Free Public Library, Campbeltown,
searched newspaper files and found a long-sought-for confirmation; Mr. Desmond Donaldson, County Librarian, Dumfriesshire,
in response to a question about another matter, sent a copy of John
Syme's obituary; Dr. Dwight Burkhardt interrupted his own work
to make Xerox copies of articles in medical journals; and my
fellow Player John Mulholland, and the Players librarian, Mr.
Louis A. Rachow, took a warm interest in providing engaging
details of Learned Pigs. For encouragement and valuable criticism
I want to thank Mr. Craig Wylie and Mrs. Daphne Ehrlich of
Houghton Mifflin Company.

A collection of useful books built up over the years, and the
magic of Xerox, made it possible to write this book in the relaxed
quiet of a New York State farmhouse. For most helpful assistance,
my thanks go to the staffs of the Widener Library, the British
Museum, the library of Brooklyn College, the New York Public

Library, the Yale University Library, the Huntington Library, and the libraries of the University of Michigan, the University of Pennsylvania, and the University of Virginia. Likewise to the staffs of *English Language Notes, University of Colorado Studies, Queens Quarterly,* and the *Dalhousie Review,* and to the Saltire Society.

A special word of appreciation is due the National Library of Scotland and the Scottish National Portrait Gallery for many courtesies, and to Hodder and Stoughton, Ltd., and the Clarendon Press for generous permissions to quote.

Finally, Brooklyn College has facilitated my work by giving me a reduced teaching load for two semesters.

ROBERT T. FITZHUGH

No Ruz Farm
Craryville, New York
January 25, 1970

CONTENTS

ILLUSTRATIONS

Endpaper — Nithdale above Ellisland, 1805
Frontispiece — Robert Burns, 1795/6, Reid

A Learned Pig
Margaret Chalmers
William Smellie
Agnes M'Lehose ("Clarinda")
Glasses given Clarinda by Burns in parting
Maria Riddell (Mrs. Walter Riddell)
Robert Riddell of Glenriddell
Hermitage at Glenriddell, near Ellisland
Francis Grose
John Syme
Alexander Cunningham
Jessie Lewars
Dr. James Maxwell

Buildings and Places Associated with Burns

Alloway Kirk, 1805
Burns' Birthplace, Alloway, 1805
Burns' Cottage
Mt. Oliphant
Lochlea
Mossgiel
Ellisland
Burns' last residence

Maps

CHRONOLOGICAL TABLE

An independent compilation, with details from the chronology prepared by DeLancey Ferguson for *Pride and Passion,* this table is designed to supplement a text in which relationships or situations are often presented entire, although they may overlap others in time.

1757 December 15, William Burnes (1721–1784) marries Agnes Broun (1737–1820).

1759 January 25, Robert Burns is born at Alloway. (His brother Gilbert is also born there, September 28, 1760; and his sisters Agnes, September 30, 1762, and Annabella, November 14, 1764.)

1765 Robert and Gilbert begin their schooling under John Murdoch.

1766 William Burnes rents Mt. Oliphant farm, moving in at Whitsunday. (William Burns is born there, July 30, 1767; John, July 10, 1769; and Isabella, June 27, 1771.)

1768 Robert and the family distressed by *Titus Andronicus.*

1772 Robert and Gilbert go in alternate weeks to study at Dalrymple.

1773 Robert studies grammar and French with Murdoch in Ayr for several weeks; he writes *Handsome Nell.*

1775 Burns attends his first dancing school; during the summer he goes to Kirkoswald.

1777 The William Burnes family moves to Lochlea Farm.

1780 The Tarbolton Bachelor's Club is organized.

1781 Burns is jilted by Alison Begbie (?); in July, he becomes a Mason; and late in the summer, he goes to Irvine, where he meets Richard Brown and suffers a severe illness. William Burnes' dispute with his Lochlea landlord begins.

1783 In January, Burns wins a £3 prize for flaxseed; in April, he begins his Commonplace Book; and in the autumn, with Gilbert, he rents Mossgiel farm.

1784 January 27, William Burnes is successful at law against his landlord. February 13, William Burnes dies. The family soon moves to Mossgiel.

1785 May 22, Elizabeth Paton bears Burns a daughter, Elizabeth. He begins to write his major poetry, and he meets Jean Armour.

1786 Burns plans emigration to Jamaica. April 3, he issues proposals for his Kilmarnock edition; he is repudiated by the Armours; May 14 (?), he takes farewell of Mary Campbell. In late July, the Kilmarnock edition is published; September 3, Jean bears twins, Robert and Jean; in October, Mary Campbell dies; November 27, Burns leaves Mauchline for Edinburgh, arriving November 29; December 14, the Edinburgh edition of the *Poems* is announced.

1787 April 17, the Edinburgh *Poems* are published; April 21, Burns sells his copyright to Creech. May 5–June 1, Burns tours the Borders; June 2 (?), he receives Meg Cameron's appeal in Dumfries; June 8, he returns to Mauchline. In late June, he tours the West Highlands, and on July 25, he reports Jean to be "in for it again." During July, Burns writes his autobiographical letter to Dr. Moore, dated August 2. August 15, he settles with Meg Cameron in Edinburgh; and August 25–September 16, he tours the Highlands with William Nicol. In early October, he visits Stirling, Harvieston, and the two Ochtertyres; and in late November, Dalswinton. December 4, back in Edinburgh, he meets Agnes M'Lehose (Clarinda), and the night of December 7/8, he dislocates his knee.

1788 January 4, Burns visits Mrs. M'Lehose for the first time; the affair grows in fervency until he leaves Edinburgh, February 18. February 25, he returns to Mauchline, after visiting Glasgow, Paisley, Dunlop, and Kilmarnock; he establishes Jean in a room in Mauchline, and goes off to visit Ellisland with John Tennant, returning March 2. March 3, Jean bears twins, one dying March 10 and one March 23. March 18, in Edinburgh, Burns signs a lease of Ellisland (the terms having been agreed on with Patrick Miller, March 13). March 20, Burns leaves Edinburgh, after taking ardent farewells of Agnes M'Lehose. (While in the city he had negotiated his Excise commission, issued officially July 14.) During April and May, Burns receives Excise instructions in Tarbolton from his friend James Findlay, and qualifies for duty. June 12, he settles at Ellisland; and August 5, he and Jean acknowledge their previous irregular marriage. In November, Jenny Clow bears Burns a son; and in December, Jean joins him at the Isle.

1789 Mid-February–February 28, Burns goes to Edinburgh to close accounts with Creech and to settle with Jenny Clow. August 19, Francis Wallace Burns is born to Jean. September, Burns begins his Excise duties, and by November 8 is ill with a "most violent cold."

1790 In July, Burns is transferred to the Dumfries 3d Division, tobacco. July 24, William Burns dies in London. December 1, Burns sends MS of *Tam o' Shanter* to Francis Grose.

1791 January 27, Burns is placed on the list of those eligible for promotion to Examiner and Supervisor. March 31, Anne Park bears Burns a daughter, Elizabeth; April 9, Jean bears him a son, William Nicol. April 11, Grose's *Antiquities* is published, with *Tam o' Shanter*. (The poem had appeared in two magazines during March.) June 19–22, Burns visits Ayrshire to attend his brother Gilbert's wedding; August 25, the Ellisland crops are sold; September 10, the Ellisland lease is renounced; early November, the Ellisland "farming things" things are sold; November 11, Burns moves to Dumfries. December 1 (?)–December 11 (?), Burns goes to Edinburgh, where he takes further farewells of Agnes M'Lehose, now planning to rejoin her husband in Jamaica.

1792 February 29, the schooner *Rosamond* is captured; April 10, Burns is made an honorary member of the Royal Company of Archers, Edinburgh; April 19, the *Rosamond's* carronades are sold; by April 26, and perhaps as early as February, Burns is promoted to the Dumfries Port Division. September 16, he writes his first letter to George Thomson; November 21, Elizabeth Riddell Burns is born to Jean; late December, and early January, 1793, the Excise Board inquires into Burns' loyalty.

1793 February 1, France declares war against England. In February, the second Edinburgh edition of *Poems* is published, with additions. May 19, Burns moves to Mill Vennel; July 27–August 2, he takes his first Galloway tour with Syme; in August, the sedition trials are held in Edinburgh; c. August 30, Burns sends *Scots Wha Hae* to Thomson. At the end of December, the party occurs which results in the Riddell quarrel.

1794 January 12, Burns returns Maria Riddell's Commonplace Book; April 21, Robert Riddell dies. June, c. 24–c. 28, Burns again tours Galloway with Syme; August 12, James Glencairn Burns is born to Jean; in late December, Burns is appointed Acting Supervisor. The final edition during Burns' life of *Poems*, Edinburgh, is published this year.

1795 In January, Burns helps organize the Dumfries Volunteers; in January (?), Mrs. Riddell seeks a reconciliation; in April, Alexander Findlater resumes his duties as Supervisor; in September, Elizabeth Riddell Burns dies. From December on, Burns is severely ill.

1796 July 3–18, Burns is at the Brow; July 21, he dies, and is buried July 25, the day his son Maxwell is born.

ROBERT BURNS
THE MAN AND THE POET

I

PROFILE

What an antithetical mind! — tenderness, roughness —
delicacy, coarseness — sentiment, sensuality —
soaring and grovelling, dirt and deity —
all mixed up in that compound of inspired clay!

LORD BYRON

Robert Burns was a witty compound of satire, sentiment, and sex, a man of "general talents" and of great personal force. One of his shrewdest admirers felt that poetry was "actually not his *forte.*" However that may have been, during a few brilliant years while he was obscure and free and sure of a sympathetic audience for Scots vernacular poetry, he created a body of work that made him one of the major poets who have written in the British Isles. Largely by following the cues of Robert Fergusson, and those of a few other minor models, Burns turned his poverty-stricken life, and the affairs of obscure Mauchline parish, into a splendid body of Poems Chiefly in the Scottish Dialect. "Where materials would have been wanting perhaps to almost every other mortal, he like an electrical kite soars aloft, & draws down etherial [fire] from heaven." Thus William Nicol, the gifted and irascible Latin master, a friend for whom Burns named a son, and from whom he once got an affectionate letter of reproof beginning "Dear Christless Bobie." *

* This facetious greeting is the only known occasion when Burns was called "Bobbie" by anyone who knew him. Affectionately, he was "Robbie," and familiarly, "Rob," "Rab," or "Robin."

When publication had brought fame, and marriage had brought a family and a government job to support it, and when the great excitement of his Mauchline years had cooled, Burns found that he had lost his freedom to speak as he wished, and had gained a more sophisticated audience with whom he felt no easy rapport. He had, moreover, said what he wanted to say, in the way he knew best how to say it, and he did not wish to repeat. With different poetic modes, both before and after his Kilmarnock and Edinburgh editions, he had only limited success. But when he turned again to the vernacular, in *Tam o' Shanter*, he wrote his finest poem. Those who advised Burns that he would not be read in Scots have been proved wrong the past hundred and seventy years.

It is said that burdensome and uncongenial work as an Exciseman during Burns' last decade interfered with his writing, but he said no, and his burden was certainly not so great then, particularly after he moved to Dumfries in 1791, as it had been when he produced his famous poems. Indeed, the *volume* of his poetic output did not decline much. He remained the vital, sociable man he had been since boyhood, alert to his times, provoked by the riddle of religion, full of irreverent delight at the human comedy, patriotic, quixotic, outraged by man's inhumanity to man, bedeviled by sex, the center of any company he was ever in. Three weeks before his death, his mind was "seldom greater." If not flush in his later years, he was not poverty-stricken, either; nor was he carefu'; and he lived simply on his income in the "hugry-mugry" fashion he was used to — at times a little in debt or behind in his rent, not frequenting his house too much latterly, but a kind and solicitous husband, and an affectionate father concerned for his children.

Burns was an honest man, a generous man, a "feeling" man (he called himself the "child of skinless sensibility"), and sometimes a pawky man, but he was never, nor did he ever want to be, a respectable bourgeois. He remained a peasant with a healthy disrespect for the "dirt o' gentry." "He knew, felt, and ardently loved what is good and great, and occasionally practiced these emotions — But too often 'his pulses maddening play' drove him headlong from these heights." So wrote his most intimate friend of the later years, John Syme. He himself had confided to his Commonplace Book, March, 1784 (age 25): "I have often coveted the acquaintance of that part of mankind commonly known by the ordinary phrase of Blackguards, . . . those who by thoughtless Prodigality, or headstrong Passions have been driven to ruin: . . . I have yet found among them, in not a few instances, some of the noblest Virtues, Magnanimity, Generosity, disinterested friendship and even modesty, in the highest perfection."

During his last six years, until his death in 1796, Burns remained essentially, and not surprisingly, much the man he had been in the previous decade. For this reason, observations of Burns in this period, like the following by Maria Riddell, his close friend, are interesting for their retrospective illumination of him throughout his mature life:

Many others, perhaps, may have ascended to prouder heights in the regions of Parnassus, but none certainly ever outshone Burns in the charms — the sorcery, I would almost call it, of fascinating conversation, the spontaneous eloquence of social argument, or the unstudied poignancy of brilliant repartee; nor was any man, I believe, ever gifted with a larger portion of the, "*vivida vis animi.*"

His personal endowments were perfectly correspondent to the qualifications of his mind: his form was manly; his action, energy itself; devoid in great measure perhaps of those graces, of that polish, acquired only in the refinement of societies where in early life he could have no opportunities of mixing; but where, such was the irresistible power of attraction that encircled him, though his appearance and manner were always peculiar, he never failed to delight and excel. His figure seemed to bear testimony to his earlier destination and employments. It seemed rather moulded by nature for the rough exercises of Agriculture, than the gentler cultivation of the Belles

Lettres. His features were stamped with the hardy character of independence, and the firmness of conscious, though not arrogant, pre-eminence; the animated expressions of countenance were almost peculiar to himself; the rapid lightnings of his eye were always the harbingers of some flash of genius, whether they darted the fiery glances of insulted and indignant superiority, or beamed with the impassioned sentiment of fervid and impetuous affections. His voice alone could improve upon the magic of his eye: sonorous, replete with the finest modulations, it alternately captivated the ear with the melody of poetic numbers, the perspicuity of nervous reasoning, or the ardent sallies of enthusiastic patriotism.

The keenness of satire was, I am almost at a loss whether to say, his forte or his foible; for though nature had endowed him with a portion of the most pointed excellence in that dangerous talent, he suffered it too often to be the vehicle of personal, and sometimes unfounded animosities. . . . The vivacity of his wishes and temper was indeed checked by almost habitual disappointments, which sat heavy on a heart, that acknowledged the ruling passion of independence, without having ever been placed beyond the grasp of penury. . . .

He was seldom, indeed never, implacable in his resentments, and sometimes it has been alleged, not inviolably faithful in his engagements of friendship. . . . His inconstancy and caprice, I am inclined to believe, originated less in levity of sentiment, than from an extreme impetuosity of feeling. . . . He was candid and manly in the avowal of his errors, and *his avowal* was a *reparation*. . . .

The penchant Burns had uniformly acknowledged for the festive pleasures of the table, and toward the fairer and softer objects of nature's creation, has been the rallying point from whence the attacks of his censors have been uniformly directed; and to these, it must be confessed, he shewed himself no stoic.

Thus runs Mrs. Riddell's famous testimony, "so discerning and impartial in understanding, that it remains the best thing written of him by a contemporary critic."

Robert Burns grew up under the influence and control of an affectionate, shrewd, and pious father, whom he revered, and whom he later described as a man of "stubborn, ungainly Integrity, and headlong ungovernable Irrascibillity." William Burnes saw life as "a continual struggle between animal instinct and controlling reason," a struggle to attain inner peace and to "exalt the mind above irregular passions," and so to give animal life pleasure and joy and thus achieve the beauty of holiness. He did not subscribe to the orthodox Calvinist belief in predestination, but felt that heaven was open to all who lived a good life and sincerely repented of their sins. Burns was deeply impressed by this teaching, and speaks of his own "idiot piety" as a child.

He also speaks of "cheerless gloom" and galley slave labor. The Burns family leased and rented land which they farmed. They were not hired farm laborers, cotters. They lived as others of their class, a no less grinding life for being common. They ate poorly and worked hard, Robert doing his full share. But William saw to it that his boys learned to write well, and Robert certainly learned to read and to understand what he read. No one has yet made a full study of Burns' reading, but its extent and acuteness are at once apparent to anyone familiar with the Eighteenth Century and with Burns' letters. He was very much a man of his time.

Upon his father's death in February, 1784, Robert became head of the family and set out earnestly with his brother to make a success of farming on his own. But as one might imagine of a young man who had been restricted as he had been, Burns' irregular passions and animal instincts asserted themselves both before his father's death, and considerably more afterward. Putting his religious beliefs to one side, he became the buoyant leader of some high-spirited young men in the community; he challenged the "auld licht" Calvinism that prevailed in his parish, voicing his father's opinions; and he fathered a bastard on Elizabeth Paton. It was not so much his challenge to the auld lichts, or his reckless general self-assertion, or his fornication, that made him notorious in a conservative rural district, as the poems he wrote rejoicing in what he had done and calling down ridicule

on worthies whom he had shocked and who wished to discipline
him. The simple result was that by 1786 when Burns (age 27)
had failed as a farmer, and had written the poems which made
him famous; when the Kirk Session had denounced him, and he
was dodging a warrant sworn out by James Armour for support
of his daughter Jean's coming child; he decided to resolve his
difficulties by emigrating to Jamaica. But before leaving Scotland
he wished to try for fame as a poet by publishing, and thought
that he might make enough money from his venture to pay his
passage. He succeeded on both counts, but he did not go to
Jamaica, and he paid some of the money to Elizabeth Paton to
settle *her* paternity claim. The warrant of James Armour was
allowed to lapse. Burns' edition brought out in nearby Kilmarnock is probably the most notable first volume of poems ever
published. It contains much of his best poetry, it made his name,
and it got him free of his Mauchline enemies. But it did not
change him much. He continued, for example, to help support
his mother, brother, and daughter at Mossgiel, even to sinking
half his Edinburgh profits in the enterprise. Burns had warm
family loyalties. He once spoke casually of his youthful correspondent, James Candlish, as "the earliest friend except my only
brother that I have on earth," and when his poor Uncle Robert
died, he took his uncle's children into his own home.

This is not the place to tell the story of Burns' loves, but it is
the place to put straight the general pattern of his life and character, in which his relations with women are both prominent and
revealing. Burns fascinated women of all classes and degrees. His
address to them was "extremely deferential, and always with a
turn either to the pathetic or humorous, which engaged their
attention particularly." He was handsome and vital. His approach no doubt varied with the station and qualities of the
woman, but essentially he regarded women as "the blood-royal
of life," and lovemaking as life's greatest pleasure. He puts it all
candidly to his correspondent George Thomson:

I am a very Poet in my enthusiasm of the Passion. — The welfare
& happiness of the beloved Object, is the *first* & *inviolate* sentiment
that pervades my soul; & whatever pleasures I might wish for, or
whatever might be the raptures they would give me, yet, if they
interfere & clash with that *first* principle, it is having these pleasures
at a dishonest price; & Justice forbids, & Generosity disdains the
purchase! — As to the herd of the Sex, who are good for little or
nothing else, I have made no such agreement with myself; but where
the Parties are capable of, & the Passion is, the true Divinity of love —
the man who can act otherwise than I have laid down, is a Villain!

A brief account of his life with Jean Armour will tell much
about him, and her, and Eighteenth Century Ayrshire.* Robert
and Jean met as village neighbors, and fell in love; and Jean
became pregnant. He offered to marry her, and indeed thought
he had done so, but her parents refused to recognize him, as too
poor, and probably too scandalous, for a son-in-law. Outraged,
he submitted to public rebuke in church for fornication in order
to receive a certificate as a bachelor from his minister. Jean bore
twins, one of whom died, Robert's mother taking the other,
Robert, Jr. After Burns' winter in Edinburgh, he returned rich
by Mauchline standards, and famous. Jean's parents made him
welcome and locked the two in a room. Burns eventually went
back to Edinburgh to settle accounts with his publisher, where
he had the famous affair with Clarinda, thinking little of Jean,
again pregnant, and when he returned to Mauchline in the spring
of 1788, he wrote to Robert Ainslie, in Edinburgh, of his meeting
with Jean, now nearly come to term.

Mauchline, 3d March, 1788

MY DEAR FRIEND,
    . . . I have been through sore tribulation, and under much buffet-
ing of the Wicked One, since I came to this country. Jean I found
banished like a martyr — forlorn, destitute, and friendless; all for the

* The attitudes and mores of the Ayrshire peasantry of that time were not those
of the Victorian and later middle class.

good old cause: I have reconciled her to her fate: I have reconciled
her to her mother: I have taken her a room: I have taken her to my
arms: I have given her a mahogany bed: I have given her a guinea;
and I have fucked her till she rejoiced with joy unspeakable and full
of glory. But — as I always am on every occasion — I have been
prudent and cautious to an astounding degree; I swore her, privately
and solemnly, never to attempt any claim on me as a husband, even
though anybody should persuade her she had such a claim, which
she has not, neither during my life, nor after my death. She did all
this like a good girl, and I took the opportunity of some dry horselitter,
and gave her such a thundering scalade that electrified the very
marrow of her bones. O, what a peacemaker is a guid weel-willy
pintle! It is the mediator, the guarantee, the umpire, the bond of
union, the solemn league and covenant, the plenipotentiary, the
Aaron's rod, the Jacob's staff, the prophet Elisha's pot of oil, the
Ahasuerus' sceptre, the sword of mercy, the philosopher's stone,
the horn of plenty, the Tree of Life between Man and Woman. . . .

Your faithful Friend,
R. B.

Despite his resolves, within a few days he had married Jean.
It was a contented marriage. She was devoted to him and cherished him, in Professor Ferguson's happy adaptation, "not weigh-
ing his merits, but pardoning his offenses." He reported the event
to his friends in a formula:

Shortly after my last return to Ayrshire, I married "my Jean." This
was not in consequence of the attachment of romance perhaps; but I
had a long and much-loved fellow creature's happiness or misery in
my determination, and I durst not trifle with so important a deposite.
Nor have I any cause to repent it. If I have not got polite tattle, modish
manners, and fashionable dress, I am not sickened and disgusted with
the multiform curse of boarding-school affectation; and I have got the
handsomest figure, the sweetest temper, the soundest constitution, and
the kindest heart in the country.

Burns and Jean had five more children,* the last born the day

---

* When Burns was farming at Ellisland, he wrote his friend and Excise Supervisor, Alexander Findlater, when sending him some eggs, "Mrs. B——, like a

of his funeral. Jean also took into her household Burns' daughter by Anne Park, and Robert Chambers reports her having said with unique authority, "Oor Robin should hae had twa wives."

Of Burns' later years, John Syme noted, "Tho Burns did not resort much to his own house yet he ever spoke affectionately & endearingly of his wife & family."

Maria Riddell wrote to Dr. Currie, December 28, 1799:

Burns said little or nothing about his Wife to me latterly, but as I believe her conduct, subsequent to their union by marriage, was exemplary towards him, so it is just to add that he always spoke of her with a high tribute of respect and esteem. He did not love her, but he was far from insensible to the indulgence and patience, "the meekness with which she bore her faculties" on many occasions very trying to the tempers of most individuals of our sex.

The "occasions" of infidelity mentioned by Mrs. Riddell are given greater significance by a letter from Thomas Telford, the engineer, to Thomas Boyd, Dumfries contractor.

Shrewsbury, 7th Decr. 1794

DEAR SIR

. . . I hope you informed my friend Robin Burns that I was very desirous of paying my respects, but tell him that unless he leaves off his baudy songs, that "he'll get his Fairen. — 'In Hell they'll roast him like a Herring.'" — Tho if he goes on in his old way not even a *she Devil* will be able to meet with a Milt* in him.

But after you have abused him properly, do tell him, that the first time I meet Mr. Alison, we will drink his health, for in case we should be consigned to a *Neuk* in his neighbourhood, it would prove some consolation to be on decent terms with one another. — Farewell — I am yours very sincerely

THOS TELFORD

---

good true wife, looking on my taste as a Standard, & knowing that she cannot give me anything — *eatable* — more agreable than a new-laid egg, she begs your acceptance of a few."
* *milt* — the secretion of the male generative organs of fishes.

Of Burns and liquor, three considerations must hold: he was a sociable man in a hard-drinking world, he had organically poor health, and he enjoyed low social position. As C. K. Sharpe, "the Scottish Walpole," remarks, "His intemperance was venial — when one considers that the gentry with whom he associated generally caroused with brandy and water whenever they met in the morning — and never dined together without getting drunk." And Catherine Carswell comments, "We need go no further than two great contemporaries of Burns who were blessed with better constitutions and kinder nurtures than fell to his share. Between them they ruled the British Empire for many years during which they were seldom sober." Like William Pitt, and Henry Dundas, his lieutenant for Scotland, Burns did his work. Unlike them, he also wrote his songs. He said, "I love drinking now and then. It defecates the standing pool of thought." He also wrote, "Occasional hard drinking is the devil to me. — Against this I have again & again bent my resolution, & have greatly succeeded. — Taverns, I have totally abandoned: it is the private parties in the family way, among the hard drinking gentlemen of this country, that does me the mischief — but even this, I have more than half given over." (January 2, 1793, to Mrs. Dunlop.)

As a young man, writing poems about Scotch Drink, Burns had little money for dissipation, and his brother reports that he was of sober habit. In Edinburgh, he seems to have enjoyed much convivial company. As he grew older, his friend Syme reports, "He loved wine and would take it freely & in considerable quantities but I never saw him brutally drunk — I have seen many *gentlemen* more drunk than ever I saw Burns — I never saw Burns drink a *dram* but as any Gentleman might." This in the Eighteenth Century might cover a good deal. Alexander Findlater comments: "That when he sat down in an evening with a few friends whom he liked, he was apt to prolong the social hour beyond the bounds which prudence would dictate, is unquestionable." Finally, on March 11, 1828, Sir Walter Scott wrote to John Lockhart, then engaged on his life of Burns, "I heard from Mr. Miller Dalswinton's [Burns' landlord's] eldest son . . . when Burns came to stay at Dalswinton all night as he often did, he used to stipulate for a bottle of brandy in his sleeping-room and drink it well nigh out before morning."

The pattern of indulgence here, and elsewhere, is clear enough. Likewise, elsewhere, the pattern of continued responsible activity as Exciseman and poet and head of a family. Likewise a record of poor health and illness all his life, and a rapid decline during his last eighteen months. He died of rheumatic fever, with possible terminal bacterial endocarditis. But there is no indication of alcoholism, and Burns no more died a drunken wastrel than Walter Scott or William Pitt. He did, however, provide a ready example for ill-informed clerical and other moralists who would not have been so active had Burns been a laird, or a lord, or obscure, or rich. An excellent case in point is that celebrated rake, Burns' neighbor James Boswell. Burns' "failings" and "follies" also made handy targets for those who noted he was not a gentleman, and who felt it unbecoming in him to hold liberal opinions on social reform, and to think and speak with improper respect of his betters.

Much of his biography, also, has been written with care not to offend the living, and particularly the upper classes, even at Burns' expense. Indeed, the patronizing tone and the class angle have been persistent elements in Burns biography since his death, mixed with dogged persistence in editing his character and selecting from his writing to fit special tastes. The present biographer, for example, was refused access to a considerable body of material in the nineteen thirties because it would "ruin the romantic concept of Burns," and he has no reason to believe that the guardian's attitude has changed.

Burns as he lived is much better than any revision, and the more fully he comes to be known, the more surely is his prediction to Jean on his deathbed being fulfilled: "Don't be afraid. I'll be more respected a hundred years after I'm dead than I am at present."

From the first, Burns wrote poetry because he wanted to say something he felt strongly about. He rhymed "for fun." His interests were men and their ways, and his own position in the world. He was bawdy, political, satiric, sentimental, impudent, humorous. He wrote of people he knew, and he spoke with the voice of men like his father, driven by landlords and oppressed by a class system. With life for his ilk short and bleak, and its only pleasures friendship and lovemaking, Burns accepted the prospect of "crazy, weary, joyless Eild [old age]" at forty, with beggary a likely prospect and death a kindly release, and he set out to enjoy his pleasures while he had youth.

He celebrated in his poems the honest man of good heart, and the sweet sonsy [jolly] lass, and the joys of friendship and love. He dignified simple life and spoke with zest of those even lower down than himself. He cried out for recognition of ability, wit, and worth, and he denounced oppression, privilege, and the unevenness of fortune. He contrasted the spontaneous, impulsive, "feeling" life with considered, dull attention to profit and advantage (what he called "Catch-the-plack"). He ridiculed pretension in religion, in politics — and in general. He depicted local life and customs. And he proclaimed that a poet should feel, should speak the language of the heart, should have a spark o' Nature's Fire.

Once he had pretty well exhausted his favorite themes in poetry, by 1787, Burns turned to an earlier enthusiasm, Scots song, becoming for a time "absolutely crazed" about it, and until his death serving as virtual editor of one famous collection and a major contributor to another. There was an Eighteenth Century vogue in both England and Scotland for Scotch folk songs and for songs in the folk manner (Professor Kinsley speaks of "more than thirty collections" between 1700 and 1782), so that here again Burns found himself writing for a sympathetic audience, in a congenial tradition, in the Scots-English mixture of his successful work, and with freedom to write as he pleased, particularly for his publisher and friend James Johnson. Moreover, instead of merely celebrating his native district as he had done in his poems, he was now celebrating all of Scotland, which pleased him. The range of human experience which he covered was much wider, also, than in his poems. And in the dramatic setting of songs he could say things which his position as a "Placeman" and head of a family would have made it ticklish to say outright. His songs were a major undertaking, requiring gifted craftsmanship and energetic devotion, and yielding rich satisfaction. Burns was busy with them until he died.

Some of his songs Burns merely collected and sent on to editors, others he ransacked from printed collections, many he modified, often building a song from a fragment or a chorus. Frequently he created songs for tunes without words. Always he composed with music in his head. He described his method to George Thomson:

Untill I am compleat master of a tune, in my own singing, (such as it is) I can never compose for it. — My way is: I consider the poetic Sentiment, correspondent to my idea of the musical expression; then I chuse my theme; begin one Stanza; when that is composed, which is generally the most difficult part of the business, I walk out, sit down now & then, look out for objects in Nature around me that are in unison or harmony with the cogitations of my fancy & workings of my bosom; humming every now & then the air with the verses I have framed: when I feel my Muse beginning to jade, I retire to the solitary fireside of my study, & there commit my effusions to paper; swinging, at intervals, on the hind-legs of my elbow-chair, by way of calling forth my own critical strictures, as my pen goes on. —
Seriously, this, at home, is almost invariably my way. — What damn'd Egotism!

Burns wrote again to Thomson on the same subject in 1794:

Whenever I want to be more than ordinary *in song;* to be in some degree equal to your diviner airs; do you imagine I fast & pray for the celestial emanation? — Tout au contraire! I have a glorious recipe, the very one that for his own use was invented by the Divinity of Healing & Poesy when erst he piped to the flocks of Admetus. — I put myself on a regimen of admiring a fine woman; & in proportion to the adorability of her charms, in proportion you are delighted with my verses.

A fuller discussion of Burns' achievement in song will be found in Section VI; many think it even greater than his achievement in poetry. Technically the songs are a virtuoso performance in marrying words to music, in fitting sentiment and illustration to melody. There is nothing comparable in our literature. Two dozen of the songs are among the finest lyrics we have, and these lyrics are true lyrics, for singing to music, not just for reading.

It should be added that since the Scots folk muse was often high-kilted, Burns created polite versions for publication, while making for himself and his friends a private collection of the choicer bawdry. "There is, there must be, some truth in original sin," he wrote to his friend Cleghorn. "My violent propensity to Bawdy convinces me of it. — Lack a day! if that species of Composition be the Sin against 'The Haly Ghaist,' 'I am the most offending soul alive.'" Here, too, he was mainly collector or improver, but sometimes also creator.

The key to any understanding of Burns is recognition of him as a complex, contradictory, and paradoxical man. In politics, for example, he recognized that the Union of Scotland and England in 1707 had brought security, economic opportunity, and relief from religious and political factionalism. But he lamented the loss of independence, he found Mary Queen of Scots more attractive than Queen Elizabeth I, and he responded better to the exiled Stuart kings than to those "obscure, beef-witted, insolent . . . foreigners" George I, II, and III. He supported the French Revolution in its early stages, and the American Revolution in retrospect. Yet he would have maintained himself to be a sturdy patriot, and so he was. His experiences with landlords and factors, a class system, and rotten borough government gave him great sympathy for the "Rights of Man" and for general social reform. Yet he joined a volunteer regiment when Great Britain was threatened by invasion from France.

Burns enjoyed attention from gentry and aristocracy, among whom he had friends and correspondents, and he was perfectly assured with them, if not always comfortable or gracious. But in general he envied those above him and spoke bitterly of patronizing superiors, privileged dullness, and class discrimination. He preferred honest worth to birth and breeding. "The rank is but the guinea's stamp, / The man's the gowd for a' that." And "gowd" Burns was more likely to find in humble circumstances. It is unfortunate that so little is on record of Burns among his own kind, and so much about his associations with his "superiors."

"He was prone to scarify, blister & reprobate timid, mean, crouching folks — but not to put himself forward as magnanimous & independent. — At times however he aimed at being the Superior — and to demolish competition." So, again, John Syme, echoing similar comments by others. But Burns could also be winning, kindly, generous, sympathetic.

Parish squabbles and windy preachers amused him, and petty parish tyranny infuriated him, especially when provoked by his own behavior. He retained a strong religious faith in a benevolent Creator, and he came to feel about Calvinist original sin that "the whole business is reversed, . . . We come in to this world with a heart & disposition to do good for it," but we soon find ourselves "under a kind of cursed necessity of turning selfish" in our own defense. "Experience of the weakness, not the strength, of human powers" made him "glad to grasp at revealed religion." Basically he felt that "The heart benevolent and kind / The most resembles God." His feelings about an afterlife varied, but he subscribed generally to this view: "All my fears & cares are of this world: if there is Another, an honest man has nothing to fear from it." And he added, "I hate a Man that wishes to be a Deist, but I fear, every fair, unprejudiced Enquirer must in some degree be a Sceptic." He continued a churchgoer and sermon critic, he led family worship at Mossgiel and Ellisland, and in his letters he was given to extended moral and theological reflections. Although he ridiculed preordained damnation, and salvation by faith alone, without good works, he wrote of the old Covenanters who had fought and died for that belief:

> The Solemn League and Covenant
>   Now brings a smile, now brings a tear.
> But sacred Freedom, too, was theirs:
>   If thou'rt a slave, indulge thy sneer.

Any effort to produce an orderly, consistent Burns must fail. He was not a man of doctrine or dogma. Like most of us, he had some loosely centered strong feelings which he expressed variously to different people in different circumstances. And like most of us he tended in his opinions to gratify his ego and relieve his distress.

One final, and summary, paradox. We can know Burns only when we see that the poetry was the man. If we rejoice in the poetry we must rejoice in the poet. Had he not been the man he was, he had not written the poetry he did. "His character," wrote his first editor and biographer, James Currie, "is displayed in almost every poem he wrote, to such as have the comprehension necessary to receive it. The very circumstance of Burns having pourtrayed himself in such vivid colours, is a decisive proof of his superior genius. . . . Inferior minds shrink from a full exposure of themselves."

II

GROWTH

And the Spring comes slowly up this way.

CHRISTABEL

Robert Burns was much like his father — intelligent, thought-ful, hard-working, kind, honest, independent, scrupulous in money matters, and fiercely proud ("the sport of strong passions"). These are disqualifying circumstances for commercial success, and as farmers, both father and son failed to prosper. A further reason for the family poverty was that during Burns' youth and young manhood, farmers without capital were hard pressed in Ayrshire. War brought inflation, depressed business, raised prices. In anticipation of more productive farming methods, landlords increased rents, taking their income out of the hides of tenants who knew only the older ways, or who had no money to improve with.

Burns' father, William Burnes (1721–1784),* was unable to rent good farms, he paid too much for those he did rent, and he tried to make a go of it by overworking himself and, later, his family. His motives were excellent and characteristic. He wished so far as possible to be his own man, and he wanted to keep his children about him so that they would grow up in a good atmosphere and not have to leave home and become farm

---

* "Burnes" was pronounced with two syllables in William's native Kincardineshire, but "Burrrns" in Ayrshire. After their father's death, Robert and his brother Gilbert adopted the spelling "Burns."

laborers or house servants, as they would have, had he continued working for wages.

William had come to Ayrshire, via Edinburgh, from Dunnotar, in the northeast, below Aberdeen, where his family of solid tenant farmers had fallen on hard times. After working for several employers as a gardener, he leased seven acres at Alloway, near Ayr, from a Dr. Campbell, and built on them with his own hands the "auld clay biggin," now one of the most famous tourist attractions in the world. On December 15, 1757, he married Agnes Broun (1732–1820), red-haired and fair and sensible, and set up housekeeping in his new cottage. There, on January 25, 1759, Robert their first child was born. William was thirty-eight.

His intention had been to set up as a nurseryman and market-gardener, but the enterprise did not prosper, and he continued employment, as gardener and overseer, for Provost William Fergusson, of Ayr, on his nearby estate of Doonholm. During the next six years, he and Agnes had another son, Gilbert, and two daughters, Agnes and Annabella, and the two-room cottage became a tight fit for the family. Needing more room, and wishing to better himself and his family, William rented from Dr. Fergusson an upland farm of seventy Scots acres named Mt. Oliphant,* about two miles away. Unable to dispose of his lease on the Alloway holding, he rented the cottage and seven acres, and borrowed £100 from his employer to stock the new farm, moving in at Whitsunday, 1766. There the family lived until Whitsunday, 1777, when they moved to Lochlea farm, ten miles away in Tarbolton parish. William and Agnes then had seven children.

The extra living space at Mt. Oliphant was probably an attic where the boys might sleep, a common feature of the "but and ben" (outer and inner room) farm cottage. Such a cottage "with its walls of stone or rammed clay, its earthen floor and thatched roof, and with the fire seldom built up except for cooking, had

---

* Gilbert Burns said later it was "almost the very poorest soil . . . in a state of cultivation." (Currie I, 69.)

a winter chill and dampness that bred tuberculosis in the young
and rheumatism in the old. . . . The stable was usually under
the same roof, and its reek mingled with the dampness and the
smell of unwashed humanity. . . . Outside the door was the
. . . glaur hole, manure heap of man and beast alike." Oatmeal
porridge supported the human inhabitants, each resident dipping
at meals with his spoon from a common bowl. Barley soup, cabbage, bread, cheese, and occasional potatoes filled out the menu.
Animals that died were eaten if possible.

We lived very sparingly [reports Gilbert Burns]. For several years
butcher's meat was a stranger in the house, while all the members of
the family exerted themselves to the utmost of their strength and
rather beyond it, in the labours of the farm. My brother, at the age of
thirteen, assisted in threshing the crop of corn, and at fifteen was the
principal labourer on the farm, for we had no hired servant, male or
female. The anguish of mind we felt at our tender years, under these
straits and difficulties, was very great. To think of our father growing
old (for he was now above fifty) broken down with the long continued fatigues of his life, with a wife and five other children, and
in a declining state of circumstances, these reflections produced in
my brother's mind and mine sensations of the deepest distress. I doubt
not but the hard labour and sorrow of this period of his life, was in
great measure the cause of that depression of spirits with which Robert
was so often afflicted through his whole life afterward. At this time
he was almost constantly afflicted in the evenings with a dull headache,
which, at a future period of his life, was exchanged for a palpitation
of the heart, and a threatening of fainting and suffocation in his bed,
in the night time. . .

Nothing could be more retired than our general manner of living
at Mt. Oliphant; we rarely saw anybody but the members of our own
family. There were no boys of our own age, or near it, in the neighbourhood. . . . My father was for some time almost the only companion we had. He conversed familiarly on all subjects with us, as if
we had been men; and was at great pains, while we accompanied him
in the labours of the farm, to lead the conversation to such subjects
as might tend to increase our knowledge, or confirm us in virtuous
habits.

Inveraray

Loch Fyne

Arrochar

Ben Lomond

Loch Lomond

River Forth

CLACKMANNAN

Harvieston

R. Devon

ARGYLL

COWAL

Dunoon

Greenock

STIRLING

Stirling

Dumbarton

Linlithgow

LINLITHGOW

Port Glasgow

Glasgow

Paisley

River Clyde

Lanark

LANARK

BUTE

FRITH OF CLYDE

Cunningham

Dunlop

Arran

Ardrossan

Irvine

Kilmarnock

Kyle

Mossgiel

Lochlea

Tarbolton

Mauchline

Ayr

Alloway

River Aye

Cumnock

New Cumnock

Campbeltown

Mt. Oliphant

AYR

Sanquhar

R. Nith

Kirkoswald

Carrick

Thornhill

Closeburn

Monaive

Friars' Carse

Ailsa Craig

Dunscore

Ellisland

Kenmuir

Loch Ken

Dumfries

Woodley

Parton

Airds

Park

KIRKCUDBRIGHT

Criffel

WIGTOWN

Wigtown

Gatehouse of Fleet

Port Patrick

Ardwell

Kirkcudbright

Wigtown Bay

PERT

0   10   20   30

Miles

Places in
Southern Scotland
Associated with
ROBERT BURNS

There are few details about Robert as a boy. He seems to have been a reserved, moody youngster, and he remarks that he was by no means a favorite with anybody, although "a good deal noted for a retentive memory and a stubborn, sturdy something" in his disposition. The midwife at his birth is reported to have said Burns was the smallest and poorest child she ever saw born — nothing but skin. And once when his teacher was called from the room and the other children broke into an uproar, Robert hid himself in a chest. Returning, the master signaled for order by striking the chest with his tawz (a strap fringed at one end, traditional symbol and instrument of authority). Poor Robbie, inside, was so upset that he screamed and had to be sent home sobbing. Another picturesque detail is that about ten days after Robert's birth, a storm blew in the gable of the cottage's clay wall above the fireplace, necessitating the removal of mother and baby to a neighbor's while repairs were made.

The one thing we do know a good deal about is Robert's schooling, and his early reading, which influenced him strongly. He learned to read and to understand what he read, and he learned to write clear, grammatical prose. The schooling began in his sixth year (1765) at Alloway Mill nearby, under a man named Campbell, who soon gave up teaching to manage the workhouse in Ayr. Subsequently, William Burnes arranged with an earnest and pedantic young man, John Murdoch, to take over the school. Murdoch's account for Currie after Burns' death of his two years at Alloway is valuable as the earliest report on Robert by an outsider, here a friendly and observant one.

In 1765, about the middle of March, Mr. W. Burnes came to Ayr, and sent to the school where I was improving in writing, . . . desiring that I would come and speak to him at a certain inn, and bring my writing-book with me. . . . In the month of May following, I was engaged by Mr. Burnes, and four of his neighbours, to teach, and accordingly began to teach the little school at Alloway. . . . My five employers undertook to board me by turns, and to make up a certain salary, at the end of the year, provided my quarterly payments from the different pupils did not amount to that sum.

My pupil Robert Burns was then between six and seven years of age; his preceptor about eighteen. Robert, and his younger brother Gilbert, had been grounded a little in English before they were put under my care. They both made a rapid progress in reading, and a tolerable progress in writing. In reading, dividing words into syllables by rule, spelling without book, parsing sentences, &c. Robert and Gilbert were generally at the upper end of the class, even when ranged with boys by far their seniors. The books most commonly used in the school were, the *Spelling Book*, the *New Testament*, the *Bible, Mason's [Masson's] Collection of Prose and Verse*, and Fisher's *English Grammar*. They committed to memory the hymns and other poems of that collection, with uncommon facility. This facility was partly owing to the method pursued by their father and me in instructing them, which was, to make them thoroughly acquainted with the meaning of every word in each sentence that was to be committed to memory. . . . As soon as they were capable of it, I taught them to turn verse into its natural prose order; sometimes to substitute synonymous expressions for poetical words, and to supply all the ellipses. . . .

Gilbert always appeared to me to possess a more lively imagination, and to be more of a wit, than Robert. I attempted to teach them a little church-music. Here they were left far behind by all the rest of the school. Robert's ear, in particular, was remarkably dull, and his voice untunable. . . . Robert's countenance was generally grave, and expressive of a serious, contemplative, and thoughtful mind.

After two years, Murdoch left the school and the neighborhood, and William Burnes undertook to teach the boys arithmetic at home by candlelight. Just before leaving, Murdoch came to say goodbye.

He brought us [says Gilbert] as a present and memorial of him, a small compendium of English Grammar, and the tragedy of *Titus Andronicus*, and by way of passing the evening, he began to read the play aloud. We were all attention for some time, till presently the whole party was dissolved in tears. A female of the play (I have but a confused remembrance of it) had her hands chopt off, and her tongue cut out, and then was insultingly desired to call for water to wash her hands.* At this, in an agony of distress, we with one voice desired he would read no more. My father observed, that if we would not hear it out, it would be needless to leave the play with us. Robert replied, that if it were left he would burn it.

Here is the second example of Robert's turbulent sensibility.

In case John Murdoch should seem unduly straitened, his exit from Ayr may be noted. Having returned to become one of the English teachers in the Ayr school, and feeling aggrieved with the Reverend Dr. Dalrymple (who had baptized Robert), Murdoch retired first to an inn and then to a private house, voicing his opinion that the doctor was as revengeful as hell and as false as the devil. He also said that the doctor was a hypocrite and a damned liar. For these slanders, he was summarily dismissed February 14, 1776, and left town. Robert remained on friendly terms with him, however, and Murdoch was chief mourner at Burns' younger brother's funeral in London some years later.

Besides arranging for the Alloway school, William sent Robert for a part of the summer of 1772, when he was thirteen years old, to a school three miles away at Dalrymple to improve his handwriting. The following summer, Murdoch having by then returned to Ayr, Robert lived with him for three weeks, studying English and French. Finally, during the summer of 1775, the boy spent some weeks with his mother's brother at Kirkoswald, near the seacoast about ten miles south, so that he might learn "Mensuration, Surveying, and Dialling, &c." at the local school. He speaks of geometry and trigonometry, and of sines and cosines.

At Kirkoswald, Burns learned more than mathematics. He made, as he says,

progress in the knowledge of mankind. — The contraband trade was at that time very successful; scenes of swaggering riot and roaring dissipation were as yet new to me; and I was no enemy to social life. —

* The stage direction reads, "Enter the Empress' sons with Lavinia, her hands cut off, and her tongue cut out, and ravished."

Here, though I learned to look unconcernedly on a large tavern-bill, and mix without fear in a drunken squabble, yet I went on with a high hand in my Geometry; till the sun entering Virgo, a month which is always carnival in my bosom, a charming Fillete who lived next door to the school overset my Trigonomertry, and set me off at a tangent from the sphere of my studies. . . . Stepping out to the garden one charming noon to take the sun's altitude, I met with my Angel. . . . It was vain to think of doing any more good at school.

At the age of eighteen, when his family moved from Mt. Oliphant to Lochlea farm, Robert had long been a "reader when he could get a book," and a reader of substantial books. "Robert read . . . with an avidity and industry scarcely to be equalled. . . . For no book was so voluminous as to slacken his industry, or so antiquated as to damp his researches." Murdoch's drill, especially his emphasis that words had precise meanings and should be used precisely, had made Robert "an excellent English scholar."

Burns' reading had given him some knowledge of Greek and Roman religion; of ancient history, and English and Scottish history;* and of the geography of the world. He knew his Bible intimately, and the popular science and astronomy used as evidence of religious truth. He was soaked in Calvinist theology, including a *Manual of Religious Belief*, the joint product of Murdoch and William Burnes, mildly liberal in its views. He had read a selection of polite letters by Eighteenth Century authors, which he used as models for his own letters. Perhaps most important, and maybe a little later, he had been enthralled by Henry Mackenzie's *Man of Feeling*, and by Laurence Sterne's *Tristram*

---

* He wrote to Dr. John Moore, author of travel books and, later, a novel: "The two first books I ever read in private, and which gave me more pleasure than any two books I ever read again, were, the life of Hannibal and the history of Sir William Wallace. — Hannibal gave my young ideas such a turn that I used to strut in raptures up and down after the recruiting drum and bagpipe, and wish myself tall enough to be a soldier; while the story of Wallace poured a Scotish prejudice in my veins which will boil along there till the flood-gates of life shut in eternal rest." (F I, #125, 106.)

Shandy, both of which greatly influenced his opinions and his prose style.

All of this reading, as well as most of the poetry he admired, was in English, which Burns learned to speak and write "with fluency, and precision, and originality . . . more particularly as he aimed at purity in his turn of expression, and avoided more successfully than most Scotchmen, the peculiarities of Scottish phraseology." It should be noted that Burns spoke English like an educated Scotsman, with Scots accent and flavor,* and wrote English, except when in his poetry he adopted a literary Scots-English largely of his own devising.

But neither Murdoch, nor William Burnes, nor Robert's reading, had much to do with his turning to poetry. He writes to Dr. Moore:

You know our country custom of coupling a man and a woman together as Partners in the labors of Harvest. — In my fifteenth autumn [1773], my Partner [Nelly Kirkpatrick] was a bewitching creature who just counted an autumn less. — My scarcity of English† denies me the power of doing her justice in that language; but you know the Scotch idiom, She was a bonie, sweet, sonsie lass. — In short, she altogether unwittingly to herself, initiated me in a certain delicious Passion, which in spite of acid Disappointment, gin-horse Prudence and bookworm Philosophy, I hold to be the first of human joys, our dearest pleasure here below. — How she caught the contagion I can't say; you medical folks talk much of infection by breathing the same air, the touch, &c. but I never expressly told her that I loved her. — Indeed I did not well know myself, why I liked so much to loiter behind with her, when returning in the evening from our labors; why the tones of her voice made my heartstrings thrill like an Eolian harp; and particularly, why my pulse beat such a furious ratann when I

---

* Burns was certainly familiar with broad Scots, and could doubtless speak it, but no evidence survives that he used it except a facetious letter to his friend William Nicol. (F I, #112, 94–95.)

† A rhetorical device and an echo from Sterne, no doubt, who frequently confesses similar inabilities, and once even supplies the reader blank pages to fill with a description to his liking. Burns had no more difficulty than Sterne in saying exactly what he wanted to in English prose.

looked and fingered over her hand, to pick out the nettle-stings and thistles. — Among her other love-inspiring qualifications, she sung sweetly; and 'twas her favorite reel to which I attempted giving an embodied vehicle in rhyme. — I was not so presumptive as to imagine that I could make verses like printed ones, composed by men who had Greek and Latin; but my girl sung a song which was said to be composed by a small country laird's son, on one of his father's maids, with whom he was in love; and I saw no reason why I might not rhyme as well as he, for excepting smearing sheep and casting peats, his father living in the moors, he had no more Scholarcraft than I had. —

Thus with me began Love and Poesy; which at times have been my only, and till within this last twelvemonth have been my highest enjoyment.

In August, 1783, Burns copied the song he wrote for Nelly into his Commonplace Book.

Song

(Tune, *I am a man unmarried*)

O once I lov'd a bonny lass
   Ay and I love her still
And whilst that virtue warms my breast
   I'll love my handsome Nell.
      Fal lal de lal &c.

As bonny lasses I hae seen,
   And mony full as braw;   *fine*
But for a modest gracefu' mien,
   The like I never saw.

A bonny lass I will confess,
   Is pleasant to the e'e;
But without some better qualities
   She's no a lass for me.

But Nelly's looks are blythe and sweet,
   And what is best of a',
Her reputation is compleat
   And fair without a flaw.

> She dresses ay sae clean and neat,
>   Both decent and genteel;
> And then there's something in her gate
>   Gars ony dress look weel.   *makes*
>
> A gaudy dress and gentle air
>   May slightly touch the heart;
> But it's innocence and modesty
>   That polisses the dart.
>
> 'Tis this in Nelly pleases me;
>   'Tis this enchants my soul;
> For absolutely in my breast
>   She reigns without controul.

In the previous April, Burns had written, "If anything on earth deserves the name of rapture or transport it is the feelings of green eighteen in the company of the mistress of his heart when she repays him with an equal return of affection." And in August he continued, "For my own part I never had the least thought or inclination of turning Poet till I got once heartily in Love, and then Rhyme and Song were, in a manner, the spontaneous language of my heart."

Of a time several years after composing *Handsome Nell*, he writes,

Poesy was still a darling walk for my mind, but 'twas only the humour of the hour. — I had usually half a dozen or more pieces on hand; I took up one or other as it suited the momentary tone of the mind, and dismissed it as it bordered on fatigue. — My Passions when once they were lighted up, raged like so many devils, till they got vent in rhyme; and then conning over my verses, like a spell, soothed all into quiet.

The tumult through which most young men pass while coming to terms with themselves began late for Burns and lasted long. Its first recorded incident fell during the year of Kirkoswald, when Burns was seventeen. He defied his father and went

to a village dancing school. (Being fond of dancing, he apparently went to another school three years later, and perhaps to
others in between.) More serious strains followed. During the
Lochlea years (1777–1784), he had a near nervous breakdown,
he suffered a religious crisis, he had girl trouble ("My heart was
compleatly tinder, and was eternally lighted up by some Goddess
or other"), he wanted to marry but could see no way to afford
a wife or family, he found his work grinding and his lot inescapable, he experienced legal oppression and class tyranny, he felt
he had abilities and he knew the futile stirrings of ambition ("The
great misfortune of my life was, never to have An Aim").

In these troubled years, he tells us, his "sole principles of action" were "vive l'amour et vive la bagatelle." He helped found
a Bachelor's Club in Tarbolton village, he became an active and
enthusiastic Mason, he continued his extensive reading, he kept
at his work, and he became known as an amusing and keen-
witted debater, particularly on religious subjects, in kirkyard,
field, or smithy. He felt he had been "sent into the world to see,
and observe," and his delight was to "study men, their manners,
and their ways," a phrase he had picked up from Alexander Pope.
Moreover, he had no intention of keeping his observations to himself; he started his Commonplace Book later to record some of
them, with a stated hope that the record might be read some day
by others.

So, despite many distresses and heavy work, Burns was a buoyant and vital young man. Gilbert says of him,

Though when young he was bashful and awkward in his intercourse
with women, yet when he approached manhood, his attachment to
their society became very strong, and he was constantly the victim
of some fair enslaver. The symptoms of his passion were often such
as nearly to equal those of the celebrated Sappho. I never indeed
knew that he *fainted, sunk, and died away;* but the agitations of his
mind and body, exceeded any thing of the kind I ever knew in real
life. He had always a particular jealousy of people who were richer

than himself, or who had more consequence in life. His love, therefore, rarely settled on persons of this description. When he selected any one out of the sovereignty of his good pleasure to whom he should pay his particular attention, she was instantly invested with a sufficient stock of charms, out of the plentiful stores of his own imagination; and there was often a great dissimilitude between his fair captivator, as she appeared to others, and as she seemed when invested with the attributes he gave her. One generally reigned paramount in his affections; . . . but . . . Robert was frequently encountering other attractions, which formed so many under-plots in the drama of his love. As these connexions were governed by the strictest rules of virtue and modesty, (from which he never deviated till he reached his 23d year,) he became anxious to be in a situation to marry.

Robert had earlier described this period of his life "[After a hard day's work] I spent the evening in the way after my own heart. — A country lad rarely carries on an amour without an assisting confident. — I possessed a curiosity, zeal and intrepid dexterity in these matters which recommended me a proper second in duels of that kind; and I dare say, I felt as much pleasure at being in the secret of half the amours in the parish, as ever did Premier at knowing the intrigues of half the courts of Europe."

The Tarbolton Bachelor's Club was founded in 1780 by young men from that village and surrounding farms, and its history, written by Burns, and its Rules, heavily influenced by him, tell much about the club and its chief instigator.

History of the Rise, Proceedings, and Regulations of the *Bachelor's Club*

> Of birth or blood we do not boast,
> Nor gentry does our club afford;
> But ploughmen and mechanics we,
> In Nature's simple dress record.

. . . By far the greater part of mankind are under the necessity *of earning the sustenance of human life by the labour of their bodies,* whereby, not only the faculties of the mind, but the nerves and sinews of the body, are so fatigued, that it is absolutely necessary to have recourse to some amusement or diversion, to relieve the wearied man, worn down by the necessary labours of life.

As the best of things, however, have been perverted to the worst of purposes, so, under the pretence of amusement and diversion, men have plunged into all the madness of riot and dissipation; and instead of attending to the grand design of human life, they have begun with extravagance and folly, and ended with guilt and wretchedness. Impressed with these considerations, we the following lads in the parish of Tarbolton, viz. Hugh Reid, Robert Burns, Gilbert Burns, Alexander Brown, Walter Mitchel, Thomas Wright, and William M'Gavin, resolved for our mutual entertainment to unite ourselves into a club or society, under such rules and regulations, that while we should forget our cares and labours in mirth and diversion, we might not transgress the bounds of innocence and decorum.

At their first meeting, with Burns presiding, they debated the topic, "Suppose a young man, bred a farmer, but without any fortune, has it in his power to marry either of two women, the one a girl of large fortune, but neither handsome in person, nor agreable in conversation, but who can manage the household affairs of a farm well enough; the other of them a girl every way agreable, in person, conversation, and behavior, but without any fortune: which of them shall he choose?"

Views on this matter are recorded in a letter from Burns to his friend John Tenant, Jr., September 13, 1784. After discussing a girl with a portion of £300, Burns continues, "We talk of air & manner, of beauty & wit, and lord knows what unmeaning nonsense; but — there — is solid charms for you — who would not be in raptures with a woman that will make him 300 £ richer? — And then to have a woman to lye with when one pleases, without running any risk of the cursed expense of bastards and all the other concomitants of that species of Smuggling — these are solid views of matrimony — "

The next year the club admitted new members. "The club being thus increased," the history continues, "we resolved to meet

at Tarbolton on the race-night, the July following, and have a
dance in honour of our society. Accordingly we did meet, each
one with a partner, and spent the evening in such innocence
and merriment, such cheerfulness and good humour, that every
brother will long remember it with pleasure and delight."

The Rules and Regulations provide for times of meeting and
procedure; for the selection of members, the choice of topics for
debate, and the maintenance of proper decorum. Fines for impropriety were to be applied to the reckoning at the inn where
the club met. Before dismissal, there was to be a "general toast
to the mistresses of the club." The 10th regulation deserves full
quotation:

Every man proper for a member of this society, must have a frank,
honest, open heart; above anything dirty or mean; and must be a
professed lover of one or more of the female sex. No haughty, self-
conceited person, who looks upon himself as superior to the rest of
the club, and especially no mean-spirited, worldly mortal, whose only
will is to heap up money, shall upon any pretense whatever be
admitted. In short, the proper person for this society is, a cheerful,
honest-hearted lad, who, if he has a friend that is true, and a mistress
that is kind, and as much wealth as genteelly to make both ends
meet — is just as happy as this world can make him.

The Bachelor's Club was short-lived, perhaps because Burns
lost interest in it when he became a Mason the next year, in
1781. A village Masonic lodge such as he joined was a sort of
convivial credit union and mutual benefit society, and Robert
seems to have been a leading spirit, becoming Depute Master in
time. Lodge St. David, Tarbolton, to which he was admitted
July 4, 1781, represented a "junchen" of Lodge St. David and
Lodge St. James which had taken place only nine days before.
In a subsequent separation, Burns chose Lodge St. James. His
Masonic activity declined after his leaving Ayrshire in 1786, but
a great moment in his life was the famous toast to him at St.
Andrew's Lodge, Edinburgh, by the Grand Master, "Caledonia,

& Caledonia's Bard, brother Burns," "which rung through the whole Assembly with multiplied honors and repeated acclamations."

His activities about Tarbolton gave Burns a seeming purpose, and relief from his problems, and entertainment; but no real settlement.

The only two doors by which I could enter the fields of fortune [he wrote] were, the most niggardly economy, or the little chicaning art of bargain-making: the first is so contracted an aperture, I never could squeeze myself into it; the last, I always hated the contamination of the threshold. — Thus, abandoned of aim or view in life; with a strong appetite for sociability, as well from native hilarity as from a pride of observation and remark; a constitutional hypochondriac taint which made me fly solitude; add to all these incentives to social life, my reputation for bookish knowledge, a certain wild, logical talent, and a strength of thought something like the rudiments of good sense, made me generally a welcome guest; so 'tis no great wonder that always "where two or three were met together, there was I in the midst of them."

In a memorandum, titled "Egotisms from my own Sensations," dated by R. H. Cromek "May," and placed between quotations from the Commonplace Book for 1784 and 1785, Robert writes, "I don't well know what is the reason of it, but somehow or other though I am, when I have a mind, pretty generally beloved; yet, I never could get the art of commanding respect. — I imagine it is owing to my being deficient in what Sterne calls 'that understrapping virtue of discretion.' — I am so apt to a *lapsus linguae*, that I sometimes think the character of a certain great man, I have read of somewhere, is very much *apropos* to myself — that he was a compound of great talents and great folly. N.B. To try if I can to discover the causes of this wretched infirmity, and, if possible, to mend it."

Burns refers to a particularly distressing incident of about this time in his letter to Dr. Moore. "A belle-fille whom I adored and who had pledged her soul to meet me in the field of matrimony, jilted me with peculiar circumstances of mortification," and helped to bring on a severe melancholia in the winter of 1781–82. It is tempting to assume that this girl was the Ellison or Alison Begbie whom Burns' youngest sister, Mrs. Begg, identified as the jilter. But his sister would have been a young girl at the time, and not necessarily too well informed about her grown brother's love affairs. Drafts of five letters seem to refer to this proposal and jilting. They are addressed merely to "A" or "E," and the first, to "A" (of which there is a manuscript), makes a proposal of marriage. The three following letters, to "my dearest E," discuss love and courtship, and the last ruefully acknowledges a rejection. They are dignified, self-conscious, and solemn. The proposal takes this form: "I hope you will forgive me when I tell you that I most sincerely & affectionately love you. — I am a stranger in these matters A———, as I assure you, that you are the first woman to whom I ever made such a declaration so I declare I am at a loss how to proceed. —

". . . I hope my inexperience of the world will plead for me — I can only say I sincerely love you & there is nothing on earth I so ardently wish for, or could possibly give me so much happiness, as one day to see you mine." Letters number two and three equate love and virtue. In letter two, he writes, "I verily believe, my dear E., that the pure genuine feelings of love are as rare in the world as the pure genuine principles of virtue and piety. . . . I have often thought that if a well-grounded affection be not really a part of virtue, 'tis something extremely akin to it. Whenever the thought of my E. warms my heart, every feeling of humanity, every principle of generosity kindles in my breast. It extinguishes every dirty spark of malice and envy which are but too apt to infest me. I grasp every creature in the arms of universal benevolence, and equally participate in the pleasures of the happy, and sympathise with the miseries of the unfortunate."

Letter number three continues the theme. "The love I have for you is founded on the sacred principles of virtue and honor. . . . Believe me, my dear, it is love like this alone which can render the marriage state happy." In letter four, he protests, "There is one rule which I have hitherto practiced, and which I shall invariably keep with you, and that is, honestly to tell you the plain truth." But, alas, in letter five, he is shocked to find that she can only wish him happiness and be his friend.

It is not even certain that Burns sent these letters to anyone, but they are similar in style and tone to one that he sent his father soon after they are presumed to have been written, and their chief biographical significance lies in their suggestion that Burns was a circumspect and proper young man so late as his twenty-second year.

A change in him, marking the arrival of his long-postponed maturity, began when he left home for seven or eight months in the summer of 1781. While marketing the flax which he and his brother raised on land taken from their father, Robert got the idea that he might improve his condition by turning flax-dresser and merchant, and so he went from Lochlea to the nearby town of Irvine to learn the trade. He also speaks of the venture as a "whim."

In Irvine he had one partner named Peacock, who may have been a relative of his mother, and one who, he says, was dishonest, but they may not have been the same. And one partner's wife set the shop afire during a New Year welcome to 1782, leaving Burns with the clothes he stood up in. But he stayed on after the misadventure for several months. Just who owned the shop which burned down is a matter of dispute, but the importance of Robert's six months in Irvine lies elsewhere than in his flax dressing and the fire. Most notably, he met a sailor, Richard Brown, and he may have read the Scotch poems of Robert Fergusson. A controversy, centering about the date of a copy of Fergusson's poems which Burns owned, has lately arisen over the occasion of his first meeting with these poems. It is obvious that the volume in question may not have provided his first acquaintance with Fergusson, and the fact that he did not begin to imitate Fergusson's poems until 1784–85 is no evidence as to when he first read them. The only significant fact in the case is Burns' statement to Dr. Moore. After mentioning that Brown had encouraged him in looser ways with women, he continues, "Here his friendship did me a mischief; and the consequence was, that soon after I resumed the plough,* I wrote the Welcome inclosed. — My reading was *only* [italics supplied] encreased by two stray volumes of Pamela, and one of Ferdinand Count Fathom, which gave me some idea of Novels. — Rhyme, except some religious pieces which are in print, I had given up; but meeting with Fergusson's Scotch Poems, I strung anew my wildly-sounding rustic lyre with emulating vigor."

The *only* italicized above suggests that Burns did not read Fergusson at Irvine, but the chronology of the passage is slurred. It is not clear just when he gave over writing poetry for a time, but it may have been before he came to Irvine. And the Welcome [*To His Bastart Wean*] celebrates a child born May 22, 1785, three years after he left Irvine, in the spring of 1782. Whatever the date, Burns' discovery of Fergusson was the chief formative influence in making him a great poet.

Richard Brown was a man of much wider experience than Burns and of considerable ability; he soon became master of a West Indiaman. He gave Burns his first thought of publication by suggesting that he send some of his poems to a magazine. Just what poems Robert showed Brown no one can say, but he may have had available *The Death and Dying Words of Poor Mailie*, and songs like *Winter, a Dirge,* or *Corn Rigs.* It may be he even showed Brown some of the religious poems he mentions to Dr. Moore. But *Corn Rigs* is a more likely choice, and an

---

* The time assigned by Gilbert for Robert's departure from "the strictest rules of virtue and modesty." (F I, #125, 113.)

excellent song.* Robert had gone far since he wrote *Handsome Nell.*

Corn Rigs

It was upon a Lammas night,
   When corn rigs are bonie,   *ridges or rows*
Beneath the moon's unclouded light,
   I held awa to Annie;
The time flew by, wi' tentless heed;   *careless*
   Till, 'tween the late and early,
Wi' sma' persuasion she agreed
   To see me thro' the barley
      Corn rigs, an' barley rigs,
       An' corn rigs are bonie:
      I'll ne'er forget that happy night,
       Amang the rigs wi' Annie.

The sky was blue, the wind was still,
   The moon was shining clearly;
I set her down, wi' right good will,
   Amang the rigs o' barley:
I ken't her heart was a' my ain;   *knew*
   I lov'd her most sincerely;
I kiss'd her owre and owre again,
   Amang the rigs o' barley.

I lock'd her in my fond embrace;
   Her heart was beating rarely:
My blessings on that happy place,
   Amang the rigs o' barley!
But by the moon and stars so bright,
   That shone that hour so clearly!
She ay shall bless that happy night
   Amang the rigs o' barley.

I had been blythe wi' comrades dear;
   I hae been merry drinking;
I had been joyfu' gath'rin gear;   *making money*
   I hae been happy thinking:

---

* In his letter to Dr. Moore, Burns places this song before his twenty-third year, although the present version may represent later emendations. (F I, #125, 112.)

> But a' the pleasures e'er I saw,
>   Tho' three times doubled fairly —
> That happy night was worth them a',
>   Amang the rigs o' barley.
>   Corn rigs, an' barley rigs,
>   An' corn rigs are bonie:
>   I'll ne'er forget that happy night,
>   Amang the rigs wi' Annie.

In Irvine, Burns also went through a religious ferment which must have been at least part cause of the desperate depression, already mentioned, which accompanied "alarming symptoms of a Pleurisy or some other dangerous disorder" that afflicted him there. The comparatively liberal theology of William Burnes was no longer satisfactory to Robert. There was a God, Burns felt sure, but what sort of a God was he, and in what relation did he stand to man? What was expected of man, with the passions God had given him? Burns never settled these matters to his satisfaction, but at Irvine he seems to have relieved himself finally of oppressive concern.

In a very early song, *Winter, a Dirge*, probably written before he went to Irvine, Burns accepts man's miserable estate and pleads to God, "Since to enjoy Thou dost deny, / Assist me to resign." But in *A Prayer in the Prospect of Death*, from the Irvine period, after admitting his human weakness and frailty, Burns finds comfort in the reflection, "But Thou art good, and goodness still / Delighteth to Forgive." And in *Stanzas Written in Prospect of Death*, on the same occasion, Burns wonders why he is loth to leave this earthly scene, which is not pleasant. He trembles before an angry God because he is guilty, and he promises never more to disobey, but he knows he is weak, and he asks for divine assistance. Neither of these poems expresses the Calvinist position.

Paraphrase of the First Psalm advances an ancient paradox. God grants peace and rest to the good, "But hath decreed that wicked men / Shall ne'er be truly blest." This decree seems harsh to Burns, and unworthy a benevolent God who created the wicked in the first place. *The Ninetieth Psalm Versified* recites the familiar theme that man is brought into the world and flourishes briefly, like the flower in beauty's pride, "But long ere night, cut down it lies / All wither'd and decay'd." He comes to no resolution, but in a later song, *Tho' Fickle Fortune,* he concludes, "Then come, Misfortune, I bid thee welcome — / I'll meet thee with undaunted mind!" And in a "wild rhapsody," *My Father Was a Farmer,* he resolves, "The past was bad, and the future hid; its good or ill untrièd, O, / But the present hour was in my pow'r, and so I would enjoy it, O."

A blank verse passage entitled *Remorse* (1783), an outgrowth of his reading Adam Smith's *Theory of Moral Sentiments,* adds complementary reflections:

> Of all the numerous ills that hurt our peace;
> That press the soul, or wring the mind with anguish;
> Beyond comparison the worst are those
> By our own folly, or our guilt brought on. . . .
> Lives there a man so firm, who, while his heart
> Feels all the bitter horrors of his crime,
> Can reason down its agonizing throbs,
> And, after proper purpose of amendment,
> Can firmly force his jarring thoughts to peace?
> O happy, happy, enviable man!
> O glorious magnanimity of soul!

It is feelings like this which led Burns to rejoice in Milton's Satan when he read *Paradise Lost.*

Some years later, a heart-wrung comment in a letter to Margaret Chalmers reveals continuing stress. "There are just two creatures I would envy, a horse in his native state traversing the forests of Asia, or an oyster on some of the desart shores of Europe. The one has not a wish without enjoyment, the other has neither wish nor fear."

A notable result of the stirrings of Burns' spirit during the confused years at Lochlea was his development of a flexible, easy, and often pungent English prose style. Most of Burns' prose is in letters, and too often his letters merely convey inflated common-places or protective politeness to social superiors, or waft senti-ment and elephantine gallantry to women. But even as he dis-covered his way in poetry, so he learned, when he was on easy terms with a correspondent and had something to say, to write forceful English prose. The pity is that there were not more such correspondents, and that we do not have more of these letters, so suggestive of Burns' conversation which everyone found enchant-ing, and almost no one recorded.

His early letters are studied compositions based on models he found in his school reader, or in a volume of "letters by the most eminent writers, with a few sensible directions for attaining an easy epistolary style." An excellent example of this early manner at its best, and a most revealing document as well, is a letter from Burns to his father, written from Irvine, December 27, 1781.

HONORED SIR,
    I have purposely delayed writing in the hope that I would have the pleasure of seeing you on Newyearday but work comes so hard upon us that I do not chuse to come, as well for that, as also for some other little reasons which I shall tell you at meeting. — My health is much about what it was when you were here only my sleep is rather sounder and on the whole I am rather better than otherwise tho it is but by very slow degrees. — The weakness of my nerves has so debilitated my mind that I dare not, either review past events, or look forward into futurity; for the least anxiety, or perturbation in my breast, produces most unhappy effects on my whole frame. — Some-times, indeed, when for an hour or two, as is sometimes the case, my spirits are a little lightened, I glimmer a little into futurity; but my principal, and indeed my only pleasurable enjoyment is looking back-wards & forwards in a moral & religious way — I am quite transported at the thought that ere long, perhaps very soon, I shall bid an eternal adiew to all the pains, & uneasiness & disquietudes of this weary life; for I assure you I am heartily tired of it, and, if I do not very much deceive myself I could contentedly & gladly resign it. —

The Soul uneasy & confin'd from home
Rests & expatiates in a life to come.

POPE

It is for this reason I am more than pleased with the 15th, 16th & 17th verses of the 7th Chapter of Rev:n* than any ten times as many verses in the whole Bible, & would not exchange the noble enthusiasm with which they inspire me, for all that this world has to offer — As for this world I despair of ever making a figure in it — I am not formed for the bustle of the busy nor the flutter of the Gay. I shall never again be capable of it. — Indeed, I am altogether unconcern'd at the thoughts of it. I foresee that very probably Poverty & Obscurity await me & I am, in some measure prepared & daily preparing to meet & welcome them. — I have but just time & paper to return you my grateful thanks for the many Lessons of Virtue & Piety you have given me — Lessons which were but too much neglected when they were given but which, I hope have been remembered ere it is yet too late — Present my dutiful respects to my Mother & my Compnts to Mr & Mrs Muir and with wishing you all a merry Newyearday I shall conclude

I am, Honored Sir, your dutiful son
ROBT BURNS

my meal is nearly out but I am going to borrow till I get more —

Four days later came the New Year party at the shop, and the fire.

Although in the latter part of the letter he is imitating and even quoting from Chapter LV of his favorite novel, *The Man of Feeling*, Burns here is obviously distressed. In his Commonplace Book, as we have seen, he speaks of a "dangerous disorder" † from which he suffered at this time, and he specifies in the letter itself his other causes for depression: religious concern, poor diet, hard work, and frustration. Certainly, also, he was lonely. It is probable that he lived by himself, and cooked his own porridge, with meal sent from home.

* A depiction of the joys of heaven.
† Possibly smallpox, then prevalent in Irvine. See Health Record, Appendix B.

The following letter, written two and a half years later, reveals a much brighter spirit, and a much lighter style, in describing to his cousin the adventures of a local orgiastic cult, the Buchanites.

Mr. James Burness   Writer   in Montrose

Mossgiel, 3d August 1784

My DEAR SIR,

I ought in gratitude to have acknowledged the receipt of your last kind letter before this time; but without troubling you with any apology I shall proceed to inform you that our family are all in health at prest and we were very happy with the unexpected favor of John Caird's company for near two weeks; & I must say it of him he is one of the most agreable, facetious warm-hearted lads I was ever acquainted with. —

We have been surprised with one of the most extraordinary Phenomena in the moral world, which, I dare say, has happened in the course of this last Century. — We have had a party of the Presbytry Relief as they call themselves, for some time in this country. A pretty thriving society of them has been in the Burgh of Irvine for some years past, till about two years ago, a Mrs Buchan from Glasgow came among them, & began to spread some fanatical notions of religion among them, & in a short time, made many converts among them, & among others their Preacher, one Mr Whyte, who upon that account has been suspended & formally deposed by his brethren; he continued however, to preach in private to his party, & was supported, both he, & their spiritual Mother as they affect to call old Buchan, by the contributions of the rest, several of whom were in good circumstances; till in spring last the Populace rose & mobbed the old leader Buchan, & put her out of the town; on which, all her followers voluntarily quitted the place likewise, & with such precipitation, that many of them never shut their doors behind them; one left a washing on the green, another a cow bellowing at the crib without meat or anybody to mind her, & after several stages, they are fixed at present in the neighbourhood of Dumfries. — Their tenets are a strange jumble of enthusiastic jargon, among others, she pretends to give them the Holy Ghost by breathing on them, which she does with postures & practices that are scandalously indecent; they have likewise disposed of all their affects & hold a community of goods, & live nearly an idle life, carrying on a great farce of pretended devotion in barns, & woods, where they lodge & lye all together, & hold likewise a community of women, as it is another of their tenets that they can commit no moral sin. — I am personally acquainted with most of them, & I can assure you the above mentioned are facts. —

This My Dr Sir, is one of the many instances of the folly of leaving the guidance of sound reason, & common sense in matters of Religion. — Whenever we neglect or despise these sacred Monitors, the whimsical notions of a perturbated brain are taken for the immediate influences of the Deity, & the wildest fanaticism, & the most inconstant absurdities, will meet with abettors & converts. —Nay, I have often thought, that the more out-of-the-way & ridiculous their fancies are, if once they are sanctified under the sacred name of Religion, the unhappy, mistaken votaries are the more firmly glued to them. —

I expect to hear from you soon, & I beg you will remember me to all friends, & believe me to be,

my Dr Sir your affectionate Cousin,
ROBERT BURNESS*

There has been much speculation about Burns' relations with the Buchanites, and with one Buchanite lass, Jean Gardner, in particular, but reliable details are lacking.

During the harsh experience of his late adolescence and early manhood, Burns also developed his views on social injustice and the need for social reform. They were personal, not theoretical. The Mt. Oliphant years had been bleak, and had ended bitterly. During the landlord's life, William Burnes had been able to make compromises on rent day, but after Provost Fergusson died, the factor did his duty, pressed for the rent, wrote threatening letters, and made the family miserable. It seemed to Burns that if honesty and hard work were not enough to make a decent living for a man and his family, then there was something wrong with the system. The Lochlea experience showed to him even more clearly the cruel disadvantage of the land system to a tenant, and the opportunities open to landlords for oppression almost without recourse for a poor man. It seemed unjust that a landed

* Burns used this spelling when writing to his cousin, who himself used it.

aristocracy and gentry should enjoy their comforts at such great burden to people like himself. And he resented the privileges of well-born dullness, and the indifference of those favored by fortune to those beneath them. "He could not well conceive of a more mortifying picture of human life than a man seeking work."

As he put it,

> See yonder poor, o'erlabor'd wight
> So abject, mean, and vile,
> Who begs a brother of the earth
> To give him leave to toil;
> And see his lordly fellow worm
> The poor petition spurn,
> Unmindful, tho' a weeping wife
> And helpless offspring mourn.

It was experience and feeling of this sort which lay behind Burns' warm response later to cries for Freedom and Liberty, for the Rights of Man, and for reform of a corrupt government managed by a privileged few for their special advantage.

The troubles which William Burnes had with his Lochlea landlord can be described simply, now that most of the legal documents have been discovered, and they are important to an understanding of both the father's integrity and the son's antipathy to moneyed gentry. When David McClure and William made their oral agreement about the Lochlea rent in 1777, McClure allowed a certain amount to William for improvements he was to make on the farm. By 1781 when McClure was desperate for money and denied the allowance which William Burnes claimed, Burnes suspended the payment of rent. On August 18, 1783, an arbitration decided in Burnes' favor, ordering him to pay McClure £231 7s 8d, which he had available, and disallowing claims against him for upward of £500. But on May 17, 1783, McClure had seized Burnes' crops and stock, to insure payment of his claims; and in the meantime, McClure's creditors had laid claims to Burnes' rent for themselves. To extricate himself from this dual demand, the harassed old man took an expensive step for one in his position: he raised an action of "multiple poinding" in the highest court in Scotland, the Court of Session, and was ordered to pay the creditors not the landlord — just two weeks before he died of tuberculosis. The expense of his defense, and the rent due, seem to have taken all his money, and the strain of the three years undoubtedly hastened his end. The family distress was acute. Their only substantial assets after William's death were claims for unpaid wages which he had allowed his children. These, rating as preferred claims, were paid before those of other creditors, and with this money the family moved promptly to Mossgiel farm, a few miles away in Mauchline parish. Robert and Gilbert, in the prospect of disaster, had sublet it even before William's death, from a friendly lawyer and fellow-Mason, Gavin Hamilton, of Mauchline.

An account of William Burnes will serve to complete the story of Robert Burns' youth and the environment from which he emerged to dazzle the world two years after his father died. The close-knit family at Lochlea felt the father's loss deeply, and Robert was particularly distressed by the old man's saying on his deathbed that he feared for his oldest son.

Testimony about William Burnes unanimously speaks of him as a superior man. Murdoch comments on his "solid reasoning, sensible remark, and a moderate seasoning of jocularity," and emphasizes the happy home life at Alloway and Mt. Oliphant, and the devotion between Agnes and her husband. Murdoch continues, "He was a tender and affectionate father; he took pleasure in leading his children in the path of virtue; not in driving them, as some parents do, to the performance of duties to which they themselves are averse. . . . He had the art of gaining the esteem and good-will of those that were labourers under him. I think I never saw him angry but twice: the one time it was with the foreman of the band, for not reaping the field as he was desired; and the other time it was with an old man, for using smutty

innuendos and *doubles entendres*. . . . As he was at no time
overbearing to inferiors, he was equally incapable of that passive,
pitiful, paltry spirit, that induces some people to *keep booing
and booing* in the presence of a great man. He always treated
superiors with a becoming respect, but he never gave the smallest encouragement to aristocratical arrogance."

Dr. Currie, citing "one who knew him toward the latter end of
his life," describes William as "above the common stature, thin,
and bent with labour, his countenance . . . serious and expressive . . . and the scanty locks on his head . . . gray." He then
quotes the famous passage describing family worship in *The Cotter's Saturday Night*, which Gilbert says was written as a picture
of his father.

> The cheerfu' supper done, wi' serious face,
>   They round the ingle, form a circle wide;   *fire*
> The sire turns o'er, wi' patriarchal grace,
>   The big ha'-Bible, ance his father's pride.
>   His bonnet rev'rently is laid aside,
> His lyart haffets wearing thin and bare;   *gray temples*
>   Those strains that once did sweet in Zion glide,
> He wales a portion with judicious care,   *selects*
> And "Let us worship God!" he says, with solemn air.

The final observation of William Burnes links him with his
sons, and is particularly interesting in its details about Robert.
Dr. John M'Kenzie, then of Mauchline, attended William Burnes
in his final illness.

When I first saw William Burns [he writes], he was in very ill health,
and his mind suffering from the embarrassed state of his affairs. His
appearance certainly made me think him inferior, both in manner and
intelligence, to the generality of those in his situation; but before
leaving him, I found that I had been led to form a very false conclusion of his mental powers. After giving a short, but distinct account, of
his indisposition, he entered upon a detail of the various causes that
had gradually led to the embarrassment of his affairs; and these he
detailed in such earnest language, and in so simple, candid, and

pathetic a manner, as to excite both my astonishment and sympathy. His wife spoke little, but struck me as being a very sagacious woman, without any appearance of forwardness, or any of that awkwardness in her manner which many of these people shew in the presence of a stranger. . . . Gilbert and Robert Burns were certainly very different in their appearance and manner, though they both possessed great abilities, and uncommon information. Gilbert partook more of the manner and appearance of the father, and Robert of the mother. Gilbert, in the first interview I had with him at Lochlea, was frank, modest, well informed, and communicative. The poet seemed distant, suspicious, and without any wish to interest or please. He kept himself very silent, in a dark corner of the room: And before he took any part in the conversation, I frequently detected him scrutinizing me during my conversation with his father and brother. . . . From the period of which I speak, I took a lively interest in Robert Burns; and, before I was acquainted with his poetical powers, I perceived that he possessed very great mental abilities, an uncommonly fertile and lively imagination, a thorough acquaintance with many of our Scottish poets, and an enthusiastic admiration of Ramsay and Fergusson. Even then, on subjects with which he was acquainted, his conversation was rich in well chosen figures, animated, and energetic. Indeed, I have always thought that no person could have a just idea of the extent of Burns's talents, who had not an opportunity to hear him converse. His discrimination of character was great beyond that of any person I ever knew; and I have often observed to him, that it seemed to be intuitive. I seldom ever knew him to make a false estimate of character, when he formed the opinion from his own observation.

Most of the poetry Burns wrote before he was twenty-five is lost. The little of his early verse we now have, and the dates are not certain, is mostly songs about Tarbolton and Mauchline girls, and mostly in English, with an occasional flavoring of Scots words. The surviving early poetry, probably from a little later, is largely religious: prayers, reflections, paraphrases of psalms. From the beginning, Burns was imitative. As he wrote to his friend Peter Hill, "It is an excellent method for improvement, and what I believe every Poet does; to place some favorite classic Author, in our own walks of study & composition, before us as a model."

The models for his songs were all around him. He heard them from friends and neighbors and sweethearts; he heard them from his mother. He also had two collections of songs, one of which he says he "pored over . . . song by song, verse by verse; carefully noting the true tender or sublime from affectation or fustian."

For his early poetry, he had the work of Allan Ramsay in vernacular Scots; Ramsay provided a model for *The Death and Dying Words of Poor Mailie,* and, later, for the verse epistles. But the poets Burns admired before 1782, and continued to admire later, were didactic, sententious, formal writers for polite readers in England, and in Scotland. A great favorite was James Thomson, a Scot, noted for his long poem, *The Seasons,* in which he drew edifying moral reflections from generalized descriptions of nature; and Alexander Pope, in whom Burns found a source of quotations second only to Thomson. He was also fond of William Shenstone, a writer of insipid elegies, *e.g., Elegy XVIII He Repeats the Song of Colin, a discerning Shepherd, Lamenting the State of the Woolen Manufactory.* Thomas Gray's *Elegy Written in a Country Churchyard* echoes throughout *The Cotter's Saturday Night,* and Oliver Goldsmith's *The Deserted Village* also provided many hints for that poem. Burns refers to both of these poets frequently. James Beattie, another Scot, was the famous author of a vapidly pleasant poem, *The Minstrel, or the Progress of Genius,* in which he condescended to native inspiration, and produced such reflections as

> And let us hope — to doubt is to rebel —
> Let us exult in hope, that all shall yet be well.

Edward Young (Hazlitt's "gloomy epigrammatist") is immortal for the line "How populous! how vital is the grave!" which comes from his *Night Thoughts on Life, Death, and Immortality.* And finally there is Robert Blair, still another Scot, who wrote *The Grave,* in which he announced

> The task be mine
> To paint the gloomy horrors of the tomb.

One finds frequent echoes of these men in Burns' poems, but not much work in their manner until after the vernacular flowering, when he was trying other modes because his success had "encouraged such a shoal of ill-spawned monsters to crawl into public notice under the name of Scots Poets, that the very term Scots Poetry borders on the burlesque." Workmanlike though his later imitations may be, Burns was unable to transmute his admired English models into poetry with his individual stamp and distinctive quality, as he had done with his vernacular models. Some of this later work has biographical interest, but as poetry, it is commonplace.

The spirit, the tone, the tune, the feel, the rhythm, the movement, the subjects, the verse forms, the conventions, and the diction of Burns' vernacular Scots poems all derived from a long tradition in Scotland, unfamiliar then and now to most readers of English literature. The suggestion that he write in this tradition was stimulated by his reading of Robert Fergusson. Burns greatly increased the dimensions of what he found. Where Fergusson wrote vividly of local occasions, scenes, and people, Burns at his best transcended the local characters and events which he described. His poems have a controlling theme, a view of life, not merely a central topic. Most important, and wholly undefinable, are the greater imagination and artistic power, the richness and flow of suggestive language, and the force of statement in Burns' work.

He developed a highly individualized style and idiom. He devised a mixture of general English and of Scots spoken in no particular area and by no particular group, to create the informal and conversational manner he wanted. He shifts back and forth from English to Scots as it suits his purpose, his rhythm, his rhyming need, his poetic mood. He tries to be simple, clear, and exciting. He speaks naturally, and to the heart.

Hearing his poetry read in proper Scots discovers grace and

rhythmic felicity and tonal sensitivity otherwise unsuspected, but he comes through well even if one cannot have that advantage. He has much to offer those who are willing to give a little for it, particularly if they have a taste for so full-blooded a poet, with so rich a zest for life. It is true that Burns' world has disappeared. But so has Chaucer's, and Shakespeare's, and Pope's, and Byron's. Great writers create their own worlds, in which those who come after find themselves.

The two years between his residence in Irvine and the death of William Burnes (1782–1784) were for Robert years of Masonic meetings, girls, reading, hard farm work, and worry, but little is known in particular of him during this time. When he became head of the family, and moved to Mossgiel farm, he and Gilbert made a vigorous effort to succeed as farmers, but bad seed and bad weather turned a meagre enterprise into a desperate one; and Robert brought other difficulties on himself, until his situation became intolerable. His personal problems as much as his meeting with Fergusson excited him to write vernacular poetry, and the poetry got him and the family out of their troubles.

III

POET

If Poetry comes not as naturally as Leaves to a tree it had
better not come at all.

John Keats

The rough material of Fine Writing is certainly the gift
of Genius; but I as firmly believe that the workmanship
is the united effort of Pains, Attention, & repeated Trial.

Burns to Henry Erskine

1. Epistles and Satires

On Robert Burns' twenty-fifth birthday (January 25, 1785),
he was known about Tarbolton and Mauchline parishes as a raff-
ish farmer whose family had had trouble with its landlord. By
January, 1789, editions of his poems had been published in Kilmarnock, Edinburgh, Belfast, Dublin, London, Philadelphia, and
New York. Although his first verse dates from 1773, when he was
fourteen, and he continued to write poetry and songs thereafter,
the poems that made his name were written between the summer of 1784 and the autumn of 1786. There survive twenty songs
of previous date, some of them excellent in the versions we have;
also a handful of solemn religious lyrics, and a few reflective
poems of small merit. This work is mostly in English, but no
doubt Burns' inner ear heard his lines pronounced with the Scots
tone and quality. There is only one vernacular poem to give a
hint of what was to follow, *The Death and Dying Words of Poor
Mailie,* in which Burns records a favorite sheep's opinions on
freedom and animal husbandry, and quotes her legacy of advice

to her son and daughter. It is an engaging comic piece in a tradition initiated by William Hamilton of Gilbertfield with *The Last Dying Words of Bonnie Heck, a Famous Grey-Hound in the Shire of Fife* and continued by Allan Ramsay and others.

Burns' productive period began in the summer of 1784, according to his brother Gilbert's recollection, with the *Epistle to Davie,** although as revised and published at Kilmarnock, the poem is dated "January," and includes references to "Jean," presumably Jean Armour, whose relations with Burns began in the summer or fall of 1785. Here, as in his earlier work, Burns is soothing his passions by writing verse, but instead of celebrating girls, he is now formulating his ideas, and he begins to reveal a striking personality as he reflects on his reading and his experience of life. Not that his opinions are original or necessarily compelling. But Burns is that rarest of rarities, a sharply perceptive man of wit and sense and imagination, who speaks out candidly, and who can magnetize his readers. Most notable of all, his poetry seems conversational while actually written in complicated rhythms and with intricate rhyming. He was a gifted metrist, and was deeply concerned with his artisanship, but he wrote for people, in a manner they could enjoy directly and understand, and about matters they had experienced.

Burns has a wide range — humor, pathos, sarcasm, bawdry, impudence, sensitivity to nature, irony, tenderness, pawky sense, satire, moral sentiment. He is not polite or deferential; the reader must take him on his own terms. He responds fully to the forces of life, and he finds that respectability is a denial of humanity and a loss of vitality. He is willing to grant that a full life may be a short one, and may seem folly to those of worldly wisdom. Certainly what makes good poetry does not please the "unco guid." He remarks simply of his tempestuous life and of the poetry that sprang from it

---

* Davie was David Sillar, member of the Bachelor's Club, fiddler, and village rhymer.

> The light that led astray
> Was light from heaven.

And after he had listened to his conscience and married Jean Armour, and had assumed family responsibilities, he observed to Sillar, "I hear you have commenced, Married Man; so much the better, though your Muse may not fare the better for it. — I know not whether the Nine Gipseys are jealous of my Lucky, but they are a good deal shier since I could boast the important relation of Husband."

Burns wrote as an Ayrshire farmer about Ayrshire men and women, but Ayrshire men and women do not differ much from men and women in other places and times, even in China, it seems. Dr. Wen Yuan-Ning, on Burns' birthday in 1944, remarked on the BBC, "Burns . . . is everybody's poet. There are in all human beings, whether Scots or Chinese, feelings and thoughts that 'lie too deep for tears.' Burns in his poems and songs expresses these elemental thoughts and feelings in a way that would strike a responsive chord even in the breast of an unlettered peasant in China, could he but understand the tongue that Burns spoke." Burns' admirer and correspondent, Mrs. Dunlop, wrote him of a Portuguese who, to soothe his soul, would repeat Burns' verses instead of saying his prayers. And Burns' epistles, which were written to friends and neighbors on purely local and personal matters, touch the concerns of men everywhere.

A famous one, the *Epistle to Davie*, opens with a brief and characteristic description of the bitter weather outside, and of the poet snug inside. Burns shifts quickly to a comparison of the rich and the poor in such weather, and then broadens his comparison:

> It's hardly in a body's pow'r,
> To keep, at times, frae being sour,
>   To see how things are shar'd;
> How best o' chiels are whyles in want,   *chaps sometimes*
> While coofs on countless thousands rant   *dolts roister*

And ken na how to ware't; *spend*
But Davie, lad, ne'er fash your head, *trouble*
  Tho' we hae little gear; *wealth*
We're fit to win our daily bread,
  As lang's we're hale and fier: *whole sound*
"Mair spier na, nor fear na," *ask not*
    Auld age ne'er mind a feg; *fig*
    The last o't, the warst o't,
    Is only but to beg.

To lie in kilns and barnes at e'en,
When banes are craz'd, and bluid is thin,
  Is, doubtless, great distress!
Yet then content could make us blest;
Ev'n then, sometimes, we'd snatch a taste
  Of truest happiness.
The honest heart that's free frae a'
  Intended fraud or guile,
However Fortune kick the ba',
  Has ay some cause to smile;
    And mind still, you'll find still,
    A comfort this nae sma';
    Nae mair then, we'll care then,
    Nae farther can we fa'.

The beggar's lot here described was no romantic fantasy, but a likely enough prospect for poor folk like Burns, and a relief from their burdens as well. In stanza five, Burns brings his comparison to its conclusion, in a statement of one of his strongest beliefs:

It's no in titles nor in rank:
It's no in wealth like Lon'on Bank,
  To purchase peace and rest.
It's no in makin muckle, mair; *much more*
It's no in books, it's no in lear, *learning*
  To make us truly blest:
If happiness hae not her seat
  An' center in the breast,
We may be wise, or rich, or great,
  But never can be blest!

> Nae treasures nor pleasures
> Can make us happy lang;
> The heart ay's the part ay
> That makes us right or wrang.

The remaining stanzas speak of the joys of love and friendship.

Burns found suggestions and models and themes for his verse epistles in similar graceful but rather empty epistles exchanged between Hamilton of Gilbertfield and Allan Ramsay. The complex fourteen-line stanza of the *Epistle to Davie* which Burns handles with such ease and felicity, dates back at least to 1597, to Alexander Montgomerie's *The Cherry and the Slae*, which Burns probably found in Ramsay's anthology, *The Ever Green*. There followed a score of similar epistles, jocular, witty, loosely constructed, some of them merely good-natured expressions of friendship and gratitude, but many loaded with careful statements of Burns' views on poetry, on the unevenness of fortune, on pretence and hypocrisy, on Ayrshire kirk affairs, and on his life and lot and love adventures. For most of them he chose the traditional six-line stanza which he uses in the *Epistle to J. Lapraik*,* where, after extending cordial greetings, he comments on poets and poetry, particularly his own.

> But, first an' foremost, I should tell,
> Amaist as soon as I could spell,
> I to the crambo-jingle fell;   *rhyming*
>   Tho' rude an' rough —
> Yet crooning to a body's sel,   *humming*
>   Does weel eneugh

> I am nae poet, in a sense;
> But just a rhymer like by chance,
> An' hae to learning nae pretence;
>   Yet, what the matter?
> Whene'er my Muse does on me glance,
>   I jingle at her.

* Lapraik was a farmer, and a rhymer like Sillar.

Your critic-folk may cock their nose,
And say, "How can you e'er propose,
You wha ken hardly verse frae prose,
    To make a sang?"
But, by your leaves, my learned foes,
    Ye're maybe wrang.

What's a' your jargon o' your Schools,
Your Latin names for horns an' stools?
If honest Nature made you fools,
    What sairs your grammers?   *serves*
Ye'd better taen up spades and shools   *shovels*
    Or knappin-hammers.   *stone-breaking*

A set o' dull, conceited hashes   *dunderheads*
Confuse their brains in college-classes,
They gang in stirks, and come out asses,   *young bullocks*
    Plain truth to speak;
An' syne they think to climb Parnassus   *then*
    By dint o' Greek!

Gie me ae spark o' Nature's fire,
That's a' the learning I desire;
Then, tho' I drudge thro' dub an' mire   *puddle*
    At pleugh or cart,
My Muse, tho' hamely in attire,
    May touch the heart.

Clearly, Burns feels that poetry is not just a matter of forms, rules, and conventions — a series of gracefully turned clichés; it must express the poet's feelings, and spring from inner compulsions. It is for both the simple and the sophisticated. Burns continues in his epistle with some personal comments, expresses a desire for friendship with Lapraik, and adds a characteristic challenge:

Awa ye selfish, warly race,   *worldly*
Wha think that havins, sense, an' grace,   *manners*
Ev'n love an' friendship should give place
        To Catch-the-Plack!   *get the money*
I dinna like to see your face,
        Nor hear your crack.

But ye whom social pleasure charms,
Whose hearts the tide of kindness warms,
Who hold your being on the terms,
    "Each aid the others,"
Come to my bowl, come to my arms,
    My friends, my brothers!

The *Second Epistle to J. Lapraik* continues the theme of the honest man which closed the *Epistle to Davie*.

My worthy friend, ne'er grudge an' carp,	
Tho' Fortune use you hard an' sharp;	
Come, kittle up your moorland harp	*tickle*
Wi' gleesome touch!	
Ne'er mind how Fortune waft an' warp;	*woof*
She's but a bitch.	

. . . .

Do ye envý the city gent,	
Behint a kist to lie an' sklent;	*counter cheat*
Or purse-proud, big wi' cent. per cent.	
An' muckle wame,	*big belly*
In some bit brugh to represent	*borough*
A bailie's name?	*magistrate's*

Or is't the paughty feudal thane,	*haughty*
Wi' ruffl'd sark an' glancing cane,	*shirt shining*
Wha thinks himsel nae sheep-shank bane,	*important*
But lordly stalks;	
While caps an' bonnets aff are taen,	
As by he walks?	

. . . .

For thus the royal mandate ran,
When first the human race began:
"The social, friendly, honest man,
    Whate'er he be,
'Tis he fulfills great Nature's plan,
    And none but he."

In *To William Simpson** *of Ochiltree,* Burns speaks at length of his desire to celebrate Ayrshire in his poems, and includes a famous comment on how poetry comes to a poet.

* A schoolmaster.

The Muse, nae poet ever fand her,   *found*
Till by himsel he learn'd to wander,
Adown some trottin burn's meander,   *brook's*
  An' no think lang:
O, sweet to stray, an' pensive ponder
  A heart-felt sang!

The warly race may drudge an' drive,   *worldly*
Hog-shouther, jundie, stretch, an' strive; *ply the elbows*
Let me fair Nature's face descrive,
  And I, wi' pleasure,
Shall let the busy, grumbling hive
  Bum owre their treasure.   *Hum*

Burns is particularly brisk in a satiric epistle which comments on the pretence and hypocrisy of his adversaries, the clergy: *To the Rev. John M'Math,* Inclosing a Copy of "Holy Willie's Prayer" which he had requested, Sept. 17, 1785.* After commenting on his shots at some clerics and clerical practices, Burns continues,

I own 'twas rash, an' rather hardy,
That I, a simple, countra Bardie,
Should meddle wi' a pack sae sturdy,
  Wha, if they ken me,
Can easy wi' a single wordie
  Louse Hell upon me.

But I gae mad at their grimaces,
Their sighin, cantin, grace-proud faces,
Their three-mile prayers an' hauf-mile graces,
  Their raxin conscience,   *elastic*
Whase greed, revenge, an' pride disgraces
  Waur nor their nonsense.   *Worst than*

 . . . .
O Pope, had I thy satire's darts
To gie the rascals their deserts,
I'd rip their rotten, hollow hearts,
  An' tell aloud
Their jugglin hocus-pocus arts
  To cheat the crowd!

* A Tarbolton clergyman.

God knows, I'm no the thing I should be,
Nor am I even the thing I could be,
But twenty times I rather would be
    An atheist clean
Than under gospel colors hid be
    Just for a screen.

An honest man may like a glass,
An honest man may like a lass;
But mean revenge an' malice fause   *false*
    He'll still disdain
An' then cry zeal for gospel laws
    Like some we ken.

The six-line stanza of the preceding epistles and of many other of Burns' poems had by his time "become the common inheritance of all such Scotsmen as could rhyme." Henley and Henderson trace it back to the trouvères. It was the vehicle for *Bonnie Heck,* and for the *Piper of Kilbarchan.* Ramsay and Fergusson were skillful in it. One of Burns' distinctions is that he could use so hackneyed a form with such vigor and freshness.

By far the most wide-ranging of the epistles is the buoyant one to James Smith,* in which Burns talks about his poetry, his views on life's burdens and rewards, his feelings about "douce folk that live by rule."

Dear Smith, the sle'est, pawkie thief,   *crafty*
That e'er attempted stealth or rief!   *plunder*
Ye surely hae some warlock-breef   *wizard-spell*
    Owre human hearts;
For ne'er a bosom yet was prief   *proof*
    Against your arts.

For me, I swear by sun an' moon,
And ev'ry star that blinks aboon,   *above*
Ye've cost me twenty pair o' shoon,   *shoes*

* Smith, a boon companion and member of the Court of Equity, kept a small draper's shop in Mauchline. He, like Richmond, found it convenient to leave the village, and eventually (1788) he emigrated to Jamaica, where he died.

Just gaun to see you;   *going*
And ev'ry ither pair that's done,
    Mair taen I'm wi' you.   *taken*

That auld, capricious carlin, Nature,   *gossip*
To mak amends for scrimpit stature,   *stunted*
She's turn'd you off, a human-creature
        On her first plan;
And in her freaks, on ev'ry feature
        She's wrote the Man.

Just now I've taen the fit o' rhyme,
My barmie noddle's working prime,   *yeasty brain is*
My fancy yerkit up sublime,
        Wi' hasty summon:
Hae ye a leisure-moment's time
        To hear what's comin?

Some rhyme a neebor's name to lash;
Some rhyme (vain thought!) for needfu' cash;
Some rhyme to court the countra clash,   *country*
        An' raise a din;
For me, an aim I never fash;   *trouble about*
        I rhyme for fun.

The star that rules my luckless lot,
Has fated me the russet coat,
An' damn'd my fortune to the groat;
        But, in requit,
Has blest me with a random-shot
        O' countra wit.

This while my notion's taen a sklent,   *turn*
To try my fate in guid, black prent;
But still the mair I'm that way bent,
        Something cries, "Hoolie!   *softly*
I red you, honest man, take tent!   *advise   heed*
        Ye'll shaw your folly:

"There's ither poets, much your betters,
Far seen in Greek, deep men o' letters,
Hae thought they had ensur'd their debtors,
        A' future ages;
Now moths deform, in shapeless tatters
        Their unknown pages."

Then farewell hopes o' laurel-boughs
To garland my poetic brows!
Henceforth I'll rove where busy ploughs
  Are whistling thrang;   *at work*
An' teach the lanely heights an' howes   *hollows*
  My rustic sang.

I'll wander on, wi' tentless heed   *careless*
How never-halting moments speed,
Till Fate shall snap the brittle thread;
  Then, all unknown,
I'll lay me with th' unglorious dead,
  Forgot and gone!

But why o' death begin a tale?
Just now we're living sound an' hale;
Then top and maintop crowd the sail,
  Heave Care o'er-side!
And large, before Enjoyment's gale,
  Let's tak the tide.

This life, sae far's I understand,
Is a' enchanted fairy-land,
Where pleasure is the magic-wand,
  That, wielded right,
Maks hours like minutes, hand in hand,
  Dance by fu' light.

The magic-wand then let us wield;
For, ance that five-an'-forty's speel'd,   *climbed*
See, crazy, weary, joyless Eild,   *Old Age*
  Wi' wrinkl'd face,
Come hostin, hirplin owre the field, *coughing* *limping*
  Wi' creepin pace.

When ance life's day draws near the gloamin,
Then fareweel vacant, careless roamin;
An' fareweel chearfu' tankards foamin,
  An' social noise:
An' fareweel dear, deluding Woman,
  The joy of joys!

. . . .

O ye douce folk that live by rule,   *sedate*
Grave, tideless-blooded, calm an' cool,
Compar'd wi' you — O fool! fool! fool!

How much unlike!
Your hearts are just a standing pool,
    Your lives a dyke!   *wall*

Nae hair-brained, sentimental traces
In your unletter'd, nameless faces!
In *arioso* trills and graces
    Ye never stray;
But *gravissimo*, solemn basses
    Ye hum away.

Ye are sae grave, nae doubt ye're wise;
Nae ferly tho' ye do despise   *wonder*
The hairum-scairum, ram-stam boys,
    The rattling squad:
I see ye upward cast your eyes —
    Ye ken the road!

Whilst I — but I shall haud me there,   *hold*
Wi' you I'll scarce gang onie where —   *go*
Then, Jamie, I shall say nae mair,
    But quat my sang,   *quit*
Content wi' you to make a pair,
    Where'er I gang.

Before noticing other poems, many of which deal with the
kirk and some of its ministers, and with Burns' love affairs, it
may be helpful to examine some background briefly. In his autobiographical letter to Dr. Moore, Burns says that even before he
had moved from Mt. Oliphant, he was fond of debating religious
topics. "Polemical divinity about this time was putting the country half-mad; and I, ambitious of shining in conversation parties
on Sundays between sermons, funerals, &c. used in a few years
more to puzzle Calvinism with so much heat and indiscretion
that I raised a hue and cry of heresy against me which has not
ceased to this hour." Sillar speaks of his friend's similar activities
in Tarbolton. "He had in his youth paid considerable attention
to the arguments for and against the doctrine of original sin, then
making considerable noise in your neighbourhood [Ayr], and
having perused Dr Taylor's work on that subject, and '*Letters on*

Religion essential to Man,' when he came to Tarbolton, his opinions were of consequence favourable to . . . the moderate side. The religion of the people of Tarbolton at that time was purely the religion of their fathers, . . . and taught by one generation to another, uncontaminated by reading, reflection, and conversation. . . . The slightest insinuation of Taylor's opinions made his neighbours suspect, and some even avoid [Burns], as an heretical and dangerous companion." Sillar also reports that Burns wore the only tied hair in the parish, and wore his plaid "wrapped in a particular manner round his shoulders."

Burns continues in the letter to Dr. Moore, speaking now of the period of his residence at Mossgiel (1784–1786). "I now began to be known in the neighbourhood as a maker of rhymes.*— The first of my poetic offspring that saw the light was a burlesque lamentation on a quarrel between two revd Calvinists, both of them dramatis person in my Holy Fair. . . . Holy Willie's Prayer next made its appearance, and alarmed the kirk-Session so much that they held three several meetings to look over their holy artillery, if any of it was pointed against profane Rhymers. Unluckily for me, my idle wanderings led me, on another side, point-blank within the reach of their heaviest metal." In other words, his having made Jean Armour pregnant gave the elders a chance to get back at him for making sport of them.

In rural Ayrshire the Kirk held high ground in Burns' day. Liberal or Conservative, it feared the Devil, felt his presence, and made every effort to counter his seductions. The instrument for opposing vice and supporting virtue was the Kirk Session, a council of parish elders presided over by the minister. This body had the right and duty to inquire into private behavior, and to recommend censure, private or public. Contumacy could bring denial of church membership, and denial meant serious loss of social standing.

But the Kirk in Ayrshire was torn by inner stress. An Auld

---

* Village rhymers were a regular feature of Scots country life, another of the poetic traditions into which Burns fitted.

Licht party clung with passion to the orthodox Calvinist faith in foreordained salvation or damnation, while a New Licht party felt that good works might help a man into heaven, and that goodness of heart was important. The bitterness distinguishing the factions was intense, and there were further complications. In some parishes the ministers were elected, and tended to be Auld Licht like the congregations. In others, the patron of the parish presented the minister, and since the patrons were gentry and the gentry were more liberal than the peasantry, the presented ministers were probably New Licht even if their congregations were not. The right of patronage was hotly debated, and was widely resented by the people.

Burns viewed these all-too-human dissensions in the ranks of the Lord with genial relish, and when, as we have seen, two Auld Licht ministers quarreled over their parish boundaries and denounced each other publicly, he wrote a poem in ironic sympathy for the Auld Licht cause, whose champions had fallen from grace and weakened its position. *The Twa Herds* [Shepherds] "met with a road of applause" from one side, and with furious resentment from the other. It is still a lively poem, but it requires too much explanation for ready enjoyment by a modern reader. Not so the three satires which followed, and which are among Burns' most famous and successful poems: *Holy Willie's Prayer, The Holy Fair,* and *Address to the Deil* [Devil].

Holy Willie's Prayer is one of the world's great and final satires. William Fisher, the speaker, was a member of the Mauchline Kirk Session which censured Burns for fornication.* Burns describes Fisher as "a rather oldish bachelor elder, in the parish of Mauchline, and much and justly famed for that polemical chattering which ends in tippling orthodoxy, and for that spiritualized

---

* Public rebuke in church by the minister of those guilty of fornication was a regular and popular feature of Sunday worship. Of this "sordid and general tyranny it is only necessary to say that the time-honoured Scottish tradition of fornication triumphantly survived all its terrors." (Edwin Muir, *John Knox,* 1930, 306–307, from Kinsley III, 1069.)

bawdry which refines to liquorish devotion." The unfortunate
man was overcome in a snowstorm on his way home, February
13, 1809, and died in a roadside ditch. Burns seized happily on
a discomfiture of Fisher and the Mauchline Kirk Session to ridicule them. In pursuit of its responsibilities, the Session had
charged Burns' landlord, Gavin Hamilton, with neglect of public
and family worship and contumacy. (His house adjoined the
churchyard.) Hamilton promptly appealed to the Presbytry of
Ayr, a superior court, which ordered the erasure of Mauchline
session minutes against him, after which "the muse overheard
Willie at his devotions." *

Originally, *Holy Willie's Prayer* was parochial, and even occasional. The "Calvinist intercession" and "language of the saints"
which it parodies are now largely historic. But the pious hypocrite exists in all times, and Holy Willie is forever his name and
symbol — in his confusion of virtue and self-interest, of piety
and persecution, of godliness and complacent self-indulgence.
Burns never printed this poem,† but it was widely circulated in
manuscript. While it delighted lawyers like Robert Aiken in Ayr,
who represented Hamilton in this matter, or clergymen like
M'Math in Tarbolton, it as certainly roused the respectable community against its author.

> O Thou that in the Heavens does dwell,
> Wha, as it pleases best Thysel,
> Sends ane to Heaven an' ten to Hell
>   A' for Thy glory,
> And no for onie guid or ill
>   They've done before Thee!
>
> I bless and praise Thy matchless might,
> When thousands Thou hast left in night,
> That I am here before Thy sight,

---

* Hamilton was sustained again when the Session appealed to a higher body
still, the Synod.
† It appeared, however, as an anonymous pamphlet in 1789. (Egerer, #16, 32.)

For gifts an' grace
A burning and a shining light
    To a' this place.

What was I, or my generation,
That I should get sic exaltation?   *such*
I, wha deserv'd most just damnation
    For broken laws,
Sax thousand years ere my creation,   *Six*
    Thro' Adam's cause!

When from my mither's womb I fell,
Thou might hae plung'd me deep in hell
To gnash my gooms, and weep, and wail
    In burning lakes,
Whare damnèd devils roar and yell,
    Chain'd to their stakes.

Yet I am here, a chosen sample,
To show Thy grace is great and ample:
I'm here a pillar o' Thy temple,
    Strong as a rock,
A guide, a buckler, and example
    To a' Thy flock!

But yet, O Lord! confess I must:
At times I'm fash'd wi' fleshly lust;   *troubled*
An' sometimes, too, in warldly trust,
    Vile self gets in;
But Thou remembers we are dust,
    Defiled wi' sin.

O Lord! yestreen, Thou kens, wi' Meg —   *last night   knowest*
Thy pardon I sincerely beg —
O, may't ne'er be a living plague
    To my dishonour!
An' I'll ne'er lift a lawless leg
    Again upon her.

Besides, I farther maun avow —   *must*
Wi' Leezie's lass, three times, I trow —
But, Lord, that Friday I was fou,
    When I cam near her,

Or else, Thou kens, Thy servant true
      Wad never steer her.   *rouse*

Maybe Thou lets this fleshly thorn
Buffet Thy servant e'en and morn,
Lest he owre proud and high should turn
      That he's sae gifted:
If sae, Thy han' maun e'en be borne
      Until Thou lift it.

Lord, bless Thy chosen in this place,
For here Thou has a chosen race!
But God confound their stubborn face
      An' blast their name,
Wha bring Thy elders to disgrace
      An' open shame!

Lord, mind Gau'n Hamilton's deserts:
He drinks, an' swears, an' plays at cartes,
Yet has sae monie takin arts
      Wi' great and sma',
Frae God's ain Priest the people's hearts
      He steals awa.

And when we chasten'd him therefore,
Thou kens how he bred sic a splore,   *row*
And set the world in a roar
      O' laughin at us:
Curse Thou his basket and his store,
      Kail an' potatoes!

Lord, hear my earnest cry and pray'r
Against that Presbyt'ry of Ayr!
Thy strong right hand, Lord, mak it bare
      Upo' their heads!
Lord, visit them, an' dinna spare,
      For their misdeeds!

O Lord, my God! that glib-tongu'd Aiken,
My vera heart and flesh are quakin
To think how we stood sweatin, shakin,
      An pish'd wi' dread,   *pissed*
While he, wi' hingin lip an' snakin,
      Held up his head.

Lord, in Thy day o' vengeance try him!
Lord, visit him wha did employ him!
And pass not in Thy mercy by them,
    Nor hear their pray'r,
But for Thy people's sake destroy them,
    An' dinna spare!

But, Lord, remember me and mine
Wi' mercies temporal and divine,
That I for grace an' gear may shine   *wealth*
    Excell'd by name;
And a' the glory shall be Thine —
    Amen, Amen!

Elizabeth Paton, the mother of Burns' first child, and the cause of his first Kirk Session rebuke, possibly in Tarbolton, had been a servant to Agnes Burnes at Lochlea, and had gone back to her home, Largieside, when the Burneses moved to Mossgiel. Betty, or Lizzie, is described as plain and of a masculine understanding. On May 22, 1785, she bore Burns a daughter, Elizabeth, whom he acknowledged, and who was eventually cared for by his mother at Mossgiel. The child grew up under the protection of her Uncle Gilbert. There is no recorded claim by Betty Paton that she had been deceived, and no claim for marriage, although there is a report that Robert's family disagreed over whether he should marry her or not. When he had raised a little money by the Kilmarnock edition of his poems, she did make a claim for "a certain sum," and on December 1, 1786, discharged "the said Robert Burns of all claims . . . against him for maintenance, cloathing and education of the said child, till it arrives at the fixed age of ten years compleat."

This affair was nothing unusual in Ayrshire peasant life. The minister's rebuke of Rab and Betty followed in due course, and the fine of a guinea, and that was that except for a delightful poem, *Welcome to a Bastart Wean,* a title more apt than the one favored by his Nineteenth Century editors, *A Poet's Welcome to His Love-Begotten Daughter.*

Thou's welcome, wean! Mishanter fa' me,   *child Mishap befall*
If thoughts o' thee or yet thy mammie
Shall ever daunton me or awe me,
      My sweet, wee lady,
Or if I blush when thou shalt ca' me
      Tyta or daddie!

What tho' they ca' me fornicator,
An' tease my name in kintra clatter?   *country chatter*
The mair they talk, I'm kend the better;
      E'en let them clash!
An auld wife's tongue's a feckless matter   *feeble*
      To gie ane fash.   *trouble*

Welcome, my bonie, sweet, wee dochter!
Tho' ye come here a wee unsought for,
And tho' your comin I hae fought for
      Baith kirk and queir;
Yet, by my faith, ye're no unwrought for —
      That I shall swear!

Sweet fruit o' monie a merry dint,   *stroke*
My funny toil is no a' tint: *lost*
Tho' thou cam to the warl' asklent,
      Which fools may scoff at,
In my last plack thy part's be in't   *coin*
      The better half o't.

Tho' I should be the waur bestead,   *worse*
Thou's be as braw and bienly clad,   *fine warmly*
And thy young years as nicely bred
      Wi' education,
As onie brat o' wedlock's bed
      In a' thy station.

Wee image o' my bonie Betty,
As fatherly I kiss and daut thee,
As dear and near my heart I set thee,
      Wi' as guid will,
As a' the priests had seen me get thee
      That's out o' Hell.

Gude grant that thou may ay inherit
Thy mither's looks an' gracefu' merit,

An' thy poor, worthless daddie's spirit
      Without his failins!
'Twill please me mair to see thee heir it
      Than stocket mailins.   *farms*

And if thou be what I wad hae thee,
An' tak the counsel I shall gie thee,
I'll never rue my trouble wi' thee —
      The cost nor shame o't —
But be a loving father to thee,
      And brag the name o't.

The second time Burns became a candidate for a Kirk Session's attention, the occasion was by no means routine. In addition to *Holy Willie's Prayer,* he had written and circulated *The Holy Fair* and *Address to the Deil;* he had led in organizing a mock Session, a Court of Equity or Fornicator's Court,* and he had boasted of his celebrity in a song, *The Fornicator.* Obviously the first rebuke had not taken.

The Fornicator

Ye jovial boys who love the joys,
      The blissful joys of Lovers,
Yet dare avow, with dauntless brow,
      When the bony lass discovers;
I pray draw near, and lend an ear,
      And welcome in a Frater,
For I've lately been on quarantine,
      A proven Fornicator.

* Designed ostensibly to discourage the desertion of girls "in trouble" by their quondam partners. The final stanza of a merry song, *Wha'll Mow* [Ride] *Me Now,* generally agreed to be by Burns (but whether his or not, no matter) will serve admirably as the motto of this sportive group.

But Deevil damn the lousy loon
      Denies the bairn he got;
Or lea's the merry arse he lo'ed   *leaves loved*
      To wear a ragged coat.

A summons and decree of this "Court," in verse and by Burns, appears in Section VI.

Before the Congregation wide,
 I passed the muster fairly,
My handsome Betsy by my side,
 We gat our ditty rarely;
But my downcast eye by chance did spy
 What made my lips to water,
Those limbs so clean where I, between,
 Commenc'd a Fornicator.

With rueful face and signs of grace
 I pay'd the buttock-hire,
But the night was dark and thro' the park   *field*
 I could not but convoy her;
A parting kiss, I could not less,
 My vows began to scatter,
My Betsy fell — lal de dal lal lal,
 I am a Fornicator.

But for her sake this vow I make,
 And solemnly I swear it,
That while I own a single crown
 She's welcome for to share it;
And my roguish boy his Mother's joy
 And the darling of his Pater,
For him I boast my pains and cost,
 Although a Fornicator.

Ye wenching blades whose hireling jades
 Have tipt you off blue-boram,   *given you the clap*
I tell you plain, I do disdain
 To rank you in the Quorum;
But a bony lass upon the grass
 To teach her esse Mater,   *to be a mother*
And no reward but for regard,
 O that's a Fornicator.

Your warlike Kings and Heros bold,
 Great Captains and Commanders;
Your mighty Caesars fam'd of old,
 And conquering Alexanders;
In fields they fought and laurels bought,
 And bulwarks strong did batter,
But still they grac'd our noble list,
 And ranked Fornicator! ! !

On the second Sunday in August, Mauchline celebrated its annual communion service. Except for the disgraced and forbidden, everybody from the parish came, and many from other parishes. Since the church could not possibly hold them all at once, a tent was erected on the church grounds from which a relay of neighboring preachers competed for the favor of those outside, while successive groups of communicants received the sacrament in the church itself. In southwestern Scotland, "sacramental occasions" like this were called popularly and aptly, "Holy Fairs."

A prose account of them published in 1759, suggests that Burns may have had it in mind as he wrote his poem in 1785 about Mauchline Holy Fair. Its title was *A Letter from a Blacksmith to the Ministers and Elders of the Church of Scotland*. A few excerpts are instructive:

In Scotland they run from kirk to kirk, and flock to see a Sacrament, and make the same use of it that the papists do of their pilgrimages and processions — that is, indulge themselves in drunkenness, folly, and idleness. . . . At the time of the administration of the Lord's Supper, upon the Thursday, Saturday, and Monday, we have preaching in the fields near the church. Allow me, then, to describe it as it really is: at first you find a great number of men and women lying upon the grass; here they are sleeping and snoring, some with their faces toward heaven, others with their faces turned downwards, or covered with their bonnets; there you find a knot of young fellows and girls making assignations to go home together in the evening, or to meet in some alehouse; in another place you see a pious circle sitting around an ale-barrel, many of which stand ready upon carts for the refreshment of the saints. . . . In this sacred assembly there is an odd mixture of religion, sleep, drinking, courtship, and a confusion of sexes, ages and characters. When you get a little nearer the speaker, so as to be within reach of the sound, tho' not of the sense of his words, for that can only reach a small circle . . . you will find some weeping and others laughing, some pressing to get nearer the tent or tub in which the parson is sweating, bawling, jumping, and beating the desk; others fainting with the stifling heat, or wrestling to extricate themselves from the crowd; one seems very devout and serious, and the next moment is scolding or cursing his neighbours for squeezing or treading on him; in an instant after, his countenance is composed to the religious gloom, and he is groaning, sighing, and weeping for his sins: in a word, there is such an absurd mixture of the serious and comick, that were we convened for any other purpose than that of worshipping the God and Governor of Nature, the scene would exceed all power of farce.

Some details from *A General View of Agriculture in the County of Ayr,* Board of Agriculture Report, 1811, by William Alton (b. 1780 — still alive 1847), suggest that there was little difference in many essentials between a holy fair and an ordinary one:

The manner in which the unmarried people, of both sexes, conduct themselves at fairs and races, is far from being decorous, and calls loudly for reformation. Great numbers of *lads* and *lasses* are collected at the fair, in the course of the afternoon, where they continue till about midnight. The country girls travel to the fair, (unless in time of frost) without shoes or stockings, with their coats tucked up, and retire to the corner of some park, near the fair, where they put on their shoes and perform the labours of the *toilette;* after which, they stalk into the fair, make *sham* calls at shops, or saunter among the crowd, till their rustic admirers, who are also on the *look-out,* invite them to the change-house. This is done by tapping the fair one on the shoulder, treading on her foot, or by some pantomimic gesture which she understands, and readily obeys, unless a swain, more to her mind, shall then make similar signals.

Nothing is so galling to the *lasses,* as to be allowed to stand long idle, in the market place, without being invited to the change-house by some young man. The place where groups of them stand, without being called upon, is termed, "the pitiful market."

A "sturdy fallow," having made his signals, struts off to the ale-house, his "clever hizzy," following at a short distance, proud of having gotten a "chance," and envied by such as have had none.

In the ale-house, the *lad* treats his *lass,* with ale, whisky, and sweet-meats, (called *fairings*), hugs her in his arms, tumbles her into a bed, if one can be found, though many persons be in the room, then, with one arm under her head, the other, and one of his legs over her, he enjoys a *tete a tete* conversation, longer or shorter, as the market happens to be brisk or slow. After a little time, they adjourn to some long-room, mason lodge, or barn, to dance reels. If the hall be much crowded at the time, they are obliged to maintain a struggle for the floor; which is done by the *lad* laying hold of his partner by the sides, and pushing her forward to the front of the crowd.

Towards night, when *John Barleycorn* has obtained possession of the *upper storey*, these struggles for the floor often lead to blows. During the affray, the weak part of the company, with the fiddler, get upon the benches, or run into a corner, while the more heroic, or those who are most intoxicated, take the post of honour. Few blows are struck in these uproars; they only pull and haul, and make a hideous noise. A few minutes exhaust their rage; — new company arrives; — the fiddler becomes arbiter; — the tattered nymphs collect their shoes, and adjust their deranged dress; — the fiddler strikes up a reel; — the dance proceeds, and the affray ends as it began, no one can tell how.

If the *lass* has already been called for, the *lad* holds by her to the utmost; but if she has not been asked for, he soon becomes indifferent and ultimately leaves her. If she has many lovers, they press into the room, and even into the bed, where she is reclining; lay hold of her by the arm, leg, or any part of her dress which they can come at; and by dint of importunity, little short of compulsion, they obtain an audience. While one is pouring out his requests, in whispers into her ear, another fixes his talons on any part of her body, which he can reach; — she listens to him, till others arrive; — they jostle each other; and all of them roar out her name, like so many auctioneers calling a roup. She continues, for a time, in a sort of passive uncertainty, yielding to the greatest force, sometimes getting upright, at other times, she is thrown upon the bed, till after enjoying several of these kind embraces, and hearing many supplications, one of the *sturdiest* of the *chiels* lays hold of her in his arms, whispers his prayer in her ear, and by main force, hurries her off holding her by the wrist, with one hand, and his other arm either round her neck or back, as a constable would keep hold of a thief, till he lodges her in a bedside, in another ale-house; at all which "she is nothing loath." — The disappointed lovers follow and renew their applications; — a similar farce is gone through, till one of them hurries her to another ale-house, and to another bed, if one can be found.

This is what they call "holding the fair," and it is continued till about midnight, when the *lads* and *lasses* begin to pair off, and return to the fair one's home, where they generally spend an hour or two by themselves, in the barn, byre, or cart shade, talking over the events of the day.

These accounts of village life, and the outraged piety which greeted Burns' poem *The Holy Fair* and other of his reflections on religious observance in his part of Ayrshire, suggest that he was but wittily clearsighted in revealing uncomfortable truth. And both Aiton and the Blacksmith give a vivid sense of what might be called the Breughel quality in Ayrshire peasant life, essential to an understanding of Burns and his poetry.

He opens his poem with a joyous salute to the summer morning, and then introduces his three allegorical maidens, Superstition, Hypocrisy, and Fun, appropriate companions with whom he sets off for the Sacramental Occasion. He gives a lively account of the country folk he meets — farmers, housewives, laborers, lasses, and then describes the churchyard scene with its mixture of piety, thirst, and lubricity, all of which find satisfaction. Then, after some shots at the local clergy, he shows the people on their way home. In *The Holy Fair*, Burns is genial, sympathetic, and deadly. He makes the most of his own dramatic situation, at once involved in the action and yet detached from it. He sets the scene and lets the actors destroy themselves. The structure of the poem manifests itself in the easy flow of events, detail strengthens tone, and style enriches theme. The poem grows to effortless perfection and dissolves with crushing simplicity.

> Upon a simmer Sunday morn,
>   When Nature's face is fair,
> I walkèd forth to view the corn,
>   An' snuff the caller air.   *fresh*

The rising sun, owre Galston Muirs,
  Wi' glorious light was glintin;
The hares were hirplin down the furs,   *hopping   furrows*
  The lav'rocks they were chantin   *larks*
    Fu' sweet that day.

As lightsomely I glowr'd abroad   *gazed*
  To see a scene sae gay,
Three hizzies, early at the road,   *young women*
  Cam skelpin up the way.   *hastening*
Twa had manteeles o' dolefu' black,
  But ane wi' lyart lining;   *gray*
The third, that gaed a wee a-back   *walked   behind a bit*
  Was in the fashion shining
    Fu' gay that day.

The twa appear'd like sisters twin,
  In feature, form, an' claes;   *clothes*
Their visage wither'd, lang an' thin,
  An' sour as onie slaes: *sloes*
The third cam up, hap-step-an'-lowp,
  As light as onie lambie,
An' wi' a curchie low did stoop,   *curtsey*
  As soon as e'er she saw me,
    Fu' kind that day.

Wi' bonnet aff, quoth I, "Sweet lass,
  I think ye seem to ken me;
I'm sure I've seen that bonie face,
  But yet I canna name ye."
Quo' she, an' laughin as she spak,
  An' taks me by the han's,
"Ye, for my sake, hae gi'en the feck   *most*
  O a' the Ten Comman's
    A screed some day.   *rip*

"My name is Fun — your cronie dear,
  The nearest friend ye hae;
An' this is Superstition here,
  An' that's Hypocrisy.
I'm gaun to Mauchline Holy Fair,   *going*
  To spend an hour in daffin: *frolic*
Gin ye'll go there, yon runkl'd pair,   *If   wrinkled*

We will get famous laughin
　　At them this day."

Quoth I, "Wi' a' my heart, I'll do't;
　　I'll get my Sunday's sark on,　　　　　　*shirt*
An' meet you on the holy spot;
　　Faith, we'se hae fine remarkin!"　　　　　*we'll*
Then I gaed home at crowdie-time,　*went*　*porridge-*
　　An' soon I made me ready;
For roads were clad, frae side to side,
　　Wi' monie a wearie body,
　　　　In droves that day.

Here farmers gash, in ridin graith,　*respectable gear*
　　Gaed hoddin by their cotters;　　　　　*jogging*
There swankies young, in braw braid-claith,　*strapping lads*
　　Are springin owre the gutters.
The lasses, skelpin barefit, thrang,　*hastening*　*in a crowd*
　　In silks an' scarlets glitter;
Wi' sweet-milk cheese, in monie a whang,　*thick slice*
　　An' farls, bak'd wi' butter,　　　　　　*cakes*
　　　　Fu' crump that day.　　　　　　　*crisp*

When by the plate we set our nose,
　　Weel heapèd up wi' ha'pence,
A greedy glowr black-bonnet throws,　*look*　*the Elder*
　　An' we maun draw our tippence.
Then in we go to see the show:
　　On ev'ry side they're gath'rin;
Some carrying dails, some chairs an' stools,　*planks*
　　An' some are busy bleth'rin　　　　　*gabbling*
　　　　Right loud that day.

Here stands a shed to fend the show'rs,
　　An' screen our countra gentry;
There Racer Jess, an' twa-three whores,
　　Are blinkin at the entry.　　　　　　*leering*
Here sits a raw o' tittlin jads,　　　*tattling jades*
　　Wi' heaving breasts an' bare neck;
An' there a batch o' wabster lads　　　　*weaver*
　　Blackguardin frae Kilmarnock,
　　　　For fun this day.

Here some are thinkin on their sins,
  An' some upo' their claes;   *clothes*
Ane curses feet that fyl'd his shins,   *soiled*
  Anither sighs an' prays:
On this hand sits a chosen swatch,   *sample*
  Wi' screw'd-up, grace-proud faces;
On that a set o' chaps, at watch,
  Thrang winkin on the lasses   *Busy*
      To chairs that day.

O happy is that man an' blest!
  Nae wonder that it pride him!
Whase ain dear lass, that he likes best,
  Comes clinkin down beside him!
Wi' arm repos'd on the chair back,
  He sweetly does compose him;
Which, by degrees, slips round her neck,
  An's loof upon her bosom,   *And his palm*
      Unkend that day.

[There follow six stanzas describing local preachers. Eventually the crowd seeks relief in taverns.]

Now butt an' ben the change-house fills,   *kitchen and parlor   tavern*
  Wi' yill-caup commentators;   *ale-cup*
Here's crying out for bakes an' gills,   *biscuits*
  An' there the pint-stowp clatters;
While thick an' thrang, an' loud an' lang,   *busy*
  Wi' logic an' wi' Scripture,
They raise a din, that in the end
  Is like to breed a rupture
      O' wrath that day.

Leeze me on drink! it gies us mair   *Blessings on*
  Than either school or college;
It kindles wit, it waukens lear   *learning*
  It pangs us fou o' knowledge: *crams*
Be't whiskey-gill or penny wheep,   *potent small beer*
  Or onie stronger potion,
It never fails, on drinkin deep,
  To kittle up our notion,
      By night or day.

The lads an' lasses, blythely bent
 To mind baith saul an' body,
Sit round the table, weel content,
 And steer about the toddy: *stir*
On this ane's dress, an' that ane's leuk,
 They're makin observations;
While some are cozie i' the neuk,   *corner*
 An' formin assignations
   To meet some day.

But now the Lord's ain trumpet touts,
 Till a' the hills are rairin,
And echoes back return the shouts;
 Black Russell is na sparin:
His piercin words, like Highlan' swords,
 Divide the joints an' marrow;
His talk o' Hell, whare devils dwell,
 Our verra "souls does harrow"
   Wi' fright that day!

A vast, unbottom'd, boundless pit,
 Fill'd fou o' lowin brunstane,   *full glowing **brimstone***
Whase ragin flame, an' scorchin heat,
 Wad melt the hardest whun-stane!
The half-asleep start up wi' fear,
 An' think they hear it roarin;
When presently it does appear,
 'Twas but some neebor snorin
   Asleep that day.

'Twad be owre lang a tale to tell,
 How monie stories past;
An' how they crowded to the yill,
 When they were a' dismist;
How drink gaed round, in cogs an' caups, *large and small wooden vessels*
 Amang the furms an' benches;
An' cheese an' bread, frae women's laps,
 Was dealt about in lunches,   *thick pieces*
   An' dawds that day.   *lumps*

In comes a gawsie, gash guidwife,   *jolly shrewd*
 An' sits down by the fire,
Syne draws her kebbuck an' her knife;   *Then cheese*
 The lasses they are shyer:

The auld guidmen, about the grace,
　　Frae side to side they bother;
Till some ane by his bonnet lays,
　　An' gies them't, like a tether,
　　　　Fu' lang that day.

Waesucks! for him that gets nae lass,　　　　　　　　　*Alas!*
　　Or lasses that hae naething!
Sma' need has he to say a grace,
　　Or melvie his braw claething!　　　　*soil with meal　fine*
O wives, be mindfu', ance yoursel,
　　How bonie lads ye wanted;
An' dinna for a kebbuck-heel
　　Let lasses be affronted
　　　　On sic a day.

Now Clinkumbell, wi' rattlin tow,　　　　　　*Bellringer　rope*
　　Begins to jow an' croon;　　　　　　　　　　*toll　boom*
Some swagger hame as best they dow,　　　　　　　　*can*
　　Some wait the afternoon.　　*[for the next round of preaching]*
At slaps the billies halt a blink,　　*gaps in fences　fellows　moment*
　　Till lasses strip their shoon:
Wi' faith an' hope, an' love an' drink,
　　They're a' in famous tune
　　　　For crack that day.　　　　　　　　　　　　*talk*

How monie hearts this day converts
　　O' sinners and o' lasses!
Their hearts o' stane, gin night, are gane　　*by nightfall　gone*
　　As saft as onie flesh is:
There's some are fou o' love divine:
　　There's some are fou o' brandy;
An' monie jobs that day begin,
　　May end in houghmagandie　　　　　　　　*fornication*
　　　　Some ither day.

In several variations, the eight-line stanza with a refrain of *The Holy Fair* had been traditional in poems of this kind for three hundred years, with its original in *Christis Kirk on the Green*. Both Ramsay and Fergusson had standardized the tag word "day" at the end of the refrain. Burns is skillful in giving this refrain an imaginative and structural variety.

Whatever may have been its relation to the Blacksmith's account of sacramental occasions quoted above, Burns' *The Holy Fair* is certainly modeled directly on Fergusson's *Leith Races* and *Hallow-Fair*. Where Ramsay was mainly quaint and humorous, Fergusson wrote vernacular poems with a spirited irreverence which Burns found congenial, and which he adopted and enriched in this poem and elsewhere. The relation of Burns' vernacular poetry to the Scots poems which suggested it is important to an understanding of what he accomplished and what he did not accomplish. A brief anthology as Appendix A will illustrate the tradition from which he worked. His originality can be appreciated only by those familiar with his sources.

Address to the Deil [Devil] is Burns' final poem of his irreverent trio, and his country neighbors must have found it little short of blasphemous. While it helped establish its author's reputation for irreligion, today it seems merely a lively recital of picturesque folklore, and its central character but a good-natured parody of Milton's Satan. Burns was no man to deny the pride and power of the Prince of Darkness, but he found only amusement in the Deil of peasant Ayrshire, and its Auld Licht clergy. The brimstone pit of pulpit oratory was for him no place even for a Devil, and he felt it was a sad comedown for Satan who had led the embattled seraphim to war, to be drowning unhappy travellers at fords and preventing cream from churning. Burns could only chuckle at such a Devil's police power over souls, especially his own. The poem was a lighthearted treatment of matters taken very seriously by some, and it incited retaliation by those offended.

> O Thou! whatever title suit thee —
> Auld Hornie, Satan, Nick, or Clootie —   *Hoofie*
> Wha in yon cavern grim an' sootie,
>   Clos'd under hatches,
> Spairges about the brunstane cootie,   *splashes tub*
>   To scaud poor wretches!   *scald*

Hear me, Auld Hangie, for a wee,   *Hangman*
An' let poor damnèd bodies be;
I'm sure sma' pleasure it can gie,
    E'en to a deil,
To skelp an' scaud poor dogs like me   *strike   scald*
    An' hear us squeel.

Great is thy pow'r an' great thy fame;
Far kend an' noted is thy name;
An' tho' yon lowin heugh's thy hame,   *flaming pit's*
    Thou travels far;
An' faith! thou's neither lag, nor lame,   *backward*
    Nor blate, nor scaur.   *bashful   afraid*

Whyles, rangin like a roarin lion   *Sometimes*
For prey, a' holes an' corners tryin;
Whyles, on the strong-wing'd tempest flyin,
    Tirlin the kirks;   *Uncovering*
Whyles, in the human bosom pryin,
    Unseen thou lurks.

. . . .

Let warlocks grim, an' wither'd hags,   *wizards*
Tell how wi' you, on ragweed nags,   *ragwort*
They skim the muirs an' dizzy crags,
    Wi' wicked speed;
And in kirk-yards renew their leagues,
    Owre howkit dead.   *exhumed*

Thence, countra wives, wi' toil an' pain,
May plunge an' plunge the kirn in vain;   *churn*
For O! the yellow treasure's taen
    By witching skill;
An' dawtit, twal-pint hawkie's gaen   *petted, twelve-pint cow's gone*
    As yell's the bill.   *dry as the bull*

Thence, mystic knots mak great abuse
On young guidmen, fond, keen an' croose;   *husbands   cocksure*
When the best wark-lume i' the house,   *tool*
    By cantraip wit,
Is instant made no worth a louse,
    Just at the bit.   *nick of time*

When thowes dissolve the snawy hoord   *thaws   snowy   hoard*
An' float the jinglin icy board,
Then, water-kelpies haunt the foord,
    By your direction,
An' nighted trav'llers are allur'd
    To their destruction.

And aft your moss-traversing spunkies   *bog   jack-o'-lanterns*
Decoy the wight that late an' drunk is:
The bleezin, curst, mischievous monkies
    Delude his eyes,
Till in some miry slough he sunk is,
    Ne'er mair to rise.

. . . .

But a' your doings to rehearse,
Your wily snares an' fechtin fierce,   *fighting*
Sin' that day Michael did you pierce
    Down to this time,
Wad ding a Lallan tongue, or Erse,   *beat   Lowland*
    In prose or rhyme.

An' now, Auld Cloots, I ken ye're thinkin,   *Hoofs*
A certain Bardie's rantin, drinkin,
Some luckless hour will send him linkin,   *hurrying*
    To your black Pit;
But, faith! he'll turn a corner jinkin,   *dodging*
    An' cheat you yet.

But fare-you-weel, Auld Nickie-Ben!
O, wad ye tak a thought an' men'!
Ye aiblins might — I dinna ken —   *perhaps*
    Still hae a stake:
I'm wae to think upo' yon den,   *sad*
    Ev'n for your sake!

2. Bard

Burns' admirers have long trumpeted his broad humanity, his championship of Freedom and Equality, his challenge to the Establishment and to Kirk tyranny. They celebrate his patriotism and his success despite a lowly origin. They lament his failure to win patronage, and his early death. And they argue about whether he is a "national" voice. But his lasting fame arises from something else entirely — his distinction as a poet. And this distinction, like so much about Burns, is paradoxical. In his poems, he is essentially a wit, a moralist, a satirist — a son of the Eighteenth Century; but his forms and style differ greatly from those of his neo-classical predecessors and contemporaries. On the other hand, he wrote of simple subjects, in natural language and a concrete style, thereby foreshadowing much in Wordsworth.

Sensitive to rhythms, tonal effects, rhetorical emphasis — Burns used language with rare force and color to give the quality and texture of life, and to urge his own feelings.* There are reaches of human experience to which his Muse does not respond. One finds irony but no tragedy; warm feeling but not the depths of Wordsworth's sonnet on Westminster Bridge or of Keats' Odes. On the other hand, Wordsworth could not have written *Tam o' Shanter* or *The Jolly Beggars,* nor Keats *Holy Willie's Prayer* or *Corn Rigs.* To each poet his own, and Burns' own is very good indeed. "Bold, graphic, variable, expressive, packed with observations and ideas, the phrases go ringing and glittering on through verse after verse, through stave after stave, through poem after poem, in a way that makes the reading of this peasant a peculiar pleasure for the student of style." (Henley.)

Burns once described poetry as "Natural ideas expressed in melodious words," a phrase suggestive of the simplicity and conversational tone of his verse, which disguise its careful finish. Burns has little in common with poets who write in an elaborate or decorative style, like Spenser, or in the grand manner, like Milton. He is what he called himself, a Bard, recording experience in a traditional way for a popular audience — "a man speaking to men." With the metaphysical and symbolist traditions he has no connection at all, except as any poetry is what Robert

---

* Sir Walter Scott wrote, "Long life to thy fame and peace to thy soul, Rob Burns! When I want to express a sentiment which I feel strongly, I find the phrase in Shakespeare — or thee." (*The Journal of Sir Walter Scott,* New York, 1890. 383–84.)

Frost called a "constant symbol," saying something in terms of something else. But even here, Burns is not much given to indirection. He speaks straightforwardly, and is distinguished among our major poets by the small expansion of artifice between the impulse which strikes poetry from experience, and the poetic statement. Like the Eighteenth Century English poets whom he admired, Burns thought to "study men, their manners, and their ways," and he agreed that "True wit is Nature to advantage dressed." In his verse, with admirable economy, he sought the memorable phrase and the apt illustration for his observation — strengthening his statement and pointing his meaning with rhythm and rhyme. Although sensitive to external nature, he felt that "Exotic rural imagery is always comparatively flat," unless it serves to enrich remark.

As we have seen, the forms and style which Burns found congenial were Scots, as was the life he wrote about; and he felt that the eclectic and irregularly used Scots vernacular was essential in giving his verse the right movement, as well as desirable in coloring characters and incidents. He agreed with Ramsay, "The *Scotticisms,* which perhaps may offend some over-nice Ear, give new Life and Grace to the Poetry, and become their Place as well as the *Doric* dialect of *Theocritus,* so much admired by the best Judges." It should be noted that in poems like *Hallowe'en* and *The Auld Farmer's New-Year Morning Salutation to his Auld Mare, Maggie,* the Doric is appropriately much richer, while in many poems it is merely an occasional coloration. The use of dialect also increases the dramatic tension between Burns' innate peasant qualities and his acquired detachment from them. One must familiarize himself with Burns' special characteristics, as is true for all poets, particularly those of another day, but with him it is largely a matter of vocabulary. The prodigies of exegesis and digestion familiar in contemporary criticism are incongruous for one of his limpid simplicity. He fiddles no harmonics, and requires no guide to his feeling or purpose.

Burns belongs with noted predecessors: Chaucer (of the *Canterbury Tales*), Henryson (of the fables and *Robene and Makyne*), and Dunbar (in his less courtly moments). His parallels with Shakespeare are often noted: modest origins and scanty formal training; "native genius"; individuality in the use of established forms and subjects; a concrete style, a lyric gift, and metrical felicity; and zest for the human comedy. In Burns' own century, he shares top honors with Pope, his fellow wit and satirist. And of his successors, he has the strongest kinship with his neighbor and contemporary, Wordsworth, and with his fellow-Scot, Byron, in the deceptively casual *Beppo* and *Don Juan.*

One of the first qualities which a reader notices in Burns' poetry is the way his "countra wit" distills observation into proverbial statement. "O wad some Power the giftie gie us / To see oursels as ithers see us!" "It's aye the cheapest lawyer's fee / To taste the barrel." "Ne'er mind how Fortune waft an' warp; / She's but a bitch." "Nursing her wrath to keep it warm." "The best-laid schemes o' mice an' men / Gang aft agley." "Feel not a want but what yourselves create." "Nae man can tether time or tide." "But facts are chiels that winna ding, / And downa be disputed." "The heart ay's the part ay / That makes us right or wrang." "Man's inhumanity to man / Makes countless thousands mourn!" "Morality, thou deadly bane / Thy tens o' thousands thou hast slain!"

> Life is all a variorum,
>   We regard not how it goes;
> Let them prate about decorum,
>   Who have characters to lose.
>
> Ye high, exalted, virtuous dames,
>   Tied up in godly laces,
> Before ye gie poor Frailty names,
>   Suppose a change o' cases:
> A dear-lov'd lad, convenience snug,
>   A treach'rous inclination —
> But, let me whisper i' your lug,   *ear*
>   Ye've aiblins nae temptation.   *maybe*

But the informality which may give zest to a proverb is likely
to blunt an epigram. Burns was fond of producing rhymed witticisms, many merely dull or strained, but a few pleasantly amusing, like his lines to Robert Ainslie's sister Rachel, in church:

> Fair maid, you need not take the hint,
>   Nor idle texts pursue;
> 'Twas guilty sinners that he meant,
>   Not angels such as you.

Many were virulent, however, and, as he told Maria Riddell,
often written on people against whom he had no enmity. One
of his best seems to have been of that kind:

On Lord Galloway

> Bright ran thy line, O Galloway,
>   Thro' many a far-famed sire!
> So ran the far-famed Roman way
>   So ended in a mire.

The subject of another has not been identified.

> Here cursing, swearing Burton lies,
> A buck, a beau, or "Dem my eyes!"
> Who in his life did little good,
> And his last words were — "Dem my blood!"

Perhaps his most famous epigram was provoked by a court duel
between Burns' friend Henry Erskine, Dean of Faculty, and Islay
Campbell, Lord Advocate — stanzas to the tune of *Killiecrankie*.

Lord Advocate

> He clench'd his pamphlets in his fist,
>   He quoted and he hinted,
> Till in a declamation-mist
>   His argument he tint it: *lost*

He gapèd for 't, he grapèd for 't,   *groped*
   He fand it was awa, man;   *found*
But what his common sense came short,
   He ekèd out wi' law, man.

Mr. Erskine

Collected, Harry stood awee,
   Then open'd out his arm, man;
His lordship sat wi' ruefu' e'e,
   And ey'd the gathering storm, man;
Like wind-driv'n hail it did assail,
   Or torrents owre a linn, man;   *cascade*
The bench sae wise, lift up their eyes,
   Hauf-wauken'd wi' the din, man.

But Burns' epigrams in general do not suggest "the ruffle's flutter and the flash of steel" so necessary to success in that difficult form. His style and language are, however, an ideal medium for his sophisticated account of mankind in the guise, largely, of Eighteenth Century Ayrshire countrymen.

It remains to suggest something of his grace at adjusting syntax and syllables to the demands of meter and rhyme, and his aptness at suiting tone, rhythm, and illustration to the matter at hand. His range and variety are happily illustrated in many of his opening stanzas.

The Holy Fair

Upon a simmer Sunday morn,
   When Nature's face is fair,
I walkèd forth to view the corn,
   An' snuff the caller air.   *fresh*
The rising sun, owre Galston Muirs,
   Wi' glorious light was glintin;
The hares were hirplin down the furs,   *furrows*
   The lav'rocks they were chantin   *larks*
      Fu' sweet that day.

To a Mouse

Wee, sleekit, cowrin, tim'rous beastie,
O, what a panic's in thy breastie!

Thou need na start awa sae hasty
     Wi' bickering brattle!   *hurrying scamper*
I wad be laith to rin an' chase thee,   *loth*
     Wi' murdering pattle!   *plough-staff*

Hallowe'en

Upon that night, when fairies light
  On Cassilis Downans dance,   [*some small hills*]
Or owre the lays, in splendid blaze,   *pastures*
  On sprightly coursers prance;
Or for Colean the rout is taen,   *road taken*
  Beneath the moon's pale beams;
There, up the Cove, to stray and rove,
  Amang the rocks and streams
    To sport that night:

. . . .

Some merry, friendly country-folks
  Together did convene,
To burn their nits, an' pou their stocks,   *nuts pull plants*
  An' haud their Hallowe'en
    Fu' blythe that night.

Death and Dr. Hornbook

Some books are lies frae end to end,
And some great lies were never penn'd:
Ev'n ministers, they had been kend   *known*
  In holy rapture,
A rousing whid at times to vend,   *lie*
  And nail't wi' Scripture.

Burns' metrical felicity is everywhere apparent, but perhaps it can be exemplified most happily by examples of the way he gives freshness and variety to the hackneyed *rime couée* which he favored.

Lines on Meeting with Lord Daer

This wot ye all whom it concerns:
I, Rhymer Rob, *alìas* Burns,
    October twenty-third,
A ne'er-to-be-forgotten day,
Sae far I sprachl'd up the brae
    I dinner'd wi' a Lord.

To a Mouse

> I'm truly sorry man's dominion
> Has broken Nature's social union,
> An' justifies that ill opinion
>   Which makes thee startle
> At me, thy poor, earth-born companion
>   An' fellow mortal!

*On the Late Captain Grose's Peregrinations Thro' Scotland,
Collecting the Antiquities of that Kingdom*

> Of Eve's first fire he has a cinder;
> Auld Tubalcain's fire-shool and fender;   *shovel*
> That which distinguishèd the gender
>   O' Balaam's ass;
> A broomstick o' the witch of Endor,
>   Weel shod wi' brass.

*The Auld Farmer's New-Year Morning Salutation to his Auld Mare,
Maggie*

> When thou and I were young and skiegh,   *skittish*
> An' stable-meals at fairs were driegh,   *tedious*
> How thou wad prance, an' snore, an' skriegh, *snort whinny*
>   An' tak the road!
> Towns-bodies ran, an' stood abeigh,
>   An' ca't thee mad.

> When thou was corn't, an' I was mellow,
> We took the road ay like a swallow:
> At brooses thou had ne'er a fellow,   *wedding-races*
>   For pith an' speed;
> But ev'ry tail thou pay't them hollow,
>   Whare'er thou gaed.

The *Cherry and the Slae* stanza of the *Epistle to Davie* provides a
more striking example of metrical virtuosity. See pp. 53–54.

In his verse, Burns normally thought and wrote concretely.

Epistle to James Smith

> My barmie noddle's working prime.   *foaming*

The Vision

> There, lanely by the ingle-cheek,   *fire-side*
> I sat and ey'd the spewing reek,
> That fill'd, wi' hoast-provoking smeek,   *cough- smoke*

The auld clay biggin;   *building*
An' heard the restless rattons squeak
About the riggin.   *rooftree*

To a Mouse

That wee bit heap o' leaves an' stibble,
Has cost thee monie a weary nibble!
Now thou's turned out, for a' thy trouble,
　　But house or hald,   *Without   holding*
To thole the winter's sleety dribble,   *endure*
　　An' cranreuch cauld!   *hoar frost*

The Twa Dogs

That merry day the year begins,
They bar the door on frosty win's;
The nappy reeks wi' mantling ream,   *cream*
An' sheds a heart-inspiring steam;
The luntin pipe, an' sneeshin mill,   *smoking   snuff box*
Are handed round wi' right guid will;
The cantie auld folks crackin crouse,
The young anes ranting thro' the house —
My heart has been sae fain to see them,
That I for joy hae barkit wi' them.

Like many a distinguished fellow-poet, Burns left much that
interests few readers. As he himself said, "He must be an excellent
poet indeed whose every performance is excellent." But the two
hundred or so pages of his best work rank among the best we
have, and it is, as Carlyle affirmed, "of Nature's own and most
cunning workmanship."

3. *Love Affairs*

During the fifteen months after August, 1785, Burns continued
to write fine poetry at a spectacular rate; he carried on intense,
complex, and disturbing love affairs — with Jean Armour, and
Mary Campbell, and perhaps Bettsy Miller; he decided to leave
Scotland, but did not; he determined to publish his poems, and
did; he achieved a substantial fame and earned a little money;
and he was prevailed upon to try another edition in Edinburgh.
It was a time of fevered activity and intense excitement, a time

of depressing failure and notable success, a time of humiliation and of bold assertion, a time of joy and deep sorrow, and of hope and perplexity.

When Burns and Jean Armour became lovers, he was twenty-six, she twenty. She must have known his reputation and the reasons for it. He was handsome and electrifying and notorious. She was shapely and willing, and he delighted in her. By February, 1786, he referred to her pregnancy as news "not the most agreable," but he gave her a paper acknowledging her in some sort as his wife or wife-to-be. The paper is not known to exist, and speculation about its contents is futile, but it probably constituted legal marriage, and Burns certainly thought of Jean as his wife, although he could by no means afford to establish a household. It was about this time that he began to consider emigrating to Jamaica and working for wages there as a slave driver, a disagreable prospect, attractive only in contrast to his desperate situation at home.

Jean's father was a master mason. When he and his wife discovered Jean's pregnancy, they forced her to surrender the paper, and sought advice from their lawyer, and Burns' friend, Robert Aiken, who "mutilated" the paper, probably cutting out the names — a maneuver of dubious legal effect on a binding contract. But James Armour regarded an illegitimate grandchild as preferable to a penniless son-in-law, and he pursued his ends in this way. In late March the Armours packed Jean off to Paisley to stay with relatives, and Mrs. Armour denied knowing of her daughter's condition to an emissary from the Kirk Session, who came to inquire officially.

Burns was thunderstruck. He felt that Jean had betrayed him, and his spirit was deeply bruised. In April he wrote a famous letter to John Arnot, to which he added a note when copying it out for Robert Riddell some years later: "The story of the letter was this — I had got deeply in love with a young Fair-One, of which proofs were every day *arising* more & more to view. — I would gladly have covered my Inamorata from the darts of Calumny with the conjugal Shield, nay had actually made up some sort of Wedlock; but I was at that time deep in the guilt of being unfortunate, for which good & lawful objection, the Lady's friends broke all our measures, & drove me au desespoir."

In the letter itself, he writes in the manner of Lawrence Sterne:

I have lost, Sir, that dearest earthly treasure, that greatest blessing here below, that last, best gift which compleated Adam's happiness in the garden of bliss, I have lost — I have lost — my trembling hand refuses its office, the frighted ink recoils up the quill — Tell it not in Gath — I have lost — a — a — a Wife!

He describes the affair with an elaborate Shandean venereal metaphor.

I rarely hit where I aim: & if I want anything, I am almost sure never to find it where I seek it. — For instance, if my pen-knife is needed, I pulled out twenty things — a plough-wedge, a horse-nail, an old letter or a tattered rhyme, in short, everything but my pen-knife; & that at last, after a painful, fruitless search, will be found in the unsuspected corner of an unsuspected pocket, as if on purpose thrust out of the way. — Still, Sir, I had long had a wishing eye to that inestimable blessing, a wife. — My mouth watered deliciously, to see a young fellow, after a few idle, common-place stories from a gentleman in black, strip & go to bed with a young girl, & no one durst say, black was his eye; while I, for just doing the same thing, only wanting that ceremony, am made a Sunday's laughing-stock, & abused like a pick-pocket. — I was well aware though, that if my ill-starred fortune got the least hint of my connubial wish, my schemes would go to nothing. — To prevent this, I determined to take my measures with such thought & forethought, such a caution & precaution, that all the malignant planets in the Hemisphere should be unable to blight my designs. — Not content with, to use the words of the celebrated Westminster Divines, "the outward & ordinary means," I left no *stone* unturned; sounded every unfathomed *depth*; stopped up every *hole* & bore of an objection; but, how shall I tell it! notwithstanding all this turning of stones, stopping of bores, &c. — whilst I, with secret pleasure, marked my project *swelling* to the proper crisis, & was singing te Deum in my own fancy; or, to change the metaphor, whilst

I was vigorously pressing on the siege; had carried the counter-scarp, & made a practicable breach behind the curtin in the gorge of the very principal bastion; nay, having mastered the covered way, I had found means to slip a choice detachment into the very citadel; while I had nothing less in view than displaying my victorious banners on the top of the walls — Heaven & Earth must I "remember"! my damned Star wheeled about to the zenith, by whose baleful rays Fortune took the alarm, & pouring in her forces on all quarters, front, flank, & rear, I was utterly routed, my baggage lost, my military chest in the hands of the enemy; & your poor devil of a humble servant, commander in chief forsooth, was obliged to scamper away, without either arms or honors of war, except his bare bayonet & cartridge-pouch; nor in all probability had he escaped even with them, had he not made a shift to hide them under the lap of his military cloak. — . . . There is a pretty large portion of bedlam in the composition of a Poet at any time; but on this occasion I was nine parts & nine tenths, out of ten, stark staring mad.

Then, after a long passage of turgid rhetoric, he reports that he is looking for another wife. This letter to Arnot was written in April.

On June 12, he writes to David Brice:

I have no news to tell you that will give me any pleasure to mention, or you, to hear. — Poor, ill-advised, ungrateful Armour came home on friday last. — You have heard all the particulars of that affair; and a black affair it is. — What she thinks of her conduct now, I don't know; one thing I know, she has made me compleatly miserable. — Never man lov'd, or rather ador'd, a woman more than I did her: and, to confess a truth between you and me, I do still love her to distraction after all, tho' I won't tell her so, tho' I see her, which I don't want to do. — My poor, dear, unfortunate Jean! how happy I have been in her arms! — It is not the losing her that makes me so unhappy; but for *her* sake I feel most severely. — I foresee she is in the road to, I am afraid, *eternal* ruin; and those who made so much noise, and showed so much grief, at the thought of her being *my wife*, may, some day, see her connected in such a manner as may give them more real cause of vexation. — I am sure I do not wish it: may Almighty God forgive her ingratitude and perjury to me, as I from my very soul forgive her! and may His grace be with her and bless her in all future life! — I can have no nearer idea of the place of eternal punishment than what I have felt in my own breast on her account. — I have tryed often to forget her: I have run into all kinds of dissipation and riot, Mason-meetings, drinking matches, and other mischief, to drive her out of my head, but all in vain: and now for a grand cure: the Ship is on her way home that is to take me out to Jamaica; and then, farewell dear old Scotland, and farewell dear, ungrateful Jean, for never, never will I see you more.

The next day, June 13, Jean wrote to the Kirk Session admitting the pregnancy and naming Robert as the father.

Since Jean would not have him, Burns determined to establish himself unquestionably as a bachelor, and was promised a certificate to that effect by his minister, the Rev. William Auld of Mauchline, if he would stand in church for three Sundays, with Jean, and be rebuked publicly. He writes on July 9 to John Richmond, "I have waited on Armour since her return home, not by — from any the least view of reconciliation, but merely to ask for her health; and — to you I will confess it, from a foolish hankering fondness — very ill-plac'd indeed. — The Mother forbade me the house; nor did Jean shew that penitence that might have been expected. — However, the Priest, I am inform'd will give me a Certificate as a single man, if I comply with the rules of the Church, which for that very reason I intend to do." He reports he is to appear that morning for the first time, and that his book will be ready in a fortnight. A letter to Brice, July 17, adds a piquant detail: "Jean and her friends insisted much that she should stand along with me in the kirk, but the minister would not allow it, which bred a great trouble I assure you, and I am blamed as the cause of it, tho' I am sure I am innocent: but I am very well pleased, for all that, not to have had her company." He made his last appearance August 6, and considered himself freed from all obligations to Jean.

Meanwhile he was seeing his Kilmarnock volume through the

press. He had issued proposals for subscribers to it on April 14, 1786, and he sent his poems to the printer June 13. The volumes were ready in late July. He was also making plans for immediate departure to Jamaica once the book was out, these having been accelerated by James Armour's swearing out a warrant against him seeking support for the coming child. He had mentioned Jamaica to Arnot in April; on July 17 he tells Brice he expects to leave in October. But on July 30 he writes to Richmond from a hiding place where Armour cannot find him:

My hour is now come. — You and I will never meet in Britain more. — I have orders within three weeks at farthest to repair aboard the Nancy, Capn Smith, from Clyde, to Jamaica, and to call at Antigua. — This, except to our friend Smith, whom God long preserve, is a secret about Mauchlin. — Would you believe it? Armour has got a warrant to throw me in jail till I find security for an enormous sum. — This they keep an entire secret, but I got it by a channel they little dream of; and I am wandering from one friend's house to another, and like a true son of the Gospel "have nowhere to lay my head." — I know you will pour an execration on her head, but spare the poor, ill-advised girl for my sake; tho', may all the Furies that rend the injured, enraged Lover's bosom, await the old harridan, her Mother, untill her latest hour!

Two days later, the distracted man writes to Smith, "Against two things however, I am as fix'd as Fate: staying at home, and owning her conjugally. — The first, by Heaven I will not do! The last, by Hell I will never do! . . . If you see Jean tell her, I will meet her, So help me Heaven in my hour of need!"

On August 14 he postpones sailing, and on September 1, he writes that he won't sail until the end of the month. But by September 27 he is thinking of a second edition of his book, and says his departure is uncertain and will probably not take place until after harvest. By October 8 he has been discussing a new edition with his Kilmarnock printer, John Wilson, and he has considered becoming an Exciseman.

Through his poems he made helpful friends, and he writes to Richmond on September 1, "The warrant is still in existence, but some of the first Gentlemen in the county have offered to befriend me; and besides, Jean will not take any step against me, without letting me know, as nothing but the most violent menaces could have forced her to sign the petition. — I have called on her once and again, of late; as she, at this moment, is threatened with the pangs of approaching travail; and I assure you, my dear Friend, I cannot help being anxious, very anxious, for her situation. — She would gladly now embrace that offer she once rejected, but it shall never more be in her power." He then urges Richmond to return and marry Jenny Surgeoner, of whom and her child by Richmond he gives touching particulars.

On September 3 he rejoices to Richmond:

A Fragment - - - -

Chorus

Green grow the rashes O
Green grow the rashes O
The lasses they hae wimble bores,   *gimlet*
The widows they hae gashes O.

1.

In sober hours I am a priest;
    A hero when I'm tipsy, O;
But I'm a king and ev'ry thing,
    When wi' a wanton Gipsey, O.
        Green grow &c.

2.

'Twas late yestreen I met wi' ane
    An' wow, but she was gentle, O!
Ae han' she pat round my cravat,
    The tither to my p - - - - - O.
        Green grow &c.

3.

I dought na speak - - yet was na fley'd - -   *afraid*
My heart play'd duntie, duntie, O;
An' ceremony laid aside,
    I fairly fun' her c-ntie, O. - - - -
        Green grow &c.

■ - - ■ - ■ - - ■ - ■ - ■

- - - Multa desunt - - -

■ - - ■ - ■ - - ■ - ■ - ■

Sept: 3d Armour has just now brought me a boy and a girl at one
throw. - - God bless them poor little dears. - -

R. B.

His volume was a success. And with James Armour checked, and his certificate as a bachelor in his pocket, and Jean safely delivered, Burns thought less and less of emigration. He had also taken legal measures against Armour. On July 22, 1786, Burns assigned his interest in Mossgiel farm, and his profits from his poems and the copyright as well, to his brother Gilbert for support of his daughter by Betty Paton. Burns' later agreement with Betty, executed December 1, 1786, superseded this agreement.

But there was another reason for Burns to postpone his departure, and perhaps this was the "other mischief" he refers to in his letter to Brice. At the same time as the Armour affair, he had been involved deeply with Mary Campbell, the girl known to history as Highland Mary.* This relationship is so hedged around with controversy that it seems best to present details about it in their full complexity. First, there is a Mary Campbell who has nothing to connect her with Burns except that she was in the right places at the right times. In 1783, she was living in Dundonald Parish, which includes Irvine; by April, 1784, she had moved to Mauchline, from which she had gone to nearby Stair by February, 1786. On April 25, 1784, when the Mauchline

---

* There is a provocative note about still another heroine of this period. A letter to Richmond, dated September 27, concludes, "Bettsy Miller awaits me." (F I, #49, 44.) She appears in his *Belles of Mauchline*, and is a character in a jolly poem, *A Mauchline Wedding*. She is also probably the "quondam Eliza" of a letter to Smith of June 11, 1787. (F I, #113, 95.)

Kirk Session questioned her, she reported one John Hay to be the father of her child. Hay denied it at the time, but confessed later.* In 1781–1782, Burns was in Irvine; by March, 1784, he had moved to Mauchline; and in May, 1786, he said goodbye to his Mary Campbell on the banks of the Ayr in Stair.

Burns' Mary Campbell became a nurse in Gavin Hamilton's family in Mauchline in July, 1785. It has been argued that the mother of an illegitimate baby could not have been so received, and hence that the Dundonald Mary was not this girl, but the Armours did not feel that their daughter in the same village would be irredeemably disgraced by having such a child, and Betty Paton married after bearing one to Burns, and lived in good odor. Either could have secured a position from the Hamiltons. It has been argued also that Burns could not have become infatuated with a woman who had born a bastard, and could not have idealized her in his poetry. But one's experience of Burns and of life is limited, indeed, for such an argument to carry much weight. And while some of Burns' comments on Mary do idealize her, many do not. However, there is no evidence permitting a final decision whether the Dundonald girl was Burns' heroine or not.

The next item relating to Highland Mary is a negligible song, *My Highland Lassie, O,* which speaks of crossing the seas and pledges faithfulness forever. R. H. Cromek printed a note about it presumably by Burns. The manuscript has disappeared, but Cromek's once-questioned reliability has been supported by the late Davidson Cook and DeLancey Ferguson. The note reads:

This was a composition of mine in very early life, before I was known at all in the world. My Highland lassie was a warm-hearted, charming young creature as ever blessed a man with generous love.

* A minute of the Session, dated "1787. December 17," is revealing. "John Hay voluntarily confessed fornication with Janet Sillar and Mary Campbell and also with Euphan Bowie from the New Town of Ayr, and the father of a child brought forth by each of them, and also confessed fornication with Margaret Ceurdie and Agnes M'Cletchie, formerly confessed by him. The Sess. appointed him to confess publicly any day he pleased." (Ch-W I, 471.)

After a pretty long tract of the most ardent reciprocal attachment, we met by appointment, on the second Sunday of May, in a sequestered spot by the Banks of Ayr, where we spent the day in taking a farewel, before she should embark for the West-Highlands, to arrange matters among her friends for our projected change of life. At the close of Autumn following she crossed the sea to meet me at Greenock, where she had scarce landed when she was seized with a malignant fever, which hurried my dear girl to the grave in a few days, before I could even hear of her illness.   .

It should be noted that the lassie of this passage is not named.

Here one must decide what Burns meant by being blessed, over a pretty long tract of most ardent reciprocal attachment, with the generous love of a warm-hearted, charming young creature. A similar decision is required about a comment he made to George Thomson when sending him *Will Ye Go To The Indes, My Mary.* "You must know, that all my earlier love-songs were the breathings of ardent Passion." And finally, what is to be made of a stanza from *Thou Lingering Star* describing the famous parting of Burns and Mary, and particularly of the line, "The flowers sprang wanton to be pressed"?

> Ayr, gurgling, kiss'd his pebbled shore,
>   O'erhung with wild woods thickening green;
> The fragrant birch and hawthorn hoar
>   'Twin'd amorous round the raptur'd scene;
> The flowers sprang wanton to be prest,
>   The birds sang love on every spray,
> Till too, too soon, the glowing west
>   Proclaim'd the speed of wingèd day.

The famous song *Highland Mary* is the only good one Burns wrote to his Mary. But does it suggest as has been maintained, that she was the one pure lily among his passion flowers?

> Ye banks and braes and streams around
>   The castle o' Montgomery,
> Green be your woods, and fair your flowers,
>   Your waters never drumlie!   *cloudy*

There Summer first unfald her robes,
   And there the langest tarry!
For there I took the last fareweel
   O' my sweet Highland Mary!

How sweetly bloom'd the gay, green birk,
   How rich the hawthorn's blossom,
As underneath their fragrant shade
   I clasp'd her to my bosom!
The golden hours on angel wings
   Flew o'er me and my dearie:
For dear to me as light and life
   Was my sweet Highland Mary.

Wi' monie a vow and lock'd embrace
   Our parting was fu' tender;
And, pledging aft to meet again,
   We tore oursels asunder.
But O, fell Death's untimely frost,
   That nipt my flower sae early!
Now green's the sod and cauld's the clay,
   That wraps my Highland Mary!

   .   .   .   .

Three years after Mary's death, Burns was moved to write some highly charged rhetoric about her to Mrs. Dunlop. Surveying his uncertainties about a life after death, he says that if there were one, he should like to meet there his father, and his friend, Robert Muir. Then he continues, "There should I, with speechless agony of rapture, again recognize my lost, my ever dear Mary, whose bosom was fraught with Truth, Honor, Constancy, & Love." Obviously, her memory is still precious to him, but one wonders why he would meet her with "speechless agony of rapture."

It seems clear that he and his Mary had a passionate love affair at the same time he was involved with Jean Armour, and that they parted with vows, exchanged in May, not long after Jean had dishonored similar ones. Before Burns and Mary could meet again, she died of fever. It is difficult to see how, in a small village, Burns' Mary could have failed to know that her affair paralleled the well-publicized one with Jean Armour.

Soon after Burns had moved to Mauchline, he found a crony in John Richmond, clerk to Gavin Hamilton, his landlord. Richmond left Mauchline under a cloud in the late autumn of 1785. During Burns' 1786–1787 winter in Edinburgh, he shared Richmond's room and bed. As late as February 7, 1788, Burns is writing to him in the old terms of intimacy, although later their relations seem to have cooled. Richmond, therefore, is an excellent source of information about Burns during the period of their close friendship. The following story, attributed to him, is undated, but it obviously relates to a time before he had left Mauchline. These notes are taken from memoranda sent by Joseph Train* to John Lockhart while Lockhart was preparing his Life of Burns, published in 1828.

Highland Mary. — Truth deprives her history of much of its charm. — Her character was loose in the extreme. — She was *kept* for some time by a Brother of Lord Eglinton's,† and even while a servant with Gavin Hamilton, and during the period of Burns' attachment it was well known that her meetings with Montgomery were open and frequent. — The friends of Burns represented to him the impropriety of his devotedness to her, but without producing any change in his sentiments. — Richmond told Mr Grierson that Montgomery & Highland Mary frequently met in a small alehouse called the Elbow — and upon one occasion he & some of Burns's friends knowing they were actually together in the Elbow — and having often in vain tried to convince Robert of her infidelity, upon this occasion they promised to give ocular proof of their assertions. — The party retired to the Elbow — Richmond (Mr Grierson's informant) was one and they took their seats in the kitchin from which two rooms branched off to the right and left — being all the accommoda-

* Collector of Excise at Castle Douglas.
† At this time the master of St. James Lodge, Tarbolton, was Captain James Montgomerie, younger brother of Colonel Hugh Montgomerie afterward Earl of Eglinton. (H & H I, 389; Kinsley III, 1080.)

tion the house contained.* They had taken their position in the kitchin, to be sure that no one could leave the other rooms without being observed. — After waiting long, and when Burns was beginning to ridicule their suspicions, at last Mary Campbell appeared from one of the rooms — was jeered by the party, in a general way — blushed and retired. — Another long interval elapsed and Burns began to rally his spirits, which were very much sunk — and Montgomery (Colonel or Capt) walked out of the same room. — Burns coloured deeply — compressed his lip — and muttered, "*damn* it." After enduring considerable bantering from his friends he soon gave way to the general hilarity of the evening, and his friends thought he had seen enough of Highland Mary but in a few days after, he returned "like the dog to its vomit."

Train adds another note:

Highland Mary. — I should have added formerly that Grierson has a facsimile of the leaf of the Bible *exchanged* by Burns with Mary containing the inscription. — in addition to what has already appeared in print the Signature of Burns is followed by his Mason's Mark which if you are a *free* mason you will understand — it is thus: >—×—→ In place of any of the commonplace facsimiles generally given of Burns' handwriting, it is likely we will give a representation of the two leaves containing these inscriptions. Mr Grierson was permitted by the surviving relations to copy these inscriptions. — One curious circumstance is worth recording. — From what motive it is now difficult to say, but one of Mary Campbell's brothers pasted a slip of paper over the *signatures* of Burns — and to read these it is necessary to hold the leaf between the eye and the light. — I saw a letter from another of her brother's to Mr Grierson stating this circumstance — and containing a lock of Mary's hair. — (It is of the true Celtic hue, and *feel*) This contains some other interesting information. — I am promised copies of it — and of several other unpublished letters of Burns, by Mr G. — These were read to me — but after some weeks exertion I have hitherto been unable to procure them. — Grierson is a curious old fellow. — He has been an enthusiastic collector of such

---

* Chambers-Wallace reports (I, 474n) that Mauchline "contained a back lane called the 'Elbow' in which was a public-house kept by a sailor, nicknamed 'The Old Tar.'"

matters connected with Burns for upwards of 20 years — during which time he has repeatedly visited the various places of the Poet's residences.

These reports raise a large probability that Burns and his Mary Campbell had begun their affair in the autumn of 1785, before Richmond left for Edinburgh, or even earlier. The "Mr. Grierson" mentioned by Train is now known to have been James Grierson of Dalgoner, a diligent collector of reliable information about Burns, and a close friend of Anthony Dunlop, son of Burns' correspondent, Mrs. Frances Dunlop.* On October 24, 1817, Grierson himself noted,

Met with   Campbell spouse to James Anderson mason in Ardrossan 1817 and sister to Highland Mary Burns friend. She says Mary was tall, fair haird with blue eyes — they were daughters of Arch. Campbell mariner who resided at Dunoon Parish & Agnes Campbell his spouse, he died in Greenock 1815 & is buried in a lair of the new burying ground he bought from widow McPherson & his widow lives there in Scots land long vennal. Their sons are Robert & Archd Carpenters there — Mrs Andersons sons possess the Bible† Burns gave her in exchange — it is printed by Alexander Kincaids assignies at Edin 1782. The booksellers mark 5/6 2 vol small 12° on each
volume is his mason mark. this son a mason works presently in Paisley. Mrs. A says her sister was buried in the old kirk ground Greenock, the new burying ground was not then begun & that widow McPherson & others know the place — during the fever she was insensible, except the last day of her life when her father asked if she knew where she was. Yes, she said, I am on my bridal bed. She died in the house of her uncle Alex Campbell, Greenock Her grandfather was tenant to Duke of Argyl but lost his farm rather than let his sons go into the army. Mrs. A showed the Bible to J. G. which she sent to Paisley to her son for, on purpose — on the first vol is in Burns hand writing "And ye shall not swear by my name falsely" — "I am the LORD" "Levit 19 Chap 12 verse" his name had been there but carefully rubed out except some letters   On the second vol

---

* Chambers-Wallace reports, also, that he knew Burns. (III, 13.)
† Further particulars of this Bible may be found in Ch-W I, 475–78. It is preserved in the Burns monument, Alloway.

there is also wrote in his hand "Thou shalt not for swear thyself but shalt perform unto the Lord thine Oath" "Matth: 35 Ch 33 verse On this vol had also been the mason mark & his name with date 1786. but papers had been pasted on & torn off so the writing is much defaced.

Leaves are folded in at or near various places as Isaiah 30 & 21. 34 & 10. 43 & 17. 55 & 16 [or 17 or 19] Jerem: x 27 [or x & 7, or Jerem 7; or Jerem 1 & 7]. 31 & 5. Ezek 18. 36 & 33. Hosea 4th 11 & 8. Zach. 13 Luke 17 & 14 John 13 & 14. 20 & 7. Rev 4 & 10* It seems evident that those two texts wrote at length in his hand, each *only* part of a verse & inscribed one in each vol. given to mary were intended strongly to alude to some secret known to them alone & it is more than probable this was some promise or Oaths he has not Oaths as in the original but *Oath* & he was not one of these men who had no meaning for what they did. — probably it was her who erased the name, conscious too of the meaning and not chusing to have the books in her possession on which were the texts connected with the name.

These memoranda of Grierson serve to identify and describe Mary Campbell, but even with them, specific proof of the nature of Burns' relations with her is lacking. One can only weigh all the available evidence and decide for himself. A further tantalizing bit is a passage from a letter to Robert Aiken, written in early October, 1786, about the time of Mary Campbell's death. "I have been feeling all the various rotations and movements within, respecting the Excise. There are many things plead strongly against it; the uncertainty of getting soon into business; the consequences of my follies, which may perhaps make it im-

* While too much should not be made of the passages marked in Mary's Bible, "Isaiah 30 & 21. 34 & 10." repeats the theme of the quotations from Leviticus and Matthew inscribed on the flyleaves of the Bible, "Jerem: 31 & 5" possibly refers to Burns' plan for taking Mary with him to the West Indes, and "Ezek 18" suggests repentance and forgiveness. "Hosea 4th 11 & 8.," "Zach. 13," "Luke 17 & 14," and "Rev 4 & 10" have a marked flavor of the Armour episode and its aftermath. In "John 13 and 14" there may be a reference to the famous ceremony of parting between Burns and Mary. But the great questions remain: Why did Mary's family preserve these references? And why did they try to obliterate Burns' name from the Bible?

practicable for me to stay at home; and besides I have for some time been pining under secret wretchedness, from causes which you pretty well know — the pang of disappointment, the sting of pride, with some wandering stabs of remorse, which never fail to settle on my vitals like vultures, when attention is not called away by the calls of society, or the vagaries of the Muse. Even in the hour of social mirth, my gaiety is the madness of an intoxicated criminal under the hands of the executioner." What, one wonders, did Aiken "pretty well know"? At this time, there would be little about Burns' edition, or his livelihood, or the Armour affair, to prompt such remarks.

He seems to have regarded Mary Campbell as a fiancée of sorts. Perhaps she was the "other wife" he was looking for when he wrote to John Arnot in April. But it is significant that, while Burns' letters are full of Jean, they say nothing of Mary either before or after she left Ayrshire. The affair with her came at the time when he was writing poems glorying in his prowess. And there is no hint throughout his life of any other "pure" romance. The evidence for one with Mary Campbell seems flimsy, indeed, while the relationship detailed and suggested in the documents above is all-too-human, and credible, and characteristic of Burns.

There has been much controversy about a child's coffin found in Mary Campbell's grave when her remains were exhumed and re-interred in 1920. It was not that of a baby born to Mary Campbell, but that of Agnes Hendry, who was born January 4, 1827 and who died February 27, 1827. These dates are taken from the Hendry family register of her brother Daniel S. Hendry, and were certified in a document in the present biographer's possession by Duncan M. Hendry on October 23, 1933.*

In mid-August, 1786, Burns had still some Kilmarnock volumes to get to their purchasers, he had an account to settle with his printer, he had a decision to make about Jamaica, he had an

* See Appendix D; also *Chronicle* 1918, 1920, 1921, 1922.

agreement to make with Betty Paton and Gilbert about little Betty's maintenance, he felt a concern for Jean, and a concern for Mary Campbell. He no longer had any concern about the Armour warrant. By late October, he had pretty well decided to print a new edition of his poems and to give up going to Jamaica; he had settled with his printer, and was negotiating a settlement with Betty Paton; Jean had born twins, and Mary was dead. Whatever the tensions and sorrows of the previous months had been, Burns was now free of compelling restraints. Friends were urging an edition in Edinburgh. Perhaps a comfortable arrangement for making a living might come to him if he went to the capital and met influential people. A new edition would probably make a good deal of money, which the family needed desperately. And the prospect of wider fame was delightful. So, on November 27, on a borrowed pony, he set out for a two day ride to Edinburgh. He had a royal reception at Covington Mains farm, near Biggar in Lanarkshire, en route, and arrived November 29 with a hangover. He had completed his career as a major poet, except for his most famous poem, *Tam o' Shanter*.

4. Kilmarnock Edition

Poems Chiefly in the Scottish Dialect, by Robert Burns, Kilmarnock, 1786, was a well-printed paper-bound volume of 240 pages, priced at three shillings. Burns and his friends had gathered over 300 subscriptions, enough to defray expenses, before printing began. In his original proposal to his subscribers, Burns had offered only Scotch poems, but he finally included half a dozen melancholy and moralizing English pieces apparently to increase the volume's appeal. And, it should be noted, although the subscribers and the presumed audience were to be almost entirely local, or at least Scottish, Burns added a liberal glossary of his Scots vocabulary. The 612 copies brought in £90, of which the printer's bill took £34/3/–; but Burns says that he cleared only £20. Perhaps the difference is accounted for partly by the

£9 passage money for Jamaica which he paid down, and may have lost. His settlement with Betty Paton took a substantial amount, and he must have given some to the family at Mossgiel. Burns cannot have had much in his pocket when he set out for Edinburgh.

The Kilmarnock volume made Burns famous at once. Review notices appeared promptly in Edinburgh and London. But Burns withheld from his book, or wrote within three months of its appearance, enough poems and songs to make another volume of the same size and quality. Some of this poetry, and a few songs, he added to his Edinburgh edition of April, 1787, but most of the poetry he never published at all. Later he sent the bulk of the songs to James Johnson and George Thomson for their collections. Of the unpublished poetry, some was too personal to appear publicly (*A Poet's Welcome*), or too likely to provoke recrimination (the epistle to John M'Math), or too broad (*The Court of Equity*), or even downright bawdy (*The Fornicator*).

Of the poems written by November, 1786, and not yet mentioned, there are five of limited interest — three moralizing and melancholy pieces (*Despondency, Lament,* and *To Ruin*), and two parochial poems that require heavy annotation (*Hallowe'en* and *The Ordination*). The opening stanzas of *Hallowe'en* are promising, but the poem progresses to a detailed account of Ayrshire folk customs, and fails to transcend its particularities. *The Ordination* concerns a Kilmarnock parish quarrel over patronage.

A song, and two minor poems, of serious social comment, are readable enough, and contain memorable passages. The song, *Man Was Made to Mourn,* is a vigorous recital of human suffering and injustice, and the inequality of human reward, with the famous lines,

> Man's inhumanity to man
> Makes countless thousands mourn.

This song concludes, in the words of the aged protagonist,

> The poor, oppressèd, honest man
>   Had never, sure, been born,
> Had there not been some recompense
>   To comfort those that mourn!
>
> O Death! the poor man's dearest friend,
>   The kindest and the best!
> Welcome the hour my agèd limbs
>   Are laid with thee, at rest!
> The great, the wealthy fear thy blow,
>   From pomp and pleasure torn;
> But, oh! a blest relief to those
>   That weary-laden mourn!

Of the two minor poems, one is bitterly ironic, with a cumbersome explanatory heading:

Address of Beelzebub: To the Right Honorable the Earl of Breadalbane, President of the Right Honorable the Highland Society, which met on the 23rd of May last, at the *Shakespeare*, Covent Garden, to concert ways and means to frustrate the desires of five hundred Highlanders who, as the Society were informed by Mr. M'Kenzie of Applecross, were so audacious as to attempt an escape from their lawful lords and masters whose property they were, by emigrating from the lands of Mr. Macdonald of Glengary to the wilds of Canada, in search of that fantastic thing — Liberty.

In this Address, the Devil, writing from Hell, urges the lords and masters to "lay aside a' tender mercies," and not merely to distrain and rob such ungrateful and troublesome tenants,

But smash them! crush them a' to spails	*chips*
An' rot the dyvors i' the jails!	*bankrupts*
The young dogs, swinge them to the labour:	*whip*
Let wark an' hunger make them sober!	
The hizzies, if they're aughtlins fawsont	*girls at all good looking*
Let them in Drury Lane be lesson'd!	*[as prostitutes]*

An' if the wives an' dirty brats
Come thiggin at your doors an' yetts,   *begging   gates*
Flaffin wi' duds an' grey wi' beas',   *flapping with vermin   fleas*
Frightin awa your deuks an' geese,
Get out a horsewhip or a jowler,   *bulldog*
The langest thong, the fiercest growler,
An' gar the tattered gypsies pack   *make   beat it*
Wi' a' their bastards on their back!

The other poem, *A Dedication to Gavin Hamilton, Esq.* like
the Author's Preface to *Tristram Shandy,* appears in the middle
of the volume. It opens with some banter, and then proceeds to
ironic sympathy. Hamilton, although he is "the poor man's friend
in need, / The gentleman in word and deed," does not satisfy his
orthodox neighbors because he is generous and kind merely from
"carnal inclination" and not because he subscribes to proper Calvinist doctrine. Burns continues,

Morality, thou deadly bane,
Thy tens o' thousands thou hast slain!
Vain is his hope, whase stay an' trust is
In moral mercy, truth, and justice!

No — stretch a point to catch a plack;   *make money*
Abuse a brother to his back;
Steal thro' the winnock frae a whore,   *window*
But point the rake that taks the door;
Be to the poor like onie whunstane,
And haud their noses to the grunstane;
Ply ev'ry art o' legal thieving;
No matter — stick to sound believing.

He adds a good deal more in the same mordant vein.
    There are also ten light-hearted and felicitous poems, laced and
graced with pungent observations, but all essentially *jeux d'esprit.*
These poems give an idea of the vivacity and salty readiness
which so delighted those who heard Burns speak. *Scotch Drink*

celebrates whiskey and Scotland, and parodies Fergusson's *Caller [Fresh] Water*, *To a Haggis* was written to amuse a gathering of Ayrshire friends, *Adam Armour's Prayer* is good-natured ridicule of his brother-in-law to be, *Poor Mailie's Elegy* pays further tribute to that immortal sheep, *The Inventory* presents a versified report to a tax gatherer, *Epistle to a Young Friend* gives "good advice" to Robert Aiken's (the tax gatherer's) son, *Tam Samson's Elegy* is rough joking on a good friend, *The Brigs of Ayr* has fun with municipal improvements pushed by Burns' friend John Ballantine, *Lines on Meeting with Lord Daer* is a bread and butter note celebrating a dinner, and *Nature's Law* bursts into joy on the birth of Jean's twins.

To this list may be added three more or less bawdy poems, one of which, *The Fornicator*, has already been quoted. The other two, *The Court of Equity* and *The Patriarch*, are given in Section VI.

Burns' songs have given him a quite different fame from that of the poems, although too often the distinction between his poetry and his songs is confused. A later section will consider the whole matter of Burns and Scottish Song, including *The Jolly Beggars — Love and Liberty*, essentially a collection of songs.

It remains to comment on a few major poems so far unnoticed but written by November 1786. First, *The Twa Dogs*, which Burns used to open the Kilmarnock volume. Here, after a famous description of the two *dogs*, not merely speakers in the guise of dogs, Burns has them discuss their masters, and the rich and the poor, and the gentles and the cotters, all with admirable good sense and humor, and then lets them part without coming to conclusions, although simple life obviously comes off the better, and the gentles are shown up for the hollow-hearted wastrels they too often are. In the central speech, dog Luath, the ploughman's collie, answers dog Caesar, the aristocratic democrat who would just as soon make love to a mongrel, and who has remarked that "surely poor-folk maun [must] be wretches!".

Luath

They're nae sae wretched's ane wad think;
Tho' constantly on poortith's brink,   *poverty's*
They're sae accustom'd wi' the sight,
The view o't gies them little fright.

Then chance an' fortune are sae guided,
They're ay in less or mair provided;
An' tho' fatigu'd wi' close employment,
A blink o' rest's a sweet enjoyment.   *snatch*

The dearest comfort o' their lives,
Their grushie weans an' faithfu' wives;   *thriving*
The prattling things are just their pride,
That sweetens a' their fire-side.

An' whyles twalpennie worth o' nappy   *ale*
Can make the bodies unco happy:
They lay aside their private cares,
To mind the Kirk and State affairs;
They'll talk o' patronage an' priests,
Wi' kindling fury i' their breasts,
Or tell what new taxation's comin,
An' ferlie at the folk in Lon'on.   *wonder*

As bleak-fac'd Hallowmass returns,   *Halloween*
They get the jovial, ranting kirns,   *harvest-homes*
When rural life, of ev'ry station,
Unite in common recreation:
Love blinks, Wit slaps, an' social Mirth   *strikes*
Forgets there's Care upo' the earth.

That merry day the year begins,
They bar the door on frosty win's;
The nappy reeks wi' mantling ream,   *cream*
An' sheds a heart-inspiring steam;
The luntin pipe, an' sneeshin mill,   *smoking   snuff-box*
Are handed round wi' right guid will;
The cantie auld folks crackin crouse,   *chatting cheerfully*
The young anes ranting thro' the house —   *romping*
My heart has been sae fain to see them,
That I for joy hae barkit wi' them.

Still it's owre true that ye hae said
Sic game is now owre aften play'd;
There's monie a creditable stock
O' decent, honest, fawsont folk,   *respectable*
Are riven out baith root an' branch,
Some rascal's pridefu' greed to quench,
Wha thinks to knit himself the faster
In favor wi' some gentle master,
Wha, aiblins thrang a parliamentin',   *perhaps busy*
For Britain's guid his saul indentin' —

The Auld Farmer's New-Year Morning Salutation to his Auld Mare, Maggie, shows Burns being kindly and warm without the sentimentality to which he was prone. He catches the old man's feeling for his work partner of many years, and he creates sure and clean the quality and tone of a farmer's life. Much of the old man's affection for Maggie, for example, comes from her having done good work on the farm, and from her having given him healthy colts to sell. Here, as in *The Twa Dogs,* the language, the feeling, the purpose, the illustrations are finely at one.

This is not true of *The Cotter's Saturday Night,* in which the style and the statement are often at odds, and the commentary seems intrusive and self-conscious rather than a natural outgrowth of the narrative. What Burns says in *The Cotter* he says in Epistles and elsewhere — the simple and natural life is better than the artificial, love and friendship are life's richest rewards, the lower classes are the strength of the country, and Scotland for Aye. The poem, a projection of Burns' father and his household, idealizes the life of poverty, family affection, and honest work, and poor is he who denies the virtues it celebrates. The father's homecoming and the family gathering, the supper, and the Bible reading, are generally touching and right, but such lines as these jar the effect of stanza five:

The parents partial eye their hopeful years;
Anticipation forward points the view.

Stanzas nine and ten begin the self-conscious intrusions. And after stanza twelve, only the satiric seventeen is more than competent; and not a few stanzas seem contrived. Burns no doubt hoped to elevate the poem by introducing the manner of his admired English models, but the result is unfortunate.

And yet the poem is still widely admired, and properly so, for a reason neatly stated by Henley and Henderson. "Burns's verse falls naturally into two main divisions. One, and that the larger, appeals with persistency and force, on the strength of some broadly human qualities, to the world in general: for the reason that the world in general is rich in sentiment but lacks the literary sense. The other, being a notable and lasting contribution to literature, is the concern of comparatively few." Yet for the few, also, *The Cotter* certainly leaves its mark and makes its point, even while they are conscious of its defects.

Three of Burns' most famous poems help further to illustrate the remark quoted above, and all follow a similar pattern — a series of narrative-descriptive stanzas which lead up to a sententious conclusion. *To a Louse* is artistically by far the best, and by far the least popular. *To a Mountain Daisy* is generally agreed to be the weakest. But *To a Mouse* has always enjoyed high popularity, and critical esteem as well. The distress of the "wee, sleekit, cowrin, tim'rous beastie" is vivid and touching; and "the best laid schemes o' mice an' men gang aft agley," surely; but what of a mouse as a symbol for brotherhood? The general experience of man is otherwise. Who feels "social union" with a mouse? In this central symbolism the poem is artificial and contrived, and sentimental. And the self-pity of its conclusion is not appealing. But for the great majority who are "rich in sentiment but lack the literary sense," these remarks are beside the point. The poem moves them, and Burns was not writing for academic critics.

Professor Sir Walter Raleigh makes a shrewd comment to this same effect. "The Scottish people feel a hearty, instinctive, and just dislike for biographers of Burns. The life of Burns, full as it was of joy and generous impulse, full also of error, disappointment, and failure, makes a perfectly devised trap for the superior person. Almost everyone is superior to Robert Burns in some one point or other — in conjugal fidelity, in worldly prudence, or in social standing. Let him be careful to forget his advantages before he approaches this graveside, or his name will be added to the roll of the failures." True, and fair enough. But it could be wished that Sir Walter had added: The story of Burns is the more moving the more fully told, and the wonder of the man and his work the more deeply felt, the more completely it is understood. Romanticizing admirers no less than "superior persons" have too often made a monstrous caricature of Burns.

To a Louse seems a perfect poem. It opens briskly, it sets a memorable scene, it tells a lively story, it maintains its tone of genial irony with a rich association of incident and image, and it moves quickly and surely to its conclusion, probably the most famous stanza Burns ever wrote. It may be remarked that one's feeling about a louse, and about the occasion, are entirely appropriate to the satiric purpose of the poem, in which not one figure or image is inept, not one line weak. And the theme is quintessential Burns — the absurdity of pretence, especially religious pretence.

To a Louse

On seeing one on a lady's bonnet at church

Ha! whare ye gaun, ye crowlin ferlie? *crawling wonder*
Your impudence protects you sairly,
I canna say but ye strunt rarely *strut*
 Owre gauze and lace,
Tho' faith! I fear ye dine but sparely
 On sic a place.

Ye ugly, creepin, blastit wonner, *marvel*
Detested, shunn'd by saunt an' sinner,
How daur ye set your fit upon her —
 Sae fine a lady!
Gae somewhere else and seek your dinner
 On some poor body.

Swith! in some beggar's hauffet squattle: *temples squat*
There ye may creep, and sprawl, and sprattle   *scramble*
Wi' ither kindred, jumping cattle,
            In shoals and nations;
Whare horn nor bane ne'er daur unsettle   *combs*
            Your thick plantations.

Now haud you there! ye're out o' sight   *hold*
Below the fatt'rils, snug an' tight;   *ribbon ends*
Na, faith ye yet! ye'll no be right,
            Till ye've got on it —
The vera tapmost, tow'ring height
            O' Miss's bonnet.

My sooth! right bauld ye set your nose out,
As plump an' grey as onie grozet: *gooseberry*
O for some rank, mercurial rozet,   *rosin*
            Or fell, red smeddum,   *insecticide*
I'd gie ye sic a hearty dose o't,
            Wad dress your droddum!   *backside*

I wad na been surpris'd to spy   *would not have*
You on an auld wife's flainen toy: *flannel cap*
Or aiblins some bit duddie boy,   *maybe* *small ragged*
            On's wyliecoat;   *undervest*
But Miss's fine Lunardi! fye!   *balloon bonnet*
            How daur ye do't?   *dare*

O Jenny, dinna toss your head,
An' set your beauties a' abread!   *abroad*
Ye little ken what cursèd speed
            The blastie's makin!
Thae winks an' finger ends, I dread,   *Those*
            Are notice takin!

O wad some Power the giftie gie us
To see oursels as ithers see us!
It wad frae monie a blunder free us,
            An' foolish notion:
What airs in dress an' gait wad lea'e us,
            An' ev'n devotion!

A stanza from the epistle to William Simpson makes an apt comment on *The Vision.*

> The Muse, nae poet ever fand her,   *found*
> Till by himsel he learn'd to wander,
> Adown some trottin' burn's meander   *brook's*
>   An' no think lang;
> O, sweet to stray, an' pensive ponder
>   A heart-felt sang!

In *The Vision,* written over a period of time, and revised, Burns "thinks lang," for forty-six stanzas, and the poem is mainly a versified record of his thoughts about Scotland, and poetry, and his place as a "rustic bard." (He makes it clear that he feels he is one of the "humbler ranks.") Here is Burns' *apologia,* his *Defence of Poesie,* his view of his calling as an honorable one and significant to his country and his people. The poem opens with stanzas describing the poet weary after a day of threshing. Stanza four continues:

> All in this mottie, misty clime,   *dusty*
> I backward mus'd on wasted time:
> How I had spent my youthfu' prime,
>   An' done naething,
> But stringing blethers up in rhyme,
>   For fools to sing.

> Had I to guid advice but harkit,
> I might, by this, hae led a market,
> Or strutted in a bank and clarkit
>   My cash-account:
> While here, half-mad, half-fed, half-sarkit,   *-shirted*
>   Is a' th' amount.

Suddenly there appears the figure of Coila, in the trim shape of Jean Armour.

> A "hair-brain'd, sentimental trace,"
> Was strongly markèd in her face;

> A wildly-witty, rustic grace
> Shone full upon her;
> Her eye, ev'n turn'd on empty space,
> Beam'd keen with honor.

The lassie wears a mantle bearing a map of Ayrshire, with pictures on it of distinguished figures, historical and contemporary. She is the spirit of the district (Kyle), and a member of a "light aerial band" which Burns invents* to inspire Scotland and Kyle. Coila speaks of patriots, soldiers, poets, improving landlords, judges, professors, rustic bards, artisans, wooers — all important in the general society; she says she has had Burns in her care since his birth, and points to what he has done under her influence:

> "When youthful Love, warm-blushing, strong,
> Keen-shivering, shot thy nerves along,
> Those accents grateful to thy tongue,
>   Th' adorèd *Name*,
> I taught thee how to pour in song
>   To soothe thy flame.

> "I saw thy pulse's maddening play,
> Wild-send thee Pleasure's devious way,
> Misled by Fancy's meteor-ray,
>   By passion driven;
> But yet the light that led astray
>   Was light from Heaven.

> "I taught thy manners-painting strains
> The loves, the ways of simple swains,
> Till now, o'er all my wide domains
>   Thy fame extends;
> And some, the pride of Coila's plains,
>   Become thy friends."

Finally she encourages him,

> "Then never murmur nor repine;
> Strive in thy humble sphere to shine;
> And trust me, not Potosi's mine,   [*of gold, silver, and copper*]

* Professor J. C. Weston feels that Burns was influenced in the creation of his troop by Pope's sylphs in *The Rape of the Lock*.

Nor king's regard,
Can give a bliss o'ermatching thine,
A rustic Bard.

"To give my counsels all in one:
Thy tuneful flame still careful fan;
Preserve the dignity of Man,
With soul erect;
And trust the Universal Plan
Will all protect."

Then she places a holly wreath on his head, and "like a passing thought" fades away. It should be noted that Coila encourages her Scots poet in purest English, as a serious-minded and thoughtful Scot should. This elaborate poem is smoothly versified, and of biographical interest, but after the opening stanzas it does not have the full force and grace of Burns at his best.

As we have seen, Burns took his position as poet seriously, and he enjoyed his success, but he recognized that it helped him little in what he called "the sober science of life." In June, 1786, he had written David Brice that his Kilmarnock edition was to be his "last foolish action," after which he intended to "turn a wise man as fast as possible." All during the exciting months which followed in Edinburgh, he was worried about his problem of a livelihood, made even greater by his more prominent position. He felt he could not live on his poetry, and fame paid no bills. His essential position was much the same after both his publications as before.

The greatest change for him was a broadening of his acquaintance. Burns responded warmly to those who offered him friendship, and he found much pleasure in three persons who were attracted to him by the Kilmarnock volume in the autumn of 1786: the Rev. George Lawrie, of Newmilns, in nearby Loudon parish; Dr. Thomas Blacklock, of Edinburgh; and Mrs. Frances Anna Wallace Dunlop, of Dunlop, a few miles north of Kilmarnock.

Before Burns left for Edinburgh, he was entertained happily by the Lawrie family at the Manse, where he left behind an appropriate poem, the prayer *O Thou Dread Power*. In the capital, he frequently saw Mr. Lawrie's son, Archibald, who was pursuing his ministerial studies, and his daughter, Christina.

Dr. Blacklock was a man of some note. Blind since infancy, he had completed his studies, nonetheless, and had become a minister, but his parishioners objecting, after a few years he retired and accepted an annuity. In Edinburgh he boarded and tutored college students, and as a musician, minor poet, and man of learning, was well enough known to be visited by Dr. Johnson on his famous visit to Scotland. Mr. Lawrie had sent him a copy of Burns' poems, and in his letter of thanks, Dr. Blacklock spoke of them with enthusiasm, and urged a second edition. This letter encouraged Burns to consider an Edinburgh edition when it was forwarded to him. In the city, he came to know Blacklock, enjoyed his company, and met interesting people through him. He wrote Mr. Lawrie, "In Dr. Blacklock, whom I see very often, I have found what I would have expected in our friend, a clear head and an excellent heart."

With Mrs. Dunlop, Burns developed a strong and lasting friendship, and one of the more notable relations in literary history. When she first read his poems, she was ill and depressed. Her husband had recently died, and her estranged oldest son had been forced to sell her beloved family estate of Craigie to pay debts incurred by fashionable living. She found such consolation in the poems, and particularly in *The Cotter's Saturday Night*, that on November 14, she wrote Burns requesting a dozen copies, and expressing pleasure that he had celebrated her ancestor, the great Sir William Wallace, in *The Vision*. Burns replied at once, citing his early enthusiasm for Wallace, and sending five copies, all he could muster.

Frances Anna Wallace (1730–1815) was proud of her family — she actually descended from an uncle of the great hero. At eighteen she had made a runaway match with John Dunlop of Dunlop (1707–1785), of a family nearly as ancient as her own.

Frances and John Dunlop had seven sons and six daughters. (Mrs. Dunlop's father added piquancy to the family by choosing as his second wife his son-in-law's sister.) After John Dunlop's death, his widow lived in semi-retirement, mainly with her son Andrew at Dunlop House, but often with her son John at his farm, Moreham Mains, near Haddington, east of Edinburgh, and occasionally at Loudon Castle, which had been rented by a son-in-law. She was a tower of strength in domestic crises, and a friendly, sensible woman not without humor, given to writing long, involved sentences and bad poetry. In any estimate of Burns, it is notable that he won and kept the friendship of Frances Dunlop.

As with most good friends, they sometimes irritated one another, but they felt at ease and maintained a remarkable candor, discussing his love affairs, the intimate family concerns of them both, politics and other topics of the day, and literature, about which Mrs. Dunlop had some knowledge and strong if often distressing opinions. Although broad-minded and occasionally broad-spoken, she objected vigorously to "improprieties" in Burns' poems. She was tedious, prolix, and repetitious in her letters, complaining that he wrote less often than she and then did not answer her because he did not read what she had written. She often spoke of the comfort his poems had given her when she first read them, and of her continuing admiration for her "dr Burns." As Professor Ferguson remarks, he seems to have felt about her as many a man does toward his mother: she often bored him, but he loved her. She in turn gave him motherly advice, loved him much like a son, and treasured his letters, which she seems to have kept private and not shared with her children. She and Burns each turned instinctively to the other in times of distress such as family deaths, or of especial happiness such as a birth of children or grandchildren. She interested herself in his family, getting to know Gilbert, calling on Jean in Mauchline, and making friends with his cousin Fanny, his uncle Robert's daughter.

She also tried to help him in a practical way. Through her he learned that Adam Smith had suggested he secure a steady income by becoming a Salt Officer, a job with less opprobrium than the Excise carried, and with light duties, paying £35 a year. She made him acquainted with Dr. John Moore, a Scot, and an M.D., Glasgow, now a fashionable author living in London. She and Dr. Moore worked hard to have Burns appointed to a newly established chair of Agriculture at the University of Edinburgh. He called it an "idle project," and felt himself unsuited for the appointment, but he did consider seriously her suggestion that he buy a commission in the army. Mrs. Dunlop thought that Burns and his family would have been better off living in the country, but when he became an Exciseman and gave up farming, she helped him through her friendships with Commissioner Robert Graham and with Collector William Corbet's wife.

After a letter from Burns of January 12, 1795, Mrs. Dunlop withheld her correspondence until eighteen months later when she heard that he was dying. Apparently his offense was writing about the execution of the king and queen in France: "What is there in the delivering over a perjured Blockhead & an unprincipled Prostitute to the hands of the hangman, that it should arrest for a moment, attention?" Although liberal, Mrs. Dunlop was no democrat. She had an early sympathy with the French Revolution, but was outraged by the later violence. She also had two daughters married to royalist refugees, and four army sons and a grandson. Burns' expression of republican sympathies, particularly in this "indelicate" way, seems to have been too much for her. A year later, he wrote in vain to ask his offense, since he had heard nothing from her, but the following letter, written a week before his death, brought an immediate response, which, unhappily has not survived.

MADAM

I have written you so often without rec.g any answer, that I would not trouble you again but for the circumstances in which I am. — An illness which has long hung about me in all probability will speedily send me beyond that bourn whence no traveller returns. — Your friendship with which for many years you honored me was a friendship dearest to my soul. — Your conversation & especially your correspondence were at once highly entertaining & instructive. — With what pleasure did I use to break up the seal! The remembrance yet adds one pulse more to my poor palpitating heart!

Farewell!!!
ROBERT BURNS

July
10th

IV

LION

I am just a poor wayfaring Pilgrim on the road to Parnassus.

BURNS TO ROBERT MUIR

I am a Bard, of no regard
Wi' gentle folks an' a' that.

Love and Liberty

1. *Edinburgh*

Burns was lionized in Edinburgh, and he enjoyed it, but he had to endure being patronized also, and he resented that. Canny pursuit of his purpose — a new edition — netted him about £450, a sum "for his relief" which Sir Walter Scott felt to be "extremely trifling." And Burns suffered tedious delays in collecting even that amount. He greatly increased his fame, a dear concern for him, but his very success hampered further poetic development. Burns finally left Edinburgh, as he had entered it, with but two practical ways of supporting himself — tenant farming and tax collecting (The Excise), both unattractive. He looked back on his venture as a "hare-brained ramble," and on Edinburgh Society as a "Greenland bay of Indifference." From the beginning he had recognized that for this small group of "Patricians" who saw too much of each other, he was merely a welcome novelty.

On his arrival in Edinburgh, Burns knew there only his old crony John Richmond, still a lawyer's clerk, with whom he was to share a room and a bed. But Burns had connections, whom he approached promptly and with dramatic results. The first was Sir

John Whitefoord, erstwhile Master of St. James Lodge, Tarbolton
(Burns was Depute Master). Formerly of Ballochmyle, near
Mauchline, Sir John had retired to Edinburgh upon selling his
estate to cover losses incurred through a bank failure. Another
Ayrshire Freemason, James Dalrymple of Orangefield, was a
friend of Burns' patron John Ballantine, the Ayr banker, and a
nephew of the Rev. Dr. William Dalrymple who had baptized
Burns. More important, Mr. Dalrymple was cousin to James
Cunningham, Lord Glencairn, a prominent member of that select
club, the Caledonian Hunt, and a friend of the leading bookseller-
publisher William Creech. Moreover, Lord Glencairn's brother
had married Miss Isabella Erskine, sister to Lord Buchan and to
Henry Erskine, Dean of the Faculty of Advocates. Within a week
of his arrival, through Dalrymple and Sir John, Burns was welcomed by the best society of the city — landed aristocracy and
gentry, and a select group of able but by no means distinguished
professional people: judges, lawyers, doctors, ministers, and university professors. Burns' Masonic affiliation certainly quickened
his progress, also. On December 7, ten days after his arrival, he
attended a meeting of the most popular Edinburgh lodge, Canongate Kilwinning, and on February 1, 1787, he was made an "assumed member" of the lodge.

The Duchess of Gordon carried him to balls and assemblies so
enthusiastically that it created a scandal heard in London. Lord
Glencairn invited Burns to his house, persuaded the Caledonian
Hunt to subscribe for 100 copies of a new edition, bestirred himself to get subscriptions from London, and seemingly introduced
Burns to Creech. Professor Dugald Stewart, who had entertained Burns at his country home near Mauchline, continued his
friendship, and brought the Kilmarnock volume to the attention
of Henry Mackenzie. On December 7, Mackenzie published a review of it in *The Lounger,* a weekly periodical he was editing,
thus supplementing reviews in the October, November, and December issues of the *Edinburgh Magazine.* Mackenzie was cor-

dial, and Burns looked to him for advice, with at least one unfortunate result in negotiations with Creech over copyright. Lord
Monboddo, Judge of the Court of Session, often had Burns to his
house, and Burns celebrated his beautiful daughter Elizabeth in
the *Address to Edinburgh.* Mr. Patrick Miller, brother of the
Lord Justice-Clerk (mentioned in *The Vision*) and later President
of the Court of Session, left a present of ten guineas, and soon
suggested that he would be pleased to have the Ploughman Poet
as a tenant on his newly bought estate of Dalswinton. The Earl
of Eglinton, at the urging of his Countess, had an agent leave ten
guineas subscription money. The young Walter Scott saw Burns at
the home of Professor Adam Fergusson. Principal William Robertson, historian and friend of Adam Smith, said that while Burns'
poems surprised him, his prose compositions were even more
wonderful, and his conversation surpassed both.

Of greater significance than his being taken up by prominent
people was an announcement on December 14 by Creech that
an edition of Burns' poems was in the press, "to be published by
subscription for the sole benefit of the author." In other words,
the poems were to be published at Burns' risk, with Creech as
his agent. The records of Burns' dealings with Creech are not
known to have survived, but the bookseller managed the details
of publication, perhaps for a commission. He also subscribed for
500 copies which he could sell at one shilling above the subscription price of five shillings.* Burns paid the printer and
binder. His relations with Creech did not remain cordial for long,
but Creech got the job done, and had the best experience and
connections in Edinburgh for it. A second Commonplace Book,
from the Edinburgh period, contains Burns' impressions of Creech.

> A little upright, pert, tart, tripping wight,
> And still his precious self his dear delight;
> Who loves his own smart shadow in the streets
> Better than e'er the fairest She he meets.

* James Grierson reports that Creech paid Burns only the "bookseller's price,"
not the subscription price for these copies. (Fitzhugh, 40.)

Much specious lore, but little understood
(Veneering oft outshines the solid wood),
His solid sense by inches you must tell,
But meet his subtle cunning by the ell!
A man of fashion, too, he made his tour,
Learn'd "vive la bagatelle et vive l'amour";
So travell'd monkies their grimace improve,
Polish their grin — nay, sigh for ladies' love!
His meddling vanity, a busy fiend,
Still making work his selfish craft must mend.

An important result of Burns' social success was that many people recorded their impressions of him, and four artists left well-authenticated likenesses of him. The Nasmyth sketch and full length painting give an accurate representation of what Burns looked like as he walked about Edinburgh. And the Nasmyth head, and particularly the Beugo engraving from it for which Burns gave additional sittings, are careful representations of his features. The Taylor portrait and the Miers silhouette supply interesting confirmation and added detail. Burns stood about five feet ten, and was strong and well knit, although not of a heavy frame, but his carriage and something about his shoulders disguised his height and his natural grace of movement. Swarthy, coarse-featured, with black hair falling over his high forehead, he tended to be moody and withdrawn in a large company, but grew animated in conversation, when his eyes would glow "like coals of living fire." Several comments of a time later than his winters in Edinburgh mention a tendency toward slovenly dress, and two speak of a pockmarked face although none of the portraits show it.

There is general agreement that Burns received adulation with dignity, and exerted himself in company because he saw it was expected of him, but was neither forward nor constrained. He was fully conscious of his abilities and depended on them and not on his situation as a ploughman poet to maintain his position. He exhibited ready wit and strong common sense, and spoke his mind independently and sometimes more forcefully than his well-bred hosts enjoyed. His conversation was frequently tinged with sarcasm, and "his deportment was plain and showed him ready to repel any insult with decision." One hostess who had not met him sent an invitation which he accepted if she would also invite a "learned pig" * then performing in a Grassmarket booth. Two observers speak of an affected rusticity, one of them the son of his printer, who describes Burns carrying a whip and cracking it in the printing shop. Two other observers felt that he had got a swelled head, but since until Burns' death he continued to speak cordially of one, David Ramsay, publisher of the *Edinburgh Courant*, it would appear that a friendship developed and continued between them nevertheless.

The general and enduring impression which Burns made on upper class Edinburgh was recorded by John Lockhart, writing thirty years later, in a biography praised by Sir Walter Scott.

There were many points in Burns's conversational habits which men, accustomed to the delicate observances of refined society, might be more willing to tolerate under the first excitement of personal curiosity, than from any very deliberate estimate of the claims of such a genius, . . . He by no means restricted his sarcastic observations on those whom he encountered in the world to the confidence of his notebook; but startled polite ears with the utterance of audacious epigrams, far too witty not to obtain general circulation in so small a society as that of the Northern capital, far too bitter not to produce a deep resentment, far too numerous not to spread fear almost as widely as admiration. . . . It needs no effort of imagination to conceive what the sensations of an isolated set of scholars (almost all either clergymen or professors) must have been in the presence of this big-boned, black-browed, brawny stranger, with his great flash-

---

* Learned pigs were a popular attraction in Burns' day. A learned pig was one trained to walk round with his proprietor inside a ring of cards and to pick up designated cards apparently by vocal direction but actually on a signal not perceived by the spectators. A common signal was the "snuffing" of the proprietor's nose. (William Frederick Pinchbeck, *The EXPOSITOR, or Many Mysteries Unraveled,* Boston, 1805.) The picture of a Learned Pig among the illustrations following page 236 is the frontispiece to Pinchbeck's book.

ing eyes, who, having forced his way among them from the plough-
tail at a single stride, manifested in the whole strain of his bearing
and conversation, a most thorough conviction that, in a society of
the most eminent men of his nation, he was exactly where he was
entitled to be; hardly deigned to flatter them by exhibiting even an
occasional symptom of being flattered by their notice; by turns calmly
measured himself against the most cultivated understandings of the
time in discussion; overpowered the *bon mots* of the most celebrated
convivialists by broad floods of merriment, impregnated with all the
burning life of genius; astounded bosoms habitually enveloped in the
thrice-piled folds of social reserve, by compelling them to tremble —
nay, to tremble visibly — beneath the fearless touch of natural pathos;
and all this without indicating the smallest willingness to be ranked
among those professional ministers of excitement, who are content
to be paid in money and smiles for doing what the spectators and
auditors would be ashamed of doing in their own persons, even if
they had the power of doing it; and, — last and probably worst of
all, — who was known to be in the habit of enlivening societies which
they would have scorned to approach, still more frequently than
their own, with eloquence no less magnificent; with wit in all likelihood still more daring; often enough, as the superiors whom he
fronted without alarm might have guessed from the beginning, and
had, ere long, no occasion to guess, with wit pointed at themselves.

An illustrative footnote to Lockhart is Henry Mackenzie's comment that Burns' admiration for Robert Fergusson was evidence
of his "propensity for coarse dissipation." But then Fergusson
had mocked Mackenzie's famous novel in a poem, *The Sow of
Feeling.* Mackenzie noted, as though it were a degrading incon-
sistency, that Burns enjoyed the attentions of important people,
but resented class distinctions. However, he does give a rare bit
of Burns' conversation. "He indulged his sarcastic humour* in
talking of men, particularly if he thought them proud, or dis-
dainful of Persons of inferior rank; his Observations were always

---

* Compare Mackenzie's observation, with Burns' comment to Mrs. Dunlop: "I
hate an ungenerous sarcasm a great deal more than I do the devil — at least as
Milton describes him; and though I may be rascally enough to be sometimes
guilty of it myself, I cannot endure it in others." (F I, #219, 205.)

acute and forcibly expressed. I was walking with him one day when we met a common Acquaintance not remarkable for Ability or intellectual Endowments. I observed how extremely fat he had lately grown. 'Yes,' said Burns, 'and when you have told that you have exhausted the subject of Mr —— Fatness is the only quality you can ascribe to him.' "

An extensive memorandum prepared for Dr. Currie by another literary man, Dr. Robert Anderson, both supports and qualifies the statements of Lockhart and Mackenzie. "I was struck with [Burns'] appearance, so different from what I had expected in an uneducated rustic. His person, though neither robust nor elegant, was manly and pleasing; and his countenance, though dark and coarse, uncommonly expressive and interesting. With an air of keen penetration and calm thoughtfulness approaching to melancholy, the usual attendant on genius, there was a kind of stern pride and supercilious elevation about him not incompatible with openness and affability, which might perhaps be properly termed a strong consciousness of intellectual excellence. His dress was plain, but genteel,* like that of a farmer of the better sort; a dark-coloured coat, light-figured waistcoat, shirt with ruffles at the breast, and boots, in which he constantly visited and walked about the Town. He wore his hair, which was black and thin, in a queue, without powder."

Anderson continues that Burns was "decent, dignified, and simple" in the large gathering where he first met him, and "perfectly easy, unembarrassed, and unassuming." As with everyone who ever met Burns, Anderson found his conversation "captivating," and "even more fascinating than his poetry." He adds the following details. "Though [Burns'] knowledge in many instances

---

* "After a brief residence in town, his plain rustic dress was exchanged for a suit of blue and buff, the livery of Fox, with buckskins and top boots." (Ch-W II, 34.) The jacket was buff, the waistcoat blue. These colors were perhaps a tribute to his Whig (Foxite) patrons. But Edinburgh was overwhelmingly Tory (Pittite). In a comment below on the ambivalence of Burns' politics, Anderson remarks that Burns supported Pitt and descried Fox. Perhaps it may be said that Burns was the prototype of the "independent liberal."

was superficial, yet he conversed on every subject in a manner that evinced the strongest marks of genius, sagacity, and acuteness, combined with the most powerful sallies of wit, sarcasm, and satire. With acuteness of intellect, which might sometimes be termed shrewdness, he possessed a still more useful talent, Good Sense, which enabled him instantly to discern what was right or wrong in literature, morality, and the general affairs of the world. He affected to despise those branches of knowledge which he had not cultivated, particularly the abstract sciences. 'I know nothing of logic, or mathematics,' I have heard him say, with great emphasis. 'I profess only poetry.' He was eager to assert the dignity and importance of poetry, which he termed the gift of heaven, though he frequently debased and degraded it by the misapplication of his own great powers to mean and unworthy purposes.* He spoke of his own productions with great complacency, and justified the faults imputed to them by loud and vehement appeals from criticism to commonsense. He recited his own beautiful Songs very readily, and with peculiar animation and feeling, though he affected † to be ignorant of the principles of music."

Anderson then proceeds to list what the polite found offensive in Burns' manner. While independent, he was the slave of "powerful, ardent, and irritable" passions. His pride sometimes showed as insolence, sometimes as resentment. "He would not condescend to practice the graces and respectful attentions of polite persons." He had strong personal, political, and religious prejudices which "misguided the rectitude of his judgment."

Burns' "morality with regard to women was lax; he transgressed the rules of sobriety openly; he was accused of ingratitude — perhaps justly, for he could not bear to conceive himself under an obligation; but his integrity in business was never questioned.

* One wishes that Anderson had listed more particularly Burns' offenses against elegant good taste. Perhaps he was one of those who advised omission of *The Jolly Beggars — Love and Liberty* from the Edinburgh volume.
† No affectation; Burns had almost no formal knowledge of music.

Though proud and revengeful, he was naturally generous and compassionate; zealous in serving those he loved, and always ready to perform offices of kindness and humanity. Though he was accustomed to admit impure and profane thoughts into his mind, yet I never heard him utter a word offensive to decency in the company of ladies; and though addicted to convivial excesses, yet I never heard that he violated the rules of sobriety in private families."

Anderson reports that he and Burns met frequently, and were on good terms, although they did not agree on many topics. "Political disputes then ran high," he remarks. "I was a Whig, attached to the principles upon which the Revolution was effected, He was a tory, an idolater of monarchy, and a Jacobite as much as he could be. I was on the side of Fox and the parliament; He adhered to Pitt and the King." Burns "was not so much elated by the distinction he obtained in Edinburgh as might be expected. He knew that it would be transient, and he neglected not the means of turning it to his advantage," even urging that some poor verses to him be published because he "thought the printing them might do him service." "It was, . . . a part of the machinery . . . of his poetical character to pass for an illiterate ploughman who wrote from pure inspiration." When Anderson "pointed out some of the evident traces of poetical imitation in his verses, privately, [Burns] readily acknowledged his obligations, and even admitted the advantages he enjoyed in poetical composition from the *copia verborum*, . . . which the knowledge and use of the English and Scottish dialects afforded him; but in company he did not suffer his pretentions to pure inspiration to be challenged, and it was seldom done where it might be supposed to affect the success of the subscription for his *Poems*."

Anderson supplies a provocative anecdote.

The vanity which led many women of rank and character to seek his acquaintance and correspondence is remarkable. One instance, not generally known, I shall mention on account of its singular romanticity, from the information of Mr. Dalzell. A Miss Car-michael,* a young poetess, who adored Burns and studied his manner, had been invited to dine with him at Mr. Ramsay's. Sometime after she took the romantic resolution of commencing a sentimental cor-respondence with him, and sent him a card requesting a meeting in the glen between Arthur's Seat and Salisbury Craigs. Though she was not handsome, he had little confidence in his own virtue, and in the delicate embarrassment of the moment he called upon Mr. Dalzell, who happened to be in Town, shewed him the card, and begged he would accompany him to the place of meeting. Dalzell readily agreed to go, and kept his appointment; but in the interval Burns changed his mind and thought proper to go alone. The end of this adventure is not known.

Burns' encounter with an eccentric clergyman will serve to close this account of his life in polite Edinburgh circles. A dis-cussion of Gray's *Elegy* having arisen during a breakfast party at the house of a High School teacher, Alexander Christinson, the minister attacked the poem generally, and Burns asked him to be more particular. Unable to quote pointedly or to make effective criticism, the minister fumbled until Burns lost patience and re-marked, "Sir, I now perceive a man may be an excellent judge of poetry by square and rule, and after all be a damned block-head!" Upon which he turned to a child sitting in Mrs. Christin-son's lap and said, "I beg your pardon, my little dear."

Burns recorded his own impressions of Edinburgh in his letters and in a Commonplace Book which he started there. At first he was amused and pleased, but troubled. "I am in a fair way of becoming as eminent as Thomas a Kempis or John Bunyan," he wrote to Gavin Hamilton. After two weeks in the city, he names his new patrons to John Ballantine, and adds, "I tremble lest I should be ruined by being dragged too suddenly into the glare of polite & learned observation." At the same time he comments

---

* Rebekah Carmichael, to whom Burns presented a copy of Fergusson's poems. (Ch-W II, 60–61.) Mr. Dalzell seems to have been Andrew Dalzell, Professor of Greek in Edinburgh University.

to Robert Aiken, "Various concurring circumstances have raised my fame as a Poet to a height which I am absolutely certain I have not merit to support; and I look down on the future as I would into the bottomless pit."

An engaging interlude is a report to Ballantine on his and Richmond's landlady, a Mrs. Carfrae.

I have just now had a visit from my Landlady who is a staid, sober, piously-disposed, sculduddry-abhoring Widow, coming on her grand climacterick. — She is at present in sore tribulation respecting some "Daughters of Belial" who are on the floor immediately above. — My Landlady who as I said is a flesh-disciplining, godly Matron, firmly believes that her husband is in Heaven; and having been happy with him on earth, she vigorously and perseveringly practices some of the most distinguishing Christian virtues, such as, attending Church, railing against vice, &c. that she may be qualified to meet her dear quondam Bedfellow in that happy place where the Unclean & the ungodly shall never enter. — This, no doubt, requires some strong exertions of Self-denial, in a hale, well-kept Widow of forty five; and as our floors are low and ill-plaistered, we can easily distinguish our laughter-loving, night-rejoicing neighbors — when they are eating, when they are drinking, when they are singing, when they are &c., my worthy Landlady tosses sleepless & unquiet, "looking for rest but finding none," the whole night. — Just now she told me, though by the by she is sometimes dubious that I am, in her own phrase, "but a rough an' roun' Christian" that "We should not be uneasy and envious because the Wicked enjoy the good things of this life; for these base jades who, in her own words, lie up gandygoin with their filthy fellows, drinking the best of wines, and singing abominable songs, they shall one day lie in hell, weeping and wailing and gnashing their teeth over a cup of God's wrath!"

An oblique expression of Burns' sentiments about the "E'nbrugh gentry" was his application to erect a headstone over Robert Fergusson's unmarked grave. All who could come by a copy of the Kilmarnock edition, or who should soon read the volume being prepared by Creech, would find the following stanza in the epistle to William Simpson:

O Fergusson! thy glorious parts
Ill suited law's dry, musty arts!
My curse upon your whunstane hearts,   *whinstone*
        Ye E'nbrugh gentry!
The tythe o' what ye waste at cartes
        Wad stow'd his pantry!   *Would have stored*

By the end of his first winter, Burns tells Dr. Moore, "I have formed many intimacies and friendships here, but I am afraid they are all of them of too tender a construction to bear carriage a hundred and fifty miles." And to Mrs. Dunlop he writes at the same time, "I know what I may expect from the world, by and by; illiberal abuse and perhaps contemptuous neglect." A more explicit statement of distaste comes in a letter of January 27, 1788, after he had been in Edinburgh a year. "Why will Great people not only deafen us with the din of their equipage, and dazzle us with their fastidious pomp, but they must also be so very dictatorially wise? I have been questioned like a child."

A little later he tells William Nicol, "My mind has been vitiated by idleness"; and to William Dunbar he writes, "My late scenes of idleness and dissipation have enervated my mind to an alarming degree." Just as he was leaving Edinburgh finally, he writes to his farmer friend, Robert Cleghorn, "My Muse has degenerated into the veriest prose-wench that ever picked cinders or followed a Tinker."

In his frustration he adopted the same attitude which he had taken when at Irvine six years before:

        Then come, Misfortune, I bid thee welcome —
        I'll meet thee with undaunted mind!

But now he had a mighty protagonist to emulate. He writes to Mrs. Dunlop, April 30, 1787, "I am resolved to study the sentiments of a very respectable Personage, Milton's Satan — 'Hail horrors! hail infernal world!'" To James Smith in June, he cries, "Give me a spirit like my favorite hero, Milton's Satan." And to

Clarinda the following January he again champions Satan's "manly fortitude in supporting what cannot be remedied."

The Reverend Hugh Blair was a famous preacher, author of a rhetoric, and a great critical eminence. He was pleased to be gracious to Burns, who wrote in his Edinburgh Commonplace Book, "I never respect him with humble veneration; but when he kindly interests himself in my welfare, or, still more, when he descends from his pinnacle, and meets me on equal ground, my heart overflows with what is called *liking*. When he neglects me for the mere carcase of greatness, or when his eye measures the difference of our points of elevation, I say to myself with scarcely any emotion — What do I care for him or his pomp either?

"It is not easy forming an exact-judging judgment of any one: but, in my opinion, Dr Blair is merely an astonishing proof of what industry and application can do. Natural parts like his are frequently to be met with — his vanity is proverbially known among his acquaintances — but he is justly at the head of what is called fine writing; and a critic of the first — the very first rank in prose; even in poesy, a good bard of Nature's making can only take the *pas* of him. He has a heart, not of the finest water, but far from being an ordinary one. In short, he is a truly worthy and most respectable character." It should be noted that a famous *gaffe* by Burns was his admitting in Blair's presence a preference for the great man's assistant, Dr. Greenfield, as a preacher. A slip in conversation, it caused Burns acute distress, and Blair was gentleman enough not to notice it.

In Edinburgh, as in Mauchline and Tarbolton, Burns preferred men who were open and free-spoken, who enjoyed a convivial evening, and preferably, men who had something to them. The city abounded in such, even if they did not grace the politer drawing rooms. But the various social strata in Edinburgh rubbed shoulders in a curiously intimate way; there was a considerable

overlap between the convivial clubs and the more elegant assemblages, and many patricians rejoiced in deep potations. In
1787, Edinburgh was a vestigial remnant of medieval times, a
noisome warren of high buildings, narrow wynds (alleys), and
packed closes, where water was delivered by cart and slops were
thrown out the window. The main street, from which the wynds
sloped down to north and south, ran along a rocky ridge, with
Edinburgh Castle at the high, west, end, and Holyrood Palace
at the bottom to the east. The city had grown upward because
there was no room to expand. In the tall tenement buildings,
porters, chimney sweeps, and their ilk inhabited the cellars; upper
class people the lower floors; merchants and clerks the middle
levels; and workmen the attics. All were served by the same
narrow staircase, adorned with accumulations of refuse. Quarters
were crowded and hygiene unthought of. Perforce much of the
city's life was carried on in the street, or in taverns, the usual
place for lawyer and client to meet, or for merchants to seal a
bargain. During the previous decades there had been some expansion of the city to the south, and by 1787 the Georgian squares
north of Princes Street were also beginning to develop. But life
still centered in the old city.

Edinburgh could boast an intellectual and social sophistication
above that common to a provincial city, which it had become on
Scotland's union with England in 1707, when the Scottish parliament was absorbed into the English. However, Scotland still had
its own system of law, centering in Edinburgh; and its presbyterian national church, whose General Assembly resembled a
national legislature. The University of Edinburgh was noted, particularly its medical school. And the self-contained and self-
satisfied Society of the old capital thought of itself as distinguished by a special canon of refinement and cultivation. In
Burns' day, it included no famous men like Hume, earlier, or
Scott, later. Burns never met his equal there, and to quote a late
Nineteenth Century Scottish biographer, "It strikes us of this day

as almost ludicrous that he should have been patronised by men of the undoubted though second-rate capacity of Dugald Stewart, Hugh Blair, and Henry Mackenzie." Indeed, it never occurred to these men and their friends that their chief if only claim to fame would be their association with Burns.

A greater irony still was their professed distaste for the vernacular which they found so delightful in Burns' poems. They wanted to speak and write English, as Burns himself did. For them, Scots had become merely a dialect of the lower classes, suitable perhaps for humorous or homely verse, but no longer a literary language. Like Burns, they admired the English poets of the Eighteenth Century, and Scots poets like Thomson and Beattie, who wrote in the English manner.

A distinguishing mark of life in the old city was the convivial clubs, for business and professional men, which met in taverns. And it was among men who enjoyed amusements of this kind that Burns found his lasting friends in Edinburgh. These clubs were usually organized around some conceit, and a sanitized account of one appears in Chapter XXXVI of *Guy Mannering*. The Crochallan Fencibles, to which Burns was introduced by his printer and Creech's partner, William Smellie, was pseudo-military, each member having rank. The "Colonel" was William Dunbar, a lawyer and Writer to the Signet. "Old sinful Smellie," as Burns called him, "that veteran of genius, wit, and Baudy," was "Adjutant." Smellie had edited the first *Encyclopaedia Britannica*, and had written many articles for it. He was author, also, of a *Philosophy of Natural History*. Burns sketched him in lines intended to be part of a long poem never completed:

> Crochallan came:
> The old cock'd hat, the brown surtout the same;
> His grisly beard just bristling in its might
> ('Twas four long nights and days to shaving night);
> His uncomb'd, hoary locks, wild-staring, thach'd
> A head for thought profound and clear unmatch'd;

Yet, tho' his caustic wit was biting rude,
His heart was warm, benevolent, and good.

Burns elsewhere speaks of Smellie as "a man positively of the first abilities & greatest strength of mind, as well as one of the best hearts & keenest wits that I have ever met with."

The name of Smellie's club came from the favorite song, *Cro Chalein* (Gaelic for "Colin's Cattle"), of the innkeeper whose tavern they frequented — Donald (Dawney) Douglas, of Anchor Close, near Smellie's shop. "Fencibles" parodied the name of the home guard fencible regiments which had been raised when the regular army was overseas during the American war. Other members of the club were Charles Hay, later, as judge, Lord Newton, the "Major" (Hay is reported to have said, "Drinking is my occupation — law my amusement"); William Craig, cousin and protector of Burns' famous heroine "Clarinda," and later, as judge, Lord Craig, the "Provost"; Hon. Henry Erskine, Dean of the Faculty of Advocates; Lord Gillies, judge of the Court of Session; Hon. Alexander Gordon, advocate; Alexander Wight; John Dundas, Edmund Bruce, and William Dallas, Writers to the Signet; Captain Matthew Henderson, subject of an elegy by Burns; John Tennant of Glenconner, farmer, one-time factor for the Dowager Countess of Glencairn, and friend of William Burnes; William Nicol, Latin master of the High School; Allan Masterton, writing master at the High School; James Johnson, an engraver; Alexander Cunningham, lawyer, and, later, jeweler; Robert Cleghorn, a farmer from just outside Edinburgh; and one Williamson of Cardrona.

Anecdotes of Williamson, and of a Dr. Gilbert Stuart, who had died the August before Burns came to Edinburgh, will serve to illustrate the quality of fellowship distinguishing these men. Stuart had been associated with Smellie in getting out the *Edinburgh Magazine and Review*, which his intemperate expressions of "indignation against vice and meanness," and his personal vendettas against prominent people, helped bring to an untimely end, despite Smellie's efforts to moderate Stuart's utterance. In the words of Robert Kerr, Smellie's biographer, Dr. Stuart

occasionally indulged in fits of extreme dissipation, which ultimately undermined his constitution, and hurried him to a premature grave.

In the course of one of his rambles, during the publication of the Edinburgh Magazine and Review, Dr Stuart came one evening to the house of Mr Smellie in a state of complete intoxication, and was immediately put to bed. Awakening in the course of the night, he conceived himself in a brothel, and alarmed the family by repeatedly vociferating *house! house!* Mr Smellie came as soon as possible to the bedside of his friend, to learn what he wanted, and endeavoured to persuade him to go quietly again to sleep. On seeing Mr Smellie almost naked, and still impressed with the idea of being in a house of bad fame, he addressed Mr Smellie with great emphasis in nearly the following words: "Smellie! I never expected to find you in such a house. Get on your clothes, and return immediately to your wife and family; and be assured I shall never mention this affair to any one."

Robert Chambers, in his *Traditions of Edinburgh*, quotes from a privately printed memoir that Williamson of Cardrona

got rather tipsy one evening after a severe *field-day*. When he came to the head of Anchor Close, it occurred to him that it was necessary that he should take possession of the castle [some half mile up the hill]. He accordingly set off for this purpose. When he got to the outer gate, he demanded immediate possession of the garrison, to which he said he was entitled. The sentinel, for a considerable time, laughed at him; he, however, became so extremely clamorous, that the man found it necessary to apprise the commanding-officer, who immediately came down to inquire into the meaning of such impertinent conduct. He at once recognized his friend Cardrona, whom he had left at the festive board of the Crochallan-Corps only a few hours before. Accordingly, humouring him in the conceit, he said: "Certainly you have every right to the command of this garrison; if you please, I will conduct you to your proper apartment." He accordingly conveyed him to a bedroom in his house. Cardrona took formal possession of the place, and immediately afterward went to bed. His feelings were indescribable when he looked out of his bedroom window next morning, and found himself surrounded with soldiers and great guns. Some time afterwards, this story came to the ears of the Crochallans; and Cardrona said he never afterward had the life of a dog, so much did they tease and harass him about his strange adventure.

Burns formed many lasting friendships among this group. Nicol became his travelling companion and spirited correspondent; Masterton and he collaborated on *Willie Brew'd a Peck o' Maut;* Cleghorn remained a most affectionate friend until Burns' death; Cunningham's devotion to Burns led him to attempt raising funds for the widow and children, an effort which drew little sympathy or response from the Patricians. With Johnson, a fellow folk-song enthusiast, Burns got out what is still the best collection of Scots traditional songs, *The Scots Musical Museum.*

By late February, 1787, when approximately the first three hundred pages of Burns' new edition had been printed,* it became evident that the number of subscriptions would require a larger edition than had been planned. As a result, these first pages were reset and additional sheets printed. The later sheets were all printed at once, together with the introductory matter. For bibliographical purists, the Edinburgh edition was then actually two editions, although the content of both is the same. Burns says that the total number of copies printed was three thousand. The book appeared April 17. Thereafter, Burns took an active interest in its distribution, at least partly to save commissions to booksellers. By early May, having done in Edinburgh what he came to do, Burns left, with no better idea of how to make a living than he had had when he arrived. Tenant farming for him had been a bitter experience, but none of his prominent new friends had offered anything at all, except Mr. Miller, who wanted him as a tenant farmer.

Burns seems to have felt that now his large edition had appeared, there would be little further demand for his poems, one

* With the famous misprint of "stinking" for "skinking" [watery] in stanza eight of the *Address to a Haggis.*

of the greatest mistakes in the history of publishing. Since Henry Mackenzie apparently agreed with him, the two of them drew up an agreement with Creech accepting Creech's offer to buy Burns' copyright for an added one hundred guineas. The agreement was made the day the poems appeared, April 17. Creech signed a note for the amount on October 23, and finally, at Burns' insistence, paid off the note without interest on May 30, 1788. But it was not until February, 1789, that Burns could report a final settlement of his account with the bookseller, and only then after frequent complaint, although Creech must have made substantial payments to Burns before that time. The delay kept Burns hanging around Edinburgh, cost him money, and hampered his reluctant plans for settling on a farm.

His feelings about Creech are revealed in the "frosty, keen" letter which he wrote him on January 24, 1788.

Sir,
    When a business, which could at any time be done in a few hours, has kept me four months without even a shadow of anything else to do but wait on it, 'tis no very favourable symptom that it will be soon done, when I am a hundred miles absent. — At any rate, I have no mind to make the experiment, but am determined to have it done before I leave Edinr — But why should I go into the country? till I clear with you, I don't know what to do, or what I have in my power to do. — You have declared yourself to the Publick at large, my friend, my Patron; at all times I gratefully own it: I beg you will continue to be so; and rather make a little exertion amid your hurried time, than trifle with a poor man in his very existence; I shall expect to hear from you tomorrow, or next day; and have the honor to be,

Sir,
your very humble ser

On March 25, 1789, Burns wrote of the final settlement to Mrs. Dunlop: "I clear about 440 or 450 £.* — To keep my brother

---

* Burns seems to have deducted from these sums his living expenses, including his tours, over about two years.

from ruin, and scattering my aged parent & three sisters comfort-
less in the world, I advanced him about 200£ of that money; this
you know was an indispensible affair, as their wellbeing is certainly to me as my own. — What money rests for myself, you will
guess is too little for my own stock; but my Master allows me
some money to build & enclose, & with that, I could have done —
if the farm would have done." In a word, by the time he got all
his much-needed money from Creech, he had found that the farm
would not do for him. What the result would have been had he
had sufficient capital is uncertain, but this is to anticipate. The
significant fact is that Creech had acted characteristically, and
for his own benefit. The *Biographical Dictionary of Eminent
Scotsmen,* originally edited by Creech's fellow townsman, Robert
Chambers, concludes its entry on Creech with the following
paragraph:

In private life Mr. Creech shone conspicuously as a pleasant companion and conversationalist, being possessed of an inexhaustible
fund of droll anecdote, which he could narrate in a characteristic
manner, and with unfailing effect. He thus secured general esteem,
in despite, it appeared, of extraordinary fondness for money, and
penuriousness of habits, which acted to the preclusion not only of
all benevolence and disposition, but even of the common honesty of
discharging his obligations when they were due.

Burns wrote nothing specifically for his new edition except the
wooden *Address to Edinburgh,* and a witty and ironic prose
*Dedication to the Noblemen and Gentlemen of the Caledonian
Hunt,* in which he assumes the role of the Ploughman Poet singing in his country's service, and addressing those who protect
her honor with conscientiousness, courage, knowledge, and public spirit.

My Lords, and Gentlemen,
A Scottish Bard, proud of the name, and whose highest ambition is
to sing in his Country's service, where shall he so properly look for

patronage as to the illustrious Names of his native Land; those who bear the honours and inherit the virtues of their Ancestors? — The Poetic Genius of my Country found me as the prophetic bard Elijah did Elisha — at the *plough*; and threw her inspiring *mantle* over me. She bade me sing the loves, the joys, the rural scenes and rural pleasures of my natal Soil, in my native tongue: I tuned my wild, artless notes, as she inspired. — She whispered me to come to this ancient metropolis of Caledonia, and lay my Songs under your honoured protection: I now obey her dictates.

Though much indebted to your goodness, I do not approach you, my Lords and Gentlemen, in the usual stile of dedication, to thank you for past favours; that path is so hackneyed by prostituted Learning, that honest Rusticity is ashamed of it. — Nor do I present this Address with the venal soul of a servile Author, looking for a continuation of those favours: I was bred to the Plough, and am independent. I come to claim the common Scottish name with you, my illustrious Countrymen; and to tell the world that I glory in the title. — I come to congratulate my Country, that the blood of her ancient heroes still runs uncontaminated; and that from your courage, knowledge, and public spirit, she may expect protection, wealth, and liberty. — In last place, I come to proffer my warmest wishes to the Great Fountain of Honour, the Monarch of the Universe, for your welfare and happiness.

When you go forth to waken the Echoes, in the ancient and favourite amusement of your Forefathers, may Pleasure ever be of your party; and may Social-joy await your return! When harassed in courts or camps with the justlings of bad men and bad measures, may the honest consciousness of injured Worth attend your return to your native Seats; and may Domestic Happiness, with a smiling welcome, meet you at your gates! May Corruption shrink at your kindling, indignant glance; and may tyranny in the Ruler and licentiousness in the People equally find you an inexorable foe!

I have the honour to be,

With the sincerest gratitude and highest respect,

My Lords and Gentlemen,

Your most devoted humble servant,

ROBERT BURNS

Edinburgh,
April 4. 1787.

It is to be wondered how many members of the ruling class group thus addressed paid much attention to the Dedication which ridiculed their aristocratic pretensions, or, paying attention, felt its sting, which was a part of Burns' response to his experience of the Patricians. Another response was resentment at being told it was customary and would be expected that he print at his own expense a thirty-six page list of subscribers' names.

To his Edinburgh edition, Burns added five of his religious poems, seven songs, and six poems of importance: *Death and Dr. Hornbook, The Brigs of Ayr, The Ordination*, the *Address to the Unco Guid, Tam Samson's Elegy*, and the *Address to a Haggis*. This last poem, a famous *tour de force*, which has become a *pièce de resistance* on Burns Nights, had been written originally to surprise a party in Ayrshire when Burns recited it as a seemingly impromptu "grace." He used it similarly, probably without the element of surprise, at the home of Andrew Bruce, merchant, in Edinburgh. By the time the Edinburgh volume appeared, the poem had already been printed in the *Caledonian Mercury* and the *Scots' Magazine*.

In the business of getting out his book, Burns was attentive and shrewd. He promoted the edition by publicizing himself as the "heaven-taught Ploughman," a role Mackenzie had assigned in his *Lounger* review. He flattered the "literati" by seeming to consult them, but he wisely paid little attention to their advice. He was prompt with copy and diligent as a proof-reader. The Edinburgh edition added little to his stature as a poet, but it spread his fame throughout the English-speaking world, largely by prompting pirated editions he probably never heard of and certainly got no return from.

But Burns' newly established position hampered his poetic development. He no longer enjoyed the freedom of relative obscurity, or that buoyancy which gives the Kilmarnock poems so much of their enduring appeal. And his very success as a vernacular poet, he wrote to the Rev. Patrick Carfrae, had "brought an inundation of nonsense over the Land. — Subscription bills for Scots Poems have so dunned and daily do so dun the Public that the very term, Scots Poetry, totters on the brink of contempt." With this in mind, he wrote a little later to Lady Elizabeth Cunningham, sister of his friend and patron, Lord Glencairn, "I am aware that though I were to give the world Performances superiour to my former works, if they were productions of the same kind, the comparative reception they would meet with would mortify me. — For this reason I wish still to secure my old friend, Novelty, on my side, by the *kind* of my performances." A year before, he had commented on his novelty to Dr. Moore: "I know that a great deal of my late eclat was owing to the singularity of my situation, and the honest prejudice of Scotsmen."

This search for novelty led Burns to try odes, Popean satires, laments, monodies, political pieces, and much else, with small success, but he never attempted what he mentioned to Lady Elizabeth — drama, and it is likely that he would have failed there, also. For he regarded drama as chiefly a vehicle for sentiments and declamations, and he shows small gift for the complex structure or the character development desirable in good plays. But certainly he secured his old friend Novelty on his side when he turned to the vernacular again in his verse tale *Tam o' Shanter*, and this may well have been a strong motive for his writing that poem.

But Burns' problems as a man were more pressing than those as a poet. The refined women of Edinburgh fascinated him. To one, Margaret Chalmers, he proposed marriage without success; another, Agnes M'Lehose, he might have married, but she was married already. And he had his living to make. Patrick Miller continued to urge that Burns rent a farm on his Dalswinton estate. While well-disposed, Mr. Miller was no Maecenas. He was looking for intelligent farmers who could restore to productivity the neglected lands he had bought, and Burns' first thought of his proposal had been, "Mr. Miller is no Judge of land; and though I dare say he means to favour me, yet he may give me, in his opinion, an advantageous bargain that may ruin me." However, on his way home from Edinburgh, and without committing himself, he stopped to see Mr. Miller's farm. Afterward, he wrote to James Smith, "I cannot settle to my mind. Farming, the only thing of which I know anything, and heaven above knows but little do I understand of that, I cannot, dare not risk on farms as they are. If I do not fix, I will go for Jamaica. Should I stay in an unsettled state at home, I would only dissipate my little fortune, and ruin what I intend shall compensate my little ones for the stigma I have brought on their names."

As a famous man, with money, Burns' position in Mauchline was far different from what it had been when he left seven months before. He wrote to William Nicol, "I never, my friend, thought Mankind very capable of anything generous; but the stateliness of the Patricians in Edinr, and the servility of my plebeian brethren, who perhaps formerly eyed me askance, since I returned home, have nearly put me out of conceit altogether with my species." He repeats his admiration for the independence and defiance of hardship of Milton's Satan. The "mean, servile compliance" of the Armour family disgusted him particularly. He wrote later to Mrs. Dunlop, "I was made very welcome to visit my girl. — The usual consequences began to betray her: and as I was at that time laid up a cripple in Edinr she was turned, literally turned out of doors, and I wrote to a friend to shelter her, till my return."

2. Tours

Before settling himself, and while awaiting a settlement from Creech, Burns took four trips which carried him over much of Scotland. The first, en route from Edinburgh back to Mauchline, was partly with a young lawyer's apprentice, Robert Ainslie, whose high spirits delighted Burns. He wrote Ainslie afterward, "There is one thing for which I set great store by you as a friend,

and it is this — that I have not a friend upon earth, besides yourself, to whom I can talk nonsense without forfeiting some degree
of his esteem." But, as we shall see, the friendship wore itself
out in a few years.

On Saturday, May 5, Burns and Ainslie rode out of Edinburgh,
and came to Ainslie's home at Dunse that night. For the next
month, Burns was busily entertained by a succession of local
worthies as he rode about the beautiful Border country, visiting
places of interest.* In his journal (one of two which he kept during his life), he notes "fine" ruins like those of Roxburgh, Jedburgh, Dryburgh, and Melrose; he jots down information about
farm practices, and prices, and rents; he speaks with enthusiasm
of particularly lovely scenery. The many entries about places
associated with Scots songs suggest that they were a major interest, for by this time Burns had agreed with James Johnson in
Edinburgh to provide him with all the songs he could find for the
Scots Musical Museum.

But, as always, Burns' chief interest was the people he met.
The journal opens with a charming account of the Ainslie family,
noting that the daughter, Rachel, was an "angel." Burns describes
the minister at Dunse as a "revd., rattling, drunken old fellow,"
and sketches the celebrated traveler, Patrick Brydone, as "a man
of quite ordinary natural abilities, ingenious but not deep, chearful but not witty, a most excellent heart, kind, joyous, & benevolent but a good deal of the French indiscriminate complaisance
— from his situation past & present an admirer of every thing
that has a splendid title or possesses a large estate."

* Besides Dunse, he mentions Kelso, Coldstream, Roxburgh, Jedburgh (where
he was made a Burgess), Melrose, Selkirk, Dryburgh, Inverleithing, Earlston,
Berwick, Eyemouth (where he went sailing), St. Abb's (where he was "made
a royal arch Mason of St. Ebbe's Lodge"), Dunbar; and after Ainslie returned
to Edinburgh, a journey across northern England to Carlisle, from which place
he returned to Scotland via Gretna, and came to Dumfries (where, also, he was
made a Burgess). North of Dumfries he visited Dalswinton, and went on to
Mauchline arriving there about June 10. On one occasion, his fame did not
excuse him from municipal censure. John Sinton reports that in Carlisle, Burns
paid a fine for release of his horse, which had been impounded for straying
off limits onto corporation grass. (Sinton, *Burns Excise Officer and Poet,* 4th
edition, Glasgow and Edinburgh, 1897. 20–21.)

After visiting a Captain Rutherford, Burns notes, "The Captn. a specious polite fellow, very fond of money in his farming way, but showed a particular respect to My Bardship . . . Miss Rutherford a beautiful girl, but too far gone woman to expose so much of so fine a swelling bosom — her face tho' very fine rather inanimately heavy." The Rev. Thomas Somerville of Jedburgh Burns found to be "a man & a gentleman, but sadly addicted to punning." (When this note was published in 1800, the good man is said "to have absolutely abandoned punning.")

Burns' adventures with Miss Isabella Lindsay, whom he met on a walking party, provide some particularly happy passages. A Mrs. Fair and a Miss Lookup, sisters, "ugly & stupid," attempted to monopolize him, but he had an eye on "Miss Lindsay, a good-humor'd amiable girl; rather short et embonpoint, but handsome and extremely graceful — beautiful hazle eyes full of spirit & sparkling with delicious moisture — an engaging face & manner, un tout ensemble that speaks her of the first order of female minds." Shaking himself free from Mrs. Fair and Miss Lookup, he "somehow or other got hold of Miss Lindsay's arm," and, he continues, "Miss seems very well pleased with my Bardship's distinguishing her, and after some slight qualms which I could easily mark, she sets the titter round at defiance, and kindly allows me to keep my hold; and when parted by the ceremony of my introduction to Mr Somerville she met me half to resume my situation — Nota Bene — the Poet within a point and a half of being damnably in love — I am afraid my bosom still nearly as much tinder as ever —

"The old, cross-grained, whiggish, ugly, slanderous hag, Miss Lookup with all the poisonous spleen of a disappointed, ancient maid, stops me very unseasonably to ease her hell-rankling bursting breast by falling abusively foul on the Miss Lindsays, particularly my Dulcinea; I hardly refrain from cursing her to her face — May she, for her pains, be curst with eternal desire and damn'd with endless disappointment." Two days later, Miss Lindsay is of a party which visited Esther Easton, "a very remarkable

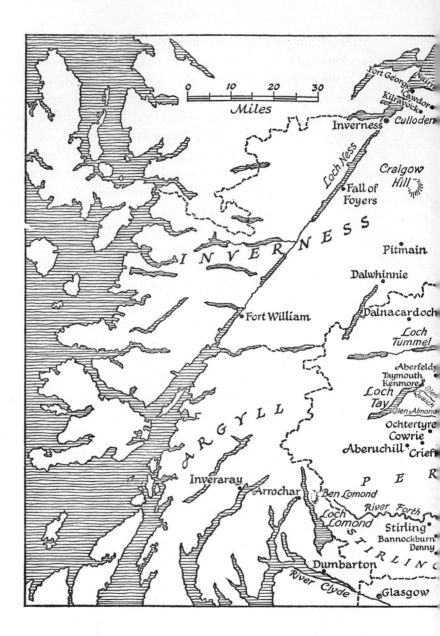

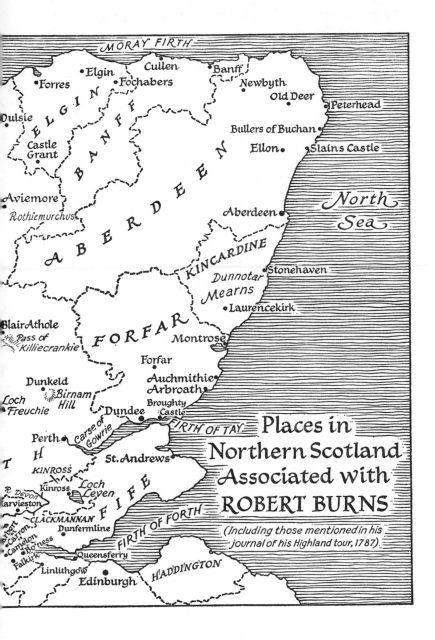

MORAY FIRTH

•Elgin   Cullen   •Banff
•Forres   •Fochabers   •Newbyth
                    Old Deer•
Oulsie   •Peterhead

ELGIN

BANFF

Castle   Bullers of Buchan•
Grant   Ellon•   •Slains Castle

Aviemore
Rothiemurchus

ABERDEEN   Aberdeen•   North Sea

                    KINCARDINE
                    Dunnotar•Stonehaven
                    Mearns
                    •Laurencekirk

BlairAthole
Pass of   FORFAR   Montrose•
Killiecrankie

        Forfar
Dunkeld   Auchmithie•
  Birnam   Arbroath•
Loch Hill
Freuchie   Dundee Broughty
                   Castle

Perth• Carse of   FIRTH OF TAY   Places in
        Gowrie   Northern Scotland
        St.Andrews•   Associated with
KINROSS   ROBERT BURNS
R.Devon Kinross Loch
arvieston   Leven   FIFE   (Including those mentioned in his
CLACKMANNAN   journal of his Highland tour, 1787)
        Dunfermline   FIRTH OF FORTH
Carron•
Camelon•Boness
Falkirk   Queensferry
  Linlithgow•   HADDINGTON
        Edinburgh

woman for reciting Poetry of all kinds, and sometimes making Scotch doggerel herself — She can repeat by heart almost every thing she has ever read, particularly Pope's Homer from end to end — has studyed Euclid by herself, and in short is a woman of very extraordinary abilities — on conversing with her I find her fully to come up to the character given of her — She is very much flattered that I send for her, and that she sees a Poet who has put out a book as she says — She is, among other things, a great Florist — and is rather past the meridian of once celebrated beauty but alas! tho very well married, before that period she was violently suspected for some of the tricks of the Cytherean Déesse."

Burns then presented Miss Lindsay with his picture, "which she accepted with something more tender than gratitude." The end of this summer idyl is tender indeed. "Took farewell of Jedburgh with some melancholy, disagreable sensations — Jed, pure be thy chrystal streams, and hallowed thy sylvan banks! Sweet Isabella Lindsay, may Peace dwell in thy bosom, uninterrupted, except by the tumultuous throbbings of rapturous Love! That love-kindling eye must beam on another, not me; that graceful form must bless another's arms, not mine!" Ten days later he met Miss Betsy Grieve and her sister at Eyemouth, and wrote, "My Bardship's heart got a brush from Miss Betsy."

The heavyweight hosts in various places led him to imagine four of them as a sturdy team of ploughhorses. He also called on a Miss Clark, "a maiden, in the Scotch phrase, 'Guid enough but no brent new,' a clever woman, with tolerable pretensions to remark and wit; while Time had blown the blushing bud of bashful modesty into the full-bosomed flower of easy confidence — She wanted to see what sort of raree show an Author was; and to let him know that though Dunbar was but a little town, yet it was not destitute of people of parts."

On one return to Berrywell, the Ainslie house at Dunse, Burns "found Miss Ainslie all alone," and reflected, "Heavenly Powers who know the weaknesses of human hearts support mine! what happiness must I see only to remind me that I cannot enjoy it!" He imagines the joys of lovemaking with Rachel, and adds later, "Charming Rachel! may thy bosom never be wrung by the evils of this life of sorrows, or by the villainy of the world's sons!" Rachel died unmarried.

Just below his apostrophe to Rachel there are two revealing comments: "I am taken extremely ill with strong feverish symptoms, & take a servant of Mr Hood's to watch me all night — embittering Remorse scares my fancy at the gloomy forebodings of death — I am determined to live for the future in such a manner as not to be scared at the approach of Death — I am sure that I could meet him with indifference, but for 'The Something beyond the grave.'

"I go with Mr Hood to see the roup [auction] of an unfortunate Farmer's stock — rigid Economy & decent Industry, do you preserve me from being the principal Dramatis Persona in such a scene of horrors!"

In Dumfries, besides the freedom of the burgh, Burns received a letter from Mrs. James Hog, Buchanan's Land, Canongate, Edinburgh, written for one Meg Cameron, who was "in trouble." Although his "sincere well-wisher," and apologetic, Meg described herself as "out of quarters, without friends," her "situation . . . really deplorable." She begged, "For God's sake, . . . write and let me know how I am to do." She did not say that Burns was the father. Burns at once wrote Ainslie a letter which reveals much of the nature of their friendship. "My first welcome to this place was the inclosed letter. — I am very sorry for it, but what is done is done. — I pay you no compliment when I say that except for my old friend Smith there is not any person in the world I would trust so far. — Please call at the Jas Hog mentioned, and send for the wench and give her ten or twelve shillings, but don't for Heaven's sake meddle with her as a *Piece*. — I insist on this, on your honor; and advise her out to some country friends. You may perhaps not like the business, but I just tax your friendship thus far. — Call immediately, or at least as soon as it is dark, for God sake, lest the poor soul be starving. — Ask her for a letter I wrote her just now, by way of token. — it is unsigned. — Write me after the meeting."

The surviving fragment of another letter to Ainslie of June 25 seems to question Burns' responsibility: "The Devil's Day-book only April 14 or fifteen so cannot yet have increased her growth much. I begin, from that, and some other circumstances, to suspect foul play." But when Meg swore out a writ against him for support of her child, he answered and paid. In view of his letter below to Ainslie of July 29, 1787, Meg is probably the "Highland wench in the Cowgate" who surprised Burns by bearing him three bastards at a birth instead of merely the "gallant half Highlander" he speaks of below to Ainslie. There is no further record of Meg Cameron or her child or children.

The occasion of the July 29 letter was the birth of Ainslie's bastard son.

Give you joy, give you joy, My dear brother! may your child be as strong a man as Samson, as wise a man as Solomon, & as honest a man as his father. I have double health & spirits at the news. Welcome, Sir, to the society, the venerable Society, of Fathers!!!

> Lo, Children are God's heritage,
> The womb's fruit his reward,
> The sons of youth as arrows are,
> In strong men's hands prepar'd.
>
> Oh, happy is the man that hath
> His quiver fill'd with those!
> He unashamed in the gate
> Shall speak unto his foes!

But truce, with the Psalmist! I shall certainly give you a congratulatory Poem on the birthday myself. My ailing child is got better, and the Mother* is certainly in for it again, and Peggy† will bring a

---

* Jean Armour. The ailing child is one of her twins, probably Jean, who died the following autumn.
† Meg Cameron.

gallant half Highlander, and I shall get a farm, and keep them all about my hand, and breed them in the fear of the Lord and an oakstick, and I shall be the happiest man upon earth.

> "Sing, Up wi't, Aily, Aily;
>   Sing down wi' kimmerland jock;
> Deil ram their lugs, quo' Willie,
>   But I hae scour'd her dock!"   Encore!

Take the following random verses to the tune of Black joke.

> "My Girl she's airy, she's buxom and gay
> Her breath is as sweet as the blossoms in May;
>   A touch of her lips it ravishes quite;
> She's always good natur'd, good humor'd and free;
> She dances, she glances, she smiles with a glee;
>   Her eyes are the lightenings of joy and delight;
> Her slender neck, her handsome waist,
> Her hair well buckl'd, her stays well lac'd,
> Her taper white leg, with an et and a, c,
> For her a,b,e,d, and her c,u,n,t,
>   And Oh for the joys of a long winter night!!!"

A letter I just got from Creech's oblidges me to be in Edinr. against this day, or tomorrow se'nnight, and then what a shaking of hands, and what coveys of *good things*, between you & I! I will call for you at Mitchelson's* the moment I arrive.

> Then, hey, for a merry good fellow;
>   And hey for a glass of good strunt;   *spirits*
> May never we sons of Apollo
>   E'er want a good friend and a ——†

Writing sense is so damn'd dry, hide-bound a business, I am determined never more to have anything to do with it. I have such an aversion to right line and method, that when I can't get over the hedges which bound the highway, I zig-zag across the road just to keep my hand in. I am going to church, and will remember you in my prayers. Farewell.

ROBT. BURNS

* Samuel Mitchelson, lawyer, whom Ainslie served as apprentice-clerk.
† These lines were Burns' concluding stanza to the ballad *I'll tell you a tale of a wife. My Girl she's airy* above, he wrote in 1784 or earlier, and copied into his Commonplace Book.

In mid-June, shortly after he had returned to Mauchline from his Border Tour, Burns set off for the West Highlands, Mary Campbell's country. His route is uncertain and his purpose unrecorded. The previously mentioned letter to Ainslie of June 25 was written from Arrochar, on Loch Long, and it mentions an earlier stop at Inverary, which produced a famous squib:

> Whoe'er he be that sojourns here,
>   I pity much his case,
> Unless he come to wait upon
>   The Lord their God, 'His Grace.'
>
> There's naething here but Highland pride
>   And Highland scab and hunger:
> If Providence has sent me here,
>   'Twas surely in an anger.

Two later records of the journey are happier. One is a ticket bearing that Mr. Burns, of Ayrshire, was "admitted and received a Burgess and Guild Brother" of Dumbarton, on June 29, 1787. The other, a letter to James Smith, reminiscent of Sterne, gives a lively account of Burns' progress down Loch Lomondside.

On our return, at a Highland gentleman's hospitable mansion, we fell in with a merry party, and danced till the ladies left us, at three in the morning. Our dancing was none of the French or English insipid formal movements; the ladies sung Scotch songs like angels, at intervals; then we flew at Bab the Bowster,* Tullochgorum, Loch Erroch Side, &c. like midges sporting in the mottie sun, or craws prognosticating a storm in a hairst day. When the dear lasses left us, we ranged round the bowl till the good-fellow hour of six; except a

---

* "*Bab the bowster* is an old favorite dance, and never omitted at penny weddings and other rustic balls. As practiced in the West of Scotland, it was rather a lengthy function. A row of men and a row of women faced each other, with one in the middle carrying a bolster. The company sang the refrain: —
>   'Wha learnt you to dance, you to dance, you to dance,
>   Wha learnt you to dance, Bab at the bowster, brawly.'
At the close of the stanza, the holder of the bolster, laid it at the feet of one of the opposite sex, and then both knelt and kissed. The process was repeated, until all had participated, or until the company tired of the game." (*The Songs of Robert Burns,* ed. J. C. Dick, London, Edinburgh, and New York, 1903. 429.)

few minutes that we went out to pay our devotions to the glorious lamp of day peering over the towering top of Benlomond. We all kneeled; our worthy landlord's son held the bowl; each man a full glass in his hand; and I, as priest, repeated some rhyming nonsense, like Thomas-a-Rhymer's prophecies I suppose. After a small refreshment of the gifts of Somnus, we proceeded to spend the day on Lochlomond, and reached Dumbarton in the evening. We dined at another good fellow's house, and consequently, pushed the bottle; when we went out to mount our horses, we found ourselves "No vera fou but gaylie yet." My two friends and I rode soberly down the Loch side, till by came a Highlandman at the gallop, on a tolerably good horse, but which had never known the ornaments of iron or leather. We scorned to be out-galloped by a Highlandman, so off we started, whip and spur. My companions, though seemingly gaily mounted, fell sadly astern; but my old mare, Jenny Geddes, one of the Rosinante family, strained past the Highlandman in spite of all his efforts with the hair halter; just as I was passing him, Donald wheeled his horse, as if to cross before me to mar my progress, when down came his horse, and threw his rider's breekless a–e in a clipt hedge; and down came Jenny Geddes over all, and my Bardship between her and the Highlandman's horse. Jenny Geddes trode over me with such cautious reverence, that matters were not so bad as might well have been expected; so I came off with a few cuts and bruises, and a thorough resolution to be a pattern of sobriety for the future.

I have yet fixed on nothing with respect to the serious business of life. I am, just as usual, a rhyming, mason-making, raking, aimless, idle fellow. However, I shall somewhere have a farm soon. I was going to say, a wife too; but that must never be my blessed lot. I am but a younger son of the house of Parnassus, and, like other younger sons of great families, I may intrigue, if I choose to run all risks, but must not marry. . . .

As for the rest of my acts, and my wars, and all my wise sayings, and why my mare was called Jenny Geddes, they shall be recorded in a few weeks hence at Linlithgow,* in the chronicles of your memory, by Robt. Burns.

* Smith had by this time moved from Mauchline to Linlithgow, where Burns planned to visit him on his contemplated Highland Tour, which he began in August. Jenny Geddes was a resolute Presbyterian vegetable seller who objected to the introduction of the new Episcopal service-book on July 23, 1637, and threw a stool at the dean who dared read from it. She aimed so well that the cleric had to duck in the pulpit to avoid being hit. (Chambers, *Traditions of Edinburgh*, 119–120.)

By July 2, Burns is again at Mauchline, having passed through Paisley on his way from Dumbarton. During July he continued the love affair with Jean Armour which had been renewed in June, and wrote his famous autobiographical letter to Dr. Moore. The recipient of this letter, Dr. John Moore (1729–1802), had published a *View of Society and Manners in France, Switzerland, and Germany* (1779), and *in Italy* (1781). He also published *Medical Sketches* (1786), and a novel, *Zeluco* (1789). Dr. Moore, it may be recalled, was a friend of Mrs. Dunlop, who sent him a copy of Burns' Kilmarnock edition, which he in turn sent to Dr. James Currie, a friend of his son Graham. Another son was the famous Sir John Moore, hero of the battle of Coruña. Dr. Moore admired Burns, and although the two men never met, they exchanged many letters. As an established author, the doctor drew from Burns more respectful address than his position and his friendly but fatuous advice warranted.

By August 7, Burns was back in Edinburgh attempting to pry more money out of Creech, settling the claim of Meg Cameron (August 15), and arranging for a trip through the Highlands with William Nicol (1744–1797), which he had hinted at in his letter of June 30 to Smith. Nicol was a man of ability, given to drink and violent explosions of temper. He caused Burns some moments of embarrassment, but they remained friends until Burns' death, and Burns named a son after him. Nicol, a witty man, irreverent to respectability like Burns, gave the Bard recognition and response and a sympathy with his social and political views, which he found in no one else. The choice of Nicol as a travelling companion was another indirect, and perhaps imprudent,* comment on the Edinburgh gentry. Henry Cockburn, who had been his student, says that Nicol, "though a good man, an intense student, and filled, but rather in the memory than the head, with knowledge, was as bad a schoolmaster as it is possible to fancy. Un-

---

* Mrs. Dunlop wrote Burns in November, 1790, of Nicol, "who, the world says, has already damned you as an author." (RB & Mrs. D, 287.)

acquainted with the nature of youth, ignorant even of the characters of his own boys, and with not a conception of the art of the duty of alluring them, he had nothing for it but to drive them; and this he did by constant and indiscriminate harshness."

There are two other contemporary accounts of Nicol, and Burns, which throw revealing light on their relationship and on the feelings of upper class Edinburgh about each of them. The first, by Alexander Young, of Harburn, W.S., is self-explanatory.

I was just entering into business when Burns came first to Edinburgh; and one of my first clients was his friend Wm. Nicol, one of the masters of the High School, who was the son of a Tailor in the village of Ecclefechan in Annandale, employed and patronized by my Grandfather and his family; which services were zealously returned to me by Mr. Nicol in the line of my profession. I considered him, and, I believe justly, as one of the greatest Latin Scholars of the Age; and when I found him & Burns over their Whiskey-punch, (which I had sometimes the honor of partaking with them) bandying *extempore* translations and imitations of English, Scotch, & Latin Epigrams, I could not help considering them as good exemplifications of the Italian *Improvisatori*.

One remarkable instance still occurs to me. When Burns gave Nicol the following strange epitaph to translate into Latin —

> "Here lies old John Hildebrode
> Have mercy on him, Gude God,
>   As he would hae on thee, if he were God
> And thou wert old John Hildebrode."

After a little consideration, Nicol gave furth a Latin edition of this nonsense; which I thought greatly superior to the original. I wrote it down, and long preserved it with some similar dogrel verses; but I now recollect the beginning only: —

> "Hic situs Hilbrodus,
>   Quo non miserabilis alter" &c.

At this time, I looked upon Nicol as a far greater Poet and genius than Burns. He had considerable, indeed constant, employment in translating the Medical & Law Theses of the graduates at the University, for which he made liberal charges, but was very ill paid. I was employed by him to recover many of these claims from English students, concerning which I corresponded with the late Mr. Roscoe, (then an Attorney in Liverpool); and on communicating to Nicol some of Mr. Roscoe's letters signifying that several of his claims were considered to be doubtful, if not desperate, he fell into an extravagant rage, swore, the most unseemly oaths & uttered the grossest blasphemies, that "if our Saviour were again on Earth and had employed him to translate a Thesis without paying him for it, he would crucify him over again!" In consequence of these and similar exhibitions, I thought it prudent to detach myself from such companions; but I never had any quarrel with them.

After reading Young's memoranda, his friend the Rt. Hon. Charles Hope, later Lord Granton, added comments of his own.

I met Burns several times at dinner in different Houses, when he first came to Edinr but I was not at all intimate with Him That visit of his to Edinr was a great misfortune to him, & led to all his after follies & misconduct, & ultimately to his ruin & premature death — to all of which his intimacy with Nicol mainly contributed — Nicoll, as you say, was a good Scholar; but I did not consider him as a *better* Scholar than Adam or Fraser — His passions were quite ungovenable, & he was altogether a most unprincipled Savage — He persecuted poor Adam* by every means in his power; & at last was guilty of a brutal Assault on him, for which the Magistrates did not expell him, as they ought to have done — As a specimen of Nicols unprincipled disposition, & at the same time of his Selfish cunning, take the following Anecdote — You Know it was at that time the Custom for the Rector once a Week to go & examine the Class of one of the other Masters, who, at the same time, came to the Rectors Class & examined it — On one of those ocasions, when I was Dux of the Rectors Class, Nicol came to examine us —. He seemed to be in particular good humour, anticipating, I have no doubt, the triumph he expected over the Rector — He went on for some time in the usual way, hearing us translate & construe — He then began to put some difficult questions, which Several of the Boys could not answer, but on putting them to me & other boys at the Head of the Class, they were all answered — At

* Rector of the High School.

last He put a question which neither I nor any other Boy could answer — On which He turned to me & said, You are a pretty fellow, Sir to be at the Head of this School — not to be able to answer this question — I'll show you that your Cousin John Hope (the late Lord Hopetoun) in my Class can answer it, & make you ashamed of yourself — He then called the Janitor & desired Him to call John Hope to come to Him — John came & the Question was put to him, but John could not answer it — Nicol was evidently very angry, but He had the Selfish Cunning not to outrage the Son of Such a Man as Old Lord Hopetoun — So He merely desired Hope to go away & send Elliott, the Herriotter, to Him — Accordingly Elliott came, & the question was repeated to him, but He did not answer it either, on which the Savage lost all command of himself, flew at poor Elliott, seized & shook by both Ears, till He almost tore them off, & quite forgetting himself, exclaimed You Scoundrel, Have I not been dunning this into you for a week past — showing that He had been leading his Boys out of their depth, & attempting to make them get by rote things that they did not understand, in hopes of having it to say, that His Boys only in the third Class were farther advanced than the Rectors — This explosion operated like Electricity on the Class — There was a universal shout & Hiss, & we all ran out of the school, leaving Nicoll frantic but stupefied with rage — So much for Nicol.*

On August 23, Burns wrote from Edinburgh, asking Ainslie to add "Burns" to any name he gave his newly born son ("Zimri Burns Ainslie or Achitophel &c, &c,") and reporting that he and Nicol intended to travel in a chaise. "Nicol thinks it more comfortable than horse-back, to which I say, Amen," he adds. The two planned to take at least three weeks for their tour, and actually spent twenty-two days, covering 600 miles. The pace was hurried at times by Nicol's impatience. Burns' correspondence shows that he would have enjoyed less haste. He had invitations to present, he wanted to collect songs for Johnson, and he particularly wanted to visit his aunts and uncles about Stonehaven and Montrose. His journal reflects his hurry, being often hardly more than staccato jottings, or an itinerary. With digressions, he

* For a more temperate view of Nicol, by Dr. J. M. Adair, see p. 170.

and Nicol went from Edinburgh to Stirling, on up the north road
to Inverness, and then east along the Moray Firth, cutting down
to Peterhead, and continuing along the coast to Aberdeen, Stonehaven, Montrose, Dundee, Perth, and Queensferry, and so back
to Edinburgh on September 16.

Lord Glencairn had given Burns a diamond stylus, and in Stirling he used it to write on a window pane his resentment that the
old royal palace had been allowed to fall into disrepair.

> Here Stewarts once in glory reign'd,
> And laws for Scotland's weal ordain'd;
> But now unroof'd their palace stands,
> Their sceptre swayed by other hands:
> Fallen indeed, and to the earth,
> Whence grovelling reptiles take their birth
> The injured Stewart line is gone,
> A race outlandish fills their throne:
> An idiot race, to honour lost —
> Who know them best despise them most.

These sentiments about the reigning house of Hanover were
hardly designed to gain Burns political favors from those who had
favors to grant.

He and his fellow Jacobite visited Bannockburn and Killiecrankie, where the Scots had slaughtered the English, and Culloden,
where the English had slaughtered Prince Charles' remaining
supporters. They visited Ossian's grave near Crieff, and at Caw-
dor were shown the bed on which King Duncan had been mur-
dered. Later they heard "that the muir where Shakespeare lays
Macbeth's witch meeting is still haunted." At Scone they viewed
a "picture of the Chevalier and his sister — Queen Mary's bed,
the hangings wrought with her own hands." They met the famous
fiddler Neil Gow and heard him play — "A short, stout-built, honest highland figure, with his grayish hair shed on his honest social
brow — an interesting face, marking strong sense, kind open-
heartedness mixed with unmistrusting simplicity."

As on his Border Tour, Burns notes lovely scenery, ruins, and details about farming, and he is interested in the people he met. At the peak of his fame, he was received in the best houses. A typical entry is that recording his visit to Blair Athole, seat of the Duke of Athole, to whom he had an introduction.

[Friday, August 31] Blair — sup with the Duchess — easy and happy from the manners of the family — confirmed in my good opinion of my friend Walker.

[Saturday, September 1] — visit the scenes round Blair — fine, but spoilt with bad taste — Tilt and Garry rivers — falls on the Tilt — heather seat — ride in company with Sir William Murray and Mr. Walker to Loch Tummel — meanderings of the [Tummel], which runs through quondam Struan-Robertson's estate from Loch Rannoch to Loch Tummel — Dine at Blair — Company — General Murray, *rien* — Captain Murray, an honest Tar — Sir W. Murray, an honest, worthy man, but tormented with the hypochondria — Mrs. Graham, *belle et amiable* — Miss Cathcart — Mrs. Murray, a painter — Mrs. King — Duchess and fine family, the Marquis, Lords James, Edward and Robert — Ladies Charlotte, Amelia and [Elizabeth] — children dance — sup — Duke — Mr. Graham of Fintray — Mr. McLaggan, Mr. and Mrs. Stewart.

Mr. Robert Graham of Fintry was to prove a firm friend to Burns the Exciseman. The poet later visited Sir William Murray at his estate of Ochtertyre. "Walker" was Josiah Walker, whom Burns had met in Edinburgh through Dr. Blacklock; he was now a tutor in the Duke's family. He speaks as do so many others of Burns' "unembarrassed, plain, firm" manner, and reports that he was delighted with the Duke's children, and in turn delighted the company with his toast to them, "honest men and bonie lasses." Of another guest, "a man of a robust but clumsy person," Burns expressed the value he entertained for him "on account of his vigorous talents, although they were clouded at times by coarseness of manners; 'in short,' he added, 'his mind is like his body, he has a confounded strong in-kneed sort of a soul.' "

The Duke was expecting an important guest, Henry Dundas,

Pitt's political lieutenant for Scotland, and wished to keep Burns as "the best dainty with which he could entertain an honored guest." But, though "easy and happy," Burns acceded to Nicol's wishes and left on Sunday, sending back a few days later *The Humble Petition of Bruar Water* to pay his "debts of honour and gratitude."

Henry Mackenzie had given Burns introductions to Sir James Grant of Grant, and to his cousin, Mrs. Elizabeth Rose, of Kilravock. He and Nicol spent half a day with Sir James, dining, and going on "through mist and darkness to Dulsie, to lie." On their way to Fort George and Inverness, they called on Mrs. Rose, and on their way back east, they had breakfast with her, when Burns was delighted to have Miss Rose sing two Gaelic songs for him. Mrs. Rose and a Mr. Grant accompanied the travellers on their way some distance, and the following winter Burns sent her a letter and a volume of the *Scots Musical Museum*. He and Nicol spent that night with a celebrated naturalist, James Brodie of Brodie, who was, as Burns notes, "truly polite, but not just the highlander's cordiality."

At Fochabers, Burns presumed on his former friendship with the Duchess of Gordon to call at Castle Gordon. The journal entry is happy, but it omits some details. "Fine palace, worthy of the noble, the polite, the generous Proprietor — Dine — Company, Duke and Duchess, Ladies Charlotte and Madelina, Colonel Abercrombie and lady, Mr. Gordon and Mr. [*blank*], a clergyman, a venerable aged figure, and Mr. Hoy, a clergyman, I suppose, a pleasant open manner — The Duke makes me happier than ever great man did — noble, princely, yet mild, condescending and affable, gay and kind — The Duchess charming, witty, kind and sensible — God bless them! Come to Cullen to lie." In a letter to James Hoy, the Duke's librarian, Burns laments having been hurried away, and continues, "May that obstinate son of Latin Prose be curst to Scotch-mile periods, and damn'd to seven league paragraphs; while Declension & Conjugation, Gender, Number, and Time, under the ragged banners of Dissonance and Disarrange-

ment eternally rank against him in hostile array!!!!!!" He goes on
to recite his connection with Johnson's *Museum,* and to request
the Duke's words to *Cauld Kail in Aberdeen,* for which he thanks
Hoy in a later letter.

His reference to the "obstinate son of Latin Prose" was, of
course, to Nicol. On arrival at Fochabers, Burns had left his companion at the inn and walked up to the castle, where he was
warmly received and pressed to join the company, just sitting
down to dinner. Burns did, but rose soon and said he must rejoin
Nicol, whereupon the Duke sent a guest with Burns to insist that
Nicol return with them and become one of the party. But Nicol,
infuriated by the seeming neglect, had ordered the chaise to be
hooked up, and stormed that if Burns did not join him, he would
set off alone. Burns joined him and they drove away. At Banff
they breakfasted with a schoolmaster friend of Nicol's, who invited a boy to be present and to serve later as messenger and
guide on a proposed visit to Duff House nearby, mansion of the
Earl of Fife. This lad later remembered that "during breakfast,
Burns played off some sportive jests at his touchy *compagnon de
voyage,* about some misunderstanding which took place between
them at Fochabers, in consequence of Burns having visited the
castle without him."

The next day, Burns notes that they passed "Lord Aberdeen's
seat — entrance denied to every body, owing to the jealousy of
three-score over a kept country-wench." In Aberdeen, which Burns
calls a "lazy town," he met "Bishop Skinner, a non-juror, son of
the author of 'Tullochgorum,' a man whose mild, venerable manner is the most marked of any in so young a man." Bishop Skinner
wrote his father a lively account of this meeting, and his father
sent Burns a rhymed epistle which opened a brief and cordial
correspondence between them. The bishop's letter follows:

Calling at the printing office the other day, whom should I meet on
the stair but the famous Burns, the Ayrshire Bard! And on Mr.
Chalmers telling him that I was the son of *Tullochgorum,* there was
no help but I must step into the inn hard by and drink a glass with

him and the printer. Our time was short, as he was just setting off for the south and his companion hurrying him; but we had fifty "auld sangs" through hand, and spent an hour or so most agreably. — "Did not your father write the *Ewie wi' the crooked horn?*" — "Yes." — "O, an I had the lown that did it!" said he, in a rapture of praise; "but tell him how I love, and esteem, and venerate his truly Scottish muse." On my mentioning *his Ewie*, and how you were delighted with it, he said it was all owing to yours, which had started the thought. He had been at Gordon Castle, and come by Peterhead. "Then," said I, "you were within four Scottish miles of *Tullochgorum's* dwelling." Had you seen the look he gave, and how expressive of vexation; — had he been your own son you could not have wished a better proof of affection. "Well," said he at parting, and shaking me by the hand as if he had been really my brother, "I am happy in having seen you, and thereby conveying my long-harboured sentiments of regard for your worthy sire; assure him of it in the heartiest manner, and that never did a devotee of the Virgin Mary go to Loretto with more fervour than I would have approached his dwelling and worshipped at his shrine." He was collecting on his tour all the "auld Scots sangs" he had not before heard of, and likewise the tunes, that he might get them set to music. "Perhaps," said he, "your father might assist me in making this collection; or, if not, I should be happy in any way to rank him among my correspondents." "Then give me your direction, and it is probable you may hear from him sometime or other." On this he wrote his direction on a slip of paper, which I have enclosed that you may see it under his own hand. As to his personal appearance, it is very much in his favour. He is a genteel looking young man of good address, and talks with as much propriety as if he had received an academical education. He has indeed a flow of language, and seems never at a loss to express himself in the strongest and most nervous manner. On my quoting with surprise some sentiments of the Ayrshire *Plowman*, "Well," said he, "and a plowman I was from youth, and till within these two years had my shoes studded with a hundred *tackets*. But even then I was a reader, and had very early made all the English poets familiar to me, not forgetting the old bards of the best of all poetical books — the Old Testament."

Burns' journal records a visit to Stonehaven, where he met his relations, noting particularly "Robert Burnes, writer . . . , one of those who love fun, a gill, a punning joke, and have not a bad heart — his wife a sweet hospitable body, without any affectation of what is called town-breeding." Burns merely mentions Montrose, where his cousin James Burness lived, a "finely-situated handsome town," but in a letter to his brother Gilbert on his return to Edinburgh, he gives many details of their uncles, aunts, and cousins. "I spent two days among our relations, and found our aunts, Jean & Isbal [his father's sisters] still alive and hale old women, John Caird [husband of Williams Burnes' sister Elspeth], though born the same year with our father, walks as vigorously as I can; they have had several letters from his son in New York. — William Brand [husband of Isbal] is likewise a stout old fellow."

This pleasant visiting was interrupted by Nicol. In a letter to James Burness, Robert laments, "Mr Nicol and Mr Carnegie have taken some freak in their head, and have wakened me just now with the rattling of the chaise to carry me to meet them at Craigie to go on our journey some other road and breakfast by the way. — I must go, which makes me very sorry." On his return to Edinburgh he sent James Burness nine copies of his book to distribute for him.

Below Montrose, Burns went sailing along the coast from Auchmithie to Arbroath, and near Perth he noted "the scene of 'Bessy Bell and Mary Gray,'" and recorded having had "Reflections in a fit of the Colic." After a night at Kinross, the journal closes bleakly, "Come through a cold barren Country to Queensferry — dine — cross the Ferry, and come to Edinburgh."

Once back in the city, Burns turned again to the business of making a living. He had, of course, to choose from the opportunities open to him. So long ago as the previous autumn he had considered the Excise as an escape from farming. The service carried a certain social opprobrium, but the duties were not heavy, the income was respectable and regular, and there was opportunity for promotion to very comfortable positions indeed. But in Burns' day, all government jobs went by political favor, and he could find no one to help him to an Excise appointment. His

Edinburgh patrons felt that the Excise was an unworthy occupation for Scotia's Bard, and that a ploughman poet should naturally return to the romantic and honorable life of a farmer. About that life, Burns was, as usual, sensible and clear-headed. He wrote Mrs. Dunlop, "As to a Laird farming his own property; sowing corn in hope, & reaping it, in spite of brittle weather, in gladness; . . . 'tis a heavenly life! — but devil take the life, of reaping the fruits that another must eat."

Since at the moment, however, he had no other practical choice, he got in touch with Patrick Miller about the farm they had discussed, expressing fear that Mr. Miller might have left Dalswinton before he could get there. "I am determined," he adds, "not to leave Edinr till I wind up my matters with Mr Creech, which I am afraid will be a tedious business."

After two weeks of waiting, he set out on another round of visits, leaving Edinburgh about October 1 with a friend of Archibald Lawrie, Dr. James McKittrick Adair. Adair seems to have been a headstrong, roving man, always off to a new start and never winning through. He wrote for Dr. Currie a pleasant narrative of his expedition with Burns, notable for the more genial picture it gives of William Nicol than that projected by Alexander Young and Lord Granton.

Burns' and Adair's destination was Harvieston, in the Devon valley, near Stirling, where Burns had gone for a day while on his tour with Nicol. The attractions there were Margaret Chalmers and her cousin Charlotte Hamilton, relatives of Gavin Hamilton. Burns' relations with Margaret were most happy, and his letters to her are among his best. She told Thomas Campbell, the poet, that Burns had proposed marriage to her, and the thought of what his life might have been with her and a comfortable income is provocative. She was not a great deal above him in station, and she was a woman of charm, intelligence, and literary taste. She and Burns remained friends after her engagement and marriage to Lewis Hay, a banker. The family connections here are complex.

Of three Murdoch sisters, Barbara had married Hamilton's father and so had become his step-mother; Euphemia had married a Mr. Chalmers and was now the widowed mother of two daughters, Cochran (Lady Mackenzie) and Margaret; and Charlotte had married John Tait of Harvieston. After her death, leaving a son and a daughter, Mr. Tait invited her sister, Mrs. Hamilton, now widowed also, to live at Harvieston with her son and her daughters Grace and Charlotte (Gavin Hamilton's half-brother and half-sisters), and manage his household until his own daughter grew up. Sometimes, Mrs. Chalmers visited there in the summer also with her daughters. In the latter years of her husband's life, the Chalmers family had lived on a farm near Mauchline, and it is probable that Burns had met Margaret Chalmers before he came to Edinburgh, where he saw her often, sometimes at Dr. Blacklock's.

Of his earlier visit to Harvieston, when Margaret had not been there, Burns had written to Gavin Hamilton, describing one of the pleasantest days of his life, "They are a family, Sir: though I had not any prior tie, though they had not been the brother & sisters of a certain generous friend of mine, I would never forget them. — I am told you have not seen them these several years, so you can have very little idea of what such young folks as they now are." He continues with a happy description of the children, reporting that he cannot speak of Charlotte "in common terms of admiration; she is not only beautiful but lovely." He reproaches Hamilton for not having seen more of such delightful relatives, and adds family gossip.

On the October visit, when Margaret was present, Burns intended to stay at Harvieston only briefly before going on to two other country houses, and then returning. But Adair stayed the fortnight, and paid successful court to Charlotte Hamilton. He reports to Dr. Currie that Burns smashed the window pane at Stirling on which he had written the couplets during his previous visit, and then goes on,

At Stirling we met with a company of travellers from Edinburgh, among whom was a character in many respects congenial with that of Burns. This was Nicol, one of the teachers of the High Grammar-School at Edinburgh — the same wit and power of conversation; the same fondness for convivial society, and thoughtlessness of to-morrow, characterized both; Jacobitical principles in politics were common to both of them; and these have been suspected, since the revolution in France, to have given place in each, to opinions apparently opposite. I regret that I have preserved no *memorabilia* of their conversation, either on this or other occasions, when I happened to meet them together. Many songs were sung; which I mention for the sake of observing, that then when Burns was called on in his turn, he was accustomed, instead of singing, to recite one or other of his own shorter poems, with a tone and emphasis, which though not correct or harmonious, were impressive and pathetic. This he did on the present occasion.

From Stirling we went next morning through the romantic and fertile vale of Devon to Harvieston, in Clackmannanshire, then inhabited by Mrs. Hamilton, with the younger part of whose family Burns had been previously acquainted. He introduced me to the family, and there was formed my first acquaintance with Mrs. Hamilton's eldest daughter, to whom I have been married for nine years. Thus was I indebted to Burns for a connexion from which I have derived, and expect further to derive, much happiness.*

Burns apparently disappointed the Harvieston party by insufficiently fervid appreciation of local scenery. But he relished two incidents which Adair describes. "A visit to Mrs. Bruce of Clackmannan a lady above ninety, the lineal descendant of that race which gave the Scottish throne its brightest ornament, interested his feelings more powerfully. This venerable dame, with characterstical dignity, informed me, on my observing that I believed

---

* Miss Hamilton and Dr. Adair were married November 16, 1789. Dr. Adair's aunt, a Mrs. Burke, writes after his death, to her niece, his sister Anne, Archibald Lawrie's wife [July 24, 1802]: "I am truly sorry to hear that my beloved James was denied the Blessing of domestic happiness . . . he never gave me the least hint of his unhappy situation." In a later letter, of February 18, 1804, she refers to "that oddaty Mrs Adair." (Volume II, *The Lawrie Family*, 60, a MS history by David Balfour Graham Langwell. Most courteously lent the present biographer by the author.)

she was descended from the family of Robert Bruce, that Robert Bruce was sprung from her family. Though almost deprived of speech by a paralytic affection, she preserved her hospitality and urbanity. She was in possession of the hero's helmet and two-handed sword, with which she conferred on Burns and myself the honour of Knighthood, remarking, that she had a better right to confer the title than *some people*."

On their way back to Edinburgh, the two men visited Dunfermline Abbey. "Here," Adair reports, "I mounted the *cutty stool,* or stool of repentence, assuming the character of a penitent for fornication; while Burns from the pulpit addressed to me a ludicrous reproof and exhortation, parodied from that which had been delivered to himself in Ayrshire, where he had, as he assured me, once been one of seven who had mounted the *seat of shame* together.

"In the court-yard, two broad flag-stones mark the grave of Robert Bruce, for whose memory Burns had more than common veneration. He knelt and kissed the stone with sacred fervour, and heartily . . . execrated the worse than Gothic neglect of the first of Scottish heroes."

While Adair was courting Charlotte Hamilton, Burns went on his intended visits to John Ramsay of Ochtertyre, near Stirling, and to Sir William Murray, at another Ochtertyre, near Crief. Ramsay he had met through Dr. Blacklock, and Sir William had been a guest at Blair Athole during Burns' stay there. By October 8, he was "exceedingly comfortably situated" at Sir William's, after a few days with Mr. Ramsay, whom he hoped to visit again on the tenth on his way back to Harvieston.

"I have been in the company of many men of genius," Mr. Ramsay wrote to Dr. Currie, "some of them poets, but never witnessed such flashes of intellectual brightness as from him, the impulse of the moment, sparks of celestial fire! I never was more delighted, therefore, than with his company for two days, tête-a-tête. In a mixed company I should have made little of him; for, in the gamester's phrase he did not always know when to play off and when to play on. . . . When I asked him whether the Edinburgh Literati had mended his poems by their criticisms, 'Sir,' said he, 'these gentlemen remind me of some spinsters in my country, who spin their thread so fine, that it is neither fit for weft or woof.'" Mr. Ramsay suggested that Burns write poetry descriptive of "beautiful landscapes of rural life and manners," or a play like the *Gentle Shepherd* "which everyone who knows our swains in the unadulterated state, instantly recognizes as true to nature."

On his return to Edinburgh, Burns had expected to go at once to Dumfries, but on October 20 he wrote to Mr. Miller that he had caught such a cold his doctors had ordered him into close confinement. He continues:

From something in your last, I would wish to explain my idea of being your Tenant. — I want to be a farmer in a small farm, about a plough-gang, in a pleasant country, under the auspices of a good landlord. — I have no foolish notion of being a Tenant on easier terms than another. — To find a farm where one can live at all, is not easy — I only mean living soberly, like an old-style farmer, and joining personal industry. — The banks of the Nith are as sweet, poetic ground as any I ever saw; and besides, Sir, 'tis but justice to the feelings of my own heart, and the opinion of my best friends, to say that I would wish to call you landlord sooner than any landed gentleman I know. — These are my views & wishes; and in whatever way you think best to lay out your farms, I shall be happy to rent one of them. — I shall certainly be able to ride to Dalswinton about the middle of next week, if I hear you are not gone.

But he did not visit Dalswinton until late November. Those familiar with Burns' sentiments about landlords may hear overtones of irony in his compliments to Mr. Miller.

3. *Clarinda*

By early December Burns was back in Edinburgh from his visit to Dumfries, and he expected to leave the city within a few days when two accidents coincided to keep him there until February and to precipitate one of the most famous episodes of his life. He met Agnes Craig M'Lehose, and he wrenched his knee so badly that he could not leave his room for a month, or travel for two months and a half. The accident, caused by a drunken coachman, also led to Burns' finally securing an appointment in the Excise, which he had hoped for on coming to Edinburgh the previous December. One of his doctors, Alexander ("Lang Sandy") Wood, learning that Burns really desired the appointment, set wheels in motion to get it for him. The person chiefly responsible for securing it seems to have been Robert Graham of Fintry, now a member of the Scottish Board of Excise.

In writing to Margaret Chalmers about his appointment, Burns said, "I have chosen this, my dear friend, after mature deliberation. The question is not at what door of fortune's palace shall we enter in; but what doors does she open to us? . . . I got this without any hanging on, or mortifying solicitation; it is immediate bread, and though poor in comparison of the last eighteen months of my existence, 'tis luxury in comparison of all my preceding life: besides, the commissioners are some of them my acquaintances, and all of them my firm friends."

When Burns and Mrs. M'Lehose met, on Tuesday, December 4, they were greatly attracted to each other, and she invited him to tea on December 6, but he found it necessary to postpone the engagement with regret until December 8, Saturday. However, on Saturday morning he suffered his accident, and they were forced to carry on their affair entirely by correspondence until January 4. Even when they began to see one another, they continued to exchange letters frequently. The affair grew fervid, and he who would savor it fully must brace himself to read the full correspondence of Sylvander (Burns) and Clarinda (Mrs. M'Lehose); the Arcadian names were her suggestion. Most of the letters are tiresome, as love letters tend to be, but they reveal a skillful and often comic game of pretence which ended in pathetic frustration. Clarinda had arranged with a friend, Miss Erskine Nimmo (a friend, in turn, of Margaret Chalmers), for an introduction to Burns, and she promptly threw herself at his head. But her orthodox Calvinism, her cautious respectability, and her vulnerable position kept her from satisfying passions she was only too willing to arouse.* She was supporting herself and two small children on two tiny annuities which she would lose in the event of scandal. Burns began the affair with obvious thoughts of another conquest, but soon found himself checked and unable either to break off or to triumph.

Mrs. M'Lehose (1759–1841) was a flirtatious sentimentalist, small, plumpish, and pretty. Having lost her mother and sister in childhood, and being a lively girl, she married at seventeen, against advice, a young law-agent of pleasing manners, James M'Lehose. In a memoir, her grandson, W. C. M'Lehose, describes the consequences of this match.

Married at so early an age, before the vivacity of youth was passed, and, indeed, before it was fully developed, possessed of considerable personal attractions, a ready flow of wit, a keen relish for society, in which her conversational powers fitted her to excel, and a strong love of admiration; she appears to have displeased her husband, because she could not at once forego those enjoyments so natural to her time of life and situation. And he, without any cause, seems to have conceived the most unworthy jealousy, which led him to treat her with a severity most injudicious, and, to one of her disposition, productive of the worst consequences.

After four and a half years of marriage, and three children, one dying in infancy, Mrs. M'Lehose found her husband's treatment unendurable, and returned to her father, Andrew Craig, a Glas-

---

* Mrs. M'Lehose seems to be the only known woman of Burns' acquaintance to meet the specifications outlined in a letter to Alexander Cunningham of September, 1792: "I remember, in my Plough-boy days, I could not conceive it possible that a noble Lord could be a Fool, or that a Godly Man could be a Knave. — How ignorant are Plough-boys! — Nay, I have since discovered that a *godly woman* may be a ———— !" (F II, #506, 120.)

gow surgeon. A fourth child was born soon thereafter. M'Lehose exercised his rights, and as soon as it was practicable, took her children from her to force her return, but she held out. Before long he exhausted his resources, suffered a period of imprisonment for debt, returned the children, and finally left the country in November, 1784. He never thereafter contributed to the support of his wife and children, except for one remittance of £50, accompanied by grandiloquent directions for his son's education. For a time, the surgeons and the writers of Glasgow each made a small annuity to the neglected wife, but withdrew them when it was found that M'Lehose had a large income in Jamaica. A judgment against him produced no results until his death in 1812, when it enabled his widow to recover funds from an account he had long maintained in London.

Upon her father's death in 1782, Mrs. M'Lehose moved to Edinburgh, where she lived under the protection of her cousin, a lawyer and Burns' fellow-Crochallan, William Craig, later Lord Craig as Judge of the Court of Session. He supplemented her annuities, and supported her after the annuities were withdrawn. Agnes Craig's education had been sketchy and frivolous, but after separation from her husband, she industriously read the best authors, and practiced a polite style. She even wrote passable verses. A woman of quick mind and lively spirit, she led an active social life, and was much concerned with religion.

Like Mrs. Dunlop, she felt distress at outspokenness in Burns' poems, *The Holy Fair* being particularly offensive to her. The temper of her meetings with Burns is suggested by a method of censorship which she says she would have exercised over certain poems had she known him when he was preparing the Kilmarnock edition. "Had Clarinda known you, she would have held you in her arms till she had your promise to suppress them." A comment on their discussions of religion and morals is similar. "If you'd caress the 'mental intelligence' as you do the corporeal frame, indeed, Sylvander, you'd make me a philosopher."

Burns obviously discussed Clarinda with his friend Ainslie, a significant detail in itself, and eventually he took Ainslie to call, thereby initiating a long and cozy relationship between the two, of which there will be more information later. As one solid mark of friendship, Ainslie later took Mrs. M'Lehose's son into his law office.

Clarinda's letters speak of bad conscience on mornings after meetings with Burns, and even report conferences with her spiritual adviser, the Rev. John Kemp, whose imagination was "rich — his feelings delicate — his discernment acute." He talked to her "in the style of a tender parent" anxious for her happiness. Sylvander fumed at the reports of Mr. Kemp. Clarinda and Sylvander exchanged verses, discussed friendship and true love, and religion. She told him of her unhappy marriage, and he told her about Jean and gave her a copy of his autobiographical letter to Dr. Moore to read.

Clarinda had been converted to orthodox Calvinism, but she could not convert Sylvander, who did, however, give her a careful, thoughtful, and sophisticated statement of his theological position, one which combined various departures from orthodoxy.

He who is our Author and Preserver, and will one day be our Judge, must be — not for His sake in the way of duty, but from the native impulse of our hearts — the object of our reverential awe and grateful adoration. He is almighty and all-bounteous, we are weak and dependent; hence prayer and every other sort of devotion. — "He is not willing that any should perish, but that all should come to everlasting life;" consequently it must be in every one's power to embrace His offer of "everlasting life;" otherwise He could not, in justice, condemn those who did not. A mind pervaded, actuated, and governed by purity, truth, and charity, though it does not *merit* heaven, yet is an absolutely necessary prerequisite, without which heaven can neither be obtained nor enjoyed; and, by Divine promise, such a mind shall never fail of attaining "everlasting life:" hence the impure, the deceiving, and the uncharitable exclude themselves from eternal bliss, by their unfitness for enjoying it. The Supreme Being has put the immediate administration of all this, for wise and good ends known to Himself, into the hands of Jesus Christ — a great Personage, whose relation to Him we cannot comprehend, but whose relation to us is that of a Guide and Saviour; and who, except for our own obstinacy and misconduct, will bring us all, through various ways, and by various means, to bliss at last.

Burns here expands his father's belief, and combines the Arminian rejection of absolute predestination with the Arian position that Christ the Son was not consubstantial with the Father, and the Socinian doctrine that denied Christ's divinity but held his birth to be a miracle.

Burns is more explicit about his feelings toward Jesus in a later letter, to Mrs. Dunlop, in which he addresses Jesus Christ as "thou amiablest of characters," and adds, "I trust thou art no Imposter, & that thy revelation of blissful scenes of existence beyond death and the grave is not one of the many impositions which time after time have been palmed off on credulous mankind." He summarizes his position to Clarinda, "My creed is pretty nearly expressed in the last clause of Jamie Deans's grace, an honest weaver in Ayrshire: 'Lord, grant that we may lead a gude life! for a gude life maks a gude end; at least it helps weel!'"

On occasion, Clarinda had to remind Sylvander that she was a married woman, and that she could stand no scandal, and he protested that she misunderstood him. By mid-February, he had promised to be hers for life, which she understood as a promise to "wait" until her husband died. But as soon as Burns got back to Ayrshire and saw Jean's desperate situation, he cleared these sentimental fantasies out of his mind and acted decisively. When she learned of his marriage to Jean, Clarinda was understandably furious, but after some tempestuous interruptions, she resumed her relations with him, and wrote in her diary, December 6, 1831, "This day I can never forget. Parted with Burns in the year 1791, never more to meet in this world. Oh, may we meet in Heaven!" The occasion of their parting was a meeting in Edinburgh before she left for Jamaica in the hope of reconciliation with her husband. But on discovery that he had a native mistress and at least one mulatto child, she returned by the same boat.

If a lyric may be taken as evidence, this final parting from Burns was warm and tender.

> O May, thy morn was ne'er sae sweet
>   As the mirk night o' December!
> For sparkling was the rosy wine,
>   And private was the chamber,
> And dear was she I dare na name,
>   But I will ay remember.

Even in good plain prose, however, Burns wrote his Nancy, no longer Clarinda, some letters after their parting which can only mean that they had returned to their old intimacy. On December 11, 1791, she is "my dearest Nancy," and a little later, "a creature very extraordinary," a lock of whose hair he is having put in a ring. On December 27, she is his "ever dearest Nancy," and he sends her the only good lines she ever inspired,

> Had we never lov'd sae kindly,
> Had we never lov'd sae blindly,
> Never met — or never parted —
> We had ne'er been broken hearted.

When Burns was finally able to leave Edinburgh on February 18, 1788, at the very height of his affair with Clarinda, he went to Glasgow "crazed with thought and anxiety," and had a happy meeting with his old Irvine friend Richard Brown, now a sea captain, and then on to Mauchline via Paisley and Kilmarnock, with a two day visit at Dunlop House. He complained of having to fight his "way severely through the savage hospitality of this country," where the object of all hosts was "to send every guest drunk to bed if they can." His letters to Clarinda became less frequent. One of February 23 from Mossgiel which reveals his impressions of Jean, and pays compliments to Clarinda, she showed

James Grierson in 1830! "I, this morning as I came home, called
for a certain woman. — I am disgusted with her; I cannot endure
her! I, while my heart smote me for the prophanity, tried to compare her with my Clarinda: 'twas setting the expiring glimmer of
a farthing taper beside the cloudless glory of the meridian sun. —
Here was tasteless insipidity, vulgarity of soul, and mercenary
fawning; there, polished good sense, heaven-born genius, and the
most generous, the most delicate, the most tender Passion. — I
have done with her, and she with me." His report of the meeting
to Ainslie, written in late February or early March reveals other
and more compelling sentiments about Jean,* of whom Burns
wrote to Brown March 7, "I found Jean — with her cargo very
well laid in; but unfortunately moor'd, almost at the mercy of
wind and tide: I have towed her into convenient harbour where
she may lie snug till she unload;† and have taken command myself — not ostensibly, but for a time in secret. — I am gratified by
your kind enquiries after her; as after all, I may say with
Othello —

> 'Excellent wretch!
> 'Perdition catch my soul but I do love thee!' "

That neither of his heroines bore too heavily on Burns' mind
is suggested by a letter he wrote to Clarinda (addressing her as
"My dear Madam") five days after leaving Edinburgh, and before
he had seen Jean. Of his visit to Paisley, he says,

My worthy, wise friend, Mr. Pattison, did not allow me a moment's
respite. — I was there ten hours; during which time I was introduced
to nine men worth six thousands; five men worth ten thousand; his
brother, richly worth twenty thousands; and a young Weaver who will
have thirty thousands good when his father, who has no more children

---

* Quoted in Profile, pp. 7–8.
† Four days before the date of this letter to Brown, on March 3, Jean had already
born a second set of twins; one of them died March 10, and the other March 22.

than the said Weaver and a Whig-kirk,* dies. — Mr P—— was bred a zealous Anti-burgher; but, during his widowerhood, he has found their strictness incompatible with certain compromises he is often obliged to make with those Powers of darkness, the devil, the world and the flesh; so he, good, merciful man! talked privately to me, of the absurdity of eternal torments, the liberality of sentiment in indulging the honest instincts of Nature, the mysteries of Concubinage, &c. He has a son, however, that at sixteen has repeatedly minted at certain priviledges, — only proper for sober, staid men, who can use the *good things* of this life without *abusing* them; but the father's parental vigilance has hitherto hedged him in, amid a corrupt and evil world. His only daughter, who, "if the beast be to the fore, and the branks [bridle] bide hale," will have seven thousand pound, when her old father steps into the dark Factory-Office of Eternity with his well-thrumm'd web of life; has put him again and again in a commendable fit of indignation by requesting a harpsichord — "O, these damn'd boarding-schools!" exclaims my prudent friend; "she was a good spinner and sower, till I was advised by her foes and mine to give her a year of Edinr!"

After two bottles more, my much-respected friend opened up to me a project, a legitimate child of Wisdom and Goodsense: 'twas no less than a long-thought-on and deeply-matur'd design to marry a girl, fully as elegant in her form as the famous Priestess whom Saul consulted in his last hours; and who had been 2d maid of honor to his deceased wife. — This, you may be sure, I highly applauded; so I hope for a pair of gloves by and by.

During the month after he left Edinburgh, Burns was much torn. There was Jean, whom he decided to marry; there was Clarinda, still delicious, with whom he must break off; there was Mr. Miller's farm to be decided about; there was his Excise commission to be negotiated; and there was William Creech. Having installed Jean in a room provided by Dr. M'kenzie, with her mother to care for her, he hurried off once more to survey the farm with his friend John Tennant of Glenconner. " 'Tis merely out of Compliment to Mr Miller," he writes Clarinda, "for I know the

* A reference to expectations from his estate of the Whig (Cameronian) Kirk.

Excise must be my lot." Before leaving Edinburgh he had written Margaret Chalmers, "I have altered all my plans of future life. A farm that I could live in, I could not find; and, indeed, after the necessary support my brother and the rest of the family required, I could not venture on farming in that style suitable to my feelings. You will condemn me for the next step I have taken: I have entered into the Excise. I stay in the West about three weeks, and then return to Edinburgh for six weeks' instructions; afterwards, for I get employ instantly, I go où il plait à Dieu — et mon Roi."

But Tennant "staggered" Burns with a favorable judgment of Ellisland farm, and he decided to rent it, keeping his Excise commission in case the farm proved a bad bargain, as he still feared it might. Tennant's judgment of the land and the lease was probably sound enough, but Burns had no stomach for the long period of development which Ellisland needed, nor the capital for it, particularly in the style suitable to his feelings. By October, 1791, he was writing to Peter Hill, Creech's old clerk, now in business for himself, that prospects for an Excise supervisorship (what he had had his eye on all the time) were good, but that he had not been so fortunate in his farming. "Mr. Miller's kindness has been just such another as Creech's was but this for your private ear."

On Monday, March 10, Burns left for Edinburgh, via Glasgow, collecting some money owed him en route; on March 13 he agreed on terms of a lease with Mr. Miller (the lease being signed March 18), and by March 17 he wrote Clarinda, "My Excise affair is just concluded." By the twentieth, after another session of "racking shop accounts with Mr Creech," he is back in Glasgow on his way to Ayrshire. During the week he had spent in Edinburgh, he told Clarinda nothing of Jean, continued fervent meetings with her (calling her his "dearest angel," and saying he loves her, has loved her, and will love her to death, through death, and forever), and gave her a pair of drinking glasses as a parting gift. It is small wonder that he writes to Richard Brown apologizing for having neglected a commission because "watching, fatigue, and a load

of Care almost too heavy for [his] shoulders, have in some degree
actually fever'd" him; by some of his experiences, probably those
with Creech, he "was convulsed with rage."

When Clarinda heard he was married — how is not known,
probably through Ainslie — she eventually wrote Sylvander ac-
cusing him of "perfidious treachery" and calling him a "villain."
He replied March 9, 1789,* that he had saved her from herself.

The letter you wrote me to Heron's carried its own answer in its
bosom: you forbade me to write you, unless I was willing to plead
guilty to a certain Indictment that you were pleased to bring against
me. — As I am convinced of my own innocence, and though conscious
of high imprudence & egregious folly, can lay my hand on my breast
and attest the rectitude of my heart; you will pardon me, Madam, if
I do not carry my complaisance so far as humbly to acquiesce in the
name of, Villain, merely out of compliment even to YOUR opinion;
much as I esteem your judgment, and warmly as I regard your worth.
— I have already told you, and I again aver it, that at the Period of
time alluded to, I was not under the smallest moral tie to Mrs B——;
nor did I, nor could I then know, all the powerful circumstances that
omnipotent Necessity was busy laying in wait for me. — When you
call over the scenes that have passed between us, you will survey the
conduct of an honest man, struggling successfully with temptations the
most powerful that ever beset humanity, and preserving untainted

* A letter written in August, 1788, has not survived, but Burns describes the
occasion of it to Ainslie, August 23. "I don't know if ever I told you some
very bad reports that Mrs Mc[Leho]se once told me of Mr Nicol. I had mentioned the affair to Mr Cruickshank, in the course of conversation about our
common friend, that a lady had said so & so, which I suspected had originated
from some malevolence of Dr Adams. — He had mentioned this story to Mr
Nicol cursorily, & there it rested; till now, a prosecution has commenced between
Dr A—— & Mr N——, & Mr N—— has press'd me over & over to give up the
lady's name. — I have refused this; & last post Mr N—— acquaints me, but in
very good natured terms, that if I persist in my refusal, I am to be served with
a summonds to compear & declare the fact. —

"Heaven knows how I should proceed! I have this moment wrote Mrs
Mc——se, telling her that I have informed you of the affair; & I shall write
Mr Nicol by Tuesday's post that I will not give up my female friend till
further consideration; but that I have acquainted you with the business & the
name; & that I have desired you to wait on him, which I intreat, my dear Sir,
you will do; & give up the name or not, as You & Mrs Mc——se's prudence shall
suggest." (F I, #266, 250.)

honor in situations where the austerest Virtue would have forgiven a
fall — Situations that I will dare to say, not a single individual of all
his kind, even with half his sensibility and passion, could have encountered without ruin; and I leave you to guess, Madam, how such a
man is likely to digest an accusation of perfidious treachery!

Was I to blame, Madam, in being the distracted victim of Charms
which, I affirm it, no man ever approached with impunity? — Had I
seen the least glimmering of hope that these Charms could ever have
been mine — or even had not iron Necessity — but these are un-
availing words. —

I would have called on you when I was in town,* indeed I could
not have resisted it, but that Mr Ainslie told me that you were determined to avoid your windows while I was in town, lest even a
glance of me should occur in the street. —

When I have regained your good opinion, perhaps I may venture
to solicit your friendship, but be that as it may, the first of her Sex I
ever knew shall always be the object of my warmest good wishes.

In February, 1790, there was an acidulous exchange of letters,
in one of which Burns sent Mrs. M'Lehose a song, *My Lovely
Nancy*. And in October, 1790, Robert Ainslie visited Burns at
Ellisland and sent a report of him to the still angry lady, with
whom Ainslie is obviously on excellent terms.

Dumfries 18th Octr. 1790

I promised to write my Dear Friend and for that End now Seat myself at Dumfries — I have been with Burns since Friday — and as
his duty as Exciseman engaged him this day, I have taken the Opportunity of coming here to Visit this Town — You desired that I
should let you hear every thing regarding him & his family and how I
was pleased — This is a difficult question as my short room here will
not permitt me to be so full as I might — and part of the question
admitts of Double Answers — I was pleased with Burns' hearty welcome of me — and it was an addition to his pleasure, that my Arrival
was upon his *Kirn* night [harvest supper], when he Expected some of

* In February, 1789, he had visited Edinburgh to settle with Creech, and for
another reason which will appear below.

his friends to help make merry, but much displeased with the Company when they arrived — They consisted of a Vulgar looking Tavern keeper from Dumfries; and his Wife more Vulgar — Mr. Miller of Dalswinton's Gardener and his Wife — and said Wife's Sister — and a little fellow from Dumfries, who had been a Clerk — These were the strangers, and the rest of the Company who are inmates of the house were Burns' Sister, and Mrs. Burns' Sister, who are Two common looking Girls who act as their Servants — and 3 Male and female cousins who had been Shearing for him — We spent the evening in the common way on Such occasions of Dancing, and Kissing the Lasses at the end of every dance — With regard to the helpmate She seems Vulgar & Common-place in a considerable degree — and pretty round & fat — She is however a kind Body in her Own way, and the husband Tolerably Attentive to her — As to the house, it is ill-contrived — and pretty Dirty, and *Hugry Mugry* — Tho last, not least Our Friend himself is as ingenious as ever, and Seem'd very happy with the Situation I have described — His Mind however now appears to me to be a great Mixture of the poet and the Excise Man — One day he Sitts down and Writes a Beautiful poem — and the Next he Seizes a cargo of Tobacco from some unfortunate Smuggler — or Roups out some poor Wretch for Selling liquors without a License From his conversation he Seems to be frequently among the Great — but No Attention is paid by people of any rank to his wife — Having found that his farm does not answer he is about to Give it up, and depend wholly on the Excise —

Now, having given you such a description of those you wished to hear of, As to myself, that Cursed melancholy, which I was complaining of, has been daily increasing — and All Burns' Jokes cannot dispell it — I sit silent & frail even amidst Mirth — and instead of that joyous Laugh which I used to have I frequently discover the Tear start into my Eyes, and Sigh most piteously — I know of no Sufficient reason for Such Misery, but the Effect of constitution, and am Sorry now to be Obliged to go among absolute Strangers — Nothing under the Sun would be so agreable as Seing you, and a letter from you would be the next Best — If you write to me, address to me to be left till called for at the post office of *Ayr*, where I shall be in a few days — and for fear of Accidents in that country, you may use the letter A or any such if you speak of Burns.

Burns & I drunk your health on Saturday at an inn & to Settle the

matter Got both Exceedingly drunk — you need say nothing of this
letter to any Body

yours most affectionately
R. AINSLIE

Mrs. M'Lehose
Lamont's Land
Canongate
Edinr.

Despite its underhandedness and patronizing tone, this letter
is certainly the best service Ainslie ever did Burns' memory. It
gives a unique and happy picture of peasant farmer Burns enjoying a party at home. The appreciative critic should never forget
that Burns was, in Henley's phrase, "essentially and unalterably
a peasant," and it is as a reminder of this cardinal fact that Ainslie's letter is of notable importance.

There are two recorded letters from Burns to Ainslie after this
date, both friendly, and a final comment on him in the last letter
from Burns to Clarinda in 1794.

My old Friend, Ainslie, has indeed been kind to you. — Tell him, that
I envy him the power of serving you. — I had a letter from him a
while ago, but it was so dry, so distant, so like a card to one of his
clients, that I could scarce bear to read it, & have not yet answered
it. — He is a good, honest fellow; and *can* write a friendly letter,
which would do equal honor to his head & his heart, as a whole sheaf
of his letters I have by me will witness; & though Fame does not blow
her trumpet at my approach *now* as she did *then,* when he first
honored me with his friendship, yet I am as proud as ever; & when I
am laid in my grave, I wish to be stretched at my full length, that I
may occupy every inch of ground I have a right to.

Mrs. M'Lehose continued to write, with some bitterness, but
she sent Burns one of her poems early in 1791. He replied wist-
fully, sending her *Sweet Sensibility how charming.* Then in November, 1791, she made a discovery which must have wrenched
her. During the delirious winter of 1788, upon leaving her, Burns

had often sought out a serving girl, one Jenny Clow, who had born him a son the following November, and whose suit for support he had answered during his visit to Edinburgh of February, 1789, when Clarinda said she would not even go near her windows for fear of seeing him. Now ill, destitute, and probably dying, this girl had found out Mrs. M'Lehose, and through her, sent an appeal to Burns for assistance. After describing Jenny's plight, Mrs. M'Lehose adds nastily, "You have now an opportunity to evince you indeed possess those fine feelings you have delineated, so as to claim the just admiration of your country. I am convinced I need add nothing farther to persuade you to act as every consideration of humanity as well as gratitude must dictate. I am, sir, your sincere well-wisher."

Burns replied November 23, with some clumsy irony, in the third person. The significant paragraph reads,

Mrs. M—— tells me a tale of the poor girl's distress that makes my very heart weep blood. I will trust that your goodness will apologize to your delicacy for me, when I beg of you, for heaven's sake, to send a porter to the poor woman — Mrs. M., it seems, knows where she is to be found — with five shillings in my name; and, as I shall be in Edinburgh on Tuesday first, for certain, make the poor wench leave a line for me, before Tuesday, at Mr. Mackay's White Hart Inn, Grassmarket, where I shall put up; and before I am two hours in town, I shall see the poor girl, and try what is to be done for her relief. I would have taken my boy from her long ago, but she would never consent.

I shall do myself the very great pleasure to call for you when I come to town, and repay you the sum your goodness shall have advanced.

There is no further information about Jenny Clow and her son.

During this visit to Edinburgh, there was a reconciliation between Burns and his "dearest Nancy," and their final meeting, when he must have learned of her intention to rejoin her husband. She sailed in February, 1792, arrived in Jamaica in April, and was back in Edinburgh by August, her health temporarily impaired. He wrote her the next spring inquiring about her health, and sending her a book;* and again in 1794 reporting that when he was asked to propose a toast, he always offered "Mrs. Mac." He is writing with a bottle by him on the table, and he has recently quarreled with Maria Riddell. Mrs. M'Lehose is still "ever dearest," and his "lovely Clarinda." The letter includes his unhappy Monody and Epigram provoked by the quarrel with Mrs. Riddell, and asks Clarinda's opinion of them.

The record does not close even here. After Burns' death, Agnes M'Lehose wanted her letters back, and on September 19, 1796, Alexander Cunningham (1763?–1812) in Edinburgh wrote John Syme in Dumfries, "I have today had another call from a Mr Ainslie W.S. *whom I suspect does* Mrs McLehose's business demanding her Letters — he wished very much to introduce me to her which I declined for two reasons — I never accept of an invitation from any Man without intending to make the retort courteous & his manners and behavior† seem quite opposite to what I would wish to meet with even in a common acquaintance besides involving me in an introduction to a Woman who for aught I know may be as chaste as Diana but who bears a quisquis‡ character in the World & which might lead to many perplexities."

Cunningham wanted permission to publish the Clarinda correspondence in the edition he and Syme were promoting to raise money for Burns' family, but Mrs. M'Lehose refused. In a further effort to secure permission, Syme asked Maria Riddell to see what she could do, and the two ladies exchanged enthusiastic letters about their "archangel," as Mrs. Riddell called him. Later,

* Burns' note to his transcript of this letter in the Glenriddell MS calls it "fustian rant of enthusiastic youth," a fair enough description but purposefully deceptive dating.
† Ainslie became for many years an elder of the Old Kirk, St. Giles, and wrote *A Father's Gift to his Children* and *Reasons for the Hope that is in us.* (*The Land of Burns*, I, 89.)
‡ In *James Currie The Entire Stranger and Robert Burns*, p. 334, Professor Robert D. Thornton prints the following footnote: "In the N.L.S., MS. 587 (1181), an undated letter from Ainslie to Mrs. M'Lehose, Ainslie speaks of the 'end of the week which you have appointed as the Termination of my Banishment.' "

she regretted her exuberance, and did not wish it known that she had corresponded with Clarinda. She writes to Dr. Currie, May 6, 1800, "I hope you have kept my correspondence with Clarinda *entre nous*. I have had the ingenuity to get back my letters, alleging their utility for furnishing information to Burns's biographer, and I have heard some circumstances of our Bard's heroine that have rather diminished my Sentimental ardour! And I was a little afraid for the future sake of those rare epistles of mine, which might, all things considered, have placed me in an awkward predicament."

Mrs. M'Lehose continued as a bright and active member of her social circle for forty years, and was described at seventy as "a well looked little woman" by James Grierson. She survived her children, all of her grandchildren except one, and most of her friends. Her grandson, W. C. M'Lehose, writes of her, "When later years thinned the ranks of her friends, and diminished the number of her invitations, it was with great difficulty she became reconciled to a more retired mode of life." In her last years her mind remained clear and alert, but she lost her memory. She died October 22, 1841, aged 82.

Although Burns had acknowledged Jean as his wife* by living with her publicly, she and he went through a ceremony of marriage in Gavin Hamilton's office, a few doors from their room, before a Justice of the Peace. And on August 5, "they both acknowledged their irregular marriage" before the Kirk Session, expressed sorrow, were rebuked, and absolved of any scandal, Burns giving a guinea for the poor on the occasion.

In June 1788 he wrote Ainslie, "Were it not for the terrors of my ticklish situation respecting provision for a family of children, I am decidedly of opinion that the step I have taken is vastly for my happiness. As it is, I look to the Excise scheme as certainty of

---

* James Grierson, in 1829, reports Clarinda as follows: "Burns in marrying Jean Armour behaved better than Jean could have expected — but B said in the situation she was and hurried out of doors by her father what could he do." (Fitzhugh, 41.) Compare Burns' letter to Clarinda of March 9, 1789, pp. 182–83.

maintenance; a maintenance, luxury, to what either Mrs. Burns or I was born to." And on September 9, he opens his mind to his old friend and fellow-student of French, the engraver John Beugo, "You do not tell me if you are going to be married. — Depend upon it, if you do not make some damned foolish choice, it will be a very great improvement on the Dish of Life. — I can speak from Experience, tho' God knows, my choice was as random as Blind-man's-buff. I like the idea of an honest country Rake of my acquaintance, who, like myself, married lately. — Speaking to me of his late step, 'L——d, man,' says he, 'a body's baith cheaper and better sair't [served]!'"

He comments in a different tone to Mrs. Dunlop. "The most placid good-nature — & sweetness of disposition; a warm heart, gratefully devoted with all its powers to love [*me* deleted] one; vigorous health & sprightly chearfulness, set off to the best advantage by a more than common handsome figure; these, I think, in a woman, may make a tolerable good wife, though she should never have read a page but the Scriptures of the Old & New Testament, nor have danced in a brighter Assembly than a Penny-pay Wedding."

After getting his appointment to the Excise and leasing his farm* and marrying Jean, Burns set vigorously and sensibly about doing what was to be done. Mr. Miller had made him an allowance for improvements, and he contracted with a Dumfries builder for a farmhouse at Ellisland. To qualify for duty as an Exciseman, he took instructions† from James Findlay, Excise officer at Tarbolton, in April and May. He busied himself securing furniture and stocking his farm. Memory of the Edinburgh excitement brought nostalgia at times, but he had foreseen that his vogue would be brief. He wrote to the "Colonel" of the Crochallans, William Dunbar, "I have dropt all conversation and all read-

---

* For 76 years, the first three at £50, the rest at £70.
† Burns' commission was dated July 14, 1788, but he did not go on duty then. (Snyder, 314–315.)

ing (prose reading) but what tends in some way or other to my serious aim," but he expresses pleasure at Dunbar's offer of correspondence.

The great days were over, and if things were now not just as he would have liked them to be, he recognized that his poetry and his fame were owing to the same causes as his discouragement and frustration — that is, to his temperament and his lot in life. In his work, as in his life, Burns is a vivid symbol of the desperation most men feel. If for him the desperation was not so quiet at times, and if he sought relief, be it noted that he lived his life forthrightly. After his death, William Nicol made a wry and pointed comment about Burns' "firmness." "The Fanatics have now got it into their heads, that dreadful bursts of penetential sorrow issued from the heart of our friend, before he expired. But if I am not much mistaken in relation to his firmness, he would disdain to have his dying moments disturbed with the sacerdotal gloom & the sacerdotal howl. He knew that he would negotiate wt. God alone, concerning his immortal interests." And Burns' friend, James Gray, echoes Maria Riddell. "Though he was often well nigh broken-hearted by the severity of his fate yet he was never heard to complain."

V

MARRIED MAN

To make a happy fireside clime
To weans and wife,
That's the true pathos and sublime
Of human life.

BURNS, *Epistle to Dr. Blacklock*
Ellisland, 21st Oct., 1789

The dramatic climax of Burns' life was the 1786–1788 period of his Kilmarnock volume and his Edinburgh residence. But the subsequent eight years offer rich biographical materials for an understanding of the private man — of his daily life, his friendships, his social and political views, his livelihood, his household, the wide range of his interests, the quality of his mind and spirit. And they reveal the irony that he lived these years under the burden of an unrecognized but debilitating and fatal illness.

Summary judgments and dramatic foreshortenings can only distort seriously, as they have done in the past, the complex truth of Robert Burns during these years. Hence the Boswellian narrative which follows.

Burns' major interest during this period was Scots song. Section VI offers a full and detailed account of his achievement, in both music and lyrics, as a song collector and song writer.

1. Aftermath

In January, 1788, while recovering from his knee injury and thinking of his prospects, Burns wrote Mrs. Dunlop, "Lately I was a sixpenny private, and, God knows, a miserable soldier enough; now I march to the campaign, a starving cadet: a little more conspicuously wretched.

"I am ashamed of all this; for though I do want bravery for the warfare of life, I could wish, like some other soldiers, to have as much fortitude or cunning as to dissemble or conceal my cowardice."

He never achieved the relatively comfortable refuge from life's "warfare" which he yearned for, and, being the man he was, he probably could not have, but during the next few years, Burns made a successful marriage, he secured a steady income, and he improved materially on his previous standard of living. With canny vigilance he continued to pursue advancement in the Excise service by recommending himself to his superiors and by soliciting favor from influential friends. His prospects for promotion to a well-paid position were good when he died. Ever mindful of his responsibilities to Jean and his children, Burns lived his last seven years as a low-grade civil servant who looked forward to an upper-grade sinecure in time. His occupation in these years was not congenial to him, but better than tenant farming, and no other choices presented themselves except an offer of work on the London *Morning Chronicle* in 1794, a position which he felt was too insecure to risk.

Burns continued to write poetry after 1786, but produced only a handful of important poems, including his most important one of all, *Tam o' Shanter*. His great interest and satisfaction lay in providing songs for two editors, James Johnson and George Thomson. Johnson, barely literate, simply and gratefully took what Burns sent him for the *Scots Musical Museum,* and between them they produced a collection which Burns correctly predicted would "defy the teeth of time."

Thomson and his book, a *Select Collection of Original Scotish Airs,* were different. He had no taste for folk song, and planned an elegant work for a polite audience, preferring English words and insisting on drawing room decorum. He was forever suggesting improvements to Burns, one of which resulted in an egregious and now forgotten version of *Scots Wha Hae*. Burns complied with Thomson's requests amiably when he could, but often refused just as amiably. "I have long ago made up my mind as to my own reputation in the Business of Authorship," he wrote Thomson, "& have nothing to be pleased, or offended at, in your adoption or rejection of my verses." By refusing all payment, Burns retained complete independence, saying that his songs might be considered "either *above*, or *below* price," and that "to talk of money, wages, fee, hire &c. would be downright Sodomy of Soul!"

The most generous term for Thomson's treatment of Burns is paltry. Once his contributor was dead, Thomson felt free to alter texts at will, as, indeed, he did harmonies which he commissioned from Beethoven. He ignored Burns' wishes and instructions, he made an unsubstantiated claim to exclusive copyright in the songs Burns had sent him, and he inked out passages in Burns' letters to him which he found unpleasant and which posterity finds revealing about his chicanery. Different rates of fading helped DeLancey Ferguson to discover this device in 1928, after Thomson had enjoyed a century and a quarter's reputation for generosity in making the correspondence available.

But Thomson left one surprising docket. When, a week before his death, Burns was being severely dunned by a tailor for the cost of his Volunteer's uniform, he turned to Thomson, among others, for help. "After all my boasted independence," he wrote, "curst necessity compels me to implore you for five pounds. — A cruel scoundrel of a Haberdasher to whom I owe an account, taking it into his head that I am dying, has commenced a process, & will infallibly put me into jail. — Do, for God's sake, send me that sum, & that by return of post. — Forgive me this earnestness, but the horrors of a jail have made me half distracted. — I do not ask all this gratuitously; for upon returning health, I hereby promise & engage to furnish you with five pounds' worth of the neatest song-genius you have seen. O I tryed my hand on Rothiemurche this morning. — The measure is so difficult, that it is impossible to infuse much genius into the lines — They are on the other side. Forgive me!"

Thomson sent the five pounds, but noted on Burns' letter, "This idea is exaggerated — he could not have been in any such danger at Dumfries nor could he be in such necessity to implore aid from *Edinr.*"

"On the other side" was

> Fairest maid on Devon banks,
>   Crystal Devon, winding Devon,
> Wilt thou lay that frown aside,
>   And smile as thou wert wont to do?
>
> Full well thou know'st I love thee dear —
> Couldst thou to malice lend an ear!
> O, did not Love exclaim: — "Forbear,
>   Nor use a faithful lover so!"
>
> Then come, thou fairest of the fair,
> Those wonted smiles, O, let me share,
> And by thy beauteous self I swear
>   No love but thine my heart shall know!

This song, reminiscent of Peggy Chalmers and days at Harvieston in the Devon valley, was his last.

Thomson capped his relations with the man who had been so generous to him by writing an ill-informed and patronizing obituary which did Burns' memory severe and lasting and gratuitous injury. But happily Burns knew nothing of that. James Johnson, a very poor man, subscribed four pounds for the relief of Burns' widow. George Thomson, two guineas.

That he should write fifty-six letters in four years to a man like Thomson illustrates one important reason why Maria Riddell should speak of Burns' habitual disappointment, and why James Gray should describe him as "broken-hearted by the severity of his fate." Where could he find, not companions, but companionship? Who shared his interest in a country where "they have as much idea of a Rhinoceros as of a Poet"? Thomson did not share Burns' tastes, and he may have been a nuisance at times, but at least he was someone Burns could write to about his central interest (the two men never met, although Thomson may have seen Burns in Edinburgh), and in whom he could find some relief from his loneliness.

This loneliness was exasperated by a temperament which made it impossible for Burns to seek and to slip into a complacent and comfortable acceptance by his superiors in station, with whom his prominence thrust him into frequent association. As he wrote to David McCulloch in 1794, "I am indeed ill at ease whenever I approach your Honorables & Right Honorables." And the more prominent he became, and the more his family depended on him, the less he could relieve his mind. As he said of himself, "Mine is the madness of an enraged Scorpion shut up in a thumb-phial." To understand Burns in his later years, one must recognize the pressure of these tensions, and the fact that his Edinburgh experience had heightened them. The letters provide ample illustration.

In one to Deborah Duff Davies, he wrote, "I remember, & 'tis almost the earliest thing I do remember, when I was quite a boy, one day at church, being enraged at seeing a young creature, one of the maids of his house, rise from the mouth of the pew to give way to a bloated son of Wealth and Dullness, who waddled surlily past her. — Indeed the girl was very pretty; and he was an ugly, stupid, purse-proud, money-loving, old monster, as you can imagine." This early resentment of snobs and snobbery, and of class distinction and social arrogance, especially that deriving from money, sharpened as Burns grew older, when his "extreme impetuosity" and his "skinless sensibility" produced notable explosions, usually private, but sometimes public. A relatively mild outburst is his ironic paragraph to Mrs. Dunlop, May 27, 1788, at the end of his Edinburgh experiences.

There are few circumstances relating to the unequal distribution of the good things of this life that give me more vexation (I mean in what I see around me) than the Importance that the Great bestow on their trifles and small matters in family affairs, compared with the same, the very same things on the contracted Scale of a Cottage. — Last afternoon I had the honor to spend an hour or two at a good woman's fireside, where the homely planks that composed the floor were decorated with a splendid Carpet, and the gay table sparkled with Silver & China. — 'Tis now about term-day, and there has been a revolution among those creatures who, tho' in appearance, Partakers & equally noble Partakers, of the same Nature with Madame; yet are from time to time, their nerves, their sinews, their health, strength, wisdom, experience, genius, time, nay a good part of their very thoughts, sold for months & years, anxious Drudges, sweating, weary slaves, not only to the necessities, the conveniences, but the Caprices of the Important Few. — We talked of the insignificant Creatures; nay, notwithstanding their general stupidity & Rascality, did some of the poor devils the honor to commend them — But, light be the turf upon his breast who taught — "Reverence Thyself!" we looked down on the unpolished Wretches, their impertinent wives and clouterly brats, as the lordly Bull does on the little, dirty Ant-hill, whose puny inhabitants he crushes in the carelessness of his ramble, or tosses in the air in the wantonness of his pride.

A variation on the theme comes in a letter to Peter Hill, January 17, 1791. Speaking of Poverty, Burns says,

Owing to thee, the Man of unfortunate dispositions & neglected education, is condemned as a fool for his dissipation; despised & shunned as a needy wretch, when his follies as usual have brought him to want; & when his unprincipled necessities drive him to dishonest practices, he is abhorred as a miscreant, & perishes by the justice of his country. — But far otherwise is the lot of the Man of Family & Fortune. — His early extravagance & folly, are fire & spirit; his consequent wants, are the embarrasments of an Honest Fellow; & when, to remedy the matter, he sets out with a legal commission to plunder distant provinces & massacre peaceful nations, he returns laden with the spoils of rapine & murder, lives wicked & respected, & dies a Villain &

a Lord. — Nay, worst of all — Alas for hapless Woman! the needy creature who was shivering at the corner of the street, waiting to earn the wages of casual prostitution, is ridden down by the chariot wheels of the Coroneted Rep, hurrying on to the adulterous assignation; she, who without the same necessities to plead, riots nightly in the same guilty trade!!!

Biographers who lament that Burns left Athole House when on his Highland Tour, a day or so before the great Henry Dundas was to arrive (and presumably be so delighted with Burns that he would "do something for him") ignore the attitude of the Dundas family to Burns which he reveals in a letter to Alexander Cunningham of March 11, 1791.

I have two or three times in my life composed from the wish, rather than from the impulse, but I never succeeded to any purpose. — One of these times I shall ever remember with gnashing of teeth. — 'Twas on the death of the late Lord President Dundas [of the Court of Session]. — My very worthy & most respected friend, Mr Alexr Wood, Surgeon, urged me to pay a compliment in the way of my trade to his Lordship's memory. — Well, to work I went, & produced a copy of Elegiac verses some of them I own rather commonplace, & others rather hidebound, but on the whole though they were far from being in my best manner, they were tolerable; & had they been the production of a Lord or a Baronet, they would have been thought very clever. — I wrote a letter, which however was in my very best manner, & inclosing my Poem, Mr Wood carried altogether to Mr Solicitor Dundas [the Lord President's son, Robert, Jr.] that then was, & not finding him at home, left the parcel for him. — His Solicitorship never took the smallest notice of the Letter, the Poem, or the Poet. — From that time, highly as I respect the talents of the Family, I never see the name, Dundas, in the column of a newspaper, but my heart seems straitened for room in my bosom; & if I am obliged to read aloud a paragraph relating to one of them, I feel my forehead flush, & my nether lip quivers. — Had I been an obscure Scribbler, as I was then in the hey-day of my fame; or had I been a dependant Hanger-on for favor or pay; or had the bearer of the letter been any other than a gentleman who has done honor to the city in which he lives, to the

Country that produced him, & to the God that created him, Mr Solicitor might have had some apology.*

A much more violent, and public, eruption resulted when the funeral procession of a Mrs. Oswald (d. December 6, 1788) displaced Burns from a comfortable inn on a wintry night. Unhappily, such exhibitions of spleen became increasingly characteristic. In a letter to Dr. Moore, to whom he sent his *Ode Sacred to the Memory of Mrs. Oswald of Auchencruive,* he describes the event, and his outrage that even the corpse of one who was rich could affront the lowly.

The inclosed Ode is a compliment to the memory of the late Mrs Oswald of Auchencruive. — You, probably, knew her personally, an honor of which I cannot boast; but I spent my early years in her neighbourhood, and among her servants and tenants I know that she was detested with the most heartfelt cordiality. — However, in the particular part of her conduct, which roused my Poetic wrath, she was much less blameable. — In January last, on my road to Ayrshire, I had put up at Bailie Whigham's in Sanquhar, the only tolerable inn in the place. — The frost was keen, and the grim evening and howling wind were ushering in a night of snow and drift. — My horse & I were both much fatigued with the labors of the day, and just as my friend the Bailie and I, were bidding defiance to the storm over a smoking bowl, in wheels the funeral pageantry of the late, great Mrs Oswald, and poor I am forced to brave all the horrors of the tempestuous night, and jade my horse, my young favorite horse whom I had just christened Pegasus, twelve miles farther on, through the wildest moors & hills of Ayrshire, to New Cumnock, the next Inn. — The powers of Poesy & Prose sink under me, when I would describe what I felt. — Suffice it to say, that when a good fire at New Cumnock had so far recovered my frozen sinews, I sat down and wrote the inclosed Ode.

The opening lines of the Ode, and the strophe are sufficient to give a sense of its bitter tone and poverty of style.

* Burns' fellow-Crochallan, and Mr. Solicitor Dundas' fellow-lawyer, Charles Hay, also urged Burns to write the poem. Lord President Dundas died December 13, 1787. (F I, #164, 147.)

Dweller in yon dungeon dark,
Hangman of creation, mark!
Who in widow-weeds appears,
Laden with unhonoured years,
Noosing with care a bursting purse,
Baited with many a deadly curse?

STROPHE

View the wither'd beldam's face:
Can thy keen inspection trace
Aught of Humanity's sweet, melting grace?
Note that eye, 'tis rheum o'erflows —
Pity's flood there never rose.
See those hands ne'er stretch'd to save,
Hands that took, but never gave.
Keeper of Mammon's iron chest,
Lo, there she goes, unpitied and unblest,
She goes, but not to realms of everlasting rest!

Burns liked this poem. He sent a copy of it to Mrs. Dunlop soon after he wrote it, and it appeared in Stuart's *Star*, London, on May 7, 1789, over an easily penetrated pseudonym. Burns also included it in his 1793 edition.

In a practical burst of resentment against privilege, Burns vigorously defended one of the "children of Dependence" against aristocratic persecution when James Clarke, schoolmaster at Moffat, was accused of undue severity by school officials with support from the Earl of Hopeton. Burns rallied his friends to Clarke's cause, wrote petitions for him to present, lent him money, and eventually won the day. Triumphantly he wrote in the Glenriddell letterbook, after a copy of one of the petitions, "Bravo! Clarke. — In spite of Hopeton & his myrmidons thou camest off victorious!"

It is often wondered at that Burns was both a Jacobite and a Jacobin, a supporter of the divine-right-of-kings Stuarts and of the French Revolution democrats, but the reason is simple enough. He wrote in Glenriddell's interleaved *Scots Musical Museum,* "Except when my passions were heated by some accidental cause, my Jacobitism was merely by way of, *Vive la bagatelle.*" When his passions were heated, he could write to Mrs. Dunlop, "Nothing can reconcile me to the common terms 'English ambassador, English court,' &c. And I am out of all patience to see that equivocal character, Hastings, impeached by 'the Commons of England.'" Essentially, the Stuart cause touched his Scots patriotism; moreover, Queen Mary was an attractive woman, and the "Scotish Muses were all Jacobites." "And, surely," he continued, "the gallant though unfortunate house of Stewart, the kings of our fathers for so many heroic ages, is a theme much more interesting than an obscure beef-witted insolent race of foreigners whom a conjuncture of circumstances kickt up into power and consequence." This comment on the Hanoverians was, at least, written in the privacy of Robert Riddell's library, unlike the indiscreet lines on the window at Stirling.

That Burns was not merely bilious in such pointed and apt comments on the Hanoverians is suggested by the historical sense revealed in a thoughtful and well-informed letter to the Editor of the *Edinburgh Evening Courant,* inspired by an anti-Stuart sermon:

I went last Wednesday to my parish church, most cordially to join in grateful acknowledgments to the Author of all Good, for the consequent blessings of the Glorious Revolution. To that auspicious event we owe no less than our liberties religious and civil — to it we are likewise indebted for the present Royal Family, the ruling features of whose administration have ever been, mildness to the subject, and tenderness of his rights. Bred and educated in revolution principles, the principles of reason and common sense, it could not be any silly political prejudice that made my heart revolt at the harsh abusive manner in which the Reverend Gentleman mentioned the House of Stuart, and which, I am afraid, was too much the language of that day. We may rejoice sufficiently in our deliverance from past evils, without cruelly raking up the ashes of those whose misfortune it was, perhaps, as much as their crimes, to be the authors of those evils; and may bless God for all his goodness to us as a nation, without, at the same time, cursing a few ruined powerless exiles, who only harboured ideas, and made attempts, that most of us would have done, had we been in their situation.

"The bloody and tyrannical house of Stuart" may be said with propriety and justice, when compared with the present Royal Family, and the liberal sentiments of our days. But is there no allowance to be made for the manners of the times? Were the royal contemporaries of the Stuarts more mildly attentive to the rights of man? Might not the epithets of "bloody and tyrannical" be with at least equal justice, applied to the house of Tudor, of York, or any other of their predecessors?

The simple state of the case, Mr. Printer, seems to me to be this — At that period the science of government — the true relation between King and subject, like other sciences, was but just in its infancy, emerging from the dark ages of ignorance and barbarism. The Stuarts only contended for prerogatives which they knew their predecessors enjoyed, and which they saw their contemporaries enjoying; but these prerogatives were inimical to the happiness of a nation and the rights of subjects. In this contest between Prince and People, the consequence of that light of science which had lately dawned over Europe, the Monarch of France, for example, was victorious over the struggling liberties of the subject: With us, luckily, the Monarch failed, and his unwarrantable pretensions fell a sacrifice to our rights and happiness. Whether it was owing to the wisdom of leading individuals, or to the justlings of party, I cannot pretend to determine; but likewise happily for us, the kingly power was shifted into another branch of the family, who, as they owed the throne solely to the call of a free people, could claim nothing inconsistent with the covenanted terms which placed them there.

The Stuarts have been condemned and laughed at for the folly and impracticability of their attempts, in 1715 and 1745. That they failed, I bless my God most fervently; but cannot join in the ridicule against them. — Who does not know that the abilities or defects of leaders and commanders are often hidden until put to the touchstone of exigence; and that there is a caprice of fortune, an omnipotence in particular accidents, and conjunctures of circumstance, which exalt us as heroes, or brand us as madmen, just as they are for or against us?

Burns then makes a telling connection between the English opposition to Stuart tyranny which ended in the Glorious Revolution of 1688, and a more recent revolution against English minis-terial and parliamentary tyranny, that of the American colonies.

Man, Mr. Printer, is a strange, weak, inconsistent being — Who would believe, Sir, that in this our Augustan age of liberality and refinement, while we seem so justly sensible and jealous of our rights and liberties, and animated with such indignation against the very memory of those who would have subverted them, who would suppose that a certain people, under our national protection, should complain, not against a Monarch and a few favourite advisers, but against our whole legislative body, of the very same imposition and oppression, the Romish religion not excepted, and almost in the very same terms as our forefathers did against the family of Stuart! I will not, I cannot, enter into the merits of the cause; but I dare say, the American Congress, in 1776, will be allowed to have been as able and as en-lightened, and, a whole empire will say, as honest, as the English Convention of 1688; and that the fourth of July will be as sacred to their posterity as the fifth of November is to us.

To conclude, Sir, let every man, who has a tear for the many miseries incident to humanity, feel for a family, illustrious as any in Europe, and unfortunate beyond historic precedent; and let every Briton, and particularly every Scotsman, who ever looked with rever-ential pity on the dotage of a parent, cast a veil over the fatal mistakes of the Kings of his forefathers.

Put in this way, Burns' sympathy for the old Scots royal house which had won independence from England, his national pride, his hatred of tyranny, and his enthusiasm for the Rights of Man and for the Promise of Liberty, Equality, and Fraternity offered by the French Revolution then developing — all form a persuasive sequence. *Scots Wha Hae* is its ringing statement, particularly stanzas Five and Six, and a noble prelude to the Jacobin cry, "A man's a man for a' that."

> For a' that, an' a' that,
> It's comin yet for a' that,
> That man to man the world o'er
> Shall brithers be for a' that.

Burns' enthusiasm for the promise held out by France was widely shared in the early 1790's in Great Britain. The English constitutional settlement of 1688 had been degraded and corrupted by a self-perpetuating oligarchy until in Burns' day there was a general eagerness and pressure for Parliamentary and other reform, and the reformers were greatly encouraged by events in France. All this bred fear of "revolution" among the ruling class, and after France declared war on England in February, 1793, the British government, to preserve "sound institutions" and aristocratic power, embarked on a savage program of repression in a series of infamous trials. In Scotland, the prosecution was even more severe, and the court procedure more scandalous, than in England. A famous orator, Thomas Muir, given a sentence in August 1793 of fourteen years transportation to Botany Bay in a notoriously rigged trial, was sent out in 1794, and rescued by an American vessel in 1796, which took him to France. In reading of certain remarks and behavior of Burns during these years, one should bear in mind the public tension and official policy illustrated by the fate of Muir and many others like him.

Burns was no doctrinaire reformer; he had no plan for improving the world. But he had suffered from poverty and oppression, and he resented the casual acceptance of inequality by the privileged. Had his income been more comfortable, he might have found his disabilities more tolerable. "The most cordial believers in a Future State," he wrote Mrs. Dunlop, "have ever been the Unfortunate." And as he remarked to Mrs. Robert Graham, "I was born a poor dog; and however I may occasionally pick a better bone than I used to do, I know that a poor dog I must live & die." The practical basis of his discouragement he voiced to Mrs. Dunlop, "I hope, if I am spared with them, to show a set of boys that will do honor to my cares & name; but I am not equal to the task of rearing girls. — Besides, I am too poor: a girl should always have a fortune." In the same spirit, he reflected to his old Crochallan Colonel, William Dunbar, "To a father who himself knows the world, the thought that he shall have Sons to usher into it, must fill him with dread; but if he have Daughters, the prospect in a thoughtful moment is apt to shock him."

When he made these comments, Burns did not know, nor could it have been known in his day, that he suffered from an infection which was soon to kill him. During his later years, Burns' normal tendency to melancholia was intensified by the pains and debility of the disease, and his mention of "blue devils" became increasingly frequent. Just when he contracted his recurring illness, rheumatic fever, is difficult to determine, but his first mention of revealing symptoms came during his residence at Irvine, 1781–1782. The earlier dull headache after days of heavy labor at Mt. Oliphant farm, of which Gilbert Burns speaks, was most likely due to the physical exhaustion of an overworked adolescent boy.

Clinical details are lacking for an assured diagnosis of Burns' final illness, but his letters, and a few other sources, provide a fairly full record, which has been examined by four physicians[*] in the last forty years. They all speak of rheumatic fever and endocarditis, and they all agree that Burns showed no signs of alcoholism. Upon examining the record, the last of these four physicians, Dr. Stanley Bardwell, of Hudson, New York, gives for the first time a full clinical analysis of available data in support of his opinion that Burns' terminal illness resulted from an original infection which produced rheumatic fever, which, in turn, may have produced bacterial endocarditis, an infection of the valves of the heart.

2. Farmer and Exciseman

The summer of 1788 was busy and often bleak for Burns. While Jean remained in Mauchline, in part receiving instruction about the duties of a farm wife under Robert's mother and sisters, he

---

[*] Sir James Crichton-Browne (*Burns From a New Point of View*, London, 1926), Harry B. Anderson (*Annals of Medical History*, X March, 1928, 47ff.), S. Watson Smith (*British Medical Journal*, December 30, 1944, 864), and Stanley Bardwell (see Appendix B).

organized his farm and superintended the building of a house
and outbuildings at Ellisland. As he wrote to Peter Hill from
Mauchline, "From Ellisland in Nithsdale* to Mauchline in Kyle†
is forty and five miles; there a house a-building, & farm enclo-
sures and improvements to tend; here a new — not so much indeed a *new* as a *young* wife." Burns rode back and forth, spending a week or ten days in each place, leaving unsupervised his
farm workers and the contractor for his buildings while he was in
Ayrshire. When at his farm, he was "a solitary Inmate of an old,
smoky 'Spence' [best room]" in the far from weathertight hut of
the outgoing tenant, David Cullie, and his wife — decent and
pious folk who were suspicious of Burns' orthodoxy and astonished at his knowledge of the Bible. In a verse epistle to Hugh
Parker, an Ayrshire friend, he describes his plight.

> In this strange land, this uncouth clime,
> A land unknown to prose or rhyme;
> Where words ne'er cross't the Muse's heckles,   *hackles*
> Nor limpit in poetic shackles:
> A land that Prose did never view it,
> Except when drunk he stacher't thro' it: *staggered*
> Here, ambush'd by the chimla cheek,   *chimney corner*
> Hid in an atmosphere of reek,
> I hear a wheel thrum i' the neuk   *spin   corner*
> I hear it — for in vain I leuk: *look*
> The red peat gleams, a fiery kernel
> Enhuskèd by a fog infernal.
> Here, for my wonted rhyming raptures,
> I sit and count my sins by chapters;
> For life and spunk like ither Christians,
> I'm dwindled down to mere existence;
> Wi' nae converse but Gallowa' bodies,
> Wi' nae kend face but Jenny Geddes.   *known*

  Burns' first day at Ellisland was June 12 (he called it "the elbow of existence"), and during the following lonely summer and

---

* Dumfriesshire
† Central Ayrshire

autumn, he wrote many letters from there and from Mauchline to old cronies in Edinburgh, letters often tinged with nostalgia. His most frequent correspondent, however, was Mrs. Dunlop, to whom he unburdened his mind, sure of her affectionate interest. That he should take time for so much letter-writing indicates something of his attitude toward his farm, and of the attention he gave it.

Professor Ferguson printed forty-six letters from the period June–December, 1788, many of them long, and they reveal an active, vigorous man who discusses books, songs, his poems, his marriage, his farm, and his general concerns. By September he was beginning to doubt the wisdom of having taken the farm at all. He wrote to Robert Graham at harvest time, on September 10, "My farm, now that I have tried it a little, tho' I think it will in time be a saving bargain, yet does by no means promise to be such a Pennyworth as I was taught to expect. — It is in the last stage of worn-out poverty, & will take some time before it pay the rent. — I might have had the Cash to supply the defficiencies of these hungry years, but I have a younger brother and three sisters, on a farm in Ayr-shire; and it took all my surplus, over what I thought necessary for my farming capital, to save not only the comfort but the very existence of that fireside family-circle from impending destruction. — This was done before I took the farm; and rather than abstract my money from my brother, a circumstance which would ruin him, I will resign the farm and enter immediately into the service of your Honours [the Excise Board]. — But I am embarked now in the farm; I have commenced married man; and I am determined to stand by my Lease, till resistless Necessity compel me to quit my ground." Ellisland became increasingly burdensome to him until he escaped from it completely into the Excise three years later.

He goes on to report that, since the Excise officer in the district surrounding Ellisland, one Leonard Smith, has recently become "quite opulent" by inheritance, perhaps the Board would consider replacing Smith with himself. Graham replied promptly on September 14, and Burns, suffering from influenza, thanked him for his "generous favor" on the twenty-third. By the following September (1789), Burns had been given the district, and reports to Mrs. Dunlop, "Five days in the week, or four at least, I must be on horseback, and very frequently ride thirty or forty miles ere I return; besides four different kinds of book-keeping to post every day." His pay was £50 a year, which compared very favorably with the incomes of ministers and school teachers. The reduced farming activity was left largely to servants, with Jean in charge of the dairying. "Burns kept twelve cows, and made butter and cheese," she reported.

The intervening year strengthened Burns' doubts about the suitability of farming for him. In March, 1789, he wrote Mrs. Dunlop,

You remember, Madam, I had two plans of life before me; The Excise & farming. — I thought, by the glimmering of my own prudence, the Excise was my most eligible scheme; but all my Great friends and particularly you, were decidedly, & therefore decided me, for farming. — My master, Mr Miller, out of real tho' mistaken benevolence, sought me industriously out, to set me on this farm, as he said to give me a lease that would make me comfortable & easy. — I was a stranger to the country, the farm and the soil, and so ventured on a bargain, that instead of being comfortable, is & will be a very, very hard bargain, if at all practicable. . . . My brother's lease is near expiring; he may be able to live by my lease as he can with propriety do things that I *now* can not do; I will plant him in this farm & throw myself on the Excise at large, where I am sure of immediate & constant bread.

Construction of the new house dragged on, but Burns wrote happily to Jean on October 14, 1788:

My dearest Love,
You need not come on Sunday to meet me on the road, for I am

engaged that day to dine with Mr Logan at Laycht, so it will be in the evening before I arrive at Mauchline. —

You must get ready for Nithsdale as fast as possible, for I have an offer of a house in the very neighbourhood with some furniture in it, all which I shall have the use of for nothing till my own house be got ready; I am determined to remove you from Ayrshire immediately, as I am a sufferer by not being on my farm myself. — We will want a Maid servant, of consequence: if you can hear of any to hire, ask after them. — The apples are all sold & gone. — I am extremely happy at the idea of your coming to Nithsdale, as it will save us from these cruel separations. — The house is one in which a Mr Newal lived during the summer, who is gone to Dumfries in Winter. — It is a large house, but we will only occupy a room or two of it. —

I am ever, my dearest Madam,
Your faithful husband & humble servt
ROBT BURNS

But Jean did not join him at this house, The Isle, until early December, and they were still there the following April 15, sometime after which they moved into the still unfinished Ellisland farmhouse. Young Robert, their only surviving child, did not follow Jean to Nithsdale for about six months, but Burns did take in his uncle Robert's children William and Fanny on their father's death in January; and his brother William spent a long time with them during the winter. William was an amiable but ineffective youth seeking employment as a saddler. Robert helped him with clothes and money, and tried without much success to get him a job. William drifted to the neighborhood of Carlisle, then across to Newcastle, and finally to London, where, in a short time, he died of a fever. Robert's letters to him are affectionate, and full of good advice, which William asked for in his own well-expressed missives to his big brother. When the family moved to Ellisland, Burns' sister Agnes joined them.

Burns' letters are full of references to his work on the farm, and to the farm's demands and worries. "Every minute," he tells

Mrs. Dunlop on April 21, 1789, "has five minutes worth of business to do, and every crown has a twenty shilling errand to run." This latter theme he expanded in December. "My poor distracted mind is so torn, so jaded, so racked & bedevil'd with the task of the superlatively Damn'd — MAKING ONE GUINEA DO THE BUSINESS OF THREE — that I detest, abhor, and swoon at the very word, Business, though no less than four letters of my very short Sirname are in it." Obviously pressed for funds, Burns was looking to active duty in the Excise for relief.

By May 13, 1789, less than a year after he had come to Ellisland, Burns is writing Robert Graham of a conversation with Collector Mitchell, and by July 31, he and Mitchell have had a long and friendly talk about removing Leonard Smith and installing Robert Burns in his place, which should "be productive of at least no disadvantage to the Revenue." If the Board agrees to the change, Burns' salary will enable him to carry on and enjoy the improvement of his farm. He has considered giving up the farm entirely, but, he adds, "The worst of it is, I know there are some respectable Characters who do me the honor to interest themselves in my welfare & behaviour, and as leaving the farm so soon may have an unsteady giddy-headed appearance, I had perhaps better lose a little money than hazard such people's esteem." By August 19 he can write Mrs. Dunlop of his appointment, and say that he expects to begin duty the first of September. He seems to have been appointed September 7, but he was not sworn in until October 27. However, his name appeared on the official list of officers October 10, and he was assigned to full duty at once without serving the customary period as an "expectant." (See addendum, p. 482.)

Illness and injury were prompt results of Burns' new activities. Two months after he went on duty, he caught a "most violent cold," and suffered severely from it (and later from a "diseased nervous system") until mid-January, 1790, having to give up his Excise-books for a time. "My nerves are in a damnable State," he wrote Gilbert on January 11. "I feel that horrid hypochondria pervading every atom of both body & soul." The following September (1790), he "was seized with a slow, illformed Fever," and also had "a most malignant Squinancy" * which nearly carried him off.

In January, 1791, he fell — "not from my horse but with my horse" † — and injured his arm and hand, but he could write with them in February. And in March his horse came down with him and broke his right arm. Waiting for him on his return home from the accident was Janet Little, a poetical milkmaid and a protégée of Mrs. Dunlop, who had come to seek encouragement. Jenny reported that he chatted "at seeming ease and good humor," but could not lie down in bed, and was obliged to sit in a chair all night, in very violent pain.

Finally, in October, 1791, he is "a poor devil nailed to an elbow chair, writhing in anguish with a bruised leg, laid on a stool before him." It was high time when, in early November, he gave up riding about and moved to Dumfries. No doubt these experiences contributed to the despondency which Mrs. Burns thought induced him to give up Ellisland.

Burns' feelings about his position as Exciseman were mixed. The extra income was welcome. To Richard Brown he wrote, "I have indeed been extremely lucky in getting an additional income of £50 a year, while, at the same time, the appointment will not cost me above £10 or £12 per annum of expenses." To Lady Elizabeth Cunningham, sister of Lord Glencairn, he remarked, "People may talk as they please of the ignominy of the Excise, but what will support my family and keep me independent of the world is to me a very important matter; I had much rather that my Profession borrowed credit from me, than that I borrowed credit from my Profession." To Robert Ainslie

---

* "Phlegonous tonsillitis." See Appendix B.
† Perhaps Jenny Geddes, although in March, 1789, he wrote to Dr. Moore of a "young favorite horse" which he had just christened Pegasus — no doubt the one celebrated in his lines *Pegasus at Wanlockhead*. (F I, #322, 315.)

he was more colorful. "For the ignominy of the Profession," he wrote, "I have the encouragement which I once heard a recruiting Sergeant give to a numerous if not a respectable audience in the Streets of Kilmarnock — 'Gentlemen, for your further & better encouragement, I can assure you that our regiment is the most blackguard corps under the crown, and consequently with us an honest fellow has the surest chance for preferment.'" After two years, he wrote to his friend Cleghorn, "The Excise, after all has been said against it, is the business for me. — I find no difficulty in being an honest man in it; the work of itself, is easy." He adds that he has been put on the Supervisor list and hopes for early promotion, which will place him in a "respectable situation."

An Exciseman's duties were complex and exacting in Burns' day, even if Burns found them easy to perform. When, the year after his death, there was published *An Abridgement of all the Statutes now in Force Relative to the Revenue of the Excise in Great Britain,* the *abridgement* ran to nine hundred octavo pages. Burns did not enjoy this convenience, but had to pore through Acts of Parliament, general orders, and memoranda to learn his job.

The following were subject to Excise duties: — Auctions, bricks and tiles, beer, candles, coaches, cocoa-nuts, coffee, cyder, perry, verjuice, glass, hops, hides and skins, malt, mead or Metheglin, paper, pepper, printed calico and silk goods, soap, British spirits, foreign spirits, starch, salt, stone bottles, sweets, tea, tobacco and snuff, wine, and wire. The duty upon these articles was, in nearly every case, charged during the manufacture, and the surveillance of the processes entailed upon the officer frequent visits by day and night, on Sunday and Saturday. For example, soap-boilers were surveyed every four hours, candlemakers every six hours, and even brick-makers had sometimes to be surveyed twice a day. Each article had several rates of duty. Tanners had to pay fourteen different rates, per lb., per skin, and per dozen skins, according to the kind of hide; and even hare and rabbit skins were not allowed to escape. There were seventy-eight rates of paper duty according to size, kind, and quality, and other similar instances could be given. Of course, no single Excise officer had all these manufactures in his station; but he generally had a number of them, and he was never allowed to forget his responsibility with regard to them all. He was expected to detect within the bounds of the district allotted to him every article upon which the king's dues had not been paid. . . . In those days a tax was levied on almost every article in daily use in the household.

A zealous officer was supposed to supplement his pay with his half-share of the fines, and of the proceeds from sales of seized goods, for which he was responsible. After he had been on active duty for a year, Burns indicates in a letter to Robert Graham that his "Decreet" will be more than his annual salary. "As my Division consists of ten large parishes, & I am sorry to say, hitherto very carelessly surveyed, I had a good deal of business for the Justices; & I believe my Decreet will amount to between fifty & sixty pounds. — I took, I fancy, rather a new way with my Frauds. — I recorded every Defaulter; but at the Court, I myself begged off every poor body that was unable to pay, which seeming candour gave me so much implicit credit with the Hon. Bench, that with high Complnts they gave me such ample vengeance on the rest, that my Decreet is double the amount of any Division in the District."

In a letter to Collector Mitchell of the same time, Burns reflects on the immutable difficulties of enforcing the law against offenders with influential friends:

I wish & pray that the goddess of Justice herself would appear tomorrow among our Honble Gentlemen, merely to give them a word in their ear, that, "Mercy to the Thief, is Injustice to the Honest Man." For my part, I have galloped over my ten parishes these four days, untill this moment that I am just alighted, or rather, that my poor jackass skeleton of a horse has let me down; for the miserable devil has been on his knees half a score of times within the last twenty miles, telling me in his own way "Behold, am not I thy faithful jade of a horse, on which thou hast ridden these many years!!!" In short, Sir, I have broke my horse's wind, & almost broke my own neck, besides some injuries in a part that shall be nameless, owing to a hard-hearted stone of a saddle; & I find that every Offender has so many Great Men to espouse his cause, that I shall not be surprised if I am committed to the strong Hold of the Law tomorrow for insolence to the dear friends of the Gentlemen of the Country.

In the letter to Graham quoted above (September 4, 1790), he expands his discontent with farming. "I am going either to give up, or subset my farm directly. — I have not liberty to subset, but if my Master will grant it me, I propose giving it just as I have it to myself, to an industrious fellow of a near relation of mine [his brother Gilbert]. — Farming this place in which I live, would just be a livelyhood to a man who would be the greatest drudge in his own family, so is no object; & living here hinders me from that knowledge of the business of Excise which it is absolutely necessary for me to attain." He goes on to hope he can get a Port Division with its easier duties and higher pay, and that he can eventually become an Examiner or Supervisor, all with the support of well-placed people, including Mr. Graham. And by January 27, 1791, he had been placed on the list of those recommended for Examiner and Supervisor. But so early as September 11, 1790, John Syme had written Alexander Cunningham of Burns, "He says he is immediately to be promoted in the Excise line," and Nicol had written to Ainslie on August 13 that Burns was already an Examiner. It would seem that he had had prematurely high hopes of advancement.

Mrs. Dunlop, ever his friend, seems to have had a hand in getting Burns' name put on the list of Supervisors, through her friendship with Robert Graham, and with the wife of General Supervisor William Corbet.* Burns wrote her in March, 1790,

* Corbet inquired of Burns' Supervisor, Alexander Findlater, about him, and received the following reply, dated December 20, 1790, an important testament to his abilities and performance as an Exciseman: "Dear Sir, Mr. Burns informs me that, in consequence of a communication between you & some of his friends, he

that the farm was a "ruinous bargain," which he must give up by Martinmas, 1791, when his rent is to rise £20, and he will consider himself "well quit" if he be no more than a hundred pounds out of pocket. He continues,

I can have in the Excise-line what they call a foot-walk whenever I chuse; that is an appointment to a Division where I am under no necessity of keeping a horse.* — There is in every Sea-port town, one or two Officers, called Port-Officers, whose income is at least seventy pounds per ann. — I will petition Mr Graham & stretch all my interest, to get one of these; and if possible on Clyde. — Greenock & Port-Glasgow are both lucrative places in that way, & to them my views are bent. — You formerly wrote me, if a Mr Corbet in the Excise could be of use to me. — If it is a Corbet who is what we call one of our General Supervisors, of which we have just two in Scotland, he can do everything for me. — Were he to interest himself properly for me, he could easily by Martinmas 1791 transport me to Port Glasgow port Division, which would be the ultimatum of my present Excise hopes. — He is a Willm Corbet, & has his home, I believe, somewhere about Stirling. — One word more, and then to have done with this most ungracious subject: all this business of my farm &c. is for your most private ear: it would be of considerable prejudice to me to have it known at present."

---

has stated his case to you by letter, & exprest his wishes on account of his family, of being translated to a more beneficial appointment: — And as at our last interview at Stirling you hinted a desire of being certified of the propriety of his Character as an officer of the Revenue; I shall, abstracted from every Consideration of his other talents, which are so universally admired, in a few words give you my Opinion of him. — He is an active, faithful, & zealous officer, gives the most unremitting attention to his office (which, by the bye is more than I at first looked for from so eccentric a Genius) and tho' his experience must as yet be small, he is capable, as you may well suppose, of achieving a much more arduous task than any difficulty that the theory or practice of our business can exhibit. — In short, — being such as I have described — and believe me, I have not 'o'erstep'd the modesty of' *truth* — he is truly worthy of your friendship; and if your recommendation can help him forward to a more eligible situation, you will have the merit of conferring an Obligation on a man who may be considered a credit to the profession." (Author's transcript of original in Burns College Museum, Alloway, published *Chronicle*, 1931.)
* He received an appointment the following July (1790) to the Dumfries third division, tobacco, but what difference this appointment may have made in his life is not clear. (Sinton, 59.)

Burns' Ellisland lease bound him to enclose the property and build "a dwelling house, Barn, byre and stable," for which improvements Mr. Miller was to advance £300. There was no provision for a sublease or for an escape. But in 1791, Mr. Miller received an offer of £1900 for the farm from a neighbor, John Morin of Laggan, which he was glad to accept because Ellisland was separated from the rest of his estate by the River Nith.* On September 10, 1791, Burns signed a release of his "Tack," and he told Robert Cleghorn that he had got "some little consideration" for his lease, but he does not say what.

He had previously sold off the crops on August 25, an occasion he described to Thomas Sloan. "I sold my crop on this day se'ennight past, & sold it very well: a guinea an acre, on an average, above value. — But such a scene of drunkenness was hardly ever seen in this country. — After the roup was over, about thirty people engaged in a battle, every man his own hand, & fought it out for three hours. — Nor was the scene much better in the house. — No fighting, indeed, but folks lying drunk on the floor, & decanting, untill both my dogs got so drunk by attending them, that they could not stand. — You will easily guess how I enjoyed the scene; as I was no further over than you used to see me. — Mrs B——& family have been in Ayr-shire these many weeks." The customary refreshment on such occasions had produced the customary results, even if somewhat more dramatic than usual.

In early November Burns sold off his "horses, cows, farming things, &c." on such terms that he could report to Mrs. Dunlop, "I have got rid of my farm with little, if any loss . . . by that peculiar Good Luck that for some years past" had attended all his motions. On November 11, 1791, he moved Jean, Robert Jr., Francis Wallace, and William Nicol into three small rooms above the Stamp Office in the Wee or Stinking or Carwart's Vennel (now Bank Street), Dumfries, within sound of the river. The

* Fourteen years later, Morin sold Ellisland for £4430.

landlord was Captain John Hamilton, of Allershaw, who proved Burns' practical friend by his considerate restraint when rent was overdue. On May 19, 1793, Burns moved to another and more comfortable of Captain Hamilton's properties, the stone house in the Mill Vennel (now Burns Street), where he died three years later, and where Jean continued to live.

With proceeds from the two sales at Ellisland, Burns paid off some obligations, including his five pound, ten shilling debt to "Mr Robert Burn, Architect, for erecting the stone over poor Ferguson." Burns wrote to Peter Hill, "He was two years in erecting it, after I commissioned him for it; & I have been two years paying him, after he sent me his account; so he & I are quits. — He had the hardiesse to ask me interest on the sum; but considering that the money was due by one Poet, for putting a tomb-stone over another, he may, with grateful surprise, thank Heaven that he ever saw a farthing of it."

Burns used other proceeds to visit Edinburgh in late November and early December, when he relieved Jenny Clow and renewed his affair with Clarinda.

Transcripts of official Excise records show that Burns succeeded to the Dumfries first, or Port, Division on April 26, 1792. He reports this promotion to Maria Riddell in a letter dated by Professor Ferguson "February, 1792." The manuscript has not been traced, and the date seems early, although here, as when Burns began his Excise duties, the official entry may have been delayed. "I am happy," he wrote Mrs. Riddell, "to inform you I have just got an appointment to the first or Port Division as it is called, which adds twenty pounds to my Salary. My Excise Income is now Cash paid Seventy pounds a year: and this I hold untill I am appointed Supervisor. . . . My Perquisites I hope to make worth 15 or 20£ more." This was Burns' last promotion, although he was made Acting Supervisor, December, 1794–April, 1795, during the illness of Supervisor Findlater.

The Board's records and Burns' own correspondence reveal

him to have been guilty of occasional small errors, inadvertence, or carelessness. That is all. He did his work conscientiously, and the Board treated him favorably. It was the emphatic opinion of Supervisor Findlater that he "would, if he had lived, have been promoted in due course; and that, at a shorter period of service than any of his predecessors." After Burns' death in July, 1796, the man below him on the list was made Examiner January 12, 1797, and Supervisor the following August 10. Burns would have received these promotions had he lived, with a salary of £120–£200.

In March, 1795, while he was Acting Supervisor, Burns replied to an offer of assistance from Patrick Heron, M.P., that the Supervisor's "business is an incessant drudgery, and would be nearly a compleat bar to every species of literary pursuit." However, he continues, the moment he is appointed Supervisor, he may be nominated on the Collector's list, "and this is always a business purely of political patronage. A Collectorship varies much, from better than two hundred a year to near a thousand. They also come forward by precedency on the list; and have, besides a handsome income, a life of complete leisure. A life of literary leisure, with a decent competence, is the summit of my wishes." Upon his promotion to Supervisor, he concludes, he would be most grateful for assistance from a politically powerful friend in securing a Collectorship.

Burns would almost certainly have been a Supervisor by the time of his letter to Heron, had his well-placed and well-intentioned friends got him into the Excise during the 1786–1787 winter, as he had wished. Had they done so, he would have avoided the exasperation of his farm, and he might well have been more comfortable financially, also.

Burns' most celebrated exploit as an Excise officer was his leading a party to board a grounded smuggling schooner, the *Rosamond*, in the Solway estuary below Dumfries. He later purchased four carronades at the sale of the seized vessel and sent them to the revolutionary government in France. The seizure is best followed in the picturesque narrative of Riding Officer Walter Crawford's journal, with a few minor emendations. The journal begins January 12, 1792. On February 26, Crawford heard of the smuggler.

26 E[vening] 4 [o'clock] Gone to Dumfries to acquent the Supervisor and Officers that a landing [of smugglers] was expected that week, In the mean time having left a person in whom I could thorowghly confide to ride Express to me on the first appearance of a landing for which he was delligently to watch.

27 E 11 My Express arrived informing me that a landing was making or about to be made, on which I set off with Mr Lewars directly, leaving Messrs. Burns, Penn & Ranking to follow as fast as possible.

By the 28 m[orning] 5 arrived at Annan and immediately sett out with the Party of Dragoons, Searched Mr M'Dowall's [a notorious smuggler] and most of the Smuglers house[s] between that and the Shore, and about Noon Rode down to the shore where I was informed that the Vessal could not gett off for want of Watter. I made an attempt to Board her with the Millitary But when wee offered to app[r]och they hailed ws that they would fire on us if wee app[r]oched any farther.

As my Party had only Pistols and were but few in number and a great number of men appearing to be on Deck I stoped the Soldiery and riding up to the Vessal allone asked liberty to Come on board which after some altercation they granted. I Boarded her and found Twenty four men under arms with fifteen round of shott each.

I returned to shore and consulting with the Officers and Millitary we agread that greater force would be absolutly necessary, In consequence of which Mr Lewars sett off for Dumfries to Bring twenty four more Dragoons while I went to Ecclefechan for the Party there with which I patroled the roads till the arrivall of Mr. Lewars with the additionall force from Dumfries.

On the 29 m 9 wee approached the Vessall with the following force, Dragoons from Dumfries Twenty Three, Annan Thirteen, Ecclefechan Eight, in all Forty four fully accoutered and on horse-back. The vessal having fallen down the Sollway Firth abouth a mill from where she was yesterday and being about a mile within sea mark, most of which space being covered with watter, and a very heavy Currant running between us and the Vessel we deemed it imposible to get at her either on foott or on horseback, so we aggread to search the coast for Boats in which to board her. But the Country People guessing our design got the start of us and staved every Boat on the Coast before we Could reach them, the vessel in the mean time keeping up a fire of grape shott and musquetry, we resolved as last resource to attempt the passage on foott as the quick sands made the riding on horseback dangerous or rather impossible.

We drew up the Millitary in three divisions determined to approach her & attact her if the s[t]ream was foardable, one party fore and aft and the Third on her Broadside, the first party being Commanded by Quarter Master Manly, the Second by my self and the Third led by Mr Burns.

Our orders to the Millitary were to reserve there fire till within eight yards of the vessel, then to pour a volley and board her with sword & Pistol. The vessel keept on firing thou without any damage to us, as from the situation of the ship they could not bring their great guns to bear on us, we in the mean time wading breast high, and in Justice to the party under my Command I must say with great alacrity; by the time we were within one hundred yards of the vessel the Crew gave up the cause, gott over side towards England which shore was for a long way dry sand. As I still supposed that there were only Country people they were putting ashore and that the Crew were keeping under Cover to make a more vigourous immediate resistance, we marched up as first concerted, but found the vessel compleatly evacuuated both of the Crew and every movable on board except as per inventory, the smugglers as their last instance of vengen[c]e having poured a six-pounder Carronade through her Broadside. She proved to be the Roseomond of Plymouth, Alexander Patty Master, and about one hundred tons burthen schooner r[igged].

This document rests in the National Library of Scotland, with two others relating to Burns and the *Rosamond*. The first, in Burns' hand, is a record of the guarding, repair, and refloating of the vessel, and her preparation for sale. The second, in the hand of Burns' fellow officer, John Lewars, is an inventory of the ship and her "furniture." Proceeds of the sale (April 19, 1792) were £166/16/6, and the expenses of preparation £45/15/4, leaving prize money of £121/1/2. The Excisemen's share of this latter sum is not recorded.

These documents were collected and supplied to Sir Walter Scott by Joseph Train, Supervisor of Excise for Castle Douglas. Train also speaks of Lewars' journal which recorded Burns' purchase of the four carronades, and of a sale catalogue with a note in Burns' hand that he had purchased them for £3. The whereabouts of Lewars' journal and of the sale catalogue are not now known; however, Sir Walter interested himself in the story, and learned that the carronades had been intercepted by the Customs at Dover. No record of this interception has come to light. For Burns to purchase the guns and despatch them to France was perfectly legal. England and France were not at war until the following February. But for an Exciseman, this expression of his feelings was dramatically reckless.

That these feelings were much excited at this time is suggested by Burns' having subscribed, November 13, 1792, to the *Gazetteer*, an Edinburgh paper just established by William Johnston, a reputable reforming politician soon to be imprisoned in the "sedition" drive. Further evidence appears in Burns' letter to Mrs. Dunlop of December 6.

We, in this country, here have many alarms of the Reform, or rather the Republican spirit, of your part of the kingdom. — Indeed, we are a good deal in commotion ourselves, & in our Theatre here, "God save the king" has met with some groans and hisses, while, Ça ira has been repeatedly called for. — For me, I am a *Placeman*, you know, a very humble one indeed, Heaven knows, but still so much so as to gag me from joining in the cry. — What my private sentiments are, you will find out without an Interpreter. — In the meantime, I have taken up the subject in another view, and the other day, for a pretty Actress's benefit-night, I wrote an address which I will give on the other page, called "The Rights of Woman."

The Rights of Woman

An Occasional Address

Spoken by Miss Fontenelle on her Benefit Night
November 26, 1792

While Europe's eye is fix'd on mighty things,
The fate of empires and the fall of kings;
While quacks of State must each produce his plan,
And even children lisp the Rights of Man;
Amid this mighty fuss just let me mention
The Rights of Woman merit some attention.

First, in the sexes' intermix'd connexion
One sacred Right of Woman is Protection:
The tender flower, that lifts its head elate,
Helpless must fall before the blasts of fate,
Sunk on the earth, defac'd its lovely form,
Unless your shelter ward th' impending storm.

Our second Right — but needless here is caution —
To keep that right inviolate's the fashion:
Each man of sense has it so full before him,
He'd die before he'd wrong it — 'tis Decorum!
There was, indeed, in far less polish'd days,
A time, when rough rude Man had naughty ways:
Would swagger, swear, get drunk, kick up a riot,
Nay, even thus invade a lady's quiet!
Now, thank our stars! these Gothic times are fled;
Now, well-bred men — and you are all well-bred —
Most justly think (and we are much the gainers)
Such conduct neither spirit, wit, nor manners.*

---

* John Syme's account (November 21, 1794) to Alexander Cunningham of the Caledonian Hunt's visit two years later to Dumfries, suggests the quality of genteel behavior ironically glanced at here. "Our Caledonian Hunt went off with dissipation without fashionable gaiety — There was not one of Noble blood at the Races if we except Maule — The exhibitions of the Bucks were splendid if we give that title to rioting. Drinking three bottles each day, disturbing the players, staggering in at the Assembly — some even dancing in boots — displayed the spirit and genius of modern manners — Baker, one of the knowing english Squires on the Turf made an elegant appearance by insulting in the

For Right the third, our last, our best, our dearest:
That right to fluttering female hearts the nearest,
Which even the Rights of Kings, in low prostration,
Most humbly own — 'tis dear, dear Admiration!
In that blest sphere alone we live and move;
There taste that life of life — Immortal Love.
Smiles, glances, sighs, tears, fits, flirtations, airs —
'Gainst such an host what flinty savage dares?
When awful Beauty joins with all her charms,
Who is so rash as rise in rebel arms?

But truce with kings, and truce with constitutions,
With bloody armaments and revolutions;
Let Majesty your first attention summon:
Ah! ça ira! the Majesty of Woman!

At unspecified times, probably during the fall of 1792, Burns is reported to have made such provocative toasts as one to the

---

grossest manner Squire Walter Riddel of this place who pursued him to Durham and made him ask pardon which is published in our papers of last week. Maule and others you would hear, pickled our friend Harry Welsh — by daubing his hair with mustard etc & sticking toothpic quills in it by way of hedgehogging the man — This lad, Cunningham, must be distracted — his behavior here has been horrible and I dare say will make a desert about him if ever he appears again in this quarter — But say nothing of this as from me — Maule, I suppose you have heard, fell in love with Patricia Gordon of Halleaths — a very beautiful & valuable young girl — and he is to marry her in the first week of Decemr — This is certainly to take place if we judge from every indication — clothes making settlement *do* etc. etc." (Author's transcript, see P.S. for p. 365.)

It will be recalled that the Caledonian Hunt had subscribed to one hundred copies of Burns' Edinburgh edition, and had received its Dedication, whose ironic sting will be more fully appreciated if it is re-read with the above account in mind. (*Cp.* pp. 143–44; see also p. 277n and pp. 10–11.) Burns left a poor if bitter epigram on Maule — "*To the Hon. Wm. R. Maule of Panmure* Extempore: On seeing the Hon. Wm. R. Maule of Panmure driving away in his fine and elegant phaeton on the race ground at Tinwald Downs, October, 1794."

Thou Fool, in thy phaeton towering,
    Art proud when that phaeton's praised?
'Tis the pride of a Thief's exhibition
    When higher his pillory's rais'd.

It should also be noted that the subject of this epigram, in 1817, twenty-one years after Burns' death, settled £50 a year on Burns' widow. Within a year and a half, however, James Glencairn Burns' improved circumstances allowed him to relieve Maule of this voluntarily assumed obligation. (Ch-W IV, 295.)

last verse of the last chapter of the last book of kings. Whatever he may have done, he had written to Mrs. Dunlop, April 3,
1789, "Politics is dangerous ground for me to tread on, and yet
I cannot for the soul of me resist an impulse of anything like
Wit." The impulse got him into trouble, for about this time he
was reported to the Excise Board as disaffected, and Collector
Mitchell was instructed to look into the matter. Burns wrote
frantically to Robert Graham, and since there has been so much
statement and counterstatement about this affair, it seems best
to present the relevant documents entire, and let Burns speak
for himself. Here is his letter to Graham, December 31, 1792.

SIR,
   I have been surprised, confounded & distracted by Mr Mitchel,
the Collector, telling me just now, that he has received an order from
your Honble Board to enquire into my political conduct, & blaming me
as a person disaffected to Government. Sir, you are a Husband — & a
father — you know what you would feel, to see the much-loved wife of
your bosom, & your helpless, prattling little ones, turned adrift
into the world, degraded & disgraced from a situation in which they
had been respectable & respected, & left almost without the necessary
support of a miserable existence. — Alas, Sir! must I think that such,
soon, will be my lot! And from the damned, dark insinuations of hellish, groundless Envy too! — I believe, Sir, I may aver it, & in the
sight of omnipotence, that I would not tell a deliberate Falsehood,
no, not though even worse horrors, if worse can be, than those I have
mentioned, hung over my head; & I say, that the allegation, whatever
villain has made it, is a Lie! To the British Constitution, on Revolution
principles, next after my God, I am most devoutly attached! —
   You, Sir, have been much & generously my Friend — Heaven knows
how warmly I have felt the obligation, & how gratefully I have thanked
you. — Fortune, Sir, has made you powerful, & me impotent; has given
you patronage, & me dependance. — I would not for my *single Self*
call on your Humanity; were such my insular, unconnected situation,
I would despise the tear that now swells in my eye — I could brave
Misfortune, I could face Ruin: for at the worst, "Death's thousand
doors stand open;" but, good God! the tender concerns that I have
mentioned, the claims & ties that I, at this moment, see & feel around

me, how they ennerve Courage, & wither Resolution! To your patronage, as a man of some genius, you have allowed me a claim; & your
esteem, as An Honest Man, I know is my due: to these, Sir, permit
me to appeal; & by these may I adjure you to save me from that
misery which threatens to overwhelm me, & which, with my latest
breath I will say it, I have not deserved.

On the same day that he wrote to Graham, he wrote to Mrs.
Dunlop that "some envious, malicious devil" had raised a little
demur about his political principles. "I have set, henceforth," he
continued, "a seal on my lips as to these unlucky politics, but to
you I must breathe my sentiments." * Unfortunately that portion
of the manuscript containing his sentiments has been torn away.
Within five days, Burns had been reassured by Robert Graham,
and had replied in a letter which stated the truth and nothing
but the truth, but perhaps not quite the whole truth.

SIR,
    I am this moment honored with your letter: with what feelings I
received this other instance of your goodness, I shall not pretend
to describe. —
    Now, to the charges which Malice & Misrepresentation have brought
against me. —
    It has been said, it seems, that I not only belong to, but head a
disaffected party in this place. — I know of no party in this place,
Republican or Reform, except an old party of Borough-Reform; with
which I never had anything to do. — Individuals, both Republican &
Reform, we have, though not many of either; but if they have associated, it is more than I have the least knowledge of: & if there exists
such an association, it must consist of such obscure, nameless beings,
as precluded any possibility of my being known to them, or they to
me. —

---

* In September, 1793, Burns presented a copy of John De Lolme's *The British
Constitution* to the Dumfries public library, with the following inscription: "Mr
Burns presents this book to the Library & begs they will take it as a Creed of
British Liberty — untill they find a better. R. B." But the day after the presentation he retrieved the volume and pasted the sheet with the inscription and
the one next to it together, to hide his indiscretion. The copy of De Lolme may
be seen in the Burns House, Dumfries. (F II, #589, 211; Ch-W IV, 55.)

I was in the playhouse one night, when Ça Ira was called for. — I was in the middle of the Pit, & from the Pit the clamour arose. — One or two individuals with whom I occasionally associate were of the party, but I neither knew of the Plot, nor joined in the Plot; nor ever opened my lips to hiss, or huzza, that or any other Political tune whatever. — I looked on myself as far too obscure a man to have any weight in quelling a Riot; at the same time as a character of higher respectability, than to yell in the howlings of a rabble. — This was the conduct of all the first Characters in this place; & these Characters know, & will avow, that such was my conduct. —

I never uttered any invectives against the king. — His private worth, it is altogether impossible that such a man as I, can appreciate; and in his Public capacity, I always revered, & ever will, with soundest loyalty, revere, the Monarch of Great Britain, as, to speak in Masonic, the sacred Keystone of our Royal Arch Constitution. —

As to Reform Principles, I look upon the British Constitution, as settled at the Revolution, to be the most glorious Constitution on earth, or that perhaps the wit of man can frame; at the same time, I think, & you know what High and distinguished Characters have for some time thought so, that we have a good deal deviated from the original principles of that Constitution; particularly, that an alarming System of Corruption has pervaded the connection between the Executive Power and the House of Commons. — This is the Truth, the Whole truth, of my Reform opinions; opinions which, before I was aware of the complection of these innovating times, I too unguardedly (now I see it) sported with: but henceforth, I seal up my lips. — However, I never dictated to, corresponded with, or had the least connection with, any political association whatever — except, that when the Magistrates & principal inhabitants of this town, met to declare their attachment to the Constitution, & their abhorrence of Riot, which declaration you would see in the Papers, I, as I thought my duty as a Subject at large, & a Citizen in particular, called upon me, subscribed the same declaratory Creed. —

Of Johnston, the publisher of the Edinr Gazetteer, I know nothing. — One evening in company with four or five friends, we met with his prospectus which we thought manly & independent; & I wrote to him, ordering his paper for us. — If you think that I act improperly in allowing his Paper to come addressed to me, I shall immediately countermand it. — I never, so judge me, God! wrote a line of prose for the Gazetteer in my life. — An occasional address, spoken by Miss Fontenelle on her benefit-night here, which I called, the Rights of Woman, I sent to the Gazetteer; as also some extempore stanzas on the Commemoration of Thomson: both of these I will subjoin for your perusal. — You will see that they have nothing whatever to do with Politics. — At the time when I sent Johnston one of these poems, but which one, I do not remember, I inclosed at the request of my warm & worthy friend, Robt Riddel Esq: of Glenriddel a prose Essay signed Cato, written by him, & addressed to the delegates for the County Reform, of which he was one for this County. — With the merits, or demerits, of that Essay, I have nothing to do, farther than transmitting it in the same Frank, which Frank he had procured me. —

As to France, I was her enthusiastic votary in the beginning of the business. — When she came to shew her old avidity for conquest, in annexing Savoy, &c. to her dominions, & invading the rights of Holland, I altered my sentiments. — A tippling Ballad which I made on the Prince of Brunswick's breaking up his camp, & sung one convivial evening, I shall likewise send you, sealed up, as it is not every body's reading. — This last is not worth your perusal; but lest Mrs Fame should, as she has already done, use, & even abuse, her old priviledge of lying, you shall be the master of everything, le pour et le contre, of my political writings & conduct.

He concludes by reporting that the Supervisor of the Galloway district has been paralyzed, and suggesting that perhaps the Board might be disposed to fill this Supervisor's place. Two days later he wrote Graham again on the subject, but he did not get the job.

On this occasion, General Supervisor Corbet came to Dumfries to inquire, an indication that the Board took the matter seriously. John Syme, in a note to Alexander Peterkin, describes the results. "Mr Corbet admonished Burns — but found no grounds, save some witty sayings — Mr Corbet, Mr Findlater Burns & I dined together once or twice on the occasion." Findlater confirms Syme in a letter to the *Glasgow Courier*, March, 1834. Burns himself reviews the event in a letter to John Francis Erskine, of Mar, who had offered him assistance on hearing that he had been dismissed. He prefixed the following explanatory note to a copy of the letter which he made in the Glenriddell letter book.

In the year 1792–3, when Royalist & Jacobin had set all Britain by the ears, because I unguardedly, rather under the temptation of being witty than disaffected, had declared my sentiments in favor of Parliamentary Reform, in the manner of that time, I was accused to the Board of Excise of being a Republican; & was very near being turned adrift in the wide world on that account. — Mr Erskine of Mar, a *gentleman indeed,* wrote to my friend Glenriddell to know if I was really out of place on account of my Political principles; & if so, he proposed a Subscription among the friends of Liberty for me, which he offered to head, that I might be no pecuniary loser by my political Integrity. —This was the more generous, as I had not the honor of being known to Mr Erskine. I wrote him as follows. —

[Dumfries, 13th April, 1793]

SIR,

Degenerate as Human Nature is said to be, &, in many instances, worthless & unprincipled it certainly is; still there are bright examples to the contrary; examples, that even in the eyes of Superiour Beings must shed a lustre on the name of Man. — Such an example have I now before me, when you, Sir, came forward to patronise & befriend a distant, obscure stranger; merely because Poverty had made him helpless, & his British hardihood of mind had provoked the arbitrary wantonness of Power. — My much-esteemed friend, Mr Riddell of Glenriddell, has just read me a paragraph of a letter he had from you. — Accept, Sir, of the silent throb of gratitude; for words would but mock the emotions of my soul. —*

You have been misinformed, as to my final dismission from the Excise: I still am in the service. — Indeed, but for the exertions of a gentleman who must be known to you, Mr Graham of Fintry, a gentleman who has ever been my warm & generous friend, I had, without so much as a hearing, or the smallest previous intimation,

---

* A few days after Burns' death, Alexander Cunningham approached Mr. Erskine for a subscription to the fund being raised in behalf of Jean and the children. He wrote Syme, "When I waited on Mr Erskine of Marr you will be surprised to hear he seem'd luck warm." (Author's transcript, see P.S. for p. 365.)

been turned adrift, with my helpless family, to all the horrors of Want. — Had I had any other resource, probably I might have saved them the trouble of a dismissal; but the little money I gained by my Publication, is almost every guinea embarked, to save from ruin an only brother; who, though one of the worthiest, is by no means one of the most fortunate of men. —

In my defence to their accusations, I said, that whatever might be my sentiments of Republics, ancient or modern, as to Britain, I abjured the idea. — That a Constitution which, in its original principles, experience had proved to be every way fitted for our happiness in society, it would be insanity to sacrifice to an untried visionary theory. — That, in consideration of my being situated in a department, however humble, immediately in the hands of the people in power, I had forborne taking any active part, either personally, or as an author, in the present business of Reform. — But that, where I must declare my sentiments, I would say that there existed a system of corruption between the Executive Power & the Representative part of the Legislature, which boded no good to our glorious Constitution; & which every patriotic Briton must wish to see amended. — Some such Sentiments as these I stated in a letter to my generous Patron, Mr Graham, which he laid before the Board at large, where it seems my last remark gave great offence; & one of our Supervisors general, a Mr Corbet, was instructed to enquire, on the spot, into my conduct, & to document me — "that *my* business was to *act,* not to think; & that whatever might be Men or Measures, it was for me to be silent & obedient." — Mr Corbet was likewise my steady friend; so between Mr Graham & him, I have been partly forgiven: only, I understand that all hopes of my getting officially forward are blasted.

But they were not blasted as we shall see. Burns' letters and songs reveal that although he did not change his sentiments, he was more careful after the inquiry. The incident closes on a lighter note. When William Nicol heard that Burns had got into trouble for speaking out of turn, he wrote in friendly reproof. Burns copied Nicol's letter into the Glenriddell letter book, with a prefatory note: "From my worthy friend Mr. Nicol of the High School, Edinr: alluding to some temeraire conduct of mine in the political opinions of that day. — "

Dear Christless Bobie,

What is become of thee? Has the Devil flown off with thee, as the glade [hawk] does with a bird? — If he should do so, there is little matter, if the reports concerning thy *imprudence* are true. — What concerns it thee whether the lousy Dumfriesian fiddlers play Cà Ira, or God save the king? Suppose you had an aversion to him, you could not, as a gentleman, wish God to use him worse than he has done. — The infliction of Ideocy is no sign of Friendship or Love;* & I am sure, damnation is a matter far beyond your wishes or ideas: — But of this kind are only the insidious suggestions of ill-minded persons; for your good sense will ever point out to you, as well as to me, a bright model of political conduct, who flourished in the victorious reign of Queen Anne viz. the vicar of Bray, who during the convulsions of Great Britain, which were without any former example, saw eight reigns, in perfect security; because he remembered that precept of the *sensible, shrewd, temporizing* Apostle — "we ought not to resist the Higher Powers — "

You will think I have gotten a pension from Government; but I assure you, no such thing has been offered me. — In this respect, my vanity prompts me to say, they have not been so *wise* as I would have wished them; for I think their Honors have employed as impotent Scribblers. —

Enough of Politics. — What is become of Mrs. Burns & the dear bairns? How is my Willie? Tell her, though I do not write often, my best wishes shall ever attend her & the family. — My wife, who is in a high devotional fit this evening, wishes that she & her children may be reckoned favorites of the Lord — and numbered with the Elect. — She indeed leaves your Honor & Me to shift for ourselves; as, as far as she can judge from the criteria laid down in Guthrie's trial of a saving interest, that both you & I are stamped with marks of Reprobation.

May all the curses from the beginning of Genesis to the end of Revelation, light, materially & effectually, on thy enemies; & may all the blessings of the Covenant be eminently exemplified in thy person, to the glory of a forgiving Deity!

Here, or elsewhere, I am always thine sincerely

Edinr 10th Febry — 93   Willm Nicol

* A reference to George III's temporary insanity.

Before copying his reply to Nicol in the letter book, Burns comments, "As my friend Nicol, though one of the worthiest, & positively the cleverest fellow I ever knew, yet no man, in his humours, having gone greater lengths in imprudence, unholiness, &c. than he; I wrote him as follows. [February 20, 1793]"

O thou, wisest among the Wise, meridian blaze of Prudence, full-moon of Discretion, & Chief of many Counsellors! — How infinitely is thy puddle-headed, rattle-headed, wrong-headed, round-headed slave indebted to thy supereminent goodness, that from the luminous path of thy own right-lined rectitude, thou lookest benignly down on an erring Wretch, of whom the zig-zag wanderings defy all the powers of Calculation, from the simple copulation of Units up to the hidden mystery of Fluxions! May one feeble ray of that light of wisdom which darts from thy sensorium, straight as the arrow of Heaven against the head of the Unrighteous, & bright as the meteor of inspiration descending on the holy & undefiled Priesthood — may it be my portion; so that I may be less unworthy of the face and favour of that father of Proverbs & master of Maxims, that antipode of Folly & magnet among the Sages, the wise & witty Willie Nicol! Amen! Amen! Yea, so be it!!! [And so on for another paragraph, finally concluding] May thy pity & thy prayer be exercised for, O thou lamp of Wisdom & mirror of Morality!

Thy devoted slave
RB

To Alexander Cunningham on the same day he sent the following dialogue:

Quere, What is Politics?
Answer, Politics is a science wherewith, by means of nefarious cunning, & hypocritical pretence, we govern civil Polities for the emolument of ourselves & our adherents. —
Quere, What is a Minister?
Answer, A Minister is an unprincipled fellow, who by the influence of hereditary, or acquired wealth; by superiour abilities; or by a lucky conjuncture of circumstances, obtains a principal place in the administration of the affairs of government. —

Q. What is a Patriot?
A. An individual exactly of the same description as a Minister, only
out of Place.

Two years later, in December, 1794, Burns was made Acting
Supervisor in Dumfries, and wrote to Mrs. Dunlop, "My Political
sins seem to be forgiven me." But in that same letter, his calling
the king and queen of France "a perjured Blockhead & an unprincipled Prostitute" so offended Mrs. Dunlop, apparently, that
she broke off the correspondence.

3. Ellisland and the Riddells

Ellisland farm lay along the west bank of the river Nith, surrounded by hills, the farmhouse on a high bank overlooking the
river. Six miles north of Dumfries and a half mile east of the road
to Kilmarnock, it was a beautiful spot, but remote, and after his
excitement of the past few years, lonely for Burns. In time he
collected and enjoyed a circle of acquaintance, but he had no
one to know him for what he was. Indeed, he had enjoyed little
enough of that recognition in Edinburgh. At Ellisland, as before
and later, galling ambiguities plagued him. He was fond of Jean
and she devoted to him. But she played only a limited part in
his life. As he wrote to Mrs. Dunlop shortly after his marriage,
"I can easily *fancy* a more agreable companion for my journey
of Life, but upon my honor, I have never *seen* the individual
Instance!" (He had looked for a more cultivated wife without
success.) "You are right," he continued, "that a Bachelor state
would have ensured me more friends; but, from a cause you will
easily guess, conscious Peace in the enjoyment of my own mind,
and unmistrusting Confidence in approaching my God, would
seldom have been of the number." He loved his children dearly,
but his family was an oppressive responsibility which limited his
utterance and burdened him, body and spirit. The struggle to
get ahead was distasteful to him, not the less because he recog-

nized that he was accepting burdens which he himself had created. He wrote his best vernacular poem at Ellisland, and many fine songs, but at the same time he was searching, unsuccessfully, for other modes. He achieved there a measure of stability and security, yet it was a time of anticlimax, restraint, and frustration.

He was both a farmer and Exciseman, yet neither the one nor the other, nor a comfortable combination of the two. He was famous for a brilliant success, which had brought him little satisfaction. He had no heart for life's "warfare," and he was often melancholy and ill, yet the immediate impression of anyone who reads his letters and notes his activities is one of buoyancy and vigor. Burns may have been at ease with his conscience at Ellisland, but his life was not in a style "suitable to his feelings," and he was no more at ease with himself than he had been at Lochlea or Mossgiel, even if for somewhat different reasons. His was not an uncommon human condition, but recognition of it is a help to understanding what he said and did.

The greatest irony of all was his position. Success had opened the way for him to enter homes of the gentry and aristocracy, but always as a tame lion. He often enjoyed it, and yet resented his reception, for the class line never disappeared between him and such people, although a few of them made him comfortable. He was usually on display, and it is too bad that so much is recorded of Burns in such circumstances, and so little when he was among cronies, or at home, or going about his business. He seldom figured among his social superiors as more than a celebrity who, although fascinating, was uncouth and awkward, and these relationships often ended in disdain or distress. With his own ilk, and among tradespeople and certain professional people, he found much good company with whom he felt comfortable; and, just as he always had, he continued to enjoy companions of "low ranks, but men of talent & humour." Never in his life, however, at Ellisland or elsewhere, except for Nicol and Smellie, perhaps, did he meet anyone of near his own calibre.

In his first year at Ellisland, Burns speaks of working with his laborers and of being tired, but his life there was certainly not the grind he had known at Lochlea or Mossgiel. After October, 1789, he devoted his efforts largely to the Excise, which was not heavy work, however tedious and time-consuming and often wearisome it may have been. One result of this change was a reduction in Burns' letter writing. Prolonged ill-health at the end of 1789, and during 1790, must have contributed to the reduction, also. But an examination of the 239 surviving and published letters of the period June, 1788–November, 1791, reveals great vigor of mind and wide interests, and the list of his correspondents is extensive and varied. He wrote most often, and with great freedom, to Mrs. Dunlop — about public events, religion, his family, his farm, his poetry, his opinions, and his general experience. She replied with many more letters than he sent her, full of affectionate concern and interest.

Correspondence with Crochallans* and similar cronies in Edinburgh was heavy, but that with "stately patricians" was light, although there is a sprinkling of letters to aristocracy and gentry. A few letters went to old Ayrshire friends like Sillar and Richard Brown, many to his brothers Gilbert and William, and one to his cousin James Burness. Dr. Moore continued to write and receive letters, and a series passed between Burns and the Grahams of Fintry. In August, 1789, by request, Burns also supplied Dr. Moore's protégée and amanuensis, Helen Maria Williams, with an elaborate critique of her poem, *The Slave Trade*, in which he found both sense and grammar wanting on occasion. Of one passage he remarks, "Either my apprehension is dull, or there is something a little confused in the apostrophe to Mr Pit. — . . . Try it in prose." Later he comments, "If you insert the word, Like, where I have placed As, you must alter Darts, to,

---

* "Many letters of Burns to Mr Smellie which remained, being totally unfit for publication, and several of them containing severe reflections on many respectable people still in life, have been burnt." (Robert Kerr, *Memoirs of the Life Writings and Correspondence of William Smellie*, 1811. II, 350.)

Darting, and Heeds, to Heeding, in order to make it grammar."
Touching homage to John Murdoch! One engaging note went to
Bruce Campbell, of Milrig, with a ballad for James Boswell,
Burns' old Mauchline neighbor, in hopes that proved vain of an
introduction; Boswell docketed the letter, "13 Novr 1788 Mr.
Robert Burns the Poet expressing very high sentiments of me."
Eight of his letters are either public or addressed to editors, and
his correspondence reveals an alert and informed interest in
public affairs.

A selection from the correspondence of these relatively quiet
years furnishes a lively record of Burns' interests, his tastes, his
good sense, his warm family feeling, his wit, the rich personality
which fascinated those who knew him, and his mode of expression. Although there are few records of Burns' electric conversation, these letters to his intimates provide a happy indication
of what it must have been like.

1. From a letter to Robert Ainslie, June 30, 1788:

I have just now been interrupted by one of my new Neighbours,
who has made himself absolutely contemptible in my eyes by his silly,
garrulous pruriency. — I know it has been a fault of my own too; but
from this moment I abjure it as I would the service of Hell!

2. From a letter to William Stewart, factor on the Closeburn
Estates north of Ellisland, with a bawdy song, July 9, 1788:

I enclose you the Plenipo. — You will see another, The Bower of bliss;
'tis the work of a Revd Doctor of the Church of Scotland — Would
to Heaven a few more of them would turn their fiery Zeal *that way!*
There, they might *spend* their Holy fury, and shew the *tree* by its
fruits! ! !

3. From a letter to Mrs. Dunlop, describing a dinner with his
landlord, Patrick Miller, August 16, 1788:

I was yesterday at Mr Miller's to dinner; the first time since I have been his Tenant. — My reception was quite to my mind: from the lady of the house, quite flattering. — I believe in my conscience that she respects me more on account of my marrying a woman in circumstances somewhat similar to her own, when she commenced Mrs Millar. — See what it is to be rich! I was going to add, & to be great; but to be rich is to be great. — She sometimes hits on a couplet or two impromptu. — She repeated one or two to the admiration of all present. — My suffrage as a professional man, was expected: I for once went, agonizing, over the belly of my conscience — Pardon me, ye, my adored Household gods, Independence of Spirit & Integrity of Soul! In the course of conversation, Johnson's musical Museum, A Collection of Scots Songs with the music, was talked of. — We got a song on the Harpsichord, beginning —

"Raving winds around her blowing" —

The Air was much admired: the Lady of the house ask'd me whose were the words — "Mine, Madam — they are my very best verses!" sacré Dieu! she took not the smallest notice of them! — The old Scots Proverb says well — "King's caff [chaff] is better than ither folks corn." — I was going to make a New Testament quotation about "casting Pearls," but that would be too virulent. — The Lady is actually a woman of sense & taste: a proof, if the subject needed, that these two said qualities, so useful & ornamental to Human Nature, are by no means inseparably of the family of Gules, Purpure, Argent, Or, &c. —

4. A letter to Jean, September 12, 1788:

MY DEAR LOVE,

I received your kind letter with a pleasure which no letter but one from you could have given me. — I dreamed of you the whole night last; but alas! I fear it will be three weeks yet, ere I can hope for the happiness of seeing you. — My harvest is going on. — I have some to cut down still, but I put in two stacks today, so I am as tired as a dog. —

You might get one of Gilbert's sweet milk cheeses [words missing] & send it to [MS torn]

On second thoughts, I believe you had best get the half of Gilbert's web of Table-linen, and make it up; tho' I think it damnable dear, but it is no out-laid money to us you know. — I have just now consulted my old Landlady about table-linen, & she thinks I may have the best for two shillings per yard; so after all, let it alone untill I return; and some day soon I will be in Dumfries, and will ask the prices there. — I expect your new gowns will be very forward, or ready to make, against I be home to get the Baiveridge [salute]. — I have written my long-thought-on letter to Mr Graham, the Commissioner of Excise; & have sent him a sheetful of Poetry besides. — Now I talk of Poetry, I had a fine Strathspey among my hands to make verses to, for Johnson's Collection which I [remainder of MS wanting]

5. From a letter to Mrs. Dunlop at Moreham Mains (her son's farm), November 13, 1788, speaking of a recent visit to Dunlop House:

I had the very great pleasure of dining at Dunlop yesterday. — Men are said to flatter women because they are weak; if it is so, Poets must be weaker still; for Misses Rachel & Keith [Mrs. Dunlop's daughters], and Miss Georgina Mckay, with their flattering attentions & artful compliments, absolutely turned my head. — I own they did not lard me over as a Poet does his Patron or still more his Patroness, nor did they sugar me up as a Cameronian Preacher does J-s-s C-st; but they so intoxicated me with their sly insinuations & delicate innuendos of Compliment that if it had not been for a lucky recollection how much additional weight & lustre your good opinion & friendship must give me in that circle, I had certainly looked on myself as a person of no small consequence.

6. From a letter to Dr. Blacklock, November 15, 1788:

A wife's head is immaterial, compared with her heart — & — Virtue's (as for Wisdom, what Poet pretends to it) — "ways are ways of pleasantness, & all her paths are peace."

7. From a letter to Mrs. Dunlop, December 7, 1788, commenting on George III, recently declared insane:

As for G. R. whom you commiserate so much in your Moreham mains epistle (you see I have read both sheets, notwithstanding your wicked

LIKENESSES OF BURNS

Robert Burns, 1787, Nasmyth. Painted for Burns' Edinburgh Edition. *Courtesy Scottish National Portrait Gallery.*

Robert Burns, 1787, Beugo, after Nasmyth, and from sittings by Burns. Probably the best likeness. Frontispiece to Edinburgh Edition.

Robert Burns drawn 1796/7. Skirving, after Nasmyth, and
not from life, but said by Sir Walter Scott to be "the only
good portrait of Burns." *Courtesy Scottish National
Portrait Gallery.*

Robert Burns, 1787 (?), Nasmyth.
Courtesy Scottish National Portrait Gallery.

Robert Burns, 1787, Miers.

Robert Burns. Painted 1828, presumably from Nasmyth drawing.
Courtesy Scottish National Portrait Gallery.

MEMBERS OF THE BURNS FAMILY

Gilbert Burns,
brother of Robert Burns.

Agnes Broun,
mother of Robert Burns.

Jean Armour Burns, 1821.
Courtesy Scottish National Portrait Gallery.

Robert Burns,
eldest son of the poet.

Elizabeth Hyslop Burns,
daughter of Robert Burns
by Anne Park.

Colonel William Nicol Burns,
son of Robert Burns.

Lieutenant Colonel
James Glencairn Burns,
son of Robert Burns.

FRIENDS OF BURNS
AND MEMORABILIA

Mrs. Frances Anna Dunlop.

Lord Glencairn.

A Learned Pig. From the John
Mulholland Magic Collection, The
Walter Hampden Memorial Library
at the Players, New York. *Courtesy
Mr. Mulholland and the Library.*

Margaret Chalmers.

William Smellie.

Agnes M'Lehose ("Clarinda").

Glasses given Clarinda by Burns in parting.

Maria Riddell (Mrs. Walter Riddell), Sir Thomas Lawrence.
Courtesy the present owner, H. J. R. Bankes, Esq.

Robert Riddell
of Glenriddell.

Hermitage at Glenriddell,
near Ellisland.

Francis Grose.

John Syme.

Alexander Cunningham.

Jessie Lewars.

Dr. James Maxwell.

BUILDINGS AND PLACES
ASSOCIATED WITH BURNS

Alloway Kirk, 1805.

Burns' Birthplace, Alloway, 1805.

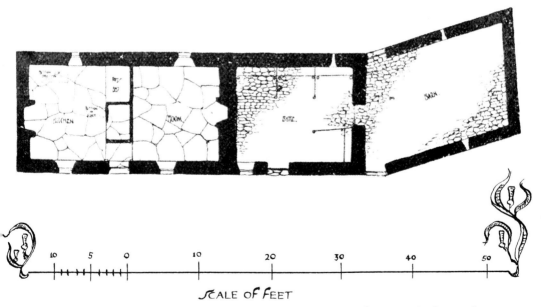

ƧCALE OF FEET

Drawings from James M'Bain, *Burns' Cottage*, 1904. The ground plan and scale show the size and William Burnes' arrangement of the but (outer room or kitchen), ben (inner room or parlor), byre (cowshed), and barn traditional in the Ayrshire farmstead.

Three farmsteads, with different arrangements
of the but, ben, barn, and byre.

Mt. Oliphant

Lochlea.

Mossgiel.

Ellisland.

Burns' last residence (house at left).

surmise) I am not sure whether he is not a gainer, by how much a Madman is a more respectable character than a Fool.

8. From a letter to Mrs. Dunlop, "New-year-day Morning, 1789":

This Day; the first Sunday of May; a breezy, blue-skied noon some time about the beginning, & a hoary morning & calm sunny day about the end, of Autumn; these, time out of mind, have been with me a kind of Holidays. — Not like the Sacramental, Executioner-face of a Kilmarnock Communion; but to laugh or cry, be chearful or pensive, moral or devout, according to the mood & tense of the Season & Myself.

9. From a letter to Robert Ainslie, January 6, 1789, congratulating him on his having become a Writer to the Signet:

I grant you enter the lists of life, to struggle for bread, business, notice, and distinction, in common with hundreds. — But who are they? Men like yourself, and of that aggregate body, your compeers, seven-tenths of them come short of your advantages natural and accidental; while two of those that remain, either neglect their parts, as flowers in a desert, or misspend their strength, like a bull goring a bramble bush.

10. A letter to his cousin, James Burness, in Montrose, February 9, 1789:

My dear Sir,
    Why I did not write to you long ago is what, even on the rack I could not answer. — If you can in your mind form an idea of indolence, dissipation, hurry, cares, change of country, entering on untried scenes of life — all combined; you will save me the trouble of a blushing apology. — It could not be want of regard for a man for whom I had a high esteem before I knew him — an esteem which has much increased since I did know him; and this caveat entered, I shall plead guilty to any other indictment with which you shall please to charge me. —
    After I parted from you, for many months, my life was one continued scene of dissipation. — Here, at last, I am become stationary, and

have taken a farm and — a wife. The farm lies beautifully situated on the Nith, a large river that runs by Dumfries, & falls into the Solway Firth. — I have gotten a lease on my farm as long as I pleased; but how it may turn out is just a guess, and it is yet to improve and inclose, &c.; however I have good hopes of my bargain on the whole. —

My Wife is, my Jean, with whose story you are partly acquainted. — I found I had a much-loved fellow-creature's happiness or misery among my hands, and I durst not trifle with so sacred a deposite. — Indeed I have not any reason to repent the step I have taken, as I have attached myself to a very good wife, & have shaken myself loose of a very bad failing. —

I have found my book, a very profitable business; and with the profits of it have begun life pretty decently. — Should Fortune not favour me in farming, as I have no great faith in her fickle Ladyship, I have provided myself in another resource, which, however some folks may affect to despise it, is still a comfortable shift in the day of misfortune. — In the heyday of my fame, a gentleman whose name at least I dare say you know, as his estate lies somewhere near Dundee, Mr Graham of Fintry, one of the Commissioners of Excise, offered me the commission of an Excise-Officer. — I thought it prudent to accept of the offer, and accordingly I took my Instructions, and have my Commission by me. — Whether I may ever do duty, or be a penny the better for it, is what I do not know; but I have this comfortable assurance that, come whatever ill fate will, I can on my simple petition to the Excise board, get into employ. —

We have lost poor uncle Robert this winter. — He had long been weak, and with very little alteration in him, he expired Janry 3d. — His Son William, has been with me this winter, & goes in May to bind himself to be a Mason with my fatherinlaw who is a pretty considerable Architect in Ayrshire. — His other Son, the eldest, John, comes to me, I expect in Summer. — They are both remarkable stout young fellows, & promise to do well. — His only daughter, Fanny, has been with me ever since her father's death and I purpose keeping her in my family till she be quite woman grown, & be fit for better service. — She is one of the cleverest girls, and has one of the most amiable dispositions, that I have ever seen. —

All friends in this country and Ayrshire are well. — Remember me to all friends in the North. — My wife joins in Compliments to your bedfellow & family. — I would write your brother-in-law, but have lost his Address. — For goodness sake don't take example by me, but write me soon. — I am ever, My dear Cousin,

yours most sincerely —
ROBT BURNS

11. From a letter to Mrs. Dunlop, April 21, 1789:

Two mornings ago as I was, at a very early hour, sowing in the fields, I heard a shot, & presently a poor little hare limped by me, apparently very much hurt. — You will easily guess, this set my humanity in tears and my indignation in arms. — The following was the result, which please read to the young ladies — I believe you may include the Major [her son], too; as whatever I have said of shooting hares, I have not spoken one irreverend word against coursing them.

He adds the first copy of *On seeing a fellow wound a hare with a shot.*

12. From a letter to the Rev. Patrick Carfrae, April 27, 1789, giving advice about a proposed edition of poems by a farmer-poet known to Mrs. Dunlop, one James Mylne:

I have, Sir, some experience of publishing; and the way in which I would proceed with Mr Mylne's Poems is this. — I would publish in two or three English & Scots Public Papers any one of his English Poems which should, by private judges, be thought the most excellent, and mention it, at the same time, as one of the many poetical productions which a Lothian Farmer of respectable character left behind him at his death. — That his friends had it in idea to publish soon, by subscription, a Collection of his Poems, for the sake of his numerous family (I think Mrs Dunlop informed me that he had a numerous family) — not in pity to that Family, but in justice to what his friends think the Poetic Merits of the deceased; and to secure in the most effectual manner, to those tender connections whose right it is, the pecuniary reward of those merits. — After thus advertising the Public of the design, I would proceed to disperse Subscription bills. — Suppose the book to be 200, a few odd pages, and that there are printed, 600 copies. — This, on elegant paper, & stitched, or in boards, will be done for less than forty pounds. — Though not above 300 Subscribers are got, that at 4sh. or even at 3sh. per Copy price to Subscribers, will more than pay costs; and thus, without risking anything, and with a probability of considerable profits as the work should succeed in the world, I would bring Mr Mylne's poetic Merits to that Bar which is alone competent to decide on them, the Voice of the public. —

From what I have seen of his works, & from what an abler Judge, my honored friend Mrs Dunlop, has often mentioned to me of those works of his which I have not seen, I have the Most sanguine hopes that Mr Mylne's Poems will be a very respectable & much esteemed addition to that species of Polite Literature.

13. From a letter to his younger brother William, then in New-castle-on-Tyne, May 5, 1789:

Your falling in love is indeed a phenomenon. To a fellow of your turn it cannot be hurtful. I am, you know, a veteran in these campaigns, so let me advise you always to pay your particular assiduities and try for intimacy as soon as you feel the first symptoms of the passion; this is not only best, as making the most of the little entertainment which the sportabilities of distant addresses always gives, but is the best preservative for one's peace. I need not caution you against guilty amours — they are bad everywhere, but in England they are the very devil.

14. A letter to James Johnson, of the *Scots Musical Museum*, June 19, 1789:

My dear friend,

What are you doing, and what is the reason that you have sent me no proof sheet to correct? Though I have been rather remiss in writing you, as I have been hurried, puzzled, plagued & confounded with some disagreable matters, yet believe me, it is not owing to the smallest neglect or forget of you, my good Sir, or your patriotic work. — Mr Clarke & I have frequent meetings & consultations on your work. — I have given him three or four songs which he is preparing for you. — One is, the Caledonian Hunt, as it seems the verses I sent you don't suit it; another is, The Braes o' Ballochmyle, to which I have likewise given him new words, & a third is, The poor Thresher. — Let me hear from you first post, and forgive this seeming neglect in a careless fellow of an indolent Poet, who is as lazy as the Packman that laid down his pack until he would f——t.

My best complnts to your father & Mr Barclay.

I am ever, dear Sir, yours sincerely,

ROBT BURNS

15. From a letter to Mrs. Dunlop, June 22, 1789:

I have just heard Mr Kirkpatrick preach a sermon. He is a man famous for his benevolence, and I revere him; but from such ideas of my Creator, good Lord, deliver me! Religion, my honored friend, is surely a simple business, as it equally concerns the ignorant and the learned, the poor and the rich. That there is an incomprehensible Great Being, to whom I owe my existence; and that He must be intimately acquainted with the operations and progress of the internal machinery, and consequent outward deportment, of this creature which He has made; these are, I think, self-evident propositions. That there is a real and eternal distinction between virtue and vice, and, consequently, that I am an accountable creature; that from the seeming nature of the human mind, as well as from the evident imperfection, nay, positive injustice, in the administration of affairs both in the natural and moral worlds, there must be a retributive scene of existence beyond the grave; must, I think, be allowed by every one who will give himself a moment's reflection. I will go further, and affirm, that from the sublimity, excellence, and purity of His doctrine and precepts, unparalleled by all the aggregated wisdom and learning of many preceding ages, though, *to appearance* He Himself was the obscurest and most illiterate of our species — therefore Jesus Christ was from God. . . .

Whatever mitigates the woes, or increases the happiness, of others, this is my criterion of goodness; and whatever injures society at large, or any individual in it, this is my measure of iniquity.

16. From a letter to Mrs. Dunlop, describing Captain Francis Grose, July 17, 1789:

Captn Grose, the well-known Author of the Antiquities of England & Wales, has been through Annandale, Nithsdale & Galloway, in the view of commencing another Publication, The Antiquities of Scot-

land. — As he has made his head-quarters with Captn Riddel, my
nearest neighbour, for these two months, I am intimately acquainted
with him; & I have never seen a man of more original observation,
anecdote & remark. — Thrown into the army from the Nursery, &
now that he is the father of a numerous family who are all settled in
respectable situations in life, he has mingled in all societies, & known
every body. — His delight is to steal thro' the country almost unknown, both as most favorable to his humour & his business. — I
have to the best of my recollection of the old buildings, &c. in the
County, given him an Itinerary thro' Ayr-shire. — I have directed
him among other places to Dunlop house, as an old building worthy
of a place in his collection. — It would have been presumption in
such a man as I, to offer an introductory letter between such folks
as Captn Grose & Major Dunlop, tho' for the honour of my native
county I could have wished that Captn Grose had been introduced
to the Dunlop family, & the Major would have been of much use to
him in directing him thro' the farther corner of Cunningham, a place
I little know, however if you discover a chearful-looking grig of an
old, fat fellow, the precise figure of Dr Slop, wheeling about your
avenue in his own carriage with a pencil & paper in his hand, you
may conclude, "Thou art the man!"

Perhaps after all I may pluck up as much impudent importance as
write to the Major by him. — He will go for Ayr-shire in four or five
days, but I have directed him thro' Carrick & Kyle first.

17. From a letter to Peter Hill, February 2, 1790, about an Edinburgh whore:

What are you doing, and how are you doing? Have you lately
seen any of my few friends? What is become of the Borough Reform,
or how is the fate of my poor Namesake Mademoiselle Burns,
decided? Which of their grave Lordships can lay his hand on his
heart and say that he has not taken advantage of such frailty; nay, if
we may judge by near six thousand years experience, can the World
do without such frailty? O man! but for thee, & thy selfish appetites
& dishonest artifices, that beauteous form, & that once innocent &
still ingenuous mind, might have shone conspicuous and lovely in the
faithful wife and the affectionate mother; and shall the unfortunate
sacrifice to thy pleasures have no claim on thy humanity? As for those
flinty-bosomed, puritannic Prosecutors of Female Frailty, & Persecu-

tors of Female Charms — I am quite sober — I am dispassionate —
to shew you that I am so I shall mend my Pen ere I proceed — It is
written, "Thou shalt not take the name of the Lord thy God in vain,"
so I shall neither say, G—— curse them! nor G—— blast them! nor
G——damn them! but may Woman curse them! May Woman blast
them! May Woman damn them! May her lovely hand inexorably shut
the Portal of Rapture to their most earnest Prayers & fondest essays
for entrance! And when many years and much port and great business
have delivered them over to Vulture Gouts and Aspen Palsies, *then*
may the dear bewitching Charmer in derision throw open the blissful
Gate to tantalize their impotent desires which like ghosts haunt their
bosoms when all their powers to give or receive enjoyment, are for
ever asleep in the sepulchre of their fathers!!!

The lady mentioned in this letter was a Miss Margaret Matthews who took "Burns" * as a *nom de guerre* because of its
celebrity on her arrival in Edinburgh. When she was proceeded
against for disorders in her "house," William Creech heard the
case as magistrate and gave her a stiff sentence. On appeal, Bailie
Creech's decision was overturned, to his intense annoyance, and
the newspapers made sport of him. One London paper announced, "Bailie Creech, of literary celebrity in Edinburgh, is
about to lead the beautiful and accomplished Miss Burns to the
hymeneal altar." When Creech threatened suit, the paper agreed
to a retraction, and printed the following: "In a former number
we noticed the intended marriage between Bailie Creech of Edinburgh, and the beautiful Miss Burns of the same place. We have
now the authority of that gentleman to say that the proposed
marriage is not to take place, matters having been otherwise
arranged to the mutual satisfaction of both parties and their respective friends."

* Throughout his life Burns enjoyed producing epigrams, epitaphs, and miscellaneous versified witticisms. One of the few to combine grace, wit, and enduring
point, was intended to be placed under the portrait of "Miss Burns."

> Cease, ye prudes, your envious railing!
> Lovely Burns had charms: confess!
> True it is she had ae failing:
> Had ae woman ever less?

18. A letter to William Nicol, February 9, 1790, in part about Nicol's mare, named "Peg Nicholson" after a mad washerwoman who had attempted to assassinate George III:

MY DEAR SIR,

That d—mned mare of yours is dead. I would freely have given her price to have saved her; she has vexed me beyond description. Indebted as I was to your goodness beyond what I can ever repay, I eagerly grasped at your offer to have the mare with me. That I might at least shew my readiness in wishing to be grateful, I took every care of her in my power. She was never crossed for riding above half a score of times by me or in my keeping. I drew her in the plough, one of three, for one poor week. I refused fifty-five shillings for her, which was the highest bode I could squeeze for her. I fed her up and had her in fine order for Dumfries fair; when four or five days before the fair, she was seized with an unaccountable disorder in the sinews, or somewhere in the bones of the neck; with a weakness or total want of power in her fillets; and, in short, the whole vertebrae of her spine seemed to be diseased and unhinged; and in eight and forty hours, in spite of the two best farriers in the country, she died and be d—mned to her! The farriers said that she had been quite strained in the fillets beyond cure before you had bought her; and that the poor devil, though she might keep a little flesh, had been jaded and quite worn out with fatigue and oppression. While she was with me, she was under my own eye, and I assure you, my much valued friend, everything was done for her that could be done; and the accident has vexed me to the heart. In fact, I could not pluck up spirits to write you on account of the unfortunate business.

There is little new in this country. Our theatrical company, of which you must have heard, leave us in a week. Their merit and character are indeed very great, both on the stage and in private life; not a worthless creature among them; and their encouragement has been accordingly. Their usual run is from eighteen to twenty-five pounds a night: seldom less than the one, and the house will hold no more than the other. There have been repeated instances of sending away six, and eight, and ten pounds a night for want of room. A new theatre is to be built by subscription; the first stone is to be laid on Friday first to come. Three hundred guineas have been raised by thirty subscribers, and thirty more might have been got if wanted.

The manager, Mr. Sutherland, was introduced to me by a friend from Ayr; and a worthier or cleverer fellow I have rarely met with. Some of our clergy have slipt in by stealth now and then; but they have got up a farce of their own. You must have heard how the Rev. Mr. Lawson of Kirkmahoe, seconded by the Rev. Mr. Kirkpatrick of Dunscore, and the rest of that faction, have accused in formal process, the unfortunate and Rev. Mr. Heron of Kirkgunzeon, that in ordaining Mr. Nelson to the cure of souls in Kirkbean he, the said Heron, feloniously and treasonably bound the said Nelson to the confession of faith, *so far as it was agreable to reason and the Word of God!*

Mrs. B. begs to be remembered most gratefully to you. Little Bobby and Frank are charmingly well and healthy. I am jaded to death with fatigue. For these two or three months, on an average, I have not ridden less than two hundred miles per week. I have done little in the poetic way. I have given Mr. Sutherland two Prologues; one of which was delivered last week. I have likewise strung four or five barbarous stanzas, to the tune of Chevy Chase, by way of Elegy on your poor unfortunate mare, beginning (the name she got here was Peg Nicholson):

> Peg Nicholson was a good bay mare
>   As ever trod on airn: *iron*
> But now she's floating down the Nith,
>   And past the mouth o' Cairn.

> Peg Nicholson was a good bay mare,
>   An' rode thro' thick an' thin;
> But now she's floating down the Nith
>   And wanting even the skin.

> Peg Nicholson was a good bay mare,
>   An' ance she bore a priest;
> But now she's floating down the Nith,
>   For Solway fish a feast.

> Peg Nicholson was a good bay mare,
>   An' the priest he rode her sair;
> An' much oppress'd an' bruis'd she was,
>   As priest-rid cattle are.

My best compliments to Mrs. Nicol, and little Neddy, and all the family. I hope Ned is a good scholar, and will come out to gather nuts and apples with me next harvest.

I am ever, my dearest Friend, yours,

ROBT BURNS

19. A letter to William Burns, February 10, 1790:

MY DEAR WILLIAM

I would have written you sooner but I have mislaid Mr Murdoch's letter, and cannot for my life lay my hand on it; so I cannot write him for want of a direction. — If I find it afterwards, I will write him & inclose it to you in London. — Now that you are setting out for that place, put on manly resolve, & determine to persevere; & in that case you will less or more be sure of success. — One or two things allow me to particularize to you. — London swarms with worthless wretches who prey on their fellow-creatures' thoughtlessness or inexperience. — Be cautious in forming connections with comrades and companions. — You can be pretty good company to yourself, & you cannot be too shy of letting anybody know you farther than to know you as a Sadler. — Another caution; I give you great credit for your sobriety with respect to that universal vice, Bad Women. — It is an impulse the hardest to be restrained, but if once a man accustoms himself to gratifications of that impulse, it is then nearly, or altogether impossible to restrain it. — Whoring is a most ruinous expensive species of dissipation; is spending a poor fellow's money with which he ought to clothe & support himself nothing? Whoring has ninety nine chances in a hundred to bring on a man the most nauseous & excrutiating diseases to which Human nature is liable; are disease & an impaired constitution trifling considerations? All this independant of the criminality of it. —

I have gotten the Excise Division in the middle of which I live. — Poor little Frank is this morning at the height in the Smallpox. — I got him inoculated, & I hope he is in a good way. —

Write me before you leave Newcastle & as soon as you reach London. — In a word, if ever you be, as perhaps you may be, in a strait for a little ready cash, you know my direction. — I shall not see you beat, while you fight like a Man.

Farewell! God bless you!

ROBT BURNS

20. From a letter to Mrs. Dunlop, April 10, 1790, in which Burns mentions his favorite novel, *The Man of Feeling:*

Still, with all my admiration of M'kenzie's writings, I do not know if they are the fittest reading for a young man who is about to set out, as the phrase is, to make his way into life. Do you not think, Madam, that among the few favored of Heaven in the structure of their minds (for such there certainly are) there may be a purity, a tenderness, a dignity, an elegance of soul, which are of no use, nay, in some degree, absolutely disqualifying, for the truly important business of making a man's way into life? If I am not much mistaken, my gallant young friend Anthony [Mrs. Dunlop's son] is very much under these disqualifications.

21. From a letter to Mrs. Dunlop, July 9, 1790, giving particulars of electioneering in Burns' neighborhood:

I have just got a summons to attend with my men-servants armed as well as we can, on Monday at one o'clock in the *morning* to escort Captn Miller from Dalswinton in to Dumfries to be a Candidate for our Boroughs which chuse their Member that day. — The Duke of Queensberry & the Nithsdale Gentlemen who are almost all friends to the Duke's Candidate, the said Captn [Patrick Miller's son], are to raise all Nithsdale on the same errand. — The Duke of Buccleugh's, Earl of Hopeton's people, in short, the Johnstons, Jardines, and all the Clans of Annandale, are to attend Sir James Johnston who is the other Candidate, on the same account. — This is no exaggeration. — On Thursday last, as chusing the Delegate for the boro' of Lochmaben, the Duke & Captn Miller's friends led a strong party, among others, upwards of two hundred Colliers from Sanquhar Coal-works & Miners from Wanlock-head; but when they appeared over a hill-top within half a mile of Lochmaben, they found such a superiour host of Annandale warriors drawn out to dispute the Day, that without striking a stroke, they turned their backs & fled with all the precipitation the horrors of blood & murther could inspire. — What will be the event, I know not. — I shall go to please my Landlord, & to see the Combustion; but instead of trusting to the strength of Man, I shall trust to the heels of my horse, which are among the best in Nithsdale.

In this election Burns, who disliked the Duke of Queensberry, supported Sir James Johnston, and wrote a series of election ballads in his behalf. *The Five Carlins*, ironically impartial, alone retains any interest.

22. A letter to Burns' old Tarbolton friend, schoolmaster John Wilson [Dr. Hornbook], September 11, 1790, in reply to a request for advice whether Wilson should try to improve his income by turning lawyer's clerk in Edinburgh:

I am truly sorry, my dear Sir, that you find yourself so uncomfortably situated in Tarbolton; the more so, as I fear you will find on trial that the remedy you propose, is worse than the disease. — The life of an Edinr Quill-driver at twopence a page, is a life I know so well — that I should be very sorry any friend of mine should ever try it. — To young lads, bred to the law, & meaning to push their way in that department & line of life, practicing as a copying Clerk is to them a necessary step; but to a gentleman who is unacquainted with the science of law, & who proposes to live merely by the drudgery of his quill, he has before him a life of many sorrows. — Pardon me, my dr Sir, this freedom: I wish only to keep you, as far as my knowledge of life can, from being misled by that seducing Slut, Fancy, under the mask of Hope. — The Excise is impracticable to you. — No man above thirty, or who has more than two children, is admissible. — However, you are the best judge of your present situation & future hopes; & as I wish to be of all the service to you that is in my scanty power, I inclose you a card to a friend of mine, the only one I have in Edinr, to whom I could with any hope of success make such a request. —

Allow me to mention one suggestion to you. — Your present appointment may be held by deputy, at least untill you go to Edinr & see what you have to expect there: let me beg of you for Mrs Wilson's sake, and your sweet little flock, not to quit the Present, poor as it is, untill you be pretty sure of your hold on the Future. —

I am afraid, too, that at this season, in vacation, you will find few of the Gentlemen of the law in town. — Had you not better defer your journey untill the Court sit down?

Mrs Burns joins me in best Complnts to Mrs Wilson. —

Farewell! & believe me to be, my dear Sir,

Yours sincerely

ROBT BURNS

Wilson took Burns' advice and gave up his Edinburgh scheme.

23. From a letter to the Rev. George Husband Baird, offering assistance to an edition of the poems of Michael Bruce, February 28, 1791:

Why did you, my dear Sir, write to me in such a hesitating style on the business of poor Bruce? Don't I know, & have I not felt, the many ills, the peculiar ills, that Poetic Flesh is heir to? — You shall have your choice of all the unpublished poems I have; & had your letter had my address, so as to have reached me in course of post (it but came to hand this morning) I should have directly put you out of suspense about it. — I suppose I need not premise, that I still reserve these my works so much in my power, as to publish them on my own account, if so the spirit move me, at any *after* period. — I only ask that some prefatory advertisement in the Book, as well as the Subscripn bills, may bear, that the Publication is solely for the behoof of Bruce's Mother: I would not leave Ignorance the least room to surmise, or Malice to insinuate, that I clubbed a share in the work from mercenary motives. . . .

I have taxed your friendship with the trouble of transmitting the enclosed letter to Dr Moore, . . . I leave it open for your perusal, I mean the printed sheet. — It is one of my latest productions [*Tam o' Shanter*]; & I dare say you may have it, if you will, to accompany Bruce's works.

The generous offer of *Tam o' Shanter* was not accepted, "in consequence of the opposition of Dr [Hugh] Blair and Dr Moore, who argued that from the moral tendency of Bruce's poetry, the insertion of Burns's . . . would be as gross a violation of propriety as the exhibition of a farce after a tragedy."

24. From the letter to Dr. John Moore enclosed in the above, also dated February 28, 1791:

What a rocky-hearted, perfidious Succubus was that Queen Elizabeth! — Judas Iscariot was a sad dog to be sure, but still his demerits shrink to insignificance, compared with the doings of the infernal Bess Tudor. — Judas did not know, at least was by no means sure, what or who that Master was; his turpitude was simply, betraying a worthy man who had ever been a good Master to him: a degree of turpitude which has even been outdone by many of his kind since. — Iscariot, poor wretch, was a man of nothing at all per Annum, & by consequence thirty pieces of silver was a very serious temptation to *him,* but to give but one instance, the Duke of Queensberry, the other day, just played the same trick on *his* kind Master, tho' His Grace is a man of thirty thousand a year, & come to that imbecille period of life when no temptation but Avarice can be supposed to affect him.

25. A letter to Alexander Findlater, Burns' Excise Supervisor, "Sunday even: [June, 1791]," about a lapse in the performance of Excise duties. The "Lorimer" of the letter was Burns' neighbor and friend, and the father of a girl he wrote songs about.

DEAR SIR,

I am both much surprised & vexed at that accident of Lorimer's Stock. — The last survey I made prior to Mr Lorimer's going to Edinr I was very particular in my inspection & the quantity was certainly in his possession as I stated it. — The surveys I have made during his absence might as well have been marked "key absent" as I never found any body but the lady, who I know is not mistress of the keys, &c. to know anything of it, and one of the times, it would have rejoiced all Hell to have seen her so drunk. I have not surveyed there since his return. — I know the gentleman's ways are, like the grace of G——, past all comprehension; but I shall give the house a severe scrutiny tomorrow morning, & send you in the naked facts. —

I know, Sir, & regret deeply that this business glances with a malign aspect on my character as an Officer; but as I am really innocent in the affair, & as the gentleman is known to be an illicit Dealer, & particularly as this is the *single* instance of the least shadow of carelessness or impropriety in my conduct as an Officer, I shall be peculiarly unfortunate if my character shall fall a sacrifice to the dark maneouvres of a Smuggler. —

I am, Sir, your oblidged & obedient humble servt
ROBT BURNS

26. A letter to David Newall, proprietor of the Isle, undated but probably in the spring of 1790:

DR SIR,

Inclosed is a state of the account between you and me and James Halliday respecting the drain. I have stated it at 2od. per rood, as in fact, even at that, they have not the wages they ought to have had, and I cannot for the soul of me see a poor devil a loser at my hand.

Humanity, I hope, as well as Charity, will cover a multitude of sins, a mantle, of which — between you and me — I have some little need.

I am, Sir, yours,
ROBT BURNS

During his last months at Ellisland, 1791, Burns' life was "chequered, joy & sorrow," by the following events:

1. He was deeply distressed by Lord Glencairn's death on January 30, which moved him to write his *Lament for James Earl of Glencairn*.

2. He had to pay a £20 bill, which he had endorsed for a friend, evidence that his credit was good if his judgment was not, and that he had funds. But the payment drained them. He wrote to David Sillar, who had asked for a loan, "It is not in my power to give you any assistance. — I am just five shillings rich at present; tho' I was considerably richer three days ago, when I was obliged to pay twenty pounds for a man who took me in, to save a rotten credit. — I heedlessly gave him my name on the back of a bill where-in I had no concern, & he — gave me the bill to pay." Burns seems not to have suffered unduly, for on June 16 he wrote Thomas Boyd, builder of his Ellisland house,

Dear Sir,

As it is high time that the account between you & me were settled, if you will take a bill of Mr Alexr Crombie's to me for twenty pounds in part, I will settle with you immediately; at least, against Wedensday se'nnight, as I am to be out of the country for a week. — Mr Crombie cannot take it amiss that I endeavour to get myself clear of his bill in this manner, as you owe him and I owe you.

3. The absence spoken of to Boyd was a visit to Kilmarnock, June 19–22, for his brother Gilbert's wedding to Jean Breckenridge.

4. Burns put aside a suggestion by Alexander Cunningham that he address a poem to the Royal Company of Archers in Edinburgh, the King's bodyguard for Scotland, who apparently were considering their fellow member Cunningham's suggestion of admitting Burns. He could not, he said, compose merely from the wish. But the select and aristocratic group admitted Burns to membership just the same, on April 10, 1792.

5. He was invited to be present at the Earl of Buchan's estate when the Earl planned to crown a bust of James Thomson, poet of *The Seasons*, with a wreath. Burns declined the invitation in a letter which began with polite irony, "Language sinks under the ardor of my feelings, when I would thank your Lordship for the honour, the very great honour, you have done me," but he sent an innocuous *Address to the Shade of Thomson*. When he learned later that the bust had been broken in a drunken frolic before the coronation, forcing the Earl to crown, instead, a volume of Thomson's poems, Burns wrote *On Some Commemorations of Thomson*, not one of his distinguished poems, but not innocuous, either.

> Dost thou not rise, indignant Shade,
>   And smile wi' spurning scorn,
> When they wha wad hae starved thy life
>   Thy senseless turf adorn?

They wha about thee mak sic fuss
  Now thou art but a name,
Wad seen thee damn'd ere they had spar'd
  Ac plack to fill thy wame.   *farthing belly*

Helpless, alane, thou clamb the brae
  Wi' meikle honest toil,
And claucht th'unfading garland there,   *clutched*
  Thy sair-won, rightful spoil.

And wear it there! and call aloud
  This axiom undoubted: —
Would thou hae Nobles' patronage?
  First learn to live without it!

"To whom hae much, more shall be given"
  Is every great man's faith;
But he, the helpless, needful wretch,
  Shall lose the mite he hath.

This was the poem Burns sent to Captain Johnston of the *Gazetteer,* cited later as evidence of his disaffection to government.

6. Finally, Burns ignored Creech's suggestion that he bring out a new edition.

At Ellisland farm, Burns' neighbor to the north was Captain Robert Riddell of Glenriddell (1755–1794), a good and amiable man recently retired at twenty-eight from the Prince of Wales Light Dragoons, and married (1784) to a Miss Elizabeth Kennedy. He enjoyed "an easy fortune," and William Smellie reported himself "sometimes *threatened* and *frightened*" with the "gigantic" Riddell's "immense *fist* and stentorian *voice*." The Captain lived as a country gentleman on his estate of Friars' Carse, pursuing an interest in folksong and local antiquities, corresponding with leading antiquaries, entertaining antiquaries and artists, and greatly enjoying convivial society. He was also an amateur musician, a church elder, and a political liberal. Although by his own account "no Draughtsman," he accompanied friends on trips to visit and sketch antiquities, and in May, 1794, after his death, there was published his *Collection of Scotch, Galwegian, and Border Tunes,* 37 pages, 7 shillings.* The University of Edinburgh in January, 1794, gave him an LL.D. in recognition of his "uncommon knowledge."

Although Riddell was widely esteemed as a man, contemporaries did not value his achievements highly. The Stenhouse edition of Johnson's *Scots Musical Museum* carries this note on Riddell's collection of tunes: "Robert Riddell of Glenriddell, Esq., was much respected, and attained some celebrity as an antiquarian, although his researches were not very profound, and some of his theories fanciful. [Mr. Charles Kirkpatrick Sharpe says,] 'Mr Riddell was an excellent man, but no musician; as I have been assured by a competent judge, whose partiality to the author would have made him very sensible of any merit his compositions might possess. . . .' Mr Riddell was member of several learned societies, and communicated various papers which were inserted in their Transactions." These latter Sir Walter Scott describes as "truly the most extravagant compositions that ever a poor Man abandoned by providence to the imaginations of his own heart had the misfortune to devise."

In commenting on Allan Cunningham's description of Robert Riddell as a "distinguished antiquarian," and much other praise, Riddell's schoolfellow, Alexander Young, of Harburn, W. S., remarks,

Robert Riddell of Glenriddell, so often mentioned in this Work with much applause, was my Schoolfellow, and in the same class with me at Dr. Chapman's in Dumfries.

In that Class also were Dr. William Charles Wills of London, Dr. James Currie of Liverpool, Dr. George Bell of Manchester, Wm. Cunningham of Enterkin &c.; and I am sure it would have astonished

* The volume was published by James Johnson, of the *Museum,* who told Burns, "I have not sold 10 copies." (Ch-W IV, 89.)

all these as much as it does me, to read such praises of the most
heavy, dull youth, the least of a Scholar, and the most incorrigible
dolt ["blockhead" deleted] in our class. He did not come much forward into the World; after we quitted school, ["and I know no ill of
him" deleted] I used to meet him at the Assizes and Dumfries Elec-
tions, when we always shook hands cordially, in remembrance of old
Class fellowship; but that he should have been commemorated, as is
done in these volumes, seems to me most extraordinary. I think the
secret must have lain in his marrying an excellent and amiable lady
of the name of Kennedy, whom all his old School fellows admired,
as much as they under-valued him.

Burns responded warmly to offers of friendship, and when
Riddell offered his, the two men grew quickly to be on excellent
terms. Burns, for example, felt free to ask if he might borrow a
laborer from Riddell to help in his first harvest. Riddell gave his
new neighbor a key to a "Hermitage" which he had had built
on his grounds, as a suitable adornment of former abbey lands.
He apparently had a romantic hope that the Bard would med-
itate in quiet there and produce poetry. Burns dutifully responded in the first month, inscribing some oracular couplets on
a Hermitage window pane, but there is no record of his frequenting the place.

Verses in Friars Carse Hermitage

June 1788

Thou whom chance may hither lead,
Be thou clad in russet weed,
Be thou deckt in silken stole,
Grave these maxims on thy soul: —

Life is but a day at most,
Sprung from night in darkness lost;
Hope not sunshine every hour,
Fear not clouds will always lour.

Happiness is but a name,
Make content and ease thy aim.
Ambition is a meteor-gleam;
Fame a restless airy dream;
Pleasures, insects on the wing
Round Peace, th' tend'rest flow'r of spring;
Those that sip the dew alone —
Make the butterflies thy own;
Those that would the bloom devour —
Crush the locusts, save the flower.
For the future be prepar'd:
Guard wherever thou can'st guard;
But, thy utmost duly done,
Welcome what thou can'st not shun.
Follies past give thou to air —
Make their consequence thy care.
Keep the name of Man in mind,
And dishonour not thy kind.
Reverence with lowly heart
Him, whose wondrous work thou art;
Keep His Goodness still in view —
Thy trust, and thy example too.

Stranger, go! Heaven be thy guide!
Quod the Beadsman on Nidside.

Of a 1792 quarto issue of this poem, apparently anonymous, with a vignette by Robert Riddell's friend Francis Grose, Stenhouse remarks, "Mr [Charles Kirkpatrick] Sharpe . . . says . . . , 'Sir Walter Scott told me that this production puzzled him — it was much too good for the one [Riddell?] and much to bad for the other [Grose?].'"

Burns rejoiced to find that Riddell was a folk-song enthusiast, and their shared interest seems to have stimulated both men, one evidence of it being an interleaved set of the first four volumes of the *Museum* with notes by Burns and Riddell — 152 by Burns (to which Riddell added ten more comments); nineteen by Riddell alone; with seventeen more by an unknown hand. (Seventeen leaves presumably with additional comments, have been excised and are now missing.) Burns ordered another interleaved *Museum* for himself, but nothing is now known of it.

Out of compliment to his friendly neighbor, Burns prepared for him a manuscript volume of some of his poems, and another of some of his letters — the letters in his own hand, but some of the poems in that of an amanuensis. The poetry volume includes also a copy in another hand of the autobiographical letter to Dr. Moore, and both volumes contain comments by Burns. In the poetry volume he wrote the following compliment to the Riddells:

As this Collection almost wholly consists of pieces local or un-finished, fragments the effusion of a poetical moment & bagatelles strung in rhyme simply pour passer le temps, the Author trusts that nobody in to whose hands it may come will without his permission give or allow to be taken, copies of anything here contained; much less to give, to the world at large, what he never meant should see the light. — At the Gentleman's requests, whose from this time it shall be, the Collection was made; and to him, & I will add, to his amiable Lady, it is presented, as a sincere though small tribute of gratitude for the many many happy hours the Author has spent under their roof. — *There*, what Poverty even though accompanied with Genius must seldom expect to meet with at the tables & in the circles of Fashionable Life, his welcome has ever been, The cordiality of Kindness, & the warmth of Friendship. — As, from the situation in which it is now placed, this M.S.S. may be preserved, & this Preface read, when the hand that now writes & the heart that now dictates it may be mouldering in the dust; let these be regarded as the genuine sentiments of a man who seldom flattered any, & never those he loved. —

　27th April 1791　　　　　　　　　　　　ROBT BURNS

Burns also wrote a song to celebrate the Riddells' wedding anniversary in 1788. R. H. Cromek prints a note by Burns on this song, but the leaf in the interleaved *Museum* opposite the printed song, which presumably carried the note, is one of those which has been removed. The sentiments, however, are substantially repeated in a letter to Riddell. The note as printed by Cromek reads, "I composed this song out of compliment to one of the happiest and worthiest married couples in the world, Robert Riddel, Esq. of Glenriddel, and his lady. At their fireside — I have enjoyed more pleasant evenings than at all the houses of fashionable people in this country put together; and to their kindness and hospitality I am indebted for many of the happiest hours of my life." There is no reason to doubt the candor of this statement, or of the note in the manuscript book of poems, or of the letter, but it should be remembered that they were all written for the Riddells to see. And subsequent events lend them irony.

Burns was much at Friars' Carse, and Riddell was pleased to have guests meet him. On such occasions, Burns felt free, when the guests had franking privileges, to ask for franks for his letters. He had access to Riddell's library, and the two of them set up the Monkland Friendly Society, a local book club, for which Burns was the managing agent, ordering books from his friend Peter Hill, acting as librarian, and in August or September of 1791, writing the account below of the enterprise for Sinclair's *The Statistical Account of Scotland, 1792.*

To store the minds of the lower classes with useful knowledge, is certainly of very great consequence, both to them as individuals, and to society at large. Giving them a turn for reading and reflection, is giving them a source of innocent and laudable amusement; and besides, raises them to a more dignified degree in the scale of rationality. Impressed with this idea, a gentleman in this parish, Robert Riddell, Esq: of Glenriddel, set on foot a species of circulating library, on a plan so simple, as to be practicable in any corner of the country; and so useful, as to deserve the notice of every country gentleman, who thinks the improvement of that part of his own species, whom chance has thrown into the humble walks of the peasant and the artisan, a matter worthy of his attention.

Mr. Riddell got a number of his own tenants, and farming neighbours, to form themselves into a society, for the purpose of having a library among themselves. They entered into a legal engagment, to abide by it for 3 years; with a saving clause or two, in cases of removal to a distance, or of death. Each member, at his entry, paid 5s.; and at each of their meetings, which were held every fourth Saturday, 6d. more. With their entry money, and the credit which they took on the faith of their future funds, they laid in a tolerable stock of books at the commencement. What authors they were to purchase, was always to be decided by the majority. At every meeting, all the books, under certain fines and forfeitures, by way of penalty, were to be produced; and the members had their choice of the volumes in rotation. He whose name stood, for that night, first on the list, had his choice of what volume he pleased in the whole collection; the second had his choice after the first; the third after the second, and so on to the last. At next meeting, he who had been first on the list at the preceding meeting, was last at this; he who had been second, was first; and so on, through the whole 3 years. At the expiration of the engagment, the books were sold by auction, but only among the members themselves; and each man had his share of the common stock, in money or in books, as he chose to be a purchaser or not.

At the breaking up of this little society,* which was formed under Mr. Riddell's patronage, what with benefactions of books from him, and what with their own purchases, they had collected together upwards of 150 volumes. It will easily be guessed, that a good deal of trash would be bought. Among the books, however, of this little library, were, Blair's Sermons, Robertson's History of Scotland, Hume's History of the Stewarts, The Spectator, Idler, Adventurer, Mirror, Lounger, Observer, Man of Feeling, Man of the World, Chrysal, Don Quixotte, Joseph Andrews, &c. A peasant who can read, and enjoy such books, is certainly a much superior being to his neighbour, who, perhaps, stalks beside his team, very little removed, except in shape, from the brutes he drives.

Another happy note in the relations of Burns and Robert Riddell is the substantial assistance Riddell gave in the campaign to

---

* "The society, though reorganized after three years, maintained its existence and supported the library until February 2, 1931, when by formal vote it was disbanded, and the books distributed to appropriate places." (Snyder, 325.)

defend the Moffat schoolmaster, James Clarke, from charges of undue severity to his pupils.

While Burns enjoyed himself frequently at Friars' Carse, there is no record of his having spent the night there, as he did at the Millers', or of Robert Riddell's having been a guest at Ellisland farmhouse. And it is certain that Friars' Carse was one of the houses Burns had in mind when he wrote Mrs. Dunlop in December of 1792, after he had moved to Dumfries, "It is the private parties in the family way, among the hard drinking gentlemen of this county, that does me the mischief." Robert Riddell's convivial tastes are given classic illustration by the "Whistle" contest.

Riddell had a family relic — a whistle, which tradition held should become the property of that competitor who could blow it when all others were under the table. Riddell agreed to contest possession of the whistle with his cousins, Alexander Fergusson of Craigdarroch, lawyer and Justice of the Peace, and Sir Robert Laurie, M. P. for Dumfriesshire. The contest, refereed by John McMurdo, Chamberlain to the Duke of Queensberry at Drumlanrig, was held October 16, 1789, and was won by Craigdarroch. "He drank upds of 5 bottles of Claret." There has been argument about whether Burns was present during the contest as a witness, and he may have been, but he certainly was amused by it, and celebrated it with a ballad, *The Whistle,* in the course of which he complimented Mrs. Riddell. Mrs. Burns thought that her husband had been present, but only as a toping spectator.

Burns' enjoyment of Robert Riddell's convivial friends had one far more happy result than *The Whistle;* it led to his writing *Tam o' Shanter.* That "dainty chield," Captain Francis Grose, the "fine fat, fodgel wight [dumpy fellow], / O' stature short but genius bright," began his extended visits to Friars' Carse in April, 1789, as he went about sketching and collecting information for his two-volume work, *The Antiquities of Scotland.* Grose was jolly and full of stories, and Burns found him a congenial companion. The poem, *On The Late Captain Grose's Peregrinations*

Thro' Scotland, a happy memorial to their friendship, jocularly notes the captain's indefatigable researches.

By some auld, houlet-haunted biggin,	*owl-haunted building*
Or kirk deserted by its riggin,	*roof*
It's ten to ane ye'll find him snug in	
Some eldritch part,	*fearful*
Wi' deils, they say, Lord saf's! colleaguin	*save us*
At some black art.	

. . . .

Of Eve's first fire he has a cinder;	
Anld Tubalcain's fire-shool and fender;	*-shovel*
That which distinguishèd the gender	
O' Balaam's ass;	
A broomstick o' the witch of Endor,	
Weel shod wi' brass.	

Forbye, he'll shape you aff fu' gleg	*Besides smartly*
The cut of Adam's philibeg;	*kilt*
The knife that nicket Abel's craig	
He'll prove you fully,	
It was a faulding jocteleg,	*clasp knife*
Or lang-kail gullie.	*cabbage knife*

But wad ye see him in his glee —
For meikle glee and fun has he —
Then set him down, and two or three
Guid fellows wi' him:
And port, O port! shine thou a wee,
And then ye'll see him!

During the association between Burns and Grose it came to be agreed that Grose would include in his book a sketch of ruined Alloway Kirk, where Burns' father was buried, and that Burns would write a poem to go with it. Before writing the poem, he sent Grose a letter recounting legends of the Kirk, some of which he later used in *Tam o' Shanter.*

Sir,
 Among the many Witch Stories I have heard relating to Aloway Kirk, I distinctly remember only two or three.

Upon a stormy night, amid whirling squalls of wind and bitter blasts of hail, in short, on such a night as the devil would chuse to take the air in, a farmer or a farmer's servant was plodding and plashing homeward with his plough-irons on his shoulder, having been getting some repairs on them at a neighbouring smithy. His way lay by the Kirk of Aloway, and being rather on the anxious look-out in approaching a place so well known to be a favorite haunt of the devil and the devil's friends and emissaries, he was struck aghast by discovering, through the horrors of the storm and stormy night, a light, which, on his nearer approach, plainly shewed itself to proceed from the haunted edifice. Whether he had been fortified from above on his devout supplication, as is customary with people when they suspect the immediate presence of Satan; or whether, according to another custom, he had got courageously drunk at the smithy, I will not pretend to determine; but so it was that he ventured to go up to, nay into the very Kirk. — As good luck would have it, his temerity came off unpunished. The members of the infernal junto were all out on some midnight business or other, and he saw nothing but a kind of kettle or caldron, depending from the roof, over the fire, simmering some heads of unchristened children, limbs of executed malefactors, &c. for the business of the night. It was, in for a penny, in for a pound, with the honest ploughman; so without ceremony he unhooked the caldron from off the fire, and pouring out the damnable ingredients, inverted it on his head, and carried it fairly home, where it remained long in the family a living evidence of the truth of the story.

Another story, which I can prove to be equally authentic, was as follows.

On a market day in the town of Ayr, a farmer from Carrick, and consequently whose way lay by the very gate of Aloway kirk-yard, in order to cross the river Doon at the old bridge, which is about two or three hundred yards farther on than the said gate, had been detained by his business till by the time he reached Aloway, it was the wizard hour, between night and morning.

Though he was terrified with a blaze streaming from the kirk, yet as it is a well known fact, that to turn back on these occasions is running by far the greatest risk of mischief, he prudently advanced on his road. When he had reached the gate of the kirk-yard, he was surprised and entertained, through the ribs and arches of an old gothic window which still faces the highway, to see a dance of witches merrily footing it round their old sooty blackguard master, who was keeping them all alive with the power of his bagpipe. The farmer stopping his horse to observe them a little, could plainly descry the faces of many old women of his acquaintance and neighbourhood. How the gentleman was dressed, tradition does not say; but the ladies were all in their smocks; and one of them happening unluckily to have a smock which was considerably too short to answer all the purpose of that piece of dress, our farmer was so tickled that he involuntarily burst out, with a loud laugh, "Weel luppen, Maggy wi' the short sark!" and recollecting himself, instantly spurred his horse to the top of his speed. I need not mention the universally known fact that no diabolical power can pursue you beyond the middle of a running stream. Lucky it was for the poor farmer that the river Doon was so near, for notwithstanding the speed of his horse, which was a good one, against he reached the middle of the arch of the bridge, and consequently the middle of the stream, the pursuing, vengeful hags were so close at his heels, that one of them actually sprung to seize him: but it was too late; nothing was on her side of the stream but the horse's tail, which immediately gave way to her infernal grip, as if blasted by a stroke of lightning; but the farmer was beyond her reach. — However, the unsightly, tailless condition of the vigorous steed was to the last hours of the noble creature's life, an awful warning to the Carrick farmers, not to stay too late in Ayr markets. —

The last relation I shall give, though equally true, is not so well identified as the two former, with regard to the scene: but as the best authorities give it for Aloway, I shall relate it. —

On a summer's evening, about the time that Nature puts on her sables to mourn the expiry of the chearful day, a shepherd boy belonging to a farmer in the immediate neighbourhood of Aloway Kirk, had just folded his charge, and was returning home. As he passed the Kirk, in the adjoining field, he fell in with a crew of men and women, who were busy pulling stems of the plant ragwort. He observed that as each person pulled a ragwort, he or she got astride of it, and called out, "Up horsie!" on which the ragwort flew off, like Pegasus, through the air with its rider. The foolish boy likewise pulled his ragwort, and cried with the rest, "Up horsie!" and, strange to tell, away he flew with the company. The first stage at which the cavalcade stopt, was a merchant's wine cellar in Bourdeaux, where, without saying, by your leave, they quaffed away at the best the cellar could afford, untill the morning, foe to the imps and works of darkness, threatened to throw light on the matter, and frightened them from their carousals. —

The poor shepherd lad, being equally a stranger to the scene and the liquor, heedlessly got himself drunk; and when the rest took horse, he fell asleep and was found so next day by some of the people belonging to the merchant. Somebody that understood Scotch, asking him what he was, he said he was such-a-one's herd in Aloway, and by some means or other getting home again, he lived long to tell the world the wondrous tale.

I am, Dr Sir,
ROBT BURNS

In addition to drawing on lore of the kind which Burns had heard from his mother and from Betty Davidson while he was a boy, the poem obviously owes a good deal to Burns' memories of his summer at Kirkoswald and the smugglers on the Carrick shore, and its hero is presumably modeled on a farmer from that district, Douglas Graham of Shanter farm, who had a boat called the *Tam o' Shanter*. Jean Burns is reported to have said that Robert composed this poem in one day while walking along the banks of the Nith, and it may well be that he composed some of it in this way. He was accustomed to composing in his head, and while walking or riding. But the poem as we know it was certainly the result of more than some hours' strolling. As Burns said, "All my poetry is the effect of easy composition, but of laborious correction." And he wrote to Lady Henrietta Don, "Though the rough material of fine writing is undoubtedly the gift of genius, the workmanship is as certainly the united effort of labor, attention and pains." (January, 22, 1789, the same day as a letter to Henry Erskine with almost the same statement. See epigraph at beginning of Section III. He had made a similar statement to Dr. Moore on January 4.) There is an even more pointed remark in a letter to Mrs. Dunlop. When she objected

at New Year, 1791, to the improprieties of *Tam,* and pronounced
it a bad poem, Burns said nothing to her about her unhappiness
until he wrote on April 11, announcing the birth on April 9 of
William Nicol Burns, who was "rather stouter but not so handsome" as Mrs. Dunlop's god-son, Francis Wallace Burns (b.
August 18, 1789). "Indeed," said Burns disarmingly, "I look on
your little Namesake to be my chef d'oeuvre in that species of
manufacture, as I look on 'Tam o' Shanter' to be my standard
performance in the Poetical line. 'Tis true, both the one & the
other discover a spice of roguish waggery that might perhaps be
as well spared; but then they also shew in my opinion a force
of genius & *a finishing polish* [italics supplied] that I despair of
ever excelling." *

So fine a critic as Hazlitt, when lecturing on Burns, said of
Tam o' Shanter, "I shall give the beginning of it, but I am afraid
I shall hardly know when to leave off." And he proceeded to
read it all. How could he have done otherwise? What need he
have said *about* it?

Like all great art, *Tam o' Shanter* delights, and defies criticism.

* This is a convenient place to record that on March 31, ten days before little
William's appearance, Anne Park, the niece of Mrs. Hyslop, hostess at the Globe
Inn, Dumfries, bore Burns a daughter, Elizabeth. This child was first taken to
Mossgiel, and then, later, was admitted to Burns' own family and raised with
his other children, by Jean. There is no further word of Anne Park, who is
presumed to have died in childbirth or soon after. Burns remained on excellent
terms with Mr. and Mrs. Hyslop, and wrote about Anne a song of which he
said, "I think it is the best love-song I ever composed in my life."

> Yestreen I had a pint o' wine,
>   A place where body saw na;
> Yestreen lay on this breast o' mine
>   The raven locks of Anna.
>
>   .   .   .   .   .
>
> Ye Monarchs take the East and West,
>   Frae Indus to Savannah!
> Gie me within my straining grasp
>   The melting form of Anna. —
>
> Then I'll despise Imperial charms,
>   An Empress or Sultana,
> While dying raptures in her arms,
>   I give and take wi' Anna.

One can notice its ambiguities and irony and ambivalence, its realism and grotesque fancy, its humor and horror, its diablerie and satire; the irresistible flow of its narrative; the force of its statement and the brilliant compulsion of its language; the wonderfully interwoven sophistication and folklore; the subtle and assured metrics; the rhetorical power, the variety of scene, the richness of texture, the vividness of detail; and the background both of form and of literary tradition — such as the wild ride; but when one has finished, as Hazlitt knew, one has done little to explain the poem's power or to increase its delight. It stands alone in our literature.[*]

Tam o' Shanter
A Tale

Of Brownyis and of Bogillis full is this Buke.
Gawin Douglas

When chapman billies leave the street,	*pedlar fellows*
And drouthy neebors neebors meet;	*thirsty*
As market-days are wearing late,	
An' folk begin to tak the gate;	*road*
While we sit bousing at the nappy,	*ale*
An' getting fou and unco happy,	*full very*
We think na on the lang Scots miles,	
The mosses, waters, slaps, and styles,	*swamps gaps in walls*
That lie between us and our hame,	
Whare sits our sulky, sullen dame,	
Gathering her brows like gathering storm,	
Nursing her wrath to keep it warm.	

[*] Note on chronology: Burns and Grose were absorbed in lore of Alloway Kirk by the summer of 1790, and Burns recited a part of *Tam o' Shanter* to Ainslie in late October. By November, Mrs. Dunlop had seen a version which apparently lacked the witch dance. Burns sent the poem to Grose December 1, and by February, Grose had returned him some proof sheets, of which he sent one to Dr. Moore on February 28 (1791). The poem appeared March 18, 1791, in the *Edinburgh Herald*, and in the *Edinburgh Magazine* for March. Grose printed it as a footnote, pp. 199–201, in his second volume, which was published April 11. (F II, #401, #437; H & H I, 439; RB & Mrs. D, 286, 289; *Chronicle*, 1935, 9; Egerer, 36; Kinsley, 1347–1364.)

This truth fand honest Tam o' Shanter   *found*
As he frae Ayr ae night did canter:
(Auld Ayr, wham ne'er a town surpasses,
For honest men and bonie lasses).

O Tam, had'st thou but been sae wise,
As taen thy ain wife Kate's advice!   *As to have taken*
She tauld thee weel thou was a skellum,   *no-count*
A blethering, blustering, drunken blellum   *chattering   babbler*
That frae November till October,
Ae market-day thou was nae sober;
That ilka melder wi' the miller,   *meal-grinding*
Thou sat as lang as thou had siller;   *silver*
That ev'ry naig was ca'd a shoe on,   *every   called*
The smith and thee gat roaring fou on;
That at the Lord's house, even on Sunday,   [*a Kirkoswald tavern*]
Thou drank wi' Kirkton Jean till Monday.   [*the hostess*]
She prophesied, that, late or soon,
Thou would be found deep drown'd in Doon,
Or catch'd wi' warlocks in the mirk   *wizards   dark*
By Alloway's auld, haunted kirk.

Ah! gentle dames, it gars me greet,   *makes me weep*
To think how monie counsels sweet,
How monie lengthen'd, sage advices
The husband frae the wife despises!

But to our tale: — Ae market-night,
Tam had got planted unco right,
Fast by an ingle, bleezing finely,   *fire*
Wi' reaming swats, that drank divinely;   *foaming new ale*
And at his elbow, Souter Johnie,   *Cobbler*
His ancient, trusty, drouthy cronie: *thirsty*
Tam lo'ed him like a very brither;
They had been fou for weeks thegither.
The night drave on wi' sangs and clatter;
And ay the ale was growing better:
The landlady and Tam grew gracious
Wi' secret favours, sweet and precious:
The Souter tauld his queerest stories;
The landlord's laugh was ready chorus:
The storm without might rair and rustle,
Tam did na mind the storm a whistle.

Care, mad to see a man sae happy,
E'en drown'd himsel amang the nappy.
As bees flee hame wi' lades o' treasure,
The minutes wing'd their way wi' pleasure:
Kings may be blest but Tam was glorious,
O'er a' the ills o' life victorious!

But pleasures are like poppies spread:
You seize the flow'r, its bloom is shed;
Or like the snow falls in the river,
A moment white — then melts forever;
Or like the borealis race,
That flit ere you can point their place;
Or like the rainbow's lovely form
Evanishing amid the storm.
Nae man can tether time or tide;
The hour approaches Tam maun ride: *must*
That hour, o' night's black arch the key-stane,
That dreary hour Tam mounts his beast in;
And sic a night he taks the road in,
As ne'er poor sinner was abroad in.

The wind blew as 'twad blawn its last;
The rattling showers rose on the blast;
The speedy gleams the darkness swallow'd;
Loud, deep, and lang the thunder bellow'd:
That night, a child might understand,
The Deil had business on his hand.

Weel mounted on his gray mare Meg,
A better never lifted leg,
Tam skelpit on thro' dub and mire,   *hurried   puddle*
Despising wind, and rain, and fire;
Whiles holding fast his guid blue bonnet,   *Now*
Whiles crooning o'er some auld Scots sonnet   *song*
Whiles glow'ring round wi' prudent cares,
Lest bogles catch him unawares: *goblins*
Kirk-Alloway was drawing nigh,
Whare ghaists and houlets nightly cry.   *owls*

By this time he was cross the ford,
Whare in the snaw the chapman smoor'd;   *smothered*

And past the birks and meikle stane,   *birches great*
Whare drunken Charlie brak's neck-bane;
And thro' the whins, and by the cairn,   *furze pile of stones*
Whare hunters fand the murder'd bairn;
And near the thorn, aboon the well,   *above*
Whare Mungo's mither hang'd hersel.
Before him Doon pours all his floods;
The doubling storm roars thro' the woods;
The lightnings flash from pole to pole;
Near and more near the thunders roll:
When, glimmering thro' the groaning trees,
Kirk-Alloway seem'd in a bleeze;
Thro' ilka bore the beams were glancing,   *every chink*
And loud resounded mirth and dancing.

Inspiring bold John Barleycorn,
What dangers thou canst make us scorn!
Wi' tippeny, we fear nae evil;   *ale*
Wi' usquabae, we'll face the Devil!   *whisky*
The swats sae ream'd in Tammie's noddle,
Fair play, he car'd na deils a boddle.   *not farthing*
But Maggie stood, right sair astonish'd,
Till, by the heel and hand admonish'd,
She ventur'd forward on the light;
And, vow! Tam saw an unco sight!

Warlocks and witches in a dance:
Nae cotillion, brent new frae France,   *brand*
But hornpipes, jigs, strathspeys, and reels,
Put life and mettle in their heels.
A winnock-bunker in the east,   *window-seat*
There sat Auld Nick, in shape o' beast;
A tousie tyke, black, grim, and large,   *shaggy dog*
To gie them music was his charge:
He screw'd the pipes and gart them skirl,   *made them squeal*
Till roof and rafters a' did dirl.   *ring*
Coffins stood round, like open presses,   *cupboards*
That shaw'd the dead in their last dresses;
And, by some devilish cantraip sleight,   *witching*
Each in his cauld hand held a light:
By which heroic Tam was able
To note upon the haly table,

A murderer's banes, in gibbet-airns;   *-irons*
Twa span-lang, wee, unchristen'd bairns;
A thief new-cutted frae a rape —
Wi' his last gasp his gab did gape;   *mouth*
Five tomahawks wi' bluid red-rusted;
Five scymitars wi' murder crusted;
A garter which a babe had strangled;
A knife a father's throat had mangled —
Whom his ain son o' life bereft —
The gray-hairs yet stack to the heft;
Wi' mair o' horrible and awefu',
Which even to name was be unlawfu'.
[Three Lawyers' tongues, turn'd inside out,
Wi' lies seam'd like a beggar's clout;
And Priests' hearts, rotten black as muck,
Lay stinking, vile, in every neuk.]*

As Tammie glowr'd, amaz'd, and curious,   *stared*
The mirth and fun grew fast and furious;
The piper loud and louder blew,
The dancers quick and quicker flew,
They reel'd, they set, they cross'd, they cleekit,†
Tililka carlin swat and reekit   *every beldam sweated and steamed*
And coost her duddies to the wark,
And linket at it in her sark!   *skipped*

Now Tam, O Tam! had thae been queans,
A' plump and strapping in their teens!
Their sarks, instead of creeshie flannen,   *greasy flannel*
Been snaw-white seventeen hunder linen! —   *fine linen*
Thir breeks o' mine, my only pair,   *These breeches*
That ance were plush, o' guid blue hair,
I wad hae gi'en them off my hurdies   *buttocks*
For ae blink o' the bonie burdies!

* These vivid and characteristic lines appeared in the first printings of *Tam o'
Shanter,* but Burns deleted them in his 1793 Edinburgh edition at the suggestion
of his friend A. F. Tytler, the elegant and celebrated minor author, critic, historian, professor, lawyer, and finally judge. Tytler, in March, 1791, wrote Burns
that he was delighted with *Tam,* but remarked that these lines "though good in
themselves, . . . derive all their merit from the satire they contain," and "are
rather misplaced among circumstances of pure horror." (Ch-W III, 256–57; F II,
#445, 70.) In December, 1792, Burns thanked Tytler for "taking the trouble
of correcting the Presswork" of the 1793 edition. (F II, #526, 138.)
† "They whirled around in the reel, faced their partners, passed across the
circle of the dance, and linked arms and turned." (Kinsley III, 1362.)

But wither'd beldams, auld and droll,
Rigwoodie hags wad spean a foal   *withered   drive a foal from the*
Louping and flinging on a crummock,   *cudgel /teat with fright*
I wonder did na turn thy stomach!

But Tam kend what was what fu' brawlie: *well*
There was ae winsome wench and wawlie,   *handsome*
That night enlisted in the core,
Lang after kend on Carrick shore
(For monie a beast to dead she shot,
An' perish'd monie a bonie boat,   *destroyed*
And shook baith meikle corn and bear,   *stole much barley*
And kept the country-side in fear).
Her cutty sark, o' Paisley harn,   *short smock coarse cloth*
That while a lassie she had worn,
In longitude tho' sorely scanty,
It was her best, and she was vauntie. —   *proud*
Ah! little kend thy reverend grannie,
That sark she coft for her wee Nannie,   *bought*
Wi' twa pund Scots ('twas a' her riches),
Wad ever grac'd a dance of witches!

But here my Muse her wing maun cour,   *fold*
Sic flights are far beyond her power:
To sing how Nannie lap and flang
(A souple jad she was and strang),
And how Tam stood like ane bewitch'd,
And thought his very e'en enrich'd;
Even Satan glowr'd, and fidg'd fu' fain,   *twitched*
And hotch'd and blew wi' might and main   *hitched*
Till first ae caper, syne anither,   *then*
Tam tint his reason a' thegither,   *lost*
And roars out: "Weel done, Cutty-sark!"
And in an instant all was dark;
And scarcely had he Maggie rallied,
When out the hellish legion sallied.

As bees bizz out wi' angry fyke,   *fuss*
When plundering herds assail their byke;   *herdboys hive*
As open pussie's mortal foes,   *the hare's*
When, pop! she starts before their nose;
As eager runs the market-crowd,
When "Catch the thief!" resounds aloud:

So Maggie runs, the witches follow,
Wi' monie an eldritch skriech and hollo.   *unearthly*

　　Ah, Tam! Ah, Tam! thou'll get thy fairin!
In hell they'll roast thee like a herrin!
In vain thy Kate awaits thy comin!
Kate soon will be a woefu' woman!
Now, do thy speedy utmost, Meg,
And win the key-stane of the brig;
There, at them thou thy tail may toss,
A running stream they dare na cross!
But ere the key-stane she could make,
The fient a tail she had to shake;   *devil*
For Nannie, far before the rest,
Hard upon noble Maggie prest,
And flew at Tam wi' furious ettle;   *purpose*
But little wist she Maggie's mettle!
Ae spring brought off her master hale,
But left behind her ain grey tail:
The carlin claught her by the rump,   *seized*
And left poor Maggie scarce a stump.

　　Now, wha this tale o' truth shall read,
Ilk man, and mother's son, take heed:
Whene'er to drink you are inclin'd,
Or cutty sarks run in your mind,
Think! ye may buy the joys o'er dear:
Remember Tam o' Shanter's mare.

Maria Riddell, wife of Robert's younger brother Walter, was literary, charming, witty, and accomplished. Daughter of William Woodley, Governor of the Leeward Isles, she had married at eighteen (September 16, 1790), at St. Kitts, the recently widowed Walter Riddell (1764–1802), who had inherited an Antiquan estate from his first and childless wife of a year. On August 31, 1791, after their return to England, Maria and Walter had a daughter, and on November 22, 1792, another, their last child. In the autumn of 1791, they came from London to the neighborhood of Dumfries, where Walter soon began to look for a country estate, and during the spring of 1792 he agreed to buy Goldilea for £16,000, paying £1000 down. He renamed it Woodley Park in honor of his wife, spent £2000 on improvements, and set up in considerable style. Burns apparently met Maria and her husband at Friars' Carse before he left Ellisland for Dumfries in early November 1791, and he became a frequent visitor to Woodley Park.

By January 22, 1792, Maria had got from Burns a letter of introduction to his Crochallan friend, the printer Smellie, author of a *Philosophy of Natural History*. Maria wanted Smellie's opinion on a book she had written, eventually published as *Voyages to the Madeira and Leeward Islands; with Sketches of the Natural History of these Islands*. Burns told Smellie that although Maria was a young lady of the first rank of fashion, and a "lively West-Indian girl of eighteen" (she was twenty), she was also a poet and a great admirer of Smellie's book. He urged that she would be a character that even in his own way "as a Naturalist & a Philosopher," would be an acquisition to his acquaintance. Smellie took to Maria, advised publication of her manuscript, and became her correspondent — solid testimony to her qualities of mind as well as to her charms.

Smellie wrote her, "When I considered your youth, and still more, your sex, the perusal of your ingenious and judicious work, if I had not previously had the pleasure of your conversation, the devil himself could not have frightened me into the belief that a female human creature could, in the bloom of youth, beauty, and consequently of giddiness, have produced a performance so much out of the line of your ladies works. Smart little poems, flippant romances, are not uncommon. But science, minute observation, accurate description, and excellent composition, are qualities seldom to be met with in the female world." Smellie then continues gallantly, "Why did you grapple with a soldier? Mr Riddell I ever will revere, though not so much as yourself must do; but if I could have had the happiness of having the company of a lady so well qualified to assist me in my favourite study, we *two* should have made a COUPLE of figures in the literary world!" In the early autumn Smellie visited the Walter Riddells at Woodley Park, and Maria took him to the Dumfries Assembly. It is perhaps anticlimax to add that Smellie printed the *Voyages,* which were dedicated to him, the book being announced in November, 1792, as for sale by Cadell in London, and by Burns' friend Peter Hill, in Edinburgh. Burns received a copy from the author, which he promised to keep "sacred."

Relations between the Walter Riddells and the Robert Riddells were soon strained. By early autumn, 1792, Burns was promising Maria that if he saw Robert Riddell he would "say nothing at all, & listen to nothing at all" about her. As he wrote her later, "Your interest with the WOMEN is, I believe, a sorry business. — So much the better! 'tis God's judgment upon you for making such despotic use of your sway over the MEN." Maria was flirtatious, even flighty, as Burns himself had ample reason to note on another occasion. "I have often told you, my Dear Friend," he once wrote her, "that you had a spice of Caprice in your composition, & you have as often disavowed it; even perhaps while your opinions were, at the moment, irrefragably proving it."

Walter Riddell, like his brother Robert, was a convivial squire, and Woodley Park was another of the country houses complained of by Burns to Mrs. Dunlop, where he was urged to drink more than he wanted. But Walter seems not to have shared his brother's interest in books, antiquities, and songs. Burns thought poorly of him, and almost never mentions him in his letters to Maria. Professor Thornton gives evidence that Walter's relatives had limited confidence in him, and he seems to have been rather a wastrel. By June, 1793, after a year at Woodley Park, Walter found it necessary to return to the West Indies, presumably to raise money, and he remained out of Great Britain for almost a year. Once he returned, unsuccessful, he forfeited his deposit and expenditures on Woodley Park, and moved Maria to "a crazy, rambling, worm-eaten, cobweb-hunting chateau of the Duke of Queensberry," Tinwald House, where their style was much reduced. From this time on, Walter was a good deal from home. He and Maria moved to Halleaths in 1795, and left Scotland in 1797. She does not mention his death, 1802, in Antiqua, in her diary.

Maria Riddell came into Burns' life just when he thought Clarinda was irrevocably leaving it, but while this new friendship provoked scandal, the twenty-four surviving letters from Burns to Maria give no indication of fervid evenings such as those with Mrs. M'Lehose. It should be noted that Mrs. Riddell carefully preserved Burns' letters to her, but was active in getting back her own letters to him after his death; none of them is known to biographers. Letters to others, however, such as those to Smellie, and to James Currie, reveal a bright, perceptive mind, and a crisp prose style.

Like Clarinda, Maria sought out Burns; like Clarinda, she was unhappily married and could write passable verse. But unlike Clarinda, she was no Calvinist, and no sentimentalist. Burns found Maria exciting. She was a sophisticated woman who could share his mind, and sympathise with his interests. He fascinated her, as he had so many women, and she played coquette with him. There are two periods in their relationship.

In the earliest surviving letter from Burns to Mrs. Riddell, she is "My Dearest Friend," whose report of better health was the welcomest letter he had ever received. He concludes, "God grant that you may live at least while I live, for were I to lose you it would leave a Vacuum in my enjoyments that nothing could fill up." Six months later he promises not to gossip about her, and "So, vive l'amour & vive la bagatelle!" A little later she is an "enviable creature," to be going to a bright party, but he begs her, "pity your melancholy friend." By January, 1793, he feels free to request her presence at the benefit night of an actor friend. In

April he is sending her a new song. "It is a trifling present, but —
'Give all thou canst' —

"Were my esteem for a certain Lady to be measured by a musical offering, that would not be less than the music of the Spheres
in score, or the Haleluias of the Hierarchies with all their accom-
paniments."

A little later, Burns sends Maria some smuggled French gloves
which his special knowledge as an Exciseman had enabled him to
procure for her. He wants to know if she will honor Thomson's
publication with a song, forwards one written to her, and adds,
"I am afraid that my song will turn out a very cold performance,
as I never can do any good with a love theme, except when I am
really & devoutly in love." The song is not particularly good, but
Burns' flimsy pretext that he was not in love can hardly have deceived Maria. Stanza III runs,

> The music of thy voice I heard,
>   Nor wist while it enslav'd me!
> I saw thine eyes, yet nothing fear'd,
>   Till fears no more had sav'd me!
> Th' unwary sailor thus, aghast
>   The wheeling torrent viewing,
> 'Mid circling horrors sinks at last
>   In overwhelming ruin.

Shortly after this letter, Mrs. Riddell accompanied her husband to
London, whence he departed abruptly for the West Indies.

In October, when Mrs. Riddell had returned alone from England, after a period of ill-health and distress, including the death
of her father, Burns sent her an epigram, and a song originally
written for Clarinda; he closed his letter, "Le bon Dieu vous
benisse!" Then in November come four letters close together, the
first jealous that she had been so surrounded by officers ("lobster-
coated Puppies") in her theatre box, that he could not get near
her; the second agreeing to visit her box "on Tuesday; when we
may arrange the business of the visit," asking advice of the "first

& fairest of Critics" about his revision of a song, calling her "Thou most amiable & most accomplished of Thy Sex," and closing with "fervent regard." The third letter complains that he is fretful and melancholy, like the Hebrew sage who foretold, "And behold, on whatsoever this man doth set his heart, it shall not prosper!" This letter concludes, "If my resentment is awakened, it is sure to be where it dare not squeak; & if in LOVE, as, God forgive me! I sometimes am; Impossibility presents an impervious barrier to the proudest daring of Presumption, & poor I, dare much sooner peep into the focus of Hell, than meet the eye of the goddess of my soul!

"Pray that Wisdom & Bliss be more frequent visitors of

RB"

By this time Maria Riddell must have known that she was playing with fire, and she had probably known it all along. The fourth November letter sends her a version of another poem, originally intended for Clarinda, which Maria had asked for. It concludes,

> By all on High, adoring mortals know!
> By all the conscious villain fears below,
> By what, Alas, much more my soul alarms,
> My doubtful hopes once more to fill thy arms!
> E'en shouldst thou, false, forswear each guilty tie,
> Thine, & thine only, I must live & die! ! !

When the inevitable explosion came, Maria chose to be insulted. Robert Riddell concluded that he must henceforth turn his back on Burns, and Burns felt himself ill-used. Just what happened, and just where, are both uncertain. But the morning after a customarily drunken evening in some country house* in late

---

* To the remarks of C. K. Sharpe (p. 10) and John Syme (p. 221–22) about genteel conviviality in and around Dumfries, may be added reminiscences of Mrs. Basil Montagu, formerly Anna Dorothea Benson, a friend of the Craiks of Arbigland, where she met Burns. Mrs. Montagu wrote to Jane Welsh Carlyle, protesting remarks which Allan Cunningham had attributed to her about Burns. "This he has put my name to, who have ever represented Burns as incapable of rudeness or vulgarity — on the contrary as gentle, modest in his manner to women, well bred and gentlemanly in all the courtesies of life, with a natural

December, 1793, Burns wrote the following letter to his hostess
of the night before. The text is Dr. Currie's, who gives the addressee as "Mrs. R * * * * *." Currie may have tinkered with the
text, but even if he did, what he printed is the closest to the incident that one can get.

MADAM,

I daresay that this is the first epistle you ever received from this
nether world. I write you from the regions of Hell, amid the horrors
of the damned. The time and manner of my leaving your earth I do
not exactly know, as I took my departure in a fever of intoxication,
contracted at your too hospitable mansion; but, on my arrival here,
I was fairly tried, and sentenced to endure the purgatorial tortures
of this infernal confine for the space of ninety-nine years, eleven
months, and twenty-nine days, and all on account of the impropriety
of my conduct yesternight under your roof. Here am I, laid on a bed
of pityless furze, with my aching head reclined on a pillow of ever-
piercing thorn, while an infernal tormentor, wrinkled, and old, and
cruel, his name I think is *Recollection,* with a whip of scorpions, forbids
peace or rest to approach me, and keeps anguish eternally awake. Still,
Madam, if I could in any measure be reinstated in the good opinion
of the fair circle whom my conduct last night so much injured, I
think it would be an alleviation to my torments. For this reason I
trouble you with this letter. To the men of the company I will make

---

politeness, poorly imitated by the artificial polish of society, since his manner
arose out of the chivalric respect and devotion he bore to the sex — a respect
that modulated his voice and veiled the flashing of his eyes, and gave a winning grace to the most trifling of his attentions; this and a thousand other
things all in commendation have I, from time to time, endeavoured to infuse
into the dense faculty of honest Allan; and, above all that, during the Carnival
of the Caledonian Hunt, 'when Universal Scotland all was drunk,' I never saw
Burns once intoxicated, though the worthy Member for Dumfries, and the good
Laird of Arbigland, and twenty more that might be named, were much more
tipsy than Tam o' Shanter, for he could see witches and warlocks, but they
could neither see or stand, and were brought home in a state of inglorious in-
sensibility. I have told him twenty times that Burns always left a dinner party,
if there were women, for the drawing room long before any other man joined
it; and this in his thick skull has produced the following brilliant remark from
Mrs. Montagu: 'He drank as other men drank.' . . . Poor Burns! Misfortune
pursues thee even to the grave! — So it is with almost all great men; reverence
keeps silent all who loved them, and Traders take up the theme." (*Chronicle*
1927, 187.)

no apology. — Your husband, who insisted on my drinking more than I chose, has no right to blame me; and the other gentlemen were partakers of my guilt. But to you, Madam, I have much to apologize. Your good opinion, I valued as one of the greatest acquisitions I had made on earth, and I was truly a beast to forfeit it. There was a Miss I—— too, a woman of fine sense, gentle and unassuming manners — do make, on my part, a miserable d—mned wretch's best apology to her. A Mrs G——, a charming woman, did me the honor to be prejudiced in my favor; this makes me hope that I have not outraged her beyond all forgiveness. — To all the other ladies please present my humblest contrition for my conduct, and my petition for their gracious pardon. O all ye powers of decency and decorum! whisper to them that my errors, though great, were involuntary — that an intoxicated man is the vilest of beasts — that it was not in my nature to be brutal to anyone — that to be rude to a woman, when in my senses, was impossible with me — but —

* * * * * *

Regret! Remorse! Shame! ye three hellhounds that ever dog my steps and bay at my heels, spare me! spare me!

Forgive the offenses, and pity the perdition of, Madam,

Your humble slave,

Since Maria Riddell's husband was out of the country, this letter could not have been addressed to her. If the addressee was, indeed, a Mrs. R * * * * *, it seems likely that she was Elizabeth Riddell (Mrs. Robert), and the terms of the letter support that attribution. Moreover, Burns' next letter to Maria seems hardly in the tone of one to a woman who had just received an abject apology from him. And he is certainly puzzled that she has cut him. He writes,

I have this very moment got the song from Sim [John Syme], & I am sorry to see that he has spoilt it a good deal. — It shall be a lesson to me how I lend him any thing again.

I have sent you Werter: truly happy to have any, the smallest, opportunity of obliging you. —

Tis true, Madam, I saw you once since I was at Woodley park; &

that once froze the very life-blood of my heart. — Your reception of me was such, that a wretch, meeting the eye of his Judge, about to pronounce sentence of death on him, could only have envied my feelings & situation. —

But I hate the theme; & never more shall write or speak of it.

One thing I shall proudly say; that I can pay Mrs R—— a higher tribute of esteem, & appreciate her amiable worth more truly, than any man whom I have seen approach her — nor will I yield the pas to any man living, in subscribing myself with sincerest truth

Her devoted humble servt
RB

It might seem from this letter that the incident, whoever the addressee of the letter from Hell may have been, took place at Woodley Park. But wherever it took place, within a fortnight, Burns is returning Maria Riddell's Common Place Book since he has forfeited her esteem. As for his unknown offense against her, he says, "To admire, esteem, prize and adore you, as the most accomplished of Women, & the first of Friends — if these are crimes, I am the most offending thing alive."

The traditional story of what happened at the dinner to produce Burns' apology is that the gentlemen over their wine began to discuss the Rape of the Sabines and decided to enact something similar when they rejoined the ladies. Mrs. Carswell, a descendant of Patrick Miller, reports a strong tradition that army officer guests planned the affair as a "rag" to humiliate Burns the Jacobin. "Such fun might have cropped up as easily at an Ellisland Hallowe'en, a Tarbolton penny bridal or an Irvine Hogmanay [New Year]. . . . But . . . this was a frolic of the gentry. . . . So when Robert had carried out his part with hearty despatch and all the latitude the occasion called for, he was stupefied to find himself alone." Possibly. The only direct account is his own, and it is not at variance. And if something of the sort took place, whom had he laid his hands on? Maria is certainly the most likely candidate.

Neighborhood gossip, as reported by Charles Kirkpatrick

Sharpe, had Maria causing a quarrel between Burns and her brother-in-law, and it held her conduct with Burns to be scandalous. But there is better information. Robert Riddell's sister-in-law, Rachel Kennedy, wrote to Burns' biographer Currie, "In the post-humous Volumes of poor Burns which y[ou edit] [MS damaged] allude to ought *not* to appear, as it refers to some circumstances of improper conduct of Burns to Mrs. Walter Riddell which she represented to Mr. Riddell, and which he thought (in his brother's absence) [he ou]ght to resent, and therefore declin'd taking a[ny f]urther notice of Burns. . . . She uniformly expressed herself *my* friend and was highly flattering in her attentions to me, but I found it quite necessary to break off all intercourse with her long before she left this Country."

Although Miss Kennedy does not refer specifically to such an incident as that described in the letter from Hell, it is unlikely that Burns would have been permitted *two* occasions for serious offense. And it is plain that Maria Riddell's conduct with him had caused family distress, wholly aside from whatever causes had led to the break with her husband's brother's wife's sister.

Some question arises whether even Robert Riddell was the husband of the letter from Hell, for in that letter, the husband is included with those who were "partakers" of his guilt. But after the incident, he continued to speak warmly of Robert Riddell. To be sure, Burns did not nourish grudges, and most of his remarks came after Riddell's death, which followed the incident by only four months. But even so, he would hardly speak so of a man who had offended him and broken their friendship. Whatever his feelings for Robert Riddell, Burns continued his low opinion of Walter, and his break with Elizabeth (Mrs. Robert) was complete. He spoke bitterly of both so late as February, 1796. If Robert Riddell was not the husband of the letter from Hell, then the letter was not addressed to his wife. And who then was the Mrs. R * * * * *? It is even possible, of course, that the party took place neither at Friars' Carse, with Elizabeth as hostess, nor at Woodley Park, and that the Mrs. R * * * * * was neither Elizabeth nor Maria. There is simply not evidence enough to make out a straightforward story. But one thing is abundantly clear. Burns' friendship with gentry had again ended in humiliation and bitterness, and he was the victim of class loyalty. Had a social equal of the Riddells so offended, there would have been an apology, perhaps, and maybe a lingering coolness, but not the ostracism which was visited on Burns. This was the sort of class-conscious treatment which infuriated him, and to which he was most sensitive, as "the sport, the miserable victim of rebellious pride, hypochondriac imagination, agonizing sensibility, and bedlam passions," of which he had written long ago to Margaret Chalmers. He responded as he had when Mrs. Oswald's funeral cortege had driven him from a comfortable fire out into the cold because he was a peasant and she had been rich gentry.

To Maria Riddell when he returned her Common Place Book, he wrote, "In a face where I used to meet the kind complacency of friendly confidence, *now* to find cold neglect & contemptuous scorn — is a wrench that my heart can ill bear. — It is however some kind of miserable good luck; that while De-haut-en-bas rigour may depress an unoffending wretch to the ground, it has a tendency to rouse a stubborn something in his bosom, which, though it cannot heal the wounds of his soul, is at least an opiate to blunt their poignancy."

During the next few months, perhaps after Robert Riddell's death on April 21, Burns wrote a *Monody on a Lady famed for her Caprice,* which he sent to Clarinda and to Mrs. Dunlop, and which Currie published in 1800, with the name Eliza substituted for Maria. The opening stanza and the Epitaph are a sufficient sample.

> How cold is that bosom which Folly once fired!
>   How pale is that cheek where the rouge lately glisten'd!
> How silent that tongue which the echoes oft tired!
>   How dull is that ear which to flatt'ry so listen'd!
>   . . . .

The Epitaph

Here lies, now a prey to insulting neglect,
  What once was a butterfly, gay in life's beam:
Want only of wisdom denied her respect,
  Want only of goodness denied her esteem.

To Mrs. Dunlop he described the subject of the Monody as "a fantastical fine-fashioned Dame of my acquaintance," and to Clarinda he wrote, "The subject of the foregoing is a woman of fashion in this country, with whom, at one period, I was well acquainted. — By some scandalous conduct to me, & two or three other gentlemen here as well as me, she steered so far to the north of my good opinion, that I have made her the theme of several illnatured things. — The following epigram struck me the other day as I passed her carriage. —

If you rattle along like your Mistress's tongue,
  Your speed will out-rival the dart:
But, a fly for your load, you'll break down on the road,
  If your stuff be as rotten's her heart."

Burns sent this epigram to Patrick Miller, Jr., in London, with the title, *Extempore Pinned to a Lady's Coach*, and signed "Nith." He asked, "How do you like the following clinch? . . . If your friends [the editors of the *Morning Post*] think this worth insertion, they are welcome." The editors did not think it worth insertion.

Sometime later, perhaps in early 1795, Burns wrote for Syme and some other cronies a parody of Pope's *Eloisa to Abelard*, called *From Esopus to Maria*, distinguished by ill-temper and general ineptitude, but containing several good lines. One line asks whether Lord Lonsdale "Must make a vast monopoly of Hell," with his villainy, and a couplet says of Maria,

"Who calls thee, pert, affected, vain coquette,
  A wit in folly, and a fool in wit!"

She probably never saw this poem, and after about a year of estrangement sought a reconciliation. In early 1795, during the late winter or spring, Burns wrote the capricious lady a third-person letter, in obvious response to an advance, requesting a book from her and asking for a sight of any poem which she might have written. Some time later, he thanks her cordially and in the first person, for the book, and tells her he is having a miniature painted of himself which she may see by calling on the painter, Reid, and mentioning that he had spoken to her of the picture. "Both the Miniature's existence & its destiny," he adds, "are an inviolable secret, & therefore very properly trusted in part *to you.*" In his next letter he says that he is sending the miniature to her, and reports he is "so ill as to be scarce able to hold this miserable pen to this miserable paper."

From the spring of 1795, Burns was a dying man, and he seems to have known it, for he writes to Mrs. Riddell in June or July, "The health you wished me in your Morning's Card is I think, flown from me forever." During the summer he advised her how to get a job in the Customs for a protégé, adding some pleasant badinage. A little later he criticizes a poem of hers in a brief note, and about the same time sends her a song of his own. That autumn, in deep distress at the death of little Elizabeth Riddell Burns (b. Nov. 21, 1792), he wishes that Maria may never experience such a loss, and he sends her a book of music. There are no more letters until June, 1796, when he excuses himself from attending her at a loyalty celebration.

I am in such miserable health as to be utterly incapable of shewing my loyalty in any way. — Rackt as I am with rheumatisms, I meet every face with a greeting like that of Balak to Balaam — "Come, curse me Jacob; & come, defy me Israel!" — So, say I, come, curse me that East-wind; & come, defy me the North!!! Would you have me in such circumstances copy you out a Love-song? No! If I must write, let it be Sedition, or Blasphemy, or something else that begins with a B, so that I may grin with the grin of iniquity, & rejoice with the rejoicing of an apostate Angel. —

— "All good to me is lost;
Evil, be thou my good!" —

I may perhaps see you on Saturday, but I will not be at the Ball. —
Why should I? — "Man delights not me, nor woman either!" Can
you supply me with the Song, "Let us all be unhappy together" —
Do, if you can, & oblige

le pauvre miserable,
RB

Burns saw Maria Riddell for the last time about two weeks before his death.

Between December, 1793, and June or July, 1794, Burns twice
wrote letters similar to the one from Hell, each resulting from an
unfortunate mixture of alcohol and politics. Both of these letters
are to men, as are two others, one earlier and one later, mere
notes of the morning after. One of these latter (from early 1792,
to John McMurdo, referee of the Whistle contest) apologizes for
undue turbulence the evening before and sends a song just composed which is convincing evidence that the turbulence has sub-
sided; the other (written, probably in February, 1794, to Samuel
Clarke, Jr.) regrets inability to keep a breakfast appointment
made convivially some hours earlier.

A letter written to Major William Robertson of Lude, December 3, 1793, before the Riddell quarrel, is self-explanatory. It
begins: "Heated as I was with wine yesternight, I was perhaps
rather seemingly impertinent in my anxious wish to be honored
with your acquaintance. — You will forgive it: 'twas the impulse
of heart-felt respect." Burns had heard Glenriddell say that
Robertson was the father of Scotch County Reform, and wished
"to take him by the hand," for, as he continues, "in times such as
these, Sir, when our Commoners are barely able, by the glimmer of
their own twilight understandings, to scrawl a frank; and when
Lords are — what gentlemen would be ashamed to be; to whom
shall a sinking Country call for help? To the *independent country gentleman!*" Several months later, he sent Robertson another

copy of *Wilt Thou be my Dearie?*, the Major having given the first
one to a lady to further his cause with her. Burns thanks him for
giving the song "first celebrity" by singing it.

A letter to Samual Clarke, Jr., of June or July, 1794, and dated
"Sunday morning," is both more serious and more amusing.

Dr Sir,

I was, I know, drunk last night, but I am sober this morning. —
From the expressions Captn Dods made use of to me, had I nobody's
welfare to care for but my own, we should certainly have come, according to the manners of the world, to the necessity of murdering
one another about the business. — The words were such as generally, I believe, end in a brace of pistols; but I am still pleased to think
that I did not ruin the peace & welfare of a wife & a family of children in a drunken squabble. — Farther, you know that the report of
certain Political opinions being mine, has already once before brought
me to the brink of destruction. — I dread lest last night's business
may be misrepresented in the same way. — You, I beg, will take
care to prevent it. — I tax your wish for Mr Burns's welfare with the
task of waiting as soon as possible, on every gentleman who was
present, & state this to him, & as you please, shew him this letter. —
What after all was the obnoxious toast? — "May our success in the
present war [against France] be equal to the justice of our cause."
— a toast that the most outrageous frenzy of loyalty cannot object to.
— I request & beg that this morning you will wait on the parties
present at the foolish dispute. — The least delay may be of unlucky
consequence to me. — I shall only add, that I am truly sorry that a
man who stood so high in my estimation as Mr Dods, should use me
in the manner in which I conceive he has done.

Presumably Clarke had no difficulty in getting a sobered Captain Dods to see the absurdity of his resentment, for nothing more
is heard of the matter.

Burns took occasion of the first letter to Samuel Clarke to protect his Excise flank. He writes,

You very oblidgingly mentioned something of your intimacy with
Mr Corbet, our Supervisor General. Some of our folks about the

Excise Office, Edinr had, & perhaps still have conceived a prejudice against me as being a drunken dissipated character. — I might be all this, you know, & yet be an honest fellow; but you know that I am an honest fellow and am nothing of this. — You may in your own way let him know that I am not unworthy of subscribing myself

My dear Clarke, YOUR FRIEND

R. BURNS

VI

SONG

He coude songes make and well endite.
Chaucer

Song — verse married to music — was Burns' earliest, his latest, his strongest, and his most enduring poetic interest. His early verse, "a darling walk" of his mind, was much of it love-songs, "the breathings of ardent Passion." "The earliest thing of Composition" to delight him was Addison's hymn, *How Are Thy Servants Blest, O Lord!* His own first composition was a song to a girl, and he notes two later songs he had composed at seventeen. As a boy and young man, Burns stored his mind with songs, some of them favorites of his mother's, some popular in the country side, some published in chapbooks, or in Ramsay's *Tea-Table Miscellany,* or in another, unidentified, collection of which he wrote, "The Collection of Songs was my vade mecum. — I pored over them, driving my cart or walking to labor, song by song, verse by verse; carefully noting the true tender or sublime from affectation and fustian. — I am convinced I owe much to this for my critic-craft such as it is." That his early interest in songs was well known is evident from a comment he made, after he had begun to assist with the *Scots Musical Museum,* to his boyhood friend James Candlish. "This, you will easily guess, is an undertaking exactly to my taste."

The relative amounts of space given to songs and to other matters in Burns' Commonplace Book of 1783–1785 emphasizes his enthusiasm. Aside from scattered references in his letters, the

Commonplace Book is the only solid evidence available of Burns' early poetic interest and production. Of its forty-two pages with entries, twenty-three contain songs, fragments of songs, or comments on songs. There are, in addition, four pages of rhymed prayers, one of epitaphs, and nine pages with three poems — *The Death and Dying Words of Poor Mailie* and two epistles to John Lapraik. The other five pages are given to varied reflections.

Great interest attaches to passages in the Commonplace Book of carefully considered comment on Scots song. It has been held hitherto that Burns reached his views independently, as a result of native good taste and perception, and it may well be so, but Professor Kinsley has recently shown that some of Burns' opinions find parallels in the published criticism of his day.

During September, 1785, he wrote,

There is a certain irregularity in the old Scotch Songs, a redundancy of syllables with respect to that exactness of accent & measure that the English Poetry requires, but which glides in, most melodiously with the respective tunes to which they are set. For instance, the fine old Song of The Mill Mill O, to give it a plain prosaic reading it halts prodigiously out of measure; on the other hand, the Song set to the same tune in Bremner's Collection* of Scotch Songs which begins "To Fanny fair I could impart &c." it is most exact measure, and yet let them both be sung before a real Critic, one above the biasses of prejudice, but a thorough Judge of Nature, — how flat & spiritless will the last appear, how trite, and tamely methodical, compared with the wild-warbling cadence, the heart-moving melody of the first. — This particularly is the case with all those airs which end in a hypermetrical syllable. — There is a degree of wild irregularity in many of the compositions & Fragments which are daily sung to them by my compeers, the common people — a certain happy arrangement of old Scotch syllables, & yet, very frequently, nothing, not even *like* rhyme, or sameness of jingle at the ends of the lines. — This has made me sometimes imagine that perhaps, it might be possible for a Scotch Poet, with a nice judicious ear, to set compositions to many of our most favorite airs, particularly that class of them mentioned above, independent of rhyme altogether.

* Robert Bremner was editor of several collections of Scots airs.

Later he comments on a song he had written,

I have even tryed to imitate, in this extempore thing, that irregularity in the rhyme which, when judiciously done, has such a fine effect on the ear. —

Fragment — Tune — Galla Water

Altho' my bed were in yon muir,
   Among the heather, in my plaidie,
Yet happy happy would I be
   Had I my dear Montgomerie's Peggy. —

When o'er the hill beat surly storms,
   And winter nights were dark and rainy;
I'd seek some dell, and in my arms
   I'd shelter dear Montgomerie's Peggy. —

Were I a Baron proud and high,
   And horse and servants waiting ready,
Then a' 'twad gie o' joy to me,
   The sharin't with Montgomerie's Peggy. –

Finally he suggests the best way to compose a song to one of the traditional tunes. "These old Scottish airs are so nobly sentimental that when one would compose to them; to south the tune, as our Scotch phrase is, over & over, is the readiest way to catch the inspiration and raise the Bard into that glorious enthusiasm so strongly characteristic of our old Scotch Poetry."

It should be noted that here Burns is expressing delight in values which he continued to cherish, and stating principles which influenced him not only in his later extensive work with songs, but in his poetry, also. He urges the primacy of melody in song, the grace of a "wild irregularity," the happy effects of escaping from the "sameness of jingle at the end of the line," the sublimity that grows from simplicity or natural expression, and the need for "Scotch syllables" to bring out the full flavor of Scotch tunes. It is important to remember that while

many of Burns' songs make charming short poems, and are often
thought of as poems, Burns wrote them as songs and considered
them to be songs. The music for a song always came first with
him; almost all the songs were written for specific tunes, and they
should be heard with tunes, preferably the tunes for which Burns
wrote them.

Further evidence of his early interest in popular songs and his
wide knowledge of them, is his famous cantata, *The Jolly Beggars*, or *Love and Liberty*. Many think it his finest production.
Said to have been inspired by a brief visit with John Richmond
and James Smith to a beggars' revel at Poosie Nansie Gibson's
dive in Mauchline, this work, like most of Burns', is derivative.
The cast, the structure, the verse forms, and the songs are all
traditional. Burns seems to have experimented with *Love and
Liberty*, and to have pruned it, as he was accustomed to do. Richmond speaks of songs by a sweep, a sailor, and Nansie's daughter
Racer Jess, all now lost; and the Merry Andrew section survives
only on a separate sheet. The cantata is structurally much better
without it. Burns wished to include *Love and Liberty* in his Edinburgh edition, but his wish was opposed by the elegant and
Reverend Dr. Hugh Blair, and the cantata was omitted. Perhaps
it should be noted that Burns had omitted the cantata from his
Kilmarnock volume, also. In September, 1793, Burns wrote to
George Thomson, "I have forgot the Cantata you allude to, as I
kept no copy, & indeed did not know that it was in existence;
however, I remember that none of the songs pleased myself, except the last — something about,

> 'Courts for cowards were erected,
> 'Churches built to please the priest' — "

This "puissant and splendid production," as Matthew Arnold
called it, was first published in a chapbook in Glasgow (1799),
as *The Jolly Beggars*, the title on the manuscript used by the
publisher. But *Love and Liberty*, the title on another manu-

script, describes the sentiments and theme of the piece far better.

The descriptive passages of *Love and Liberty* (which Burns called "recitativos," an odd term for him to use in describing Scots vernacular verse) are some of the most vivid and memorable poetry he ever wrote, and they give the songs a great lift. The songs themselves are lively, and appropriate for their singers, but one can easily understand Burns' dissatisfaction with them. The soldier, his doxy, the female thief, the bullying tinker, and the ballad singer in his second song all use a moderately polite English which is out of character and out of key with the introduction and the setting. If in successful art every element must combine to strengthen the central effect, then, despite the vigor of these songs, Burns was right that they are in some degree unsatisfactory. The fiddler's song, only, is tinged with the Doric and quite in character, with its refrain "Whistle owre the Lave o't" (a traditional cant phrase of bawdy ambiguity — roughly equivalent to "Let's not worry about that").

The Anglified songs are picturesque, but they lack the realistic vulgarity appropriate to the occasion and the singers. Moreover, the cantata is not well-suited to performance, although it is performed from time to time, and the songs give a good effect as detached pieces, particularly *John Highlandman.* The recitativos are something else again — pungent, humorous, dramatic — done with an assured brevity that gives vitality to a stale convention. They bring the group in Poosie Nansie's grimy hostel sharply alive. And here again, as in all of Burns' great poems, there is the rich, fresh language, the memorable phrasing, the swift finality of style.

Despite its unevenness, *Love and Liberty* moves irresistibly from the initial tableau of the ragged veteran and his doxy through the increasingly dramatic conflicts involving the fiddler, the trull, and the tinker, to the thunderously received first song of the Bard, and then to his fiery second, when, literally, all Hell breaks loose.

There are other verse tales than *Tam o' Shanter* in our literature, if few so good, and none in the Eighteenth Century. Where at all, however, is there anything to approach *Love and Liberty*?

Love and Liberty

A Cantata

1

RECITATIVO

When lyart leaves bestrow the yird,   *gray*
Or wavering like the Bauckie-bird,   *bat*
  Bedim cauld Boreas' blast;
When hailstanes drive wi' bitter skyte   *slanting stroke*
And infant Frosts begin to bite,
  In hoary cranreuch drest;   *hoarfrost*
Ae night at e'en a merry core
  O' randie, gangrel bodies,
In poosie-Nansie's held the splore,   *riotous frolic*
  To drink their orra dudies: *extra rags*
    Wi' quaffing, and laughing,
      They ranted an' they sang;
    Wi' jumping, and thumping,
      The vera girdle rang.   *griddle*

First, niest the fire, in auld, red rags,   *next*
Ane sat; weel brac'd wi' mealy bags,
  And knapsack a' in order;
His doxy lay within his arm;
Wi' usquebae an' blankets warm,   *whisky*
  She blinket on her Sodger;
An' ay he gies the tozie drab   *tipsy*
  The tither skelpan kiss,   *another smacking*
While she held up her greedy gab   *mouth*
  Just like an aumous dish: *beggar's bowl for alms*
    Ilk smack still, did crack still,
      Just like a cadger's whip;   *horse driver's*
    Then staggering, an' swaggering,
      He roar'd this ditty up —

1

SONG

Tune: *Soldier's Joy*

I am a Son of Mars who have been in many wars,
    And show my cuts and scars wherever I come;
This here was for a Wench, and that other in a trench,
    When welcoming the French at the sound of the drum.
        Lal de daudle &c.

My Prenticeship I past where my Leader breath'd his last,
    When the bloody die was cast on the heights of Abram;
And I served out my TRADE when the gallant GAME was play'd,
    And the MORO low was laid at the sound of the drum.

I lastly was with Curtis among the FLOATING BATT'RIES,
    And there I left for witness, an arm and a limb;
Yet let my Country need me, with Elliot to head me,
    I'd clatter on my stumps at the sound of a drum.

And now tho' I must beg, with a wooden arm and leg,
    And many a tatter'd rag hanging over my bum,
I'm as happy with my wallet my bottle and my Callet,   *woman*
    As when I us'd in scarlet to follow a drum.

What tho', with hoary locks, I must stand the winter shocks,
    Beneath the woods and rocks, oftentimes for a home,
When the tother bag I sell and the tother bottle tell,
    I could meet a troop of Hell at the sound of the drum.

2

RECITATIVO

He ended; and the kebars sheuk,   *rafters shook*
    Aboon the chorus roar;   *above*
While frighted rattons backward leuk,   *rats*
    An' seek the benmost bore;   *inmost hole*

A fairy FIDDLER frae the neuk   *from the corner,*
    He skirl'd out, ENCORE,   *shrilled out*
But up arose the martial CHUCK,   *wench*
    An' laid the loud uproar —

2

SONG
Tune: *Sodger Laddie*

I once was a Maid tho' I cannot tell when,
And still my delight is in proper young men:
Some one of a troop of DRAGOONS was my dadie,
No wonder I'm fond of a SODGER LADDIE.
      Sing lal de dal &c.

The first of my LOVES was a swaggering blade,
To rattle the thundering drum was his trade;
His leg was so tight and his cheek was so ruddy,
Transported I was with my SODGER LADDIE.

But the godly old Chaplain left him in the lurch;
The sword I forsook for the sake of the church;
He ventur'd the SOUL, and I risked the BODY,
'Twas then I prov'd false to my SODGER LADDIE.

Full soon I grew sick of my sanctified Sot,
The Regiment at large for a husband I got;
From the gilded SPONTOON to the FIFE I was ready,   *pike*
I asked no more but a SODGER LADDIE.

But the PEACE it reduc'd me to beg in despair,
Till I met my old boy in a CUNNINGHAM fair;
His RAGS REGIMENTAL they flutter'd so gaudy,
My heart it rejoic'd at a SODGER LADDIE.

And now I have lived — I know not how long,
And still I can join in a cup and a song;
But whilst with both hands I can hold the glass steady,
Here's to thee, MY HERO MY SODGER LADDIE.

3

RECITATIVO

Then niest outspak a raucle Carlin   *next*   *coarse old woman*
Who ken't fu' weel to cleek the Sterlin;   *knew how*   *snatch*
For mony a pursie she had hooked,
An' had in mony a well been douked: *ducked*

Her LOVE had been a HIGHLAND LADDIE,
But weary fa' the waefu' woodie!   *ill betide*   *noose*
Wi' sighs an' sobs she thus began
To wail her braw JOHN HIGHLANDMAN.   *fine*

3
SONG
Tune: O, an' ye were dead, Gudeman

A highland lad my Love was born,
The lalland laws he held in scorn: *lowland*
But he still was faithfu' to his clan,
My gallant, braw John Highlandman.

Chorus
Sing hey my braw John Highlandman!
Sing ho my braw John Highlandman!
There's not a lad in a' the lan'
Was match for my John Highlandman.

With his philibeg, an' tartan plaid,   *kilt*
An' guid Claymore down by his side,   *Highland sword*
The ladies' hearts he did trepan   *beguile*
My gallant, braw John Highlandman.
        Sing hey &c.

We ranged a' from Tweed to Spey,
An' liv'd like lords an' ladies gay:
For a lalland face he feared none,
My gallant, braw John Highlandman.
        Sing hey &c.

They banish'd him beyond the sea,
But ere the bud was on the tree,
Adown my cheeks the pearls ran,
Embracing my John Highlandman.
        Sing hey &c.

But Och! they catch'd him at the last,
And bound him in a dungeon fast,
My curse upon them every one,
They've hang'd my braw John Highlandman.
        Sing hey &c.

And now a widow I must mourn
The pleasures that will ne'er return;
No comfort but a hearty can,
When I think on John Highlandman.
   Sing hey &c.

4

RECITATIVO

A pigmy Scraper wi' his Fiddle,
Wha us'd to trystes an' fairs to driddle, *cattle markets* *totter*
Her strappan limb an' gausy middle,   *buxom*
  (He reach'd nae higher)
Had hol'd his heartie like a riddle   *sieve*
  An' blawn't on fire.

Wi' hand on hainch, and upward e'e,   *haunch*
He croon'd his gamut, ONE, TWO, THREE,
Then in an ARIOSO key,
  The wee Apollo
Set off wi' ALLEGRETTO glee
  His GIGA SOLO —   *jig-song*

4

SONG
Tune: *Whistle owre the lave o't*

Let me ryke up to dight that tear,   *reach* *wipe*
An' go with me an' be my DEAR;
An' then your every CARE an' FEAR
  May whistle owre the lave o't.   *rest of it*

Chorus

I am a Fiddler to my trade,
An' a' the tunes that e'er I play'd,
The sweetest still to WIFE or MAID,
  Was whistle owre the lave o't.

At KIRNS an' WEDDINS we'se be there, *harvest homes* *we'll*
An' O sae nicely's we will fare!
We'll bowse about till Dadie CARE   *boose*
  Sing whistle owre the lave o't.
    I am &c.

Sae merrily's the banes we'll pyke,   *bones   pick*
An' sun oursells about the dyke;
An' at our leisure when ye like
    We'll whistle owre the lave o't.
      I am &c.

But bless me wi' your heav'n o' charms,
An' while I kittle hair on thairms   *tickle   gut strings*
HUNGER, CAULD, an' a' sic harms
    May whistle owre the lave o't.
      I am &c.

5

RECITATIVO

Her charms had struck a sturdy CAIRD,   *tinker*
    As weel as poor GUTSCRAPER;
He taks the Fiddler by the beard,
    An' draws a roosty rapier —   *rusty*
He swoor by a' was swearing worth
    To speet him like a Pliver,   *spit   Plover*
Unless he would from that time forth
    Relinquish her forever:
Wi' ghastly e'e poor Tweedledee
    Upon his hunkers bended,   *haunches*
An' pray'd for grace wi' ruefu' face,
    An' so the quarrel ended;
But tho' his little heart did grieve,
    When round the TINKLER prest her,
He feign'd to snirtle in his sleeve   *snigger*
    When thus the CAIRD address'd her —

5

SONG
Tune: *Clout the Caudron*   *Mend   Cauldron*

My bonie lass I work in brass,
    A TINKLER is my station;   *tinker*
I've travell'd round all Christian ground
    In this my occupation;

I've ta'en the gold an' been enroll'd
  In many a noble squadron;
But vain they search'd when off I march'd
  To go an' clout the CAUDRON.
      I've ta'en the gold &c.

Despite that SHRIMP, that withered IMP,
  With a' his noise an' cap'rin;
An' take a share with those that bare
  The BUDGET and the APRON!   *leather bag*
And *by* that STOWP! my faith and houpe,   *pot   hope*
  And *by* that dear KEILBAIGIE,   *whiskey*
If e'er ye want, or meet with scant,
  May I ne'er WEET MY CRAIGIE!   *wet my throat*
      And by that Stowp, &c.

6

RECITATIVO

The Caird prevail'd — th'unblushing fair
  In his embraces sunk;
Partly wi' LOVE o'ercome saw sair,   *sore*
  An' partly she was drunk:
SIR VIOLINO with an air
  That show'd a man o' spunk,
Wish'd UNISON between the pair,
  An' made the bottle clunk
      To their health that night.

But hurchin Cupid shot a shaft,   *urchin*
  That play'd a DAME a shavie —   *trick*
The Fiddler RAK'd her fore and aft,
  Behint the Chicken cavie: *coop*
Her lord, a Wight of Homer's craft,
  Tho' limpan wi' the Spavie,   *Spavin*
He hirpl'd up an' lap like daft,   *hobbled   leapt*
  An' shor'd them DAINTY DAVIE *offered them a night of it*
      O' boot that night.

He was a care-defying blade,
  As ever Bacchus listed!   *enlisted*
Tho' Fortune sair upon him laid,
  His heart she ever miss'd it.

He had no WISH but — to be glad,
  Nor WANT but — when he thristed: *thirsted*
He hated nought but — to be sad,
  And thus the Muse suggested
    His sang that night.

6

SONG
Tune: *For a' that an' a' that*

I am a BARD of no regard,
  Wi' gentle folks an' a' that;
But HOMER LIKE the glowran byke,   *staring crowd*
  Frae town to town I draw that.

Chorus

For a' that an' a' that,
  An' twice as muckle's a' that
I've lost but ANE, I've TWA behin',
  I've WIFE ENEUGH for a' that.

I never drank the Muses' STANK,   *pond*
  Castalia's burn an' a' that,   *stream*
But there it streams an' richly reams,   *froths*
  My HELICON I ca' that.
    For a' that &c.

Great love I bear to all the FAIR,
  Their humble slave and a' that;
But lordly WILL, I hold it still   *sexual appetite*
  A mortal sin to thraw that.   *thwart*
    For a' that &c.

In raptures sweet this hour we meet,
  Wi' mutual love an' a' that;
But for how lang the FLIE MAY STANG   *desire   sting*
  Let INCLINATION law that.   *determine*
    For a' that &c.

Their tricks an' craft hae put me daft,
  They've ta'en me in, an' a' that,

But clear your decks an' here's the SEX
  I like the jads for a' that.   *jades*
     For a' that an' a' that,
       An' twice as muckle's a' that,
     My DEAREST BLUID to do them guid
       They're welcome till't for a' that.   *to it*

7

RECITATIVO

So sung the BARD — and Nansie's waws   *walls*
Shook with a thunder of applause
  Re'echo'd from each mouth!
They toom'd their pocks, they pawn'd their duds, *emptied their bags*
They scarcely left to coor their fuds,   *cover their buttocks*
  To quench their lowan drouth: *burning*
Then owre again the jovial thrang   *throng*
  The Poet did request,
To lowse his PACK an' wale a sang,   *loose   choose a song*
  A BALLAD o' the best.
     He, rising, rejoicing,
       Between his twa DEBORAHS,
     Looks round him an' found them
       Impatient for the Chorus.

7

SONG
Tune: *Jolly Mortals, fill your glasses*

See the smoking bowl before us,
  Mark our jovial, ragged ring!
Round and round take up the Chorus,
  And in raptures let us sing —

Chorus

A fig for those by law protected!
  LIBERTY's a glorious feast!
Courts for Cowards were erected,
  Churches built to please the PRIEST.

What is TITLE, what is TREASURE,
  What is REPUTATION's care?
If we lead a life of pleasure,
  'Tis no matter HOW or WHERE.
      A fig for &c.

With the ready trick and fable
  Round we wander all the day;
And at night, in barn or stable,
  Hug our doxies on the hay.
      A fig for &c.

Does the train-attended CARRIAGE
  Thro' the country lighter rove?
Does the sober bed of MARRIAGE
  Witness brighter scenes of love?
      A fig for &c.

Life is all a VARIORUM,
  We regard not how it goes;
Let them cant about DECORUM,
  Who have character to lose.
      A fig for &c.

Here's to BUDGETS, BAGS and WALLETS!
  Here's to all the wandering train!
Here's our ragged BRATS and CALLETS!
  One and all cry out, AMEN!

A fig for those by law protected,
  LIBERTY's a glorious FEAST!
COURTS for Cowards were erected,
  CHURCHES built to please the priest.

Just how much Burns knew about music is puzzling. In September, 1785, he wrote, "I set about composing an air in the old Scotch style. I am not Musical Scholar enough to prick down my tune properly, so that it can never see the light, and perhaps 'tis no great matter." However, Burns learned to read music after a fashion, and became intimately familiar with many books of Scotch airs. In 1791, he told Johnson that he had "all the music of the country," except one collection, which he wished to have. It should be mentioned also that church instruction in music was customary in Burns' day, and we have seen that John Murdoch attempted some elementary musical training at the Alloway school.* As a young man, Burns bought a fiddle, on which he learned to play slow tunes.

He often mentioned having had songs played or sung for him, particularly after his association with James Johnson had begun. The journals of his tours record his being sung to with pleasure, and during his winter with William Cruikshank while he was nursing his injured knee, he enjoyed hours of listening to young Janet Cruikshank play on her harpsichord. He mentions his wife's singing many times, and when he lived at Ellisland he had as neighbor one Kirsty Flint, whose lusty voice was at his service. At Ellisland also, he speaks of having had "an able Fiddler" with him, and in Dumfries he thanks Johnson for making him acquainted with Nathaniel Gow, another fiddler. Later during the Dumfries years he mentions "Fraser, the Hautboy player," a "musical Highlander," and a "Singing Master." And there is frequent mention in his letters of Stephen Clarke, the Edinburgh organist and musical editor of the Museum, who was often about Dumfries professionally. From these and other sources Burns learned with precision, and carried in his head, the body of Scotch folk tunes, and many others as well.

Although he won his first fame with poems on his life, and opinions, and conflict with the Kirk, his Edinburgh experience did not divert him from a main interest in vernacular poetry. Rather, his discovery that in Edinburgh the patricians, the gentry, the literati, the Crochallans — all were enthusiasts about folk songs, served to encourage him in returning to his earlier and still strong interest. We have seen, also, that after his great

---

* He found Robert's voice untunable. In later life Burns responded to calls for his songs by reciting them. His mature singing voice was harsh. (See Anderson, 147; Adair, 189; and Syme, 413.)

success, he felt "Scots poetry" had become "contemptible" through the rush of petty and often imitative Scots versifiers into print, and that he feared mortification if he continued to write even superior poetry of that sort since it no longer offered novelty. Songs, however, were another matter.

The task he set himself was to provide words for all the tunes which he liked and felt were worth preserving. When, as often was true with dance tunes, there were no words, he wrote them, frequently taking hints from titles or other songs; when there were fragments, he expanded or combined them; when there were good verses, he adopted them; and when existing songs seemed faulty, he mended them. He took no money for his work, and he did not acknowledge authorship. He rhymed for fun, and for Scotland, and his great enthusiasm extended far beyond merely composing words for tunes. In January 1793, for example, he wrote to Thomson, "Lochaber and the braes of Ballenden, excepted, so far as the locality either from the title of the air, or the tenor of the Song, could be ascertained, I have paid my devotions at the particular shrine of every Scots Muse." In simple language, he had visited the site associated with every Scots song that he knew except two. And, more important, after he began his association with Johnson in 1787, Burns was alert and active in collecting unpublished songs *and tunes*. He was as much concerned with the music of the *Scots Musical Museum* as with the song texts.

Burns did not live to publish his projected volume of the songs he wished to acknowledge, or his notes on Scots song, although many of the notes do survive in the interleaved *Museum* which he prepared for Robert Riddell, and on sheets in the Laing collection of the University of Edinburgh. The extent of Burns' knowledge and the scope of his activity, and often even the fact or proportion of his authorship of individual songs, must be determined largely from these notes, or from letters. But anyone who examines this material recognizes at once that Burns had, as he said, "paid more attention to every description of Scots songs than perhaps any body living has done." Fortunately, Thomson preserved Burns' letters to him (they are now in the Morgan library); and the Johnson letters and memoranda for volumes I–IV of the *Museum* are in the British Museum, with others known and in private hands. In addition, Burns' general correspondence is full of songs and comments on songs.

James Johnson was content to take what Burns sent him, but George Thomson chose to suggest melodies for which Burns should write lyrics, and then to suggest changes in the lyrics. Thomson can be indexed quickly as a man who objected to *Comin' Thro' the Rye* because young ladies might not like to sing about kissing. A typical proposal from him was that Burns substitute "Ne'er made sic anither" in the lines, "For Nature made her what she is / And never made anither." Burns refused the suggestion. For "mammie's wark" [work], Thomson preferred "mother's wark," and Burns remarked cryptically, "If you think this last is better, you may adopt it." Thomson demurred at the tune for which Burns wrote *Scots Wha Hae,* and at the third line of the first stanza:

> Scots wha hae wi' Wallace bled,
> Scots, wham Bruce has often led,
> Welcome to your gory bed, —
> Or to victorie.

Burns replied, "Your idea, 'honour's bed,' is, though a beautiful, a hacknied idea; so, if you please, we will let the line stand as it is. I have altered the song as follows." He repeats the stanza, modifying the last line to read "Or to glorious victorie" so that it might accommodate Thomson's tune. The two additional syllables in each fourth line produced such results as "Traitor! Coward! turn & flie!" "Caledonian! on wi' me!" and "But they shall be — shall be free!" Public disapproval forced Thomson to restore Burns' original lines when Currie printed them in his biography in 1800.

Without extensive background, the mass of detailed comment about lines, phrases, titles, and tunes in the Burns-Thomson correspondence is tiresome, but there are frequent passages in Burns' letters which reveal his knowledge, his taste, and his concern about the relation of words to music. Salty comments also enliven his letters. For example, "I have begun anew, Let me in this ae night. — Do you think that we ought to retain the old Chorus? I think we must retain both the old chorus & the first Stanza of the old Song. — I do not altogether like the third line of the first Stanza, but cannot alter it to please myself. — I am just three stanzas deep in it.

[Here he quotes the stanzas.]

How do you like this? and would you have the denouement to be successful or otherwise? Should she 'let him in,' or not?" In the song as printed she does not.

Burns and Thomson disagreed about what Burns called "simplicity," and about the related desirability of a Scots vocabulary. Thomson was for English elegance, English words, and propriety. But Burns wrote to him, "Let me tell you, that you are too fastidious in your ideas of Songs & ballads." And later, "Give me leave to criticize your taste in the only thing in which it is in my opinion reprehensible: (you know I ought to know something of my own trade) of Pathos, Sentiment, & Point, you are a compleat judge; but there is a quality more necessary than either, in a Song, & which is the very essence of a Ballad, I mean Simplicity — now, if I mistake not, this last feature you are a little apt to sacrifice to the foregoing." Elsewhere he writes, "There is a pastoral simplicity, a something that one may call, the Doric style & dialect of vocal music, to which a dash of our native tongue & manners is particularly, nay peculiarly apposite."

He later gives an example. "There is a naïveté, a pastoral simplicity, in a slight intermixture of Scots words & phraseology, which is more in unison (at least to my taste, & I will add, to

every genuine Caledonian taste,) with the simple pathos, or
rustic sprightliness, of our native music, than any English verses
whatever. — For instance, in my Auld Rob Morris, you propose
instead of the word, 'descriving,' to substitute the phrase 'all telling', which would spoil the rusticity, the pastoral, of the stanza."
In the interleaved *Museum*, Burns cites lines from *There's Nae
Luck about the House* as "unequalled almost by anything I ever
heard or read." In the stanza he admired, the sailor's wife, on
hearing of her husband's return, sings,

> His very foot has music in't
>   As he comes up the stair.
> And will I see his face again?
>   And will I hear him speak?
> I'm downright dizzy wi' the thought —
>   In truth I'm like to greet!   *weep*

Burns continues to emphasize this critical principle in letters
to Thomson. "I still have several M. S. S. Scots airs by me, which
I have pickt up, mostly from the singing of country lasses. —
They please me vastly; but your learned lugs [ears] would perhaps be displeased with the very features for which I like them.
— I call them Simple; you would pronounce them Silly." And
elsewhere, "Now let me declare off from your taste. — Toddlin
hame is a song that to my taste is an exquisite production of
genius. — That very Stanza you dislike

> 'My kimmer & I lay down to sleep   *gossip (girl)*
>   [And twa pint stoups at our bed feet   *tankards*
> And ay when we waken'd we drank them dry;
>   What think you of my wee kimmer and I?']

is to me a piece of charming native humour. — What pleases
me, as simple & naive, disgusts you as ludicrous & low."
  Apparently Thomson was not alone in his feelings. "The legion
of Scotish Poetasters of the day," Burns wrote, "whom your
brother Editor, Mr Ritson, ranks with me as my coevals, have

always mistaken vulgarity for simplicity; whereas Simplicity is as much eloignée from vulgarity, on the one hand, as from affected point & puerile conceit, on the other." Thomson proved obdurate, however, and his niggling moved Burns to his famous outburst, "These English Songs gravel me to death." However, he continued to supply a good many of them at Thomson's insistence, acceding to Thomson's requests when he could, and noting once, "The rhythm of the song is abused as you desired."

In the matter of revision, Burns made a distinction between traditional songs and the work of individual poets. He wrote of some tampering by his acquaintance, Josiah Walker, "Let a Poet, if he chuses, take up the idea of another, & work it into a piece of his own; but to mangle the works of the poor Bard whose tuneful tongue is now mute forever in the dark & narrow house, by Heaven 'twould be Sacriledge! I grant that Mr Walker's version is an improvement; but, I know Mr Walker well, & esteem him much; let him mend the Song as the Highlander mended his gun: he gave it a new stock, a new lock, & a new barrel."

Burns also had strong objections to elegant modification of Scots folk music. Of Thomson's musical editor, Joseph Pleyel, he exclaims, "Whatever Mr Pleyel does, let him not alter one iota of the original Scots Air [of the tune for *Highland Mary*]; . . . Let our National Music preserve its native features. They are, I own, frequently wild, & unreducable to the modern rules; but on that very eccentricity, perhaps, depends a great part of their effect."

Of sophisticated formal music, Burns had little or no understanding, but the "nobly sentimental" Scotch airs delighted him as much as the songs for them. Here he found no response from the improving Thomson, to whom he wrote, "I am sensible that my taste in Music must be inelegant & vulgar, because people of undisputed & cultivated taste can find no merit in many of my favorite tunes. — Still, because I am cheaply pleased, is that any reason why I should deny myself that pleasure? — Many of our Strathspeys, ancient & modern, give me most exquisite enjoyment, where you & other judges would probably be shewing signs of disgust. — For instance, I am just now making verses for Rothemurche's Rant, an air which puts me in raptures: & in fact, unless I be pleased with the tune, I never can make verses to it." This final statement should be noted most particularly, since Burns speaks often of trying with small success to write for tunes suggested by Thomson which he had no liking for.

Elsewhere he comments, "You know that my pretensions to musical taste, are merely a few of Nature's instincts, untaught & untutored by Art. — For this reason, many musical compositions, particularly where much of the merit lies in Counterpoint, however they may transport & ravish the ears of you, Connoisseurs, affect my simple lug no otherwise than merely as melodious Din."

Burns felt that no tune was complete without words to sing it by. "I think that it is better," he wrote, "to have mediocre verses to a favorite air than none at all." Indeed, the very quality of the music made it difficult, often, to provide words at all. "If you mean, my dear Sir," he wrote Thomson in his third letter to him, "that all the Songs in your Collection shall be Poetry of the first merit, I am afraid you will find difficulty in the undertaking more than you are aware of. — There is a peculiar rhythmus in many of our airs, and a necessity of adapting syllables to the emphasis, or what I would call, the *feature notes,* of the tune, that cramps the Poet, & lays him under almost insuperable difficulties." But Burns did not reconcile himself to a merely utilitarian mediocrity. He "had rather be the author of five well-written songs than of ten otherwise," and he suppressed songs which he did not feel were tolerable, or told Thomson to do so.

It is with these difficulties in mind that Burns wrote to the Rev. John Skinner, "The world may think slightingly of the craft of song-making, if they please, but as Job says — 'O that mine adversary had written a book!' — let them try. There is a certain something in the old Scotch songs, a wild happiness of thought and expression, which peculiarly marks them, not only from English songs, but also from the modern efforts of song-wrights, in our native manner and language."

It was Burns' ability to surmount the difficulties he mentions, and to capture the "certain something in the old Scotch songs" which is his distinguishing achievement. He knew that many of his songs were "trifling enough perhaps, but they served as a vehicle to the music." As he said elsewhere, of the *Museum,* "Once for all, let me apologize for many silly compositions of mine in this work. Many beautiful airs wanted words; in the hurry of other avocations, if I could string a parcel of rhymes together any thing near tolerable, I was fain to let them pass." It is, however, an illuminating experience to compare Burns' songs with those he worked from, or with the common fare of the song books. His standards were high, and his achievement unsurpassed in technical skill, and in working within the spirit and manner of the folk songs he loved.

On another difficulty, that of keeping fresh and original, Burns makes a brilliant and bawdy comment to Thomson.

Originality is a coy feature, in composition, & in a multiplicity of efforts in the same style disappears entirely. . . . Some years ago, when I was young, & by no means the saint I am now, I was looking over, in company with a belle lettre friend, a Magazine Ode to Spring, when my friend fell foul of the recurrence of the same thoughts, & offered me a bet that it was impossible to produce an Ode to Spring on an original plan. — I accepted it, & pledged myself to bring in the verdant fields, — the budding flowers, — the chrystal streams, — the melody of the groves, — & a love-story into the bargain, & yet be original. Here follows the piece, & wrote for music too!

Ode to Spring — Tune — The tither morn. —

When maukin bucks, at early fucks,	*hare*
In dewy grass are seen, Sir,	
And birds, on boughs, take off their mows	*coits*
Among the leaves sae green, Sir;	

Latona's sun looks liquorish on
    Dame Nature's grand impètus
Till his prick go rise, then westward flies
    To roger Madame Thetis.

Yon wandering rill that marks the hill,
    And glances o'er the brae, Sir,
Slides by a bower where many a flower
    Sheds fragrance on the day, Sir;
There Damon lay, with Sylvia gay,
    To love they thought no crime, Sir;
The wild-birds sang, the echoes rang,
    While Damon's arse beat time, Sir. —

First, wi' the thrush, his thrust & push
    Had compass large & long, Sir;
The blackbird next, his tuneful text,
    Was bolder, clear & strong, Sir:
The linnet's lay then came in play,
    And the lark that soar'd aboon, Sir;   *above*
Till Damon fierce, mistimed his arse,
    And fucked quite out of tune, Sir.

Now for decency. — A great critic, Aikin on songs, says that love & wine are the exclusive themes for song-writing. — The following is on neither subject, & consequently is no Song; but will be allowed, I think, to be two or three pretty good *prose* thoughts inverted into rhyme.

Is There for Honest Poverty follows. The rapid shift in tone and spirit is highly characteristic of Burns' letters.

Those to Johnson and Thomson also teem with detailed and precise directions for fitting words to melodies. In these instructions there is much to indicate that he had come to understand musical notation. Of *O Saw Ye Bonie Lesley,* he writes to Thomson in November, 1792,

Every seventh line ends with three syllables, in place of the two in the other lines, but you will see in the sixth bar of the second part, the place where these three syllables will always recur, that the four semiquavers usually sung as one syllable will with the greatest propriety divide into two — thus

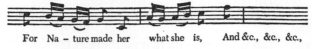

For Na - ture made her   what she   is,   And &c., &c., &c.,

Characteristic later comments show both Burns' concern over musical settings, and the extent and kind of his musical knowledge. For example, "The bonie brucket [soot-marked] lassie — I enclose you a song to it, as I think it should be set; & with a better effect than the modulation in the Museum." To Johnson he wrote of *Turn Again, Thou Fair Eliza,* "The song will not sing to your tune; but there is a Perthshire tune in McDonald's collection of *Highland Airs* which is much admired in this country; I intended the verses to sing to that air. . . . There is another air in the same collection, an Argyleshire air, which with a trifling alteration will do charmingly. . . . The alterations are: in the fourth bar of the first and third strains, which are to be the tune, instead of the crotchet C, and the quavers G and E, at the beginning of the bar make an entire minim in E, I mean E, the lowest line."

Again, to Thomson, he comments on an air for the Jacobite verses, *There'll Never Be Peace Till Jamie Comes Hame.* "It is a little irregular in the flow of the lines; but where two short syllables, that is to say, one syllable more than regular feet, if those two syllables fall to the space of one, crotchet-time, composed of two different quavers under a slur, it has, I think, no bad effect, to divide them." And of another song, he says, "If you honor my verses by setting the air to it, I will vamp up the old Song, & make it English enough to be understood. — I have sent you my song noted down to the air, in the way I think that it should go; I believe you will find my set of the air to be one of the best."

These comments on music may be concluded with a touching analogy. "Conjugal love is a Passion which I deeply feel, & highly venerate; but somehow it does not make such a figure in Poesy as that other species of the Passion —

'Where Love is Liberty & Nature law. — '

Musically speaking, the first is an instrument of which the gamut is scanty & confined, but the tones inexpressibly sweet; while the last has powers equal to all the intellectual Modulation of the Human Soul."

For one with Burns' rhythmic sense, it is not surprising to find that with him composition was often accompanied by physical action. During his years at Ellisland he speaks of having composed while on horseback, and in Dumfries there are frequent references to songs which were the result of walks. He no doubt also welcomed a respite on these walks from the healthy confusion of his household. Once he writes of having tried out a song *viva voce* ("I sat, & raved, under the shade of an old thorn, till I wrote one to suit the measure"). We have already seen that he could not make verses for a tune unless he liked it and could feel it. Moreover, he was a pragmatist, noting, "Making a poem is like begetting a son: you cannot know whether you have a wise man or a fool, untill you produce him to the world & try him."

For convenience, Burns' two famous statements about his methods of composition are herewith repeated. In connection with the second, it may be noted that though his early songs were "breathings of ardent passion," he had to adopt a formula to raise his spirits at age thirty-five. Both comments are addressed to George Thomson, the first in 1793, the second in 1794.

1. "Untill I am compleat master of a tune, in my own singing, (such as it is) I never can compose for it. — My way is: I consider the poetic Sentiment, correspondent to my idea of the musical expression; then chuse my theme; begin one Stanza; when that is composed, which is generally the most difficult part

of the business, I walk out, sit down now & then, look out for objects in Nature around me that are in unison or harmony with the cogitations of my fancy & workings of my bosom; humming every now & then the air with the verses I have framed: when I feel my Muse beginning to jade, I retire to the solitary fireside of my study, & there commit my effusions to paper; swinging, at intervals, on the hindlegs of my elbow-chair, by way of calling forth my own critical strictures, as my pen goes on."

2. "Do you think that the sober, gin-horse routine of existence could inspire a man with life, & love, & joy — could fire him with enthusiasm, or melt him with pathos, equal to the genius of your Book? — No! No!!! — Whenever I want to be more than ordinary *in song;* to be in some degree equal to your diviner airs; do you imagine I fast & pray for the celestial emanation? — Tout au contraire! I have a glorious recipe, the very one that for his own use was invented by the Divinity of Healing & Poesy when erst he piped to the flocks of Admetus. — I put myself on a regimen of admiring a fine woman; & in proportion to the adorability of her charms, in proportion you are delighted with my verses."

J. C. Dick notes than Burns recorded "about forty" tunes not published before, and provided songs for them; and that he edited many airs in instrumental collections for singing. "Very few of the tunes of Burns' songs had been printed with words until they were set to his verses." Dick estimates that only about 200 Scots tunes were available in publications when Burns began his work, and reports that Johnson had appropriated most of the best ones for the first of his volumes. In all, Burns sent some 350 songs to Johnson and Thomson, and for them he "embodied the whole cycle of Scottish Song, both as a writer of original songs, and as, for want of a better definition, a reconstructor of the songs of the past." Burns was no mere collector like David Herd, and certainly no scholar-antiquarian like Joseph Ritson; more than anything else he was a greatly gifted folk-artist, working among traditional materials and making them his own, often turning commonplace work into "living, emotional song."

As Sir Walter Scott has put it, few songs, "whether serious or humourous, passed through his hands without receiving some of those magic touches which, without greatly altering the song, restored its original spirit, or gave it more than it had ever possessed. So dexterously are these touches combined with the ancient structure that the *rifacciamento,* in many instances, could scarcely have been detected without the avowal of the bard himself."

Among the songs which Burns sent to Johnson, two of the happiest combinations of "poetic sentiment," "musical expression," "theme," and illustrations in harmony, are *Sweet Tibbie Dunbar* and *Ay Waukin, O.* Like many other excellent songs in the canon, they have great charm when sung, but only limited appeal when read. *Ay Waukin, O* is especially fine.

Sweet Tibbie Dunbar

O, wilt thou go wi' me, sweet Tibbie Dunbar?
O, wilt thou go wi' me, sweet Tibbie Dunbar?
Wilt thou ride on a horse, or be drawn in a car,
Or walk by my side, O sweet Tibbie Dunbar?

I care na thy daddie, his lands and his money;
I care na thy kin, sae high and sae lordly;
But say that thou'lt hae me for better or waur,   *worse*
And come in thy coatie, sweet Tibbie Dunbar.   *short petticoat*

Ay Waukin, O

Chorus

Ay waukin, O,   *wakeful*
    Waukin still and weary:
Sleep I can get nane
    For thinking on my dearie.

Simmer's a pleasant time:
  Flowers of every colour,
The water rins owre the heugh,   *crag*
  And I long for my true lover.

When I sleep I dream,
  When I wauk I'm eerie,   *apprehensive*
Sleep I can get nane
  For thinkin on my dearie.

Lanely night comes on,
  A' the lave are sleepin,   *rest*
I think on my bonie lad,
  And I bleer my een wi' greetin.   *eyes   weeping*

Ay waukin, O,
  Waukin still and weary:
Sleep I can get nane
  For thinking on my dearie.

Although Burns was widely familiar with ballads, he had little interest in them. But in his letters it was his common practice to use the words "ballad" and "song" almost interchangeably, a practice which reveals that he thought of songs as situation pieces, little stories, like ballads only shorter. Burns in his songs did not weave gossamer threads into mood pieces. Rather, he used concrete language and a compact style to develop human relationships. Most of his early songs, and some of the later ones, grew out of personal experience — often passionate, but they are not private or particular or confessional. While they may reflect Burns' experience, and feelings, and sense of life, the songs depict experience transmuted into art that is representative and general. And many of them, it should be noted, are for women to sing. As Burns wrote to Jean McMurdo of a song he had written about her, "Every composition of this kind must have a series of Dramatic incident in it, so I have had recourse to my invention." Many of these songs make charming little poems, but when they

are read, if they have choruses* or refrains, these pleasant adornments of a song grow monotonous. There follows a brief selection
of these "dramatic lyrics."

Last May a Braw Wooer

Last May a braw wooer cam down the lang glen,
   And sair wi' his love he did deave me.   *deafen*
I said there was naething I hated like men:
   The deuce gae wi'm to believe me, believe me —
   The deuce gae wi'm to believe me!

He spak o' the darts in my bonie black een,
   And vow'd for my love he was diein.
I said, he might die when he liket for Jean:
   The Lord forgie me for liein, for liein —
   The Lord forgie me for liein!

A weel-stocket mailen, himsel for the laird,   *farm*
   And marriage aff-hand were his proffers:
I never loot on that I kenn'd it, or car'd,   *let*
   But I thought I might hae waur offers, waur offers —   *worse*
   But I thought I might hae waur offers.

But what wad ye think? In a fortnight or less
   (The Deil tak his taste to gae near her!)
He up the Gate-Slack to my black cousin, Bess!
   Guess ye how, the jad! I could bear her, could bear her —
   Guess ye how, the jad! I could bear her.

But a' the niest week, as I petted wi' care,   *next*
   I gaed to the tryste o' Dalgarnock,   *cattle-fair*
And wha but my fine fickle lover was there?
   I glowr'd as I'd seen a warlock, a warlock —   *stared*
   I glowr'd as I'd seen a warlock.

But owre my left shouther I gae him a blink,
   Lest neebours might say I was saucy.

* Burns told George Thomson, "I am not fond of choruses to songs." (F II,
#580, 193.)

My wooer he caper'd as he'd been in drink,
   And vow'd I was his dear lassie, dear lassie —
   And vow'd I was his dear lassie!

I spier'd for my cousin fu' couthy and sweet;   *asked   loving*
   Gin she had recover'd her hearin?
And how her new shoon fit her auld, shachl'd feet?   *shoes shapeless*
   But heavens! how he fell a swearin, a swearin —
   But heavens! how he fell a swearin!

He beggèd, for gudesake, I wad be his wife,
   Or else I wad kill him wi' sorrow;
So e'en to preserve the poor body in life,
   I think I maun wed him to-morrow, to-morrow —   *must*
   I think I maun wed him to-morrow!

Duncan Gray

Weary fa' you, Duncan Gray!   *woe befall*
   (Ha, ha, the girdin o't!)   *girthing*
Wae gae by you, Duncan Gray   *Woe go with*
   (Ha, ha, the girdin o't!)
When a' the lave gae to their play,   *rest*
Then I maun sit the lee-lang day,   *must live-long*
And jeeg the cradle wi' my tae,   *jog toe*
   And a' for the girdin o't!

Bonie was the Lammas moon
   (Ha, ha, the girdin o't!),
Glowrin a' the hills aboon   *above*
   (Ha, ha, the girdin o't!).
The girdin brak, the beast cam down,
I tint my curch and baith my shoon, *lost kerchief shoes*
And, Duncan, ye're an unco loon   *rogue*
   Wae on the bad girdin o't!

But Duncan, gin ye'll keep your aith   *if oath*
   (Ha, ha, the girdin o't!),
I'se bless you wi' my hindmost breath   *I'll*
   (Ha, ha, the girdin o't!).
Duncan, gin ye'll keep your aith,

The beast again can bear us baith,
And auld Mess John will mend the skaith   *damage*
And clout the bad girdin o't.   *patch*

Willie Wastle

Willie Wastle dwalt on Tweed,
  The spot they ca'd it Linkumdoddie.
Willie was a wabster guid   *weaver*
  Could stown a clue wi' onie bodie.   *have stolen   skein*
He had a wife was dour and din,   *sullen   dark*
  O, Tinkler Madgie was her mither!   *Tinker*
Sic a wife as Willie had,   *Such*
  I wad na gie a button for her.

She has an e'e (she has but ane),
  The cat has twa the very colour,
Five rusty teeth, forbye a stump,   *besides*
  A clapper-tongue wad deave a miller;   *deafen*
A whiskin beard about her mou,
  Her nose and chin they threaten ither: *each other*
Sic a wife as Willie had,
  I wad na gie a button for her.

She's bow-hough'd, she's hem-shin'd   *bandy-legged   haim-shinned*
  Ae limpin leg a hand-breed shorter;   *one   hand-breadth*
She's twisted right, she's twisted left,
  To balance fair in ilka quarter;   *either*
She has a hump upon her breast,
  The twin o' that upon her shouther: *shoulder*
Sic a wife as Willie had,
  I wad na gie a button for her.

Auld baudrans by the ingle sits,   *Auld pussie*
  An' wi' her loof her face a-washin;   *paw*
But Willie's wife is nae sae trig,
  She dights her grunzie wi' a hushion;   *wipes snout footless stocking*
Her walie nieves like midden-creels,   *ample fists manure-baskets*
  Her face wad fyle the Logan Water: *foul*
Sic a wife as Willie had,
  I wad na gie a button for her.

Wha Is That at My Bower Door

"Wha is that at my bower door?"
   "O, wha is it but Findlay!"
"Then gae your gate, ye'se nae be here."   *go your way*   *you'll*
   "Indeed maun I!" quo' Findlay.   *must*
"What mak ye, sae like a thief?"
   "O, come and see!" quo' Findlay.
"Before the morn ye'll work mischief?"
   "Indeed will I!" quo' Findlay.

"Gif I rise and let you in" —   *If*
   "Let me in!" quo' Findlay —
"Ye'll keep me wauken wi' your din?"
   "Indeed will I!" quo' Findlay.
"In my bower if ye should stay" —
   "Let me stay!" quo' Findlay —
"I fear ye'll bide till break o' day?"
   "Indeed will I!" quo' Findlay.

"Here this night if ye remain" —
   "I'll remain!" quo' Findlay —
"I dread ye'll learn the gate again?"   *way*
   "Indeed will I!" quo' Findlay.
"What may pass within this bower"
   ("Let it pass!" quo' Findlay!)
"Ye maun conceal till your last hour" —
   "Indeed will I!" quo' Findlay.

Tam Glen

My heart is a-breaking, dear tittie,   *sister,*
   Some counsel unto me come len':
To anger them a' is a pity,
   But what will I do wi' Tam Glen?

I'm thinking, wi' sic a braw fellow   *such*   *fine*
   In poortith I might mak a fen'.   *poverty* *shift*
What care I in riches to wallow,
   If I mauna marry Tam Glen?   *must not*

There's Lowrie the laird o' Dumeller:
    "Guid day to you, brute!" he comes ben.   *in*
He brags and he blaws o' his siller,   *money*
    But when will he dance like Tam Glen?

My minnie does constantly deave me,   *mother deafen*
    And bids me beware o' young men.
They flatter, she says, to deceive me —
    But wha can think sae o' Tam Glen?

My daddie says, gin I'll forsake him,   *if*
    He'd gie me guid hunder marks ten.
But if it's ordain'd I maun take him,
    O, wha will I get but Tam Glen?

Yestreen at the valentine's dealing,   *Last night*
    My heart to my mou gied a sten,   *mouth leap*
For thrice I drew ane without failing,
    And thrice it was written "Tam Glen"!

The last Halloween I was waukin   *wakefully watching*
    My droukit sark-sleeve, as ye ken —   *wetted shift-*
His likeness came up the house staukin,   *stalking*
    And the very grey breeks o' Tam Glen!   *breeches*

Come, counsel, dear tittie, don't tarry!
    I'll gie ye my bonie black hen,
Gif ye will advise me to marry   *If*
    The lad I lo'e dearly, Tam Glen.

I'm O'er Young to Marry Yet

Chorus

I'm o'er young, I'm o'er young,
    I'm o'er young to marry yet!
I'm o'er young, 'twad be a sin
    To tak me frae my mammie yet.

I am my mammie's ae bairn,   *only child*
    Wi' unco folk I weary, Sir,   *strange*
And lying in a man's bed,
    I'm fley'd it make me eerie, Sir.   *afraid apprehensive*

Hallowmass is come and gane,
   The nights are lang in winter, Sir,
And you an' I in ae bed —
   In trowth, I dare na venture, Sir!

Fu' loud and shrill the frosty wind
   Blaws thro' the leafless timmer, Sir,   *timber*
But if ye come this gate again,   *way*
   I'll aulder be gin simmer, Sir.   *older be by summer*

Chorus
I'm o'er young, I'm o'er young,
   I'm o'er young to marry yet!
I'm o'er young, 'twad be a sin
   To tak me frae my mammie yet.

What Can a Young Lassie

What can a young lassie,
What shall a young lassie,
What can a young lassie
   Do wi' an auld man?
Bad luck on the penny
That tempted my minnie   *mother*
To sell her puir Jenny
   For siller an' lan'!   *money*

He's always compleenin
Frae mornin to eenin;
He hoasts and he hirples   *coughs hobbles*
   The weary day lang;
He's doylt and he's dozin;   *muddled impotent*
His blude it is frozen —
O, dreary's the night
   Wi' a crazy auld man!

He hums and he hankers,
He frets and he cankers,
I never can please him
   Do a' that I can.

He's peevish an' jealous
Of a' the young fellows —
O, dool on the day   *woe*
    I met wi' an auld man!

My auld auntie Katie
Upon me taks pity,
I'll do my endeavour
    To follow her plan:
I'll cross him an' wrack him
Until I heartbreak him,
And then his auld brass
    Will buy me a new pan.

O, Steer Her Up, an' Haud Her Gaun

O, steer her up, an' haud her gaun —   *rouse*   *keep her going*
    Her mither's at the mill, jo,
An' gin she winna tak a man,   *if*   *will not*
    E'en let her tak her will, jo.
First shore her wi' a gentle kiss,   *threaten*
    Then ca' another gill, jo,   *call for*
An' gin she tak the thing amiss,   *if she should take*
    E'en let her flyte her fill, jo.   *scold*

O, steer her up, an' be na blate,   *bashful*
    An' gin she take it ill, jo,
Then leave the lassie till her fate,
    And time nae langer spill, jo!   *waste*
Ne'er break your heart for ae rebute,   *one rebuff*
    But think upon it still, jo,
That gin the lassie winna do't,
    Ye'll fin' anither will, jo.

It goes without saying that one's delight in productions like these is greatly increased when they are sung.

Of course, songs inseparably linked to melodies in the public mind are among Burns' most famous.

Ye Banks and Braes

Ye banks and braes o' bonie Doon,
    How can ye bloom sae fresh and fair;
How can ye chant, ye little birds,
    And I sae weary, fu' o' care!
Thou'll break my heart, thou warbling bird,
    That wantons thro' the flowering thorn:
Thou minds me o' departed joys,
    Departed, never to return. —

Oft hae I rov'd by bonie Doon,
    To see the rose and woodbine twine;
And lika bird sang o' its Luve,
    And fondly sae did I o' mine. —
Wi' lightsome heart I pu'd a rose,
    Fu' sweet upon its thorny tree;
And my fause Luver staw my rose,   *stole*
    But, ah! he left the thorn wi' me. —

A comparison of this song with an earlier version, *Ye Flowery Banks o' Bonie Doon*, generally agreed to be poetically superior, illustrates simply the special requirement of song. When the song quoted above "is sung to the melody forever associated with it," says Professor T. Crawford, "the extra syllables cease to be redundant, and the song emerges as quite different in mood from the other. . . . When considered as a *song*, and not merely as a verbal pattern, it becomes a beautifully poignant expression of love's melancholy, . . . When associated with the music, the repetition of 'departed' and the stock expression 'never to return' add immeasurably to the pathos."

Green Grow the Rashes, O

Chorus

Green grow the rashes, O;
Green grow the rashes, O;
The sweetest hours that e'er I spend,
Are spent among the lasses, O.

There's nought but care on ev'ry han',
    In every hour that passes, O:
What signifies the life o' man,
    An' 'twere na for the lasses, O.

The war'ly race may riches chase,   *worldly*
    An' riches still may fly them, O;
An' tho' at last they catch them fast,
    Their hearts can ne'er enjoy them, O.

But gie me a cannie hour at e'en,
    My arms about my dearie, O;
An' war'ly cares an' war'ly men,
    May a' gae tapsalteerie, O!   *topsy-turvy*

For you sae douce, ye sneer at this;   *grave*
    Ye're nought but senseless asses, O:
The wisest man the warl' e'er saw,   *world*
    He dearly lov'd the lasses, O.

Auld nature swears, the lovely dears
    Her noblest work she classes, O:
Her prentice han' she try'd on man,
    An' then she made the lasses, O.

Chorus

Green grow the rashes, O;
    Green grow the rashes, O;
The sweetest hours that e'er I spend,
    Are spent among the lasses, O.

Comin Thro' the Rye

Chorus

O, Jenny's a' weet, poor body,   *wet*
    Jenny's seldom dry:
She draigl't a' her petticoatie,   *draggled*
    Comin thro' the rye!

Comin thro' the rye, poor body,
    Comin thro' the rye,

She draigl't a' her petticoatie,
Comin thro' the rye!

Gin a body meet a body
Comin thro' the rye,
Gin a body kiss a body,
Need a body cry?

Gin a body meet a body
Comin thro' the glen,
Gin a body kiss a body,
Need the warld ken?

Chorus

O, Jenny's a' weet, poor body,
Jenny's seldom dry:
She draigl't a' her petticoatie,
Comin thro' the rye!

The popular lines below derive from a second set (#418) in the *Museum,* which Professor Kinsley feels Burns had nothing to do with.

Ilka lassie hae her laddie,
Nane they say hae I;
But a' the lads they smile at me
When comin' thro' the rye.

The bawdy possibilities in this theme, Burns explored elsewhere.

Sweet Afton

Flow gently, sweet Afton, among thy green braes!
Flow gently, I'll sing thee a song in thy praise!
My Mary's asleep by thy murmuring stream —
Flow gently, sweet Afton, disturb not her dream!

Thou stock dove whose echo resounds thro' the glen,
Ye wild whistling blackbirds in yon thorny den,

Thou green-crested lapwing, thy screaming forbear —
I charge you, disturb not my slumbering fair!

How lofty, sweet Afton, thy neighbouring hills,
Far mark'd with the courses of clear, winding rills!
There daily I wander, as noon rises high,
My flocks and my Mary's sweet cot in my eye.

How pleasant thy banks and green vallies below,
Where wild in the woodlands the primroses blow;
There oft, as mild Ev'ning weeps over the lea,
The sweet-scented birk shades my Mary and me.

Thy crystal stream, Afton, how lovely it glides,
And winds by the cot where my Mary resides!
How wanton thy waters her snowy feet lave,
As, gathering sweet flowerets, she stems thy clear wave!

Flow gently, sweet Afton, among thy green braes!
Flow gently, sweet river, the theme of my lays!
My Mary's asleep by thy murmuring stream —
Flow gently, sweet Afton, disturb not her dream!

Auld Lang Syne

Chorus

For auld lang syne, my dear,
For auld lang syne,
We'll tak a cup o' kindness yet
For auld lang syne!

Should auld acquaintance be forgot,
And never brought to mind?
Should auld acquaintance be forgot,
And auld lang syne!

And surely ye'll be your pint-stowp,   *pay for*
And surely I'll be mine,
And we'll tak a cup o' kindness yet
For auld lang syne!

We twa hae run about the braes,
    And pou'd the gowans fine,   *pulled   daisies*
But we've wander'd monie a weary fit   *foot*
    Sin' auld lang syne.

We twa hae paidl'd in the burn   *paddled   brook*
    Frae morning sun till dine,   *noon*
But seas between us braid hae roar'd   *broad*
    Sin' auld lang syne.

And there's a hand, my trusty fiere,   *comrade*
    And gie's a hand o' thine,
And we'll tak a right guid-willie waught   *draught*
    For auld lang syne!

Chorus
For auld lang syne, my dear,
    For auld lang syne,
We'll tak a cup o' kindness yet
    For auld lang syne!

There were many "auld lang syne" songs before Burns', and he said he took down this one "from an old man's singing." Professor Kinsley discusses possible revisions, but comes to the conclusion that, "There remains no good evidence on which to question Burns's story that he got *Auld Lang Syne* from oral tradition." The air to which it is now sung was selected by George Thomson, possibly after consultation with Burns.

Burns once complained to Thomson that it was difficult "to ascertain the truth respecting our Poesy & Music." "I myself," he continued, "have lately seen a couple of Ballads sung through the streets of Dumfries, with my name at the head of them as the Author, though it was the first time ever I had seen them." But he tried to collect all the information he could about Scots song, recording much of it in Riddell's interleaved *Museum,* and more in the Laing collection notes. He gives the authorship of songs, assigns their native regions or the occasion of their composition, quotes fragments or versions of traditional songs, makes critical comments, and records engaging anecdotes. The ensuing legend about *The Kirk Wad Let Me Be* is in the Laing notes.

Tradition in the Western parts of Scotland tells this old song . . . once saved a Covenanting Clergyman out of a scrape. It was a little prior to the Revolution, a period when being a Scots Covenanter was being a Felon, one of their clergy who was at that very time hunted by the merciless soldiery, fell in, by accident, with a party of the military. The soldiers were not exactly acquainted with the person of the Rev. gentleman of whom they were in search; but from some suspicious circumstances they fancied that they had got one of that cloth and opprobious persuasion among them in the person of this stranger. "Mass John," to extricate himself, assumed such a freedom of manners (very unlike the gloomy strictness of his sect), and among other convivial exhibitions, sung (and, some traditions say, composed on the spur of the occasion) "Kirk wad let me be," with such effect, that the soldiers swore he was a d——d honest fellow, and that it was impossible *he* could belong to these hellish conventicles, and so gave him his liberty.

In the interleaved *Museum,* Burns records the source of *O'er the Moor Amang the Heather.* "This song is the composition of a Jean Glover, a girl who was not only a whore, but also a thief; and in one or other character has visited most of the Correction Houses in the West. She was born, I believe, in Kilmarnock. I took down the song from her singing as she was strolling through the country, with a slight-of-hand blackguard." Of *The Bush Aboon Traquair,* he notes, "This, another beautiful song of Mr. Crawford's composition. In the neighbourhood of Traquair, tradition still shows the old 'bush'; which, when I saw it in the year '87, was composed of eight or nine ragged birches. The Earl of Traquair has planted a clump of trees near by, which he calls *The new bush.*"

Burns attaches one of his regional notes to *Dumbarton's Drums Beat Bonny, O!* "This is the last of the West Highland airs; and from it, over the whole tract of country to the confines of Tweed-side, there is hardly a tune or song that one can say has taken its origin from any place or transaction in that part of Scotland. The oldest Ayr Shire reel is *Stewarton lasses,* which was made by the father of the present Sir Walter Montgomery Cunning-ham, alias Lord Lyle; since which period there has indeed been local music in that country in great plenty. *Johnnie Faa* is the only old song which I could ever trace as belonging to the ex-tensive county of Ayr."

Burns was evidently delighted with the following anecdote, which will serve to conclude this brief selection from his memo-randa. *"Kate of Aberdeen,* is, I believe, the work of poor Cunning-ham the player; of whom the following anecdote, though told before, deserves a recital. A fat dignitary of the Church coming past Cunningham one Sunday as the poor poet was busy plying a fishing-rod in some stream near Durham, his native country, his reverence reprimanded Cunningham very severely for such an occupation on such a day. The poor poet, with that inoffensive gentleness of manners which was his peculiar characteristic, re-plied, that he hoped God and his reverence would forgive his seeming profanity of that sacred day, 'as he had no dinner to eat, but what lay in the bottom of that pool.' This, Mr. Woods, the player who knew Cunningham well and esteemed him much, assured me was true."

It is ironic that Burns' heroic efforts to "embody" Scots folk song should have helped to inhibit its continued "localizing," and hence should have straitened its vitality. The whole Eighteenth Century movement toward collection and publication of folk songs hastened their translation from songs for singing into songs for performance and listening. And when a poet like Burns, or one of his lesser contemporaries like Lady Nairne, the Rev. John Skinner, Lady Anne Barnard, or Jane Eliot took a hand in the process, the result of these publications was art song as well. This is not to say that all of Burns' songs were of high quality, or even always better than the materials he worked from. Some were not, and he knew it. But his towering achievement served to stabilize his own localizings as the common forms, although independent development did continue, particularly with the bawdy songs of which he produced polite versions.

On the whole, it seems fair to say that the *Scottish Musical Museum* soon became what it has remained, the standard repository of traditional songs and airs in its day as formulated by Burns, and that, to quote Gavin Greig, "The songs of Robert Burns have never been sung by our peasantry in general; or, putting it more widely, we may say that Scottish book-songs have never been the songs of the mass of the Scottish people. This statement, so far as we know, is made for the first time in good black print. It is to me quite astounding that the Scottish people themselves should put forward the songs of Burns, Lady Nairne, Tannahill, Hogg, and Scott, as their own authentic native minstrelsy — as the songs that are and have been all along sung by swain and maid in the field and by the fireside; and that speakers and writers should work themselves into a fine frenzy over what is largely a delusion."

For Scots, of course, Burns' songs have special interest as expressions of national character and feeling, and country dwellers nowadays are said to find them more appealing than city folk. But even in Scotland, changing tastes, and particularly the "pop" hit tune as promoted by recordings and broadcasts, have reduced the popularity of Burns' songs. From the sophisticated, on the other hand, there is complaint that Burns stands in the way of a contemporary flowering of Scots poetry.

For the larger audience, as for Scotsmen, the two-score famous songs of Burns whether they are sung, or read as poems, provide a lively gallery of characters and strong appeal to a wide range of human feeling. Gaiety, bawdry, tenderness, humor, patriotism, passion, despair, bacchanalianism, and much else, in a variety of moods and voices, are common to all times and countries, no matter what their local dress.

And for those interested in the technique of suiting poetry to sentiment, and sentiment to melody, and of felicitously developing theme and situation with economy, Burns offers never ending excitement.

It remains to discuss *The Merry Muses* and related matters, and the first of these matters to understand plainly is that Scotland possesses "a wonderful quantity of indecorous traditionary verse, not of an inflammatory character, but simply expressive of a profound sense of the ludicrous in connection with the sexual affections. Such things, usually kept from public view, oozed out in merry companies such as Burns loved to frequent." So wrote Robert Chambers in 1851, in his life of Burns. And the contemporary expert on pornography, Mr. G. Legman, reports a "truly remarkable" body of such verse still to be circulating in Scotland, credit for stimulating which is customarily given to the repressions of the Calvinist Kirk. Sydney Goodsir Smith and Hugh MacDiarmid both vouch for the comparative superiority of Scots to other bawdry.

As we have seen, Burns wrote down a bawdy song in the 1783–85 Commonplace Book (*My Girl She's Airy*), and his correspondence is full of "uninflammatory" bawdry thereafter, particularly references to and quotations from songs. Alexander Cunningham summarized the matter nicely: "His poetry & letters were often so blended with Religion Politics Love & Bawdry that the greatest care must be taken" to edit them carefully. Some blander bawdry has long been regularly printed in editions of Burns — *Here's His Health in Water, The Rantin Dog, Wha Is That at My Bower Door*, songs from *The Jolly Beggars* — *Love and Liberty*. And a large number of Burns' contributions to Johnson and Thomson had their origins in popular bawdy songs. Publication in the *Museum* and the *Select Collection* of polite songs

to the familiar bawdy tunes must have created widespread tension, probably agreeable. Some of the more notable derivations
from bawdy originals are *Green Grow the Rashes, O, Duncan
Gray, Duncan Davison, John Anderson,* and *Tho' Women's
Minds.*

The Crochallans and similar groups specialized in bawdy songs,
and rejoiced in Burns with his wide knowledge of them. He
mentions in several of his letters a private collection of what he
called "cloaciniad verse," and he promised to send Andrew
Erskine a copy of some clandestine poems, on Erskine's request.
Just what form Burns' collection took is not clear; perhaps a notebook, but more likely single sheets. In 1815 Allan Cunningham
copied some songs from a MS belonging to a Mr. I. Gracie of
Dumfries, who had received it from his father, the Dumfries
banker James Gracie, who in turn had received it from Burns
himself. The whereabouts of any MSS sent to Erskine, or of the
Gracie MS, are not known.

Textual, bibliographical, editorial, and historical problems relating to Burns and bawdy songs are "riddling, perplexed, and
labyrinthical" in the extreme. Just what Burns' collection contained is not known; what Allan Cunningham saw is not certain;
and what, if anything, Burns sent to Erskine is also unknown.
But that Burns was familiar with such materials and delighted in
them is plain enough; and with bawdy songs he followed the
same courses as with more polite ones. He worked as a folk artist
with familiar materials, "localizing" what he found. It remains
conjectural much of the time whether a particular version of a
bawdy song is "by" Burns, or "mended by" him, or merely "old."
From the Mauchline days on, he had many friends who shared
the national taste for bawdry with him, and to them he sent
bawdy songs or poems when he came upon them or composed
them.

After Burns' death there appeared a pamphlet of 128 pages
(122 pages of text), with a date of 1799, and with some pages

watermarked 1799, and some 1800. It bore the title: *"The MERRY MUSES of Caledonia*; a Collection of FAVOURITE SCOTS SONGS, ANCIENT and MODERN: selected for the use of the CROCHALLAN FENCIBLES.

> Say Puritan, can it be wrong,
> To dress plain truth in witty song?
> What honest Nature says, we should do,
> What every lady does, — or would do."

It is not known who edited this pamphlet, or who printed it, or from what sources the contents were derived, but it does contain some songs by Burns, and others probably by him, together with many traditional songs; all of the kind described by Robert Chambers. During the Nineteenth Century, many clandestine volumes appeared with the *Merry Muses* title, but not until 1843 was Burns' name connected with one.* These later volumes present a great variety of English and Scots bawdry — most of it wholly unconnected with Burns, or with the original collection. A popular issue, much "copied," bore the date 1827 (the date of it was probably 1872), and the phrase on the title page, "Not for maids, ministers, or striplings." The Burns Federation sponsored a *Merry Muses* in 1909, edited by its Secretary, Duncan McNaught ("Vindex"), with the ostensible purpose of showing that Burns was chiefly interested in providing purified versions of the national minstrelsy. Only since 1959 in Great Britain, and 1964 in the United States, have reliable texts, and detailed, plain discussions of the whole area, been available. Those who would inform themselves more fully are cordially referred to the Postscript to this section.

Some of Burns' bawdry has already been introduced into this volume where it was appropriate. A selection follows, both of

---

* A gathering published as *The Giblet Pie* in 1806 claimed that some of its songs were "taken from the Original Manuscripts of R. Burns." (Legman, *Merry Muses*, 269.)

items by Burns, and of items which he refers to or knew and liked.

1. By all tests of style and sentiments, *Wha'll Mow Me Now?* is Burns' song, although there is no direct evidence of authorship.

O, I hae tint my rosy cheek,   *lost*
 Likewise my waste sae sma';
O wae gae by the sodger lown   *woe,*
 The sodger did it a'.

Chorus

O wha'll mow me now, my jo,   *ride sweetheart*
 And wha'll mow me now:
A soldier wi' his bandileers
 Has bang'd my belly fu'.

Now I maun thole the scornfu' sneer *must endure*
 O' mony a saucy quine;   *wench*
When, curse upon her godly face!
 Her cunt's as merry's mine.

Our dame hauds up her wanton tail,
 As due as she gaes lie;
An' yet misca's a young thing,   *abuses*
 The trade if she but try.

Our dame can lae her ain gudeman,
 An' mow for glutton greed;
An' yet misca' a poor thing,   *abuse*
 That's mowin' for its bread.

Alake! sae sweet a tree as love,
 Sic bitter fruit should bear!
Alake, that e'er a merry arse,
 Should draw a sa'tty tear.   *salty*

But deevil damn the lousy loon,
 Denies the bairn he got!
Or lea's the merry arse he lo'ed,
 To wear a ragged coat!

2. *The Case of Conscience,* a parody of Calvinist morality, was sent by Burns to his friend, Provost Robert Maxwell of Lochmaben, December 20, 1789.

I'll tell you a tale of a Wife,
  And she was a Whig and a Saunt;   *Hypocrite   Saint*
She liv'd a most sanctify'd life,
  But whyles she was fash'd wi her cunt.   *at times   troubled*

Poor woman! she gaed to the Priest   *went*
  And till him she made her complaint;   *to*
"There's naething that troubles my breast
  Sae sair as the sins o' my cunt.

"Sin that I was herdin at hame,   *Since*
  Till now I'm three score and ayont,
I own it wi' sin and wi' shame,
  I've led a sad life wi' my cunt."

He bade her to clear up her brow,
  And no be discourag'd upon 't;
For holy gude women enow   *enough*
  Were mony times waur't wi' their cunt.   *worsted*

It's naught but Beelzebub's art,
  But that's the mair sign of a saunt,   *more*
He kens that ye're pure at the heart,
  Sae levels his darts at your cunt.

What signifies Morals and Works,
  Our works are no wordy a runt!   *worth   cabbage stalk*
It's Faith that is sound, orthodox,
  That covers the fauts o' your cunt.   *faults*

Were ye o' the Reprobate race
  Created to sin and be brunt,   *burned*
O then it would alter the case
  If ye should gae wrang wi' your cunt.

But you that is Called and Free
  Elekit and chosen a saunt,
Will't break the Eternal Decree
  Whatever ye do wi' your cunt?

And now with a sancify'd kiss
   Let's kneel and renew covenant:
It's this — and it's this — and it's this —
   That settles the pride o' your cunt.

Devotion blew up to a flame;
   No words can do justice upon't;
The honest auld woman gaed hame
   Rejoicing and clawin her cunt.

Then high to her memory charge;
   And may he who takes it affront,
Still ride in Love's channel at large,
   And never make port in a cunt! ! !

3. After reviewing grounds for ascribing *The Patriarch* to Burns,
Professor Kinsley says, "I am inclined . . . to accept this attribution."

As honest Jacob on a night,
   Wi' his beloved beauty,
Was duly laid on wedlock's bed,
   And noddin' at his duty:
      Tal de dal, &c.

"How lang," she says, "ye fumblin' wretch,
   Will ye be fucking at it?
My eldest wean might die of age,   *child*
   Before that ye could get it.

"Ye pegh, and grane, and groazle there,   *puff   grunt*
   And make an unco splutter,
And I maun ly and thole you here,   *must endure*
   And fient a hair the better."   *devil a*

Then he, in wrath, put up his graith,   *tool*
   "The deevil's in the hizzie!   *wench*
I mow you as I mow the lave,   *rest*
   And night and day I'm bisy.

"I've bairn'd the servant gypsies baith,   *got with child*
   Forbye your titty, Leah;   *Also   sister*

Ye barren jad, ye put me mad,
    What mair can I do wi' you.

"There's ne'er a mow I've gi'en the lave,
    But ye ha'e got a dizzen;
And damned a ane ye'se get again,   one you'll
    Altho' your cunt should gizzen."   wither

Then Rachel calm, as ony lamb,
    She claps him on the waulies,   genitals
Quo' she, "Ne'er fash a woman's clash, pay heed to chatter
    In trowth, ye mow me braulies.   admirably

"My dear 'tis true, for mony a mow,
    I'm your ungratefu' debtor;
But ance again, I dinna ken,
    We'll aiblens happen better."   perhaps

Then honest man! wi' little wark,   work
    He soon forgat his ire;
The patriarch, he coost the sark,   cast   shirt
    And up and till't like fire! ! !   to it

4. Both Professor Ferguson and Professor Kinsley accept *Nine Inch Will Please a Lady* as Burns' song.

"Come rede me, dame, come tell me, dame,   advise
    My dame come tell me truly,
What length o' graith, when weel ca'd hame, gear   driven
    Will sair a woman duly?"   serve
The carlin clew her wanton tail,   scratched
    Her wanton tail sae ready —
"I learn'd a sang in Annandale,
    Nine inch will please a lady. —

"But for a koontrie cunt like mine,   country
    In sooth, we're nae sae gentle;
We'll tak tway thumb-bred to the nine,   two thumb-breadths
    And that's a sonsy pintle: comely penis
O leeze me on my Charlie lad,   I take delight in
    I'll ne'er forget my Charlie!
Tway roarin' handful's and a daud   lump
    He nidge't it in fu' rarely. —   thrust

"But weary fa' the laithron doup,   *lazy rump*
   And may it ne'er be thrivin!
It's no the length that maks me loup,   *jump*
   But it's the double drivin. —
Come nidge me, Tam, come nudge me, Tam,
   Come nidge me o'er the nyvel!   *navel*
Come lowse & lug your battering ram,   *loose   draw out*
   And thrash him at my gyvel!"   *gabel*

5. The parody ballad, *Grim Grizzel,* is authentic Burns, and according to Professor Kinsley, authentic Scots rustic humor.

Grim Grizzel was a mighty Dame
   Weel kend on Cluden-side:
Grim Grizzel was a mighty Dame
   O' meikle fame and pride.   *great*

When gentles met in gentle bowers
   And nobles in the ha',
Grim Grizzel was a mighty Dame,
   The loudest o' them a'.

When lawless Riot rag'd the night
   And Beauty durst na gang,   *go about*
Grim Grizzel was a mighty Dame
   Wham nae man e'er wad wrang.

Nor had Grim Grizzel skill alane
   What bower and ha' require;
But she had skill, and meikle skill,
   In barn and eke in byre.   *also   cowshed*

Ae day Grim Grizzel walkèd forth,
   As she was wont to do,
Alang the banks o' Cluden fair,
   Her cattle for to view.

The cattle shit o'er hill and dale
   As cattle will incline,
And sair it grieved Grim Grizzel's heart
   Sae muckle muck tae tine.   *much   lose*

And she has ca'd on John o' Clods,
   Of her herdsmen the chief,

And she has ca'd on John o' Clods,
   And tell'd him a' her grief: —

"Now wae betide thee, John o' Clods!
   I gie thee meal and fee,   *give*
And yet sae meickle muck ye tine
   Might a' be gear to me!   *wealth*

"Ye claut my byre, ye sweep my byre,   *clean out*
   The like was never seen;
The very chamber I lie in
   Was never half sae clean.

"Ye ca' my kye adown the loan   *call my cattle   lane*
   And there they a' discharge:
My Tammie's hat, wig, head and a'
   Was never half sae large!

"But mind my words now, John o' Clods,
   And tent me what I say: *heed*
My kye shall shit ere they gae out,
   That shall they ilka day.   *every*

"And mind my words now, John o' Clods,
   And tent now wha ye serve;
Or back ye'se to the Colonel gang,   *you'll*
   Either to steal or starve."

Then John o' Clods he lookèd up
   And syne he lookèd down;   *then*
He lookèd east, he lookèd west,
   He lookèd roun' and roun'.

His bonnet and his rowantree club   *mountain ash*
   Frae either hand did fa';
Wi' lifted een and open mouth
   He naething said at a'.

At length he found his trembling tongue,
   Within his mouth was fauld: *enfolded*
"Ae silly word frae me, madám,
   Gin I daur be sae bauld.   *If   dare   bold*

"Your kye will at nae bidding shit,
 Let me do what I can;
Your kye will at nae bidding shit,
 Of onie earthly man.

"Tho' ye are great Lady Glaur-hole,   *mud-hole*
 For a' your power and art
Tho' ye are great Lady Glaur-hole,
 They winna let a fart."

"Now wae betide thee, John o' Clods!
 An ill death may ye die!
My kye shall at my bidding shit,
 And that ye soon shall see."

Then she's ta'en Hawkie by the tail,   *Bossy*
 And wrung wi' might and main,
Till Hawkie rowted through the woods   *bellowed*
 Wi' agonizing pain.

"Shit, shit, ye bitch," Grim Grizzel roar'd,
 Till hill and valley rang;
"And shit, ye bitch," the echoes roar'd
 Lincluden wa's amang.   *walls* [*of ruined Lincluden abbey*]

6. Burns wrote to his fellow-Crochallan, Robert Cleghorn, on October 25, 1793, sending him the song below: "From my late hours last night, & the dripping fogs & damn'd east-wind of this stupid day, I have left me as little soul as an oyster. — 'Sir John, you are so fretful, you cannot live long.' — 'Why, there is it! Come, sing me a Baudy-song to make me merry!!!' "

Act Sederunt of the Session —
A Scots Ballad —

In Edinburgh town they've made a law,
 In Edinburgh at the Court o' Session,
That standing pricks are fauteors a',   *offenders*
 And guilty of a high transgression. —

Chorus

Act Sederunt o' the Session,   *official act*
Decreet o' the Court o' Session,
That standing pricks are fauteors a',
And guilty of a high transgression.

And they've provided dungeons deep.
  Ilk lass has ane in her possession;   *each*
Until the wretches wail and weep,
  They there shall lie for their transgression. —

Chorus

Act Sederunt o' the Session,
Decreet o' the Court o' Session,
The rogues in pouring tears shall weep,
By act Sederunt o' the Session. —

7. Burns' experience with kirk session discipline obviously lay behind his burlesque called variously *Libel Summons* or *The Court of Equity*.

In Truth and Honour's name — Amen —
Know all men by these Presents plain: —

This fourth o' June, at Mauchline given,
The year 'tween eighty five and seven,
We, Fornicators by profession,
As per extractum from each Session,   *by authentic document*
In way and manner here narrated,
Pro bono Amor congregated;
And by our brethren constituted,
A Court of Equity deputed. —
With special authoris'd direction
To take beneath our strict protection,
The stays-out-bursting, quondam maiden,
With Growing Life and anguish laden;
Who by the rascal is deny'd,
That led her thoughtless steps aside. —
He who disowns the ruin'd Fair-one,
And for her wants and woes does care none;

The wretch that can refuse subsistence
To those whom he has given existence;
He who when at a lass's by-job,   *side-line (fornication)*
Defrauds her with a frig or dry-bob;   *cheats her of orgasm*
The coof that stands on clishmaclavers   *dolt   palavering*
When women haflins offer favors: —   *halfway*
All who in any way or manner
Distain the Fornicator's honor,
We take cognisance thereanent,
The proper Judges competent. —

First, Poet Burns he takes the chair;
Allow'd by a', his title's fair;
And pass'd nem. con. without dissension,
He has a Duplicate pretension. —   *[Betty Paton & Jean Armour]*
Next Merchant Smith, our worthy Fiscal,
To cow each pertinaceous rascal;
In this, as every other state,
His merit is conspicuous great:
Richmond the third, our trusty Clerk,*
The minutes regular to mark,
And sit dispenser of the law,
In absence of the former twa;
The fourth our Messenger at Arms,
When failing all the milder terms,
Hunter, a hearty, willing brother,
Weel skill'd in dead and living leather. — *shoeleather pudenda*
Without Preamble less or more said,
We, body politic aforesaid,
With legal, due Whereas, and Wherefore,
We are appointed here to care for
The interests of our constituents,
And punish contraveening truants,
Keeping a proper regulation
Within the lists of Fornication. —

Whereas, our Fiscal, by petition,
Informs us there is strong suspicion,
You Coachman Dow and Clockie Brown,   *Clockmaker*
Baith residenters of this town;   *Both*

* Richmond had left Mauchline for Edinburgh before this poem was written. His inclusion on the Court was part of the fun.

In other words, you, Jock, and, Sandy,
Hae been at wark at Houghmagandie;   *Fornication*
And now when facts are come to light,
The matter ye deny outright. —

First, You, John Brown, there's witness borne,
And affidavit made and sworn,
That ye hae bred a hurly-burly
'Bout Jeany Mitchel's tirlie-whirlie,
And blooster'd at her regulator,   *blustered*
Till a' her wheels gang clitter-clatter. —   *go*
And farther still, ye cruel Vandal,
A tale might even in hell be scandal!
That ye hae made repeated trials
Wi' drugs and draps in doctor's phials,
Mixt, as ye thought, wi' fell infusion,
Your ain begotten wean to poosion. —
And yet ye are sae scant o' grace,
Ye daur to lift your brazen face,   *dare*
And offer for to take your aith,   *oath*
Ye never lifted Jeany's claith. —   *dress*
But tho' ye should yoursel manswear,
Laird Wilson's sclates can witness bear,   *slates*
Ae e'ening of a Mauchline fair,
That Jeany's masts they saw them bare;
For ye had furl'd up her sails,
And was at play — at heads and tails. —   *maidenhead*   *penis*

Next, Sandy Dow, you're here indicted
To have, as publickly you're wyted,   *charged*
Been clandestinely upward whirlin
The petticoats o' Maggy Borelan,
And giein her canister a rattle,
That months to come it winna settle. —
And yet, ye offer your protest,
Ye never herried Maggy's nest;
Tho', it's weel ken'd that at her gyvel   *gabel*
Ye hae gien mony a kytch and kyvel. —   *jerk and thump*

Then Brown and Dow, before design'd,
For clags and clauses there subjoin'd,   *incumbrances*
We, Court aforesaid, cite and summon,
That on the fifth o' July comin,

The hour o' cause, in our Court-ha',
At Whitefoord's arms, ye answer Law!*

This, mark'd before the date and place is,
Sigillum est, per,
             Burns the Preses.

This Summons and the signet mark,
Extractum est, per,
             Richmond, Clerk.

At Mauchline, idem date of June,
'Tween six and seven, the afternoon,
You twa, in propria personae,
Within design'd, Sandy and Johny,
This Summons legally have got,
As vide witness underwrote:
Within the house of John Dow, vintner,
Nunc facio hoc
             Gullelmus Hunter.

There follow certain traditional bawdy songs in which Burns rejoiced.

8. *Andrew an' his Cuttie Gun* Burns called "the work of a Master."

Blythe, blythe, blythe was she,	
Blythe was she but and ben;	*out and in*
An' weel she lo'ed it in her nieve,	*fist*
But better when it slippit in.	
When a' the lave gaed to their bed,	*rest went*
And I sat up to clean the shoon,	
O wha think ye cam jumpin' ben,	
But Andrew an' his cuttie gun?	*little*
Or e'er I wist he laid me back,	
And up my gamon to my chin;	*petticoat*

* At this point in several MSS, there are 59 lines of adjuration from the court to the culprits, omitted by Burns in revision.

And ne'er a word to me he spak,
    But liltit out his cuttie gun.

The bawsent bitch she left the whalps,   *with white stripe on face*
    And hunted round us at the fun,
As Andrew fodgel'd wi his arse,   *fidgeted*
    And fir'd at me the cuttie gun.

O some delights in cuttie stoup,   *little tankards*
    And some delights in cuttie-mun,   *old song*
But my delight's an areselins coup,   *tumble*
    Wi' Andrew an' his cuttie gun.

Blythe, blythe, blythe was she,
Blythe was she but and ben;
An' weel she lo'ed it in her nieve,
But better when it slippit in.

9. Burns called *The Grey Goose and the Gled,* "a droll Scots song, more famous for its humor than delicacy."

As I look'd o'er yon castle wa',
    I spied a grey goose an' a gled;   *hawk*
They had a feight between them twa,   *fight*
    An' o' as their twa hurdies gaed.   *buttocks went*

Wi' a hey ding it in, an' a how ding it in,
    An' a hey ding it in, it's lang today.
Fal lary tele, tale, lary tale,
    Fal lary tal, lal lary tay.

She heav'd up, and he strack down,
    Between them twa they made a mow;
That ilka fart that the carlin gae,   *every*   *woman gave*
    It's four o' them wad fill'd a bowe.   *six bushels*
        With a hey, &c.

Temper your tail, the carlin cried,
    Temper your tail by Venus' law;
Gird hame your gear, gudeman, she cried,   *Push*   *tool*
    Wha the deil can hinder the wind to blaw?   *blow*
        With a hey, &c.

For were ye on my saddle set,
    An' were ye weel girt in my gear,   *equipment*
Gin the wind o' my arse blew ye out o' my cunt,
    Ye'll never be reckon'd a man o' wier.   *valor*
        With a hey, &c.

He plac'd his Jacob whare she did piss,
    And his bollocks whare the wind did blaw,
An' he grippet her fast by the gushet o' her arse,   *crack*
    And he gave her cunt the common law.
        With a hey, &c.

10. *As I Cam o'er the Cairney Mount*, "an excellent but somewhat licentious song," appeared with asterisks, and purified, in the *Museum* (#577 in Professor Kinsley's edition of Burns). Herewith an older version.

As I cam o'er the Cairney mount,
    And down amang the blooming heather,
The Highland laddie drew his durk
    And sheath'd it in my wanton leather.

        O my bonnie, bonnie Highland lad,
        My handsome, charming Highland laddie;
        When I am sick and like to die,
        He'll row me in his Highland plaidie.   *roll*

With me he play'd his warlike pranks,
    And on me boldly did adventure,
He did attack me on both flanks,
    And push'd me fiercely in the centre.

A furious battle then began,
    Wi' equal courage and desire,
Altho' he struck me three to one,
    I stood my ground and receiv'd his fire.

But our ammunition being spent,
    And we quite out o' breath an' sweating,
We did agree with ae consent,
    To fight it out at the next meeting.

11. Versions of *John Anderson, My Jo* go back at least until 1630. Burns seems to have adapted his famous song from the set below which was printed in the *Merry Muses*.

<table>
<tr><td>John Anderson, my jo, John,</td><td>sweetheart</td></tr>
<tr><td>   I wonder what ye mean,</td><td></td></tr>
</table>

John Anderson, my jo, John,
   I wonder what ye mean,
To lie sae lang i' the mornin'
   And sit sae late at e'en?
Ye'll bleer a' your een, John,   *eyes*
   And why do ye so?
Come sooner to your bed at e'en,
   John Anderson, my jo.

John Anderson, my jo, John,
   When first that ye began,
Ye had as good a tail-tree
   As ony ither man;
But now its waxen wan, John,
   And wrinkles to and fro;
I've twa gae-ups for ae gae-down,
   John Anderson, my jo.

I'm backit like a salmon,
   I'm breastit like a swan;
My wame it is a down-cod,   *belly   down pillow*
   My middle ye may span:
Frae my tap-knot to my tae, John,
   I'm like the new-fa'n snow;
And it's a' for your convenience,
   John Anderson, my jo.

O it is a fine thing
   To keep out o'er the dyke;   *wall*
But its a meikle finer thing,
   To see your hurdies fyke;   *buttocks   fidget*
To see your hurdies fyke, John,
   And hit the rising blow;
It's then I like your chanter-pipe,   *fingering stem of bagpipe*
   John Anderson, my jo.

When you come on before, John,
   See that ye do your best;

When ye begin to haud me,
   See that ye grip me fast;
See that ye grip me fast, John,
   Until that I cry "Oh!"
Your back shall crack or I do that,
   John Anderson, my jo.

John Anderson, my jo, John,
   Ye're welcome when ye please;
It's either in the warm bed
   Or else aboon the claes: *above   clothes*
Or ye shall hae the horns, John,
   Upon your head to grow;
An' that's the cuckold's mallison   *curse*
   John Anderson, my jo.

With the matter now plainly before them, readers may well ponder why *The Merry Muses* remained clandestine for so long, and, indeed, whether Burns' taste for bawdry merits the celebrity which suppression has given it.

VII

LAST YEARS

Alas! Alas! a devilish change indeed.

Burns to John Rankine

During Burns' last four years, his political and social opinions offended many, his sarcasms continued to wound people, and his reputation for irreligion endured. His temperament grew more explosive as his health worsened, and as he grew less hopeful of recognition, reward, and security. He continued to enjoy bawdry and convivial parties, and to relish low caste company when it was amusing, and he was held to have loose ways with women. Burns in Dumfries was simply Rab Mossgiel grown older and more experienced in the world.

He did his work as before, he loved his family and supported it in modest comfort,* he was ready with assistance to the less fortunate, and he lived within his income. But John Syme said,

---

* In December, 1793, he writes Mrs. Dunlop of his daughter Elizabeth by Jean, "these four months a sweet little girl, my youngest child, has been so ill, that every day, a week or less threatened to terminate her existence." Then he continues, "There had much need be many pleasures annexed to the states of husband & father, for God knows, they have many peculiar cares. — I cannot describe to you, the anxious, sleepless hours these ties frequently give me. I see a train of helpless little folks: me, & my exertions, all their stay; & on what a brittle thread does the life of man hang! If I am nipt off at the command of Fate; even in all the vigour of manhood as I am, such things happen every day — gracious God! what would become of my little flock! — 'Tis here that I envy your people of fortune. A Father on his deathbed, taking an everlasting leave of his children, is indeed woe enough; but the man of competent fortune leaves his sons and daughters independency & friends; while I — but my God, I shall run distracted if I think any longer on the subject!" (F II, #605, 223.)

"Robin's heart and temper are not cold and frugal." He did not hain up [save] the bawbees [ha'pence]. There was obviously little spare cash.

Burns enjoyed respect and status in Dumfries. Both his correspondence and other evidence show him on good terms with many solid and prominent people. He remained creative, and a fascinating companion, until the end. The only noteworthy change in him during this period was that his illness grew more severe and his depression plagued him more frequently.

Despite increasing illness and distress, Burns retained his pungency and zest until his health finally broke completely. The February after he moved to Dumfries (1792), he sent Mrs. Dunlop a jar of brandy, with a letter in which he remarked that he knew better how to find smugglers than she did. By late summer of that year, he is busy "correcting the Press-work of two Publications," presumably a volume of the *Museum,* and the 1793 edition of his poems. The latter burden he soon turned over to Alexander Fraser Tytler,* but Professor Ross Roy has discovered that Burns himself superintended the edition which Creech brought out in 1794.

On September 10, 1792, he wrote an extensive letter to Alexander Cunningham, continuing the following reflections on religion and marriage:

But of all Nonsense, Religious Nonsense is the most nonsensical; so enough, & more than enough of it. — Only, by the bye, will you, or can you tell me, my dear Cunningham, why a religioso turn of mind has always a tendency to narrow & illiberalize the heart? They are orderly; they may be just; nay, I have known them merciful: but still your children of Sanctity move among their fellow-creatures with a nostril snuffing putrescence, & a foot spurning filth, in short, with that conceited dignity which your titled Douglases, Hamiltons,

---

* Burns had supplied Creech with added material for this volume, including *Tam o' Shanter,* asking in return only some copies to give his friends. Even to get these, he had to dun Creech. (F II, #538, 151.)

Gordons, or any other of your Scots lordlings of seven centuries standing, display when they accidentally mix among the many-aproned Sons of Mechanical Life. . . .

Apropos, how do you like, I mean *really* like, the Married Life? — Ah, my Friend! Matrimony is quite a different thing from what your love-sick youths & sighing girls take it to be! — But Marriage, we are told, is appointed by G — & I shall never quarrel with any of HIS Institutions. — I am a husband of older standing than you, & I shall give you *my* ideas of the Conjugal State — (En passant, you know I am no Latin, is not "Conjugal" derived from "Jugum" a yoke?). — Well then, the scale of Good-wifeship I divide into ten parts — Good-Nature, four; Good-Sense two; Wit, one; Personal Charms, viz. a sweet face, eloquent eyes, fine limbs, graceful carriage (I would add a fine waist too, but that is so soon spoiled you know), all these one: as for the other qualities belonging to, or attending on, a Wife, such as fortune, connections, education, (I mean, education extraordinary), family-blood, &c. divide the two remaining degrees among them as you please; only, remember that all these minor properties must be expressed by *fractions;* for there is not any one of them in the aforesaid scale entitled to the dignity of an Integer.

A letter (dated January, 1793, by Professor Ferguson) to Provost David Staig of Dumfries, made detailed suggestions for improving the Burgh's revenue from ale. Shortly thereafter Burns requested a Burgess's privilege of free schooling for his children in the Dumfries academy. After pointing out that a good deal of ale comes into Dumfries untaxed, Burns continues, "I know that our Collector has a percentage on the Collection; but as it is no great object to him he gives himself no concern about what is *brought in* to the town. — The Supervisor would suit you better. — He is an abler & a keener man; &, what is all-important in the business, such is his official influence over, & power among, his Offrs that were he to signify that such was his wish, not a 'pennie' would be left uncollected. — It is by no means the case with the Collector. — The Offrs are not so immediately among his hands, & they would not pay the same attention to his mandates."

Not only would the reforms he suggests benefit the Burgh

revenue, they would also protect respectable Dumfries brewers from unfair competition. The reforms, Burns estimates, would increase revenue from this source by one third. Burns concludes, "These crude hints, Sir, are entirely for your private use. — I have by no means any wish to take a sixpence from Mr Mitchel's income: nor do I wish to serve Mr Findlater: I wish to shew any attempt I can, to do anything that might declare with what sincerity I have the honor to be,

Sir, your obliged humble servt

Robt Burns"

Sometime, apparently, before his break with Mrs. Riddell, she and Burns had found amusement in creating "armorial bearings" for him.* He first speaks of this project in a letter of March 3, 1794, to Cunningham. Burns was particularly concerned that the "pipe" in his design should be the true "stock & horn" of a Scottish shepherd.

There is one commission that I must trouble you with. — I lately lost a valuable Seal, a present from a departed friend, which vexes me much. — I have gotten one of your Highland pebbles,† which I fancy would make a very decent one; & I want to cut my armorial bearings on it: will you be so obliging as enquire what will be the expence of such a business? — I do not know that my name is matriculated, as the Heralds call it, at all; but I have invented one for myself; so, you know, I will be chief of the Name; & by courtesy of Scotland, will likewise be entitled to Supporters. — These, however, I do not intend having on my Seal. — I am a bit of a Herald; & shall give you, Secundum artem, my Arms. — On a field, azure, a holly-bush, seeded, proper, in base; a Shepherd's pipe & crook, Saltier-wise, also proper, in chief. — On a wreath of the colors, a woodlark perching on a sprig of bay-tree, proper, for Crest. — Two Mottoes: Round the top of the

---

* While in Edinburgh Burns had visited the Herald's Office to see if the name "Burns" was included in "that granary of Honors." It was not. (F I, #125, 105.)

† From Mrs. Riddell, though he does not mention it, the quarrel being at its height.

Crest — "Wood-notes wild" — At the bottom of the Shield, in the usual place —

"Better a wee bush than nae bield." —   *shelter*

By the Shepherd's pipe & crook, I do not mean the nonsense of Painters of Arcadia, but a Stock-&-horn, & a Club; such as you see at the head of Allan Ramsay, in [David] Allan's quarto Edition of the Gentle Shepherd. — By the bye, do you know Allan? — He must be a man of very great genius. — Why is he not more known? Has he no Patrons; or do "Poverty's cold wind & crushing rain beat keen & heavy" on him? — I once, & but once, got a glance of that noble editn of the noblest Pastoral in the world, & dear as it was; I mean, dear as to my pocket, I would have bought it; but I was told that it was printed & engraved for Subscribers only. — He is the *only* Artist who has hit *genuine* Pastoral costume. — What my dear Cunningham, is there in riches, that they narrow & encallous the heart so? — I think, that were I as rich as the sun, I would be as generous as day; but as I have no reason to imagine my soul a nobler one than every other man's, I must conclude that wealth imparts a bird-lime quality to the Possessor, at which the man, in native poverty, would have revolted.

By May, he is writing to Thomson in delight about illustrations for *The Cotter's Saturday Night* which David Allan is doing, and he also comments on the seal. Of the illustrations he says, "I would humbly propose that in No 1st instead of the Younker knitting stockings, I would, in preference to your 'Trump', to put a stock & horn among his hands, as if he were screwing & adjusting it." At the end of his letter, commenting on the seal, he says, "My 'seal' is all well, except that my 'Holly' must be a *bush,* not a *tree,* as in the present shield. — I also enclose it, & will send the pebble by the first opportunity."

In November he writes to Thomson again with concern that Allan get the "stock & horn" right, giving explicit details.

Tell my friend, Allen (for I am sure that we only want the trifling circumstance of being known to one another, to be the best friends on earth) that I much suspect he has, in his plates, mistaken the figure of the stock & horn. — I have, *at last,* gotten one; but it is a very rude instrument. — It is composed of three parts; the stock, which is the hinder thigh-bone of a sheep, such as you see in a mutton-ham: the horn, which is a common Highland cow's horn, cut off at the smaller end, untill the aperture be large enough to admit the "stock" to be pushed up through the horn, untill it be held by the thicker or hip-end of the thigh-bone; & lastly, an oaten reed exactly cut & notched like that which you see every shepherd-boy have when the corn-stems are green & full-grown. — The reed is not made fast in the bone, but is held by the lips, & plays loose in the smaller end of the "stock;" while the "stock," & the horn hanging on its larger end, is held by the hands in playing. — The "stock" has six, or seven, ventiges on the upper side, & one back-ventige, like the common flute. — This of mine was made by a man from the braes of Athole, & is exactly what the shepherds wont to use in that country. — However, either it is not quite properly bored in the holes, or else we have not the art of blowing it rightly; for we can make little of it. — If Mr Allen chuses, I will send him a sight of mine; as I look on my-self to be a kind of brother-brush with him. — "Pride in Poets is nae sin," & I will say it, that I look on Mr Allen & Mr Burns to be the only genuine & real Painters of Scottish Costume in the world. —

Farewell!

R. BURNS

Something of Burns' position in Dumfries is suggested by the recognition he was granted. On November 30, 1792, he was elected senior warden of the Dumfries Lodge of Masons. On March 5, 1793, the committee in charge of the public library in Dumfries, "by a great majority resolved to offer to Mr Robert Burns a share in the library, free of any admission-money and the quarterly contributions to this date, out of respect and esteem for his abilities as a literary man; and they directed the secretary to make this known to Mr Burns as soon as possible, that the application which they understood he was about to make in the ordinary way might be anticipated." A few months later, Burns was, by vote, appointed a member of the committee.

In March of 1793, Burns reminded "the Lord Provost, Bailies, & Town Council of Dumfries" that they had made him an Honorary Burgess in 1787, and requested that they grant him the Burgess's privilege of free schooling in the town academy. The request was granted. In January, 1795, he was one of the organizers of the Royal Dumfries Volunteers, and for some months he served as a member of the directing committee. The Corps included many of Dumfries' most respected people, and membership was a social distinction.

A fellow Volunteer was James Gray, Latin Master and Rector at the Dumfries Academy 1794–1801, and then Latin Master at the Edinburgh High School 1801–1822. His second wife was Clarinda's friend and Burns' correspondent, Mary Peacock. In 1822, accompanied by his wife, Gray went to India as chaplain for the East India Company. He and Burns were friends in Dumfries, and in 1814 Gray wrote a defense of Burns for Alexander Peterkin, which he recast for Gilbert Burns in 1820. These statements have a good deal of special pleading in them, and the passages below are the more convincing, therefore, in their admissions.

In his letter to Peterkin, Gray writes of Burns,

It is not, however, denied that he sometimes mingled with society unworthy of him. He was of a social and convivial nature. He was courted by all classes of men for the fascinating powers of his conversation, but over his social scene uncontrolled passion never presided. Over the social bowl, his wit flashed for hours together, penetrating whatever it struck, like the fire from heaven; but even in the hour of thoughtless gaiety and merriment, I never knew it tainted by indecency. It was playful or caustic by turns, following an allusion through all its windings; astonishing by its rapidity, or amusing by its wild originality, and grotesque yet natural combinations, but never, within my observation, disgusting by its grossness.

Gray's redaction for Gilbert is more detailed.

It was my good fortune to be introduced to [Burns] soon after I went to Dumfries. This was early in 1794, and I saw him often and intimately during the remainder of his life. I sometimes met him in the scene of conviviality, and there, if any where, I must have received conviction of that intellectual and moral degredation of which we have heard so much; but no such impression was made on my mind. He seemed to me to frequent convivial parties from the same feelings with which he wrote poetry, because nature had eminently qualified him to shine there, and he never on any occasion indulged in solitary drinking. He was always the living spirit of the company, and by the communications of his genius, seemed to animate every one present with a portion of his own fire. He indulged in the sally of wit or humour, of striking originality, and sometimes of bitter sarcasm, but always free from the least taint of grossness. I was, from the commencement of my acquaintance with him, struck with his aversion to all kinds of indelicacy, and have seen him dazzle and delight a party for hours together by the brilliancy and rapidity of his flashes, without even an allusion that could give offense to vestal purity. I never saw him intoxicated; and, indeed, I am convinced, that though his company was courted by men of all ranks, and he was much in society of a convivial nature, that he was very seldom in a state of inebriation.

I often met him at breakfast parties, which were then customary in Dumfries, and sometimes enjoyed a morning walk with him; and on these occasions, if he had been suffering from midnight excesses, it must have been apparent. On the contrary, his whole air was that of one who had enjoyed refreshing slumbers, and who arose happy in himself, and to diffuse happiness on all around him; his complexion was fresh and clear, his eye brilliant, his whole frame vigorous and elastic, and his imagination ever on the wing. His morning conversations were marked by an impassioned eloquence, that seemed to flow from immediate inspiration, and shed an atmosphere of light and beauty around every thing it touched, alternately melting and elevating the soul of all who heard him. He had read much, and possessed a most powerful memory, which never exhibited any symptoms of that decay, which must have been the consequence of habitual intoxication; so far from it, he gleaned all that was valuable from every book he perused, which he could either quote in the words of the original, or make the ideas his own, and embody them in a more beautiful form.

Charles Kirkpatrick Sharpe (1780?–1851) was the third son of Burns' correspondent Charles Sharpe of Hoddam, in Annandale, east of Dumfries. During his boyhood, C. K. Sharpe became familiar with Burns' appearance, and he knew those who knew Burns well. Later, as "The Scottish Walpole," he met almost everyone of importance in Scotland. The following memorandum of his, dated January 8, 1808, appears on the back of a receipt from his father's agents, Walker and Gordon.

I do not choose to remember — or rather to record — Burns's frailties, however such things might amuse the public — he was exactly like other people as to his faults — these, however, bore no proportion to his genius.

He was very unlucky in his position — tho those called his superiors pretended at first to relish his compositions and conversation, they were not fitted, for the greater part, to do so — he must quickly have discovered this — hence his rudeness in conversation, which was much complained of.

Mr Riddell was a man of very limited understanding — Mr MacMurdo, and perhaps one gentleman more, were the only people in Dumfriesshire who really could understand his merit.

Some of his gentle friends were foolish, crack brained Whigs, democrats who, I have no doubt, egged him on, nay inspired, his extravagant notions, which did him so much harm — this was suggested to me by a person, who though he entertained very different political notions from Burns, loved, admired, and befriended him to the last.

Archibald Lawrie (1768–1837), son of the Rev. George Lawrie of Loudon, at whose home Burns had been a welcome guest, saw something of Burns in Edinburgh. In 1794, Archibald married Anne M'Kittrick Adair, sister of Burns' friend and fellow-traveller, Dr. Adair, who married Charlotte Hamilton. He met Miss Adair at Dunlop House, and Mrs. Dunlop actively promoted the match. Archibald was appointed assistant to his father at Loudon, became an officer, not a chaplain, of a militia regiment, and won a reputation as a sporting parson. In 1793, while on his way a-courting — unsuccessfully — in England, Lawrie passed through Dumfries, and sought out his old friend Burns. He recorded their meeting in his journal:

Before supper I sent for Mr Burns the poet, who came soon after I sent for him, but could not sup with me. He came into the room where I was supping with a number of strangers, and there he sat from 11 at night till 3 next morning. I left them about 12, and had a most confounded and extravagant Bill to pay next morning, which I grudged exceedingly, as I had very little of Burns's company; he was half drunk when he came, and completely drunk before he went away in the morning. . . . Thursday, 20th. After breakfast called on Mr B., found him at home, took a plateful of broth with him, and afterwards he took a walk with me thro the town of Dumfries, and along the banks of the Nith, which was extremely pleasant. After having walked some time with Mr B., I returned again with him to his house, where I stayed and dined and spent the day; after dinner we had some charming music from a Mr Fraser, master of a band of soldiers raised by and belonging to Lord Breadalbane; having drunk tea, we went to a wood upon the banks of the river Nith, where Mr Fraser took out his [haut boy] and played a few tunes most delightfully, which had a very pleasing effect in the wood. We then left this rural retirement, walked back to the town where I parted with Mr B., and continued my walk with a Mr Lewis [Lewars], a friend of Burns, who dined in company with me. The night coming on, I went with Mr Lewis and supped with him on cold mutton and eggs, at 12 o'clock left his house; went to the Inn, King's Arms, and ordered the chambermaid to show me to bed; having rested my mare one day more, which she had not the slightest occasion for, but the temptation of Burns company I could not withstand.

When Burns' acquaintance, Josiah Walker, wrote a biographical preface to Morison's *Burns* in 1811, he included an account of a visit to Burns in Dumfries.

Dr Currie is under a mistake when he says that Burns was confined in the house from October 1795 to the January following; for, in the month of November, I passed two days with him, when I observed no unfavorable change in his looks, his spirits, or his appetite.

Circumstances having, at that time, led me to Scotland, after an absence of eight years, during which my intercourse with Burns had been almost suspended, I felt myself strongly prompted to visit him. For this purpose, I went to Dumfries, and called upon him early in the forenoon. I found him in a small house of one story. He was sitting on a window-seat reading, with the doors open, and the family arrangements going on in his presence, and altogether without that appearance of snugness and seclusion which a student requires. After conversing with him for some time, he proposed a walk, and promised to conduct me through some of his favourite haunts. We accordingly quitted the town, and wandered a considerable way up the beautiful banks of the Nith. Here he gave me an account of his latest productions, and repeated some satirical ballads which he had composed, to favour one of the candidates at the last borough election. These I thought inferior to his other pieces, though they had some lines in which vigour compensated for coarseness. He repeated also his fragment of an *Ode to Liberty*, with marked and peculiar energy, and shewed a disposition which, however, was easily repressed, to throw out political remarks, of the same nature with those for which he had been reprehended. On finishing our walk, he passed some time with me at the inn, and I left him early in the evening to make another visit at some distance from Dumfries.

On the second morning after, I returned with a friend, who was acquainted with the poet, and we found him ready to pass a part of the day with us at the inn. On this occasion I did not think him quite so interesting as he had appeared at his outset. His conversation was too elaborate; and his expression weakened by a frequent endeavour to give it artificial strength. He had been accustomed to speak for applause, in the circles which he frequented, and seemed to think it necessary, in making the most common remark, to depart a little from the ordinary simplicity of language, and to couch it in something of epigrammatic point. In his praise and censure he was so decisive, as to render a dissent from his judgment, difficult to be reconciled with the laws of good breeding. His wit was not more licentious than is unhappily too venial in higher circles, though I thought him rather unnecessarily free in the avowal of his excesses. Such were the clouds by which the pleasures of the evening were partially shaded, but frequent corruscations of genius were visible between them. When it began to grow late, he shewed no disposition to retire, but called for fresh supplies of liquor, with a freedom which might be excusable, as we were in an inn, and no condition had been distinctly made, though it might easily have been inferred, had the inference been welcome, that he was to consider himself as our guest; nor was it till he saw us worn out, that he departed, about three in the morning, with a reluctance which probably proceeded less from being deprived of our company, than from being confined to his own. Upon the whole, I found this last interview not quite so gratifying as I had expected; although I discovered in his conduct no errors which I had not seen in men who stand high in the favour of society, or sufficient to account for the mysterious insinuations which I heard against his character. He, on this occasion, drank freely without being intoxicated, a circumstance from which I concluded, not only that his constitution was still unbroken, but that he was not addicted to solitary cordials; for if he had tasted liquor in the morning, he must have easily yielded to the excess of the evening.

Burns had a warm friend in young David McCulloch of Ardwell, near Gatehouse, and when he was ready to set out on a trip to that country in the summer of 1794, he wrote McCulloch on June 21:*

MY DEAR SIR,

My long projected journey through your country is at last fixed; & on Wednesday next, if you have nothing of more importance than take a saunter down to Gatehouse, about two or three o'clock, I shall be happy to take a draught of Mckune's best with you. — Collector Syme will be at Glens about that time, & will meet us about dish-of-tea-hour. — Syme goes also to Kiroughtree; & let me remind you of your kind promise to accompany me there. — I will need all the friends I can muster, for I am indeed ill at ease whenever I approach your Honorables & Right Honorables. —

> Yours sincerely
> ROBT BURNS

At an undetermined date, but probably on the king's birthday, May 24, 1794, McCulloch encountered Burns in Dumfries; he

* McCulloch had been admitted a member of the Dumfries St. Andrews Lodge of Masons the previous May 6. (Ch-W IV, 121.)

later reported the meeting to John Lockhart when Lockhart was writing his *Life of Burns.** According to Lockhart,

McCulloch was seldom more grieved, than when, riding into Dumfries one fine summer's evening to attend a country ball, he saw Burns walking alone, on the shady side of the principal street of the town, while the opposite part was gay with successive groups of gentlemen and ladies, all drawn together for the festivities of the night, not one of whom appeared willing to recognize him. The horseman dismounted and joined Burns, who, on his proposing to him to cross the street, said: "Nay, nay, my young friend — that's all over now;" and quoted after a pause some verses of Lady Grizel Baillie's pathetic ballad:

> His bonnet stood ance fu' fair on his brow,
> His auld ane look'd better than mony ane's new;
> But now he lets't wear ony gate it will hing,   *any way   hang*
> And casts himsel' dowie upon the corn-bing.   *sad   -heap*

> Oh, were we young, as we ance hae been,
> We sud hae been galloping down on yon green,   *should*
> And linking it ower the lily-white lea, —   *tripping*
> *And werena my heart light, I wad die.*

It was little in Burns's character to let his feelings on certain subjects escape in this fashion. He, immediately after citing these verses, assumed the sprightliness of his most pleasing manner; and taking his young friend home with him, entertained him very agreably until the hour of the ball arrived, with a bowl of his usual potation, and bonie Jean's singing some verses which he had recently composed.

In the spring of 1796, when Burns' illness was much advanced, Grace Aiken, a daughter of Burns' early friend, Robert Aiken, of Ayr, had occasion to pass through Dumfries, on her way to pay a visit in Liverpool.

Walking along the street towards the residence of her friend, Mrs Copland, she passed a tall, slovenly-looking man, of sickly aspect, who

---

* McCulloch's sister Elizabeth was the wife of Sir Walter Scott's brother Thomas. Lockhart was, of course, married to Sir Walter Scott's daughter Sophia. (Lockhart, Scott Douglas edition, 103.)

presently uttered an exclamation which made her turn round. It was Burns, but so changed from his former self that she could hardly have recognized him, except by his voice. When she asked him playfully if he had been going to pass her by without notice, he spoke as if he felt that it was proper for him, nowadays, to let his old friends be the first to hold forth the hand of friendship. At her pressing request he accompanied her to Mrs Copland's house; he even consented, after much entreaty, to go home and dress, so that he might return at four to dinner. He spent the evening cheerfully, and retired about midnight. The circumstance is worthy of notice, because neither Mrs Copland nor any of her friends — all members of the best society in Dumfries — had any objection to entertaining or meeting Burns. The hostess had not seen him for a considerable time, but from no cause affecting his reputation.

Burns' Dumfries neighbor Jesse Lewars, sister of his fellow-Exciseman John Lewars, helped nurse the poet during his final illness. She has left some pleasant reminiscences of Burns' and Jean's household.

As far as Burns was left to be guided by his own inclinations, his personal domestic habits were generally simple and temperate. As he was often detained by company from the dinner provided for him by his wife, she sometimes, if she thought he was likely to be absent, would not prepare that meal for him. When he chanced to come home and find no dinner ready, he was never in the least irritated, but would address himself with the greatest cheerfulness to any make-shift set before him. They generally had abundance of good Dunlop cheese, sent to them by their Ayrshire friends. The poet would sit down to bread and cheese, with his book by his side, and seem to the casual visitor as happy as a courtier at the feast of kings. He was always anxious that his wife should be well and neatly dressed, and did his utmost to counteract any tendency to carelessness — which she sometimes excused by alleging the duties of a nurse and mother — not only by gentle remonstrance, but by buying for her the best clothes he could afford. He rarely omitted to get for her any little novelty in female dress. She was, for instance, one of the first persons in Dumfries to wear a dress of gingham — a stuff which was at its first introduction rather costly, and used almost exclusively by the well-to-do.

John Syme (1755–1831), Distributor of Stamps in Dumfries, has been mentioned often in this book. In 1826, Dr. Robert Chambers found Syme to be "essentially a Scottish gentleman of 'the old school' — a well-bred *bon-vivant*," and he reports Syme's delight that when a host hesitated to draw the cork from another bottle, "Burns transfixed him by a comparison of his present position with that of Abraham lingering over the filial sacrifice." Syme's obituary in the *Dumfries Weekly Journal* spoke of him as "this talented, vivacious, peculiar, and most remarkable gentleman, whose memory deserves more than a passing notice," and went on to report that he "applied diligently to business, acted as factor for various gentlemen, and dispensed the rights of hospitality on a scale, certainly within his means, but still beyond the health and strength of almost any other human being. No man in the South of Scotland had half so extensive a circle of friends, and no man, it may be added, ever gave so many social parties. Mr. Syme hated to dine alone; and to him social converse, over a modicum of port, books, and a rubber, were the *summum bonum* of human happiness."

After Burns' death, Syme and Gilbert Burns went to Liverpool to stay with Dr. James Currie, in order to help him with the biography he was to write. "In those days there were no steam boats, and while returning to the Nith in an ordinary packet, a very terrible storm arose which appears to have alarmed even the boldest mariners. The excellent Gilbert, sick and frightened, hid himself below and spent his hours in prayer; but Mr. Syme, who was made of sterner stuff, who possessed nerves of iron and sinews of steel, remained on deck and assisted the crew as far as he could, until the vessel rounded St. Bees Head, and found temporary shelter in Whitehaven or Maryport."

In 1797, Maria Riddell wrote to James Currie, Syme's friend and employer (as factor on his estate), "I know Syme to be a careless & a very unsuspicious character. . . . He has a good head, united to an excellent heart, but I know that in matters of business he wants method; he is always in a labyrinth of papers and accounts, and, somewhat like the cuttlefish, he obscures himself altogether in a mist of his own creating." Syme himself provides a footnote to this comment. In a letter to Alexander Cunningham, he reports with shamefaced amusement that at the end of a long journey to go hunting, he discovered that he had not brought his dogs.

It will be remembered that Robert Chambers described Syme as a *bon-vivant*. In 1804, Mrs. Riddell wrote to Dr. Currie of Syme's marriage, "I think Syme did right, and has mended His *peccada* in the best possible way. I fancy the Lady never had beauty to allure, but merely, as Falstaff said, 'Rebellion came in his way, and he found it.'"

Syme's record of his intimacy with Burns has a candor rare in the documents available to Burns' biographers. Most of it survives in letters to his and Burns' friend Alexander Cunningham, in Edinburgh, but a valuable addition consists of comments on passages from early critics and biographers of Burns which Syme supplied to Alexander Peterkin when Peterkin was preparing his counterblast to them in 1815. Syme's account of a tour with Burns through Galloway in 1793* is particularly revealing.

> From my Cabin at Troqueer near Dumfries
> 3d August 1793 — evening —

DEAR CUNNINGHAM

I had the distinguished favor and high gratification of receiving a large packet of choice pamphlets with your very acceptable letter of 24th July — They reached me on the 26th the evening before I set out with Burns on a tour thro the wilds and cultivated plains of Galloway some account of which tour I am so disposed to give you, and perhaps you are so disposed to receive that I trust you will graciously undertake to read to the end of this (to be) very long extended epistle —

I got Burns a grey Highland shelty to ride on — we dined the first

---

* As we have seen from Burns' letter to David McCulloch, he and Syme also toured southwestern Scotland again in 1794.

day of our Tour at Glendonwynnes of Parton — a beautiful situation on the banks of the Dee — in the evening we walked up a *bonny know* and had as grand a view of alpine scenery as can well be found — a delightful soft evening gave it all its great graces. Immediately opposite & within a mile of us we saw *Airds* a charming romantic place where dwelt Low the author of Mary weep no more for me — This was classical ground for Burns — He viewed the "highest hill which rises o'er the source of Dee" — He would have staid till "the passing spirit" had appeared had we not resolved to reach Kenmure that night — We arrived as Mr. & Mrs. Gordon were sitting down to Supper — *

Here is a genuine Baron's seat — the Castle, an old building stands on a large natural moat — In front the river Ken winds for miles thro the most fertile and beautiful Holm until it expands into a Loch 12 miles long, the banks of which on the South present a fine and soft landskape of green knolls, natural wood, and here and there a gray rock — In short I cannot conceive a scene more terribly romantic than the Castle of Kenmore, Burns thinks so much of it that he has long meditated on putting his thoughts in poetry descriptive of it — Indeed I take it he has begun the work — I should be very curious to see how his mind views it — We spent 3 days with Mr. Gordon whose polished hospitality is of an original and endearing kind. It is not only ask and it shall be given, seek & ye shall find but here is what you may wish to have, take it as you incline — Mrs. Gordon's lap dog Echo was dead — she would have an Epitaph — Several had been made — Burns was asked for one — He did not like the subject but to please the Lady he made the following —

> In wood & wild ye warbling throng
> Your heavy loss deplore
> Now half extinct your powers of Song
> Sweet Echo is no more
>
> Ye jarring screeching things around
> Scream your discordant joys,
> Now half your din of tuneless sound
> With Echo silent lies —

* During his late teens, while serving as an ensign in the 72nd regiment, Syme had formed a friendship which lasted until his death with a fellow officer, John Gordon, later Viscount Kenmure.

I don't give you this as a great thing — He does not like it — But I may give you one or two better things before I am done writing —

We left Kenmore and went to Gatehouse — I took him the moor road where savage & desolate regions extended wide around — The sky turned sympathetic with the wretchedness of the soil and treated the poor travellers to the full with a flood of misery — For 3 hours did the wild Elements "rumble their bellyful upon our defenseless heads — O, ho, twas foul" — we were utterly wet and we got vengeance at Gatehouse by getting utterly drunk — there is not such a scene of delightful beauty in Scotland as Gatehouse — As it is a stage on the road to Ireland I will not describe it — Tis well known to travellers and you likely have, or will see it —

From Gatehouse we went to Kirkcudb[righ]t thro a fine country but before I bring you there I must tell you Burns had got a pair of *jimmy* boots, which the wetness had rendered it an impossible task to get on — the brawny poet tried force & tore them in shreds — a whiffling vexation like this is more trying to the temper than a serious calamity — we were going to the *Isle* — Lord Selkirks and the forlorn Burns was quite discomfited — a sick stomach, headache &c lent their forces & the man of verse was quite *accablé*. Mercy on me how he did fume & rage — nothing would restore him in temper — I tried all I could think of, at length I got a lucky hit — across the bay of Wigton I showed him Ld. Galloway's house — he expectorated his spleen against the aristocratic elf, and regained a most agreeable temper — I have about half a dozen of capital extempores which I dare not write — But I may *repeat* and you shall hear them some time — I declare they possess as much point and classical *terseness* if I may so express myself, as anything I can imagine. O, he was in an epigrammatic humour indeed — I told him it was rash to crucify Ld. G—— in the way he was doing for tho he might not receive any favours at his hands yet he might suffer an injury — He struck up immediately

> Spare me thy vengeance G—— — ay
> In quiet let me live;
> I ask no kindness at thy hand
> For thou hast none to give.

A Laird not very respectable is safer game — He does not love one Morrin* — He therefore gives a blow to him

* Purchaser of Ellisland.

When Morrin, deceased to the devil went down
Twas nothing would serve him but Satan's own crown;
Thy Fool-head, quoth Satan, that crown shall wear never:
I grant thou'rt as wicked, — but not quite so clever —

14th Augt.

The Interval from the first date to this has passed without my having time or word to finish what I have still to say in continuation of
our Tour. I am to bring you to Kirkcudbt along with our Poet without
boots. I carried the torn ruins across my saddle in despight of his
fulminations and in contempt of apperances — and whats more Lord
Selkirk carried them in his coach to Dumfries — & insisted they were
worth the mending —

We reached Kirkcudbt about one, oclock — I had engaged us to
dine with one of the first men in our Country L. Dalzell — But Burns'
obstreperous independence would not dine but where he should as
he said, eat like a Turk, drink like a fish & swear like the Devil —
Since he would not dine with Dalzell in his own house he had nothing for it but (Dalzell) to dine with us in the Inn — we had a very
agreeable party. In the evening we went to the *Isle* — Robert had not
absolutely regained the milkiness of good temper, and it occurred
once or twice to him that the Isle was the seat of a *Lord,* yet that
Lord was not an *Aristocrate* He knew the family a little* — At length
we got there about 8, as they were at tea & coffee — It is one of the
most delightful places formed by the assemblage of every soft, but not
tame object which constitutes natural and cultivated beauty But not
to speak of its external graces let me tell you that we found all the
female family (all beautiful) and some strangers at the Isle — and
who else but Urbani — It is impossible to pay due respect to the
family by putting them forward as principal figures on this paper when
I have to tell you that *Urbani* sung us many Scotch Songs accompanied
with music — The two young Ladies of Selkirk sung also — We had
the song Lord Gregory which I asked for to have occasion to call
upon Burns to *speak* his words to that tune — He *did speak* them —
and such was the effect, that a dead silence ensued — Twas such a
silence as a mind of feeling must necessarily preserve when it is
touched, as I think sometimes & will happen, with that sacred en-

* Lord Daer with whom he had dined at Dugald Stewart's in 1786 was second
son of the fourth Earl of Selkirk.

thusiasm which banishes every other thought than the contemplation and indulgence of the sympathy produced. . . .

We enjoyed a very happy evening — we had really a treat of mental and sensual delights — the latter consisting in abundance & variety of delicious fruits &c — the former you may conceive from our society — a company of 15 or 16 very agreeable young people.

We got to Dumfries next day — so Ends our Tour — I shall not dwell longer upon it, yet I could give you many other circumstances — but recollecting how Boswell treats of his Tour with Johnson & how he tells you of his, etc, etc, etc, I fear I might incur similar contempt. I have not seen Robert since.

I anxiously hope & pray that you Mrs. Cunningham and the dear little one will meet with all the happy things of this world — I remain Dear Cunningham —

Your old & affectionate companion & friend
John Syme

At this point in the manuscript, Cunningham has inserted the following note: "Either on this ride to Dumfries or next day Burns I believe composed Scots wha hae with Wallace bled — the sublime address of Bruce to his troops. — Burns sent it soon after to J. Dalzell. He shewed it next day to J.S. in the stamp office." Burns, however, in a letter to George Thomson, dated by Professor Ferguson "About 30 August 1793," gives other particulars of *Scots Wha Hae.*

I am delighted with many little melodies which the learned Musician despises as silly & insipid. — I do not know whether the old air, "Hey tutti taitie," may rank among this number; but well I know that, with Fraser's Hautboy, it has often filled my eyes with tears. — There is a tradition, which I have met with in many places of Scotland, that it was Robert Bruce's March at the battle of Bannock-burn. — This thought, in my yesternight's evening walk, warmed me to a pitch of enthusiasm on the theme of Liberty & Independence, which I threw into a kind of Scots Ode, fitted to the Air, that one might suppose to be the gallant Royal Scot's address to his heroic followers on that eventful morning. —

Robert Bruce's march to BANNOCKBURN —
To its ain tune —

Scots, wha hae wi' WALLACE bled,
Scots, wham BRUCE has aften led,
Welcome to your gory bed, —
Or to victorie.—

Now's the day & now's the hour;
See the front o' battle lower;
See approach proud EDWARD's power,
Chains & Slaverie. —

Wha will be a traitor-knave?
Wha can fill a coward's grave?
Wha sae base as be a Slave?
— Let him turn & flie: —

Wha for SCOTLAND's king & law,
Freedom's sword will strongly draw,
FREE-MAN stand or FREE-MAN fa',
Let him follow me. —

By Oppression's woes & pains!
By your Sons in servile chains!
We will drain our dearest veins,
But they *shall* be free!

Lay the proud Usurpers low!
Tyrants fall in every foe!
LIBERTY's in every blow!
Let us DO — or DIE!!!

So may God ever defend the cause of Truth and Liberty, as he did
that day! — Amen.!

RB

P.S. I shewed the air to Urbani, who was highly pleased with it, &
begged me to make soft verses for it; but I had no idea of giving myself any trouble on the subject till the accidental recollection of that
glorious struggle for Freedom, associated with the glowing ideas of

some other struggles of the same nature, *not quite so ancient,* roused
my rhyming mania.

Burns had seen Urbani at Lord Selkirk's on July 31 or August 1, and the gestation of *Scots Wha Hae* may well have been
the result of that meeting, as Cunningham suggests, with the
song taking final form as Burns reports to Thomson. The song
is flaming evidence that Burns did not lighten his sympathies
with the French Revolution in the summer of 1793, even though
he may have become more discreet.

Robert Chambers quotes a Mr. Carson as source of the following anecdote, which forms an engaging supplement to Syme's
account of the 1793 Galloway tour.

The only friends of the host and hostess invited to meet the travellers, Burns and Syme, at Kenmure, were the Rev John Gillespie, the
highly esteemed minister of the parish, and myself.

On the evening preceding their departure, the bard having expressed
his intention of climbing to the top of "the highest hill that rises o'er
the source of Dee," there to see the arbour of Lowe, the author of
the celebrated song "Mary's Dream," Mr Gordon proposed that they
should all sail down the loch in his barge *Glenkens,* to the Airds Hill
below Lowe's seat. Seeing that this proposal was intended in compliment by the worthy host both to the bard and to Mr Gillespie, who
had been the patron of Lowe, the gentlemen all concurred; and the
weather proving propitious next morning, the vessel soon dropt down
to the foot of Loch Ken with all the party on board. Meanwhile, Mr
Gordon's groom led the travellers' horses round to the Boat-o'-Rhone,
saddled and bridled, that each rider might mount on descending from
the poet's seat; but the barge unfortunately grounded before reaching
the proposed landing-place — an obstruction not anticipated by any
of the party. Mr Gordon, with the assistance of an oar, vaulted from
the prow of the little vessel to the beach, and was soon followed in
like manner by Mr Syme and myself; thus leaving only the venerable
pastor of Kells and the bard on board. The former, being too feeble
to jump, as we had done, to land, expressed a desire to remain in the
vessel till Mr Gordon and I returned; upon hearing which, the
generous bard instantly slipt into the water, which was, however, so

deep as to wet him to the knees. After a short entreaty, he succeeded in getting the clergyman on his shoulders; on observing which, Mr Syme raised his hands, laughed immoderately and exclaimed: "Well, Burns, of all men on earth, you are the last I would have expected to see *priest-ridden!*" We laughed also, but Burns did not seem to enjoy the joke. He made no reply, but carried his load silently through the reeds to land.

When Mr Syme's account of this excursion with the bard into Galloway appeared in Dr Currie's first edition of the *Life and Works of Robert Burns,** the Glenkens people, who were actors in this part of the drama, were very much surprised to find the above incident not even alluded to. . . . We were all fully satisfied that it was by the bard's wading into the loch that his *new boots* were so thoroughly wet, and that the choler or independence next day manifested by him to Syme was only the result of his wounded feelings at having been made such a laughing-stock by his friend for merely rendering assistance due by common humanity to old age or infirmity, which Mr Gordon and myself charged ourselves afterward for having overlooked in that instance.

In giving excerpts from the following letter of Syme's, the *Burns Chronicle* (1934) omits the colorful account of Eighteenth Century "toasting."

DEAR CUNNINGHAM
. . . [Burns] says he cannot possibly be in Edinr where he should enjoy much happiness — particularly with you — He is confined here by his business and I dare say in part by his finances, for Robin's heart and temper are not cold and frugal — My Irish friend (Mr Large) filled him and me etc very *fu* last friday — A downright Irish Native & Robt. Burns in co — I defy apathy itself to escape a doze — Bi Jasus says the first & is that the way you fill in Scotland — arrah now we drink every good toast a bumper with us, & bad luck to him who shews daylight at the brim to a toast I give for *bi* the holy they are all of the vary best at all at all — now here's his majesty etc etc etc and many fine fellows in succession, to each of whom a bumper was necessary — other ways a pistol shot.

* Considerably embroidered by Currie.

It then became Robin to make a bumper — & hang the fellow for his toast made 13 — He gave — not a man — but a nation — Ireland — on which bi the holy says my friend we must have a round dozen to her before another toast be given — So that you see Cunningham how impossible it was to get free — . . .

I still am resolved upon paying you a visit before August — . . . I need not write the particulars I wish to communicate relative to Burns's production etc for I will regale you in conversation with some of these.

But the wild Bard has just now popped in while I was writing this and no less than a very elegant female figure of good rank reading a book aside me (She is the wife of an intimate acquaintance of mine — a writer in Kirkuidbr a very clever respectable woman whom I much esteem & so does Robin) Her husband was out — & Robin's confounding wit began to play — He remained all day — and was according to use & wont charming company. The wicked fellow had read a vehemently loyal advertisement by a Club of bucks here who call themselves the loyal *Native* Club — The individuals who compose it are neither Robins favorites nor mine, but we are far from differing from them on sentiments of loyalty — we differ on *sentiment* abstractedly considered — They know scarcely the meaning of the word sentiment & their Society consists mainly in roaring & drinking. Robin spouts the following — on the advertisement of the *Loyal Natives*

> Pray who are these *Natives* the rabble so ven'rate?
> They're our true ancient natives, and the breed unregen'rate:
> The ignorant savage that weather'd the storm,
> When the Man and the Brute differed but in the form.

Dont let any Dumfries person see this for one of the Savages if he heard it, might cut Robins pipe —

The following two passages from letters give pleasant details of Burns and Syme together. The first is from about May 1, 1795. "Burns and I are one and indivisible — but what with his occupation and mine we meet only by starts — or at least occasionally — & we drink as many *cups* of tea as *bottles* of wine together. We are two of the best *privates* in the Dumfries Royal Volunteers — But not to flatter myself or him, I would say that hang me if I should know how to be happy were he not in the way of making me so at times — " The second is dated February 24, 1796.

Burns tells me he had (if I did not misunderstand him) a long letter very lately from you — About a month ago he mentioned a scheme he was to follow which, if he accomplishes, will prove a very agreeable treat to you — He is to sit down as the spirit moves him and write you prose & poetry on every subject which strikes him — to form a sort of Journal business of it — and when it grows thro' two or three sheets to send the foliage — This will surely be a very valuable and entertaining farrago or Burnsana (is this a right term?)   I have prompted him to execute the design & shall not miss giving him the spur — He and I dined tete a tete last Sunday in my Cabin — quite sober — only one bottle of port betwixt us — I like this better than a debauch even in an Inn — Yet when two or three are gathered together in the name of friendship & *nostri-generis* — why, I would as soon have a bottle or a bottle & a half as a share of that quantity — We have a very superior fellow here — Dr Maxwell — who to an uncommon if not wonderful science in Physic adds the perfect manners and mind of a gentle man — you would be much attached him — without him & Burns I should find this place very blank & dreary —

The story draws very near its close in the next letter, of July 17, 1796. That of July 19 will be found later in the account of Burns' death.

My dear Cunningham
    I had your favour covering letter to the Bard which I delivered personally. He poor fellow is in a very bad state of health — I really am extremely alarmed, not only by the cadaverous aspect and shaken frame of Burns, but from the accounts which I have heard from the first faculty here — But I entertain strong hopes that the vigour of his former stamina will conquer his present illness, and that by care & the attention & advice he receives from Dr Maxwell he will recover — I do not mean to alarm you but really poor Burns is very ill — However do not say whence you heard so — You are doing him a great

kindness & benefit, and I am sure it is well bestowed — I cannot allow myself to imagine the business will fail, for God forbid there should be any rule of office that could not be dispensed with on such an occasion as the present.

Cunningham had urged the Excise Board to continue Burns at full pay even though he could not perform his duties. The Board felt that it must hold to its rule of granting only half pay in such circumstances, but Currie reports that Burns' "full emoluments were continued to him by the kindness of Mr [Adam] Stobbie, a young expectant in the Excise, who performed the duties of the office without fee or reward." Commissioner Graham sent a private contribution of £5.

Burns left an estate of approximately £300, and debts not above £20. But there were no liquid assets except the sums sent him in his last two weeks by James Burness and George Thomson, £15 in all, and the £5 from Robert Graham. James Burness sent another £5 for immediate necessities.

After Burns' death Cunningham undertook to raise a subscription in Edinburgh for the benefit of Jean and the children, but the response was discouraging. He wrote Syme August 9, 1796, "The truth is my dear Syme the poor Bards frailties excuse this vile word were not only so well known here but often I believe exaggerated that even the admirers of genius cannot be prevailed on to do what we all ought 'to forget and forgive' — "

On September 19, in discussing a proposed edition of Burns' poems and letters, Cunningham again writes to Syme, "To select & arrange what ought to be published of Burns's will be no easy task when you consider the variety of taste & opinions which obtain among men — and the necessity there is for the strictest delicacy being ever kept in View — His poetry & letters were often so blended with Religion Politics Love & Bawdry that the greatest care must be taken to render his thoughts & opinions consistent — "

In preparing for the extensive correctional comment in his

Preface to an 1815 edition of Currie (the copyright having expired), Alexander Peterkin had passages from several biographers and critics of Burns set in type, from which he pulled proofsheets. Three sheets survive which he sent to John Syme for comment. 2 1/3 sheets in 1935 were in possession of the Editor of the *Burns Chronicle*, with whose permission transcripts were prepared which are the basis of quotations here. 2/3 of the third sheet was then in the Watson Collection (1190) in the National Library of Scotland. Excerpts from these documents have appeared *ante*. Remaining items of interest follow.

Currie. "His temper now became more irritable and gloomy: he fled from himself into society, often of the lowest kind."

Syme deletes "the lowest kind" and substitutes "a low rank."

Syme: "Burns was fastidious on the point of going to meet strangers in a Tavern to shew himself as a Toy or wonder — when I had occasion to exhibit the Poet to a man of distinction who courted the favor, I wrote him a proper card of solicitation."

David Irvine: "His habits gradually became more pernicious."

Syme deletes "pernicious" and substitutes "inexcusable." *

Irvine: "Often did he acknowledge his numerous breaches of the duties of a husband and a father."

* An illustration of Syme's comment is the rhymed apology below from Burns to Mr. S. M'kenzie of Dumfries, which carries the following docket: "Mr. Robt Burns with a pretended excuse for having used my character ill — 1796 — Delivered to me by Mr. Syme, opposite the Inn possessed by Mrs. Riddick, in Bank Street." (Kinsley II, #520, 814.)

> The friend who wild from Wisdom's way
>   The fumes of wine infuriate send,
> (Not moony madness more astray)
>   Who but deplores that hapless friend?

> Mine was th'insensate, frenzied part,
>   (Ah! why did I those scenes outlive,
> Scenes so abhorrent to my heart!)
>   'Tis thine to pity and forgive. —
>   RB

Peterkin: "Ask Mrs Burns what were the breaches of Duty of which he was guilty."

The reply, in the margin, is neatly torn away. The proofsheet containing this material belonged to the late editor of the *Burns Chronicle*.

Syme: "Burns had much collision with world — could penetrate & appreciate character well & could acquit himself as well as any Lord of high & courtly race & experience."

Syme: "I conceived Burns to have been highly chivalrous & polite — quite devoid of vulgarity or meanness."

Sir Walter Scott: "To lay before him his errors, or to point out their consequences, was to touch a string that jarred every feeling with him. . . . It is a dreadful truth, that when racked and tortured by the well-meant and warm expostulations of an intimate friend, he at length started up in a paroxysm of frenzy, and, drawing a sword cane, which he usually wore, made an attempt to plunge it into the body of his adviser: in the next instant, he was with difficulty witheld from suicide."

Syme: "This happened to me — In my parlour at Rydale one afternoon Burns & I were very gracious & confidential — I did advise him to be temperate in all things — I might have spoken Daggers but I did not mean them — He shook to the inmost fibre of his frame, drew the sword cane, when I exclaimed, What! wilt thou thus, & in my own house? The poor fellow was so stung with remorse &c, that he dashed himself down on the floor — (which is a flagged floor) and beat his face against it — He shunned me during some weeks after from remorse and self-reproach — But we became better friends ever after."

As already mentioned by John Syme, Burns' chief physician in his terminal illness was his friend Dr. James Maxwell, whose father, Kirkonnel Maxwell, had followed Prince Charles in 1745.

Maxwell had studied medicine in France, had joined the Republican Army, and had helped guard the scaffold on which Louis XVI had been executed, dipping his handkerchief in the royal blood. Maxwell and Burns shared a combined Jacobitism and Jacobinism, and they and Syme and perhaps a few others were used to converse behind closed doors in violently loyalist Dumfries. Dr. Maxwell enjoyed high professional reputation, and he was most devoted in his attendance on Burns, but means were lacking at that time to diagnose Burns' illness, and Dr. Maxwell's advice to seek rest in pleasant surroundings, and gentle exercise, and sea bathing, was worthless at best. Nonetheless Burns tried to follow it, and went to Brow, on the Solway, near Dumfries, in early July, 1796. Brow is well described by Sir James Crichton-Browne:

Ten miles south-east of Dumfries, on the Solway shore, stands the meanest, shabbiest little spa in all the world. It consists of three whitewashed cottages; a tank the size of a dining-table and lined with red-stone, into which, through an iron pipe, the mineral water trickles; an esplanade a score of yards long, of coarse tufted grass; and the pump-room, a dilapidated wooden shed, the walls and benches of which are graven over and over again with the initials of those who have sought healing at the Well. The country immediately around is flat and uninteresting. Inland there are a few stunted plantations of gnarled oaks and shaggy Scotch firs, which by their bent backs bear witness to the rough usage of the western winds, while in front there is a broad, flat, hillocky expanse, studded with bent grass and furze, and ending in the sea-beach, consisting of a mixture of sand and clay known locally as *sleetch*. This uninviting substance extends for several miles into the Solway Firth, with so slight a declination that the tide at low water recedes entirely out of sight and leaves to the eye a barren and cheerless waste.

On a dull day, with the skies draped in cloud and at low water, a more forlorn and desolate place than the Brow-Well — for that is how this spa is named, no one knows how or why — it would be difficult to imagine; but when the sun shines and the skies clear and the tide is in, it becomes a fascinating spot, for a magnificent panorama is disclosed to view. On the horizon on the east stretches the long range of the Cumberland and Westmoreland mountains, Skiddaw, Saddleback, Helvellyn, and the rest of them in an outline of fantastic beauty, and ending in the "sapphire promontory which men name St. Bees"; to the south "huge Criffel's hoary top ascends"; to the west, tier on tier, run the rugged Galloway hills, and then the ample woodlands that surround Comlongan Castle, while in the foreground sparkle the last ripples of the Atlantic flow.

But whatever its physical features may be, the Brow-Well must be regarded as a sacred precinct by all Scotsmen, for it was the scene of the last act of a memorable and deeply moving Scottish tragedy. It was the Gethsemane of Robert Burns.

Once at the Brow, removed from his friends and family, almost entirely alone, Burns sat under a hawthorne tree and saw his strength gradually slip away. Each day he waded out until the cold water came up to his armpits, and then waded back to sit under the hawthorne again and think of his daily more apparent end. Finally, on July 18, after he had become entirely certain the end was not far off, he climbed wearily into a carriage and was driven back to Dumfries.

At this time Maria Riddell was staying near Brow, and, hearing that Burns was there, she invited him to dinner and sent her carriage for him.

I was struck [she writes] with his appearance on entering the room. The stamp of death was impressed on his features. He seemed already touching the brink of eternity. His first salutation was "Well, Madam, have you any commands for the other world?" I replied, that it seemed a doubtful case which of us should be there soonest, and that I hoped he would yet live to write my epitaph. (I was then in a poor state of health.) He looked in my face with an air of great kindness, and expressed his concern at seeing me look so ill, with his accustomed sensibility. At table he ate little or nothing, and he complained of having entirely lost the tone of his stomach. We had a long and serious conversation about his present situation, and the approaching termination of all his earthly prospects. He spoke of his death without any of the ostentation of philosophy, but with firmness as well as feeling — as an event likely to happen very soon, and which gave him concern chiefly from leaving his four children so young and un-protected, and his wife in so interesting a situation — in hourly ex-pectation of lying-in of a fifth. He mentioned, with seeming pride and satisfaction, the promising genius of his eldest son, and the flattering marks of approbation he had received from his teachers, and dwelt particularly on his hopes of that boy's future conduct and merit. His anxiety for his family seemed to hang heavy upon him, and the more perhaps from the reflection that he had not done them all the justice he was so well qualified to do. Passing from this subject, he shewed great concern about the care of his literary fame, and particularly the publication of his posthumous works. He said he was well aware that his death would occasion some noise, and that every scrap of his writing would be revived against him to the injury of his future repu-tation: that letters and verses written with unguarded and improper freedom, and which he earnestly wished to have buried in oblivion, would be handed about by idle vanity or malevolence, when no dread of his resentment would restrain them, or prevent the censures of shrill-tongued malice, or the insidious sarcasms of envy, from pouring forth all their venom to blast his fame.

He lamented that he had written many epigrams on persons against whom he entertained no enmity, and whose characters he should be sorry to wound; and many indifferent poetical pieces, which he feared would now, with all their imperfections on their head, be thrust upon the world. On this account he deeply regretted having deferred to put his papers into a state of arrangement, as he was now quite incapable of the exertion. . . . The conversation was kept up with great evenness and animation on his side. I had seldom seen his mind greater or more collected. There was frequently a considerable degree of vivacity in his sallies, and they would probably have had a greater share, had not the concern and dejection I could not disguise, damped the spirit of pleasantry he seemed not unwilling to indulge.

We parted about sun-set on the evening of that day (the 5th of July, 1796); the next day I saw him again, and we parted to meet no more!

Burns left a moving record of his last days in letters which he wrote to friends and members of his family and to Jean. After his return to Dumfries, two days before his death, John Syme visited him and described the visit to Alexander Cunningham. Burns' first letter from Brow, written soon after his arrival, was to George Thomson.

Brow 4th July

My dear Sir,
I recd your songs: but my health being so precarious nay dangerously situated, that as a last effort I am here at a sea-bathing quarters. — Besides my inveterate rheumatism, my appetite is quite gone, & I am so emaciated as to be scarce able to support myself on my own legs. — Alas! is this a time for me to woo the Muses? However, I am still anxiously willing to serve your work; & if possible shall try: — I would not like to see another employed, unless you could lay your hand upon a poet whose productions would be equal to the rest. — You will see my alterations & remarks on the margin of each song. — You may think it hard as to "Cauld kail in Aberdeen," but I cannot help it. — My address is still Dumfries.

Farewell! & God bless you!
RBurns

There follow letters to Alexander Cunningham, to his father-in-law James Armour, to his brother Gilbert, to his cousin James Burness, to Jean, and to a friend begging the use of a gig to take him back to Dumfries. A letter to Mrs. Dunlop has already been quoted at the close of Section III, and one to George Thomson at the opening of Section V.

Brow-Sea-bathing quarters
July 7th

My dear Cunningham
I received yours here this moment and am indeed highly flattered with the approbation of the literary circle you mention; a literary circle inferiour to none in the two kingdoms. — Alas! my friend, I fear the voice of the Bard will soon be heard among you no more! For those eight or ten months I have been ailing, sometimes bedfast & sometimes not; but these last three months I have been tortured with an excruciating rheumatism, which has reduced me to nearly the last

stage. — You actually would not know me if you saw me. — Pale, emaciated, & so feeble as occasionally to need help from my chair — my spirits are fled! fled! — but I can no more on the subject — only the Medical folks tell me that my last & only chance is bathing & country quarters & riding. — The deuce of the matter is this; when an Excise-man is off duty, his salary is reduced to 35£ instead of 50£. — What way, in the name of thrift, shall I maintain myself & keep a horse in Country-quarters — with a wife & five children at home, on 35£? I mention this, because I had intended to beg your utmost interest & all friends you can muster, to move our Commissrs of Excise to grant me the full salary. — I dare say you know them all personally. — If they do not grant it me, I must lay my account with an exit truly en poëte, if I die not of disease I must perish with hunger. —

I have sent you one of the songs: the other, my memory does not serve me with, & I have no copy here; but I shall be at home soon, when I will send it you. — Apropos to being at home, Mrs Burns threatens in a week or two to add one more to my Paternal charge, which if of the right gender, I intend shall be introduced to the world by the respectable designation of Alexr Cunningham Burns. My last was James Glencairn, so you can have no objection to the company of Nobility. —

Farewell —
RB

Mr Jas Armour *Mason   Mauchline*

For Heaven's sake & as you value the welfare of your daughter, & my wife, do, my dearest Sir, write to Fife to Mrs Armour to come if possible. — My wife thinks she can yet reckon upon a fortnight. — The Medical people order me *as I value my existence,* to fly to sea-bathing & country quarters, so it is ten thousand chances to one that I shall not be within a dozen miles of her when her hour comes. — What a situation for her, poor girl, without a single friend by her on such a serious moment. —

I have now been a week at salt water, & though I think I have got some good by it, yet I have some secret fears that this business will be dangerous if not fatal. —

Your affectionate son —

July 10th

RBurns

DEAR BROTHER

It will be no very pleasing news to you to be told that I am dangerously ill, & not likely to get better. — An inveterate rheumatism has reduced me to such a state of debility, and my appetite is tottaly gone, so that I can scarcely stand on my legs. — I have been a week at sea-bathing, & I will continue there or in a friend's house in the country all the summer. — God help my wife & children if I am taken from their head! — They will be poor indeed. — I have contracted one or two serious debts, partly from my illness these many months & partly from too much thoughtlessness as to expense when I came to town that will cut in too much on the little I leave them in your hands. — Remember me to my Mother. —

Yours

July 10th   RBURNS

Mr James Burness *Writer Montrose*
MY DEAREST COUSIN,

When you offered me money-assistance little did I think I should want it so soon. — A rascal of a Haberdasher to whom I owe a considerable bill taking it into his head that I am dying, has commenced a process against me, & will infallibly put my emaciated body into jail. — Will you be so good as to accomodate me, & that by return of post, with ten pound. — O, James, did you know the pride of my heart, you would feel doubly for me! Alas! I am not used to beg! The worst of it is, my health was coming about finely; you know & my Physician assures me that melancholy & low spirits are half my disease, guess then my horrors since this business began. — If I had it settled, I would be I think quite well in a manner. — How shall I use the language to you, O do not disappoint me! but strong Necessity's curst command. —

I have been thinking over & over my brother's affairs, & I fear I must cut him up; but on this I will correspond at another time, particularly as I shall need your advice. —

Forgive me once more for mentioning by return of Post. — Save me from the horrors of a jail!

My Compliments to my friend James, & to all the rest. — I do not know what I have written. The subject is so horrible, I dare not look it over again. —

Farewel

July 12th   RBURNS

The threat of jail, though real enough for delinquent debtors in Burns' day, was probably not serious for him, but his melancholy was understandably deep, and it was sharpened by this prospect which he felt to be ominous. In his last letter to Jean, he makes an effort to be hopeful.

Brow, Thursday [14th]

MY DEAREST LOVE,

I delayed writing until I could tell you what effect sea-bathing was likely to produce. It would be injustice to deny that it has eased my pains, and I think has strengthened me; but my appetite is still extremely bad. No flesh nor fish can I swallow: porridge and milk are the only things I can taste. I am very happy to hear by Miss Jessy Lewars that you are all well. My very best and kindest compliments to her, and to all the children. I will see you on Sunday.

Your affectionate Husband,
R. BURNS

The next letter arranged for his return to Dumfries.

John Clark   Esquire   *Locherwoods*

Saturd: nⁿ[16th]

MY DEAR SIR,

my hours of bathing have interfered so unluckily as to have put it out of my power to wait on you. — In the meantime, as the tides are over I anxiously wish to return to town, as I have not heard any news of Mrs Burns these two days. — Dare I be so bold as to borrow your Gig? I have a horse at command, but it threatens to rain, & getting wet is perdition. Any time about three in the afternoon, will suit me exactly. —

Your most gratefully & sincerely
RBURNS

Burns' last letter was to his father-in-law.

Mr James Armour   *Mauchline*

Dumfries, 18th July 1796

MY DEAR SIR,

Do for Heaven's sake, send Mrs Armour here immediately. My wife is hourly expecting to be put to bed. Good God! what a situation for her to be in, poor girl, without a friend! I returned from sea-bathing quarters today, and my medical friends would almost persuade me I am better; but I think and feel that my strength is so gone that the disorder will prove fatal to me.

Your Son-in-law,
R. BURNS

The day after Burns returned from Brow, John Syme went to see him, and wrote at once to Cunningham.

Dumfries 19th July — 1796 — noon —

MY DEAR CUNNINGHAM

I wrote you last Sunday and mentioned that our friend Burns was very ill — I conceive it to be a task (you would not forgive me did I omit it) to mention now, that I believe it is all over with him. I am this minute come from the mournful chambers in which I have seen the expiring genius of Scotland departing with Burns. Dr. Maxwell told me yesterday he had no hopes — today the hand of Death is visibly fixed upon him. I cannot dwell on the scene — It overpowers me — yet Gracious God were it thy will to recover him! He had life enough to acknowledge me — and Mrs. Burns said he had been calling on you and me continually — He made a wonderful exertion when I took him by the hand — with a strong voice he said, "I am much better today, — "I shall soon be well again for I command my spirits & my mind. But yesterday I resigned myself to death" — Alas it will not do. . . .

I will write you whenever any alteration of the case takes place — Meantime I feel from my soul I can give you no hopes.

Excuse the irregularity of this if necessary

Yours truly
J SYME

The illness is — the whole system
debilitated & gone, beyond the power
(perhaps) of man to restore —

Burns died Thursday, July 21, 1796, at five o'clock in the morning.

Of many ironies in Burns' career, his funeral was certainly not the least. Too late, it did him impressive honor, and of a sort he would not have relished. It was arranged by his devoted friend, John Syme, and during it a son was born to Jean, who, unaware of the promise her husband had made to Cunningham, named him Maxwell Burns. It would certainly have astonished many at the funeral to know that Burns would become a towering world figure, part of whose history would be the failure of such as they to recognize his worth.

The funeral was held on Monday, July 25, at the Dumfries Town Hall, from which the procession moved more than half a mile to the cemetery through streets lined by troops from the Angusshire Fencibles and the Cinque Ports Cavalry, both commands being then stationed in Dumfries. At the head marched a firing party of Burns' fellow-volunteers, and, behind them, the Cinque Ports Cavalry band playing the Dead March from *Saul*. Then came the bier supported by Volunteers, who changed at intervals. There followed Burns' relatives and "a number of the respectable inhabitants of the town and country." The remaining Volunteers came next, and a guard of Fencibles closed the procession. "A vast concourse of persons assembled, some of them from a considerable distance," and "the great bells of the churches tolled at intervals during the time of the procession. When arrived at the churchyard gate, the funeral party formed two lines and leaned their heads on their firelocks pointed to the ground. Through this space the corpse was carried and borne to the grave. The party then drew up alongside of it, and fired three volleys over the coffin when deposited in the earth."

Two stanzas from the poem with which Burns closed the Kilmarnock volume are his best epitaph.

> Is there a whim-inspirèd fool,
> Owre fast for thought, owre hot for rule,
> Owre blate to seek, owre proud to snool? —   *modest   cringe*

> Let him draw near;
> And owre this grassy heap sing dool,   *woe*
> And drap a tear.
>
> . . . .
>
> The poor inhabitant below
> Was quick to learn and wise to know,
> And keenly felt the friendly glow
> And softer flame;
> But thoughtless follies laid him low
> And stain'd his name.

Efforts of Cunningham in Edinburgh and Syme in Dumfries to collect funds for the benefit of Jean and the children met with limited success. In Liverpool, Dr. James Currie, a Dumfriesshire native and an early admirer of Burns, raised £70, and a London subscription produced £700. In all, £1200 was raised, invested, and turned over to the Bailies and Provost of Ayr; and Dr. Currie's four volumes in 1800, which he edited without compensation, raised £1400. On the income from these funds, Jean continued to live as a widow, quietly and sensibly, in the house where her husband had died. In later years, when her sons could assist her, she was most comfortable. She survived until March 26, 1834.

She refused offers to have her children educated away from her when they were young; eventually the three boys who grew to maturity received a good schooling. Robert (1786–1857), known in his family as "The Laird," got an appointment in the Stamp Office, London. He left an illegitimate son, who in turn left a son, who is reported to have died without issue. Burns has no known descendants by the male line. Maxwell Burns died in 1799, and Francis Wallace in 1803. William Nicol (1791–1872) and James Glencairn (1794–1865) became cadets in the East India Company's service, retiring as Colonel and Lieutenant Colonel. Burns' only direct descendants by Jean Armour are issue of James Glencairn's daughter Sarah.

Burns' daughter by Betty Paton, and his daughter by Anne

Park, each received £200 on marriage, from the subscription funds. Mrs. Carswell reports (1931) of Betty Paton, "Later she married happily and was respected by all. Today the wealthiest of all the blood of Burns, and the only one to reach the peerage of the United Kingdom, is descended from the child she bore the poet."

The caricature of Burns as a Heaven-Taught Ploughman who rose to meteoric fame and declined into dissipated poverty and neglect has faded, happily. But unfortunate ironies remain. His appeal to Scotsmen has served to foster the notion that he is but a local or national poet, and persistent fascination with his personality and his dramatic career, and with his all too human frailties, continues to shift interest from his having been a poet at all. Moreover this very interest in the man tends to ignore the complexity of his character; his good sense and candor and self-knowledge; and his share of that loneliness which is the lot of all great men, and particularly of great artists. The understanding which Burns foresaw would come to him eventually is possible only for those who have lived with him. To make this as nearly possible as can be today, this book has been written.

APPENDICES

APPENDIX A

SCOTS VERNACULAR POEMS WHICH INFLUENCED BURNS

The Life and Death of Habbie Simson, the Piper of Kilbarchan

Kilbarchan now may say alas!
For she hath lost her game and grace,
Both *Trixie* and *The Maiden Trace;*   *[tunes]*
   But what remead?
For no man can supply his place:
   Hab Simson's dead.

Now who shall play *The Day it Dawis,*
Or *Hunt's Up,* when the cock he craws?
Or who can for our kirk-town cause
   Stand us in stead?
On bagpipes now nobody blaws
   Sen Habbie's dead.   *since*

Or wha will cause our shearers sheer?
Wha will bend up the brags of weir,   *raise war*
Bring in the bells, or good play-meir   *hobby-horse*
   In time of need?
Hab Simson could, what needs you speir?   *ask*
   But now he's dead.

So kindly to his neighbours neist   *next*
At Beltan and St. Barchan's feast
He blew, and then held up his breast,
   As he were weid: *mad*
But now we need not him arrest,
   For Habbie's dead.

At fairs he play'd before the spear-men,
All gaily graithed in their gear men: *accoutered*
Steel bonnets, jacks, and swords so clear then
   Like any bead:
Now wha shall play before such weir-men   *warriors*
   Sen Habbie's dead?

At clark-plays when he wont to come,
His pipe played trimly to the drum;
Like bikes of bees he gart it bum,   *hives made hum*
   And tun'd his reed:
Now all our pipers may sing dumb,
   Sen Habbie's dead.

And at horse races many a day,
Before the black, the brown, the gray,
He gart his pipe, when he did play,
   Baith skirl and skreed: *scream shriek*
Now all such pastime's quite away
   Sen Habbie's dead.

He counted was a waled wight-man,   *chosen strong-*
And fiercely at football he ran:
At every game the gree he wan   *prize*
   For pith and speed.
The like of Habbie was na than,
   But now he's dead.

And then, besides his valiant acts,
At bridals he wan many placks;
He bobbit ay behind folk's backs
   And shook his head.
Now we want many merry cracks
   Sen Habbie's dead.

He was convoyer of the bride,
With Kittock hinging at his side;
About the kirk he thought a pride
   The ring to lead: *bridal procession*
But now we may gae but a guide,   *go without*
   For Habbie's dead.

So well's he keepèd his decorum,
And all the stots of *Whip-meg-morum;*   *bouncing turns*

He slew a man, and wae's me for him,
    And bure the feid!   *feud*
But yet the man wan hame before him,
    And was not dead.

Ay whan he play'd the lasses leugh
To see him teethless, auld, and teugh,
He wan his pipes besides Barcleugh,
    Withouten dread!
Which after wan him gear eneugh;   *wealth*
    But now he's dead.

Ay when he play'd the gaitlings gedder'd,   *children*
And when he spake the carl bleddered, *old man* *babbled*
On Sabbath days his cap was fedder'd,
    A seemly weid;
In the kirk-yeard his mare stood tedder'd
    Where he lies dead.

Alas! for him my heart is sair,
For of his spring I gat a skair,   *a quick air* *share*
At every play, race, feast, and fair,
    But guile or greed;
We need not look for piping mair,
    Sen Habbie's dead.

                            Robert Sempill of Beltrees

The Last Dying Words of Bonnie Heck, A Famous Grey-hound in the Shire of Fife

Alas, alas, quo' bonnie Heck,
On former days when I reflec';
I was a dog much in respec'
    For doughty deed:
But now I must hing by the neck
    Without remeid.

O fy, sirs, for black burning shame,
Ye'll bring a blunder on your name?
Pray tell me wherein I'm to blame.
    Is't in offoc'

Because I'm cripple, auld, and lame?
    Quo' bonnie Heck.

What great feats have I done mysel
Within clink of Kilrenny bell,
When I was souple, young, and fell,   *strong*
    But fear or dread;   *Without*
John Ness and Paterson can tell,
    Whose hearts may bleed.

They'll witness that I was the vier   *rival*
Of all the dogs within the shire;
I'd run all day and never tire;
    But now my neck,
It must be stretchèd for my hire,
    Quo' bonnie Heck.

How nimbly could I turn the hare,
Then serve myself; that was but fair;
For still it was my constant care
    The van to lead.
Now what could sery Heck do mair?
    Syne kill her dead.

At the King's-muir and Kelly-law,
Where good stout hares gang fast awa',   *went*
So cleverly I did it claw,
    With pith and speed;
I bure the bell before them a'
    As clear's a bead.

I ran alike on a' kind grunds;
Yea, in the midst of Ardry whins,   *furze*
I gripped the maukins by the buns,   *hares*
    Or by the neck;
When naething could slay them but guns,
    Save bonnie Heck.

I wily, witty, was, and gash,   *lively*
With my auld fellin pawky pash;   *very sly head*
Nae man might ance buy me for cash
    In some respec';
Are they not then confounded rash,
    That hangs poor Heck?

I was a hardy tyke, and bauld;   *dog*   *bold*
Tho' my beard's grey, I'm not so auld.
Can any man to me unfauld
      What is the feid,   *feud*
To stane me ere I be well cauld?
      A cruel deed!

Now honesty was ay my drift;
An innocent and harmless shift,
A kail-pot lid gently to lift,
      Or aumrie sneck,   *cupboard latch*
Shame fa' the chafts dare call that thift, *jaws*   *theft*
      Quo' bonnie Heck.

So well's I cou'd play Hocus-Pocus,
And of the servants mak Jodocus,
And this I did in every Locus
      Throw their neglec':
And was not this a merry Jocus?
      Quo' bonnie Heck.

But now, good sirs, this day is lost
The best dog in the East-Neuk coast;
For never ane durst brag nor boast
      Me, for their neck,
But now I must yield up the ghost,
      Quo' bonnie Heck.

And put a period to my talking;
For I'm unto my exit making:
Sirs, ye may a' gae to the hawking,
      And there reflec'
Ye'll ne'er get sic a dog for maukin   *hare*
      As bonnie Heck.

But if my puppies ance were ready,
Which I gat on a bonnie lady,
They'll be baith clever, keen, and beddy,
      And ne'er neglec'
To clink it like their ancient daddy,
      The famous Heck.

William Hamilton of Gilbertfield

An Elegy on John Cowper*

I warn ye a' to greet and drone;	*weep*
John Cowper's dead — Ohon! Ohon!	
To fill his post alake there's none	
That with sic speed	
Could sa'r sculdudry out like John,	*smell whoring*
But now he 's deid.	

He was right nacky in this way,	*clever*
And eydent baith be night and day,	*diligent*
He wi' the lads his part could play,	
When right sair fleed,	
He gart them good bill-siller pay;	*stud fees*
But now he 's dead.	

Of whore-hunting he gat his fill,
And made be 't mony a pint and gill;
Of his braw post he thought nae ill,
Nor didna need;
Now they may mak a kirk and mill
O 't, since he 's dead.

Altho' he was nae man of weir,	*war*
Yet mony a ane, wi' quaking fear,	
Durst scarce afore his face appear,	
But hide their head;	

* It is necessary, for the illustration of this clergy to strangers, to let them a little into the history of the kirk-treasurer and his man. The treasurer is chosen every year, a citizen respected for riches and honesty; he is vested with an absolute power to seize and imprison the girls that are too impatient to have their green gown before it is hemmed. Them he strictly examines, but no liberty is to be granted till a fair account be given of those persons they have obliged: it must be so; a list is frequently given, sometimes of a dozen or thereby, of married or unmarried unfair traders, whom they secretly assisted in running their goods: these his lordship makes pay to some purpose, according to their ability, for the use of the poor. If the lads be obstreperous, the kirk-sessions, and worst of all, the stool of repentance, are threatened, a punishment which few of any spirit can bear. The treasurer, being changed every year, never comes to be perfectly acquainted with the affair; but their general servant, continuing for a long time, is more expert at discovering such persons, and the places of their resort, which makes him capable to do himself and customers both a good and ill turn. John Cowper maintained this post with activity, and good success, for several years. *Ramsay's note.*

The wylie carle, he gather'd gear,   *fellow*
    And yet he's dead.

Ay, now to some part far awa',
Alas he's gane and left it a';
May be to some sad whilliwha   *deceitful fellow*
    Of fremit blood;   *not akin*
'Tis an ill wind that disna blaw
    Somebody good.

Fy upon Death! he was to blame,
To whirl poor John to his lang hame;
But tho' his arse be cauld, yet fame,
    Wi' tout of trumpet,
Shall tell how Cowper's awfu' name
    Could flie a strumpet.

Shame fa' ye'r chandler-chafts',* O Death!
For stapping of John Cowper's breath,
The loss of him is public skaith.   *loss*
    I dare well say,
To quat the grip he was right laith
    This mony a day.

POSTSCRIPT.

Of umquhile John to lie or bann,   *denounce*
Shaws but ill will, and looks right shan,   *pitiful*
But some tell odd tales of the man;
    For fifty head
Can gie their aith they've seen him gawn†
    Since he was dead.

Keek but up thro' the Stinking Stile,‡
On Sunday morning a wee while,
At the kirk door, out frae an aisle,
    It will appear:
But tak good tent ye dinna file   *foul*
    Ye'r breeks for fear.   *breeches*

---

* Lean or meagre cheeked; when the bones appear like the sides or corners of a candlestick, which in Scots we call a chandler. *Ramsay's note.*
† The common people, when they tell their tales of ghosts appearing, say, he has been seen "gawn," or stalking. *Ramsay's note.*
‡ Opposite to this place is the door of the church, which he attended, being a beadle. *Ramsay's note.*

For well we wat it is his ghaist:
Wow, wad some fouk that can do't best,*
Speak til't, and hear what it confest;
      'Tis a good deed
To send a wand'ring saul to rest
      Amang the deid.

He ken'd the bawds and louns fou well,
And where they used to rant and reel,
He pawkily on them could steal,
      And spoil their sport;
Aft did they wish the muckle deil
      Might take him for 't.

But ne'er a ane of them be spar'd,
E'en tho' there was a drunken laird
To draw his sword, and make a faird,   *bullying bustle*
      In their defence;
John quietly put them in the guard,
      To learn mair sense:

There maun they lie till sober grown,
The lad neist day his fault maun own;
And to keep a' things hush and lown
      He minds the poor;†
Syne after a' his ready's shown,
      He damns the whore.

And she, poor jade, withoutten din,
Is sent to Leith-wynd-fit‡ to spin,
With heavy heart, and cleathing thin,
      And hungry wame,
And ilka month a well-paid skin,   *beating*
      To make her tame.

But now they may scour up and down,
And safely gang their wakes aroun,
Spreading their claps thro' a' the town,

* It is another vulgar notion that a ghost will not be laid to rest till some priest speak to it, and get an account of what disturbs it. *Ramsay's note.*
† Pays hush-money to the treasurer. *Ramsay's note.*
‡ The house of correction at the foot of Leith-wynd. *Ramsay's note.*

But fear or dread;   *without*
For that great kow to bawd and lown,   *goblin   rogue*
John Cowper's dead.

Allan Ramsay

Familiar Epistles

WHICH PASSED BETWEEN LIEUT. HAMILTON*

AND ALLAN RAMSAY

EPISTLE I.

Gilbertfield, June 20th, 1719.

O fam'd and celebrated Allan!
Renown'd Ramsay! canty callan!
There's nowther Highland-man nor Lawlan,
  In poetrie,
But may as soon ding down Tamtallan,   [*castle*]
  As match wi' thee.

For ten times ten, and that's a hunder,
I ha'e been made to gaze and wonder,
When frae Parnassus thou didst thunder,
  Wi' wit and skill;
Wherefore I'll soberly knock under,
  And quat my quill.

Of poetry the hail quintescence
Thou hast suck'd up, left nae excrescence
To petty poets, or sic messens,   *lap-dogs*
  Tho' round thy stool
They may pick crumbs, and lear some lessons
  At Ramsay's school.

Tho' Ben and Dryden of renown   *Ben Jonson*
Were yet alive in London town,
Like kings contending for a crown,
   'Twad be a pingle,   *hard task*
Whilk o' you three wad gar words sound
  And best to gingle.

* Hamilton was a retired officer on half pay.

Transform'd may I be to a rat,
Wer't in my power, but I'd create
Thee upo' sight the laureat
        Of this our age,
Since thou may'st fairly claim to that
        As thy just wage.

Let modern poets bear the blame,
Gin they respect not Ramsay's name,
Wha soon can gar them greet for shame,   *make   weep*
        To their great loss,
And send them a' right sneaking hame
        Be Weeping-cross.

Wha bourds wi' thee had need be wary,   *jests*
And lear wi' skill thy thrust to parry,
When thou consults thy dictionary
        Of ancient words,
Which come from thy poetic quarry
        As sharp as swords.

Now tho' I should baith reel and rottle,
And be as light as Aristotle,
At Ed'nburgh we sall ha'e a bottle
        Of reaming claret
Gin that my half-pay siller shottle   *drawer*
        Can safely spare it.

At crambo then we'll rack our brain,   *a rhyming game*
Drown ilk dull care and aching pain,   *each*
Whilk aften does our spirits drain   *which*
        Of true content;
Woy, woy! but we's be wonder fain,   *we'll   merry*
        When thus acquaint.

Wi' wine we'll gargarize our craig,   *throat*
Then enter in a lasting league,
Free of ill aspect or intrigue;
        And, gin you please it,   *if*
Like princes when met at the Hague,
        We'll solemnize it.

Accept of this, and look upon it
With favour, tho' poor I've done it:

Sae I conclude and end my sonnet,
  Who am most fully,
While I do wear a hat or bonnet,
    Yours,
     Wanton Willy.

POSTSCRIPT.

By this my postscript I incline
To let you ken my hail design   *know whole*
Of sic a long imperfect line   *such*
    Lies in this sentence,
To cultivate my dull engine
    By your acquaintance.

Your answer therefore I expect;
And to your friend you may direct
At Gilbertfield; do not neglect,   *[near Glasgow]*
    When ye have leisure,
Which I'll embrace with great respect,
    And perfect pleasure.

ANSWER 1.

       Edinburgh, July 10th, 1719.
Sonse fa' me, witty, Wanton Willy, *good fortune*
Gin blyth I was na as a filly;   *If*
Not a fou pint, nor short-hought gilly,
    Or wine that's better,
Could please sae meikle, my dear Billy, *much*
    As thy kind letter.

Before a lord and eik a knight,
In gossy Don's be candle-light,
There first I saw't, and ca'd it right,
    And the maist feck   *part*
Wha's seen't sinsyne, they ca'd as tight *since then*
    As that on Heck.

Ha, heh! thought I, I canna say
But I may cock my nose the day,
When Hamilton the bauld and gay
    Lends me a heezy,   *good lift*

In verse that slides sae smooth away,
            Well tell'd and easy.

Sae roos'd by ane of well-kend mettle,
Nae sma' did my ambition pettle,
My canker'd critics it will nettle,
            And e'en sae be 't:
This month I'm sure I winna settle,
            Sae proud I 'm wi't.

When I begoud first to cun verse,   *began*
And could your Ardry whins rehearse,
Where Bonny Heck ran fast and fierce,
            It warm'd my breast;
Then emulation did me pierce,
            Whilk since ne'er ceast.

May I be licket wi' a bittle,   *fuller's club*
Gin of your numbers I think little;   *If*
Ye're never rugget, shan, nor kittle,   *silly   knotty*
            But blyth and gabby,
And hit the spirit to a tittle
            Of standard Habby.

Ye'll quat your quill! — that were ill, Willy,
Ye's sing some mair yet, nill ye will ye,
O'er meikle haining wad but spill ye,   *saving   spoil*
            And gar ye sour;   *make*
Then up and war them a' yet, Willy,   *excel*
            'Tis in your pow'r.

To knit up dollars in a clout,
And then to card them round about,
Syne to tell up, they downa lont   *Then   bow down*
            To lift the gear;   *money*
The malison lights on that rout,
            Is plain and clear.

The chiels of London, Cam, and Ox,
Ha'e rais'd up great poetic stocks
Of Rapes, of Buckets, Sarks, and Locks,
            While we neglect
To shaw their betters; this provokes
            Me to reflect

On the learn'd days of Gawn Dunkell;*
Our country then a tale could tell,
Europe had nane mair snack and snell   *clever*   *sharp*
     At verse or prose:
Our kings† were poets too themsell,
     Bauld and jocose.

To Ed'nburgh, Sir, whene'er ye come,
I'll wait upon ye, there's my thumb,
Were't frae the gill-bells to the drum‡
     And tak' a bout,
And faith I hope we'll not sit dumb,
     Nor yet cast out.

Hallow-Fair

At *Hallowmas*, whan nights grow lang,
   And *starnies* shine fu' clear,   *little stars*
When fock, the nippin cald to bang,   *folk*   *defeat*
   Their winter *hap-warms* wear,   *mantles*
Near Edinbrough a fair there hads,   *holds*
   I wat there 's nane whase name is,
For strappin dames and sturdy lads,
   And cap and stoup, mair famous   *cup*   *tankard*   *more*
     Than it that day.

Upo' the tap o' ilka lum   *every chimney*
   The sun began to keek,   *peep*
And bad the trig made maidens come
   A sightly joe to seek   *lover*
At *Hallow-fair*, whare browsters rare   *brewers*
   Keep gude ale on the gantries,   *stands*
And dinna scrimp ye o' a skair   *do not*   *share*
   O' kebbucks frae their pantries,   *cheeses*
     Fu' saut that day.

* Gavin Douglas (1475?–1522), bishop of Dunkeld, and translator of the *Aeneid*.
† James the First and Fifth. *Ramsay's note.*
‡ From half an hour before twelve, at noon, when the music-bells begin to play, (frequently called the gill-bells, from people taking a whetting dram at that time,) to the drum at ten o'clock at night; when the drum goes round to warn sober folks to call for a bill. *Ramsay's note.*

Here country John in bonnet blue,
   An' eke his Sunday claise on,   *also*
Rins efter Meg wi' *rokelay* new,
   An' sappy kisses lays on;
She'll tauntin say, Ye silly coof!
   Be o' your gab mair spairin;
He'll tak the hint, and criesh her loof   *grease   palm*
   Wi' what will buy her fairin,   *lunch*
      To chow that day.

Here chapman billies tak their stand,   *pedlar fellows*
   An' shaw their *bonny wallies;*   *wares*
Wow, but they lie fu' gleg aff hand   *readily*
   To trick the silly fallows:
Heh, Sirs! what cairds and tinklers come, *gypsies and tinkers*
   An' *ne'er-do-weel* horse-coupers,
An' spae-wives fenzying to be dumb,   *fortune-tellers*
   Wi' a' siclike landloupers,   *vagabonds*
      To thrive that day.

Here Sawny cries, frae Aberdeen;
   "Come ye to me fa need: *who*
The brawest *shanks* that e'er were seen   *hose*
   I'll sell ye cheap an' guid.
I wyt they are as protty hose
   As come fae *weyr* or *leem*:   *wire   loom*
Here tak a rug, and shaw's your pose: *bargain   money*
   Forseeth, my ain's but teem   *own's   empty*
      An' light this day."

Ye wives, as ye gang thro' the fair,   *go*
   O mak your bargains hooly!
O' a' thir wylie lowns beware,   *these   rogues*
   Or fegs they will ye spulzie.   *figs   spoil*
For fairn-year *Meg Thamson* got,   *last-year*
   Frae thir mischievous villains,   *these*
A scaw'd bit o' a penny note,   *worthless*
   That lost a score o' shillins
      To her that day.

The dinlin drums alarm our ears,
   The serjeant screechs fu' loud,
"A' gentlemen and volunteers

That wish your country gude,
Come here to me, and I shall gie
   Twa guineas and a crown,
A bowl o' *punch*, that like the sea
   Will soum a lang dragoon   *swim*
      Wi' ease this day."

Without the cuissers prance and nicker,   *lancers*
   An' our the ley-rig scud;   *grass-field   drive*
In tents the carles bend the bicker, *old men   tankard*
   An' rant an' roar like wud.   *mad*
Then there's sic yellowchin and din,   *yelling*
   Wi' wives and wee-anes gablin,   *children*
That ane might true they were a-kin   *believe*
    To a' the tongues at Babylon,
      Confus'd that day.

Whan *Phoebus* ligs in *Thetis* lap,
   Auld Reekie gies them shelter,   *Edinburgh*
Whare cadgily they kiss the cap,   *gaily   cup*
   An' ca't round helter-skelter.
Jock Bell gaed furth to play his freaks,   *pranks*
   Great cause he had to rue it,
For frae a stark Lochaber aix   *strong*
   He gat a *clamihewit*   *heavy blow*
      Fu' sair that night.

"Ohon!" quo' he, "I'd rather be
   By *sword* or *bagnet* stickit,   *bayonet*
Than hae my crown or body wi'
   Sic deadly weapons nicket."
Wi' that he gat anither straik   *stroke*
   Mair weighty than before,
That gar'd his feckless body aik, *made   useless   ache*
   An' spew the reikin gore,
      Fu' red that night.

He peching on the cawsey lay, *breathing hard   pavement*
   O' kicks and cuffs weel sair'd;   *served*
A *Highland* aith the serjeant gae,   *oath   gave*
   "She maun pe see our guard." *must be seeing*
Out spak the weirlike corporal,   *warlike*
   "Pring in ta drunken sot."

They trail'd him ben, an' by my saul,   *in*
 He paid his drunken groat,
  For that neist day.   *next*

Good fock, as ye come frae the fair,   *folk*
 Bide yont frae this black squad;   *keep away from*
There's nae sic savages elsewhere
 Allow'd to wear cockade.
Than the strong lion's hungry maw,
 Or tusk o' Russian bear,
Frae their wanruly fellin paw   *unruly*
 Mair cause ye hae to fear
  Your death that day.

A wee soup drink dis unco weel   *very well*
 To had the heart aboon;   *hold   above*
It's good as lang's a canny chiel
 Can stand steeve in his shoon.   *upright*
But gin a birkie's owr weel sair'd,   *chap's*
 It gars him aften stammer   *makes*
To *pleys* that bring him to the guard,
 An' eke the *Council-chawmir*,
  Wi' shame that day.

         Robert Fergusson

The Farmer's Ingle

Whan gloming grey out o'er the welkin keeks,   *peeps*
 Whan Batie ca's his owsen to the byre,   *oxen*
Whan Thrasher John, sair dung, his barn-door steeks,   *beaten*
 And lusty lasses at the dighting tire: *winnowing*
What bangs fu' leal the e'enings coming cauld,   *defeats   truly*
 And gars snaw-tapit winter freeze in vain;
Gars dowie mortals looks baith blyth and bauld,   *melancholy*
 Nor fley'd wi' a' the poortith o' the plain;   *frightened   poverty*
 Begin, my Muse, and chant in hamely strain.

Frae the big stack, weel winnow't on the hill,
 Wi' divets theekit frae the weet and drift,   *sods   thatched*
Sods, peats, and heath'ry trufs the chimley fill,   *turfs*
 And gar their thick'ning smeek salute the lift;   *make   smoke   sky*

The gudeman, new come hame, is blyth to find,
  Whan he out o'er the halland flings his een,   *partition*
That ilka turn is handled to his mind,   *every*
    That a' his housie looks sae cosh and clean;   *snug*
    For cleanly house looes he, tho' e'er sae mean.

Weel kens the gudewife that the pleughs require   *ploughmen*
  A heartsome meltith, and refreshing synd   *meal* *wash down*
O' nappy liquor, o'er a bleezing fire: *heady*
  Sair wark and poortith douna weel be join'd. . .*poverty* *cannot*
Wi' buttered bannocks now the girdle reeks,   *griddle*
  I' the far nook the bowie briskly reams *wooden milk-vessel* *foams*
The readied kail stand by the chimley cheeks,   *broth* *chimney side*
  And had the riggin het wi' welcome steams,   *holds* *roof*
  Whilk than the daintiest kitchen nicer seems.   *Which*

Frae this lat gentler gabs a lesson lear;   *mouths* *learn*
  Wad they to labouring lend an eidant hand,   *diligent*
They'd rax fell strang upo' the simplest fare,   *grow*
  Nor find their stamacks ever at a stand.
Fu' hale and healthy wad they pass the day,
  At night in calmest slumbers dose fu' sound,
Nor doctor need their weary life to spae,   *foretell*
  Nor drogs their noddle and their sense confound, *drugs*
  Till death slip sleely on, and gi'e the hindmost wound.

On sicken food has mony a doughty deed   *such*
  By Caledonia's ancestors been done;
By this did mony wight fu' weirlike bleed   *warlike*
  In brulzies frae the dawn to set o' sun: *broils*
'Twas this that brac'd their gardies, stiff and strang, *arms*
  That bent the deidly yew in antient days,
Laid Denmark's daring sons on yird alang,   *earth*
  Gar'd Scottish thristles bang the Roman bays;
  For near our crest their heads they doughtna raise.

The couthy cracks begin whan supper's o'er,   *sociable gossip*
  The cheering bicker gars them glibly gash *beaker* *makes* *talk*
O' simmer's showery blinks and winters sour,
  Whase floods did erst their mailins produce hash: *farms*
'Bout kirk and market eke their tales gae on,
  How Jock woo'd Jenny here to be his bride,

And there how Marion, for a bastard son,
   Upo' the cutty-stool was forc'd to ride,   *stool of repentence*
   The waefu' scald o' our Mess John to bide.   *scolding Clergyman*

The fient a chiep's amang the bairnies now;   *murmur's children*
   For a' their anger's wi' their hunger gane:
Ay maun the childer, wi' a fastin mou',   *children*
   Grumble and greet, and make an unco mane,   *cry moan*
In rangles round before the ingle's low: *clusters fire's glow*
   Frae gudame's mouth auld warld tale they hear,
O' Warlocks louping round the Wirrikow,   *Goblin*
   O' gaists that win in glen and kirk-yard drear,   *dwell*
   Whilk touzles a' their tap, and gars them shak wi' fear. *rumple top*
                                     makes

For weel she trows that fiends and fairies be
   Sent frae the de'il to fleetch us to our ill;   *flatter*
That ky hae tint their milk wi' evil eie,   *cows lost*
   And corn been scowder'd on the glowing kill.   *scorched kiln*
O mock na this, my friends ! but rather mourn,
   Ye in life's brawest spring wi' reason clear,
Wi' eild our idle fancies a' return,   *age*
   And dim our dolefu' days wi' bairnly fear;   *childish*
   The mind's ay cradled whan the grave is near.

Yet thrift, industrious, bides her latest days,
   Tho' age her sair dow'd front wi' runcles wave, *faded wrinkles*
Yet frae the russet lap the spindle plays,
   Her e'enin stent reels she as weel's the lave.   *stint rest*
On some feast-day, the wee-things buskit braw   *dressed finely*
   Shall heeze her heart up wi' a silent joy,   *lift up*
Fu' cadgie that her head was up and saw   *happy*
   Her ain spun cleething on a darling oy,   *own grandchild*
   Careless tho' death shou'd make the feast her foy. *farewell feast*

In its auld lerroch yet the deas remains,   *site dais*
   Whare the gudeman aft streeks him at his ease, *stretches*
A warm and canny lean for weary banes
   O' lab'rers doil'd upo' the wintry leas: *sore-worn*
Round him will badrins and the colly come,   *puss*
   To wag their tail, and cast a thankfu' eie
To him who kindly flings them mony a crum
   O' kebbock whang'd, and dainty fadge to prie; *cheese sliced thick cake*
   This a' the boon they crave, and a' the fee.

Frae him the lads their morning counsel tak,
   What stacks he wants to thrash, what rigs to till;   *ridges*
How big a birn maun lie on bassie's back,   *burden   old horse's*
   For meal and multure to the thirling mill.   *toll of meal*
Niest the gudewife her hireling damsels bids
   Glowr thro' the byre, and see the hawkies bound, *Look cowshed cows*
Take tent case Crummy tak her wonted tids,   *tantrums*
   And ca' the leglin's treasure on the ground,   *milking pails*
   Whilk spills a kebbuck nice, or yellow pound.   *cheese*

Then a' the house for sleep begin to grien,   *yearn*
   Their joints to slack frae industry a while;
The leaden God fa's heavy on their ein,
   And halflins steeks them frae their daily toil: *half-way shuts*
The cruizy too can only blink and bleer,   *rush-light*
   The restit ingle's done the maist it dow;   *fire's can*
Tacksman and cottar eke to bed maun steer,   *Tenant*
   Upo' the cod to clear their drumly pow,   *pillow muddled head*
   Till wauken'd by the dawning's ruddy glow.

Peace to the husbandman and a' his tribe,
   Whase care fells a' our wants frae year to year;
Lang may his sock and couter turn the gleyb,   *ploughshare coulter*
   And bauks o' corn bend down wi' laded ear.   *strips /glebe*
May Scotia's simmers ay look gay and green,
   Her yellow har'sts frae scowry blasts decreed;   *showery*
May a' her tenants sit fu' snug and bien,   *comfortable*
   Frae the hard grip of ails and poortith freed,   *poverty*
   And a lang lasting train o' peaceful hours succeed.

Robert Fergusson

Leith Races

In July month, ae bonny morn,
   Whan Nature's rokelay green   *mantle*
Was spread o'er ilka rigg o' corn   *every ridge*
   To charm our roving een;   *eyes*
Glouring about I saw a quean,   *Staring lass*
   The fairest 'neath the lift;   *sky*
Her EEN ware o' the siller sheen,
   Her SKIN like snawy drift,
      Sae white that day.

Quod she, "I ferly unco sair,   *wonder*
    That ye sud musand gae,   *should   musing go*
Ye wha hae sung o' HALLOW-FAIR,
    Her winter's pranks and play:
Whan on LEITH-SANDS the racers rare,
    Wi' Jocky louns are met,   *rogues*
Their orro pennies there to ware,   *extra   waste*
    And drown themsel's in debt
            Fu' deep that day."

An' wha are ye, my winsome dear,
    That takes the gate sae early?   *yay*
Whare do ye win, gin ane may spier,   *dwell   if   ask*
    For I right meikle ferly,   *much   wonder*
That sic braw buskit laughing lass   *such   finely   dressed*
    Thir bonny blinks shou'd gi'e,   *These   glances   give*
An' loup like HEBE o'er the grass,   *leap*
    As wanton and as free
            Frae dule this day.   *From sorrow*

"I dwall amang the caller springs   *fresh*
    That weet the LAND o' CAKES,
And aften tune my canty strings   *merry*
    At BRIDALS and LATE-WAKES:
They ca' me MIRTH; I ne'er was kend   *known*
    To grumble or look sour,
But blyth wad be a lift to lend,
    Gif ye wad sey my pow'r   *try*
            An' pith this day."

A bargain be't, and, by my feggs,   *truly*
    Gif ye will be my mate,   *If*
Wi' you I'll screw the cheery pegs,
    Ye shanna find me blate;   *bashful*
We'll reel an' ramble thro' the sands,
    And jeer wi' a' we meet;
Nor hip the daft and gleesome bands   *miss*
    That fill EDINA's street
            Sae thrang this day.   *busy*

Ere servant maids had wont to rise
    To seeth the breakfast kettle,   *boil*
Ilk dame her brawest ribbons tries,   *Each   finest*

To put her on her mettle,
Wi' wiles some silly chiel to trap,   *fellow*
    (And troth he's fain to get her,)   *glad*
But she'll craw kniefly in his crap,   *crow briskly*
    Whan, wow! he canna flit her   *fly*
        Frae hame that day.

Now, mony a scaw'd and bare-ars'd lown
    Rise early to their wark,
Enough to fley a muckle town,   *frighten   large*
    Wi' dinsome squeel and bark.
"Here is the true an' faithfu' list
    O' Noblemen and Horses;
Their eild, their weight, their height, their grist,   *age   contents*
    That rin for PLATES or PURSES
        Fu' fleet this day."

To WHISKEY PLOOKS that brunt for wooks   *Pimples   burned   weeks*
    On town-guard soldiers faces,
Their barber bauld his whittle crooks,   *razor*
    An' scrapes them for the races:
Their STUMPS erst us'd to *filipegs*,   *kilts*
    Are dight in spaterdashes
Whase barkent hides scarce fend their legs   *encrusted   protect*
    Frae weet, and weary plashes
        O' dirt that day.

"Come, hafe a care (the captain cries),
    On guns your bagnets thraw;   *twist*
Now mind your manual exercise,
    An' marsh down raw by raw."
And as they march he'll glowr about,
    'Tent a' their cuts and scars: *Note*
'Mang them fell mony a gausy snout   *very big*
    Has gusht in birth-day wars,
        Wi' blude that day.

Her *Nanesel* maun be carefu' now,   *[The Captain himself]*
    Nor maun she pe misleard,   *must   unmannerly*
Sin baxter lads hae seal'd a vow   *baker*
    To skelp and clout the guard:
I'm sure AULD REIKIE kens o' nane   *Edinburgh knows   none*
    That wou'd be sorry at it,

Tho' they should dearly pay the kane,   *rent*
  An' get their tails weel sautit
      And sair thir days.   *sore*

The tinkler billies i' the Bow   *tinker fellows*
  Are now less eidant clinking,   *diligently*
As lang's their pith or siller dow,   *silver allows*
  They're daffin', and they're drinking.
Bedown LEITH-WALK what burrochs reel
  Of ilka trade and station,   *every*
That gar their wives an' childer feel   *make   children*
  Toom weyms for their libation   *Empty stomachs*
      O' drink thir days.

The browster wives thegither harl   *brewer   drag*
  A' trash that they can fa' on;
They rake the grounds o' ilka barrel,
  To profit by the lawen: *reckoning*
For weel wat they a skin leal het   *know   truly hot*
  For drinking needs nae hire;
At drumbly gear they take nae pet;   *muddy goods*
  Foul WATER slockens FIRE
      And drouth thir days.

They say, ill ale has been the deid   *death*
  O' mony a beirdly lown;   *stout fellow*
Then dinna gape like gleds wi' greed   *kites*
  To sweel hail bickers down;   *swill whole tankards*
Gin Lord send mony ane the morn,   *If   many a one next day*
  They'll ban fu' sair the time   *curse   sore*
That e'er they toutit aff the horn   *blew the horn (drank)*
  Which wambles thro' their weym   *belly*
      Wi' pain that day.

The Buchan bodies thro' the beech
  Their bunch of *Findrums* cry,   *fish*
An' skirl out baul', in Norland speech,   *scream   bold   Northland*
  "Gueed speldings, fa will buy."   *good dried fish   who*
An' by my saul, they're nae wrang gear   *goods*
  To gust a stirrah's mow;   *give taste to a man's mouth*
Weel staw'd wi' them, he'll never spear   *stowed   ask*
  The price o' being fu'
      Wi' drink that day.

Now wyly wights at Rowly Powl,
   An' flingin' o' the Dice,
Here brake the banes o' mony a soul   *bones*
   Wi' fa's upo' the ice:
At first the gate seems fair an' straught,   *way*
   So they had fairly till her;   *hold   to*
But wow! in spite o' a' their maught,   *might*
   They're rookit o' their siller   *cheated   silver*
      An' goud that day.   *gold*

Around whare'er ye fling your een,
   The Haiks like wind are scourin';   *Horses*
Some chaises honest folk contain,
   An' some hae mony a Whore in;
Wi' rose and lilly, red and white,
   They gie themselves sic fit airs,
Like Dian, they will seem perfite;   *perfect*
   But its nae goud that glitters   *gold*
      Wi' them thir days.

The LYON here, wi' open paw,
   May cleek in mony hunder,   *hook   hundreds*
Wha geck at Scotland and her law,   *toss the head in disdain*
   His wyly talons under;   *cunning*
For ken, tho' Jamie's laws are auld,
   (Thanks to the wise recorder),
His Lyon yet roars loud and bawld,   *bold*
   To had the Whigs in order   *keep   Hypocrites*
      Sae prime this day.   *prim*

To town-guard Drum of clangor clear,
   Baith men and steeds are raingit;   *ranged*
Some liveries red or yellow wear,
   And some are tartan spraingit: *striped*
And now the red, the blue e'en-now
   Bids fairest for the market;
But, 'ere the sport be done, I trow
   Their skins are gayly yarkit
      And peel'd thir days.

Siclike in Robinhood debates,   *Thus*
   Whan twa chiels hae a pingle;   *chaps   argument*
E'en-now some couli gets his aits,

An' dirt wi' words they mingle,
Till up loups he, wi' diction fu',
   There's lang and dreech contesting,   *dreary*
For now they're near the point in view;
   Now ten miles frae the question
         In hand that night.

The races o'er, they hale the dools,   *sorrows*
   Wi' drink o' a' kin-kind;
Great feck gae hirpling hame like fools,   *most*   *limping*
   The cripple lead the blind.
May ne'er the canker o' the drink
   E'er make out spirits thrawart,   *bad tempered*
'Case we git wharewitha' to wink
   Wi' een as BLUE'S a BLAWART   [*a plant*]
         Wi' *straiks* thir days!

Auld Reike, July 21. [*1773*]   *Edinburgh*

                                                   Robert Fergusson

APPENDIX B

MEDICAL OPINION AND DATA
UPON WHICH IT IS BASED

*Dr. Stanley Bardwell has written especially for this biography the follow-
ing clinical analysis of the health record of Robert Burns to be found below.*

1. One of the outstanding characteristics of rheumatic fever is its clinical
variability. Usual complaints include malaise,* prostration,* feverishness,*
loss of appetite,* and migrating joint pain,* redness, and swelling. Once a
person is victimized by rheumatic fever, recurrences are the rule. It is apt to
wax and wane. Death due to rheumatic fever is a consequence of carditis,
an infection of the lining, or the body, or the containing sac of the heart.

2. Rheumatic fever is caused by a preceding infection with a ubiquitous bacteria called beta-hemolytic streptococcus.

3. Assured diagnosis of rheumatic fever and carditis may be established only
with a careful history, physical examination, and electro-cardiagraphic,
X-ray, and laboratory studies.

4. In the vast majority of instances, bacterial endocarditis occurs in a setting in which a heart valve has been previously damaged by rheumatic fever.
Therefore, it can be distinguished from rheumatic fever only by the use of
blood culture studies, although it is manifested as well by skin hemorrhages,†
enlargement of a painful spleen,† blood in the urine,† and paralysis† due to
breaking off of vegetations which occur on the affected heart valve.

5. Bacterial endocarditis has as its principal symptoms: weakness,‡ malaise,‡
feverishness,‡ sweating, weight loss,‡ skin hemorrhages,‡ large tender spleen,
occasional joint pains‡ (1/3 of patients), and paralysis.

There is nothing in the record to suggest either venereal disease or the
usual stigma of alcoholism. Almost certainly Burns had recurrent attacks of

* Burns mentions all of these symptoms. RTF.
† There is no mention of any of these symptoms in the record. RTF.
‡ Burns mentions these symptoms. RTF.

rheumatic fever. Bacterial endocarditis may have been present terminally, but not necessarily. If rheumatic heart disease is not granted, then endocarditis as a diagnosis is not justified.

Prompt recognition of symptoms, and assessment of the clinical situation would today lead to appropiate treatment with penicillin, or other suitable antibiotics, and possibly cortisone or one of its derivatives.

THE HEALTH RECORD OF ROBERT BURNS
Compiled from his correspondence and other sources

1. Burns in adolescence, as reported later by his brother Gilbert: "My brother, at the age of thirteen, assisted in threshing the crop of corn, and at fifteen was the principal labourer on the farm, for we had no hired servant, male or female. The anguish of mind we felt at our tender years, under these straits and difficulties, was very great. To think of our father growing old (for he was now above fifty) broken down with the long continued fatigues of his life, with a wife and five other children, and in a declining state of circumstances, these reflections produced in my brother's mind and mine sensations of the deepest distress. I doubt not but the hard labour and sorrow of this period of his life, was in a great measure the cause of that depression of spirits with which Robert was so often afflicted through his whole life afterwards. At this time he was almost constantly afflicted in the evenings with a dull headache, which, at a future period of his life, was exchanged for a palpitation of the heart, and a threatening of fainting and suffocation in his bed, in the night time." (Currie I, 70.)

2. Burns at 22, to his father, December 27, 1781: "My health is much about what it was when you were here only my sleep is rather sounder and on the whole I am rather better than otherwise tho it is but by very slow degrees. — The weakness of my nerves has so debilitated my mind that I dare not, either review past events, or look forward into futurity." He goes on to say that he is weary of life, sees nothing ahead for him, and would welcome death. (F I, #4, 40.)

3. "Previous to his leaving Ayrshire," 1786: "At that early period these nocturnal faintings and suffocations were so frequent he always kept a large tub filled with cold water in the place where he slept, and often during the night he rose and plunged himself among the cold water which gave instant relief." Reported by a "bedfellow," to James Grierson of Dalgoner. (*Robert Burns His Associates and Contemporaries*, Chapel Hill, 1953. 54.) See below, no. 45.

4. Burns to his former schoolmaster, John Murdoch, January 15, 1783: "Though indolent, yet so far as an extremely delicate constitution permits, I am not lazy." (F I, #13, 14.)

5. Burns in his Commonplace Book, "March — 84": "There was a certain period in my life that my spirit was broke by repeated losses & disasters, which threatened, & indeed effected the utter ruin of my fortune. My body too was attacked by that most dreadful distemper, a Hypochondria, or confirmed Melancholy." (*Robert Burns's Commonplace Book*, eds. J. C. Ewing and W. Cook, Glasgow, 1938. 8.)

6. Of the same period Burns writes to Dr. Moore: "The finishing evil that brought up the rear of this internal file was my hypochondriac complaint being irritated to such a degree, that for three months I was in a diseased state of body and mind, scarcely to be envied by the hopeless wretches who have just got their mittimus." (F I, #125, 112.)

7. Burns' headnote in his Commonplace Book, August, 1784, to a versified prayer probably written in 1781: "A prayer when fainting fits & other alarming symptoms of a Pleurisy or some other dangerous disorder, which indeed still threaten me, first put Nature on the alarm." (Ewing and Cook, 18.)

8. Burns to John Tennant, Jr., September 13, 1784: "My unlucky illness on friday last did not do me a greater disservice than in disappointing me of the pleasure I had promised myself in spending an hour with you." (F I, #18, 19.)

9. Burns to John Ballantine of Ayr, December 13, 1786, describing his arrival in Edinburgh after a convivial party en route: "I have suffered ever since I came to town [he had been there two weeks] with a miserable head-ach & stomach complaint; but am now a good deal better." (F I, #63, 56.)

10. Burns after his first winter in Edinburgh, 1786–1787; comment by Dugald Stewart: "I should have concluded in favour of his habits of sobriety, from all of him that ever fell under my own observation. He told me indeed himself, that the weakness of his stomach was such as to deprive him entirely of any merit in his temperance. I was however somewhat alarmed about the effect of his now comparatively sedentary and luxurious life, when he confessed to me, the first night he spent in my house after his winter's campaign in town, that he had been much disturbed when in bed, by a palpitation at his heart, which, he said, was a complaint to which he had of late become subject." (Currie I, 141.)

11. Burns in his Journal of his Border Tour, May 23–24, 1787: "I am taken

extremely ill with strong feverish symptoms, & take a servant of Mr Hood's to watch me all night — embittering Remorse scares my fancy at the gloomy forebodings of death — I am determined to live for the future in such a manner as not to be scared at the approach of Death." By the 25th he was about and active. (*Robert Burns His Associates and Contemporaries,* Chapel Hill, 1953. 118.)

12. Burns to William Nicol, July 29, 1787: "A lingering indisposition has hung about me for some time and has beaten me out of the use of pen and ink." (F I, #123, 103.)

13. Burns to Mrs. Dunlop, July 31, 1787: "I have indeed been ailing." (F I, # 124, 104.)

14. Burns to Dr. John Moore, August 2, 1787: "Of late I have been confined with some lingering complaints originating as I take it in the stomach. — To divert my spirits a little in this miserable fog of Ennui, I have taken a whim to give you a history of Myself." (F I, #125, 104.)

15. Burns in his Journal of his Highland Tour, September 15, 1787, at Kinross: "A fit of the Colic." (*Journal of a Tour in the Highlands made in the Year 1787,* ed. J. C. Ewing, London and Glasgow, 1927. 17.)

16. Burns to Patrick Miller, October 20, 1787: "I was still more unlucky in catching a miserable cold for which the medical gentlemen have ordered me into close confinement, 'under pain of Death!' the severest of penalties. — In two or three days, if I get better, . . . I will take a ride to Dumfries directly." (F I, #144, 131.)

17. From a poem, *Address to the Toothache,* probably of this period: "Thou hell of a' diseases." Burns continued to suffer from the toothache. See below, no. 54, 56.

18. Burns to Robert Ainslie, November 23, 1787: "You will think it romantic when I tell you, that I find the idea of your friendship almost necessary to my existence. You assume a proper length of face in my bitter hours of blue devilism, and you laugh fully up to my highest wishes at my good things." (F I, #153, 140.)

19. Burns to John Beugo, December 4?, 1787: "A certain sour-faced old acquaintance called Glauber's salts hinders me from my lesson tonight." Burns and Beugo were taking French lessons together. (F I, #156, 142.)

20. Burns to various correspondents, early December, 1787, to early March, 1788, about an injury to his knee:
a. To Agnes M'Lehose (Clarinda), December 8, 1787: "Tonight I was to have had the very great pleasure [of seeing you] — I was intoxicated with

the idea. — but an unlucky fall from a coach has so bruised one of my knees, that I can't stir my leg off the cushion." (F I, #159, 143.)

b. To Margaret Chalmers, December 12, 1787: "I am here under the care of a surgeon, with a bruised limb extended on a cushion; and the tints of my mind vying with the livid horror preceding a midnight thunderstorm. A drunken coachman was the cause of the first, and incomparably the lightest evil; misfortune, bodily constitution, hell and myself, have formed a 'Quadruple Alliance' to guarantee the other. I got my fall on Saturday, and am getting slowly better." (F I, #160, 144.)

c. To Clarinda, December 12, 1787: "I stretch a point indeed, my dearest Madam, when I answer your card on the rack of my present agony." (F I, #161, 145.)

d. To Margaret Chalmers, December 19, 1787: "The atmosphere of my soul is vastly clearer than when I wrote you last. For the first time, yesterday I crossed the room on crutches. It would do your heart good to see my bardship, not on my *poetic*, but on my *oaken* stilts; throwing my best leg with an air." (F I, #162, 145.)

e. To Clarinda, December 20, 1787: "My limb now allows me to sit in some peace; to walk I have yet no prospect of, as I can't mark it to the ground." (F I, #162, 147.)

f. To Clarinda, December 27(?), 1788: "My limb is vastly better; but I have not any use of it without my crutches. Monday, for the first time, I dine at a neighbour's, next door. As soon as I can go so far, *even in a coach,* my first visit shall be to you." The dating of this letter is discussed in *Studies in Scottish Literature*, VI, 4, April 1969, 260–262. (F I, # 169, 153.)

g. To Clarinda, January 4, 1788: "Tomorrow evening I intend taking a chair, and paying a visit at Park-Place to a much valued old friend." If Clarinda is to be at home, he will call on her. (F I, #170, 155.)

h. To John Ballantine, January, 1788: "Some weeks bypast indeed I have been a cripple in one of my legs, owing to a fall by the drunken stupidity of a coachman. — I am got a good deal better, but can walk little yet without my crutches." (F I, #173, 158.)

i. To Clarinda, January 14, 1788: "My limb has been so well today that I have gone up and down stairs often without my staff. Tomorrow, I hope to walk once again on my own legs to dinner. It is only next street." (F I, #178, 164.)

j. To Clarinda, January 20, 1788: "The impertinence of fools has joined with a return of an old indisposition to make me good for nothing today. . . . A little alarm last night and today that I am mortal, has made such a revolution in my spirits! . . . I can scarce hold up my head." Next day, he writes, "I am, my lovely friend, much better this morning, on the whole; but I have a horrid languor on my spirits." (F I, #182, 168.)

k. To Mrs. Dunlop, January 21, 1788: "After six weeks' confinement, I am beginning to walk across the room. They have been six horrible weeks; anguish and low spirits made me unfit to read, write, or think." (F I, #184, 171.)

l. To Margaret Chalmers, January 29, 1788: "Now for that wayward unfortunate thing, myself. . . . The sport, the miserable victim of rebellious pride, hypochondriac imagination, agonizing sensibility, and bedlam passions! . . . Seriously though, life presents me with but a melancholy path: but my limb will soon be sound, and I shall struggle on." (Date corrected by Professor G. Ross Roy, PBSA, 1967. 357.) (F I, #185, 177.)

m. To John Tennant, February 7, 1788: "I met with an ugly accident about ten weeks ago, by the drunkeness of a Coachman; I fell and dislocated the cap of my knee, which laid me up a cripple, that I have but just lately laid aside my crutches. — I shall not have the use of my limb as formerly, for some months, perhaps years to come." (F I, #197, 183.)

n. To John Richmond, February 7, 1788: "I have not got, nor will not for some time, get the better of my bruised knee; but I have laid aside my crutches." (F I, #196, 182.)

o. To the Rev. John Skinner, February 14, 1788: "I have been a cripple now near three months, though I am getting vastly better." (F I, #203, 188.)

p. To William Cruikshank, March 3, 1788: (Burns has left Edinburgh where the accident occurred, and where he lived with Cruikshank.) "My unlucky knee is rather worse, and I fear for some time will scarcely stand the fatigue of my Excise instructions." (F I, #214, 199.)

21. Burns to Richard Brown, March 20, 1788: "Watching, fatigue, and a load of Care almost too heavy for my shoulders, have in some degree actually fever'd me." (F I, #228, 212.)

22. Burns to Mrs. Dunlop, April 28, 1788: "I prepared with the sincerest pleasure to meet you at the Mount, and came to my brother's on Saturday night, to set out on Sunday, but for some nights preceding I had slept in an apartment where the force of the winds and rains was mitigated by being sifted through numberless apertures in the windows, walls, &c. In consequence I was on Sunday, Monday, and part of Tuesday, unable to stir out of bed, with all the miserable effects of a violent cold." (F I, #238, 220.)

23. Burns to John Ballantine, July, 1788: He would transcribe a poem for Ballantine except that he has a "bruised finger." A brief note only. (F I, 259, 240.)

24. Burns to Robert Graham of Fintry, September 23, 1788: "Though I am scarce able to hold up my head with this fashionable influenza, which

is just now the rage hereabouts, yet with half a spark of life, I would thank you for your most generous favor of the 14th." (Burns is now living in a far from weathertight hut on a newly rented farm while the farmstead is abuilding.) (F I, #273, 259.)

25. Burns to Dr. James Mundell(?), October, 1788: "As my symptoms are continuing milder, I have not waited on you; but my liquid drug has failed. — You will please send me by my servant the bearer, a recruit of the g —— d D —— n. — I am still using the unction, tho' thank Heaven, not extreme unction." (F I, #277, 265.)

26. Burns to William Cruikshank, December, 1788: "My knee, I believe, never will be entirely well; and an unlucky fall this winter has made it still worse." (F I, #292, 281.)

27. Burns to Mrs. Dunlop, June 21, and July 7, 1789: "Will you take the effusions, the miserable effusions, of low spirits, just as they flow from their bitter spring? I know not of any particular cause for this worst of all my foes besetting me; but for some time my soul has been beclouded with a thickening atmosphere of evil imaginations and gloomy presages." "As I mentioned to you in a letter you will by this time have received, I have since I was at Dunlop been rather hurried and out of spirits." (F I, #350, 341, 343.)

28. Burns to Mrs. Dunlop, November 8, 1789: (He is now riding thirty to forty miles a day in all weathers as an Exciseman.) "I have somehow got a most violent cold; and in the stupid, disagreable predicament of a stuffed, aching head and an unsound, sickly crassis [temperament, disposition], do I sit down to thank you for yours of the nineteenth." (F I, #371, 368.)

29. Burns to Mrs. Dunlop, December 13, 1789: "I am groaning under the miseries of a diseased nervous System; . . . For now near three weeks I have been so ill with a nervous head-ach, that I have been obliged to give up for a time my Excise-books, being scarce able to lift my head, much less to ride once a week over ten muir Parishes." He continues with comments on the rapid shifts between health and illness, and adds reflections on death and immortality. (F I, #374, 372.)

30. Burns to William Nicol, December 13, 1789: "I have been so ill, my ever dear Friend, that I have not been able to go over the threshold of my door since I saw you." (F I, #375, 375.)

31. Burns to Lady Winifred Maxwell Constable, December 16, 1789: He speaks of an "unlucky indisposition" which had prevented his keeping an engagement. (F I, #377, 376.)

32. Burns to Lady Elizabeth Cunningham, December 23, 1789: He thanks her for a letter which "came very seasonably to his aid amid the cheerless gloom and sinking despondency of December weather and diseased nerves." (F I, #379, 378.)

33. Burns to his brother Gilbert, January 11, 1790: "I have not in my present frame of mind much appetite for exertion in writing. — My nerves are in a damnable State. — I feel that horrid hypochondria pervading every atom of my body & soul. — This Farm has undone my enjoyment of myself. — It is a ruinous affair on all hands. — But let it go to hell! I'll fight it out and be off with it." (F II, #381, 1.)

34. Burns to William Dunbar, January 14, 1790: "I have had a tract of bad health most part of this winter, else you had heard from me ere now. — Thank Heaven, I am now got so much better as to be able to partake a little in the enjoyments of life." (F II, #382, 2.)

35. Letter to Mrs. Dunlop, January 25, 1790: "My health is greatly better, and I now begin once more to share in satisfaction and enjoyment with the rest of my fellow-creatures." (F II, #385, 4.)

36. Burns to Clarinda, February ?, 1790: "I have indeed been ill, Madam, the whole winter. An incessant head-ache, depression of spirits, and all the truly miserable consequences of a deranged nervous system, have made dreadful havoc of my health and peace. Add to all this, a line of life into which I have lately entered obliges me to ride, on the average, at least 200 miles each week. However, thank Heaven, I am now greatly better in my health." (F II, #388, 7–8.)

37. Burns to Alexander Dalziel, October 5, 1790: "A few days after I received yours I was seized with a slow, illformed fever from which I am just risen out of a weary bed of Sickness; & if this is not apology enough, I must inform you farther that I have likewise had a most malignant Squinancy [subacute phlegonous tonsillitis] which had me very near the precincts of the Grave. — I am now got greatly better, though by no means in a confirmed state of health. — Yesterday, for the first time, I rode as far as Dumfries [from Ellisland, about six miles]." (F II, #422, 43–44.) Dr. Douglas Guthrie of Edinburgh was kind enough to search out the definition of "squinancy."

38. Burns to Mrs. Dunlop, October 6, 1790: "I was just beginning to get the better of a malignant squinancy & slow fever which had tormented me for three weeks & had actually brought me to the brink of the grave." (F II, #423, 45.)

39. Burns to Mrs. Dunlop, February 7, 1791: "When I tell you, Madam,

that by a fall, not from my horse but with my horse, I have been a cripple some time, & that this is the first day my arm & hand have been able to serve me in writing, you will allow that it is too good an apology for my seemingly ungrateful silence." (F II, #435, 55.)

40. Burns to Peter Hill, March, 1791: "I have been this week plagued with an indigestion." (F II, #440, 62.)

41. Burns to Mrs. Dunlop, April 11, 1791: "This is the greatest effort my broken arm has yet made." (F II, #443, 69.) Burns refers here, apparently, to a later accident than the one mentioned in no. 38 above.

42. Burns to A. F. Tytler, April, 1791: He speaks of "the unfortunate accident I have met with," and adds later, "A day or two after I received your letter my horse came down with me and broke my right arm." (F II, #445, 70.)

43. Burns to Lady Winifred Maxwell Constable, April 25, 1791: He speaks of "the unlucky accident of having lately broken my right arm." (F II, #448, 72.)

44. Burns to Peter Hill, October, 1791: "A poor devil nailed to an elbow chair, writhing in anguish with a bruised leg, laid on a stool before him, is in a fine situation truly for saying bright things." (F II, #475, 95.) This accident is Burns' fourth since moving to Ellisland farm in June, 1788, and his third in 1791.

45. Mrs. Dunlop to Burns, December 30, 1792 and March 16, 1793: "[Dec. 30] I was so ill that morning you left us I could not leave my bed till towards dinner time. It was no cordial for my disappointment in not seeing you when I heard from Keith how much you were complaining yourself, and when Adair on his arrival confirmed the continuance of your still doing the same as long as he and you were together." [Burns and Adair had made a visit to Harvieston, in the Devon Valley, in the autumn of 1787.] "[March 16] How does the cold bath suit this weather? We are in snow here." (*Robert Burns and Mrs. Dunlop*, London, 1898. 371 and 380.) These references seem to say that Burns had continued his cold baths at Harvieston in 1787, and at Dunlop in 1792. See above, no. 3.

46. Burns to Mrs. Dunlop, January 2, 1793: "I am better, though not quite free of my complaint." (F II, #529, 190.)

47. Burns to Robert Graham of Fintry, January 5, 1793: (Graham was on the Excise Board and Burns is trying to get a better post.) He urges his "hardy constitution." Burns obviously considers himself a vigorous and

active man who has suffered from bouts of illness. And he leads, as he always has done, a vigorous and active life. (F II, #530, 145.)

48. Burns to Maria Riddell, November, 1793: "Here I sit, altogether Novemberish, a damn'd melange of Fretfulness & melancholy; not enough of the one to rouse me to passion, nor of the other to repose me in torpor; my soul flouncing & fluttering round her tenement, like a wild Finch caught amid the horrors of winter & newly thrust into a cage. (F II, #596, 217.)

49. Burns to James Johnson, February, 1794: "I have, all this winter, been plagued with low spirits & blue devils, so that I have almost hung my harp upon the willow trees." (F II, #616, 233.)

50. Burns to Alexander Cunningham, February 25, 1794: "For these two months I have not been able to lift a pen. My constitution and frame were, ab origine, blasted with a deep incurable taint of hypochondria, which poisons my existence." (F II, #619, 234–35.)

51. Burns to Mrs. Dunlop, June 25, 1794: After an apology for neglect of his correspondence, he writes, "To tell you that I have been in poor health, will not be excuse enough, though it is true. I am afraid that I am about to suffer for the follies of my youth. My medical friends threaten me with a flying gout; but I trust they are mistaken." (F II, #628, 246.) Burns is now 35. The following definition of "flying gout" received through the courtesy of Dr. Douglas Guthrie of Edinburgh: "a term applied to gouty or rheumatic cases in which there is no swelling of the joints, but pain in their interior, which frequently changes its seat."

52. Burns to Mrs. Dunlop, September, 1794: "I am so poorly today as to be scarce able to hold my pen." (F II, #638, 258.)

53. Burns to Maria Riddell, Spring, 1795: "I am so ill as to be scarce able to hold this miserable pen to this miserable paper." (F II, #668, 299.)

54. Burns to William Creech, May 30, 1795: "At present the delightful sensations of an omnipotent Tooth-ach so engross all my inner man, as to put it out of my power even to write Nonsense." (F II, #671, 302.)

55. Burns to Maria Riddell, June or July, 1795: "The health you wished me in your Morning's Card is I think, flown from me forever. — I have not been able to leave my bed today, till about an hour ago." (F II, #674, 304.)

56. Burns to George Thomson, July 3, 1795: "I am at present quite occupied with the charming sensations of the Tooth-Ach." (F II, #673, 303.)

57. Burns to Mrs. Dunlop, January 31, 1796: "The Autumn robbed me of my only daughter & darling child, & that at a distance too & so rapidly as to put it out of my power to pay the last duties to her. — I had scarcely begun to recover from that shock, when I became myself the victim of a most severe Rheumatic fever, & long the die spun doubtful; until after many weeks of sick-bed, it seems to have turned up more life, & I am beginning to crawl across my room, & once indeed have been before my own door in the street." (F II, #688, 316.)

58. Burns to George Thomson, April, 1796: "Alas! my dear Thomson, I fear it will be some time ere I tune my lyre again! . . . Almost ever since I wrote you last [in February], I have only known Existence by the pressure of the heavy hand of Sickness; & have counted time by the repercussions of Pain! Rheumatism, Cold, & Fever have formed, to me, a terrible Trinity in Unity, which makes me close my eyes in misery, & open them without hope." (F II, 693, 319.)

59. Burns to George Thomson, May, 1796: "I cannot boast of returning health. I have now reason to believe that my complaint is a flying gout: — a damnable business!" (F II, #694, 321.)

60. Letter to James Johnson, about June 1, 1796: "How are you, my dear Friend? & how comes on yr fifth volume? — You may probably think that for some time past I have neglected you & your work; but, Alas, the hand of pain, & sorrow, & care has these many months lain heavy on me! — Personal & domestic affliction have almost entirely banished that alacrity & life with which I used to woo the rural Muse of Scotia. — In the meantime let us finish what we have so well begun. — . . . Many a merry meeting this Publication has given us, & possibly it may give us more, though, alas! I fear it — This protracting, slow, consuming illness which hangs over me, will, I doubt much, my ever dear friend, arrest my sun before he has well reached his middle carreer, & will turn over the Poet to far other and more important concerns than studying the brilliancy of Wit or the pathos of Sentiment. — However, Hope is the cordial of the human heart, & I endeavour to cherish it as well as I can." (F II, #696, 322.)

61. Burns to Maria Riddell, June 1, 1796: "I am in such miserable health as to be utterly incapable of shewing my loyalty in any way. — . . . Would you have me in such circumstances copy you out a Love-song? No! if I must write, let it be Sedition, or Blasphemy, or something else that begins with B [Bawdy?], so that I may grin with the grin of iniquity, & rejoice with the rejoicing of an apostate Angel." (F II, #697, 323.)

62. Burns to James Clarke, June 26, 1796: (Burns had helped Clarke with

a loan, which Clarke was repaying in installments.) "Still, still the victim
of affliction; were you to see the emaciated figure who now holds the
pen to you, you would not know your old friend. — Whether I shall ever
get about again, is only known to Him, the Great Unknown, whose
creature I am. — Alas, Clarke, I begin to fear the Worst! As to my individual Self, I am tranquil; — I would despise myself if I were not: but
Burns's poor widow! & half a dozen of his dear little ones, helpless orphans,
there I am weak as a woman's tear." (F II, #698, 323–24.)

63. Burns to George Thomson, July 4, 1796: "I recd. your songs: but
my health being so precarious nay dangerously situated, that as a last
effort I am here at a sea-bathing quarters. — Besides inveterate rheumatism, my appetite is quite gone, & I am so emaciated as to be scarce
able to support myself on my own legs. — Alas! is this a time for me to
woo the Muses? However, I am still anxiously willing to serve your work;
& if possible I shall try." (F II, #699, 324.)

64. Burns to Alexander Cunningham, from Brow, July 7, 1796: "Alas!
my friend, I fear the voice of the Bard will soon be heard among you
no more! For these eight or ten months I have been ailing, sometimes
bedfast & sometimes not; but these last three months I have been tortured
with an excruciating rheumatism, which has reduced me to nearly the
last stage. — You actually would not know me if you saw me. — Pale,
emaciated, & so feeble as occasionally to need help from my chair — my
spirits fled! fled! — but I can no more on the subject — only the Medical
folks tell me that my last & only chance is bathing & country quarters
& riding." He continues, asking how he can afford it, with his pay reduced
and his family to support. (F II, #700, 325.)

65. Burns to James Armour, his father-in-law, July 10, 1796: "I have now
been a week at salt water, & though I think I have got some good by it,
yet I have some secret fears that this business will be dangerous if not
fatal." (F II, #701, 326.)

66. Burns to his brother Gilbert, July 10, 1796: "It will be no very
pleasing news to you to be told that I am dangerously ill, & not likely
to get better. — An inveterate rheumatism has reduced me to such a state
of debility, & my appetite is tottaly gone, so that I can scarcely stand on
my legs. — I have been a week at sea-bathing, & I will continue there
or in a friend's house in the country all summer." (F II, #703, 326–27.)

67. Burns to his cousin, James Burness, of Montrose, July 12, 1796: (He
is being dunned by a tailor, partly for the expense of his volunteer's uniform, and asks his cousin for ten pounds.) "The worst of it is, my health
was coming about finely; you know & my Physician assures me that

melancholy & low spirits are half my disease, guess then my horrors since this business began." (F II, #705, 328.)

68. Burns to James Gracie, July 13, 1796: "It would be doing high injustice to this place not to acknowledge that my rheumatisms have derived great benefit from it already; but, alas, my loss of appetite still continues." (F II, #707, 329.)

69. Burns to his wife, July 14, 1796: "I have delayed writing until I could tell you what effect sea-bathing was likely to produce. It would be injustice to deny that it has eased my pains, and I think has strengthened me; but my appetite is still extremely bad. No flesh nor fish can I swallow: porridge and milk are the only things I can taste." (F II, #708, 329.)

70. Maria Riddell, describing her last meeting with Burns, during the time he was at Brow: "I was struck with his appearance on entering the room. The stamp of death was imprinted on his features. He seemed already touching the brink of eternity. His first salutation was, 'Well, Madam, have you any commands for the other world?' I replied that it seemed a doubtful case which of us should be there soonest, and that I hoped he would yet live to write my epitaph. (I was then in a bad state of health.) He looked in my face with an air of great kindness, and expressed his concern at seeing me look so ill, with his accustomed sensibility. At table he ate little or nothing, and he complained of having entirely lost the tone of his stomach. We had a long and serious conversation. . . . I had seldom seen his mind greater or more collected. There was frequently a considerable vivacity in his sallies, and they would probably have had a greater share, had not concern and dejection I could not disguise, damped the spirit of pleasantry he seemed not unwilling to indulge." (Currie I, 221, 223.)

71. John Syme to Alexander Cunningham, July 17, 1796: "I have your favour covering letter to the Bard which I delivered personally. He poor fellow is in a very bad state of health — I am extremely alarmed, not only by the cadaverous aspect and shaken frame of Burns, but from the accounts which I have heard from the first Faculty here — But I entertain strong hopes that the vigor of his former stamina will conquer his present illness, and that by care & the attention & advice he receives from Dr Maxwell he will recover — I do not mean to alarm you but really poor Burns is very ill — " (From author's transcript. See P. S. for p. 365.)

72. John Syme to Alexander Cunningham, July 19, 1796: "The illness is — the whole system debilitated & gone." (Author's transcript.)

73. Notes taken down from Mrs. Burns by John M'Diarmid: "Burns

thought himself dying before he went to the Brow. He seemed afraid however of dwelling on the subject, considering Mrs. B's situation [momentarily expecting a baby]. On one occasion he said distinctly, 'Dont be afraid: I'll be more respected a hundred years after I'm dead than I am at present.' He was not above a week at the Brow when he returned. [It was 15 days.] Mrs. Burns was so struck with the change in his appearance, that she became almost speechless. From this period he was closely confined to bed, and was scarcely *'himself'* for half an hour together. By this, it is meant that his mind wandered, and that his nervous system was completely unhinged. He was aware of the infirmity himself, and told his wife that she was to touch him, and remind him that he was going wrong. The day before he died, he called very quickly and with a hale voice, 'Gilbert! Gilbert!' Three days before he died, he got out of bed, and his wife found him sitting in a corner of the room with the bed clothes around him. Mrs. B got assistance, and he suffered himself to be gently led back to bed. But for the fit, his strength would have been unequal to such an exertion." (*Life and Works of Robert Burns*, ed. P. Hately Waddell, Glasgow, 1867. II, xxiv.)

74. John Syme to Alexander Cunningham, July 21, 1796: "Burns departed this morning at 5 oClock." (Author's transcript. See P. S. for p. 365.)

75. "According to popular tradition, 'early in the month of January [1796], when his health was in the course of improvement, Burns tarried too late at a jovial party in the Globe Tavern. Before returning home, he unluckily remained for some time in the open air and, overpowered by the effects of the liquor he had drunk, fell asleep. In these circumstances and in the peculiar condition to which a severe medicine had reduced his constitution, a fatal chill penetrated to his bones; he reached home with the seeds of a rheumatic fever already in possession of his weakened frame.'" (*The Life and Works of Robert Burns*, ed. Robert Chambers, rev. William Wallace, Edinburgh and London, 1896. IV, 254.)

76. "From October 1795, to the January following, an accidental complaint confined him to the house. A few days after he began to go abroad, he dined at a tavern, and returned home about three o'clock in a very cold morning, benumbed and intoxicated. This was followed by an attack of rheumatism, which confined him about a week." (Currie I, 219.) But Josiah Walker, who visited Burns in November, 1795, "observed no unfavorable change in his looks," and found him active, and happy to go on walks. However, Burns wrote to Robert Cleghorn, January, 1796: "Since I saw you, I have been much the child of disaster. — Scarcely began to recover the loss of an only daughter & darling child,* I became

---

* Elizabeth Riddell Burns died in September, 1795.

myself a victim of a rheumatic fever, which brought me to the borders of the grave. — After many weeks of a sick-bed, I am just beginning to crawl about." (F II, #687, 315.) The record above reveals that Burns had fallen victim to a rheumatic fever long before the exposure mentioned by Currie and Chambers, if indeed, it did occur. There is no substantiated source for the story.

77. Hately Waddell quotes both a Gilbert Baird and a Mrs. Marion Hunter, who claimed to have known Burns, as saying he was pockmarked. (II, xxvii and xxxix.) This is the only suggestion that he may have had smallpox. There was an epidemic of it in Irvine the winter Burns was there. (Strawhorn, *Ayrshire at the Time of Burns,* 1959, 20.)

APPENDIX C

BURNS' AUTOBIOGRAPHICAL
LETTER TO DR. JOHN MOORE

Sɪʀ

For some months past I have been rambling over the country, partly on account of some little business I have to settle in various places; but of late I have been confined with some lingering complaints originating as I take it in the stomach. — To divert my spirits a little in this miserable fog of Ennui, I have taken a whim to give you a history of MYSELF. — My name has made a small noise in the country; you have done me the honor to interest yourself very warmly in my behalf; and I think a faithful account of, what character of a man I am, and how I came by that character, may perhaps amuse you in an idle moment. — I will give you an honest narrative, though I know it will be at the expence of frequently being laughed at; for I assure you, Sir, I have, like Solomon whose character, excepting the trifling affair of WISDOM, I sometimes think I resemble, I have, I say, like him "Turned my eyes to behold Madness and Folly;" and like him too, frequently shaken hands with their intoxicating friendship. — In the very polite letter Miss Williams did me the honor to write me, she tells me you have got a complaint in your eyes. — I pray God that it may be removed; for considering that lady and you are my common friends, you will probably employ her to read this letter; and then goodnight to that esteem with which she was pleased to honor the Scotch Bard. — After you have perused these pages, should you think them trifling and impertinent, I only beg leave to tell you that the poor Author wrote them under some very twitching qualms of conscience, that, perhaps he was doing what he ought not to do: a predicament he has more than once been in before. —

I have not the most distant pretensions to what the pye-coated guardians of escutcheons call, A Gentleman. — When at Edinr last winter, I got acquainted in the Herald's Office, and looking through that granary of Honors I there found almost every name in the kingdom; but for me,

" — My ancient, but ignoble blood
Has crept thro' Scoundrels ever since the flood" —

Gules, Purpure, Argent, &c. quite disowned me. — My Fathers rented land
of the noble Kieths of Marshal, and had the honor to share their fate. — I
do not use the word, Honor, with any reference to Political principles;
loyal and disloyal I take to be merely relative terms in that ancient and
formidable court known in this Country by the name of CLUB-LAW. —
Those who dare welcome Ruin and shake hands with Infamy for what they
sincerely believe to be the cause of their God or their King — "Brutus and
Cassius are honorable men." — I mention this circumstance because it
threw my father on the world at large; where after many years' wanderings
and sojournings he pickt up a pretty large quantity of Observation and
Experience, to which I am indebted for most of my little pretensions to
wisdom. — I have met with few who understood "Men, their manners and
their ways" equal to him; but stubborn, ungainly Integrity, and headlong,
ungovernable Irrascibillity are disqualifying circumstances: consequently I
was born a very poor man's son. — For the first six or seven years of my
life, my father was gardiner to a worthy gentleman of small estate in the
neighbourhood of Ayr. — Had my father continued in that situation, I must
have marched off to be one of the little underlings about a farm-house;
but it was his dearest wish and prayer to have it in his power to keep his
children under his own eye till they could discern between good and evil;
so with the assistance of his generous Master my father ventured on a
small farm in his estate. — At these years I was by no means a favorite
with any body. — I was a good deal noted for a retentive memory, a
stubborn, sturdy something in my disposition, and an enthusiastic, idiot
piety. — I say idiot piety, because I was then but a child. — Though I
cost the schoolmaster some thrashings, I made an excellent English scholar;
and against the years of ten or eleven, I was absolutely a Critic in sub-
stantives, verbs and particles. — In my infant and boyish days too, I
owed much to an old Maid of my Mother's, remarkable for her ignorance,
credulity and superstition. — She had, I suppose, the largest collection in
the county of tales and songs concerning devils, ghosts, fairies, brownies,
witches, warlocks, spunkies, kelpies, elf-candles, dead-lights, wraiths, ap-
paritions, cantraips, giants, inchanted towers, dragons and other trumpery.
— This cultivated the latent seeds of Poesy; but had so strong an effect on
my imagination that to this hour, in my nocturnal rambles, I sometimes keep
a sharp look-out in suspicious places; and though nobody can be more
sceptical in these matters than I, yet it often takes an effort of Philosophy
to shake off these idle terrors. — The earliest thing of Composition that I
recollect taking pleasure in was, The vision of Mirza and a hymn of

Addison's beginning — "How are Thy servants blest, O Lord!" I particularly
remember one half-stanza which was music to my boyish ear —

> "For though in dreadful whirls we hung,
> "High on the broken wave" —

I met with these pieces in Mas[s]on's English Collection, one of my
school-books. — The two first books I ever read in private, and which gave
me more pleasure than any two books I ever read again, were, the life of
Hannibal and the history of Sir William Wallace. — Hannibal gave my
young ideas such a turn that I used to strut in raptures up and down after
the recruiting drum and bagpipe, and wish myself tall enough to be a
soldier; while the story of Wallace poured a Scotish prejudice in my veins
which will boil along there till the flood-gates of life shut in eternal rest. —
Polemical divinity about this time was putting the country half-mad; and
I, ambitious of shining in conversation parties on Sundays between sermons,
funerals, &c. used in a few years more to puzzle Calvinism with so much
heat and indiscretion that I raised a hue and cry of heresy against me
which has not ceased to this hour. —

My vicinity to Ayr was of great advantage to me. — My social disposition,
when not checked by some modification of spited pride, like our catechism
definition of Infinitude, was "without bounds or limits." — I formed many
connections with other Youngkers who possessed superiour advantages; the
youngling Actors who were busy with the rehearsal of PARTS in which they
were shortly to appear on that STAGE where, Alas! I was destined to
drudge behind the SCENES. — It is not commonly at these green years that
the young Noblesse and Gentry have a just sense of the immense distance
between them and their ragged Playfellows. — It takes a few dashes into
the world to give the young Great man that proper, decent, unnoticing disregard for the poor, insignificant, stupid devils, the mechanics and peasantry
around him; who perhaps were born in the same village. — My young
Superiours never insulted the clouterly appearance of my ploughboy carcase, the two extremes of which were often exposed to all the inclemencies
of all the seasons. — They would give me stray volumes of books; among
them, even then, I could pick up some observations; and ONE, whose heart
I am sure not even the MUNNY BEGUM's scenes have tainted, helped me
to a little French. — Parting with these, my young friends and benefactors,
as they dropped off for the east or west Indies, was often to me a sore
affliction; but I was soon called to more serious evils. — My father's generous Master died; the farm proved a ruinous bargain; and, to clench the
curse, we fell into the hands of a Factor who sat for the picture I have
drawn of one in my Tale of two dogs. — My father was advanced in life
when he married; I was the eldest of seven children; and he, worn out by
early hardship, was unfit for labour. — My father's spirit was soon irritated,
but not easily broken. — There was a freedom in his lease in two years

more, and to weather these two years we retrenched expences. — We lived very poorly; I was a dextrous Ploughman for my years; and the next eldest to me was a brother, who could drive the plough very well and help me to thrash. — A Novel-Writer might perhaps have viewed these scenes with some satisfaction, but so did not I: my indignation yet boils at the recollection of the scoundrel tyrant's insolent, threatening epistles, which used to set us all in tears. —

This kind of life, the chearless gloom of a hermit with the unceasing moil of a galley-slave, brought me to my sixteenth year; a little before which period I first committed the sin of RHYME. — You know our country custom of coupling a man and woman together as Partners in the labors of Harvest. — In my fifteenth autumn, my Partner was a bewitching creature who just counted an autumn less. — My scarcity of English denies me the power of doing her justice in that language; but you know the Scotch idiom, She was a bonie, sweet, sonsie lass. — In short, she altogether unwittingly to herself, initiated me in a certain delicious Passion, which in spite of acid Disappointment, gin-horse Prudence and bookworm Philosophy, I hold to be the first of human joys, our dearest pleasure here below. — How she caught the contagion I can't say; you medical folks talk much of infection by breathing the same air, the touch, &c. but I never expressly told her that I loved her. — Indeed I did not well know myself, why I liked so much to loiter behind with her, when returning in the evening from our labors; why the tones of her voice made my heartstrings thrill like an Eolian harp; and particularly, why my pulse beat such a furious ratann when I looked and fingered over her hand, to pick out the nettle-stings and thistles. — Among her other love-inspiring qualifications, she sung sweetly; and 'twas her favorite reel to which I attempted giving an embodied vehicle in rhyme. — I was not so presumtive as to imagine that I could make verses like printed ones, composed by men who had Greek and Latin; but my girl sung a song which was said to be composed by a small country laird's son, on one of his father's maids, with whom he was in love; and I saw no reason why I might not rhyme as well as he, for excepting smearing sheep and casting peats, his father living in the moors, he had no more Scholar-craft than I had. —

Thus with me began Love and Poesy; which at times have been my only, and till within this last twelvemonth have been my highest enjoyment. — My father struggled on till he reached the freedom in his lease, when he entered on a larger farm about ten miles farther in the country. — The nature of the bargain was such as to throw a little ready money in his hand at the commencement, otherwise the affair would have been impractible. — For four years we lived comfortably here; but a lawsuit between him and his Landlord commencing, after three years tossing and whirling in the vortex of Litigation, my father was just saved from absorption in a jail by phthisical consumption, which after two years promises, kindly stept in and snatch'd him away — "To where the wicked cease from troubling, and where the weary be at rest."

It is during this climacterick that my little story is most eventful. — I was, at the beginning of this period, perhaps the most ungainly, aukward being in the parish. — No Solitaire was less acquainted with the ways of the world. — My knowledge of ancient story was gathered from Salmon's and Guthrie's geographical grammars; my knowledge of modern manners, and of literature and criticism, I got from the Spectator. — These, with Pope's works, some plays of Shakespear, Tull and Dickson on Agriculture, The Pantheon, Locke's Essay on the human understanding, Stackhouse's history of the bible, Justice's British Gardiner's directory, Boyle's lectures, Allan Ramsay's works, Taylor's scripture doctrine of original sin, a select Collection of English songs, and Hervey's meditations had been the extent of my reading. — The Collection of Songs was my vade mecum. — I pored over them, driving my cart or walking to labor, song by song, verse by verse; carefully noting the true tender or sublime from affectation and fustian. — I am convinced I owe much to this for my critic-craft such as it is. —

In my seventeenth year, to give my manners a brush, I went to a country dancing school. — My father had an unaccountable antipathy [to (deleted)] against these meetings; and my going was, what to this hour I repent, in absolute defiance of his commands. — My father, as I said before, was the sport of strong passions: from that instance of rebellion he took a kind of dislike to me, which, I believe was one cause of that dissipation which marked my future years. — I only say, Dissipation, comparative with the strictness and sobriety of Presbyterean country life; for though the will-o'-wisp meteors of thoughtless Whim were almost the sole lights of my path, yet early ingrained Piety and Virtue never failed to point me out the line of Innocence. — The great misfortune of my life was, never to have AN AIM. — I had felt early some stirrings of Ambition, but they were the blind gropins of Homer's Cyclops round the walls of his cave: I saw my father's situation entailed on me perpetual labor. — The only two doors by which I could enter the fields of fortune were, the most niggardly economy, or the little chicaning art of bargain-making: the first is so contracted an aperture, I never could squeeze myself into it; the last, I always hated the contamination of the threshold. — Thus, abandoned of [every (deleted)] aim or view in life; with a strong appetite for sociability, as well from native hilarity as from a pride of observation and remark; a constitutional hypochondriac taint which made me fly solitude; add to all these incentives to social life, my reputation for bookish knowledge, a certain wild, logical talent, and a strength of thought something like the rudiments of good sense, made me generally a welcome guest; so 'tis no great wonder that always "where two or three were met together, there was I in the midst of them." — But far beyond all the other impulses of my heart was, un penchant á l'adorable moitiée du genre humain. — My heart was compleatly tinder, and was eternally lighted up by some Goddess or other: and like every warfare in this world, I was sometimes crowned with success, and sometimes mortified with defeat. — At the plough, scythe or reap-hook I feared no competitor, and set Want at defiance; and as I never cared farther for my labors than while I was in actual exercise, I spent the evening in the way after my own heart. — A country lad rarely carries on an amour without an assisting confident. — I possessed a curiosity, zeal and intrepid dexterity in these matters which recommended me a proper Second in duels of that kind; and I dare say, I felt as much pleasure at being in the secret of half the amours in the parish, as ever did Premier at knowing the intrigues of half the courts of Europe. —

The very goosefeather in my hand seems instinctively to know the well-worn path of my imagination, the favorite theme of my song, and is with difficulty restrained from giving you a couple of paragraphs on the amours of my Compeers, the humble Inmates of the farm-house and cottage; but the grave sons of Science, Ambition or Avarice baptize these things by the name of Follies. — To the sons and daughters of labor and poverty they are matters of the most serious nature: to them, the ardent hope, the stolen interview, the tender farewell, are the greatest and most delicious part of their enjoyments. —

Another circumstance in my life which made very considerable alterations in my mind and manners was, I spent my seventeeth summer on a smuggling [coast] a good distance from home at a noted school, to learn Mensuration, Surveying, Dialling, &c. in which I made a pretty good progress. — But I made greater progress in the knowledge of mankind. — The contraband trade was at that time very successful; scenes of swaggering riot and roaring dissipation were as yet new to me; and I was no enemy to social life. — Here, though I learned to look unconcernedly on a large tavern-bill, and mix without fear in a drunken squabble, yet I went on with a high hand in my Geometry; till the sun entered Virgo, a month which is always a carnival in my bosom, a charming Fillette who lived next door to the school overset my Trigonomertry, and set me off in a tangent from the sphere of my studies. — I struggled on with my Sines and Co-sines for a few days more; but stepping out to the garden one charming noon, to take the sun's altitude, I met with my Angel,

> ——"Like Proserpine gathering flowers,
> "Herself a fairer flower" —

It was vain to think of doing any more good at school. — The remaining week I staid, I did nothing but craze the faculties of my soul about her, or steal out to meet with her; and the two last nights of my stay in the country, had sleep been a mortal sin, I was innocent. —

I returned home very considerably improved. — My reading was enlarged with the very important addition of Thomson's and Shenstone's works; I had seen mankind in a new phasis; and I engaged several of my schoolfellows to keep up a literary correspondence with me. — This last helped me much on in composition. — I had met with a collection of letters by the Wits of Queen Ann's reign, and I pored over them most devoutly. — I kept copies of any of my own letters that pleased me, and a comparison between them and the composition of most of my correspondents flattered my vanity. — I carried this whim so far that though I had not three farthings worth of business in the world, yet every post brought me as many letters as if I had been a broad, plodding son of Day-book & Ledger. —

My life flowed on much in the same tenor till my twenty third year. — Vive l'amour et vive la bagatelle, were my sole principles of action. — The addition of two more Authors to my library gave me great pleasure; Sterne and Mckenzie. — Tristram Shandy and the Man of Feeling were my bosom favorites. — Poesy was still a darling walk for my mind, but 'twas only the humour of the hour. — I had usually half a dozen or more pieces on hand; I took up one or other as it suited the momentary tone of the mind, and dismissed it as it bordered on fatigue. — My Passions when once they were lighted up, raged like so many devils, till they got vent in rhyme; and then conning over my verses, like a spell, soothed all into quiet. — None of the rhymes of those days are in print except, Winter, a dirge, the eldest of my printed pieces; The Death of Poor Mailie, John Barleycorn, And songs first, second and third: song second was the ebullition of that passion which ended the forementioned school-business. —

My twenty third year was to me an important era. — Partly thro' whim, and partly that I wished to set about doing something in life, I joined with a flax-dresser in a neighbouring town, to learn his trade and carry on the business of manufacturing and retailing flax. — This turned out a sadly unlucky affair. — My Partner was a scoundrel of the first water who made money by the mystery of thieving; and to finish the whole, while we were giving a welcoming carousal to the New year, our shop, by the drunken carelessness of my Partner's wife, took fire and was burnt to ashes; and left me like a true Poet, not worth sixpence. — I was obliged to give up business; the clouds of misfortune were gathering thick round my father's head, the darkest of which was, he was visibly far gone in a consumption; and to crown all, a belle-fille whom I adored and who had pledged her soul to meet me in the field of matrimony, jilted me with peculiar circumstances of mortification. — The finishing evil that brought up the rear of this infernal file with my hypochondriac complaint being irritated to such a degree, that for three months I was in [a] diseased state of body and mind, scarcely to be envied by the hopeless wretches who have just got their mittimus, "Depart from me, ye Cursed." —

From this adventure I learned something of a town-life. — But the principal thing which gave my mind a turn was, I formed a bosom-friendship with a young fellow, the first created being I had ever seen, but a hapless son of misfortune. — He was the son of a plain mechanic; but a great Man in the neighbourhood taking him under his patronage gave him a genteel education with a view to bettering his situation in life. — The Patron dieing just as he was ready to launch forth into the world, the poor fellow in despair went to sea; where after a variety of good and bad fortune, a little before I was acquainted with him, he had been set ashore by an American Privateer on the wild coast of Connaught, stript of every thing. — I cannot quit this poor fellow's story without adding that he is at this moment Captain of a large westindiaman belonging to the Thames. —

This gentleman's mind was fraught with courage, independance, Magnanimity, and every noble, manly virtue. — I loved him, I admired him, to a degree of enthusiasm; and I strove to imitate him. — In some measure I succeeded: I had the pride before, but he taught it to flow in proper channels. — His knowledge of the world was vastly superiour to mine, and I was all attention to learn. — He was the only man I ever saw who was a greater fool than myself when WOMAN was the presiding star; but he spoke of a certain fashionable failing with levity, which hitherto I had regarded with horror. — Here his friendship did me a mischief; and the consequence was, that soon after I resumed the plough, I wrote the WELCOME inclosed. — My reading was only encreased by two stray volumes of Pamela, and one of Ferdinand Count Fathom, which gave me some idea of Novels. — Rhyme, except some religious pieces which are in print, I had given up; but meeting with Fergusson's Scotch Poems, I strung anew my wildly-sounding, rustic lyre with emulating vigour. — When my father died, his all went among the rapacious hell-hounds that growl in the kennel of justice; but we made a shift to scrape a little money in the family amongst us, with which, to keep us together, my brother and I took a neighbouring farm. — My brother wanted my harebrained imagination as well as my social and amorous madness, but in good sense and every sober qualification he was far my superiour. —

I entered on this farm with a full resolution, "Come, go to, I will be wise!" — I read farming books; I calculated crops; I attended markets; and in short, in spite of "The devil, the world and the flesh," I believe I would have been a wise man; but the first year from unfortunately buying in bad seed, the second from a late harvest, we lost half of both our crops: this overset all my wisdom, and I returned "Like the dog to his vomit, and the sow that was washed to her wallowing in the mire. — "

I now began to be known in the neighbourhood as a maker of rhymes. — The first of my poetic offspring that saw the light was a burlesque lamentation on a quarrel between two revd Calvinists, both of them dramatis person in my Holy Fair. — I had an idea myself that the piece had some merit; but to prevent the worst, I gave a copy of it to a friend who was very fond of these things, and told him I could not guess who was the Author of it, but that I thought it pretty clever. — With a certain side of both clergy and laity it met with a roar of applause. — Holy Willie's Prayer next made its appearance, and alarmed the kirk-Session so much that they held three several meetings to look over their holy artillery, if any of it was pointed against profane Rhymers. Unluckily for me, my idle wanderings led me, on another side, point-blank within the reach of their heaviest metal. — This is the unfortunate story alluded to in my printed poem, The Lament. — 'Twas a shocking affair, which I cannot yet bear to recollect; and had very nearly given [me] one or two of the principal qualifications for a place among those who have lost the chart and mistake the reckoning of Rationality. — I gave up my part of the farm to my brother, as in truth it was only nominally mine; and made what little preparation was in my power for Jamaica. — Before leaving my native country for ever, I resolved to publish my Poems. — I weighed my productions as impartially as in my power; I thought they had merit; and 'twas a delicious idea that I would be called a clever fellow, even though it should never reach my ears a poor Negro-driver, or perhaps a victim to that inhospitable clime gone to the world of Spirits. — I can truly say that pauvre Inconnu as I then was, I had pretty nearly as high an idea of myself and my works as I have at this moment. — It [is] ever my opinion that the great, unhappy mistakes and blunders, both in a rational and religious point of view, of which we see thousands daily guilty, are owing to their ignorance, or mistaken notions of themselves. — To know myself had been all along my constant study. — I weighed myself alone; I balanced myself with others; I watched every means of information how much ground I occupied both as a Man and as a Poet: I studied assiduously Nature's DESIGN where she seem'd to have intended the various LIGHTS and SHADES in my character. — I was pretty sure my Poems would meet with some applause; but at the worst, the roar of the Atlantic would deafen the voice of Censure, and the novelty of west-Indian scenes make me forget Neglect. —

I threw off six hundred copies, of which I had got subscriptions for about three hundred and fifty. — My vanity was highly gratified by the reception I met with from the Publick; besides pocketing, all expences deducted, near twenty pounds. — This last came very seasonable, as I was about to indent myself for want of money to pay my freight. — So soon as I was master of nine guineas, the price of wafting me to the torrid zone, I bespoke a passage in the very first ship that was to sail, for

Hungry ruin had me in the wind —
I had for some time been sculking from covert to covert under all the terrors of a Jail; as some ill-advised, ungrateful people had uncoupled the merciless legal Pack at my heels. — I had taken the last farewel of my few friends; my chest was on the road to Greenock; I had composed my last song I should ever measure in Caledonia, "The gloomy night is gathering fast," when a letter from Dr Blacklock to a friend of mine overthrew all my schemes by rousing my poetic ambition. — The Doctor belonged to a set of Critics for whose applause I had not even dared to hope. — His idea that I would meet with every encouragement for a second edition fired me so much that away I posted to Edinburgh without a single acquaintance in town, or a single letter of introduction in my pocket. — The baneful Star that had so long shed its blasting influence in my Zenith, for once made a revolution to the Nadir; and the providential care of a good God placed me under the patronage of one of his noblest creatures, the Earl of Glencairn: "Oublie moi, Grand Dieu, si jamais je l'oublie!" —

I need relate no farther. — At Edinr I was in a new world: I mingled among many classes of men, but all of them new to me; and I was all attention "to catch the manners living as they rise." —

You can now, Sir, form a pretty near guess what sort of a Wight he is whom for some time you have honored with your correspondence. — That Fancy & Whim, keen Sensibility and riotous Passions may still make him zig-zag in his future path of life, is far from being improbable; but come what will, I shall answer for him the most determinate integrity and honor; and though his evil star should again blaze in his meridian with tenfold more direful influence, he may reluctantly tax Friendship with Pity but no more. —

My most respectful Compliments to Miss Williams. — Her very elegant and friendly letter I cannot answer at present, as my presence is requisite in Edinburgh, and I set off tomorrow. —

If you will oblidge me so highly and do me so much honor as now and then to drop me a letter, Please direct to me at Mauchline, Ayrshire. —

I have the honor to be, Sir,
your ever grateful humble servt

Mauchline 2d August ⎱
　　　　1787 ⎰

ROBT BURNS

APPENDIX D

THE CHILD IN HIGHLAND
MARY'S GRAVE

A letter from Mr. W. Hillhouse Carmichael, J.P., in reply to an inquiry, and a memorandum by Mr. Carmichael and Mr. Archibald MacPhail, quoted below, provide additional details of the exhumation of Mary Campbell's remains.

76 Finnart St
Greenock
Scotland
30th Octr. 1933

Robert T. Fitzhugh Esq.
College Park
Maryland U.S.A.

DEAR MR. FITZHUGH,

I duly received your letter of Septr 5th. I regret not having been able to see you when in Greenock. My friend Mr. Archibald McPhail and myself have collaborated in drawing up a report of what happened at the removal of *all* the contents of the three lairs, in one of which Burns' Highland Mary was interred, in the Old West Burying Ground. When permission had been given by Parliament to include the ground where a Church and Burying Ground existed, into the site of a shipbuilding yard, it was agreed, in certain ways, as to the disposal of the old tombstones and what was below them. The owners of the shipbuilding yard had to transfer *all* the contents of the three lairs, in one of which Highland Mary was buried, to suitable ground in the New Cemetery, along with the Memorial Stone. This was done as stated in the report enclosed herewith. At the date (Novr. 8th 1920) of the removal of the contents of the three lairs, I was convener or chairman of the Cemetery and Parks Committee of the Greenock Corporation and was present in that capacity. Mr. McPhail, who is a student of Burns, was present at my invitation. It is within our knowledge, that in 1827, an infant aged 6 weeks, was buried in one of the lairs, as per enclosed document.* You are quite at liberty to print anything sent you herewith. With regards,

I am,

Yours faithfully,

W. HILLHOUSE CARMICHAEL

Mr. Carmichael also supplied the following supplementary details:

Removal of the contents of the three lairs in Old West Church Burying Ground, Greenock, Scotland (Novr. 8th 1920) in one of which Burns' Highland Mary was buried. All the contents of the three lairs (earth bones and wood) were taken up to the New Cemetery, where a suitable excavation had been made, to receive the contents of the three lairs. The Memorial Stone† was re-erected in New Cemetery. Suitable receptacles to contain, separately, bones, wood and earth having been provided, the excavation was proceeded with. There were three lairs, lying approximately North & South. The lairs were four feet deep, when what was taken for the old shore consisting of clay and gravel was reached. There were some springs of water visible at this level draining into the river Clyde, which flows not far from the Old Burying Ground. The excavation was carried out decently and in order. When a certain depth had been reached, bones, wood of the old coffins (the wood rotten and in small pieces) and what were evidently small pieces of human remains, black flecked with small white spots, "chemicalized" by mother earth. Three skulls were found and one jaw bone with teeth in a good state of preservation. *All* the bones and skulls were those of grown people. In the north lair and in the northwest corner, lying on the old shore, was found (lying in spring water) the bottom board of an infant's coffin, perfect in shape in good condition but sodden with water. No infant's bones, so far as we saw, were exposed. When the earth, wood, bones &c. were thrown up each was placed separately in different receptacles for transferrence to New Cemetery. All the bones found were placed in a coffin and were reverently interred in New Cemetery.

(signed)   W. HILLHOUSE CARMICHAEL J. P.

ARCHIBALD MACPHAIL

Past-Presidents
of Greenock (the mother) Burns Club.

    After correspondence, on July 23, 1934, Mr. Carmichael added the following details: "There is no doubt that the place of Highland Mary's burial was known. She was buried in McPherson's ground (McP. was a ship's carpenter) for the same reason that the Hendry child was i.e. either

* The Duncan M. Hendry memorandum of October 23, 1933.
† Permission to mark the grave had been asked by the Greenock Burns Club, February 23, 1803.

poverty precluding buying ground or else a neighbourly obligation. This sort of thing is done in Scotland among folk not very well off."

The late James D. Sloan of Ayr generously supplied a transcript from the *Campbeltown Courier*, October 25, 1930 containing information about the Hendry burial from Miss J. Hendry, 2 Margaret Street, Greenock:

The suggestion that the baby found in Highland Mary's grave was Mary Campbell's child is utter rubbish. The baby was Agnes Hendry my father's sister. Of that there is not the slightest doubt. The baby's father, my grandfather, was Captn. Duncan Hendry, a Campbeltown man, who came to reside in Greenock, where the child was born.

My grandfather had no burial ground in Greenock. The family burial ground was in Campbeltown, and, being a friend and neighbour of the McPherson's he was allowed to bury the child in the same grave as Highland Mary. That was the custom in those days.

Had it been a grown-up person, of course, a new lair would have been taken, but not in the case of a baby. I have often heard my father talk about it.

Shortly after Highland Mary's remains were re-interred in Greenock Cemetery, ten years ago, it was recorded in the local paper, the "Greenock Telegraph" that the coffin found in Highland Mary's grave was that which had contained the baby Hendry. The first suggestion that the child was Highland Mary's was made in an American newspaper. I paid no attention to that at the time, but now that it has cropped up again in Mrs. Carswell's book I feel bound to state the true facts of the case.

Another point which proves that Mrs. Carswell's book is wrong, is that if the child had been Mary Campbell's, it would have been laid in the same coffin with her.

All our family have been keenly interested in the controversy, and only the other day I had a letter from my cousin in Tarbrax, in which she said, — "I see that woman slandering our Highland Mary. Oh! that mistake of burying our wee auntie in her grave."

LIST OF
MAJOR SOURCES

POST SCRIPTS

INDEX

LIST OF
MAJOR SOURCES

Currie   *The Works of Robert Burns, with an account of his life,* by James Currie, 4 volumes, was first published in Liverpool in 1800, and reissued many times, with revisions. I have used the London, 1806 edition, which includes the revisions.

Museum   *The Scots Musical Museum.* James Johnson. Edinburgh 1787–1803. 6 volumes. I have used the facsimile reprint of William Stenhouse's 1853 annotated edition in 4 volumes, issued by Folklore Associates, Hatboro, Pennsylvania, 1962.

M'Lehose   *The Correspondence between Burns and Clarinda,* ed. W. C. M'Lehose. Edinburgh and Dublin, 1843. Also New York, 1843. I have used the New York edition.

Scott Douglas   *The Works of Robert Burns,* ed. William Scott Douglas. Edinburgh, 1877–79. 6 volumes.

Chronicle   *The Annual Burns Chronicle and Club Directory,* Kilmarnock, 1892, and annually thereafter under several variations of title.

Chambers–   *The Life and Works of Robert Burns,* ed. Robert
Wallace   Chambers, rev. William Wallace. Edinburgh and London,
or Ch–W   1896. 4 volumes.

H & H   *The Poetry of Burns,* ed. William Ernest Henley and Thomas F. Henderson. Edinburgh, 1896. 4 volumes. In the interest of providing an agreeable text for general readers, quotations from Burns' poems and songs in this volume have been taken largely from H & H. Those readers who prefer a text edited on more recent and more rigorous principles, and without a marginal gloss, are urged to consult Professor Kinsley's excellent edition. See "Kinsley" below.

RB & Mrs. D   *Robert Burns and Mrs Dunlop.* Correspondence, ed. William Wallace. London, 1898.

Dick   *The Songs of Robert Burns,* ed. James C. Dick. London, Edinburgh, Glasgow, New York, 1903.

Dick I M   *Notes on Scottish Song by Robert Burns,* ed. J. C. Dick. London, Edinburgh, Glasgow, New York, and Toronto, 1908. (The Interleaved *Museum*)

Carswell   *The Life of Robert Burns,* by Catherine Carswell. London, 1930; New York, 1931. I have used the New York edition.

F   *The Letters of Robert Burns,* ed. J. DeLancey Ferguson. Oxford, 1931. 2 volumes. References to this edition are so arranged that they may be used with the revised edition now in preparation by Professor G. Ross Roy.

Snyder   *The Life of Robert Burns,* by Franklyn Bliss Snyder. New York, 1932.

P & P   *Pride and Passion, Robert Burns,* by DeLancey Ferguson. New York, 1939.

Fitzhugh   *Robert Burns His Associates and Contemporaries,* ed. Robert T. Fitzhugh, and *The Journal of the Border Tour,* ed. DeLancey Ferguson. Chapel Hill, 1943.

Daiches   *Robert Burns,* by David Daiches. New York, 1950.

Skinner   *Burns: Authentic Likenesses,* by Basil Skinner. Edinburgh and London, 1963.

Crawford   *Burns, A Study of the Poems and Songs,* by T. Crawford. Edinburgh and London, 1960. Second edition, 1965. I have used the second edition.

Egerer   *A Bibliography of Robert Burns,* by J. W. Egerer. Edinburgh and London, 1964. Corrected and reprinted 1965. I have used the 1965 edition.

Kinsley   *The Poems and Songs of Robert Burns,* ed. James Kinsley. Oxford, 1968. 3 volumes.

Supplementary List
of Books on Burns

Readers of Burns may find interest in the following books not mentioned elsewhere in this volume.

Barke, James, *Immortal Memory,* a novelized life of Burns in five volumes, 1946–1954:
    The Wind That Shakes the Barley, early years.
    The Song in the Green Thorn Tree, creative period.
    The Wonder of All the Gay World, Edinburgh sojourn.
    The Crest of the Broken Wave, post Edinburgh period.
    The Well of the Silent Harp, final years and death.

Craig, David, *Scottish Literature and the Scottish People 1680–1830.* London, 1961.

Gibbon, Lewis Grassic, (pseud. for J. Leslie Mitchell), *Sunset Song.* 1932. A novel of country people in the Mearns, the district from which William Burnes came.

Hecht, Hans, *Robert Burns: The Man and His Work.* London, Edinburgh, Glasgow, 1936. Translated by Jane Lymburn.

Kinsley, James, ed., *Scottish Poetry: A Critical Study.* London, 1955.

Reid, J. B., *A Complete Word and Phrase Concordance to the Poems and Songs of Robert Burns.* Glasgow, 1889. Reissued, New York, 1968.

Speirs, John, *The Scots Literary Tradition.* London, 1940; rev. 1962.

Wilson, Sir James, *The Dialect of Robert Burns.* Oxford, 1923.

Wilson, Sir James, *The Scottish Poems of Robert Burns in his Native Dialect.* Oxford, 1924.

Wittig, Kurt, *The Scottish Tradition in Literature.* London and Edinburgh, 1958.

POST SCRIPTS

Preface

Epigraph. From *Thoughts suggested . . . near the Poet's residence.*

I. Profile

Page 1

Epigraph. L. A. Marchand, *Byron*, New York, 1957. I, 426.

"not his *forte.*" Maria Riddell, Currie I, 253.

Nicol. From author's transcript of original in library of Edinburgh University. See author's unpublished dissertation, 1935, Cornell University Library, 240–43. See also, R. D. Thornton, *James Currie, The Entire Stranger, and Robert Burns*, Edinburgh and London, 1963. 332.

Page 2

sophisticated audience. cp. J. W. Egerer, "Burns and 'Guid Black Prent,'" *The Age of Johnson*, New Haven, 1949. 269–79.

no wish to repeat. F I, #379, 379; also #319, 312; #333, 326.

burden. F I, #373, 370; II, #473, 93; #610, 228. Also, McDiarmid Notes, P. Hately Waddell, *The Life and Works of Robert Burns*, 2 vols., Glasgow, 1867. II, xxi–xxv. See dissertation, 525–47.

Page 3

Syme. Author's transcript of original in Nat. Lib. of Scotland (Watson Collection, 1190). See dissertation, 339.

Commonplace Book. *Robert Burns's Commonplace Book*, eds. J. C. Ewing and D. Cook, Glasgow, 1938. 7–8.

Maria Riddell. Currie I, 253ff. See also, J. C. Weston, "The Text of Maria Riddell's Sketch of Burns," *Studies in Scottish Literature*, V, 3 (January, 1968). 194–97.

Page 4

"so discerning." H & H II, 421.

Page 5

"continual struggle." Crawford, 40, 41.

Page 6

"earliest friend." F II, #440, 63.
"extremely deferential." J. G. Lockhart, *The Life of Robert Burns*, ed. W.
Scott Douglas, London, 1882. 113.
"blood-royal." F II, #556A, 165.
lovemaking. Gilbert Burns, Currie I, 71.

Page 7

"a very Poet." F II, #646, 271–72.
locked in a room. Fitzhugh, 44.
To Ainslie. F I, #215, 199–200; also *The Merry Muses of Caledonia*, published for the Burns Federation, 1911. 137–38.

Page 8

formula. F I, #272, 257.
eggs. F II, #393, 13–14.

Page 9

"twa wives." Ch-W III, 365n.
Syme. Author's transcript of original, then the property of the late J. C.
Ewing. See dissertation, 335.
Maria Riddell to Currie. *Chronicle* 1921, 108.
Telford letter. R. T. Fitzhugh, "The Paradox of Burns' Character," *Studies in Philology*, XXXII, 1 (January, 1935). 113–14.

Page 10

Sharpe. *Chronicle* 1903, 100.
Carswell. Copy in author's library of *Outlook* I, 5 (Aug., 1936). 60.
"defecates." Ch-W IV, 428n.
"occasional hard drinking." F II, #529, 140.
Syme. Author's transcript. See dissertation, 331.
Findlater. J. Currie, *The Life and Works of Robert Burns*, ed. Alexander
Peterkin, Edinburgh, 1815. I, xcv.

Page 11

Scott. *The Letters of Sir Walter Scott*, ed. H. J. C. Grierson, London, 1936.
X, 401.

Page 12

"more respected." Waddell II, xxiv; also Fitzhugh, 41.

Nature's Fire. See F, index, under "Scots Poetry."

"absolutely crazed." F I, #147, 134.

Kinsley. J. Kinsley, "The Music of the Heart," *Renaissance and Modern Studies*, V, iii (1964). 33.

Page 13

To Thomson. F II, #586, 200.

To Thomson. F II, #644, 265.

Page 14

Bawdy. F II, #592, 213.

Page 15

Syme. Author's transcript. See dissertation, 336; also P.S. for p. 9.

religion. Waddell II, xxiii–iv; F I, #261, 242; II, #395, 16; I, #353, 348; #89, 79; #252, 231; II, #392, 13. Also F I, # 350, 343; #221, 207; #374, 373; II, #506, 120; #649, 281. See also F, index, under "Religion."

Page 16

Currie. *Chronicle* 1919, 14.

II. Growth

Although often sparse, the details of Burns' early life are well established, except for a few relating to his stay in Irvine; but one does wish that original texts of material printed by Dr. Currie were available. The story of Burns' development as a poet, however, remains obscure, and must be reconstructed from hints in his letters and his Commonplace Book. It is greatly to be regretted that we cannot follow this growth as we can that of John Keats, for example, in similarly unpromising circumstances.

Page 18

"auld clay biggin." A building with two rooms, outer, "but," and inner, "ben," hence a but and ben. See P & P. 11; and *Ayrshire at the Time of Burns,* ed. John Strawhorn, 1959. 34–94; also index for Dr. Alexander Campbell and William Fergusson (Doonholm).

Page 19

"lived very sparingly." Currie I, 69–70; 62–63.

Page 22

"retentive memory."   F I, #125, 106.
midwife.   J. M. Murdoch, *Familiar Links with Robert Burns*, Ayr, 1933. 58.
chest.   Fitzhugh, 59.
gable blown in.   Currie I, 378.

Page 23

Murdoch.   Currie I, 87–89.
Titus Andronicus.   Currie I, 61–62.

Page 24

Dr. Dalrymple.   Ch-W I, 34n.
further schooling.   Currie I, 65, 66.
Kirkoswald.   F I, #125, 111.

Page 25

"reader when he could get a book."   Currie I, 60; also 64.

Page 26

"fluency and precision."   Dugald Stewart, Currie I, 137.
harvest partner.   F I, #125, 108.

Page 28

young love.   *Commonplace Book*, Ewing and Cook, 3.
"a darling walk."   F I, #125, 112.

Page 29

dancing school.   F I, #125, 109; Snyder, 93, n. 9.
"tinder."   F I, #125, 110.
"An Aim." F I, #125, 109.
"vive l'amour."   F I, #125, 111.
"to see and observe."   F I, #13, 13–14.
"Though when young."   Currie I, 71.

Page 30

Robert.   F I, #125, 110.
Bachelor's Club Rules.   Currie I, 104–6.

Page 31

"views of matrimony."   F I, #18, 20.
new members.   Currie I, 107.

Page 32

Rules. Currie I, appendix, 363–67.
July 4, 1781. *Chronicle* 1929, 139.
subsequent separation. *Chronicle* 1929, 141.

Page 33

"Caledonia's Bard." F I, #77, 67. *Chronicle* 1937, 94–102; 1947, 37–43.
"two doors." F I, #125, 109–10.
"Egotisms." *Reliques of Robert Burns*, ed. R. H. Cromek, London, 1808.
   339. See also J. D. Ferguson, "In Defense of R. H. Cromek," *Philological*
   Quarterly, IX. 239–48; and D. Cook, *Chronicle* 1922, 1–21.

Page 34

"jilted." F I, #125, 112.
five drafts. F I, #5, 6, 7, 8, 9, 5–11.

Page 35

ownership of shop. *Chronicle* 1905, 33–42.
Robert Fergusson. F I, #125, 113; *Chronicle* 1956, 1–2.
To Dr. Moore. F I, #125, 113.

Page 38

religious ferment. *Commonplace Book*, Ewing and Cook, 8, 18; Crawford,
   12–16.

Page 39

Adam Smith. *Commonplace Book*, 5.
heart-wrung comment. F I, #162, 146.

Page 40

early letters. Currie I, 64.
To William Burns. F I, #4, 4–5.

Page 41

"dangerous disorder." *Commonplace Book*, 18. (Heading to prayer)

Page 42

To James Burness. F I, #17, 18–19.

Page 44

"man seeking work." Currie III, Appendix, 382.
Lochlea troubles. McVie, *Chronicle* 1935, 69–87. See also Snyder, 77–83;
   Strawhorn, *Ayrshire*, 133.

Page 45

Murdoch.   Currie I, 94, 95.

Page 46

Currie.   Currie I, 82.
M'Kenzie.   *Poems of Robert Burns,* Edinburgh, 1811. (Morison's Burns) II, 261–62.

Page 47

early poetry.   F I, #125, 112.
To Peter Hill.   F I, #276, 263.

Page 48

collection of songs.   *Chronicle* 1935, 12; F I, #125, 109.

Page 49

"ill-spawned monsters."   F I, #319, 311–12; see also F I, #333, 326.
Burns' diction.   Crawford, ix–xv, and discussions of individual poems, *passim;* Raymond Bentman, "Robert Burns's Use of Scottish Diction," *From Sensibility to Romanticism,* New York, 1965; and R. Crombie Saunders, "Burns in Two Tongues," *Saltire Review* I, 3 (1954). 41–45; also a review of Crawford: McD. Emslie, "Burns and the Alien Diction," *Essays in Criticism* X, 4 (Oct., 1960). 451–61.

III. Poet

By his early twenties, the record of Robert Burns has become fairly full, but little poetry of these years has survived. Apparently he destroyed it when he thought he was going to Jamaica in 1786. A representative selection of poetry which influenced Burns is offered in Appendix A — poems not easily available for the general reader. They will illustrate Burns' freely acknowledged debt, and the irony of his being at once a highly imitative and a highly original poet.

Knowledge of the quality and tone of peasant life in Ayrshire is important for an understanding of his poems. It also reveals that Burns was a fairly normal product of his environment. Section III seeks to provide some lively evidence on this point.

Mary Campbell (the "Highland Mary" of much romantic confusion) had minor importance for Burns before her death (see P & P. 144–50). The extended section on Mary is presented to give full and circumstantial information about her from reliable sources, which readers may interpret for

themselves. At very least it establishes the girl as a flesh and blood person —
tall, fair-haired, blue-eyed, a native of Cowal, and victim of a fever. It
should be noted that the Lord Eglinton mentioned by Train did, indeed,
have a brother, despite claims to the contrary (McVie, *Chronicle* 1956.
107). Also that the Hendry response to Mrs. Carswell's story of the coffin
found in Mary's grave (Appendix D) was prompt, and not suspiciously
delayed as has been charged.

Page 51

Epigraphs.   Aileen Ward, *John Keats,* New York, 1963. 275. F I, #299, 292.

Page 52

Gilbert's recollection.   Currie III, 378–79.
To Sillar.   F I, #355, 350.
Wen Yuang-Ning, *Chronicle* 1945, 6.

Page 55

models and themes for epistles. See J. C. Weston, "Robert Burns' Use of the
Scots Verse-Epistle Form," *Philological Quarterly,* April, 1970.

Page 59

six-line stanza.   H & H I, 336–42.

Page 62

"Polemical divinity."   F I, #125, 107.
Sillar's comment.   Morison's Burns II, Appendix I, 259–60.

Page 63

To Dr. Moore.   F I, #125, 113–14.

Page 64

Kirk dissension.   Crawford, 25–48; for auld lichts and new lichts, see Kinsley
III, 1045; also R. W. Chambers, *The Life and Works of Robert Burns,*
4 vols., Edinburgh and London, 1880. I, 122–23.
Fisher.   H & H II, 321; *The Glenriddell Manuscripts of Robert Burns,*
printed not published, John Gribbel, Philadelphia, 1914. Facsimile, 2 vols.
 (1 verse, 1 letters).

Page 65

Hamilton.   Synder, 110–11, and 146, n.18; see also Kinsley III, 1047–53.

Page 68

Elizabeth Burns.   Ch-W I, 119–20.
Betty Paton's settlement.   *Scribners Magazine,* Dec. 1933. 383–84.

Page 72

The blacksmith.   Synder. 175–76, 185, n.35.

Page 73

Aiton.   Strawhorn, *Ayrshire,* "Holding the Fair." 73–75.

Page 84

Henley.   H & H IV, 274.
"Natural ideas."   Ch-W II, 129.

Page 85

"study men."   F I, #13, 14.
"rural imagery."   F II, #557, 168.
vernacular.   cp. F II, #507, 122; #511, 126.
Ramsay.   Quoted by D. Daiches, "Eighteenth Century Vernacular Poetry,"
    Scottish Poetry, a Critical Study, ed. J. Kinsley, London, 1955. 159. Burns
    mentions "Theocrites" in his Kilmarnock preface.

Page 92

news "not the most agreable."   F I, #21, 22.
legal marriage.   James Smith may have been a witness. In F I, #251, 230.
    Burns asks Smith to write a letter which can be shown, saying that "such
    things are" about his marriage.
To Arnot.   F I, #29, 26–30; see also Strawhorn, 137.

Page 94

To Brice.   F I, #31, 30–31.
Jean writes to Kirk Session.   Ch-W I, 344n.
To Richmond.   F I, #33, 32.

Page 95

To Brice.   F I, #34, 33.

Page 96

To Richmond.   F I, #36, 35.
To Smith.   F I, #37, 36.
dates.   F I, #40, 37, 38; #43, 40; #49, 44.
new edition.   F I, #53, 46–47.

Page 97

To Richmond, Sept. 1.   F I, #43, 40.
To Richmond, Sept. 3.   From transcript supplied the author by the late
DeLancey Ferguson. See also, Kinsley #124, I. 294.

Page 98

assignment.   F I, #35, 33–34.
Dundonald Mary Campbell.   Ch-W I, Appendix VIII. 470–75.

Page 99

Cromek.   *Reliques,* 237.

Page 100

To George Thomson.   F II, #511, 127. October 26, 1792.

Page 101

To Mrs. Dunlop.   F I, #374, 373.

Page 102

Train MS.   Fitzhugh, 54–55.

Page 103

another note.   Fitzhugh, 57–58.

Page 104

Anthony Dunlop.   RB & Mrs. D, xxv–xxvi; also xxvi n.
Grierson notes.   Fitzhugh, 34–36; p. 36, Grierson adds, "Highland from
Dunoon Parish Cowal." See map of Northern Scotland.

Page 105

"texts connected with the name."   Those who wish to pursue the matter of
Mary Campbell further are referred to Snyder, 129–46.

Page 106

Aiken.   F I, #53, 47.

Page 107

Returns from Kilmarnock edition.   Ch-W I, 468–70.

Page 108

Review notices.   Egerer, 4.

Page 114

"Burns's verse."   H & H I, v.
Raleigh.   Walter Raleigh, *Some Authors, A Collection of Literary Essays,
1896–1916,* Oxford, 1923. 221–22.

Page 119
"sober science."   F I, #31, 31.
"last foolish action."   F I, #31, 31.

Page 120
Blacklock.   F I, #80, 71.
dozen copies.   Thornton, *Currie,* 26on. Also, *Chronicle* 1939, 50, #276 (2).

Page 121
candor.   RB & Mrs. D, 48; 108–11; 175; 286–87; 296–97.
sympathy.   RB & Mrs. D, 179; 264; 271–72; 275; 365.

Page 122
"idle project."   F I, #330, 325; #351, 344.
commission.   F I, #90, 82.
Dunlop quarrel.   F II, #649, 281; also 349.
Last letter to Mrs. Dunlop.   F II, #702, 326.

IV. *Lion*

Much of the information in Section IV is standard, but Burns' own feelings about his Edinburgh patrons, and about his publisher, William Creech, have been emphasized. His friendship with William Nicol has been clarified, also. Details of the gentry's carousing provide a background against which Burns' own exploits seem modest. Indeed, as Professor Ferguson has remarked, Burns was not so much a conspicuous sinner as one who sinned conspicuously. The upper social class of many Crochallan Fencibles should be noted. (McVie, *Chronicle* 1964, 10.)

The Clarinda affair is given full coverage, but perhaps the best comment on it is Jean's, to John M'Diarmid. Allan Cunningham identified the heroine of "Had we never lov'd sae kindly" as a "frail dame of Dumfriesshire," but M'Diarmid adds (Waddell II, xxiv), "Mrs. Burns thinks it was no one but Clarinda."

Details about Learned Pigs are a novelty in Burns scholarship.

Page 124
Epigraph.   To Muir. F I, #64, 57.
Scott.   J. D. Lockhart, *The Life of Robert Burns,* ed. W. Scott Douglas, London, 1882. 113.
"hare-brained ramble." F I, #309, 300.
"Greenland bay."   Fitzhugh, 111.

Page 125

Duchess.   Ch-W II, 60.

Page 126

advertisement.   Ch-W II, 22.

Page 127

appearance.   Lockhart, Scott Douglas edition. 112; Currie I, 230–31; *Chronicle* 1906, 75–76.
"like coals."   Ch-W IV, 218. John Syme to H. Constable, Nov. 1829; quoted in Syme's obituary, *Dumfries Weekly Journal,* Dec. 16, 1831.
pock-marked.   Waddell II, xxvii, xxxix.

Page 128

"his deportment."   Morison's Burns I, lxv–vi.
learned pig.   Fitzhugh, 32.
rusticity.   Ch-W II, 137.
whip.   R. Kerr, *Memoirs of the Life, Writings, and Correspondence* of *William Smellie,* Edinburgh, 1811. II, 350–51.
swelled head.   Author's transcript of original (National Library of Scotland, Ms. number 22.4.17). See also F, index, under "David Ramsay."
Lockhart.   Scott Douglas edition, 126ff.

Page 129

Mackenzie.   *The Anecdotes and Egotisms of Henry Mackenzie,* ed. H. W. Thompson, London, 1927. 151–52.

Page 130

Anderson.   *Chronicle* 1925, 14ff.

Page 132

poor verses.   *Chronicle* 1925, 12.

Page 133

eccentric clergyman.   Ch-W II, 76–77.
To Hamilton.   F I, #62, 55.
To Ballantine.   F I, #63, 57.

Page 134

To Aiken.   F I, #65, 58.
Mrs. Carfrae.   F I, #77, 67–68.

Page 135

To Dr. Moore. F I, #97, 85.
To Mrs. Dunlop. F I, #98, 86.
"Great people." F I, #189, 175.
To Nicol. F I, #216, 201.
To Dunbar. F I, #236, 217.
To Cleghorn. F I, #230, 214.
To Mrs. Dunlop. F I, #98, 86.
To Smith. F I, #113, 95.

Page 136

To Clarinda. F I, #171, 156.
Blair. *The Works of Robert Burns,* ed. W. Scott Douglas, 6 vols., Edin-
    burgh, 1877–79. VI, 391.
gaffe. Ch-W II, 76.

Page 138

"ludicrous." Ch-W II, 23.
Smellie. F II, #440, 63.

Page 139

Crochallans. McVie, *Chronicle* 1964, 10.
Dr. Stuart. Kerr, *Smellie,* I, 502–3.

Page 140

Williamson. Robert Chambers, *Traditions of Edinburgh,* rev., Edinburgh
    and London, 1868. 182–83.

Page 141

Edinburgh edition. Edwin Wolf, 2nd, " 'Skinking' or 'Stinking'?", *Library
    Chronicle of . . . University of Penna.* xiv (April, 1947). 3–14.

Page 142

agreement. Reproduced, Snyder, 224.
To Creech. Text printed by Professor G. Ross Roy, *Papers of the Biblio-
    graphical Society of America,* 1965. 358. He writes that Currie probably
    had the letter but did not print it for fear of offending Burns' "superiors."
    See also S. Parks, PBSA, 1966. 453–64.
final settlement F I, #315, 308.
To Mrs. Dunlop. F I, #324, 317.

Page 145

To a Haggis. Fitzhugh, 37–38.
pirated editions. J. W. Egerer, "Burns and 'Guild Black Prent,'" *The Age of Johnson*, New Haven, 1949. 269–79.

Page 146

"inundation of nonsense." F I, #333, 326; see also F I, #319, 312.
To Lady Elizabeth Cunningham. F I, #379, 379.
To Dr. Moore. F I, #291, 284.
Drama. J. D. Ferguson, "Burns and the Drama," *Scots Magazine* XXI (1934). 278–86.
"Mr. Miller." F I, #77, 67.

Page 147

To Smith. F I, #113, 95–96.
To Nicol. F I, #114, 96.
Milton's Satan. F I, #113, 95.
To Mrs. Dunlop. F I, #254, 234.
To Ainslie. F I, #122, 102.

Page 148

Border Tour. Fitzhugh, Journal text edited by DeLancey Ferguson. 108–22.
People Burns met. Journal: Minister at Dunse, Dr. Bowmaker, 107, 117; Brydone, 109; Rutherford, 110–11.

Page 149

Somerville. Ch-W II, 105.
Miss Lindsay. Journal, 111ff.
Esther Easton. Journal, 113.

Page 152

plough horses. Journal, 115.
Ladies. Betsy Grieve, 116; Miss Clarke, 117; Rachel Ainslie, 118; also Ch-W II, 116n.

Page 153

illness. Journal, 118.
roup. Journal, 119.
Meg Cameron. Ch-W II, 121. For "Meg," not "May," see DeLancey Ferguson, "Some New Burns Letters," PMLA LI, 4 (Dec., 1936). 979.
To Ainslie. F I, #246, 226. Here dated "about 1 June, 1788," which is a year too late.

Page 154

To Ainslie.   F I, #116, 98.
To Ainslie, July 29, 1787.   See "Meg Cameron" above.
"Highland wench."   F II, #586, 203.

Page 156

Dumbarton.   *Chronicle* 1927, 82–84.
To Smith.   F I, #117, 98–100.
Sterne.   *Tristram Shandy* II, 9.

Page 158

Creech.   Ch-W II, 141; 145–46; F I, #294, 285.
Meg Cameron.   Ch-W II, 145–46.
Cockburn.   *Memorials of His Time*, Edinburgh, 1856. 4.

Page 159

Nicol.   Fitzhugh, 65–67; 97–98.

Page 161

To Ainslie.   F I, #130, 119–20.
three weeks.   F I, #131, 120.
Journal.   *Journal of a Tour in the Highlands . . . by Robert Burns*, ed. J. C. Ewing, London and Glasgow, 1927. Transcript pp. 11–17.

Page 163

Burns at Blair Athole.   Ch-W II, 162; Currie I, 178–82; cp. *post* xxx–xx and F II, #441, 64–65.

Page 164

"debts."   F I, #135, 123.
"obstinate son of Latin Prose."   F I, #145, 131.

Page 165

later letter.   F I, #149, 136.
messenger and guide.   Ch-W II, 172.
Bishop Skinner.   *Chronicle* 1944, 35.

Page 167

To Gilbert.   F I, #137, 125.

Page 168

Edinburgh patrons.   F I, #324, 317.
To Mrs. Dunlop.   F II, #510, 125.
To Mr. Miller.   F I, #139, 126–27.
Adair.   Currie I, 168–72.
proposal.   F II, 334.

Page 169

Murdoch sisters.   Ch-W II, 153.
To Hamilton.   F I, #132, 121–22.
Burns' itinerary.   F I, #140, 128; #141 and #142, 128–29.

Page 170

Marriage of Adair and Charlotte Hamilton.   Ch-W II, 188 n.

Page 171

Ramsay.   Currie I, 188–89.

Page 172

To Mr. Miller.   F I, #144, 130, 131.
return from Dumfries.   F I, #155, 141.

Page 173

To Margaret Chalmers.   F I, #207, 192.
Clarinda.   *Burns and Clarinda,* ed. W. C. M'Lehose, New York, 1843.
   (Originally published in Edinburgh the same year); see also R. L. Brown,
   Clarinda, Dewsbury, England, 1968.

Page 174

Mrs. M'Lehose and her husband.   M'Lehose, 17, 28.

Page 175

method of censorship.   M'Lehose, 186.
caress.   M'Lehose, 176.

Page 176

Mr. Kemp.   M'Lehose, 174.
theological position.   F I, #174, 159.

Page 177

To Mrs. Dunlop.   F I, #374, 374.
mid-February.   F I, #204, 189.
diary.   M'Lehose, 53.

Page 178

mulatto child.   Brown, *Clarinda,* 64–65.
1791 letters.   F II, #484, 101; #485, 101; #486, 102.
Feb. 1788 letters.   F I, #197, 183; #207 and #208, 192.
trip to Mauchline.   F I, #209, 194; #211, 195; #214, 198.

Page 179

"disgusted." Fitzhugh, 43; F I, #210, 194.
To Ainslie. F I, #215, 199–200.
To Brown. F I, #220, 206.
Mr. Pattison. F I, #209, 193–94.

Page 180

"Compliment to Mr. Miller." F I, #210, 195.

Page 181

To Margaret Chalmers. F I, #207, 192.
To Hill. F II, #475, 95.
lease. F I, #223, 208; lease reprinted by Snyder, 503–7.
To Clarinda. F I, #225, 210.
Creech. F I, #228, 212.
"dearest angel." F I, #225, 210.
loves her. F I, #224, 209.
To Brown. F I, #228, 212.

Page 182

To Clarinda. F I, #320, 312.

Page 183

acidulous exchange. F II, #388 and #389, 7 and 8.
Ainslie to Clarinda. R. Fitzhugh, "Burns at Ellisland," *Modern Language Notes*, LII (Nov. 1938). 525–26.

Page 185

To Clarinda, 1794. F II, #629, 247–48.
Sweet Sensibility. F II, #462, 82.

Page 186

Jenny Clow's appeal. M'Lehose, 262–63.
Burns' reply. F II, #483, 100.

Page 187

To Clarinda. F II, #544, 155; #629, 247.
Cunningham to Syme. Author's transcript of original; see P.S. for p. 365.
For details of Cunningham, see *Chronicle* 1933, 94ff.

Page 188

Maria Riddell. *Chronicle* 1923, 76.
Mrs. M'Lehose. Fitzhugh, 40; M'Lehose, 52.

details of Burns' marriage.   Fitzhugh, 58; F I, #251, 230; Snyder, 303.
To Ainslie.   F I, #249, 229.

Page 189

To Beugo.   F I, #268, 252.
To Mrs. Dunlop.   F I, #247, 227.
To Dunbar.   F I, #236, 217.

Page 190

From Nicol.   Author's transcript. See P.S. for p. 1.
Gray.   J. Currie, *The Works of Robert Burns,* with additions by Gilbert
Burns, London, 1820. I, 439.

V. Married Man

The anticlimax of Burns' later years is rendered more poignant by his unrecognized infection. From a biographer's point of view, there is almost too
much information about Burns during these years when his life was less interesting than before, and his poetic output generally less striking. It should
be noted that Burns himself eagerly sought employment in the Excise, which
offered a desirable and steady income, and good prospects for promotion.
He was a faithful officer, and a brave one, as the *Rosamond* incident reveals.

The full truth of Burns' life in Dumfries is probably not known, but from
comments such as those by Syme, Cunningham, Thomas Telford, James
Gray, and C. K. Sharpe, the outline is clear enough. Some relatively fresh
details appear here about Burns' friend Robert Riddell, but the puzzle of the
Riddell quarrel cannot be solved on the basis of presently available information. It is hoped the note on Jenny Little will be of interest. And one of the
rich adornments of the book, certainly, is Mrs. Walter Riddell's portrait.

Page 191

To Mrs. Dunlop.   F I, #184, 171.

Page 192

"defy the teeth of time." F I, #288, 275.

Page 193

To Thomson.   F II, #511, 126; #507, 123.
George Thomson.   J. Cuthbert Hadden, *George Thomson, The Friend of
Burns,* London, 1898; J. D. Ferguson, "Cancelled Passages in the Letters
of Robert Burns to George Thomson," PMLA XLIII (1928). 1110–20;
see also *passim,* Dick (Historical Notes), Kinsley (Notes and Commentary), and R. D. Thornton, unpublished Harvard dissertation.
docket.   F II, #706, 328–29.

Page 194

Thomson's contribution.   J. G. Lockhart, *The Life of Robert Burns,* ed. W. Scott Douglas, London, 1882. 277.

Page 195

"Rhinoceros."   F I, #268, 251.
Did Thomson meet Burns?   Hadden, 134–38.
"ill at ease."   F II, #627, 245.
"thumb-phial."   F I, #290, 277.
To Deborah Davies.   F II, #556A, 165.
To Mrs. Dunlop.   F I, #244, 224.

Page 196

To Hill.   F II, #430, 51–52.

Page 197

To Cunningham.   F II, #441, 64–65.

Page 198

To Dr. Moore.   F I, #322, 315.

Page 199

Glenriddell Collection.   *The Glenriddell Manuscripts of Robert Burns,* printed not published, John Gribbel, Philadelphia, 1914. Facsimile, 2vols. (1 verse, 1 letters).

Page 200

"Jacobitism." Dick I M, 27.
To Mrs. Dunlop.   F II, #397, 18.
"beef-witted." Dick I M, 5.
Edinburgh Evening Courant.   F I, #283, 269–71.

Page 203

To Mrs. Dunlop, 1.   F II, #403, 26.
To Mrs. Graham.   F II, #402, 25.
To Mrs. Dunlop, 2.   F II, #510, 125.
To Dunbar.   F II, #382, 2.

Page 205

To Hill.   F I, #255, 235.
Ellisland.   F I, #247, 226; #272, 257.
"elbow of existence."   F I, 381.

Page 206

To Graham.   F I, #269, 253.

Excise.   John Sinton, *Burns, Excise Officer and Poet,* Glasgow and Edinburgh, 4th edition, 1897; R. W. Macfadzean, "Burns's Excise Duties and
Emoluments," *Chronicle* 1898, 53ff.; J. Macfadzean, "Robert Burns and
the Scotch Excise Board," *Chronicle* 1903, 26ff.; B. R. Leftwich, "Burns
and the Excise," *Chronicle* 1936, 65ff.

Page 207

To Graham.   F I, #273, 259.
To Mrs. Dunlop, 1.   F I, #363, 360.
Twelve cows.   M'Diarmid Notes, Waddell II, xxii.
To Mrs. Dunlop, 2.   F I, #324, 317–18.
To Jean.   F I, #278, 265.

Page 208

uncle Robert.   F I, #314, 307–8.
Agnes.   M'Diarmid Notes, Waddell II, xxii.

Page 209

To Mrs. Dunlop.   F I, #330, 324.
"business."   F I, #378, 377.
To Graham.   F I, #341, 335; #353, 347.
To Mrs. Dunlop.   F I, #359, 356.
September 7.   *Chronicle* 1936, 68.
October 27.   Snyder, 317.
October 10.   Ch-W III, 96; Snyder, 316.
"expectant."   F I, #367, 364.
"most violent cold."   F I, #371, 368.
"diseased nervous system."   F I, #374, 372.

Page 210

"hypochondria."   F II, #381, 1.
"slow, illformed Fever."   F II, #422, 44.
"with my horse."   F II, #435, 55.
broken arm.   F II, #445, 70.
Janet Little.   RB & Mrs. D, see index; Hilton Brown, *Chronicle* 1950, 15–
20; *The Poetical Works of Janet Little, the Scotch Milkmaid,* Air, 1792.
This volume carries a subscription list of nearly 700 names, among them,
Dr. Adair, Edinburgh; Mr. Robert Ainsley, writer, Edinburgh; Mr. Robert Burns, Dumfries; and James Boswell, Esq., of Auchinleck. Hilton

Brown, who cites no authority, reports that "Jenny is said to have made fifty pounds" from her volume. She wrote in English, and preferred quatrains and couplets.

Mrs. Dunlop's letters to Burns contain many references to Janet, or Jenny, Little, and her poetry, with quotations. While Mrs. Dunlop did not rate Jenny's work highly, she offered the woman encouragement in her benevolent-officious way, and tried to engage Burns' interest and assistance. Jenny herself sought Burns' patronage by addressing an epistle to him in his favorite stanza, her only use of that form. A few stanzas will suffice:

> To hear thy song, all ranks desire;
> Sae well thou strik'st the dormant lyre.
> Apollo, wi' poetic fire,
>   Thy breast did warm,
> An' critics silently admire
>   Thy art to charm.
>
> .   .   .   .
>
> When slighted love becomes thy theme,
> An' woman's faithless vows you blame,
> With so much pathos you exclaim,
>   In your Lament,
> But glanc'd by the most frigid dame,
>   She wad relent.
>
> .   .   .   .
>
> Did Addison or Pope but hear,
> Or Sam, that critic most severe,
> A plough-boy sing, wi' throat sae clear,
>   They, in a rage,
> Their works wad a' in pieces tear
>   An' curse your page.

This salutation prompted Burns to write Mrs. Dunlop (F I, #362, 359), calling it "a very ingenious but modest composition." Nothing daunted by Burns' silence, Jenny presented herself at Ellisland on the day of his accident, which she celebrated with another modest composition. It begins by reciting her disappointment at not having been able to see him earlier, and bursts out as he comes into view:

> Hark! now he comes, a dire alarm
>   Re-echoes through his hall!
> Pegasus kneel'd, his rider's arm
>   Was broken by a fall.
>
> The doleful tidings to my ears
>   Were in harsh notes convey'd;
> His lovely wife stood drown'd in tears,
>   While thus I pond'ring said:

"No cheering draught, with ills unmix'd,
Can mortals taste below;
All human fate by heav'n is fix'd,
Alternate joy and wo."

With beating breast I view'd the bard;
All trembling did him greet:
With sighs bewail'd his fate so hard,
Whose notes were ever sweet.

A year later, however, (F II, #491, 106) Burns gallantly assures Mrs. Dunlop, "I am glad to hear so good an account of Jenny Little's affairs. I have done next to nothing for her yet, but I shall now set about & fill up my Subscription bill."

"elbow chair." F II, #475, 95.
despondency. M'Diarmid Notes, Waddell II, xxii.
To Brown. F I, #369, 365–66.
To Lady Elizabeth Cunningham. F I, #379, 379.
To Ainslie. F I, #367, 364.

Page 211

To Cleghorn. F II, #473, 93.
Exciseman's duties. *Chronicle* 1898, 53ff.

Page 212

To Graham. F II, #419, 40–41.
To Mitchell. F II, #417, 38.
To Cleghorn. F II, #473, 94.

Page 213

Syme to Cunningham. Author's transcript. See P.S. for p. 365.
Nicol to Ainslie. Ch-W III, 200.
Mrs. Dunlop. RB & Mrs. D, 155; 241, 245, 249.
To Mrs. Dunlop. F II, #396, 17.

Page 215

Ellisland lease. Snyder, 503–7; Ch-W III, 296.
To Cleghorn. F II, #473, 93.
sale of crops. F II, #466, 87.
sale of "farming things." F II, #481, 98.
To Mrs. Dunlop. F II, #491, 105.
Nov. 11, 1791. P & P, xviii.

Page 216

To Hill.　F II, #495, 109.
Excise records.　Sinton, 59.
Maria Riddell.　F II, #497, 110.
Burns' Excise record.　F, index; *Chronicle* 1936, 66–69; Sinton, *passim.*
promotion.　Sinton, 60.

Page 217

Findlater. *Glasgow Courier,* March, 1834.
To Heron.　F II, #660, 292.
Rosamond.　*Scotsman,* and *Glasgow Herald,* Nov. 11, 1932; *Chronicle* 1934,
　43–52.

Page 220

Gazetteer.　P & P, xviii.
To Mrs. Dunlop.　F II, #524, 137.

Page 223

To Mrs. Dunlop.　F I, #376, 321.
To Graham.　F I, #528, 139–40.

Page 224

To Mrs. Dunlop.　F II, #529, 140.
To Graham.　F II, #530, 143–45.

Page 226

"tippling Ballad."　*When Princes and Prelates.*
Syme to Peterkin.　Author's transcript. See dissertation, 334; also P.S. for
　p. 9.
Findlater.　Author's Cornell Univ. dissertation, 234–37.
To Erskine of Mar.　F II, #558, 169–70.

Page 228

Nicol.　Gribbel facsimile, Glenriddell letter book. See P.S. for p. 64.

Page 230

To Nicol.　F II, #537, 150–51.
To Cunningham.　F II, #536, 149–50.

Page 231

To Mrs. Dunlop.　F II, #649, 281.
To Mrs. Dunlop.　F I, #254, 234.
"suitable to his feelings."　F I, #207, 192.

Page 232

"talent and humour." Author's transcript. See dissertation, 332; also P.S. for p. 9.

Page 233

Ellisland. F I, #270, 254; #271, 255–56; and M'Diarmid Notes, Waddell II, xxi–xxii.
list of correspondents. *Chronicle* 1933; 1939.
Helen Maria Williams. F I, #358, 352–55.

Page 234

To Bruce Campbell. F I, #284, 271–72.
To Ainslie. F I, #252, 231.
To Stewart. F I, #253, 232–33.
To Mrs. Dunlop. F I, #264, 245.

Page 235

To Jean. F I, #270, 254–55.

Page 236

To Mrs. Dunlop. F I, #285, 272–75.
To Dr. Blacklock. F I, #287, 274.
To Mrs. Dunlop. F I, #290, 277.

Page 237

To Mrs. Dunlop. F I, #293, 282–83.
To Ainslie. F I, #295, 286–87.
To James Burness. F I, #314, 307–8.

Page 239

To Mrs. Dunlop. F I, #330, 324.
To Rev. Patrick Carfrae. F I, #333, 327.

Page 240

To William Burns. F I, #337, 332.
To James Johnson. F I, #348, 340; see *The Scots Musical Museum,* originally published by James Johnson, with illustrations by William Stenhouse, reissued by Folklore Associates, Hatboro, Penna. 1962.

Page 241

To Mrs. Dunlop. F I, #350, 342.
To Mrs. Dunlop. F I, #352, 346.

Page 242

To Hill. F II, #387, 6–7.

Page 243

Creech. Ch-W III, 164n.

Page 244

To Nicol. F II, #390, 8–10.

Page 246

To William Burns. F II, #391, 10–11.

Page 247

To Mrs. Dunlop. F II, #403, 27–28.

Page 248

To John Wilson. F II, #420, 42–43.

Page 249

To Rev. George Husband Baird. F II, #438, 60–61.
Blair and Moore. Ch-W III, 240.
To Dr. Moore. F II, #437, 58.

Page 250

To Findlater. F II, #460, 81–82.

Page 251

To Newall. F II, #398, 20.
"chequered." F II, #443, 68.
To Sillar. F II, #461, 82.
To Boyd. F II, #458, 80.

Page 252

Gilbert's wedding. F II, #457, 79; P & P, xviii.
Archers. F II, #441, 64–65.
Lord Buchan. F II, #465, 85.

Page 253

Creech. F II, #475, 95.
Robert Riddell. See account of Riddell in DNB; Dick. xliii; Kerr, *Smellie*,
    II. 364, 365; R. D. Thornton, *Chronicle* 1953, 44–67; Stenhouse, *Museum*,
    I, lxxvi.
Friars' Carse. For punctuation see Gribbel, Glenriddell letter book, p. 6.

Page 254

degree. Under date of January 23, 1794, the minutes of "Edin. Coll." record, "A report was made to the Meeting that Robert Riddell Esqr. of Glenriddell F. S. A. of London & of Edinburgh had been judged by the Law Faculty a proper candidate for receiving the Degree of Doctor of Laws; and he was recommended as a Gentleman of uncommon knowledge as an Antiquarian.

"The Senatus Academicus having considered the Said Report & recommendation, unanimously consented to confer the Said Degree upon Mr. Riddell, and ordered his Diploma to be issued in the usual form." From a Xerox copy of the Minutes, courtesy C. P. Finlayson, Esq., Keeper of MSS, The University Library, Edinburgh.

Stenhouse, *Museum*, I, lxxvi.

Scott. P & P, 121.

Young. Fitzhugh, 77.

Page 255

borrow a laborer. F I, #271, 255.

Page 256

1792 quarto. Not listed in H & H, Egerer, or Kinsley.

interleaved set. Dick I M; F II, #513, 129.

Page 257

Glenriddell Collection. See P.S. for p. 64.

wedding anniversary song. Cromek, *Reliques*, 269.

Page 258

To Riddell. F I, #271, 255.

Cromek. Dick I M, 73; Cook, *Chronicle* 1922, 1–22; J. D. Ferguson, "In Defense of R. H. Cromek," *Philological Quarterly*, IX (1930). 239–48.

librarian. M'Diarmid Notes, Waddell II, xxiv.

Statistical Account. F II, #469, 89–90.

Page 260

drinking. F II, #529, 140.

Whistle contest. Ch-W III, 102–9; M'Diarmid Notes, Waddell II, xxiii.

Page 261

To Grose. F II, #401, 22–24.

Page 264

Douglas Graham. H & H I, 437.

Pages 264–65

composition of *Tam o' Shanter.* H & H I, 438; Morison's Burns II, 340;
F II, #443, 68; Egerer, 16on. 4 and 5; F I, #298, 289; #294, 284;
#299, 272.

Page 265

Anne Park. Ch-W III, 364–65; Snyder, 307; Maria Riddell to Currie,
Chronicle 1921, 108.
"Yestreen I had . . ." *The Merry Muses of Caledonia,* ed. G. Legman,
New Hyde Park, N.Y., 1965. 9–10.
Tam o' Shanter. See H & H I, 433–41; Kinsley III, 1347–64.

Page 273

Walter Riddell and Woodley Park. F II, #626, 244.
To Smellie. F II, #492, 106–7.
Smellie to Maria Riddell. Kerr, *Smellie* II, 361–63; 366–67.

Page 274

Maria Riddell's *Voyages.* Ch-W III, 313n; F II, #517, 132.
strained relations. F II, #509, 124.
To Maria Riddell. F II, #675, 306; #555, 163.
Thornton. R. D. Thornton, *Currie,* 293–94 & 304; see also Kerr, *Smellie*
II, 390.

Page 275

Maria Riddell. See Sharpe, *Chronicle* 1903, 100; *Chronicle* 1920, 1921,
1923, 1924; Kerr, *Smellie, passim.*
"Dearest Friend." F II, #497, 110.
"vive l'amour." F II, #509, 124.
"enviable creature." F II, #520, 133–34; see also *Chronicle* 1935, 4.
request. F II, #516, 131.

Page 276

"trifling present." F II, #556, 163.
French gloves. D. Ferguson, "Some New Burns Letters," PMLA LI, 4
(Dec. 1936). 982.
"The music of thy voice." *Farewell, thou stream;* H & H III, 235.
Walter Riddell to West Indies. Thornton, *Currie,* 294; Kerr, *Smellie* II,
371–73.
epigram. F II, #590, 211.
four letters. F II, #594, 215; #595, 216; #596, 216–17; #597, 217.

Page 278

letter from Hell. F II, #608, 226–27.
Walter Riddell away. Thornton, *Currie*, 294.
"Mrs. R*****" Currie II, 449.

Page 279

To Maria Riddell. F II, #609, 227–28.

Page 280

returning Common Place Book. F II, #611, 229–30.
"rag." Carswell, 367–68; see also Ainslie, *ante*, 205–7.

Page 281

Sharpe. *Chronicle* 1903, 100.
Rachel Kennedy. Thornton, *Currie*, 296–97.
Robert Riddell. F II, #621, 239; #623, 241; #626, 244; #630, 249.
Walter Riddell. F II, #689, 317.

Page 282

To Margaret Chalmers. F I, #185, 172.
To Maria Riddell. F II, #611, 230.
To Mrs. Dunlop. F II, #634, 254.
To Clarinda. F II, #629, 248.
Epigram to Patrick Miller, Jr. F II, #622, 240.

Page 284

To Maria Riddell. F II, #650, 282; #658, 289–90; #668, 299; #674, 304; #675, 305–6; #679, 309; #681, 310; #683, 314; #697, 323.

Page 285

politics and alcohol. F II, #501, 113; #600, 220 (*Chronicle* 1968, 30); #617, 333–34; #618, 234; #631, 249–50.

VI. *Song*

This section attempts to give a comprehensive account of Burns' work in Scots song. If it seems detailed, that in turn has seemed the only way to make clear what Burns achieved, and also the limits of his accomplishment. The section owes much, of course, to Burns' correspondence with George Thomson, and to the Stenhouse edition of Johnson's *Museum* (Folklore Associates reissue, 1962), but without the work of Henley and Henderson, J. C. Dick, and James Kinsley, it could not have been written.

Page 288

Epigraph. Prologue to the *Canterbury Tales*, l. 95.

early interest in song. F I, #125, 106, 112; II, #511, 127; Dick I M, 28, 29.

"vade mecum." F I, #125, 109.

To Candlish. F I, #193, 179.

Page 289

comment on song. J. Kinsley, "Music of the Heart," *Renaissance and Modern Studies* VIII (1964). 5–52, particularly 27, 28, & 36.

"Scotch Songs." *Commonplace Book*, Ewing and Cook, 37–38, 39. See P.S. for p. 3.

Page 290

Later he comments. Ewing and Cook, 39–40.

Finally. Ewing and Cook, 41.

Page 291

Love and Liberty. H & H II, 291–313; Kinsley III, 1148–62; Crawford, 130–46; *The Jolly Beggars,* ed. J. C. Weston, Northampton, Mass., 1963; J. C. Weston, "The Text of Burns' 'The Jolly Beggars,'" *Studies in Biography* 13 (1960). 239–47; D. Daiches, *Robert Burns,* New York, 1950. 215–32. (Also later revisions.)

"dissuaded." J. D. Ferguson, "Burns and Hugh Blair," *Modern Language Notes* XLV (Nov., 1930). 440–46.

To Thomson. F II, #586, 202.

Page 302

"I set about composing." Ewing and Cook, 42.

"all the music." F II, #452, 75.

Page 303

musicians. Janet Cruikshank, Morison's Burns I, lxxxi. Kirsty Flint, Dick I M, xlvii. "an able fiddler," F I, #258, 239. Nathaniel Gow, F II, #591, 212. "a musical Highlander," F II, #576, 189. Fraser, F II, #567, 179. "Singing Master," F II, #684, 313.

Page 304

fading interest in vernacular poetry. F I, #379, 379; #333, 326; #319, 311–12.

songs. Dick I M; Dick (Historical Notes); Kinsley (Notes and Commentary); and H & H (Notes); all *passim*.

tunes and music.   Dick I M, xlviii, liii.

notes on song.   Dick I M; Cook, *Chronicle* 1922; Ferguson, "Cromek," *Philological Quarterly* IX. 239–48.

"paid more attention."   Dick I M, 5.

Page 305

letters.   Dick (Historical Notes) makes full use of the Johnson material.

Thomson.   Dick I M (xxxix n.), acknowledges a debt to Hadden's *George Thomson, the Friend of Burns,* but asks, "Why the friend of Burns?" See also R. D. Thornton's unpublished Harvard dissertation; and F II, #522, 134; #575, 188; and for *Scots Wha Hae,* F II, #584, 197.

Page 306

"Let me in this ae night."   F II, #637, 257.

Simplicity.   F II, #511, 126; #554, 161; #507, 122; #535, 148; #554, 162; #588, 210; Dick I M, 15.

Page 307

To Thomson.   F II, #647, 276.

Page 308

Thomson's niggling.   F II, #644, 268; #647, 277.

tampering.   F II, #554, 161.

elegant modification of music.   F II, #559, 172.

formal knowledge of music.   *Commonplace Book,* Ewing and Cook, 42; F II, #637, 256; #582, 194.

need for a tune.   F II, #637, 256; #514, 129; #694, 321.

Page 309

To Rev. John Skinner.   F I, #147, 133–34.

Page 310

apologies   Dick I M, 24, 26.

originality.   F II, #651, 283.

Pages 311–12

To Thomson on music.   F II, #515, 130; #586, 202; #569, 182; #644, 268; #646, 271. For Johnson, see Dick (Historical Notes), 368, #48.

Page 313

methods of composing.   F II, #577, 190; #637, 256; #636, 255; #506, 200–201; #644, 265.

Page 314

Dick.   Dick I M, xlviii & xliii–iv; also Dick, Preface, xiii.

"whole cycle." Dick I M, l; Dick (Historical Notes), #152, 403–4; see also Kinsley, commentary on songs, III.

Page 315

Scott.   Review of Cromek's *Reliques, Quarterly Review,* Feb. 1, 1809.

Page 316

To Jean McMurdo.   F II, #572, 185.

Page 324

"extra syllables."   Crawford, 290–91.

Page 328

Auld Lang Syne.   Kinsley, #240, III, 1289–91; Dick (Historical Notes), #234, 438–40.

To Thomson.   F II, #646, 274.

Page 329

"a Covenanting Clergyman."   *Chronicle* 1922, 6–7.

Jean Glover.   Dick I M, 57.

Bush.   Dick I M, 20.

Dumbarton's Drums.   Dick I M, 31.

Page 330

Cunningham the player.   Dick I M, 13.

Page 331

polite versions.   Legman, *Merry Muses,* xli–xlii.

Gavin Greig.   *Chronicle* 1950, 28.

Page 332

"indecorous traditionary verse." Quoted by S. G. Smith in "Robert Burns and the Merry Muses of Caledonia," *Hudson Review* VII, 3 (Autumn, 1954). 334.

"truly remarkable."   G. Legman, *The Horn Book,* New Hyde Park, N.Y., 1964 (2nd printing 1966). 163.

Cunningham.   Author's transcript. See P.S. for p. 365.

origins in . . . bawdy songs.   See notes in H & H, Dick, Kinsley, and Legman's *Merry Muses.* Also *The Merry Muses of Caledonia,* ed. James Barke and Sydney Goodsir Smith, with preface by J. DeLancey Ferguson, Edinburgh, 1959. Also, New York, 1964.

Page 333

Mr. Gracie.   Legman, *Horn Book,* 132–34.

Page 334

Merry Muses.   See Egerer, #311, 154–56; also Legman, *Merry Muses,* 260–97.

Page 341

To Cleghorn.   F II, #592, 212.

Page 346

"A droll Scots song."   F II, #637, 257.

VII. Last Years

Burns' friendship with John Syme began before he had moved to Dumfries from Ellisland in 1791, and continued until his death. Although remarks by Syme have appeared from time to time throughout the earlier parts of this book, it has seemed best to continue here the general principle of presenting relationships as a whole. And since this one began late in Burns' life and really continued beyond his death, the appropriate place for the main part of this vivid record is near the end of the book, even though certain events in it, chronologically, fall earlier than some already presented. See the Chronological Table, pp. xv–xviii.

Page 350

convivial parties.   Syme to Cunningham, author's transcript. See P.S. for p. 365.
assistance.   Peterkin's Currie I, lxxxix–xc.
"cold and frugal."   Author's transcript. See dissertation, 390.

Page 351

jar of brandy.   F II, #493, 107–8.
To Cunningham.   F II, #506, 120.

Page 352

To Provost Staig.   F II, #534, 147–48.

Page 353

Maria Riddell and seal.   *Chronicle* 1921, 100. See representation of Burns' seal on title page.
To Cunningham.   F II, #620, 237–38.
"a bit of a Herald."   see McVie, *Chronicle* 1952, 56–63.

Page 354

To Thomson. F II, 625, 243.
To Thomson. F II, #642, 278.

Page 355

Burns' position in Dumfries. *Chronicle* 1937, 102; Ch-W IV, 54–55; F II, #542, 154; Snyder, 372.

Page 356

James Gray. Snyder, 378; 438 (n. 40); F II, 364. Peterkin's Currie I, lxxxv–vi; Gilbert Burns' Currie I, 433–34.

Page 358

Sharpe. *Chronicle* 1903, 99–100.
Archibald Lawrie. F II, 357; Ch-W IV, 14.

Page 359

Josiah Walker. Morison's Burns I, cxii–v.

Page 361

David McCulloch. F II, #627, 245.
king's birthday, May 24. This date kindly supplied by Mrs. Isobel Dewar of the Nat. Lib. of Scotland; see Lockhart, Scott Douglas edition, 224; and Ch-W IV, 121–22.

Page 362

Grace Aiken. Ch-W IV, 262.

Page 363

Jesse Lewars. Ch-W IV, 119.

Page 364

John Syme. Ch-W IV, 217–18; *Chronicle* 1920, 115–16. I am deeply indebted to Mr. Desmond Donaldson, County Librarian, Dumfriesshire, for sending me a copy of Syme's obituary in the *Dumfries Weekly Journal* of December 6, 1833. Syme had died November 24, after an illness of two days.
Syme to Cunningham. Author's transcript. See P.S. for p. 365.
Maria Riddell and Currie. *Chronicle* 1924, 86.

Page 365

Syme-Cunningham correspondence. The originals of this correspondence, then in the Burns Cottage Museum, Alloway, were kindly made available to the author in 1933 by the late Lieut. Col. T. C. Dunlop, head of the

Trustees. For selections, see *Chronicle* 1934, 1935, 1936, 1938, 1939, 1940. The author's transcript is in his doctoral dissertation, in the Library of Cornell University.

Syme to Cunningham. Author's transcript. See above.

Page 369

To Thomson. F II, #582, 194–96.

Page 371

Mr. Carson. Ch-W IV, 20–21.

Page 372

Syme to Cunningham. Author's transcript. See above.

Page 373

two passages. Author's transcript. See above.

Page 374

Syme to Cunningham. Author's transcript. See above.

Page 375

Stobbie. Currie I, 229.

financial details. Ch-W IV, 264n; Peterkin's Currie I, xc.

estate. Money owed him by his brother Gilbert (*Chronicle* 1900, 77–90), and personal property, including his library which was appraised after his death at £90 (Alloway Cottage document 184).

Cunningham to Syme. Author's transcript. See above p. 365.

Page 376

Peterkin proof sheets. Author's transcript. See above p. 365.

Page 378

Brow. Sir James Crichton-Browne, *Burns from a New Point of View*, London, 1926. 1–3. Courtesy of the publishers, Hodder and Stoughton, Ltd.

Page 379

Maria Riddell. Currie I, 221–23.

Page 381

To Thomson. F II, #699, 324.

To Cunningham. F II, #700, 325.

Page 382

To James Armour. F II, #701, 326.

Page 383
To Gilbert Burns.   F II, #703, 326–27.
To James Burness.   F II, #705, 327–28.

Page 384
To Jean.   F II, #708, 329.
To John Clark.   F II, #709, 330.
To James Armour.   F II, #710, 330.

Page 385
Syme to Cunningham.   Author's transcript. See above, p. 365.

Page 386
funeral.   Currie I, 224–25; D. Ferguson, "The Earliest Obituary of Burns,"
Modern Philology, XXXII (Nov. 1934). 179–84. Also dissertation, 237–
40.

Page 387
subscription.   Chambers (1880) IV, 306–9; and Syme-Cunningham correspondence.
returns from Currie edition.   T. Besterman, *The Publishing Firm of Cadell
and Davies*, 1938. xxi.

Page 388
Betty Paton.   Some details of Betty Paton's descendants may be found in
Chronicle 1922, 114.

Addendum to Page 209
Dr. James Currie kept a notebook in which he made entries to assist him
in writing his Life of Burns. The following entry is further evidence that
Robert Burns had discussed giving up Ellisland with his brother Gilbert even
before he went on active Excise duty:

Gilbert Burns to Rob[t]
6 Aug 89
—Not that I would have you give up your farm which I am afraid may be
your idea, as I knew that you are a little disgusted with the cares of farming, & your poetic sensibility & love of ease makes you think that you cannot
too much avoid that which gives you uneasiness" he goes on to argue very
sensibly ag[t]. giving it up.

R. D. Thornton, "Burns Letters and
the Currie Notebook," Studies in
Scottish Literature, VII, 1 & 2 (1970).

INDEX